RESEARCH HANDBOOK ON MOTIVATION IN PUBLIC ADMINISTRATION

ELGAR HANDBOOKS IN PUBLIC ADMINISTRATION AND MANAGEMENT

This series provides a comprehensive overview of recent research in all matters relating to public administration and management, serving as a definitive guide to the field. Covering a wide range of research areas including national and international methods of public administration, theories of public administration and management, and technological developments in public administration and management, the series produces influential works of lasting significance. Each *Handbook* will consist of original contributions by preeminent authors, selected by an esteemed editor internationally recognized as a leading scholar within the field. Taking an international approach, these *Handbooks* serve as an essential reference point for all students of public administration and management, emphasizing both the expansion of current debates, and an indication of the likely research agendas for the future.

Titles in the series include:

Handbook on Corruption, Ethics and Integrity in Public Administration
Edited by Adam Graycar

Handbook of Research Methods in Public Administration, Management and Policy
Edited by Eran Vigoda-Gadot and Dana R. Vashdi

Handbook of Collaborative Public Management
Edited by Jack Wayne Meek

Handbook on Performance Management in the Public Sector
Edited by Deborah Blackman

Research Handbook on E-Government
Edited by Eric W. Welch

Handbook of Theories of Public Administration and Management
Edited by Thomas A. Bryer

Research Handbook on HRM in the Public Sector
Edited by Bram Steijn and Eva Knies

Handbook on Gender and Public Administration
Edited by Patricia M. Shields and Nicole M. Elias

Research Handbook on Motivation in Public Administration
Edited by Edmund C. Stazyk and Randall S. Davis

Research Handbook on Motivation in Public Administration

Edited by

Edmund C. Stazyk

Associate Professor, Rockefeller College of Public Affairs & Policy, Department of Public Administration and Policy, University at Albany, State University of New York, USA

Randall S. Davis

Associate Professor, School of Management and Marketing, College of Business and Analytics, Southern Illinois University, USA

ELGAR HANDBOOKS IN PUBLIC ADMINISTRATION AND MANAGEMENT

Cheltenham, UK • Northampton, MA, USA

© Edmund C. Stazyk and Randall S. Davis 2022

All rights reserved. No part of this publication may be reproduced, stored in a retrieval system or transmitted in any form or by any means, electronic, mechanical or photocopying, recording, or otherwise without the prior permission of the publisher.

Published by
Edward Elgar Publishing Limited
The Lypiatts
15 Lansdown Road
Cheltenham
Glos GL50 2JA
UK

Edward Elgar Publishing, Inc.
William Pratt House
9 Dewey Court
Northampton
Massachusetts 01060
USA

A catalogue record for this book
is available from the British Library

Library of Congress Control Number: 2022931166

This book is available electronically in the Elgaronline
Political Science and Public Policy subject collection
http://dx.doi.org/10.4337/9781789906806

Printed on elemental chlorine free (ECF)
recycled paper containing 30% Post-Consumer Waste

ISBN 978 1 78990 679 0 (cased)
ISBN 978 1 78990 680 6 (eBook)

Printed and bound in the USA

Contents

List of contributors   viii

1   Introduction to the *Research Handbook on Motivation in Public Administration*   1
     Edmund C. Stazyk and Randall S. Davis

PART I   THEORY AND FOUNDATIONS

2   The political economy of bureaucratic motivation   10
     Yongjin Ahn and William G. Resh

3   Behavioral public administration and employee motivation   27
     Carina Schott

4   The ins and outs of motivational crowding   39
     Trent Engbers

5   Self-determination theory and public employee motivation research   57
     Justin M. Stritch, Ulrich Thy Jensen and Michelle Allgood

6   Goals as a driver of public sector motivation   71
     Edmund C. Stazyk and Jisang Kim

7   What do we know yet about public service motivation in Latin America? A review of the evolution of empirical research   89
     Pablo Sanabria-Pulido and Cristian Pliscoff

8   Experiments and qualitative methods: towards a methodological framework   105
     Kai Xiang Kwa

PART II   MOTIVATION AS A DRIVER OF SECTOR DECISIONS

9   Employee motivation across job sectors   122
     Jaclyn Piatak

10   Monetary and non-monetary compensation in for-profit, nonprofit, and public organizations: comparison and competition   137
     Laura Langbein and Fei W. Roberts

11   Unionization and the motivational context in public management   154
     Randall S. Davis and Warefta Rahman

12   Public pensions and employment in the public sector   168
     Gang Chen and Hyewon Kang

13	Unreserved fund balance management practices in US counties *John A. Hamman, LaShonda M. Stewart, Brian C. Chapman and Jeremy N. Phillips*	183

PART III FACTORS AFFECTING RECRUITMENT, SELECTION, AND RETENTION

14	Responsibility toward others is vital in public and non-profit organizations: can we recruit, hire, and cultivate it? *Neil M. Boyd and Branda Nowell*	201
15	Merit system integrity and public service motivation in the US federal civil service: evidence on the importance of merit principles *Gene A. Brewer, J. Edward Kellough and Hal G. Rainey*	219
16	Job design and motivation: crafting the work of the public sector *Alexander C. Henderson and Jessica E. Sowa*	234
17	Job design and public employee work motivation: towards an institutional reading *David Giauque and Rafaël Weissbrodt*	249
18	For the children? Teachers' motivation and systems for recruitment, retention, and evaluation *Stephen B. Holt*	264
19	Public service motivation education and government career preferences: a teaching agenda *Leonard Bright*	284

PART IV MOTIVATION AND EMPLOYEE BEHAVIOR

20	Linking justice and employee performance in public organizations *Ellen V. Rubin and Minsung Michael Kang*	293
21	Ethics, prosocial and public service motivation: disentangling their relationship and identifying the implications for the public and nonprofit sectors *Jessica Breaugh and Guillem Ripoll*	307
22	Organizational identity orientation: a public sector research agenda *Julie Langer and Mary K. Feeney*	321
23	Change-oriented organizational citizenship behavior in public organizations: appropriateness, opportunity, risk, and public service motivation *Jesse W. Campbell*	336

24	Stressed versus motivated public employees: a systematic review of the motivation and stress literatures through a contextualized job demands-resources model *Rick T. Borst*	354
25	Worked to a crisp: 'realistic' and 'symbolic' stressor effects on burnout *Adam C. Green*	377
26	What happened to you? Understanding trauma and motivation in the public service workplace *Heather Getha-Taylor and Morgan D. Farnworth*	387

PART V   CONCLUSION

27	Conclusions: where does motivation research in public administration go from here? *Randall S. Davis and Edmund C. Stazyk*	402
Index		410

Contributors

Yongjin Ahn is a doctoral candidate at the Sol Price School of Public Policy in the University of Southern California, USA. He is interested in bureaucratic politics and public management, and specifically in behavioral measures of bureaucratic motivation. His research focuses on human resource management, organizational behavior, and citizen-state interaction.

Michelle Allgood is a doctoral student in the School of Public Affairs at Arizona State University, USA. Her research focuses on public management, workplace coping and stress, and equity and access issues, especially for members of the disability community.

Rick T. Borst is an Assistant Professor at the Utrecht University School of Governance, the Netherlands. His research focuses on the behavior, attitudes, and psychological characteristics of public sector and semi-public sector employees, taking into account the role of (human resource) management and institutional contexts.

Neil M. Boyd is the David J. & Deborah West Professor of Management, and Chair of the Management & Organizations Department in the Freeman College of Management at Bucknell University, USA. His published work examines topics in human resource management, organization development, and managing for sustainability. His work has appeared in leading publication outlets in the fields of management, public management, and community psychology. His recent work examines community experiences at work and how employees and organizations can benefit when a workplace is infused with a culture of community. He is also well known for his extensive research at the intersection of organization studies and community psychology, and his work on 'other-regarding' motivation constructs (i.e., public service motivation, sense of community responsibility, prosocial motivation, and altruism) is leading to new discoveries in behavioral public management.

Jessica Breaugh is a post-doctoral researcher at the Hertie School in Berlin, Germany. Her research focuses on public management, with an emphasis on employee outcomes, work motivation, engagement, and public service motivation conceptualizations. She has worked as a public service practitioner for the Canadian federal, provincial, and municipal governments, with the most research position as an advisor in the area of human resources management. Her latest research related to public service motivation is published in *Public Management Review*.

Gene A. Brewer is a Professor of Public Administration and Policy, School of Public and International Affairs, the University of Georgia, USA. He is an internationally recognized scholar, researcher, and consultant with expertise in public administration, management, and the policy process. Brewer holds several secondary appointments at universities and research institutes internationally. He is a fellow of the National Academy of Public Administration and a senior Fulbright specialist for the US Department of State.

Leonard Bright is an Associate Professor at Texas A&M University's Bush School of Government and Public Service, USA. His research contributions have been recognized through publications in the leading academic journals in his specialty of public management.

His publications have had a measurable impact on his field of study as illustrated by the frequent citation of his research. He is considered to be a top national expert in his field on motivation for public service employees.

Jesse W. Campbell is an Associate Professor in the Department of Public Administration at Incheon National University in South Korea. Currently, he is researching topics in comparative public administration, and specifically how the adoption of public sector reform affects the performance and well-being of public servants. A second stream of research focuses on questions with unique relevance to the Korean administrative context.

Brian C. Chapman is a retired university administrator and adjunct faculty member in the Master of Public Administration at Southern Illinois University, USA. His research focuses on leadership, ethics, and budgeting in public administration.

Gang Chen is an Associate Professor in Public Administration at the University of Albany, State University of New York, USA. He is also the co-director of the State and Local Government Finance Project (SLGF) at the Center for Policy Research at Rockefeller College. His research focuses on state and local budgeting, financial management, and public pension governance.

Randall S. Davis is an Associate Professor in the School of Management and Marketing, College of Business and Analytics at Southern Illinois University, USA. He primarily examines the social and psychological mechanisms that contribute to individual performance in the public workplace. His research focuses on several themes in public management including organizational behavior, human resource management, employee motivation, work stress, and goal setting.

Trent Engbers is an Associate Professor of Political Science and Public Administration and Director of the Master of Public Administration program at the University of Southern Indiana, USA. His research focuses on public and nonprofit management, social capital, and leadership. He is an award-winning nonprofit leader, consultant and educator and lives in Evansville, Indiana, with his wife and four children.

Morgan D. Farnworth is a doctoral student in the School of Public Affairs and Administration, University of Kansas, USA, and a 2020 Robert Wood Johnson Foundation Health Policy Fellow. Her work focuses on the role of government in advancing health equity and, particularly, how public organizations can improve health outcomes for marginalized communities. Her research spans several policy and administrative areas, including addiction and substance use treatment, behavioral health, housing, and education.

Mary K. Feeney is a Professor and Lincoln Professor of Ethics in Public Affairs at the School of Public Affairs at Arizona State University, USA, and is currently serving as Program Officer for the Science of Science program in the Directorate for Social, Behavioral and Economic Sciences at the US National Science Foundation. Her research is on public and nonprofit management and science and technology policy. Her most recent public management research focuses on technology use in local governments in the United States.

Heather Getha-Taylor is a Professor in the School of Public Affairs and Administration at the University of Kansas, USA. Her work focuses on public and nonprofit management, with specific emphasis on human resource management, collaborative governance, and public service leadership topics.

David Giauque is an Associate Professor of Human Resource Management at the Swiss Graduate School of Public Administration, University of Lausanne, Switzerland. His publications and research interests include: values and ethics in the public sector; health in public organizations; new public management reforms; motivation of public agents; human resources management; sociology of organizations and public administrations; sociology of political-administrative actors. He has published numerous articles and books on these different topics.

Adam C. Green is a doctoral candidate in the School of Psychological and Behavioral Sciences at Southern Illinois University, USA. His research focuses on interaction between ideological groups, moral debate, and organizational ethics. The goal of his research is to promote intergroup dialogue and to foster open communication in organizations.

John A. Hamman is an Associate Professor in the School of Management and Marketing, College of Business and Analytics at Southern Illinois University, USA. His current research focuses on incentives and motivations influencing public financial management practices and decisions and administrative decision making and performance more broadly. He has published articles in many journals including *Public Administration Review*, *Public Budgeting and Finance*, *Journal of Public Management and Social Policy*, *American Review of Public Administration*, *International Review of Public Administration*, *Review of Public Personnel Administration*, and chapters in edited volumes.

Alexander C. Henderson is an Associate Professor in the School of Management at Marist College, USA. His research focuses on organizational behavior, human resource management, and administrative discretion. He previously served as an operational officer, director, and chief administrative officer in several emergency services agencies.

Stephen B. Holt is an Assistant Professor in the Department of Public Administration and Policy, Rockefeller College of Public Affairs and Policy at the University at Albany, State University of New York, USA. His research focuses on public sector workforce dynamics, public organization performance, and education policy and administration. The themes of his work center on the impacts of public workers' demographics and motivation on government performance and equity.

Ulrich Thy Jensen is an Assistant Professor in the School of Public Affairs and a faculty affiliate at the Center for Organizational Research and Design at Arizona State University, USA. His research interests span issues of leadership, motivation, values and performance in public service. His research builds on new and innovative ways to understand the importance of leadership in shaping the attitudes of public service providers and the performance of their organizations.

Hyewon Kang is a Visiting Assistant Professor in the Department of Public Administration and Policy at the State University of New York, USA. Her research interest intersects public management, public budgeting, and financial management using quantitative and experimental methods. Specific topics of interest are fiscal transparency, fiscal stress, and state-local governments' relationship.

Minsung Michael Kang is a PhD candidate in Public Administration at Rockefeller College, University at Albany, State University of New York, USA. His research interests in public and personnel management include organization theory and behavior, bureaucratic whistleblowing, frontline employment, and organizational justice.

J. Edward Kellough is a Professor in the Department of Public Administration and Policy, School of Public and International Affairs, at the University of Georgia (UGA), USA. He served previously as the Head of the Department of Public Administration and Policy at UGA and as MPA and PhD program director. Kellough specializes in the field of public sector human resources management. He is an elected Fellow of the National Academy of Public Administration (NAPA), and is past President of NASPAA, the Network of Schools of Public Policy, Affairs, and Administration. His books include *The New Public Personnel Administration*, seventh edition, with Lloyd G. Nigro (Wadsworth, Cengage Learning, 2014) and *Understanding Affirmative Action: Politics, Discrimination, and the Search for Justice* (Georgetown University Press, 2007). His research has appeared in numerous academic journals. He has lectured or made research presentations in Australia, Canada, China, Denmark, Germany, Italy, the Republic of Georgia, the Netherlands, Russia, Saudi Arabia, South Korea, Ukraine, and the United Arab Emirates.

Jisang Kim is a PhD candidate in the Department of Public Administration and Policy at the University at Albany's Rockefeller College of Public Affairs and Policy, State University of New York, USA, and a Research Associate at the Center for Women in Government and Civil Society. His primary research interests involve public accountability in government organizations and how accountability affects the public safety and well-being of communities.

Kai Xiang Kwa is currently a Lecturer at the School of Social Sciences, Nanyang Technological University, Singapore. He has published in the *Asian Journal of Political Science* and the *International Review of Public Administration* and is the co-author of *Exploring Public–Private Partnerships in Singapore: The Success–Failure Continuum* (Routledge, 2019). His research interests include the dynamics of motivation, ethics, philosophy and politics in public administration, climate change policy, and artificial intelligence policy. His research on public administration and policy governance has been supported by the Ministry of Education in Singapore and the National Research Foundation of the Republic of Korea.

Laura Langbein teaches policy analysis and program evaluation at American University, Department of Public Administration and Policy Analysis, USA. She studies bureaucratic discretion, intrinsic motivation and pay, with applications to corruption and environment and education policy. She authored *Program Evaluation: A Statistical Guide* (ME Sharpe, 2012). Her recent publications appear in *Journal of Comparative Policy Analysis*, *Public Administration*, *International Public Management Journal*, *Sexuality Research and Social Policy*, and *Administration and Society*.

Julie Langer is an Assistant Professor in the Department of Public Administration at Northern Illinois University, USA. She studies how organizations are used as vehicles for the expression of identity and what this means for their ability to both create and destroy value in society. Langer's work has received best paper award recognition from the Academy of Management, public and nonprofit division, as well as the editor's prize for best scholarly paper from the journal *Nonprofit Management and Leadership*. Her research has been published in

Perspectives on Public Management and Governance, Administration & Society, Nonprofit and Voluntary Sector Quarterly and the *American Review of Public Administration*.

Branda Nowell is a Professor in the School of Public and International Affairs and Director of the Doctoral Program in Public Administration at North Carolina State University, USA. Trained as an organizational-community psychologist, Nowell's research focuses on interorganizational networks including the design of governance systems in complex problem domains and the psychological experience of community within networked settings. She teaches graduate courses in network governance, organizational theory, research methods, change management, and program evaluation.

Jeremy N. Phillips is an Associate Professor of Public Policy and Administration in the College of Business and Public Affairs at West Chester University of Pennsylvania, USA, where he primarily teaches courses related to nonprofit management, program evaluation, research design, quantitative analysis, and financial decision making. His research focuses on taxing and spending decisions at the state and local levels.

Jaclyn Piatak is an Associate Professor in the Department of Political Science and Public Administration at the University of North Carolina at Charlotte, USA, and teaches courses in the Gerald G. Fox Master of Public Administration Program. Her work centers on understanding and managing public service, both at the organizational and individual level. She focuses on several areas in public and nonprofit management, including human resource management, motivation, and public service delivery.

Cristian Pliscoff is Director of the Undergraduate Program in Public Administration at the School of Government, Catholic University of Chile. His areas of interest are public administration, State reform, and ethics in public administration.

Warefta Rahman is an MPA student in the School of Management and Marketing within the College of Business and Analytics at Southern Illinois University, USA. She received her BSS & MSS in Public Administration from the University of Dhaka. Her research interests focus on public management themes including organizational behavior, employee performance, work motivation, human resources management and development, and political-economic factors influencing governance.

Hal G. Rainey is Professor Emeritus in the Department of Public Administration and Policy, School of Public and International Affairs, at the University of Georgia, USA. He teaches courses and conducts research on the application of organizational theory and behavior in government organizations. Jossey-Bass/Wiley has recently published the sixth edition of the book, *Understanding and Managing Public Organizations*, that he has coauthored with Sergio Fernandez and Deanna Malatesta of Indiana University.

William G. Resh is the C.C. Crawford Associate Professor of Management and Performance and Associate Professor at the University of Southern California's Sol Price School of Public Policy, USA. Bill's work focuses on executive politics and public management. His scholarship is published in respected peer-reviewed journals and academic presses across the fields of public administration, political science, and public policy. His book, *Rethinking the Administrative Presidency* (Johns Hopkins University Press), was awarded the Herbert Simon

Best Book Award for its lasting contribution to the study of public administration by the American Political Science Association in 2019.

Guillem Ripoll is an Assistant Professor at the University of Navarra, Spain. He obtained his PhD at the Autonomous University of Barcelona (Programme: Politics, Policies and International Relations). His research revolves around the expansion of the concept of public service motivation; specifically, he investigates the relationship between motivation and ethics.

Fei W. Roberts is a Professorial Lecturer in the Department of Public Administration and Policy at American University, USA. Her research focuses on democratic governance, bureaucratic discretion, employee motivation, and public-private comparisons.

Ellen V. Rubin is an Associate Professor of Public Administration and Policy at the University at Albany, State University of New York, USA. Her research interests in public personnel management include organizational justice, performance management, and civil service reforms.

Pablo Sanabria-Pulido is an Associate Professor and Director of Graduate Programs at the School of Government, Universidad de los Andes, Colombia, and Affiliate Professor of the Public Administration Division of Centro de Investigación y Docencia Económicas, CIDE México. His areas of interest are public management and policy analysis, organizational behavior, corruption and transparency, local government, and public affairs education.

Carina Schott is an Assistant Professor at the Utrecht University School of Governance (USG), the Netherlands. She conducts research at the interface of Public Management and HRM in the public sector where she concentrates on the individual level. Specifically, her research focuses on employee motivation and well-being; the implications of a changing work environment for professionals; and leadership in various public sectors (in particular, education, healthcare, and inspection services).

Jessica E. Sowa is a Professor in the Joseph R. Biden Jr. School of Public Policy & Administration at the University of Delaware, USA. Her research focuses on human resource management in government and nonprofit organizations, volunteer management, leadership, and organizational effectiveness. She is the editor-in-chief of the *Review of Public Personnel Administration*.

Edmund C. Stazyk is an Associate Professor in the Department of Public Administration and Policy at the University at Albany, State University of New York, USA. His research focuses on the application of organization theory and behavior to public management, public administration theory, and human resource management. His primary areas of interest include bureaucracy, organizational and individual performance, and employee motivation.

LaShonda M. Stewart received her PhD from Mississippi State University in May 2008. Her general research area focuses on local governments' financial management practices, state's rainy-day funds, global budgeting, participatory budgeting, and health information technology. She is, however, most recognized for her research on local governments' unreserved fund balances with research appearing in *Public Budgeting and Finance, Public Finance and Management, Journal of Public Budgeting, Accounting & Financial Management; Financial Management,* and *Administration & Society; Society*. In her current research, she seeks to develop a model to explain how local governments accumulate savings. She teaches courses in public administration which include public budgeting, financial management, research methods for public administrators and statistics. She also serves as Director of the Chancellor's Scholars Program.

Justin M. Stritch is an Associate Professor at Arizona State University's School of Public Affairs, USA, and a Senior Research Affiliate at the Center for Organization Research and Design (CORD). His research focuses on public employee attitudes and motivations, quality of work life, organizational fairness and equity, decision making, and public sector sustainability.

Rafaël Weissbrodt is an Associate Professor at the School of Health Sciences, HES-SO Valais-Wallis, Sion, Switzerland. He holds a PhD in Political Science, a Master's degree in Work and Organizational Psychology, and the European Ergonomist title. His publications and research interests include organizational resilience in the context of new and emerging risks, occupational health and safety management, human factors and ergonomics, and organizational design and management. He is the author of several peer-reviewed publications on these topics.

1. Introduction to the *Research Handbook on Motivation in Public Administration*

Edmund C. Stazyk and Randall S. Davis

TAKING STOCK OF THE STATE OF PUBLIC AND NONPROFIT MOTIVATION RESEARCH

Existing books and handbooks on motivation in the field of public administration are rare and, yet, few research topics have received as much direct and sustained scholarly attention as that of motivation. In fact, one of the field's few homegrown theories—a theory known as public service motivation (PSM)—has produced well over 250 articles since the concept was originally articulated by Perry and Wise in 1990. Moreover, with the advent of the behavioral public administration movement, efforts to understand employee motivation have only grown in recent years and are likely to continue. As such, it is surprising that relatively few scholarly efforts have been undertaken to compile the broad body of research addressing and encompassing employee motivation and closely related topics.

Notably, a handful of important attempts have been made in recent years—mainly, over the last two decades—to assemble discrete theories of motivation into something resembling a coherent whole, and then disseminate this material to relevant public administration and management audiences. One such example is Perry and Hondeghem's (2008) *Motivation in Public Management: The Call of Public Service*, which has become one of the primary works tracing the intellectual development and evolution of PSM since Perry and Wise first took steps to formalize the concept.

While efforts like Perry and Hondeghem's have certainly expanded the dialogue on motivation in public administration, such efforts have also been limited and narrow in scope, focused almost entirely on the concept of PSM. Yet, as decades of research conducted both in- and outside of public administration have demonstrated, PSM is only one factor in, and aspect of, employee motivation. Other factors (e.g., socio-demographic characteristics, personal preferences, the instrumental facets of jobs, goals, co-worker relations, leadership, and organizational climate) shape the motives and motivation of workers and the subsequent performance of public organizations.

As our discussion so far illustrates, what is missing and desperately needed in the field of public administration is a *Handbook* that compiles and incorporates these broader perspectives into something that approaches a coherent whole; a *Handbook* that addresses the wider, more diverse intellectual terrain of public and nonprofit employee motivation (as opposed to the narrower slice that, at present, frequently dominates much of the field's attention and focus).

To this end, the current Handbook features leading and emerging voices on employee motivation in an attempt to offer a comprehensive scholarly review of the field and practice of motivation research in public administration. Our aim has been to assemble a slate of researchers and topics that are likely to be appealing to both national and international audiences, and it is our deepest hope that our *Handbook* provides a strong research foundation that offers academics, researchers, and doctoral students a snapshot of the terrain of public administration motivation scholarship. We further hope that this approach will offer our readers an in-depth, broad-based review of cutting-edge academic research on motivation in public administration that both is informative for those looking for new insights into employee motivation, and, simultaneously, will serve as a springboard for new and more nuanced research on the topics presented by our authors.

To this end, *Handbook* contributors were afforded significant latitude in writing their chapters. They were simply asked to (1) provide a detailed review and discussion on a topic widely viewed as central to the study of motivation in public administration, and (2) map out a research agenda for future attention and work on their chosen topic. It is our hope that this dual approach will offer readers an interesting and thought-provoking review on employee motivation, both as it stands currently and as it may evolve in the coming years.

Finally, we specifically set out to include a mix of senior, junior, and emerging scholars in the *Handbook*. Our aim was to ensure a diversity of perspectives was present across our chapters as well as to encourage a healthy dialogue across the chapters about the current and future state of research on employee motivation. As our contributors demonstrate across their chapters, we have learned much yet many pressing and important issues remain. We hope our efforts here will catalyze new, creative research that fills these research gaps.

OUTLINE OF THE *HANDBOOK*

In the remainder of this introduction, we outline the basic structure of our *Handbook* and briefly describe each chapter. We divided the book into four primary parts. Each part contains several chapters addressing different topics and subjects, all loosely related. It is clear that this division is rough at best, and many of our chapters touch on themes discussed in other parts of the book. The parts should, therefore, be treated as reflecting the general thrust and direction of a given chapter, but our readers are likely to find much of value in chapters regardless of the specific part they appear in. These parts include the following

- Theory and Foundations
- Motivation as a Driver of Sector Decisions
- Factors Affecting Recruitment, Selection, and Retention
- Motivation and Employee Behavior.

Part I: Theory and Foundations

The opening part of the *Handbook* is intended to provide a brief review of some of the core, foundational concerns and theoretical concepts associated with employee motivation in public and nonprofit sector organizations. It begins with Chapter 2, penned by Yongjin Ahn and Bill Resh addressing the political economy of bureaucratic motivation. Public administration scholars have long contended that the political environment of public sector organizations distinguishes government agencies from private firms and, as a consequence, limits the efficacy of certain motivators (e.g., money) for public employees. Ahn and Resh review and explore what we know about motivation from the research on the political control of bureaucracy.

Chapter 3, written by Carina Schott, provides an overview of the emerging literature exploring the motivation of public sector employees from the viewpoint of behavioral public administration (BPA). BPA is an emerging subfield in public administration and management that draws heavily on approaches commonly utilized in psychology (and, particularly, the use of experiments and experimental designs) in an effort to understand the psychological processes that produce or enhance employee motivation. Schott reviews the development of BPA and considers the impact of this emerging subfield on our understanding of employee motivation.

In Chapter 4, Trent Engbers reviews motivational crowding theory. As Engbers notes, motivational crowding theory considers what effect, if any, extrinsic interventions (e.g., money and performance-related pay) have on intrinsic motivation (e.g., public service motivation). Engbers reviews the research on motivational crowding as well as various factors that help explain when motivational crowding is most likely to occur. He then considers how motivational and structural differences within the public sector make motivational crowding particularly concerning, before proposing an agenda for future research on crowding.

Next, Justin Stritch, Ulrich Thy Jensen, and Michelle Allgood review Deci and Ryan's (1985) Self-Determination Theory (SDT). SDT is one of the most prominent theoretical frameworks in the field of psychology and in the study of human motivation. The theory has evolved, over time, into a 'metatheory' for understanding human motivation, well-being and wellness in a wide variety of contexts, including the public and nonprofit workplace. Strich and colleagues explore the core theoretical perspectives that underpin SDT, before evaluating its usefulness as a device for explaining the behavioral consequences of different motivations and motivational processes in the public workplace.

In Chapter 6, Edmund Stazyk and Jisang Kim review the history of goal-setting theory, its adoption and adaptation into the field of public management, and its current status in the field. They explore how the discussion and debate around goals as a motivational tool have evolved in the public sector setting as well as in the broader social sciences. They then present a series of key issues and questions that warrant additional study and consideration as researchers work to understand and capitalize on the benefits of goals as a motivational device capable of improving employee and organizational outcomes.

Next, Pablo Sanabria-Pulido and Cristian Pliscoff consider the current state of PSM research in Latin America. As their chapter illustrates, other countries and settings have unique institutional contexts that have important implications for the performance of their public institutions as well as on the motives of their workers. Sanabria-Pulido and Pliscoff review what we know about PSM in Latin America and, in doing so, illuminate the strengths and weaknesses of PSM's applicability generally and theoretically. Similar efforts have been undertaken in other countries and settings, partly because it has become increasingly clear that PSM's applicability and generalizability are, at least partly, determined by contextual factors. Given its diversity and size, Latin America presents a unique opportunity to consider how PSM intersects with other, largely unexplored challenges unique to developing countries.

The final chapter in this part, written by Kai Xiang Kwa, explores different methodological approaches that could be employed to understand the motives and motivation of public and nonprofit sector workers. More specifically, Kwa reviews the weaknesses of the various dominant methodological approaches (i.e., survey and experimental research) typically used to determine what motivates workers as well as some of the weaknesses associated with qualitative approaches. Kwa calls for researchers to pursue more mixed methods-based research in an effort to overcome the respective weaknesses of each approach (quantitative and qualitative), then proposes a framework combining quantitative and qualitative methodological approaches in motivation scholarship.

Part II: Motivation as a Driver of Sector Decisions

Part II of the *Handbook* turns to a discussion of sector-based characteristics and factors that appear to steer employees into particular job sectors: public, private, or nonprofit. Public administration scholars have long argued that public and nonprofit organizations confront certain structural and institutional disadvantages that limit the ability to attract and motivate particular workers (e.g., limited financial incentives). Yet, conversely, PSM research, in particular, points to numerous unique factors that may draw other individuals into the public and nonprofit realms (e.g., altruistic motives, familial socialization). Much of the research written about sector differences—as is the case with the chapters included in this *Handbook*—attempts to uncover conditions that drive sector selection decisions among workers.

In the opening chapter of this part, Jaclyn Piatak directly embraces the challenge of articulating what we know about sector choices and motivation. More specifically, she considers several key questions throughout her chapter, including (1) how PSM relates to other job sector motives, (2) how the blurring of sectoral boundaries has influenced employees' willingness to work in specific job sectors, (3) what motivates individuals to join the government, nonprofit, and for-profit sectors, and (4) what can government and nonprofit managers do to recruit and retain future generations? She concludes by offering suggestions on where scholars should look next in their efforts to understand how sector decisions and employee motives intersect.

Next, in Chapter 10, Laura Langbein and Fei Roberts note that both monetary and non-monetary compensation play an integral role in enhancing employee work motivation. They then review how one extrinsic motivator, money, is likely to remain important to employees regardless of their sector preferences and decisions. To this end, the authors review core aspects of wage determination theory, then consider how employees' monetary compensation is likely to differ between and within each employment sector. In the second half of their chapter, Langbein and Roberts consider the various ways monetary and non-monetary aspects of compensation (including intrinsic incentives and public service motivation) are likely to interact and, in turn, to effect public sector motivation.

Turning to Chapter 11, Randy Davis and Warefta Rahman argue that theories hoping to shed light on employee work motivation and, in turn, individual and organizational performance must account for the various ways in which exogenous factors shape the institutional context of job sectors and organizations. They further suggest that unionization represents one salient factor for many public organizations with the capacity to influence the motivational process. The authors then unpack the various ways that unions can influence employee-member attitudes, organizational structure, and external environmental demands, which then shape employees' motives and motivation. They conclude by suggesting models of public sector motivation would do well to account for unionization when studying public sector motivation and performance.

In 'Public Pensions and Employment in the Public Sector,' Gang Chen and Hyewon Kang consider the various ways in which pensions and pension systems have attracted workers to the public sector. They begin by exploring many of the theoretical and practical explanations for the reasons why pensions would or would not affect public employees' motivations and sector decisions. Then, they conduct a comprehensive literature review and summarize the empirical findings on the impact of pensions on employees' decisions. They conclude that pension plan design, benefit changes, and plan types affect turnover rates, retirement decisions, and composition of the public workforce, each of which has direct and indirect effects on employee motivation.

Part II concludes with a chapter written by John Hamman and colleagues. Like Chen and Kang, Hamman and colleagues consider how the management of financial resources, particularly slack resources, affect the motivation of public sector employees. As other *Handbook* authors note, the public sector is subject to unique rules, laws, and restrictions that can make management and motivation more challenging. Hamman and colleagues offer a glimpse into how slack resources and unreserved fund balances among US county governments intersect with management strategies generally, then how both may impact employee motivation. In doing so, they demonstrate how powerful best practices and management decisions can be in shaping motivation.

Part III: Factors Affecting Recruitment, Selection, and Retention

Part III of the *Handbook* turns to an exploration of the many ways in which employee motivation intersects with organizational recruitment, selection, and retention processes. As decades of research demonstrate, public and nonprofit employment systems are significantly different than those found in the private sector. At a minimum, they tend to be much more rigid and structured. Moreover, in some cases, employee motivation may be enhanced or inhibited by an organization's recruitment, selection, and retention strategies. In fact, some public administration scholars encourage practitioners to design human resource management (HRM) systems in ways that are more likely to attract and motivate public and nonprofit employees. Yet, in other cases, an employee's personal preferences and expectations of their job and work may be a more important driver of motivation than HRM or administrative systems. Here, redesigning HRM practices may have little or no impact on employee motivation. The collection of chapters in this part highlight many of these complexities and tensions.

Leading the discussion is this part is a chapter prepared by Neil Boyd and Branda Nowell. As Boyd and Nowell suggest, public management scholars have focused almost exclusively on the importance of PSM as a core ingredient in producing a highly motivated public and nonprofit sector workforce. However, in our narrow efforts to better understand PSM, Boyd and Nowell suggest that the field has learned of the importance of many other, closely related concepts and theories—especially altruism, prosocial motivation, and a community-oriented sense of responsibility—that should inform how we think about employee motivation. They go on to encourage researchers to study and evaluate PSM within the milieu of a broader conceptual and theoretical landscape across related disciplines (i.e., primarily management and the social sciences) to better understand how to hire, train, and cultivate cultures of responsibility toward others.

Chapter 15, penned by Gene Brewer, Ed Kellough, and Hal Rainey, examines the importance of merit principles in public employment. The authors suggest that four decades of reforms—reforms intended to expand managerial discretion and enhance political accountability—have weakened the normative foundation of civil service systems, which requires that employees be hired, promoted, and retained based on their ability to perform a job rather than on their political connections or other non-job-related criteria. They go on to test this claim using data from the US Merit Systems Protection Board (MSPB). Their results suggest that an erosion in merit principles appears, in fact, to be occurring. They further suggest that we may be witnessing a decline in PSM as a consequence, and they call for reformers to exercise greater caution when tinkering with public personnel systems.

Next, Alex Henderson and Jessica Sowa directly take up the issue of job design as it relates to motivation. Some of the earliest studies on motivation outside of the field of public administration attempted to determine how jobs could be designed and structured to improve employee motivation and performance. Henderson and Sowa apply this approach, with a modern twist, to suggest that how jobs are designed serves as the foundation for how individuals evaluate, consider, and understand their work. Applying this perspective, they then consider which factors are most likely to impact employee job fit, motivation, and performance. They conclude their chapter by considering how (1) new challenges in the 21st century, including the role of technology and user experiences, (2) the necessity of collaboration within and across agencies, and (3) individual expectations for work experiences may impact public organizations and employees in the coming decades.

Chapter 17, like the previous chapter, considers the importance of job design and job design strategies in securing high levels of motivation from workers. In it, David Giauque and Rafaël Weissbrodt offer their own definition of job and work design, before presenting five distinct streams of research on the topic and then examining what this body of research tells us about the relationships between work characteristics and work outcomes. They then focus on six elements that can be used to understand the importance of job design for workers, including (1) the cultural and institutional context; (2) the organizational climate; (3) changes and reforms; (4) role ambiguity, political interference, and administrative constraints; (5) relational work; and (6) human resource management (HRM) in the public sector. The authors conclude by proposing areas for future research.

Chapters 18 and 19 consider the relationship between motivation and education. In Chapter 18, Stephen Holt outlines the theoretical assumptions about motivation behind the various policy interventions aimed at improving teacher performance. He then reviews the literature on the most common policies—pay-for-performance, budgetary and employment stakes, teacher selection practices, professional development, and mentoring—and links the evidence from these policies back to broad theories of motivation. Finally, he presents descriptive evidence from a national cohort of high school students that shows students who later become teachers have higher levels of public service motivation and family-related motivation and are less motivated by money than their peers.

In Chapter 19, Leonard Bright reiterates many of the themes Holt presents, particularly in his discussion of the importance of education as well as PSM as a feeder for careers into the public and nonprofit sectors. Bright's chapter differs from Holt's, however, in that he is primarily interested in graduate education as a tool for recruiting students into the public and nonprofit sectors. To this end, he offers a set of recommendations that can help guide the development of teaching pedagogy aimed at increasing graduate students' interest in government careers, especially students with high levels of PSM, and calls on scholars to be proactive in their efforts to overcome the stereotypes and weaknesses associated with public sector employment.

Part IV: Motivation and Employee Behavior

In Part IV of the *Handbook*, we turn finally to a discussion on the various ways that employee motivation and behavior intersect. This is, perhaps, the most thoroughly studied area of motivation research in public administration, with findings clearly demonstrating that employee motivation both shapes and is itself shaped by other important employee behaviors as well as by management initiatives.

In the opening chapter of this part, Ellen Rubin and Michael Kang explore how fairness, a core value of public administration and public personnel management, might influence employee motivation and performance. Organizational justice scholars, mainly in psychology, suggest fairness is tremendously important, but they offer two different explanations for the link between fairness and performance. The first perspective, the social exchange approach, argues that concepts like leader-member exchange, affect, and trust mediate the relationship between justice perceptions and employee motivation and performance. The second perspective, the relational approach, suggests fair treatment heightens identification with work groups, which in turn inspires cooperation among workers. Rubin and Kang apply these two dominant theoretical approaches to describe how organizational justice enhances motivation and performance and to argue that fairness, motivation, and performance are deeply intertwined concepts.

Chapter 21, written by Jessica Breaugh and Guillem Ripoll, addresses a similar set of themes. As the authors argue, public management scholars are increasingly looking for ways to conceptually disentangle PSM and prosocial motivation, both of which focus on individuals' altruistic motives and motivations. The authors develop a theoretical framework that is intended to explore whether PSM and prosocial motivation, as theoretical constructs, are similarly related to employees' ethical attitudes and behaviors. Next, they consider whether these same conclusions are likely to hold simultaneously in both the public and nonprofit sectors, before concluding with recommendations for future research.

In Chapter 22, Julie Langer and Mary Feeney argue that Organizational Identity Orientation (or OIO) can be useful in determining how organizational members come to understand their organization's primary motivations and values—an important factor in determining whether employees believe they fit well with their work environment and will then exert additional time, energy, and effort on its behalf. Langer and Feeney employ qualitative OIO research to generate a set of new questionnaire items capturing collectivistic, relational, and individualistic OIO. They then report the results of three studies testing the OIO measures: (1) two pilot studies to develop the measures, (2) a test of the measures in the National Cross Sector Organizational Studies Project (NCSOSP), and (3) a national online survey administered to a sample of local government managers. The authors conclude by discussing how OIO and their new measures can advance our understanding of identity and motivation in public organizations.

Turning to Chapter 23, Jesse Campbell suggests change-oriented organizational citizenship behavior (OCB) can help public organizations adapt to evolving environmental conditions, mitigate resource scarcity, assimilate promising new technologies, and combat the perception that public servants are indifferent to actual citizen needs. Campbell proceeds to note that public servants often lack incentives to pursue change and that the cultural, structural, and interpersonal dimensions of organizational experience can reduce the perceived appropriateness of, and opportunities for, change-oriented OCB. The author then argues that PSM, if applied carefully, can act as a countervailing force in organizational contexts that are otherwise hostile to change.

In Chapter 24, Rick Borst notes that a burgeoning body of scholarship in public administration indicates job stress and PSM are interrelated. These findings can be attributed, at least partly, to the application of Job Demands-Resources (JD-R) theory to public administration studies. JD-R theory was developed in the context of organizational psychology, but it can be applied across most work environments. Borst presents a summary of JD-R, with an emphasis on the various job stressors and motivators that impact workers and why. The chapter ends with a discussion of the relevance of JD-R theory to the field.

Chapter 25, titled 'Worked to a Crisp: 'Realistic' and 'Symbolic' Stressor Effects on Burnout,' raises themes similar to those presented by Borst, ultimately emphasizing how harmful stress can be to employee motivation. However, the chapter author, Adam Green, approaches the links between stress and motivation differently than Borst by applying Integrated Threat Theory (ITT) to distinguish between 'realistic' and 'symbolic' stressors. ITT posits that realistic and symbolic stress occur and contribute to burnout differently. Green begins his chapter by summarizing the core tenets of ITT, before examining potential stressors in the public sector context. He concludes with potential directions for future research.

Heather Getha-Taylor and Morgan Farnworth close out Part IV with a chapter that introduces the concept of trauma and explores its potential implications for PSM. The authors argue that trauma may influence PSM through multiple pathways (e.g., because traumatic events can draw individuals to public work and/or because public employees may, themselves, experience trauma through their interactions with citizens and clients). As such, they review existing conceptualizations of trauma, and then consider how trauma is likely to impact public employees and their PSM. Based on the authors' assessment, they provide a theoretical framework useful for informing future trauma-related scholarship.

Finally, the *Handbook* concludes with a summary chapter penned by Davis and Stazyk in the final part, discussing the future of research about motivation in public administration based on the knowledge generated by their colleagues and co-authors, to whom they owe an enormous debt of gratitude for their time and work on this *Handbook*.

ACKNOWLEDGEMENTS

The *Handbook* editors give special thanks to Heeun Kim and Josh McCray for their valuable assistance in preparing the final version of this volume.

REFERENCES

Perry, J.L., and Hondeghem, A. (2008). *Motivation in public management: The call of public service.* New York, NY: Oxford University Press.
Perry, J.L., and Wise, L. (1990). The motivational bases of public service. *Public Administration Review*, *50*, 367–373.

PART I

THEORY AND FOUNDATIONS

2. The political economy of bureaucratic motivation

Yongjin Ahn and William G. Resh

INTRODUCTION

In a fragmented and decentralized political system like the United States, power and autonomy are not based solely on technical expertise or constitutional/legal authority as in the world of Weber's bureaucracy. Indeed, even centralized and autocratic states depend on local and professional autonomy to govern effectively. As Norton Long puts it, 'the lifeblood of administration is power' (Long, 1949, p. 263). That is, bureaucrats are political actors whose power is dependent on how well they mobilize political support (Heclo, 1978; Kingdon, 1984; Moe, 1989; Carpenter, 2001). Thus, research must consider that civil servants are motivated to secure legitimacy of their core functions/activities. By that very nature, bureaucrats engage in politics. By the nature of delegation and the autonomy inherent in that delegation, civil servants decide on an increasingly frequent basis 'who gets what, when, and how'—the very essence of politics (Lasswell, 2018). However, the extent to which civil service institutions are treated theoretically or empirically as political institutions in and of themselves is lacking. Bureaucratic motivation is acknowledged as a 'function of a constellation of conditions or factors' (Golden, 2000, p. 154). But have political science or public administration, two disciplines where public bureaucracies are widely studied, adequately accommodated the extent to which political considerations motivate bureaucrats? We start with this problem.

This chapter consists of three sections. First, we describe how political science and public administration study the bureaucracy with a focus on the 'political control' of the bureaucracy. We give an overview of key theories and fundamental assumptions in establishing bureaucratic behavior/motivation in this literature. Second, we point out some controversial assumptions that undergird this scholarship and assess the validity of these critiques. Third, we evaluate the political economy approach of bureaucratic politics. We show how the literature has contributed to developing a scientific study of bureaucracy and provide examples and suggestions for complementing its weaknesses. We argue that a behavioral approach, albeit with its limitations, can complement the weaknesses of the political economic approach of studying bureaucratic motivations (and vice versa). But a more integrated approach is necessary.

THE POLITICAL ECONOMY OF BUREAUCRACY

In political science and public administration, there are largely two streams of research on bureaucracy—those interested in institutions and those interested in behavior (Meier and O'Toole, 2006). The former is commonly referred to as the 'political control' literature. It is also known as rational choice institutionalism (Zegart, 2010) or the political economy approach (hereafter we use political economy) to understanding public bureaucracies. This perspective stems from a normative view of top-down political accountability (e.g., Finer, 1941). As a result, the political economy approach to studying bureaucratic behavior is not actually an account of behavior within a bureaucracy, but is predominantly a story of how political principals control the bureaucratic agents (Moe, 1987). As a result, little attention is paid to incentives operating within organizations; rather they treat inner workings of bureaucracies as a black-box, unconditionally questioning the legitimacy of bureaucratic actions that are not direct reflections of principal preferences as 'agency loss' (Meier and O'Toole, 2006, p. 95).

Why are bureaucracies depicted this way in the political economy literature? Scholars are certainly not naive enough to believe that bureaucrats are submissive actors who lack strategic actions when confronted by political stimuli. It is also clear empirically that actors in the policy process are motivated by more than simply maximizing some sort of outcome; votes for politicians (Downs, 1957; Mayhew, 1974; Fiorina, 1981), budget (Niskanen, 1971) or career advancement (Downs, 1967) for bureaucrats, and efficiency of the executive branch for presidents (e.g., Moe and Wilson, 1994). Instead, bureaucrats and politicians operate with a portfolio of motivations that are stimulated by various incentives that often come in conflict with one another. Bureaucrats wish to avoid embarrassment (Kaufman, 1981); they are incentivized to build expertise (Gailmard and Patty, 2007); they value reputations (Carpenter, 2001; Carpenter and Krause, 2012) and professional norms (Friedrich, 1940; Wilson, 1989; Miller and Whitford, 2016); they are public service motivated (Perry and Wise, 1990; Dilulio, 1994) and heavily influenced by organizational identification (Simon, 1947; March and Simon, 1958; Akerlof and Kranton, 2005); as well as their desire to make an impact on policy (Downs, 1967).

Such diversity and ambiguity of individual motivations present a modeling problem because there is no simple measure that can reasonably be thought to capture a given utility maximization. What is especially troubling in modeling bureaucratic behavior is that they may not be as motivated by factors commonly found in the private sector, that is, profits, efficiency, and wages (Moe, 1984). By making explicit the assumptions about goals and motivations of actors—what is referred to as 'thick-rational models' (Green and Shapiro, 1996, p. 18)—rational choice theorists ease the modeling problem. That is, an analytical convenience is achieved by making strong (but in many cases reasonable) assumptions and by relying on the normative view of top-down democratic responsiveness.

Making sweeping assumptions about individual motivations is important in modeling the relationship between the bureaucracy and its political masters. After all, the political economy approach's main interest lies in institutional behavior, though it is ironically derived from assumptions at the micro-level. That is, their main unit of analysis is the perceived organizational or institutional output, but little knowledge or actual observation is produced about the individuals who comprise those institutions. Based on these assumptions, scholars began to adopt economic approaches such as principal–agent theory (Miller, 2005), transaction cost theory (Moe, 1984; Krause, 2010), and rational choice institutionalism (Zegart, 2010). Among these, principal–agent theory (hereafter PAT) served as a strong theory to claim that bureaucracies are under control of its political principals.

PAT was suitable in refuting the perceptions of an uncontrollable bureaucracy (e.g., Lowi, 1969; Redford, 1969) by viewing the bureaucracy-president/Congress relationship as a form of contract. It became widely used as a theoretical foundation for building theories of delegation that are compatible with the framers' view of legislative supremacy (Frederickson et al., 2015; Workman, Jones, and Jochim, 2010). As PAT became widely adopted to studies of bureaucratic politics, the emphasis was put on the principal's strategies to incentivize or sanction the bureaucracy in order to pursue its goals of reelection. Particularly, the congressional dominance school of thought (Weingast and Moran, 1983; McCubbins, Noll, and Weingast, 1987, 1989) put an overt focus on Congress's capacity to control the bureaucracy.

This school of thought applied PAT as its main methodology to demonstrate that Congress creates incentives to elicit bureaucrats' compliance, even in the absence of monitoring and punishment (McCubbins and Schwartz, 1984). Control mechanisms in this line of research focus on minimizing costs of information asymmetry and transaction costs. They focus on the trade-offs between controlling (or decreasing discretion) and granting bureaucratic flexibility when designing administrative procedures, that is, information gains and distributive losses. For instance, the amount of discretionary authority that Congress grants to the bureaucracy depends on the similarity of policy preferences, the level of political uncertainty, Congress's level of confidence in controlling the agenda, the level of informational asymmetry, and the level of congressional-executive conflict (Epstein and O'Halloran, 1994). These theories, perhaps too deterministically, suggest that agency discretion is dependent upon Congress's choice of delegation. Therefore, it is difficult to infer anything about bureaucratic motivation from these studies. At best, the behaviors of bureaucrats are inferred by understanding the intents of congressional committees and evidence is based almost entirely on counterfactuals.

MOTIVATION IN EXECUTIVE POLITICS

How are the motivations of presidents and their appointees, along with career bureaucrats, depicted in the political economy literature? As in legislative politics, there are several preconceived notions of the motivations of presidents. Compared to members of Congress, presidents think about national problems. The primary motivation of the chief executive does not lie in reelection, but is rather incentivized to create a coherent and centralized bureaucracy that can advance his policy agenda (Moe and Wilson, 1994). Behavioral assumptions about the president stem largely from a normative approach that presidents are interested primarily in solving national problems—those that Congress cannot solve due to collective action problems. Nonetheless, presidents are structurally constrained by congressional opposition, bureaucratic resistance, and institutional inertia. They also have knowledge problems; no systematic body of knowledge is available to presidents taking office, forcing them to rely on experience and popular belief systems. And they face time constraints, just as many other politicians, but are sensitive about their legacy (Howell and Moe, 2016). Therefore, the president's motivation with respect to controlling the bureaucracy is to prioritize 'responsive competence' over 'neutral competence' to achieve his policy goals (Moe, 1985, p. 239).

Despite the president's set of constraints, scholars began to propose a theory of a strong presidency (Moe, 1985), arguing that president has advantages over other political institutions (mainly Congress) in utilizing the bureaucracy to advance his policy agenda. Early work on the presidency focused primarily on the Reagan administration's various strategies to bring career bureaucrats to their knees. Subsequently, this line of research developed into what is referred to as the administrative presidency (Nathan, 1983). There are unilateral tools at the president's disposal such as executive orders, presidential proclamations, presidential bill signing statements, executive agreements, and national security directives, and contextual tools such as the power to reorganize the bureaucracy, appointment powers, and budgetary powers (Durant, 1992). Furthermore, the unitary executive theory moves the presidential power beyond constitutional boundaries to control the bureaucracy (Waterman, 2009). We can easily witness that concerns of democratic backsliding based on such unitary executive theory became a reality in the Trump administration (e.g., Moynihan, 2020). Also, presidents advance their policy agenda by imposing regulatory delay, that is, postponing policy implementation promulgated during the previous administration. For instance, Thrower (2018) finds that liberal agencies under the Obama administration were targeted for policy disruption under the Trump administration and that regulatory delays were more common among highly politicized agencies. That is, presidential motivation to engage in such 'policy disruption' is largely derived from ideological conflict with the current administration's policy goals.

How do bureaucrats then react to a president's administrative strategies? Motivations of bureaucrats with respect to the president's administrative strategies are found mostly in the appointee-careerist relationship literature. Since Hugh Heclo's (1977) *A Government of Strangers*, presidency scholars have separated the two types of officials by three issues: political ideology, time horizon, and loyalty (Brewer and Maranto, 2000, pp. 71–2). Historically, since the Eisenhower and Nixon administrations, clashes between conservative administrations and the liberal career bureaucracy emerged as a phenomenon of interest in presidential studies. Conflicts were particularly exacerbated during the Reagan administration. Maranto (1993) argued that the way Reagan managed the executive branch was twofold—borrowing from McGregor's (1960) management terminology, career bureaucrats were managed under Theory-X (assuming externally motivated employees), while political appointees were managed under Theory-Y (assuming internally motivated employees). Ever since, politicizing through appointment powers has been considered one of the most frequently used and effective strategies (e.g., Wood and Waterman, 1991, 1993) among various executive tools.

Particularly frequently examined in this line of research was the ideological divide between conservative appointees and liberal career bureaucrats. The motivations of conservative appointees gravitated towards controlling the career bureaucracy in fear that they would not faithfully carry out policies of their conservative presidents. On the other hand, careerists were motivated towards concerns that they would fall into a lethargic bureaucracy that would soullessly implement policies that contradicted their political ideology. That is, the motivational gap between these two groups was considered as concerns of bureaucratic drift for conservatives, and concerns of 'bureaucratic passivity' for liberals (Rourke, 1992).

However, a longitudinal study covering the Nixon (1970), Reagan (1986–87), and Bush (1991–92) administrations, all of which were conservative administrations in a divided government (except for a short period during the Reagan administration), demonstrated that party affiliations and political ideology of career executives were malleable over time (Aberbach and Rockman, 1995). This implies that the Civil Service Reform Act of 1978 gave political appointees flexibility to control their agencies by especially using Senior Executive Service (SES) appointments, and that there was motivational variation among presidents to match the ideological composition of their career bureaucrats.

Such variations and ambiguity in presidential goals are one of the (among many) factors that make 'a mockery of most efforts to apply principal–agent theory in the study of the administrative presidency' (Durant and Resh, 2010, p. 2). As such, more recently, scholars are reconsidering the previous PAT-oriented view regarding politicization and centralization strategies as control mechanisms (Lewis and Richardson, 2021). Nevertheless, early studies of the administrative presidency have strived to apply the president-bureaucrat relationship under the canonical PAT framework. Moe and Wilson (1994) suggested that rational choice theory has the capacity to bring in presidents in modeling executive politics. Based on the underlying assumption that presidents come to office with a distrust of the career bureaucracy, much of the initial work of administrative presidency tried to fit the president-bureaucrat relationship into key assumptions of canonical PAT; there is goal conflict and information asymmetry between the bureaucracy and the president, hence, presidents strive to dominate the bureaucracy.

Therefore, a similar critique of the political control of the bureaucracy literature can be applied to studies of the administrative presidency. Although there was much progress in this line of research of unpacking bureaucratic motivations and is relatively new to bureaucratic politics overall compared to legislative politics, much of the research struggles from the same weaknesses such as unitary-actor assumptions and simplified motivations of careerists/appointees/and presidents. However, the line of research on the political appointee-careerist relationship has been making steady progress in unpacking the black-box of federal agencies (Golden, 2000; O'Leary, 2010; Resh, 2015; Hollibaugh, Miles, and Newswander, 2020; Waterman and Ouyang, 2020), and more studies are starting to incorporate various motivations of presidents other than national interests (e.g., Kriner and Reeves, 2015). We elaborate on this in the following sections.

PROBLEMATIC ASSUMPTIONS

As mentioned briefly in the previous section, there are a number of problematic assumptions in the political economy approach. The approach of using PAT has its strength in achieving model parsimony by using a minimal number of variables to explain the bureaucracy-politics relationship. However, this comes at the cost of losing context and neglecting the social embeddedness of administrative phenomena. As a result, one major critique of this literature is the lack of explanatory power of how bureaucrats gain autonomy or discretion additional to their statutory authority. There is little accommodation made for bureaucrats' autonomic/endogenous actions in these models (but see Gailmard and Patty, 2012). Instead, a latent assumption seems to be that bureaucrats accept structural characteristics political principals create in pursuing their self-interests.

Take Terry Moe's seminal theory of structural politics, for example. Moe (1989) expounds on how powerful interest groups influence bureaucratic motivation not by telling exactly what to do, but by choosing and placing the right types of bureaucrats. He nicely characterizes the underlying motivations of each actor. Career bureaucrats want autonomy and seek to demonstrate their expertise in the long run; interest groups face political uncertainty and engage in political compromise, hence winning groups want to be politically insulated while losing groups desire for a structure that works against effective performance; politicians, as always, seek reelection and are sensitive to the needs of potential winning groups; and presidents are motivated to structure an effective bureaucracy in pursuing national interests. The theory is powerful and opened up a road for empirical testing in the realm of structural politics (Wood and Bohte, 2004; Selin, 2015; Carrigan, 2017). However, the problem with Moe's (1989) approach is that it leaves no room for endogenous changes within bureaucracies. It may be powerful in explaining cases of policy failure or ineffective bureaucracies, but would not do a great job in analyzing evolutions or policy innovations that happen frequently (e.g.,

Teodoro, 2011). Also, it is often the case where delegation occurs in existing agencies rather than agencies created (Carpenter, 2001, p. 358). This is in line with Zegart's (2010) critique that rational choice institutionalism focuses entirely on agency creation rather than evolution, leaving adaptation dynamics weakly explained. Besides, although Moe's (1989) model distinguishes between career bureaucrats and political appointees, it does not account for diverse preferences among bureaucrats and pays attention entirely to the gains and losses of their political principals. That is, the theory explains bureaucracies in the absence of self-sustaining processes and does not allow for implications of bureaucratic motivation other than carrying out their mandated roles.

Another major flaw of the political economic approach is its tendency to infer behaviors/motivations of individual bureaucrats based on observations at the institutional level, which constitutes an ecological fallacy. This happens when we don't have enough information for both levels of analysis, which is most often the case.

Therefore, we often conclude that an unresponsive bureaucracy is attributable to shirking bureaucrats; a politically insulated agency consists of bureaucrats with more discretion; bureaucrats are more responsive to powerful interest groups, and so on. The opposite case is also easily spotted, the atomistic fallacy, which is making incorrect inferences at the group level based on information on the individual level. An example would be Niskanen's (1971) famous budget-maximizing theory. The problem of merely aggregating up (inaccurate) individual preferences to make a theory at the institutional level would be problematic. Indeed, subsequent studies show that budget maximizing is not always the case. For instance, Golden's (2000) study argues that proposing more budget would imply a full-face challenge to the president and his appointees' policy agenda. That is, increasing regulation and social welfare programs, especially in a conservative administration, might not always fulfill federal employees' self-interests. In this case, it makes more sense that budget-cutting or budget-minimizing instead of -maximizing would better advance one's self-interests through career advancement and job security (also Bowling, Cho, and Wright, 2004; Arapis and Bowling, 2020).

Along with problems of not accounting for endogenous changes within agencies and ecological/atomistic fallacies, there are problematic assumptions related to applying PAT to the bureaucracy-politics relationship. Some elements of the canonical PAT are (1) agent impact, (2) information asymmetry, (3) goal conflict, (4) a unified principal with a first-mover advantage, (5) a principal who knows the agent's rationality by backward induction, and (6) ultimatum bargaining (Miller, 2005, pp. 205–6). Among those, scholars of bureaucracy focused mostly on adverse selection, moral hazard, and goal conflict. However, Waterman and Meier (1998) argue that the reason the political control literature is obsessed with identifying control mechanisms is that it is the most problematic situation, that is, when the agent has more information than the principal in a high conflict situation. However, they argue that this is only one special case among various possible relationships. For instance, there might be a case where the principal has more information than the agent under high goal conflict situation, that is, patronage system; when both have enough information under goal conflict, that is, advocacy coalition; when both have enough information under goal consensus, that is, policy subsystems (Waterman and Meier, 1998, p. 188). Therefore, when considering information and goal conflict as a variable instead of a constant, there is room for accommodating a much more complex and dynamic model of bureaucratic control. A rich literature in organizational studies provides both theoretical and empirical evidence that these conditions provide contextual elements that can lead to varying behaviors, particularly based on the level of professionalism, mission, and task-orientation.

Subsequent studies that use PAT as their main framework became aware of its critiques (e.g., Moe, 1984) and considered relaxing the assumptions and modifying the theory from a different perspective. For instance, the transactional authority perspective views the principal–agent relationship not from a principal authority perspective, but from a dynamic cooperative relationship based on reciprocity and mutual agreement (Carpenter and Krause, 2015). Rather than focusing on the principal's control problem, a transactional authority framework considers both informal control mechanisms (e.g., peer pressure, organizational socialization, and trust) and formal mechanisms (e.g., budgets, rules and procedures, legislation, and appointments). Accounting for mutuality and reciprocity between the legislature and the bureaucracy is persuasive for several reasons. First, considering that public bureaucracies lack explicit incentive mechanisms (e.g., pecuniary rewards), the role of implicit incentives increases in inducing intrinsic motivation such as internal/external reputation (Carpenter, 2001) and career advancement opportunities (Teodoro, 2011). Second, they consider the legislative-bureaucratic relationship as a continuous and repeated interaction, while many delegation studies treat the relationship as a non-cooperative one-shot game. Treating the relationship as a dynamic rather than a static model does a better job reflecting the reality of mutual bargaining and exchange over multiple periods. Third, Carpenter and Krause's (2015) emphasis that bureaucratic politics literature should extend from institutional/constitutional theories to incorporating interdisciplinary studies (e.g., organizational theory and social psychology) is a valid point. Thus, the transactional authority theory as a modified version of PAT is compatible with behavioral theories of organizations, yet under-researched in bureaucratic politics.

When applied to presidential studies, Pfiffner (1987) shows that presidents and their appointees can get along well with career bureaucrats, that is, the 'cycle of accommodation thesis.' He argues that unlike the widely held belief that presidents come into office with distrust and fear of sabotage from the career bureaucracy, both appointees and careerists learn how to work with each other. By examining a longitudinal survey of presidential appointees between 1964 and 1984, the study confirms that most career bureaucrats are competent and responsive to their president (Pfiffner, 1987, p. 61). Such a cooperative relationship would be hard to explain under the assumptions of goal conflict and information asymmetry, that is, canonical PAT assumptions.

Finally, another weakness of the political economy approach that applies to early research is the lack of empirical evidence supporting the theory. This seems perfectly natural since most theories are built on deductive reasoning, but they also tend to overly rely on case studies, mostly a handful of regulatory agencies (Huber and Shipan, 2000). Moe (1989) shows how his theory applies to three agencies: the Consumer Product Safety Commission (CPSC), the Occupational Safety and Health Administration (OSHA), and the Environmental Protection Administration (EPA).

In an effort to generalize their theory of procedural politics, McNollgast also focused only on several agencies such as the Federal Trade Commission (Weingast and Moran, 1983), EPA (McCubbins, Noll, and Weingast, 1989), and the Federal Communications Commission (McCubbins, Noll, and Weingast, 1987). Take McCubbins and Schwartz's (1984) famous oversight theory as another example. The theory was built on a persuasive argument that oversight functions of Congress properly work through two different forms—police-patrol (direct sanctioning) and fire-alarms (indirect mechanism through interest groups)—however, without any form of evidence. These examples show how rational choice theorists attempted to formulate universal propositions based on scant empirical evidence (Zegart, 2010, p. 212).

A CRITICAL ASSESSMENT

So far, we have pointed out as weaknesses of the political economy approach (1) the lack of attention to autonomous action within agencies, (2) ecological/atomistic fallacies, (3) problematic assumptions when applying PAT to the bureaucracy-politics relationship, and (4) the lack of empirical evidence in building theory. These are all valid critiques of the literature. Strong assumptions of individual bureaucrats resulted in simplistic models of bureaucratic motivation. By treating the inner workings of organizations as black-boxes and dummying out many variables that get in the way of a principal's pursuit of self-interests, the political economic approach led to a lack of knowledge of what actually happens inside bureaucracies. Also, by neglecting psychological foundations, rational choice theorists downplayed the role of socialization critical in forming bureaucrats' values and workplace attitudes (e.g., Lipsky, 1980; Kaufman, 2006).

However, it would be unfair to overlook the political economy's contributions to bureaucratic politics. There are certainly strengths of political economic models that assume rationality and clearly define the actors' motivations and goals. When we acknowledge the trade-off between model parsimony and empirical realism, theories derived from political economic approaches can be excused for their oversimplification of the real world. In this way, it is possible to produce generalizable knowledge of bureaucratic-politics relationships. Multiple examples can be found of how the deductive approach serves as a foundation for following studies to inductively accumulate empirical evidence. In the previous section, we critiqued on how deductively driven theories lack empirical evidence. However, it is also true that such theories serve as testing grounds and foundations for theory advancement. For instance, Moe's (1989) structural politics theory has been widely tested among scholars (Wood and Bohte, 2004; Selin, 2015; Carrigan, 2017). Similarly, Balla (1998) tested McNollgast's theory of procedural politics on the Health Care Financing Administration to show that the notice-and-comment procedure is not an effective tool for controlling agencies. Likewise, Shipan (2004) developed a spatial model of agency policymaking and tested it on the Food and Drug Administration to find that preferences of Congress members do not influence agency action. Although their way of presenting the results might be problematic (e.g., arguing the lack of congressional influence on agencies based on null results) and their results contradict McNollgast's theory, it is still encouraging to see how subsequent studies can build and refine previous theories. Indeed, mixed results can be evidence of theory development.

In a similar vein, more studies are reinforcing empirical evidence on top of their deductive theory. Based on a game-theoretical model, Lavertu and Moynihan (2012) developed a statistical model that explains the role of leadership in performance management systems. They argue for an approach that links formal theorizing and empirical analyses. Particularly, the National Science Foundation's Empirical Implications of Theoretical Models initiative encourages political science to accumulate empirical knowledge.

Another encouraging aspect of accumulating empirical evidence is found in presidential studies. Notably, an increasing amount of studies are starting to uncover the mechanisms of which presidential strategies enhance or deteriorate bureaucratic effectiveness. For instance, does more politicization and centralization increase responsiveness, as in the world of the canonical PAT? Recent research suggests it might not always be the case. Appointments can be counterproductive under extreme ideological conflict and policy preference mismatches (Golden, 2000; Durant and Resh, 2010). Presidents, being conscious of other constraints (e.g., interest groups and Congress), occasionally decide to deliberately appoint those who are ideologically distant from themselves (Bertelli and Feldmann, 2007). They also strategically place different types of appointees according to the agency's characteristics (Hollibaugh, Horton, and Lewis, 2014; Waterman and Ouyang, 2020) and use recess appointments to prioritize loyalty and responsiveness over competence (Miller, 2015). These imply that we should treat presidential appointments as a political resource, which diverts from the traditional view of regarding appointments as a control mechanism. Importantly, an appointee's relative professional orientation, public service experience, and 'the information and expertise they acquire from actual job experience' can also be important resources that deserve a more granular empirical analysis than PAT studies typically provide (Krause and O'Connell, 2016, p. 914).

More recently, there is increasing efforts to further examine micro-level foundations behind appointee-careerist relationships. In line with studies that determine that bureaucrats do not always behave as in the world of rational choice theory, Resh (2015) finds that trust and organizational learning mechanisms are critical elements for a president and his appointees to manage agencies successfully. Uncovering psychological mechanisms such as dyadic trust (trust between appointees and managers) and stratified trust (trust between appointees and executive careerists) bring light to the black-box of what actually happens within bureaucracies. Studies that attempt to measure actual micro-level perceptions across multiple agencies are scant, but increasing with more administrative data sets (Fernandez et al., 2015) becoming widely available and applying psychological theories to administrative settings (Grimmelikhuijsen et al., 2017). We come back to this point.

With respect to the downsides of applying PAT, subsequent studies have tried to find a better approach that can complement its previous flaws. For instance, Brehm and Gates (1999) point out that the political economy approach leaves many unanswered questions such as what and how bureaucrats maximize, what type of sanctions or rewards are effective in a subordinate-supervisor relationship, and how professionalism plays out. To get a better understanding of bureaucratic behavior, they bridge the political economy approach with organizational theory to find that predispositions of subordinates are much more influential on performance than are supervisors' sanctions. While previous studies that apply the canonical PAT focus mostly on the agent's moral hazard, Brehm and Gates's (1999) study reversed the angle by showing that adverse selection matters.

Likewise, Golden (2000) shows that the appointee-careerist relationship cannot be simply defined under a PAT framework and finds that the widely accepted loyalty-competence trade-off in the public administration literature does not always hold when the relationship is based on trust and respect. She focuses particularly on the various tools that President Reagan employed during his term—strategic appointments, centralization strategies such as empowering the Office of Management and Budget (OMB) and Office of Information and Regulatory Affairs (OIRA), micromanagement techniques such as reorganization and personnel management (e.g., jigsaw management)—to find that the Reagan administration used largely two types of strategies to change the motivation and behaviors of career bureaucrats. First, jigsaw management, a strategy to alienate career bureaucrats from the decision-making process, made it difficult for careerists to resist their political principals. Under jigsaw management, 'careerists become unable to use their expertise, autonomy, line responsibility, institutional memory, and program knowledge to resist presidential agendas' (p. 79). Second, centralization (e.g., the OMB threatening agencies with budget cuts), politicization (e.g., inserting appointees, empowering the secretary's office), and threats of reduction in force (RIF) changed career bureaucrats' utility function in a way that benefited more from cooperating rather than resisting. However, these strategies did not uniformly apply to all agencies. Still, the consequences varied depending on agency factors such as service-oriented culture and professionalism, ideological composition, agency history (collective memory), cohesiveness about policy among members within the agency, and esprit de corps.

Additionally, Dilulio (1994) presents the concept of principled agents that transcend the canonical PAT. Critiques on how previous studies neglected the principal–agent problems 'within' agencies—how supervisors elicit cooperation from their subordinates (agents) in promoting organizational mission/goals. Following James Q. Wilson's (1989), Philip Selznick's (1966), and Herbert Kaufman's (2006) emphasis on leadership-organizational culture, he examined the leader's role in cultivating social/moral/psychological rewards for bureaucrats in the Federal Bureau of Prisons. Dilulio's findings shed light on how self-interested subordinates cooperate in the absence of pecuniary incentives. He also critiques rational choice theorists who neglect social sentiments and moral motivations as 'half-baked Barnadians' in that they can only explain shirking and subverting behaviors. In line with the studies of Brehm and Gates (1999) and Carpenter (2001), his findings show that effective leadership enables members to 'redefine their self-interest in terms of the preferences of leaders they respect, the well-being of co-workers they care about, and the survival and reputation of organizations they labor for' (Dilulio, 1994, p. 316).

Similarly, Miller and Whitford's (2016) work reversed the lens by focusing on the principal's moral hazard, which is also a twist from the previous literature's application of PAT. Under their modified PAT model, bureaucrats play a more proactive role by serving as a trustee. A trustee differs from an agent in the canonical PAT in that she is free from the principal's pressure in decision-making and granted authority that credibly constrains the principal. On the other hand, the trustee is constrained by her professional norms (e.g., reputation and peer evaluation) as well as rules and procedures. By binding both parties to a credible commitment, Miller and Whitford's (2016) model suggests that a bureaucracy as a trustee can guarantee long-term social efficiency. The principals' and agents' motivations in such a trustee model are much more flexible and realistic compared to the canonical PAT. As Knott and Miller (2008, p. 409) put it, 'the resilience of the American political system is based not on congressional dominance or the administrative presidency but on a complex system of Madisonian checks and balances, which collectively make public agencies subordinate to the laws, not dependent on lawmakers.' Such extensions and adaptations in the political economy literature provide promising directions for bureaucratic politics research.

Indeed, a transactional authority perspective (Carpenter and Krause, 2015) builds on Moe's (2005) argument that cooperation and power are 'two sides of the same coin,' accounting for mutual bargaining and exchange over multiple periods. They rightly point out that bureaucratic politics literature should embrace theories from organizational theory and social psychology to explain the informal components of the contract.

FUTURE AGENDA

As we noted earlier, public administration research has diverged into two streams—public management on the one hand, and bureaucratic politics (or the political economy approach of bureaucracy) on the other (Meier and O'Toole, 2006; Frederickson et al., 2015; Jilke et al., 2019). The former focuses on organizational behavior and general management in developing theories of public organizations, while the latter develops theories based on economic approaches of comprehensive rationality (e.g., PAT). While the political economic approach has been criticized for its lack of empirical evidence at the individual level, the public management approach has also been criticized for neglecting big questions related to state capacity and government legitimacy (Milward et al., 2016; Moynihan, 2018; Resh, 2019). More recently, the emergence of behavioral public administration (BPA) has raised concerns that public administration research is becoming excessively method-driven towards using experiments rather than being question/theory-driven, and that the field is becoming overly narrow in using perspectives other than a limited range of cognitive psychological theories and their applications (Bhanot and Linos, 2020; Hassan and Wright, 2020). More importantly, the behavioral approach is limited in that institutional embeddedness is extremely difficult to manipulate in an experimental context (Bertelli and Riccucci, 2020).

Despite its critiques, we see the potential of BPA to compensate for the weaknesses of the political economic approach. Public administration scholars have done a good job developing concepts/theories that bridge bureaucratic politics and public management using a behavioral approach, for example, administrative burden, street-level bureaucracy, and guerrilla government. Additionally, examining how personality traits and emotions influence bureaucratic behavior can imbue more sophistication to comprehensive rationality in modeling bureaucratic motivation (Nørgaard, 2018). However, we argue that this is valuable to the extent that politics and institutional embeddedness are appropriately considered, regardless of whether the method employed is experimental or not. We suggest three recent articles that serve the two ends of using a behavioral approach without sacrificing political/institutional context. The studies use various methods including conjoint survey experiments via innovative sampling approaches (Hollibaugh, Miles, and Newswander, 2020), FOIA requests of political appointees' resumes to construct a continuous measure of loyalty-competence (Waterman and Ouyang, 2020), and machine learning to measure organizational reputation (Anastasopoulos and Whitford, 2019). We examine how these studies contribute to the overall bureaucratic politics literature.

To begin with, Hollibaugh, Miles, and Newswander (2020), using a behavioral approach, build on the concept of guerrilla government (O'Leary, 2010) and unpack the mechanisms behind public employees' dissent. They use the federal salary database to construct their sampling frame and employ a conjoint survey experiment to see how different factors of guerrilla tactics interact with each other. Findings show that several factors drive guerrilla behavior. Those factors include an individual code of ethics, a view of policy relevance, the probability of facing retribution, the likelihood of the public being harmed by the proposed policy (policy scope), the rank of the person making the request, and the severity of retribution for dissent. They find that among these factors, the strongest predictor of guerrilla tactics is the individual's code of ethics, followed by the view of policy relevance. On the other hand, they find little evidence of the effect of punishment or the type of retribution. Overall, the results provide empirical evidence to support the fundamental assumptions of guerrilla government;

traditional views of public administration such as the politics-administration dichotomy are an inaccurate depiction of the bureaucracy.

Waterman and Ouyang's (2020) research asks 'to what extent (as the PAT suggests) do presidents prefer loyalty over competence?' Their problem of awareness comes from the fact that few studies focus on lower-level presidential appointments that do not require Senate confirmation, or what Lewis and Waterman (2013) refer to as 'invisible presidential appointments.' Also, previous studies employ dichotomous measures of loyalty and competence to simply see whether a trade-off exists, but do not reveal much about the extent. Based on such gaps in the literature, they distinguish between four types of presidential appointments—Senate confirmation appointments (PAS), Senior Executive Service (SES), Schedule C, and other presidential appointments (PA)—to examine how a president's political/institutional constraints affect choosing different types of appointments as an attempt to strategically balance between loyalty and competence. To construct a continuous measure of loyalty and competence (rather than a dichotomous variable as in most previous studies), they examined the resumes of appointees in the Bush and Obama administrations via FOIA requests. By estimating the level of loyalty and competence and displaying the distributions of each type of appointment, they find that trade-offs exist, but are contingent on the types of appointment and type of administration. For instance, constitutional constraints in PAS appointments incentivized presidents to reward competence over loyalty, while PA and Schedule Cs were more likely to be loyal compared to SES appointees. By developing a continuous measure of loyalty and competence, they approximate reality compared to simply dichotomizing and see the extent and scope conditions of which presidents are willing to make trade-offs.

Also, recent works of Jason Anastasopoulos are examples of how machine learning (ML) is becoming a method used to bridge behavioral studies with bureaucratic politics. For example, Anastasopoulos and Whitford (2018) used supervised ML, a technique that uses a response variable that can supervise prediction or inference (James et al., 2013, p. 26). They examined federal agencies' moral reputation, one among Carpenter and Krause's (2012) four types of organizational reputation. They analyzed tweets from federal agencies to identify how agencies communicate reputational information to the public. First, they identified textual content in Twitter and coded tweets (the unit of analysis) into the four types of reputation. Second, among the collected tweets, they randomly sampled 200 tweets and tasked research assistants and MTurkers with coding them into a reputational category. Based on their coding scheme, they built an ML classifier with the training data set (70 percent of the data). They then applied the trained model to the remaining tweets (i.e., testing data set) to predict whether a tweet contained contents related to moral reputation. Ultimately, they find the percentage of each agency's use of moral reputation tweets. One important point we see from this research is that despite the limitations (e.g., concerns related to the data and coding quality in building a classifier), a promising feature of ML is that it can reduce a substantial amount of labor in conducting textual analyses. This would be particularly intriguing to students of bureaucratic politics who spend a large amount of time constructing original data sets by extracting information from various sources of government reports.

CONCLUSION

The purpose of this chapter is to make a critical review of how bureaucratic behavior/motivation is modeled in political economic research. We particularly focused on the principal–agent theory since it is arguably the most popular framework applied in this area. We have pointed out problematic assumptions as well as the potential to refine and advance theories of bureaucratic politics. We have also noted the problem of treating political institutions as a unitary actor and the threats of ecological/atomistic fallacies. Despite the criticisms, it is hard to deny that political economic studies have massively contributed to the scientific study of bureaucracy. Formal modeling and deductive theory building have established foundations for inductive theory testing. Also, models of rational choice theories have the potential to incorporate behaviorism and bounded rationality. We show how this can be done by introducing several recent studies that strive to examine the micro-foundations of bureaucratic behavior/motivations within the context of bureaucratic politics.

Nevertheless, we still know little about policy processes within agencies and what happens inside the heads of bureaucrats. As Herbert Kaufman (2001, p. 26) puts it, 'public servants are a fractionated mélange of heterogeneous groups, not a disciplined, coherent, coordinated body of like-minded members.' In order to account for such heterogeneity, more theory refinement using an interdisciplinary approach (e.g., incorporating social psychology and organizational behavior) along with rigorous empirical testing is required to narrow the current gap in bureaucratic politics.

REFERENCES

Aberbach, J.D., and Rockman, B.A. (1995). The political views of US senior federal executives, 1970–1992. *The Journal of Politics, 57*, 838–852.

Akerlof, G.A., and Kranton, R.E. (2005). Identity and the economics of organizations. *Journal of Economic Perspectives, 19*, 9–32.

Anastasopoulos, L.J., and Whitford, A.B. (2019). Machine learning for public administration research, with application to organizational reputation. *Journal of Public Administration Research and Theory, 29*, 491–510.

Arapis, T., and Bowling, C. (2020). From maximizing to minimizing: A national study of state bureaucrats and their budget preferences. *Journal of Public Administration Research and Theory, 30*, 144–160.

Balla, S.J. (1998). Administrative procedures and political control of the bureaucracy. *American Political Science Review, 92*, 663–673.

Bertelli, A., and Feldmann, S.E. (2007). Strategic appointments. *Journal of Public Administration Research and Theory, 17*, 19–38.

Bertelli, A.M., and Riccucci, N.M. (2020). What is behavioral public administration good for? *Public Administration Review*, first published online on August 8, 2020 at doi: https://doi.org/10.1111/puar.13283.

Bhanot, S.P., and Linos, E. (2020). Behavioral public administration: Past, present, and future. *Public Administration Review, 80*, 168–171.

Bowling, C.J., Cho, C.L., and Wright, D.S. (2004). Establishing a continuum from minimizing to maximizing bureaucrats: State agency head preferences for governmental expansion—a typology of administrator growth postures, 1964–98. *Public Administration Review, 64*, 489–499.

Brehm, J.O., and Gates, S. (1999). *Working, shirking, and sabotage: Bureaucratic response to a democratic public*. Ann Arbor, MI: University of Michigan Press.

Brewer, G.A., and Maranto, R.A. (2000). Comparing the roles of political appointees and career executives in the US federal executive branch. *The American Review of Public Administration*, *30*, 69–86.

Carpenter, D. (2001). *The forging of bureaucratic autonomy: Reputations, networks, and policy innovation in executive agencies, 1862–1928*. Princeton, NJ: Princeton University Press.

Carpenter, D.P., and Krause, G.A. (2012). Reputation and public administration. *Public Administration Review*, *72*, 26–32.

Carpenter, D., and Krause, G.A. (2015). Transactional authority and bureaucratic politics. *Journal of Public Administration Research and Theory*, *25*, 5–25.

Carrigan, C. (2017). *Structured to fail? Regulatory performance under competing mandates*. New York, NY: Cambridge University Press.

Downs, A. (1957). *An economic theory of democracy*. New York, NY: Harper and Row.

Downs A. (1967). *Inside bureaucracy*. Boston: Little, Brown, and Company.

Dilulio Jr, J.D. (1994). Principled agents: The cultural bases of behavior in a federal government bureaucracy. *Journal of Public Administration Research and Theory*, *4*, 277–318.

Durant, R.F. (1992). *The administrative presidency revisited: Public lands, the BLM, and the Reagan revolution*. Albany, NY: State University of New York Press.

Durant, R.F., and Resh, W.G. (2010). 'Presidentializing' the bureaucracy. In Robert F. Durant (ed.), *The Oxford handbook of American bureaucracy*. New York, NY: Oxford University Press, pp. 545–568.

Epstein, D., and O'Halloran, S. (1994). Administrative procedures, information, and agency discretion. *American Journal of Political Science*, *38*, 697–722.

Fernandez, S., Resh, W.G., Moldogaziev, T., and Oberfield, Z.W. (2015). Assessing the past and promise of the Federal Employee Viewpoint Survey for public management research: A research synthesis. *Public Administration Review*, *75*, 382–394.

Finer, Herman. (1941). Administrative responsibility in democratic government. *Public Administration Review*, *1*, 335–350.

Fiorina, Morris. (1981). Congressional control of the bureaucracy: A mismatch of incentives and capabilities. In Lawrence Dodd and Bruce Oppenheimer (eds), *Congress reconsidered*. Washington, DC: Congressional Quarterly, pp. 332–348.

Frederickson, H.G., Smith, K.B., Larimer, C.W., and Licari, M.J. (2015). *The public administration theory primer* (3rd edn). Boulder, CO: Westview Press.

Friedrich, Carl J. (1940). Public policy and the nature of administrative responsibility. *Public Policy*, *1*, 3–24.

Gailmard, Sean, and Patty, John. (2007). Slackers and zealots: Civil service, policy discretion, and bureaucratic expertise. *American Journal of Political Science*, *51*, 873–889.

Gailmard, Sean, and Patty, John. (2012). *Learning while governing: Expertise and accountability in the executive branch*. Chicago, IL: University of Chicago Press.

Golden, M.M. (2000). *What motivates bureaucrats? Politics and administration during the Reagan years*. New York, NY: Columbia University Press.

Green, D., and Shapiro, I. (1996). *Pathologies of rational choice theory: A critique of applications in political science*. New Haven, CT: Yale University Press.

Grimmelikhuijsen, S., Jilke, S., Olsen, A.L., and Tummers, L. (2017). Behavioral public administration: Combining insights from public administration and psychology. *Public Administration Review*, *77*, 45–56.

Hassan, S., and Wright, B.E. (2020). The behavioral public administration movement: A critical reflection. *Public Administration Review*, *80*, 163–167.

Heclo, H. (1977). *A government of strangers*. Washington, DC: Brookings Institution.

Heclo, H. (1978). Issue networks and the executive establishment. In A. King (ed.), *The new American political system*. Washington, DC: American Enterprise Institute, pp. 262–287.

Hollibaugh Jr, G.E., Horton, G., and Lewis, D.E. (2014). Presidents and patronage. *American Journal of Political Science*, *58*, 1024–1042.

Hollibaugh Jr, G.E., Miles, M.R., and Newswander, C.B. (2020). Why public employees rebel: Guerrilla government in the public sector. *Public Administration Review*, *80*, 64–74.

Howell, W., and Moe, T. (2016). *Relic: How our constitution undermines effective government, and why we need a more powerful presidency*. New York, NY: Basic Books.

Huber, J.D., and Shipan, C.R. (2000). The costs of control: Legislators, agencies, and transaction costs. *Legislative Studies Quarterly, 25*, 25–52.
James, G., Witten, D., Hastie, T., and Tibshirani, R. (2013). *An introduction to statistical learning*. New York, NY: Springer.
Jilke, S., Olsen, A.L., Resh, W., and Siddiki, S. (2019). Microbrook, mesobrook, macrobrook. *Perspectives on Public Management and Governance, 2*, 245–253.
Kaufman, H. (1981). Fear of bureaucracy: A raging pandemic. *Public Administration Review, 41*, 1–9.
Kaufman, H. (2006). *The forest ranger: A study in administrative behavior*. Washington, DC: Resources for the Future.
Kaufman, H. (2001). Major players: Bureaucracies in American government. *Public Administration Review, 61*, 18–42.
Kingdon, J.W. (1984). *Agendas, alternatives, and public policies*. Boston: Little, Brown.
Knott, J.H., and Miller, G.J. (2008). When ambition checks ambition: Bureaucratic trustees and the separation of powers. *The American Review of Public Administration, 38*, 387–411.
Krause, G.A. (2010). Legislative delegation of authority to bureaucratic agencies. In Robert F. Durant (ed.), *The Oxford handbook of American bureaucracy*. New York, NY: Oxford University Press, pp. 521–544.
Krause, G.A., and O'Connell, A.J. (2016). Experiential learning and presidential management of the US federal bureaucracy: Logic and evidence from agency leadership appointments. *American Journal of Political Science, 60*, 914–931.
Kriner, D.L., and Reeves, A. (2015). *The particularistic president: Executive branch politics and political inequality*. Cambridge, MA: Cambridge University Press.
Lasswell, Harold D. (2018). *Politics: Who gets what, when, how*. Plano, TX: Pickle Partners Publishing.
Lavertu, S., and Moynihan, D.P. (2012). The empirical implications of theoretical models: A description of the method and an application to the study of performance management implementation. *Journal of Public Administration Research and Theory, 23*, 333–360.
Lewis, D.E., and Richardson, M.D. (2021). The very best people: President Trump and the management of executive personnel. *Presidential Studies Quarterly, 51*, 51–70.
Lewis, David E., and Richard W. Waterman. (2013). The invisible presidential appointments: An Eexamination of appointments to the Department of Labor, 2001–11. *Presidential Studies Quarterly, 43*, 35–57.
Lipsky, M. (1980). *Street-level bureaucracy: Dilemmas of the individual in public services*. New York, NY: Russell Sage Foundation.
Long, N.E. (1949). Power and administration. *Public Administration Review, 9*, 257–264.
Lowi, T.J. (1969). *The end of liberalism; ideology, policy, and the crisis of public authority*. New York, NY: Norton.
Maranto, R. (1993). Still clashing after all these years: Ideological conflict in the Reagan executive. *American Journal of Political Science, 37*, 681–698.
March, J., and Simon, H. (1958). *Organizations*. New York, NY: Wiley.
Mayhew, D.R. (1974). *Congress: The electoral connection*. New Haven, CT: Yale University Press.
McCubbins, M.D., and Schwartz, T. (1984). Congressional oversight overlooked: Police patrols versus fire alarms. *American Journal of Political Science, 28*, 165–179.
McCubbins, M.D., Noll, R.G., and Weingast, B.R. (1987). Administrative procedures as instruments of political control. *Journal of Law, Economics, and Organization, 3*, 243–277.
McCubbins, M.D., Noll, R.G., and Weingast, B.R. (1989). Structure and process, politics and policy: Administrative arrangements and the political control of agencies. *Virginia Law Review, 75*, 431–482.
McGregor, D. (1960). *The human side of enterprise*. New York, NY: McGraw-Hill.
Meier, K.J., and O'Toole Jr, L.J. (2006). *Bureaucracy in a democratic state: A governance perspective*. Baltimore, MD: Johns Hopkins University Press.
Miller, G.J. (2005). The political evolution of principal–agent models. *Annual Review of Political Science, 8*, 203–225.
Miller, G.J., and Whitford, A.B. (2016). *Above politics*. New York, NY: Cambridge University Press.
Miller, S.M. (2015). The relationship between short-term political appointments and bureaucratic performance: The case of recess appointments in the United States. *Journal of Public Administration Research and Theory, 25*, 777–796.

Milward, B., Jensen, L., Roberts, A., Dussauge-Laguna, M.I., Junjan, V., Torenvlied, R., and Durant, R. (2016). Is public management neglecting the state? *Governance*, *29*, 311–334.

Moe, T.M. (1984). The new economics of organization. *American Journal of Political Science*, *28*, 739–777.

Moe, T.M. (1985). The politicized presidency. In John E. Chubb and Paul E. Peterson (eds), *The new direction in American politics*. Washington, DC: Brookings Institution, pp. 235–271.

Moe, T.M. (1987). An assessment of the positive theory of 'congressional dominance'. *Legislative Studies Quarterly*, *12*, 475–520.

Moe, Terry. (1989). The politics of bureaucratic structure. In John E. Chubb and Paul E. Peterson (eds), *Can the government govern?*, Washington, DC: Brookings Institution Press, pp. 267–329.

Moe, T.M. (2005). Power and political institutions. *Perspectives on Politics*, *3*(2), 215–233.

Moe, T M., and Wilson, S.A. (1994). Presidents and the politics of structure. *Law and Contemporary Problems*, *57*, 1–44.

Moynihan, D.P. (2018). A great schism approaching? Towards a micro and macro public administration. *Journal of Behavioral Public Administration*, *1*, first published online on February 22, 2018 at https://doi.org/10.30636/jbpa.11.15.

Moynihan, Donald P. (2020). Populism and the deep state: The attack on public service under Trump, first published online on May 21, 2020 at SSRN: https://ssrn.com/abstract=3607309 or http://dx.doi.org/10.2139/ssrn.3607309.

Nathan, R.P. (1983). *The administrative presidency*. New York, NY: John Wiley and Sons.

Niskanen, W.A. (1971). *Bureaucracy and representative government*. Piscataway, NJ: Transaction Publishers.

Nørgaard, A.S. (2018). Human behavior inside and outside bureaucracy: Lessons from psychology. *Journal of Behavioral Public Administration*, *1*, first published online on February 26, 2018 at https://doi.org/10.30636/jbpa.11.13.

O'Leary, R. (2010). Guerrilla employees: Should managers nurture, tolerate, or terminate them? *Public Administration Review*, *70*, 8–19.

Perry, J.L., and Wise, L.R. (1990). The motivational bases of public service. *Public Administration Review*, *50*, 367–373.

Pfiffner, J.P. (1987). Political appointees and career executives: The democracy-bureaucracy nexus in the third century. *Public Administration Review*, *47*(1), 57–65. https://doi.org/10.2307/975472.

Redford, E.S. (1969). *Democracy in the administrative state*. New York, NY: Oxford University Press.

Resh, W.G. (2015). *Rethinking the administrative presidency: Trust, intellectual capital, and appointee-careerist relations in the George W. Bush administration*. Baltimore, MD: Johns Hopkins University Press.

Resh, W.G. (2019). The disarticulation of the administrative state (and public administration). *Administration and Society*, *51*, 347–370.

Rourke, Francis E. (1992). Responsiveness and neutral competence in American bureaucracy. *Public Administration Review*, *52*, 539–546.

Selin, J.L. (2015). What makes an agency independent? *American Journal of Political Science*, *59*, 971–987.

Selznick, P. (1966). *TVA and the grass roots; a study in the sociology of formal organization*. New York, NY: Harper and Row.

Simon, H.A. (1947). *Administrative behavior—a study of decision-making*. New York, NY: The Free Press.

Shipan, C.R. (2004). Regulatory regimes, agency actions, and the conditional nature of congressional influence. *American Political Science Review*, *98*, 467–480.

Teodoro, M.P. (2011). *Bureaucratic ambition: Careers, motives, and the innovative administrator*. Baltimore, MD: Johns Hopkins University Press.

Thrower, S. (2018). Policy disruption through regulatory delay in the Trump administration. *Presidential Studies Quarterly*, *48*(3), 517–536.

Waterman, R.W. (2009). The administrative presidency, unilateral power, and the unitary executive theory. *Presidential Studies Quarterly*, *39*, 5–9.

Waterman, R.W., and Meier, K.J. (1998). Principal–agent models: An expansion? *Journal of Public Administration Research and Theory*, *8*, 173–202.

Waterman, R.W., and Ouyang, Y. (2020). Rethinking loyalty and competence in presidential appointments. *Public Administration Review*, first published online on June 1, 2020 at https://doi.org/10.1111/puar.13212.

Weingast, B.R., and Moran, M.J. (1983). Bureaucratic discretion or congressional control? Regulatory policymaking by the Federal Trade Commission. *Journal of Political Economy*, *91*, 765–800.

Wilson, J.Q. (1989). *Bureaucracy: What government agencies do and why they do it*. New York, NY: Basic.

Wood, B.D., and Bohte, J. (2004). Political transaction costs and the politics of administrative design. *The Journal of Politics*, *66*, 176–202.

Wood, B.D., and Waterman, R.W. (1991). The dynamics of political control of the bureaucracy. *American Political Science Review*, *85*, 801–828.

Wood, B.D., and Waterman, R.W. (1993). The dynamics of political-bureaucratic adaptation. *American Journal of Political Science*, *37*, 497–528.

Workman, Samuel, Jones, Bryan D., and Jochim, Ashley E. (2010). Policymaking, discretion, and overhead democracy. In Robert F. Durant (ed.), *The Oxford handbook of American bureaucracy*. New York, NY: Oxford University Press, pp. 612–637.

Zegart, A.B. (2010). Agency design and evolution. In Robert F. Durant (ed.), *The Oxford handbook of American bureaucracy*. New York, NY: Oxford University Press, pp. 207–230.

3. Behavioral public administration and employee motivation
Carina Schott

INTRODUCING BEHAVIORAL PUBLIC ADMINISTRATION AND VARIOUS TYPES OF EMPLOYEE MOTIVATION

Understanding the nature of human behavior and attitudes is not only central to the study of psychology (Weiner, Healy and Proctor 2012), but also some of the founding fathers of public administration—in particular, Herbert Simon (1947), Robert Dahl (1947) and Dwight Waldo (1948 [2017])—stressed the importance of understanding the behavior of humans already more than half a century ago. Driven by the ambition to ensure an ongoing dialogue and cross-fertilization of knowledge between public administration and psychological research, Grimmelikhuijsen and colleagues (2017) introduced the interdisciplinary research field of *Behavioral Public Administration* (BPA), which presents a micro-perspective of individual behavior and attitudes.

Grimmelikhuijsen and colleagues (2017) argue that the behavioral approach is beneficial to the field of public administration because of potential advancements in both theory and methodology. Theoretically, the discipline of public administration is thought to benefit from connecting macro-level theories with psychological micro-level foundations as is illustrated by research on institutional theories of government transparency and citizens' attitudes (e.g., Tetlock et al. 2000). Methodologically, the added value of BPA is expected to result from psychological insights on experimental research designs and measurement techniques. While experimental designs help to overcome endogeneity problems (Druckman 2011; Pearl 2009), psychological insights on scale development can help to overcome measurement errors and allow inferences to be drawn across contexts and studies.

As a driver of behavior, the concept of motivation and the question of what motivates people to do their job and to perform well still presents a 'big question' in public management research (Behn 1995; Perry and Hondeghem 2008). A specific type of employee motivation that continues to attract attention from both public administration scholars and policy makers across the globe is that of *public service motivation* (PSM) (Ritz, Brewer and Neumann 2016), which refers to 'an individual's orientation to delivering services to people with a purpose to do good for others and society' (Perry and Hondeghem 2008, p. vii). Continuing interest in this specific type of motivation can be explained by the strong evidence of PSM being associated with work-related outcomes, such as job satisfaction and public sector attraction provided by recently published meta-analyses (Homberg, McCarthy and Tabvuma 2015).

However, PSM is certainly not the only type of employee motivation. *Prosocial motivation*, which can be defined as 'the desire to expend effort to benefit other people' (Grant 2008, 48), is a second type of other-regarding motivation increasingly discussed and studied in the public administration literature. For example, Van der Voet, Steijn and Kuipers (2017) found that both prosocial motivation and client meaningfulness are sufficient, but not necessary, conditions for commitment to change among youth care professionals. In another study, Steijn and Van der Voet (2019) found evidence that highly prosocially motivated child welfare workers are more sensitive to burdensome rules and procedures than their colleagues who do not score high on this type of work motivation. Burdensome rules and regulations seem to threaten the realization of prosocial aspirations, thereby negatively affecting the employees' job satisfaction. When comparing PSM and prosocial motivation we see overlap but also differences. Both concepts look out for beneficiaries and can therefore be considered as other-oriented types of motivation. However, while PSM is directed at society at large, prosocial motivation is concerned with particular individuals and groups in one's direct contact (Corduneau, Dudau and Kominis 2020; Ritz et al. 2020; Schott et al. 2019).

Next to this, it is important to be aware of the fact that—regardless of the large body of research providing evidence for public sector workers being driven by other-regarding types of motivation—employees are likely to be driven by several *coexisting motives*. Rather than assuming that employees are pure knights who are solely driven by a desire to contribute to society (PSM) or to help others (prosocial motivation), a more realistic picture is that their behavior is also initiated by external rewards and/or the experienced need to comply with common norms and standards. Applied to the working context of public servants, this means that they may be motivated to perform well because of a combination of the societal and personal impact they can generate, but also because good performance is the norm and/or a requirement to keep the job. In line with this, French and Emerson (2014) found that typical extrinsic motives such as job security, fringe benefits and wages—also referred to as *public sector motivation* (Perry and Hondeghem 2008)—were considered as highly important by a number of public sector employees next to the opportunity to fulfill higher order needs. Similarly, Stazyk (2013) argued that 'performance-related pay and public service motivation may work in tandem—at least in some cases—to motivate employees' (p.265), suggesting that employee motivation is a highly complex and multifaceted concept (Weske and Schott 2018). The remainder of this chapter, however, will focus on PSM as it presents one of the few endogenous concepts being developed and refined by public administration scholars on their own (Moynihan, Vandenabeele and Blom-Hansen 2013).

PSYCHOLOGICAL THEORIES IN RESEARCH ON PUBLIC SERVICE MOTIVATION

The study of motivation has a long history among psychologists (Kanfer 1990). During the 1930s and 1940s, experimental psychologists conducted numerous studies to test drive-based learning theories. In the 1950s and 1960s, the interest in motivation shifted towards personality, social, clinical, and industrial and organizational psychologists who emphasized and studied the role of individuals' aspirations, expectations and affect. A well-known theory from this period is Aktinson's (1957) theory of achievement motivation. Fundamental to this theory is the idea that individuals engage in behavior with the expectation that their performance will be evaluated against a standard of excellence. Consequently, behavior is thought to result from the willingness to achieve this standard and the tendency to avoid failure. Around the same time, social psychologist McGregor (1960) developed his classical Theory X and Theory Y on human work motivation. This theory presents two different perspectives on how employees can be motivated to perform well. Theory X assumes that employees are lazy and need to be stimulated by external incentives such as salary, reputation and close supervision. Theory Y, in contrast, assumes that employees are intrinsically motivated to perform well and to develop themselves. From this perspective, it is the manager's job to ensure that employees have everything needed to do their work.

The concept of intrinsic motivation also plays an important role in modern psychological theories on (employee) motivation such as *Self-Determination Theory* (SDT) (Deci and Ryan 1985; Deci, Olafsen and Ryan 2017). In particular, SDT suggests that employees' performance and wellbeing are affected by the type of motivation they have for their work. SDT differentiates types of motivation on a continuum ranging from controlled (extrinsic) to autonomous (intrinsic), depending on the degree of internalization of external pressures, which depends on the satisfaction of three basic psychological needs: the need for autonomy, competence and relatedness. Within this motivational continuum, five types of motivation are situated: (1) *intrinsic motivation* resulting from people's interest in the activity itself and presenting the most autonomous or self-determined type of motivation; (2) *external regulation* resulting from behavioral engagement on the basis of external pressures and demands presenting the most controlled or prototypical extrinsic type of motivation; (3) *introjected regulation* represents the weakest form of internalization—this regulation has been taken in by the person, but has not been accepted as his or her own; (4) *identified regulation* indicates that people identify with the value of a behavior for their own self-selected goals; and (5) *integrated regulation* is a truly autonomous type of motivation, involving the integration of one's own identification with other norms, interests and values.

Although often treated interchangeably, this regulation is different from intrinsic motivation because the activity is instrumentally important for personal goals rather than being purely enjoyable. This difference becomes clear when considering the activity of donating blood. Most people would agree that they are entirely free in their choice to donate blood and they do so because it reflects who they are and how they want to be seen by others. At the same time, the act of donating blood itself is not considered as joyful (it may even be a painful activity), therefore representing an integrated rather than intrinsic type of motivation.

When turning to PSM—the most frequently studied type of employee motivation in the field of public administration—we see that scholars frequently use insights from *self-determination theory* to explain, for instance, the relationship between PSM and its antecedent. Viewing PSM as an autonomous type of motivation, Schott and Pronk (2014) hypothesize and find evidence that specific HR practices (e.g., job characteristics, training and consultation) contribute to the satisfaction of the three basic psychological needs (for autonomy, competence and relatedness) and that the satisfaction of these needs, in turn, is positively associated with PSM. At a theoretical level, Vandenabeele (2007) used insights from self-determination theory to explain how PSM originates from institutions. He argues that certain basic psychological needs are satisfied within these institutions thereby stimulating the internalization of public values and, as a consequence hereof, the foundation of PSM.

A different line of research draws on SDT to map the factors that may explain the complex relationship between performance-related rewards and PSM. While some previous studies have found support for the crowding out hypothesis, that is, performance-related pay reduces PSM (Georgellis, Iossa and Tabvuma 2011), others found that performance-related pay is associated with greater job satisfaction for employees with higher PSM (Stazyk 2013). Using insights from SDT, Corduneau et al. (2020) map out a conceptual model specifying the contextual and personal factors leading to the internalization of extrinsic rewards through the satisfaction of the basic psychological needs, thereby stimulating rather than reducing PSM. Although sound empirical research is needed in testing the entire conceptual model, previous research supports parts of it. The results of a statistical analyses based on a sample of more than 3000 Danish school teachers showcases that perceiving obligatory student plans as controlling is negatively associated with PSM, supporting the idea that motivation crowding can occur if basic needs are not satisfied (Jacobsen, Hvitved and Andersen 2014).

A second contemporary psychological theory that is frequently used in PSM research is that of *Person-Environment Fit Theory* (Kristof 1996; Kristof-Brown and Guay 2011). A core argument of this theory is that an incompatibility between the characteristics and values of an individual and his/her work environment can cause negative effects. Research on the so-called 'dark sides' of PSM draws heavily on this theory (Schott and Ritz 2018). Scholars argue and find evidence that if public service-motivated individuals cannot fulfill their desire to provide public services this is likely to negatively affect attitudinal outcomes of job satisfaction (Van Loon, Vandenabeele and Leisink 2015), physical wellbeing (Liu, Yang and Yu 2015) and intentions to stay in the current job (Quratulain and Kahn 2015).

In addition, person-environment fit theory has been used to explain inconsistent findings between PSM and job performance. Following, amongst others, Wright and Pandey (2008) and (Bright 2007) one potential reason for the mixed findings is that many studies test for direct outcomes of PSM while assuming that public service organizations are characterized by values and norms that resemble the ones considered as important by public service-motivated individuals. High levels of red tape are often found in the public sector (Pandey and Kingsley 2000) and the increasing focus on business-like values caused by the rise of managerialism (Frederickson 2005) and economic individualism (Bozeman 2007) may, however, prevent a self-evident employee–organizational value congruence in the public sector. Empirical evidence supports the notion that value congruence—or the fit between the person and the environment are crucial for the relationship between PSM and positive work-related outcomes (e.g., Christensen and Wright 2011; Van Loon et al. 2018).

To sum up, SDT theory and person-environment fit theory played an important role in the advancement of PSM research. However, although being most influential, they certainly do not present the only psychological theories used by public administration scholars interested in employee motivation. Schott, Van Kleef and Steen (2015), for example, introduced identity theory (Burke and Stets 2009) to the study of PSM to explain variations in the behavior and decision-making of highly public service-motivated individuals in the context of dilemma situations. In addition, scholars have argued that insights from construal-level theory of psychological distance (Trope and Liberman 2010) and Heckhausen and Gollwitzer's (1987) Rubicon model of stages of human action are useful to conceptually separate PSM from prosocial motivation (Ritz et al. 2020; Schott et al. 2019) and Bakker (2015) integrates PSM with job demands-resources theory in order to explain how employees in the public sector deal with their daily job demands and resources.

EXPERIMENTS IN RESEARCH ON PUBLIC SERVICE MOTIVATION

When considering the fact that Wright and Grant (2010) called for more experimental research on PSM already ten years ago, the number of studies using an experimental design is still limited though rising. To date, three topics can be identified using different types of experimental designs. Table 3.1 provides an overview of these studies summarizing the main findings, type of experimental design and research sample.

Early experimental research focused on the relationship between PSM and performance. Although not studying PSM directly, to my knowledge, Brewer and Brewer (2011) were the first who took this route. The authors find that respondents are significantly faster, more accurate and more vigilant in performing a simple task on the computer when they were told that the research they were participating in was being funded by a 'government agency' compared to respondents who were told that the funding comes from a 'business firm.' Two years later, Bellé (2013) showed that exposure to contact with beneficiaries and self-persuasion interventions had a positive effect on actual job performance and that PSM strengthened these effects. His study took place in a real hospital setting, suggesting that the external validity of his study can be considered as high. Again, two years later, Pedersen (2015) found evidence that PSM can be activated by a low-intensity randomized survey experiment among students. Also, in this study PSM was found to cause better performance. However, the generalizability of this finding, just like the findings of the Brewer and Brewer (2011) study, may at least be questioned because performance was measured by the number of minutes students were willing to spend on completing a future research survey (rather than by more real-live indicators of attitudes and/or behavior).

Next to experimental studies on PSM and performance, two very recent streams of experimental PSM research can be identified: research focusing on ethical behavior and research focusing on employee recruiting. Drawing on a large sample of over 5000 Chilean government employees, Meyer-Sahling, Mikkelsen and Schuster (2019) find that PSM activation increases the likelihood to report ethical problems to management. The experimental design of this study is based on the assumption that asking about PSM can render salient PSM-orientations of respondents. Therefore, the order of PSM and outcome questions is randomized in this survey experiment. However, Meyer-Sahlinger and colleagues' (2019) finding that PSM can be activated or primed could not be replicated in two lab and one survey experiment conducted by Christensen and Wright (2018) who used data from student samples. The authors, therefore, draw less optimistic conclusions and point out that although PSM may increase ethical behavior somehow, the influence of public managers is likely to be limited. The recent study by Olsen et al. (2019) presents a different approach towards the relationship between PSM and (un)ethical behavior. Rather than activating the concept of PSM, Olsen et al. (2019) studied the influence of PSM on behavioral dishonesty measured by a simple dice game in which participants have the opportunity to cheat without anybody (except for the researcher on the basis of statistical analysis) noticing. The author finds that higher levels of PSM are associated with less dishonest behavior among students who desire a public service career.

Interestingly also, experimental research on PSM and employer branding reports inconsistent findings. Asseburg et al. (2020) found PSM to moderate the relationship between experimentally manipulated prosocial employment attributes and the intentions to apply for a public sector job among non-students. Weske et al. (2020) and Linos (2017), in contrast, did not find any evidence that public-service motivated students and police officers, respectively, were attracted to public values in employer branding. The experimental stimuli in the Asseburg et al. (2020) and Weske et al. (2020) studies were hypothetical job advertisements either stressing or not stressing typical public values related to PSM, thereby presenting two examples of

Table 3.1 Overview of experimental studies on PSM

Focus of study	Author(s), year of publication	Experimental design	Sample	Main finding
PSM and performance	Brewer and Brewer 2011*	Lab experiment	Students	Sig. relationship found
	Bellé 2013	Field experiment	Nurses	Sig. relationship found
	Pedersen 2015	Survey experiment	Students	Sig. relationship found
PSM and (un)ethical behaviour	Christensen and Wright 2018	Survey experiment, lab experiments	Students	Sig. relationship NOT found
	Olsen et al. 2019	Survey experiment	Students	Sig. relationship found
	Meyer-Sahling, Mikkelsen and Schuster 2019	Survey experiment	Chilean government employees	Sig. relationship found
PSM and employer branding	Asseburg et al. 2020	Survey experiment (vignette study)	Students and non-students	Sig. relationship found
	Weske et al. 2020	Survey experiment (vignette study)	Students	Sig. relationship NOT found
	Linos 2017	Field experiment	Police officers	Sig. relationship NOT found

Note: * This study does not study PSM directly.

experimental vignette studies. Linos (2017) applied a field experiment to test which messages are most effective at attracting different and new police recruits.

HOW NEW IS THE INTEGRATION OF MOTIVATIONAL RESEARCH WITH METHODS AND THEORIES FROM PSYCHOLOGY?

The review of the use of psychological theories and experimental methods in research on employee motivation showcases that the critical observation of BPA scholars stressing the limited use of these theories and methods in the field of public administration (Grimmelikhuijsen et al. 2017) only partly holds for research on employee motivation. While experimental research designs have indeed been scarce until very recently, the use of psychological theories dates back to the beginning of PSM research (see also Hassan and Wright 2020). As such, the research topic of employee motivation in general and the topic of PSM in particular seems to have been characterized by the theoretical aspect of BPA for quite some time now and, more recently, also by its methodological aspects.

In particular, the review of studies integrating the topic of employee motivation with psychological theories (especially SDT theory and person-environment fit theory) illustrated that using insights from these theories helped the research field of PSM to move forward in at least three ways. First, this integration stimulated research on the origins of PSM. Second, it inspired researchers to take a more skeptical stance on PSM as illustrated by research on the 'dark sides' of PSM. Third, it helped to find explanations for inconsistent findings of previous studies concerning the PSM-performance relationship.

When turning to the overview of motivational studies applying experimental methods, then we see a slightly different picture. Also, while some PSM research has been devoted to the development of a measurement instrument (e.g., Kim 2017; Kim et al. 2013; Perry 1997; Vandenabeele 2008; Wright, Christensen and Pandey 2013), experimental research on PSM remains relatively small in number and one-sided in the variety of experimental methods. This conclusion is somewhat surprising given the fact that, already in 2010, Wright and Grant called for more experimental research on PSM, because this type of research 'can provide researchers with greater levels of control that demonstrate causal effects in organizational contexts while ruling out alternative explanations' (p. 692).

UNANSWERED QUESTIONS ABOUT BEHAVIORAL PUBLIC ADMINISTRATION AND EMPLOYEE MOTIVATION

The review of (empirical) studies on employee motivation and psychological theories and experimental methods, on the one hand and the reflection on the novelty of the integration of psychological theories and methods with public administration research on employee motivation, on the other, has shown that important questions have been answered, but it also raises some new questions. These sections illustrate that PSM researchers are pioneers in using psychological theories and also increasingly make use of experimental research designs as advocated by BPA scholars. At the same time, the review showcases where progress can be made, thereby providing avenues for future research.

First, it is interesting to note that almost all experimental studies on employee motivation are survey experiments. Only one study presents a field experiment (Bellé 2013) and two studies present classic lab experiments (Brewer and Brewer 2011; Christensen and Wright 2018), thereby presenting less than half of all studies included in the review. This suggests that experimental survey research designs are employed even more frequently in research on employee motivation if compared to the general body of published public administration research. Estimates suggest that between 30 and 50 percent of all experiments published in Public Administration and Public Policy journals can be categorized as survey experiments (Bouwman and Grimmelikhuijsen 2016). Each experimental research design has its own advantages and disadvantages. Following Hansen and Tummers (2020), experimental realism is an important benefit distinguishing field experiments from survey and lab experiments, which are better suited to ensure internal validity. Given the fact that PSM is often associated with practical implication, such as the advice to use PSM in selection decisions or the need to think about alternative reward systems instead of pay-for-performance (Ritz et al. 2016), more field experimental research may be necessary as this type of research design allows us to draw conclusions about causal effects in realistic settings.

Second, the review showcases that findings from experimental studies on PSM are inconsistent. Differences in the sample characteristics may present one explanation for the mixed findings of studies on PSM and employer branding and PSM and ethical behavior.[1] This highlights the need for replication studies which, in contrast to natural sciences, have never been an integral part of public management and public administration research in general (Pedersen and Stritch 2018; Walker, James and Brewer 2017) and research on employee motivation in particular. Replication serves the important purpose that stronger conclusions may be drawn as the probability of Type I and Type II errors is reduced. True replication studies employing not only the same methods, but also using data from comparable respondents should therefore be high on the research agenda. This advice fits well with the worldwide open science movement stressing the need to share data and research tools and publishing open access.

Third, the overview of the frequently studied psychological theories in research on employee motivation showed that this type of research is—not exclusively but strongly—shaped by self-determination and person-environment fit theory. This is not a bad thing per se, but I believe that it may be worthwhile to also look more systematically at different theoretical psychological perspectives in order to open up new research streams. A promising candidate is that of moral licensing theory (Mullen and Monin 2016), which just like consistency theories (e.g., Festinger's (1957) cognitive dissonance theory, Bem's (1972) self-perception theory), belongs to a group of theories that can be categorized as sequential behavioral paradigms. Central to these paradigms is the idea that behavior should not be studied in isolation. Rather, it should be investigated in the context of relevant previous behavior. To the best of my knowledge, public administration scholars have not yet integrated these paradigms into the study of employee motivation. This is unfortunate as decades of social psychological research have supported the notion that individuals drive towards consistency (Mullen and Monin 2016). At the same time, numerous studies have demonstrated what seems like the reverse phenomenon: 'Acting in one direction enables actors to later do just the opposite' (Mullen and Monin 2016, 364), also called moral licensing behavior. An interesting question for future research would be whether PSM serves as a potential buffer of moral licensing behavior (i.e., feeling free to perform morally quotational behavior because of previous good deeds). Because lab experiments, which usually take one of two forms—classroom experiments and computerized experiments—enable us to test how individuals react to their own choices and previous behavior (Bouwman 2020), this type of experimental research provides a suitable method to answer this question. In both cases, a specific room is equipped to run the experimental session in order to eliminate external influences.

CONCLUDING REMARKS

Using insights from psychological theories stands at the core of public administration research focusing on employee motivation. In particular, research on the concept of public service motivation (PSM) strongly benefited from the integration with self-determination and person-environment fit theory, thereby shedding light on the underlying mechanisms linking PSM with its antecedents and outcomes. This means important questions have been answered. However, PSM may also benefit from making use of psychological theories that stress the need to study behaviors, attitudes and motivations in the context of previous behaviors, attitudes and motivations, such as moral licensing theory. Next to making use of psychological insights, PSM research employs experimental research designs as advocated by proponents of behavioral public administration (BPA). This trend, however, is more recent, strongly dominated by survey experiments, and showcases inconsistent findings regarding the relationship between PSM and (un)ethical behavior, on the one hand, and PSM and employer branding, on the other hand. Summing up, this chapter illustrates that the critique of BPA scholars highlighting the limited use of psychological theories and methods is only partly justified when it comes to PSM research. At the same time, it uncovers new avenues for future motivational research based on the principles of BPA. It is my hope that it spurs more research into these areas.

NOTE

1. Please remember, some studies were based on student samples, while others used data of employees (see Table 3.1).

REFERENCES

Asseburg, J., and Homberg, F. (2020). Public service motivation or sector rewards? Two studies on the determinants of sector attraction. *Review of Public Personnel Administration*, *40*, 82–111.
Asseburg, J., Hattke, J., Hensel, D., Homberg, F., and Vogel, R. (2020). The tacit dimension of public sector attraction in multi-incentive settings. *Journal of Public Administration Research and Theory*, *30*, 41–59.
Atkinson, J.W. (1957). Motivational determinants of risk-taking behavior. *Psychological Review*, *64*, 359–372.
Bakker, A.B. (2015). A job demands—resources approach to public service motivation. *Public Administration Review*, *75*, 723–732.
Behn, R.D. (1995). The big questions of public management. *Public Administration Review*, *55*, 313–324.
Bellé, N. (2013). Experimental evidence on the relationship between public service motivation and job performance. *Public Administration Review*, *73*, 143–153.
Bem, D.J. (1972). Self-perception theory. *Advances in Experimental Social Psychology*, *6*, 1–62.
Bouwman, R. (2020) Experimental methods B: Laboratory experiments. In E. Vigoda-Gadot and D.R. Vashdi (eds), *Handbook of research methods in public administration, management and policy: Breaking new frontiers*, Cheltenham, UK and Northampton, MA, USA: Edward Elgar Publishing, pp. 234–253.
Bouwman, R., and Grimmelikhuijsen, S. (2016). Experimental public administration from 1992 to 2014: A systematic literature review and ways forward. *International Journal of Public Sector Management*, *29*, 110–131.
Bozeman, B. (2007). *Public values and public interest: Counterbalancing economic individualism*, Washington, DC: Georgetown University Press.
Brewer, G.A., and Brewer Jr., G.A. (2011). Parsing public/private differences in work motivation and performance: An experimental study. *Journal of Public Administration Research and Theory*, *21*, 347–362.
Bright, L. (2007). Does person-organization fit mediate the relationship between public service motivation and the job performance of public employees? *Review of Public Personnel Administration*, *27*, 361–379.
Burke, P. J., and Stets, J. E. (2009). *Identity theory*, Oxford: Oxford University Press.
Corduneanu, R., Dudau, A., and Kominis, G. (2020). Crowding-in or crowding-out: The contribution of self-determination theory to public service motivation. *Public Management Review*, first published online on April 30, 2020 at https://doi.org/10.1080/14719037.2020.1740303.
Christensen, R.K., and Wright, B.E. (2011). The effects of public service motivation on job choice decisions: Disentangling the contributions of person-organization fit and person-job fit. *Journal of Public Administration Research and Theory*, *21*, 723–743.
Christensen, R., and Wright, B. (2018). Public service motivation and ethical behavior: Evidence from three experiments. *Journal of Behavioral Public Administration*, *1*, 1–8.
Dahl, R.A. (1947). The science of public administration: Three problems. *Public Administration Review*, *7*(1), 1–11.

Deci, E.L., and Ryan, R.M. (1985). The general causality orientations scale: Self-determination in personality. *Journal of Research in Personality*, *19*, 109–134.

Deci, E.L., Olafsen, A.H., and Ryan, R.M. (2017). Self-determination theory in work organizations: The state of a science. *Annual Review of Organizational Psychology and Organizational Behavior*, *4*, 19–43.

Druckman, J. (2011). *Cambridge handbook of experimental political science*, New York, NY: Cambridge University Press.

Festinger, L. (1957). *A theory of cognitive dissonance*, Stanford, CA: Stanford University Press.

Frederickson, H.G. (2005). Public ethics and the new managerialism: An axiomatic theory. In H.G. Frederickson and R.K. Ghere (eds), *Ethics in public management*, New York, NY: M.E. Sharpe, pp. 165–183.

French, P.E., and Emerson, M.C. (2014). Assessing the variations in reward preference for local government employees in terms of position, public service motivation, and public sector motivation. *Public Performance and Management Review*, *37*, 552–576.

Georgellis, Y., Iossa, E., and Tabvuma, V. (2011). Crowding out intrinsic motivation in the public sector. *Journal of Public Administration Research and Theory*, *21*, 473–493.

Grant, A.M. (2008). Does intrinsic motivation fuel the prosocial fire? Motivational synergy in predicting persistence, performance, and productivity. *Journal of Applied Psychology January*, *93*, 48–58.

Grimmelikhuijsen, S., Jilke, S., Olsen, A.L., and Tummers, L. (2017). Behavioral public administration: Combining insights from public administration and psychology. *Public Administration Review*, *77*, 45–56.

Hansen, J.A., and Tummers, L. (2020). A systematic review of field experiments in public administration. *Public Administration Review*, *80*, 921–931.

Hassan, S., and Wright, B.E. (2020). The behavioral public administration movement: A critical reflection. *Public Administration Review*, *80*, 163–167.

Heckhausen, H., and Gollwitzer, P.M. (1987). Thought contents and cognitive functioning in motivational versus volitional states of mind. *Motivation and Emotion*, *11*, 101–120.

Homberg, F., McCarthy, D., and Tabvuma, V. (2015). A meta-analysis of the relationship between public service motivation and job satisfaction. *Public Administration Review*, *75*, 711–722.

Jacobsen, C.B., Hvitved, J., and Andersen, L.B. (2014). Command and motivation: How the perception of external interventions relates to intrinsic motivation and public service motivation. *Public Administration*, *92*, 790–806.

Kanfer, R. (1990). Motivation theory and industrial and organizational psychology. In M.D. Dunnette and Hough (eds), *Handbook of industrial and organizational psychology. Volume I: Theory in industrial and organizational psychology*, Palo Alto, CA: Consulting Psychologists Press, pp. 75–130.

Kim, S. (2017). Comparison of a multidimensional to a unidimensional measure of public service motivation: Predicting work attitudes. *International Journal of Public Administration*, *40*, 504–515.

Kim, S., Vandenabeele, W., Wright, B.E., Andersen, L.B., Cerase, F.P., Christensen, R.K., Desmarais, C., Koumenta, M., Leisink, P., Liu, B., Palidauskaite, J., Pedersen, L.H., Perry, J.L., Ritz, A., Taylor, J., and De Vivo, P. (2013). Investigating the structure and meaning of public service motivation across populations: Developing an international instrument and addressing issues of measurement invariance. *Journal of Public Administration Research and Theory*, *23*(1), 79–102.

Kristof, A.L. (1996). Person-organization fit: An integrative review of its conceptualizations, measurement, and implications. *Personnel Psychology*, *49*, 1–49.

Kristof-Brown, A., and Guay, R.P. (2011). Person–environment fit. In S. Zedeck (ed.), *APA handbook of industrial and organizational psychology, Vol 3: Maintaining, expanding, and contracting the organization*, Washington, DC: American Psychological Association, pp. 3–50.

Linos, E. (2018). More than public service: A field experiment on job advertisements and diversity in the police. *Journal of Public Administration Research and Theory*, *28*(1), 67–85.

Liu, B., Yang, K., and Yu, W. (2015). Work-related stressors and health-related outcomes in public service: Examining the role of public service motivation. *The American Review of Public Administration*, *45*(6), 653–673.

McGregor, D. (1960). *The human side of enterprise*, New York, NY: McGraw-Hill.

Meyer-Sahling, J.H., Mikkelsen, K.S., and Schuster, C. (2019). The causal effect of public service motivation on ethical behavior in the public sector: Evidence from a large-scale survey experiment. *Journal of Public Administration Research and Theory, 29*, 445–459.

Moynihan, D.P., Vandenabeele, W., and Blom-Hansen, J. (2013). Debate: Advancing public service motivation research. *Public Money and Management, 33*, 288–289.

Mullen, E., and Monin, B. (2016). Consistency versus licensing effects of past moral behavior. *Annual Review of Psychology, 67*, 363–385.

Olsen, A.L., Hjorth, F., Harmon, N., and Barfort, S. (2019). Behavioral dishonesty in the public sector. *Journal of Public Administration Research and Theory, 29*, 572–590.

Pandey, S.K., and Kingsley, G.A. (2000). Examining red tape in public and private organizations: Alternative explanations form a social psychological model. *Journal of Public Administration Research and Theory, 10*, 779–799.

Pearl, J. (2009). *Causality.* Cambridge: Cambridge University Press.

Pedersen, M.J. (2015). Activating the forces of public service motivation: Evidence from a low-intensity randomized survey experiment. *Public Administration Review, 75*, 734–746.

Pedersen, M.J., and Stritch, J.M. (2018). RNICE Model: Evaluating the contribution of replication studies in public administration and management research. *Public Administration Review, 78*, 606–612.

Perry, J.L. (1997). Antecedents of public service motivation. *Journal of Public Administration Research and Theory, 7*(2), 181–197.

Perry, J.L., and Hondeghem, A. (2008). *Motivation in public management: The call of public service*, New York, NY: Oxford University Press.

Quratulain, Samina, and Khan, Abdul K. (2015). How does employees' public service motivation get affected? A conditional process analysis of the effects of person–job fit and work pressure. *Public Personnel Management, 44*, 266–289.

Ritz, A., Brewer, G.A., and Neumann, O. (2016). Public service motivation: A systematic literature review and outlook. *Public Administration Review, 76*, 414–426.

Ritz, A., Schott, C., Nitzl, C., and Alfes, K. (2020). Public service motivation and prosocial motivation: Two sides of the same coin? *Public Management Review, 22*, 974e–998.

Schott, C., and Pronk, J.L.J. (2014). Investigating and explaining organizational antecedents of PSM. *Evidence-based HRM: A Global Forum for Empirical Scholarship, 2*, 28–56.

Schott, C., and Ritz, A. (2018). The dark sides of public service motivation: A multi-level theoretical framework. *Perspectives on Public Management and Governance, 1*(1), 29–42.

Schott, C., van Kleef, D.D., and Steen, T. (2015). What does it mean and imply to be public service motivated? *The American Review of Public Administration, 45*, 689–707.

Schott, C., Neumann, O., Baertschi, M., and Ritz, A. (2019). Public service motivation, prosocial motivation and altruism: Towards disentanglement and conceptual clarity. *International Journal of Public Administration, 42*, 1200–1211.

Simon, H.A. (1947). *Administrative behavior: A study of decision-making processes in administrative organization*, New York: Macmillan.

Stazyk, E.C. (2013). Crowding out public service motivation? Comparing theoretical expectations with empirical findings on the influence of performance-related pay. *Review of Public Personnel Administration, 33*, 252–274.

Steijn, B., and Van der Voet, J. (2019). Relational job characteristics and job satisfaction of public sector employees: When prosocial motivation and red tape collide. *Public Administration, 97*, 64–80.

Tetlock, P.E., Kristel, O.V., Elson, S.B., Green, M.C., and Lerner, J.S. (2000). The psychology of the unthinkable: taboo trade-offs, forbidden base rates, and heretical counterfactuals. *Journal of Personality and Social Psychology, 78*, 853–870.

Trope, Y., and Liberman, N. (2010). Construal-level theory of psychological distance. *Psychological Review, 117*, 440–463.

Van der Voet, J., Steijn, B., and Kuipers, B.S. (2017). What's in it for others? The relationship between prosocial motivation and commitment to change among youth care professionals. *Public Management Review, 19*, 443–462.

Van Loon, N., Kjeldsen, A.M., Andersen, L.B., Vandenabeele, W., and Leisink, P. (2018). Only when the societal impact potential is high? A panel study of the relationship between public service motivation and perceived performance. *Review of Public Personnel Administration, 38*, 139–166.

Van Loon, N.M., Vandenabeele, W., and Leisink, P. (2015). On the bright and dark side of public service motivation: The relationship between PSM and employee wellbeing. *Public Money and Management*, *35*, 349–356.

Vandenabeele, W. (2007). Toward a public administration theory of public service motivation: An institutional approach. *Public Management Review*, *9*, 545–556.

Vandenabeele, W. (2008). Development of a public service motivation measurement scale: Corroborating and extending Perry's measurement instrument. *International Public Management Journal*, *11*, 143–167.

Waldo, D. (2017). *The administrative state: A study of the political theory of American public administration*, with an introduction by H.T. Miller, Abingdon, UK and New York: Routledge.

Walker, R.M., James, O., and Brewer, G.A. (2017). Replication, experiments and knowledge in public management research. *Public Management Review*, *19*, 1221–1234.

Weiner, I.B., Healy, A.F., and Proctor, R.W. (2012). *Handbook of psychology, experimental psychology*. Hoboken, NJ: John Wiley and Sons.

Weske, U., and Schott, C. (2018). What motivates different groups of public employees working for Dutch municipalities? Combining autonomous and controlled types of motivation. *Review of Public Personnel Administration*, *38*, 415–430.

Weske, U., Ritz, A., Schott, C., and Neumann, O. (2020). Attracting future civil servants with public values? An experimental study on employer branding. *International Public Management Journal*, *23*, 677–695.

Wright, B.E., and Grant, A.M. (2010). Unanswered questions about public service motivation: Designing research to address key issues of emergence and effects. *Public Administration Review*, *70*(5), 691–700.

Wright, B.E., and Pandey, S.K. (2008). Public service motivation and the assumption of person—organization fit: Testing the mediating effect of value congruence. *Administration and Society*, *40*, 502–521.

Wright, B.E., Christensen, R.K., and Pandey, S.K. (2013). Measuring public service motivation: Exploring the equivalence of existing global measures. *International Public Management Journal*, *16*, 197–223.

4. The ins and outs of motivational crowding
Trent Engbers

WHAT IS MOTIVATIONAL CROWDING

The intrinsic desire to serve others, while not unique to the public sector, is an oft cited distinction of public sector employment (Rainey, 2014). Deci (1971) states that 'one is said to be intrinsically motivated to perform an activity when one receives no apparent reward except the activity itself' (105). Thus, the reward that motivates the activity on the task is some internal drive related to the activity such as pleasure, challenge, altruism, self-determination or some other inherent personal proclivity. This contrasts with extrinsic rewards such as financial compensation, recognition or feedback which motivates action from outside of the individual. Given that employees who are intrinsically motivated tend to exhibit higher levels of organizational commitment, productivity and performance (Crewson, 1997), attracting and retaining intrinsically motivated public sector employees strengthens the public sector.

One hypothesized threat to intrinsic motivation is motivational crowding. Motivational crowding occurs when individuals who are intrinsically motivated are exposed to external rewards in such a way and under such conditions that their level of intrinsic motivation changes (Frey, 1997). This could include instances of 'crowding in' in which external stimuli serve to reinforce and strengthen internal motivation such as when public employees experience greater awareness of the benefits of their service through client contact (Bellé, 2015). More commonly, motivational crowding refers to 'crowding out' effects by which external incentives serve to decrease intrinsic motivation. These extrinsic incentives serve to replace intrinsic desires through a number of causal mechanisms.

This chapter will begin by reviewing these mechanisms and the theoretical concepts underlying motivational crowding. It will then discuss empirical findings on motivational crowding and its determinants in the public sector. The latter half of the chapter will focus specifically on differences that make motivational crowding particularly relevant to the public sector and the impact of motivational crowding on public administration. The chapter will conclude with suggestions for future research.

EARLY THEORETICAL CONCEPTIONS

Frey (and Jegen, 2001) contribute the theoretical foundations of motivational crowding theory to two sources. First, the now over 50-year-old economic research by Titmuss (2018) which argued that incentivizing blood donations with financial compensation actually reduced willingness to give because it removed the selfless motivation of giving of oneself to others without return. The empirical support of Titmuss's thesis has been somewhat mixed with the most recent meta-analysis suggesting that financial incentives do not crowd out blood donations (Niza, Tung and Marteau, 2013). However, some experimental studies continue to find an effect that extrinsic rewards lead to detrimental donating behavior (Mellström and Johannesson, 2008).

Second, early conceptions of motivational crowding theory were built upon the work of a number of cognitive social psychologists in the 1970s whose work demonstrates that under certain conditions where the individual engages in an intrinsically motivational task, financial rewards decrease rather than increase motivation because of their negative effect on intrinsic motivation (Deci, 1972a; Deci and Ryan, 1964; Lepper and Green, 1978). Early studies suggested that there are two potential sources that lead to this loss of motivation. (1) According to Adams's (1963) equity theory, individuals seek balance between rewards and effort. In those instances, in which reward and effort are mismatched, individuals will either increase effort to a level appropriate for the reward or employers will decrease rewards to the level appropriate for the effort. When individuals are intrinsically motivated and then receive external motivation through compensation, there is a disconnect between effort and reward. The individual perceives that the totality of the intrinsic and extrinsic reward is too great for their effort and thus decreases their intrinsic motivation to bring reward and effort into alignment (Deci, 1972b). (2) An alternative perspective is that external rewards cause the internalization of a message that the work being completed is not sufficiently interesting as to merit intrinsic motivation. Deci (1971) argues the point in this way

> [M]oney is frequently used as a means of 'buying' services which would probably not otherwise be rendered. Perhaps, then, the presence of money as an external reward suggests to the subjects that they 'should probably not render this activity with-out pay,' that is, they should not be so intrinsically motivated to do the activity. This could lead the subjects to a process of cognitive reevaluation of the activity from one which is intrinsically motivated to one which is motivated by the anticipation of money. (107)

As such, the task comes to be seen as something for which there should not be an intrinsic motivation and thus the intrinsic motivation disappears.

Based on these two conceptualizations of cognitive social psychology, the theoretical basis for crowding out (or for that matter crowding in) can be justified by either (a) a change in preferences associated with an external motivation or (b) a change in the perceived nature of the task being completed (Frey, 1997). In the prior case, there is an assumption that external interventions (be they financial compensation, praise or other sticks and carrots) may influence internal motivation and that 'the external motivation may crowd-out or crowd-in intrinsic motivation (or leave it unaffected)' (Frey, 1997, 592).

RECENT THEORETICAL CONCEPTIONS

In most recent research, the theoretical basis has shifted toward three major effects: impaired self-determination, impaired self-esteem and impaired expression possibility. Of these three, self-determination has received the greatest amount of attention in recent empirical studies (Jacobsen and Jensen, 2017; Lohmann, Houlfort and De Allegri, 2016). Self-determination Theory suggests that employee performance is affected by the type of motivation provided in a work context and that intrinsic motivation arises out of three basic motivation drivers: competence, relatedness and autonomy. Competence reflects the desire to control the outcome of effort and to develop mastery in the task. Relatedness refers to the desire to interact and cooperate with others and autonomy flows from the desire to control one's own life and the task at hand (Ryan and Deci, 2017). Thus, motivational crowding interferes with the intrinsic desires for competence, relatedness and autonomy by exerting external control and shifting the locus of control from the inside to the outside with the use of material incentives.

Regarding impaired self-esteem, the introduction of external incentives threatens altruistically driven self-esteem. Intrinsic desires to do good for others are minimally ignored and potentially rejected when extrinsic offers or commands are produced (Frey, 1997; Reeson and Tisdell, 2008). By providing an external incentive, the individual's self-esteem associated with personal drive is diminished as psychological questions are raised as to the true source (internal vs external) of the motivation (Frey, 1997).

Lastly, motivational crowding may decrease intrinsic motivation through the impaired possibility of expression. Like with impaired self-esteem, by providing an extrinsic reward of command, individuals lose the opportunity to manifest intrinsic motivation. However, the theoretical argument is that the loss of motivation comes not only from the threat to psychological self-esteem, but from the opportunity to demonstrate that commitment in a behavioral and public way (Frey, 1997).

EMPIRICAL FINDINGS

Over the past five decades many reviews have been conducted on crowding effects with fairly consistent support that motivational crowding is real and has an effect on motivation, effort and performance (Cerasoli, Nicklin and Ford, 2014; Deci, Koestner and Ryan, 1999; Rummel and Feinberg, 1988; Tang and Hall, 1995; Wiersma, 1992). The most recent meta-analysis of this data, examining 128 well-controlled experiments, was completed in 1999 and included both a reanalysis of the previous four meta-analyses on motivational crowding and new research on motivational crowding published in the late 1990s. In general, the results of this meta-analysis found that the introduction of external incentives ranging from cash to marshmallows reduced the intrinsic motivation as measured by both free choice activity (i.e., the willingness to engage in the activity without compensation) and self-reported interest in the task across age groups (Deci, Koestner and Ryan, 1999).

The exceptions to these findings were with regard to verbal incentives and unexpected incentives. The results of the meta-analysis showed that the presence of positive feedback had a positive and not negative impact on intrinsic motivation. Likewise, when the tangible rewards were unexpected or not contingent on performance, there was no effect on intrinsic motivation (Deci, Koestner and Ryan, 1999). This suggests that the introduction of what Daniel Pink (2011) calls 'now that' rewards (as distinguished from 'if then' rewards) are not detrimental to motivational crowding.

This section will take off where the 1999 meta-analysis ended and review the most important studies of the past two decades with special emphasis on the empirical investigation of motivational crowding in the public sector.

The goal of this section is not to suggest that public employees should not be paid well. Few government workers would work were they not paid. Rather, the purpose is to explore different approaches to compensation and their effect on intrinsic motivation. One study found that while both wage levels and intrinsic motivation increased effort, a 0.2 percent increase in wages resulted in 1 percent increase in effort but a 0.68 percent increase of intrinsic motivation resulted in a 1 percent increase in effort (Taylor and Taylor, 2011). Thus, structuring wages in such a way to not negatively impact intrinsic motivation is important.

Using the framework established by Deci and colleagues (1999), this section will examine three types of contingent rewards. Engagement contingent rewards where individuals received extrinsic rewards for engaging in the task. Completion rewards where the reward was contingent on completing the task within a particular time frame. Lastly, performance rewards where the external reward was variable and based on achieving a specified level of performance.

Engagement-contingent Attempting a Task

The compensation strategy which has received the least attention and the one which has received no public sector attention in the past 20 years is engagement-contingent rewards by which the employee is compensated merely for attempting the task. In one of few studies on engagement-contingent rewards undertaken since 1999, Selart and colleagues (Selart et al., 2008) examine how the offering of a reward to participate in a 'psychological study' affected the use of creativity in that study. Students were recruited under three conditions (no compensation, engagement-contingent compensation and performance-contingent compensation). The researcher found that those students who received a reward for participating were no less creative than those who received no compensation and both groups outperformed those who received a performance-contingent reward.

Completion-contingent Finishing the Task

The volume of completion-contingent research is not much better. One well-designed study looked at the willingness of software programmers to participate in and complete open-source software development. The findings from this study are interesting in that they suggest a somewhat contingent result. The authors find payment norms moderate the effect of compensation on programmer completion. For those tasks for which a payment norm existed, the introduction of extrinsic rewards reduced completion relative to the control group. Alternatively, when no payment norm existed, then the introduction of the incentive reduced performance (Alexy and Leitner, 2011).

This has practical implications for public administration with a particular focus on the nonprofit sector. Nonprofit employees are regularly asked to volunteer for their organization outside of the responsibilities of their job. The logic behind the Alexy and Leitner (2011) study would suggest that completion-contingent payments would have little effect on the willingness to complete regular job requirements for which pay is a norm but would have negative effects on those responsibilities which are generally considered to be voluntary.

Performance-contingent: Meeting Performance Objectives

Unlike engagement- and completion-contingent research, there has been a robust study of performance-contingent compensation over the past 20 years. This research has been particularly robust in the areas of performance and innovation.

In a series of experiments in Italy, Bellé and Cantarelli (Bellé, 2015; Bellé and Cantarelli, 2015) found significant but moderated effects of performance-contingent rewards that suggest motivational crowding. In the first study (Bellé, 2015), 300 nurses were involved in a controlled experiment where they were asked to assemble surgical kits. They were rewarded with either fixed pay, fixed pay with a performance bonus or fixed pay with a symbolic bonus (a certificate to the top five producers). In one condition the nurses were told that they would be privately told of their productivity and in the other condition that their productivity would be public. Lastly, the conditions were manipulated in terms of whether they had the opportunity to meet a program beneficiary. Performance-contingent rewards were most effective in those situations where the rewards were private, and the presence of a symbolic reward had no effect on performance. Most interestingly, the exposure of the nurses to program beneficiaries magnified the crowding out effects of pay for performance. Since beneficiary contact is assumed to increase intrinsic motivation, these findings are consistent with those theoretical arguments that extrinsic motivation crowds out intrinsic motivation. This finding is also interesting because it conflicts with much of the other research that suggests that mundane tasks, such as assembling surgical kits, would be immune from motivational crowding.

Unlike the nurses' study, Bellé and Cantarelli (2015) looked at executives and the impact of incentives on their motivational structure using survey data. The survey experiment of 256 executives in 9 or 13 central government departments used randomly manipulated vignettes along with measures of extrinsic, intrinsic and public service motivation. While the study found no effect related to public service motivation, the original intrinsic/extrinsic level of motivation influenced the impact of the performance-contingent reward. For those employees who were originally extrinsically motivated, the reward increased effort. However, for those employees who were originally more intrinsically motivated, rewards of any level (5, 10, 25 or 50 percent bonus) decreased effort.

One finds an interesting but less simple set of results in terms of the relationship between extrinsic motivators and innovation. Jacobsen and Andersen (2014) find that performance-contingent rewards can positively impact innovation by looking at the introduction of incentives over time on the productivity of patents by Danish researchers in public sector organizations. In a series of four studies, publication incentives are found to sometimes impact innovation positively as measured by patent production. However, this effect was moderated by perception of the incentive as shaped by the manager. When the manager's presentation of the incentives was such that the manager was seen as supportive, then the incentive increased innovation. If the incentives were seen as punishment or controlling, then they had a less desirable effect.

Verbal Crowding

The preponderance of research on motivational crowding has focused on financial compensation as the main factor in loss of intrinsic motivation. However, there has been some limited exploration of the crowding effects of other forms of extrinsic motivators such as feedback or supervision. This research seems to suggest that there are important motivational differences between extrinsic verbal and tangible rewards (Deci, Koestner and Ryan, 1999). In particular, critical feedback and the command environment have shown to decrease intrinsic motivation when the verbal feedback is perceived as controlling. Based on a logic of self-determination, a significant command environment or one in which feedback is seen as discipline has been shown to reduce intrinsic feedback as employees are seen as losing autonomy (Frey and Jegen, 2001; Frey and Osterloh, 2006). Likewise, there is also reason to believe that even positive feedback has the potential for motivational crowding over the long term if recipients come to expect it. In fact, there is some evidence that suggests that when individuals are simply told that they will be given performance feedback that it negatively impacts intrinsic motivation (Harackiewicz and Manderlink, 1984).

DETERMINANTS OF MOTIVATIONAL CROWDING

Given these findings, it is likely that motivational crowding is highly contingent. In a 2016 study of health care workers, Lohmann and colleagues suggest that the research presented above is perhaps not as dire as it seems upon initial review. Rather their study finds that extrinsic motivators can have both positive and negative effects depending on the specific design and implication of the policy and its perception and evaluation by the employee (Lohmann, Houlfort and De Allegri, 2016). To make broad claims that extrinsic rewards diminish intrinsic motivation should be pursued with caution. Alternatively, one might think about a contingent approach whereby motivational crowding occurs under certain circumstances including the interpersonal context, the perception of the employee, nature of the task performed and individual-level characteristics.

Probably the earliest and most cited determinant of motivational crowding is the perception of the extrinsic reward by the employee (Andersen and Pallesen, 2008; Frey, 1997; Frey and Jegen, 2001). Given the strong theoretical argument that motivational crowding works through a loss of self-determination and autonomy, it should not be surprising that many scholars believe that the likelihood of motivational crowding is contingent on how the extrinsic reward is perceived. If the reward is perceived as controlling, then it is likely to crowd out the intrinsic motivation since it reduces the individual's perception that they can determine their own course of action. Likewise, a perception of command is more likely to distract from the 'warm glow' feeling of self-sacrifice to help others (Jacobsen, Hvitved and Andersen, 2014). Similarly, the effect of external interventions on self-esteem and thus intrinsic motivation are negative when they seem to ignore the worker's motivation, but positive when perceived as support (Frey and Jegen, 2001).

While related to perception, but distinct in important ways, is the interpersonal context within the organization. Interpersonal context refers to the degree to which the environment in which the task is completed influences autonomy, competence or relatedness. Like the research on motivator perception, much of the findings on interpersonal context focus on the degree to which the environment is seen as controlling versus non-controlling (Deci, Koestner and Ryan, 1999). However, it is likely that a wider range of environmental factors could foster or detract from a sense of autonomy, competence and relatedness. Factors such as supervisory support, healthy culture, client interaction and other environmental factors shape the employee experience.

With regards to job design, most scholars now agree that the nature of the job is an important determinant in the effect of external incentives on internal motivation. For tasks which are highly structured and routine, there appears to be minimal effect of extrinsic incentives in crowding out motivation. Empirically speaking, when the task under investigation is dull, the effects of the introduction of external incentives is much weaker (Deci, Koestner and Ryan, 1999). Alternatively, those tasks that are unstructured, complex, require creativity or are personally or socially meaningful are most susceptible to crowding out (Eisenberger, Pierce and Cameron, 1999; Pink, 2011; Wiersma, 1992). As one example, taking advantage of a natural experiment in which performance-based pay was introduced at the Internal Revenue Service (IRS), but not at the Office of the Comptroller of the Currency (OCC), Bertelli (2006) examined how performance-contingent pay affected intrinsic motivation as measured by the Employee Viewpoint Survey. Bertelli found that performance pay had the effect of increasing motivation for non-supervisory employees and decreasing it for supervisory employees. This is consistent with a situation in which more complex and interesting work would have less negative effect.

It is also possible that there may be some demographic differences that explain employee responses to extrinsic motivation. There appear to be consistent differences in terms of how intrinsic and extrinsic motivation play out between the sexes and this difference tends to hold in terms of the effect of motivational crowding. Consistent with stereotypes, women tend to place higher value on other-oriented reputational concerns than do men. As a result, in the absence of extrinsic rewards, women are more likely to engage in socially beneficial activity than men (Bénabou and Tirole, 2006). While too few studies have included sex as a moderator in examining motivational crowding, those that do have tended to find that women are more receptive to crowding out effects than men. When looking at the issue of blood donation, not only do women donate at higher rates than men, but the introduction of financial incentives to donate leads to a disproportionate drop in donations among women. When given the opportunity to donate the extrinsic reward to charity, rates of donation return to normal levels for women, but not for men (Mellström and Johannesson, 2008). Likewise, men and women in the British system demonstrate significantly different motives for public service and responses to extrinsic motivators (Georgellis, Iossma and Tabvuma, 2011). Most provoking among the findings is the conclusion that higher public sector wages in Britain reduces the likelihood of women moving to the public sector as a result of motivation crowding.

Lastly, there also appears to be age effects with younger people experiencing greater motivational crowding effects than older people. This is likely the effect of two factors. First, young people are more likely to be subject to external influences as a means of regulating behavior and thus more sensitive to external interventions. Second, older participants have greater cognitive capacity. Greater cognitive capacity results in an enhanced ability to separate the informational from controlling stimuli and a greater likelihood to interpret stimuli as a reflection of goal-oriented performance (Deci, Koestner and Ryan, 1999).

These contingent factors appear to be broadly relevant across sectors. However, there is also reason to believe that there might be factors unique to the public sector which influence the impact of extrinsic motivation.

MOTIVATIONAL CROWDING AND THE PUBLIC SECTOR

The debate as to how or if public sector organizations differ from private sector organizations is perennial if not unending. Since the 1960s there have been individuals who have minimized the differences between public and nonprofit organizations (Hall, Johnson and Haas, 1967) and this perspective continues to today among scholars who point out that clear distinctions are difficult to identify because of the often overlapping nature of the public and private sector (Cooper, 2002; Kettl, 2015). Despite this skepticism, decades of public administration research have identified a range of differences that have a potential to influence our understanding of public sector motivation. A small sampling of these differences includes the presence of constraints, administrative authority constrained by law, expectations of fairness and public values, goal ambiguity and multiplicity and different motivational incentives (Malatesta and Carboni, 2015).

Employing intrinsically motivated workers has been proposed as a way of strengthening organizational performance in the public sector and thus the issue of motivational crowding has particular relevance for public and nonprofit organizations. Employees are attracted to the public sector because of higher satisfaction with work characteristics and because it offers greater opportunity for altruistic behaviors (Georgellis, Iossa and Tabvuma, 2011).

Likewise, many governments seek out employees who exhibit high levels of altruistic motivation. Government organizations that have ethical or public service objectives seek to attract workers who share these goals (Dixit, 2002). This is true both because of the shared interest but also because it reduces the need of governments to invest in high-powered incentives (Besley and Ghatak, 2005). This is especially true for public organizations where the preferences of government and the client are well aligned such as in education, health care and many public works. Interestingly, Prendergast (2007) finds that there is a disincentive to hiring such public-spirited individuals when the goals of clients and government are not aligned as with criminal proceedings. This section will highlight differences in motivation and structure within the public sector which are important for understanding motivational crowding.

Motivational Differences

Public sector employees demonstrate a higher commitment to altruistic behaviors than private sector employees (Rainey, 2014) and place greater emphasis on intrinsic over extrinsic rewards (Crewson, 1997). This preference tends to hold up for both caring and uncaring occupations (Georgellis, Iossa and Tabvuma, 2011). This is not to say that extrinsic rewards are not valued by public sector employees (Lyons, Duxbury and Higgins, 2006). Rather, it is to say that many public sector employees exhibit higher levels of intrinsic motivation toward their work responsibilities.

This finding that public sector employees are less extrinsically motivated than private sector employees has held up in a wide range of contexts (Buelens and Van den Broeck, 2007). However, there are important differences in this finding based on hierarchy and job characteristics (Buelens and Van den Broeck, 2007). The differences between public and private sector work motivation may arise (1) because the nature of the public sector environment and tasks are such that it causes individuals to exhibit higher levels of intrinsic motivation or (2) because individuals with higher levels of intrinsic motivation are drawn toward the public sector (Feeney, 2008; Houston, 2006).

Structural Differences

In addition to motivational preferences, there are a variety of structural differences that one might expect to influence the impact of extrinsic incentives. Some of which would include pay structures, transparency issues and the presence of rule-based systems.

Public and nonprofit organizations experience different wage structures as a means of compensating employees. At the federal level, these compensation structures are in many ways Janus-faced. On the one hand, the majority of public employees are overcompensated relative to their private sector counterparts (Falk, 2012; Georgellis, Iossa and Tabvuma, 2011). This is especially true when calculations are inclusive of both wages and benefits and is especially true for entry-level and low-skilled workers (Falk, 2012). On the other hand, critics of pay for performance point to the fact that the public sector has insufficient funds to use external motivation in an effective way (Dowling and Richardson, 1997; Heinrich, 2007). These limits to external motivation are rooted in three causes: (1) the standardization of pay under civil service and other pay band systems, (2) budget constraints associated with tax-based revenue streams (Miller and Whitford, 2007), and (3) public opinion mandates that restrict policy makers' willingness to provide impactful external incentives (Perry, Engbers and Jun, 2009). As a result, the issue of motivational crowding becomes particularly relevant as public employees face a risk of having intrinsic motivation crowded out by external incentives, while at the same time are unlikely to experience enough external compensation to offset the loss of intrinsic motivation with a similar volume of extrinsic motivation.

As a result of a myriad of state and national laws, most western democracies have adopted rules requiring standardized pay systems or transparency requirements for public workers (Albano and Leaver, 2004). The pay of public sector workers is widely known with two-thirds of public sector workers reporting that their pay information is publicly available and only 16.2 percent suggesting any restrictions on discussing pay at work (Hegewisch, Williams and Drago, 2011). Consequently, public sector wage transparency increases the likelihood that pay differentials will result in motivational crowding. Under the precepts of equity theory, individual calculations associated with personal motivation, perception of contribution and reward structures become more evident when greater pay information is available. Empirically, this can be found in a 1993 study of college and university faculty which found that greater differences in wages resulted in decreased productivity, collaboration and satisfaction at public colleges where pay is widely known, but not at private colleges and universities where pay is more secretive (Pfeffer and Langton, 1993).

Public organizations are more likely to use rule-based systems than financial incentives as a means of directing individual behavior (Miller and Whitford, 2007). This is true for two reasons. First, as mentioned above, public organizations often do not have the resources necessary to impose effective external financial incentives. Second, the normal solution for inefficient incentives is to rely on penalization or ownership structures such as joint ownership to address the problem of incentives. These solutions are generally unavailable in the public sector. Moreover, the ambiguous goals, uncontrollable environmental factors and level of team production found in many public sector jobs further exacerbate the ability of public employers to effectively use financial incentives, thus shifting toward rule-based control mechanisms (Miller and Whitford, 2007). At the same time, heightened levels of supervision independent of pay has a negative effect on intrinsic motivation (Schulze and Frank, 2003). This leaves public sector managers with somewhat of a 'Sophie's choice' with both pay and supervision decreasing intrinsic motivation under certain circumstances.

IMPLICATIONS FOR PUBLIC SECTOR MANAGEMENT

Based on these motivational and structural factors, motivational crowding has some unique applications to the public sector such as in the areas of public service motivation, pay for performance, human resource administration and public policy implementation.

Public Service Motivation

Given the tenants of motivational crowding theory which suggest that external interventions can serve to crowd out or crowd in intrinsic motivation, the concept of public service motivation represents an important alternative to public management strategies that stress material compensation (Perry and Hondeghem, 2008; Perry and Wise, 1990). While the majority of motivational crowding research has tended to focus on the loss of intrinsic motivation generally, it is important to understand the effects on specific types of intrinsic motivation such as public service motivation which reflects the motive to help others and society (Delfgaauw and Dur, 2008; Hondeghem and Perry, 2009). Public employers have an incentive to retain public service motivation as it is associated with lower cost motivational strategies and has been found to predict a wide range of desirable workplace outcomes, a select sample of which would include job satisfaction, organizational commitment, person-organization fit, mission valence and quality of work (see review of this literature in Ritz, Brewer and Neumann, 2016).

In terms of the relationship between motivational crowding and public service motivation, one might consider both the effects of financial incentives and command incentives. With regard to the effect of financial incentives, the preponderance of the scholarly community has aligned with the dangers of pay incentives for public service motivation. A recent systematic review of the literature on public service motivation found that warning against financial incentives was one of the most cited practical implications among public service motivation research (Ritz, Brewer and Neumann, 2016). At the same time, much of the literature was theoretical or failed to measure motivational crowding in a specific way. In contrast, one local government study found that pay incentives were associated with greater job satisfaction for those employees who possessed the most public service motivation (Stazyk, 2013). Like motivational crowding, the relationship between pay and public service motivation is likely contingent on perception and job characteristics.

The effects of external factors on public service motivation are not limited to financial incentives but include command systems as well. In a study of Danish school teachers, it was found that the use of command structures reduced public service motivation when the commands were perceived as controlling. Theoretically, Jacobsen and colleagues (2014) argued that the perception of command detracts from autonomy and interferes with the relationship structure in ways that shift the motivation from public service to an extrinsic controlled motivation. While the effect of command perception was found across all aspects of public service motivation, it had the greatest negative effect on commitment to public interest and attraction to policy making (Jacobsen, Hvitved and Andersen, 2014).

Pay for Performance

Perhaps more than any other area, the research on motivational crowding has come into conflict with the dominant economic paradigm of pay for performance. The basic premise of pay for performance is that subordinate effort and performance is greatest if it is aligned with pay (Frey and Jegen, 2001). Pay for performance has become very popular within the public sector largely because of its symbolic value which is associated with responsible stewardship of public resources (Taylor and Taylor, 2011). However, the preponderance of research on the efficacy of pay for performance is not optimistic (Perry, Engbers and Jun, 2009). In particular, the effect of contingent compensation on motivational crowding is particularly pessimistic (Bellé, 2015; Bellé and Cantarelli, 2015; Jacobsen and Andersen, 2014).

That is not to say that pay for performance is never appropriate for the public sector. Pay for performance has a place. Under the right circumstances (clear goals, adequate compensation, employee support for merit pay), pay for performance has a positive and substantive effect on employee performance (Greiner et al., 1977). Likewise, the area of public service appears to moderate the likelihood that motivational crowding will occur with pay for performance. Studies within the health care sector tend to find that pay for performance has a largely positive effect (Andersen, 2007; Shaw et al., 2003). In contrast, more traditional government services such as regulatory organizations generally report that pay for performance was more divisive (Bertelli, 2006; Marsden, 2004). At the local government level, the results are likewise mixed. Studies of teacher pay for performance have consistently (though not universally) shown a negative effect on intrinsic motivation and employee job attitudes (Andersen and Pallesen, 2008; Heneman and Young, 1991). Likewise, some early studies of police officers demonstrate a positive effect when clear goals are present (Greiner et al., 1997). More recent research has been less optimistic finding that rarely does pay for performance have a positive impact on agency performance outputs (Johnson, 2012).

Consistent with the argument presented above that motivational crowding is most likely to occur in the face of tasks which are ambiguous and require creativity, so too does the research on pay for performance suggest that merit-based pay systems are likely to be most detrimental to intrinsic motivation when the job task requires interpretation and ambiguity. In the face of well-structured, non-managerial tasks, pay for performance research is more optimistic (Milkovich and Wigdor, 1991; Perry, Engbers and Jun, 2009), but research on managers tends to find a detrimental effect despite conventional wisdom that pay for performance will be most effective at higher levels of organizational leadership (Risher and Fay, 2007).

While this section is critical of pay for performance as a compensation strategy, not all extrinsic motivators have a negative effect. Unexpected and non-contingent financial rewards have been shown to have a positive effect (Deci, Koestner and Ryan, 1999). Likewise, other forms of extrinsic compensation such as job security and lower work hours both have been shown to have a positive effect on government employment without crowding out effects (Georgellis, Iossa and Tabvuma, 2011). Consequently, a holistic approach to compensation is necessary.

Human Resource Functions Implications

There are motivational crowding implications for a wide range of human resource functions ranging from recruitment to performance evaluation. With regard to recruitment, external incentives in the employee recruitment domain do increase the quantity of applicants applying for a position, but can result in decreased quality of those applicants as they lower the level of intrinsic motivation of those who apply (Delfgaauw and Dur, 2007). At the same time, they may reduce the likelihood of individuals choosing the organization based on similarity of values and organizational characteristics (Bretz, Boudreau and Judge, 1994). This is evidenced by the fact that higher levels of predicted earnings reduce the likelihood of accepting employment in the public sector for current private sector employees in the British health and education sectors (though not necessarily in other sectors) (Georgellis, Iossa and Tabvuma, 2011).

Opportunities for interesting work are important in understanding job attraction and recruitment (Georgellis, Iossa and Tabvuma, 2011). To this end, job design is important for reinforcing intrinsic motivation. While over 40 years old, the Hackman and Oldham (1976) job characteristics model continues to provide insight into job design for human motivation (Barrick, Mount and Li, 2013). The theory suggests that by designing jobs to manifest five characteristics (skill variety, task variety, task significance, autonomy and feedback) employees will be better motivated by intrinsic desires such as satisfaction or feelings of contribution. These characteristics are intrinsically impactful because they trigger internal reactions to experience meaningfulness, responsibility for outcomes and knowledge of results (Hackman and Oldham, 1976).

These job design characteristics are consistent with many of the leadership strategies identified in a review of public service motivation. Paarlberg and Lavigna (2010) argue that motivation can be stimulated using a number of non-compensatory strategies. These include (1) aligning employee values and organizational ideology, (2) communicating inspirational ideology, (3) creating value congruence through orientation, (4) setting clear and important public service goals, (5) clarifying the 'line of sight' between work, beneficiaries and the social significance of the job, (6) creating work structures that empower employee participation, and (7) modeling prosocial motivation. Given that motivational crowding is most likely in those tasks that are complex and creative (Bertelli, 2006), aligning job design and compensation is a critical task for avoiding motivational crowding.

Lastly, in terms of performance evaluation, there is reason to believe that the way that performance feedback is provided will have a significant effect on how it influences motivation. When negative performance feedback is perceived as being provided informationally (as opposed to evaluative or controlling), there is a greater likelihood of it having a positive effect on motivation. Alternatively, positive performance feedback has a positive impact regardless of intent on motivation (Deci, Koestner and Ryan, 1999). This suggests that good feedback minimizes authoritative language, acknowledges good performance without rewards, provides choice in terms of how to move forward and emphasizes the intrinsically motivating aspects of work (e.g., interest or challenge).

Public Policy Implications

While the primary focus of this *Handbook* is on the management subfield of public administration, it is worth acknowledging that motivational crowding has implications for how public administrators shape public policy. A number of studies have found that some tax and incentive structures crowd out desirable citizen behavior. For example, economists agree that the high rate of tax compliance in the United States should be understood, at least partially, by citizens' perceived trust by their government and thus subsequent respect for the rule of law (Graetz and Wilde, 1985). Studies in other countries find that those governments in which citizens have the greatest level of participation, thus crowding in the rule of law, exhibit higher levels of tax compliance where more controlling governments exhibit lower levels of compliance (Pommerehne and Weck-Hannemann, 1996).

Another example illustrates how financial incentives might motivate citizens to avoid contributing to public good. Research in Switzerland studying the placement of a nuclear storage facility finds that compensating residents of a community decreases their willingness to accept the undesirable amenity. Without a financial incentive 50.8 percent of residents expressed a willingness to host the undesirable amenity, likely because of a belief that someone must or that they are contributing to the public good. However, when citizens of the same community were told that they would be compensated, the level of acceptance dropped to 24.6 percent because the altruistic motivation was stripped away (Frey and Oberholzer-Gee, 1997). Likewise, research in Columbia, South America, found that external regulation led to greater deforestation than internal self-governance as self-determination and self-esteem declined (Ostmann, 1998).

DIRECTION OF THE FIELD

As this chapter hopefully suggests, a lot is known about motivational crowding. At the same time, it is clear there remain areas of disagreement and relationships that are far from simple, unidirectional causation. This section outlines four research agendas that should be prioritized in subsequent studies of motivational crowding.

Agenda One: Field Experiments

There have been lots of experimental lab studies, but few rigorous random assignment studies in a natural context. This is not to say that there are no field studies. Frey and Gotte (1999) and Barkema (1995) both execute well-designed field studies that compare organizations across an industry and attempt to draw conclusions about motivational crowding based on their management structure and compensation. In both cases the field research validates the consistent findings of laboratory experiments. However, neither of these studies truly can account for the exogenous factors that affect organizational selection and which may affect the impact of extrinsic motivation. As early as 1999, Prendergast expressed skepticism that the empirical research on motivational crowding would hold up in workplace settings in the same way that it has in laboratory studies. Consequently, there remains a need to apply experimental methods to natural contexts to determine how much of the findings of motivational crowding research are constrained by their methodological design.

Agenda Two: Crowding In

This chapter began as an attempt to review the broad literature on motivational crowding as it applies to the public sector. However, it quickly became clear that the overwhelming preponderance of public sector research on motivational crowding is on 'crowding out' and not 'crowding in.' There have been a number of good works that have looked at fostering public service motivation (Moynihan and Pandey, 2007; Pandey and Stazyk, 2008; Wright, Moynihan and Pandey, 2012). However, most research on fostering public service motivation does not directly address motivational crowding and how managerial strategies might reinforce existing levels of public service motivation. Implicit in the study of motivational crowding is the idea that intrinsic motivation is desirable, consequently, research should be as focused on reinforcing its presence as it is on avoiding its loss.

Agenda Three: Comparison of Contingent Structures

As the reviews of motivational crowding make clear, extrinsic rewards are not all the same (Cerasoli, Nicklin and Ford, 2014; Deci, Koestner and Ryan, 1999; Rummel and Feinberg, 1988; Tang and Hall, 1995; Wiersma, 1992). Verbal rewards differ from financial and symbolic rewards. Contingent rewards differ from non-contingent rewards. Most importantly, contingent rewards appear to differ based on whether they are engagement, completion or performance based (Deci, Koestner and Ryan, 1999). However, the overwhelming preponderance of research, especially public sector research has been performance based (Cerasoli, Nicklin and Ford, 2014). Given that past research suggests that engagement and completion contingent rewards appear to be less detrimental to intrinsic motivation, more research should be conducted as to determine their effect in the public sector.

Agenda Four: Contingent Models

This review of motivational crowding takes a very pessimistic view of the effect of extrinsic rewards on intrinsic motivation. However, the effect is likely highly contingent on the person, organization, task and reward structure in terms of the ultimate effect. While a number of well-executed studies have looked at various contingencies such as sex (Georgellis, Iossa and Tabvuma, 2011), age (Deci, Koestner and Ryan, 1999), task (Eisenberger, Pierce and Cameron, 1999), perception (Jacobsen, Hvitved and Andersen, 2014), industry and policy design (Lohmann, Houlfort and De Allegri, 2016), few studies have investigated multiple contingent factors and no one has yet put forth a full contingency model. There is a tremendous need to undertake motivational crowding research that examines multiple industries and considers intervening, moderating and mediating effects. Without such a model, motivational crowding research is doomed to oversimplification.

CONCLUSION

The findings on motivational crowding are rich with implications for public management including the insight they provide on employee recruitment, making selection decisions based on public service motivation, using organizational strategies to increase intrinsic motivation and designing compensation systems (Ritz, Brewer and Neumann, 2016). This review finds that extrinsic rewards do have the potential to negatively impact intrinsic motivation, but that various contingencies moderate that effect. The relevance of this research informs public management scholars with specific focus on pay for performance, public service motivation, human resource management and policy design. However, new research approaches are needed to address the unanswered questions of motivational crowding.

REFERENCES

Adams, J.S. (1963). Towards an understanding of inequity, *The Journal of Abnormal and Social Psychology*, *67*, 422–436.

Albano, G.L. and Leaver, C. (2004), *Transparency, recruitment and retention in the public sector*, Bristol, UK: Centre for Market and Public Organization.

Alexy, O. and Leitner, M. (2011). A fistful of dollars: Are financial rewards a suitable management practice for distributed models of innovation? *European Management Review*, *8*, 165–185.
Andersen, L.B. (2007). Professional norms, public service motivation and economic incentives: What motivates public employees?, paper presented at *EGPA Conference*, Madrid, Spain.
Andersen, L.B. and Pallesen, T. (2008). Not just for the money? How financial incentives affect the number of publications at Danish research institutions, *International Public Management Journal*, *11*, 28–47.
Barkema, H.G. (1995). Do job executives work harder when they are monitored?, *Kyklos*, *48*, 19–42.
Barrick, M.R., Mount, M.K., and Li, N. (2013). The theory of purposeful work behavior: The role of personality, higher-order goals, and job characteristics, *Academy of Management Review*, *38*, 132–153.
Bellé, N. (2015). Performance-related pay and the crowding out of motivation in the public sector: A randomized field experiment, *Public Administration Review*, *75*, 230–241.
Bellé, N. and Cantarelli, P. (2015). Monetary incentives, motivation, and job effort in the public sector: An experimental study with Italian government executives, *Review of Public Personnel Administration*, *35*, 99–123.
Bénabou, R. and Tirole, J. (2006). Incentives and prosocial behavior, *American Economic Review*, *96*, 1652–1678.
Bertelli, A.M. (2006). Motivation crowding and the federal civil servant: Evidence from the US Internal Revenue Service, *International Public Management Journal*, *9*, 3–23.
Besley, T. and Ghatak, M. (2005). Competition and incentives with motivated agents, *American Economic Review*, *95*, 616–636.
Bretz Jr, R.D., Boudreau, J.W., and Judge, T.W. (1994). Job search behavior of employed managers, *Personnel Psychology*, *47*, 275–301.
Buelens, M. and Van den Broeck, H. (2007). An analysis of differences in work motivation between public and private sector organizations. *Public Administration Review*, *67*(1), 65–74.
Cerasoli, C.P., Nicklin, J.M., and Ford, M.T. (2014). Intrinsic motivation and extrinsic incentives jointly predict performance: A 40-year meta-analysis, *Psychological Bulletin*, *140*, 980–1008.
Cooper, P.J. (2002). *Governing by contract: Challenges and opportunities for public managers*, Washington, DC: CQ Press.
Crewson, P.E. (1997). Public-service motivation: Building empirical evidence of incidence and effect, *Journal of Public Administration Research and Theory*, *7*, 499–518.
Deci, E. L. (1971). Effects of externally mediated rewards on intrinsic motivation, *Journal of Personality and Social Psychology*, *18*, 105–115.
Deci, E.L. (1972a). The effects of contingent and noncontingent rewards and controls on intrinsic motivation, *Organizational Behavior and Human Performance*, *8*, 217–229.
Deci, E.L. (1972b). Intrinsic motivation, extrinsic reinforcement, and inequity, *Journal of Personality and Social Psychology*, *22*, 113–120.
Deci, E.L. and Ryan, R.M. (1964). The empirical exploration of intrinsic motivation, *Advances in Experimental Social Psychology*, *13*, 39–76.
Deci, E.L., Koestner, R., and Ryan, R.M. (1999). A meta-analytic review of experiments examining the effects of extrinsic rewards on intrinsic motivation, *Psychological Bulletin*, *125*, 627–668.
Delfgaauw, J. and Dur, R. (2008). Incentives and workers' motivation in the public sector, *The Economic Journal*, *118*, 171–191.
Dixit, A. (2002). Incentives and organizations in the public sector: An interpretative review, *Journal of Human Resources*, *37*, 696–727.
Dowling, B. and Richardson, R. (1997). Evaluating performance-related pay for managers in the National Health Service. *International Journal of Human Resource Management*, *8*(3), 348–366.
Eisenberger, R., Pierce, W.D., and Cameron, J. (1999). Effects of reward on intrinsic motivation—negative, neutral, and positive: Comment on Deci, Koestner, and Ryan, *Psychological Bulletin*, *125*, 677–691.
Falk, J.R. (2012). *Comparing the compensation of federal and private-sector employees*, Washington, DC: Congress of the United States, Congressional Budget Office.
Feeney, M.K. (2008). Sector perceptions among state-level public managers, *Journal of Public Administration Research and Theory*, *18*, 465–494.

Frey, B.S. (1997). *Not just for the money: An economic theory of human behavior*, Cheltenham, UK and Northampton, MA, USA: Edward Elgar Publishing.
Frey, B.S. and Gotte, L. (1999). Does pay motivate volunteers? Unpublished manuscript, Institute for Empirical Economic Research, University of Zurich.
Frey, B.S. and Jegen, R. (2001). Motivation crowding theory, *Journal of Economic Surveys*, *15*, 589–611.
Frey, B. and Oberholzer-Gee, F. (1997). The cost of price incentives: An empirical analysis of motivation crowding-out. *The American Economic Review*, *87*(4), 746–755.
Frey, B.S. and Osterloh, M. (2006). Evaluations: Hidden costs, questionable benefits, and superior alternatives, *University of Zurich IEW Working Paper*, 302.
Georgellis, Y., Iossa, E., and Tabvuma, V. (2011). Crowding out intrinsic motivation in the public sector, *Journal of Public Administration Research and Theory*, *21*, 473–493.
Graetz, M.J. and Wilde, L.L. (1985). The economics of tax compliance: Facts and fantasy, *National Tax Journal*, *38*, 355–363.
Greiner, J.M., Dahl, R.E., Hatry, H.P., and Millar, A.P. (1977). *Monetary incentives and work standards in five cities: Impacts and implications for management and labor*, Washington, DC: The Urban Institute.
Hackman, J.R. and Oldham, G. (1976). Motivation through the design of work: Test of a theory, *Organizational Behavior and Human Performance*, *16*, 250–279.
Hall, R.H., Johnson, N.J., and Haas, J.E. (1967). Organizational size, complexity, and formalization, *American Sociological Review*, *36*, 903–912.
Harackiewicz, J.M. and Manderlink, G. (1984). A process analysis of the effects of performance-contingent rewards on intrinsic motivation, *Journal of Experimental Social Psychology*, *20*, 531–551.
Hegewisch, A., Williams, C., and Drago, R. (2011). *Pay secrecy and wage discrimination*, Washington, DC: Institute for Women's Policy Research.
Heinrich, C.J. (2007). Evidence-based policy and performance management: Challenges and prospects in two parallel movements. *American Review of Public Administration*, *37*(3), 255–277.
Heneman, H.G. and Young, I.P. (1991). Assessment of a merit pay program for school district administrators, *Public Personnel Management*, *20*, 35–48.
Hondeghem, A. and Perry, J.L. (2009). EGPA symposium on public service motivation and performance: Introduction, *International Review of Administrative Sciences*, *75*, 5–9.
Houston, D.J. (2006), Walking the walk of public service motivation: Public employees and charitable gifts of time, blood, and money, *Journal of Public Administration Research and Theory*, *16*, 67–86.
Jacobsen, C.B. and Andersen, L.B. (2014). Performance management in the public sector: Does it decrease or increase innovation and performance? *International Journal of Public Administration*, *37*(14), 1011–1023.
Jacobsen, C.B. and Jensen, L.E. (2017). Why not just for the money? An experimental vignette study of the cognitive price effects and crowding effects of performance-related pay, *Public Performance and Management Review*, *40*, 551–580.
Jacobsen, C.B., Hvitved, J., and Andersen, L.B. (2014) Command and motivation: How the perception of external interventions relates to intrinsic motivation and public service motivation, *Public Administration*, *92*, 790–806.
Johnson, R.R. (2012). Police officer salaries and agency performance outputs, *Criminal Justice Studies*, *25*, 191–203.
Kettl, D.F. (2015). *The transformation of governance: Public administration for the twenty-first century*, Baltimore, MD: Johns Hopkins University Press.
Lepper, M. and Green, D. (1978). *The hidden cost of reward*, Hillsdale, NJ: Laurence Earlbaum Associates.
Lohmann, J., Houlfort, N., and De Allegri, M. (2016). Crowding out or no crowding out? A Self-Determination Theory approach to health worker motivation in performance-based financing, *Social Science and Medicine*, *169*, 1–8.
Lyons, S.T., Duxbury, L.E., and Higgins, C.A. (2006). A comparison of the values and commitment of private sector, public sector, and parapublic sector employees, *Public Administration Review*, *66*, 605–618.
Malatesta, D. and Carboni, J.L. (2015). The public–private distinction: Insights for public administration from the state action doctrine, *Public Administration Review*, *75*, 63–74.

Marsden, D. (2004). The role of performance-related pay in renegotiating the 'effort bargain': The case of the British public service. *ILR Review*, *57*(3), 350–370.

Mellström, C. and Johannesson, M. (2008). Crowding out in blood donation: Was Titmuss right?, *Journal of the European Economic Association*, *6*, 845–863.

Milkovich, G.T. and Wigdor, A.K. (1991). *Pay for performance: Evaluating performance appraisal and merit pay*, Washington, DC: National Academy Press.

Miller, G.J. and Whitford, A.B. (2007). The principal's moral hazard: Constraints on the use of incentives in hierarchy, *Journal of Public Administration Research and Theory*, *17*, 213–233.

Moynihan, D.P. and Pandey, S.K. (2007). The role of organizations in fostering public service motivation, *Public Administration Review*, *67*, 40–53.

Niza, C., Tung, B., and Marteau, T.M. (2013). Incentivizing blood donation: Systematic review and meta-analysis to test Titmuss' hypotheses, *Health Psychology*, *32*, 941–949.

Ostmann, A. (1998). External control may destroy the commons, *Rationality and Society*, *10*, 103–122.

Paarlberg, L. and Lavigna, B. (2010). Transformational leadership and public service motivation: Driving individual and organizational performance, *Public Administration Review*, *70*, 710–718.

Pandey, S.K. and Stazyk, E.C. (2008). Antecedents and correlates of public service motivation. In J.L. Perry and A. Hondeghem (eds), *Motivation in public management: The call of public service*, London: Oxford University Press, pp. 101–117.

Perry, J L. and Hondeghem, A. (2008). Building theory and empirical evidence about public service motivation, *International Public Management Journal*, *11*, 3–12.

Perry, J.L. and Wise, L.R. (1990). The motivational bases of public service, *Public Administration Review*, *50*, 367–373.

Perry, J.L., Engbers, T.A., and Jun, S.Y. (2009). Back to the future? Performance-related pay, empirical research, and the perils of persistence, *Public Administration Review*, *69*, 39–51.

Pfeffer, J. and Langton, N. (1993). The effect of wage dispersion on satisfaction, productivity, and working collaboratively: Evidence from college and university faculty, *Administrative Science Quarterly*, *38*, 382–407.

Pink, D.H. (2011). *Drive: The surprising truth about what motivates us*, London: Penguin.

Pommerehne, W.W. and Weck-Hannemann, H. (1996). Tax rates, tax administration and income tax evasion in Switzerland, *Public Choice*, *88*, 161–170.

Prendergast, C. (1999). The provision of incentives in firms, *Journal of Economic Literature*, *37*, 7–63.

Prendergast, C. (2007). The motivation and bias of bureaucrats, *American Economic Review*, *97*, 180–196.

Rainey, H.G. (2014). *Understanding and managing public organizations*, San Francisco, CA: Jossey Bass.

Reeson, A.F. and Tisdell, J.G. (2008). Institutions, motivations and public goods: An experimental test of motivational crowding, *Journal of Economic Behavior and Organization*, *68*, 273–281.

Risher, H. and Fay, C.H. (2007). *Managing for better performance: Enhancing federal performance management practices*, Washington, DC: IBM Center for the Business of Government.

Ritz, A., Brewer, G.A., and Neumann, O. (2016). Public service motivation: A systematic literature review and outlook, *Public Administration Review*, *76*, 414–426.

Rummel, A., and Feinberg, R. (1988). Cognitive evaluation theory: A meta-analytic review of the literature. *Social Behavior and Personality: An International Journal*, *16*(2), 147–164.

Ryan, R.M. and Deci, E.L. (2017). *Self-determination theory: Basic psychological needs in motivation, development, and wellness*, New York, NY: Guilford Publications.

Selart, M., Nordström, T., Kuvaas, B., and Takemura, K. (2008). Effects of reward on self-regulation, intrinsic motivation and creativity, *Scandinavian Journal of Educational Research*, *52*, 439–458.

Shaw, J.D., Duffy, M.K., Mitra, A., Lockhart, D.E., and Bowler, M. (2003). Reactions to merit pay increases: A longitudinal test of a signal sensitivity perspective, *Journal of Applied Psychology*, *88*, 538–544.

Schulze, G.G. and Frank, B. (2003). Deterrence versus intrinsic motivation: Experimental evidence on the determinants of corruptibility, *Economics of Governance*, *4*, 143–160.

Stazyk, E.C. (2013). Crowding out public service motivation? Comparing theoretical expectations with empirical findings on the influence of performance-related pay, *Review of Public Personnel Administration*, *33*, 252–274.

Tang, S.H. and Hall, V.C. (1995). The overjustification effect: A meta-analysis. *Applied Cognitive Psychology*, 9(5), 365–404.
Taylor, J. and Taylor, R. (2011). Working hard for more money or working hard to make a difference? Efficiency wages, public service motivation, and effort, *Review of Public Personnel Administration*, 31, 67–86.
Titmuss, R. (2018). *The gift relationship (reissue): From human blood to social policy*, Bristol, UK: Policy Press.
Wiersma, U.J. (1992). The effects of extrinsic rewards in intrinsic motivation: A meta-analysis, *Journal of Occupational and Organizational Psychology*, 65, 101–114.
Wright, B.E., Moynihan, D.P., and Pandey, S.K. (2012). Pulling the levers: Transformational leadership, public service motivation, and mission valence, *Public Administration Review*, 72, 206–215.

5. Self-determination theory and public employee motivation research
Justin M. Stritch, Ulrich Thy Jensen and Michelle Allgood

INTRODUCTION

According to Deci and Ryan (2008), self-determination theory (SDT) is a macrotheory of human motivation that 'addresses such basic issues as personality development, self-regulation, universal psychological needs, life goals and aspirations, energy and vitality, nonconscious processes, the relations of culture to motivation, and the impact of social environments on motivation, affect, behavior, and well-being' (p. 182). Vansteenkiste, Niemiec, and Soenens (2010) describe SDT as 'similar to the construction of a puzzle. Over the years, new pieces have been added to the theory once their fit was determined' (p. 105).

As such, there are many different interconnected dimensions of the SDT macrotheory and streams of research that have followed. While SDT developed initially to enhance our understanding of intrinsic and extrinsic motivations, SDT research has expanded well beyond its initial scope. SDT must be presented as a discussion of its constituent parts (or mini-theories): (1) Cognitive Evaluation Theory (CET), (2) Organismic Integration Theory (OIT), (3) Causality Integrations Theory (CIT), (4) Basic Psychological Needs Theory (BPNT), and (5) Goal Contents Theory (GCT).[1] One of the drawbacks of such a macro-theoretical approach is that it does not lead to a parsimonious explanation of key variables and theoretical mechanisms describing relationships. While book-length treatments of all SDT perspectives can be found elsewhere (Deci and Ryan, 2004; Gagné, 2014), our goal in this chapter is to outline the key constructs and propositions and discuss how they have been used to enhance our understanding of workplace motivation, paying particular attention to their role in public management research.

SDT has been credited for greatly enhancing our understanding of human motivation in a wide range of social settings. SDT research has considered the link between motivation and performance in education (Reeve, 2002), athletics and physical competition (Hagger and Chatzisarantis, 2007), as well as in studies of mental health and behavioral change (Wild, Cunningham, and Ryan, 2006). In the early 2000s, Gagné and Deci (2005) brought renewed attention to the importance of SDT and its mini-theories to scholars in business and management. In discussing the importance of SDT to the study of workplace motivation, Gagné and Deci (2005) note that 'The primary difference between SDT and most other work motivation theories is that the novel contribution of SDT is on the relative strength of autonomous versus controlled motivation, rather than on the total amount of motivation' (pp. 340–341). Such perspectives are critical when considering the effects of extrinsic incentives, such as pay and control regimes (e.g., pay for performance systems), on individual employee motivation. As we will discuss further, the SDT approach allows for considerable nuance in understanding how extrinsic motives might function in individuals.

Public administration and management researchers have also drawn from SDT and its constituent parts to enhance our understanding of motivation in the public workplace (Chen and Bozeman, 2013; Fernandez and Moldogaziev, 2015). While discussed in greater detail in the pages that follow, Cognitive Evaluation Theory has proven useful in explaining motivation crowding in public sector organizations and the effects of different types of motives (e.g., extrinsic and intrinsic) on employee behaviors and outcomes (Bellé, 2015; Georgellis, Iossa, and Tabvuma, 2011; Jacobsen and Andersen, 2014). Similarly, Organismic Integration Theory has provided a more nuanced way of understanding external controls in relation to extrinsic motives and their subsequent effects on motivation (e.g., Pedersen, 2015). Indeed, given the prominence of intrinsic and extrinsically oriented motives, values and belief systems and mechanisms of external control and accountability in public administration and management research, it is natural that scholars have turned to SDT for insights.

The goal of this chapter is twofold. First, we want to give the reader a better sense of what exactly constitutes SDT. To do so, we discuss the initial conceptualization and development of SDT along with its central constructs. We do this by providing a description of the key facets of five SDT 'mini-theories.' We hope to paint a more nuanced picture of the different theoretical perspectives that exist and what is conveyed when people simply refer to SDT. Second, we intend to show how the theory has been used to enhance public administration and management research.

SELF-DETERMINATION THEORY

Background and Overview

Ryan, Kuhl, and Deci (1997) describe SDT as using empirical methods to study motivation and personality while employing an organismic metatheory that emphasizes the role of humans' evolved inner resources for personality development and behavioral self-regulation (cited in Ryan and Deci, 2000, p. 68). In some ways, SDT was a reaction to the behaviorism and emphasis on external controls prevalent in psychological research in the late 1960s. Given the orientation towards growth, well-being and the enhancement of life experiences, SDT is frequently considered an important part of the positive psychology movement, which emphasizes human well-being and flourishing as opposed to an orientation that focuses on the psychological abnormalities in individuals (Gagné and Vansteenkiste, 2013; Patterson and Joseph, 2007; Sheldon and Ryan, 2011).

The emergence of SDT can be traced to early studies on the effects of extrinsic rewards on an individual's intrinsic motivations when researchers started to observe that extrinsic rewards would have a deleterious effect on intrinsic motivation (Deci and Ryan, 2012). According to Gagné and Deci (2005), SDT offers additional theoretical insights borne out of initial formulations of intrinsic and extrinsic motivations that simply treated extrinsic and intrinsic rewards as additive in nature (Porter and Lawler, 1968; Vroom, 1964). As the authors observe:

> one strand of research concerning the additivity of intrinsic and extrinsic motivation was potentially problematic and controversial. Specifically, early studies testing the additivity hypothesis found that tangible extrinsic rewards undermined intrinsic motivation whereas verbal rewards enhanced it (Deci, 1971), thus implying that intrinsic and extrinsic motivation can be positively and negatively interactive rather than additive. (Gagné and Deci, 2005, p. 332)

According to Deci and Ryan (2008), 'the type or quality of a person's motivation would be more important than the total amount of motivation for predicting many important outcomes such as psychological health and well-being, effective performance, creative problem solving, and deep or conceptual learning' (p. 182). These early observations paved the way for the first generation of SDT research and the initial formulations of Cognitive Evaluation Theory, Organismic Integration Theory and Causality Orientations Theory (Deci and Ryan, 1985b).

Traditionally, *intrinsic motivation* is described as doing work because of the enjoyment and fulfillment that comes from completing the work itself. In contrast, *extrinsic motivation* requires instrumentality between the completion of the task and separable consequences, such as monetary or verbal rewards (Gagné and Deci, 2005, p. 331). However, from an SDT perspective, intrinsic motivation is more than simply enjoyment and fulfillment—intrinsic motivation is part of human nature and is reflected in the ways humans challenge themselves, the pursuit of new experiences and perspectives and engagement in behaviors that demonstrate curiosity such as search and exploration (Deci, 1975). As Vansteenkiste, Niemiec, and Soenens (2010) note, within the SDT framework, intrinsic motivation is not the active pursuit of enjoyment prior to initiating an activity or behavior, but, in contrast, 'enjoyment is the byproduct of full immersion in the activity' (p. 107).

A critical contribution of SDT to motivation research is the distinction the perspective makes regarding *autonomous* and *controlled* motivations. Building on work suggesting an extrinsic/intrinsic categorization of motives, the SDT framework considers differences between autonomy and control within extrinsic motives. According to Deci and Ryan (2008), by considering extrinsic motives with different levels of external regulation, the theory allows for an integration of internalized, external motives (p. 182). In doing so, SDT provides a much more complex vision of extrinsic motives and creates a path through which external forces can be internalized and become a part of one's sense of self.

At its core, SDT considers the primacy of an individual's need for autonomy, competence and relatedness. *Autonomy* refers to the ability of an individual to act as the causal agent. *Competence* refers to an individual's ability to complete a task effectively (or efficiently). *Relatedness* refers to an individual's willingness to interact, cooperate and care for others (Ryan and Deci, 2000). According to the SDT perspective, these three innate psychological needs facilitate natural propensities for growth and integration, as well as social development and personal well-being (Ryan and Deci, 2000, p. 68). SDT holds that these three basic needs must be satisfied in order to foster individual growth and well-being.

SDT, as just described at the broadest level, identifies broad constructs and relationships; the SDT framework relies on what scholars refer to as its mini-theories for more specific identification of theoretical relationships among variables and discussions of key constructs. Indeed, as a collective endeavor, SDT researchers have adopted an approach to modify and evolve the SDT framework in the face of inconsistent or unexpected findings, facilitating the development of different mini-theories. Prior to our discussion of SDT in public management research on the topic of employee motivation, we provide a brief overview of the theories that fall within the SDT framework.

Cognitive Evaluation Theory

Cognitive Evaluation Theory (CET) was the first of the mini-theories within the SDT framework to emerge (Deci, 1975). CET was developed as a means of understanding how extrinsic

Table 5.1   Deci and Ryan's (1985b) propositions for Cognitive Evaluation Theory

Proposition 1: 'External events relevant to the initiation or regulation of behavior will affect a person's intrinsic motivation to the extent that the events affect the perceived locus of causality of that behavior. Events that promote a more external perceived locus of causality will undermine intrinsic motivation. Whereas those that promote a more internal perceived locus of causality will enhance intrinsic motivation.' (p. 62)
Proposition 2: 'External events will affect a person's intrinsic motivation for an optimally challenging activity to the extent they influence the person's perceived competence within the context of some self-determination. Events that promote greater perceived competence will enhance intrinsic motivation, whereas those that diminish perceived competence will decrease intrinsic motivation.' (p. 63)
Proposition 3: 'Events relevant to the initiation and regulation of behavior have three potential aspects, each with functional significance. The informational aspect facilitates an internal perceived locus of causality and perceived competence, thus enhancing intrinsic motivation. The controlling aspect facilitates an external perceived locus of causality, thus undermining intrinsic motivation and promoting extrinsic compliance or defiance. The amotivating aspect facilitates perceived incompetence, thus undermining intrinsic motivation and promoting amotivation. The relative salience of these three aspects to a person determines the functional significance of an event.' (p. 64)

rewards could diminish levels of intrinsic motivation (Deci, 1971). Central to CET is the concept of *locus of causality*, which is a construct that 'reflects the degree to which one is self-determining with respect to their own behavior' (Deci and Ryan, 1985b, p. 62). The theoretical propositions of CET outlined by Deci and Ryan (1985b, pp. 62–4) are presented in Table 5.1.

According to Rummel and Feinberg (1988), individuals who are intrinsically motivated attribute 'the cause of their behavior to internal needs and performed those behaviors for intrinsic rewards and satisfaction' (p. 147). In contrast, externally controlling events (e.g., performance requirements, monetary incentives, etc.) pressure people to think or behave in certain ways that can undermine intrinsic motivation. According to Deci (1971), individuals who are working under conditions of extrinsic rewards engage in a cognitive re-evaluation process of the activity—and a shift from an intrinsically oriented motivation of the work to one that is extrinsic in nature. The shift in the perceived locus of causality—from an internal, intrinsic motivation to one that is external in nature—would lead to a decline in a person's intrinsic motivation due to decreases of volition and interest.

In addition to the locus of causality, individual competence and self-determination play a critical role in CET, as well as information. Deci (1971) characterizes rewards as either informational or controlling in nature. According to Rummel and Feinberg (1988), 'After receiving controlling rewards, an intrinsically motivated person's locus of causality was hypothesized to shift from internal to external causing the individual to perform only if he/she expects future external rewards' (p. 148). Information provides a mechanism through which individuals can assess their competence on the rewarded activity. Depending on whether competence or incompetence is conveyed, self-determination is subsequently affected and will result in either increases or decreases of intrinsic motivations (p. 148). Such perspectives allow for CET to consider how external events, such as receiving information regarding competence, can facilitate both interest and enjoyment of tasks (Vansteenkiste, Niemiec, and Soenens, 2010).

Organismic Integration Theory

Early motivation research typically considered external motivation and intrinsic motivation as separate constructs. However, SDT scholars take a differentiated view of extrinsic motivation. Indeed, rather than thinking of extrinsic and intrinsic motivation as inherently separate, researchers began to think of the degree to which extrinsic motivation might be experienced as either autonomous versus controlled, suggesting a continuum along which scholars might distinguish different extrinsic motivations (Ryan and Connell, 1989). A second important facet of Organismic Integration Theory (OIT) relates to how individuals internalize externally motivated behaviors that are socially important and self-initiated, but not intrinsically motivated. *Internalization* is a process through which individuals become socialized and endorse various societal norms and values; the internalization process is one that promotes social responsibility (Ryan and Deci, 2000). Internalization is an active process, transforming outer regulation to one that becomes driven internally. According to Deci and Ryan (1985b), internalization is a natural process and allows for an understanding of how 'behaviors an organism would not do naturally will have to be extrinsically motivated, but that these behaviors may be integrated into the realm of self-determination (i.e., they can be valued and done willingly), even though they will never become intrinsically motivated' (p. 131).

Based on experimental findings that were originally conceived as extensions of CET (e.g., Koestner et al., 1984; Ryan, 1982), the OIT distinguishes among four types of extrinsic regulatory styles in addition to amotivation (or helplessness) and intrinsic motivation (see Vansteenkiste, Niemiec, and Soenens, 2010, pp. 114–17). These different extrinsic regulations are:

1. *External regulation* allows for the least amount of individual autonomy as behaviors are incentivized by rewards and punishments. Externally regulated motivation allows only for compliance with external demands and there is no value internalization that occurs.
2. *Introjected regulation* occurs when individuals perform a behavior that is partially internalized as a means of garnering pride and self-esteem, or to avoid feelings such as guilt. Thus, introjected regulation involves a low-level internalization.
3. *Identified regulation* is when individuals both understand the personal value and significance of a particular behavior. Both personal values and endorsements drive identified regulation, increasing the level of internalization of the behavior—although the behavior is not fully internalized.
4. *Integrated regulation* occurs when the values and the goals of the behavior are fully internalized in the individual and are fully aligned with an individual's conception of self. At this level of regulation, there is a complete internalization of the value of the behavior.

OIT allows for an understanding of external events that can be experienced as both autonomous and volitional. The essential premise of OIT is that individuals can develop interests in behaviors that once did not interest them. Through the process, individuals develop towards self-determined regulation of those behaviors (Deci and Ryan, 1985b, p. 133). Furthermore, research has shown that higher levels of internalization and more autonomous motivations are associated with a range of positive outcomes such as persistence, performance and social functioning, whereas increases in controlled motivation can have deleterious effects on these outcomes (Vansteenkiste, Niemiec, and Soenens, 2010).

Causality Orientations Theory

Deci and Ryan (1985a) argue that differences exist in individuals' orientations towards the environment, and these interpersonal differences will drive variation in individuals' experiences and how they interpret and understand events. Causality Orientations Theory (COT) distinguishes among the *autonomous*, *controlled* and *impersonal* as three broad classes of behavior and motivationally relevant psychological processes. Deci and Ryan (1985a) developed a general measure of causality orientations, which provides measures of an individual's orientations towards autonomous, control-determined and impersonal functioning. Knowing individual orientations could then help us understand an individual's motivational responses to various interventions and environmental contexts.

Koestner and Zuckerman (1994) point to the frequent confusion between the terms 'locus of causality' and 'locus of control' (p. 324). The authors cite Deci and Ryan's (1991) distinction among these key constructs:

> Locus of control being internal versus external refers to whether a person believes that outcomes can (versus cannot) be reliably attained: in other words it refers to contingency expectation, with efficacy expectations implicit within them. Thus locus of control allows one to predict whether a person is likely to engage in motivated action. In contrast, locus of causality being internal versus external refers to whether the experienced locus of initiation for a motivated action is internal versus external to one's self. (Deci and Ryan, 1991, p. 249; quoted in Koestner and Zuckerman, 1994 on p. 324)

As such, COT considers variation in the locus of causality. According to Koestner and Zuckerman (1994), individuals who have an orientation towards autonomous functioning are predicted to be more likely to seek out various choices and experience their actions and behaviors as self-initiated and self-determined. In contrast, individuals with an orientation towards controlled functioning are expected to seek out controls and interpret events and their environmental context as controlling—using verbiage such as *should*, *need to*, *must* and *ought to* (Deci and Ryan, 1985b, p. 157). Finally, individuals with impersonal orientations view themselves as having no control over their own behaviors and no ability to obtain different outcomes, leading some to call this orientation amotivational (Koestner and Zuckerman, 1994, pp. 322–3).

Following Deci and Ryan (1985a), both autonomy and control orientations should increase the belief in an individual's internal locus of control. In contrast, the impersonal orientation should increase belief in external locus of control. In research, the control-determined and autonomous orientations were found to be orthogonal, as Knee and Zuckerman (1996) observe, 'implying that the degree to which one generally perceives situations as fostering growth and learning says little about the degree to which one perceives them as imposing pressure and control' (p. 77). According to Hagger and Chatzisarantis (2011), 'causality orientations can be viewed as reflecting a continuum ranging from high to low levels of generalized perceptions of self-determination with respect to action' (p. 486).

Researchers have consistently found a positive relationship between autonomy orientation and positive self-evaluations, including self-efficacy, private self-consciousness and ego-development (Deci and Ryan, 1985a; Koestner and Zuckerman, 1994; Scherhorn and Grunert, 1988), as well as positive relationships between autonomy and internal locus of control. In contrast, Deci and Ryan (1985a) found control orientation to be related to an extrinsic orientation towards activities. Individuals with higher control orientations are more likely to report that it is important to perform well and have a greater time conscientiousness. Individuals with higher control orientations are also more likely to experience hostile feelings. The control orientation has no relationship (positive or negative) with self-evaluations. In summarizing research regarding achievement, Koestner and Zuckerman (1994) note that 'control orientation appears to be related to the adoption of a pressured extrinsic orientation toward activities' (p. 323). An impersonal orientation is associated with low self-esteem, and individuals with this orientation have an external locus of control (Deci and Ryan, 1985a).

Basic Psychological Needs Theory

Basic psychological needs theory (BPNT) posits that innate psychological nutriments are necessary for psychological and physical health as well as social wellness (Vansteenkiste, Niemiec, and Soenens, 2010, p. 131). These psychological needs are autonomy, competence and relatedness and, as noted earlier, they lie at the heart of the SDT framework. While psychological needs are not new to motivation research, Van den Broeck et al. (2016) point to two unique contributions of BPNT. First, these needs are viewed as innate in the individual and are not acquired through socialization. Second, needs enable individuals' natural inclinations towards growth, internalization and well-being.

Autonomy refers to the need for one to act with a sense of ownership over their behavior and the need to feel psychologically free. It is important to note, however, that autonomy does not mean to act independently of the desires of others. Rather, it means to act with a sense of choice and volition, even if the action is consistent with the wishes or preferences of others. *Competence* refers to a sense of command over one's own skills and abilities, as well as being able to learn and develop new skills. Finally, *relatedness* refers to the need to feel connected to others, and the need to both care for and feel cared for by others (Van den Broeck et al., 2016, pp. 1198–9).

Following the identification of the needs themselves, BPNT specifies three dimensions of the social environment that can support or thwart the satisfaction of autonomy, competence and relatedness. First, an autonomy supportive context can promote the exercise of volition by organizational members. Second, a structured environment can promote competence, in contrast to an environment that is disorganized and chaotic. Finally, social contexts characterized by warmth and concern for others can facilitate relatedness (Vansteenkiste, Niemiec, and Soenens, 2010, pp. 131–2). Often, however, there are times when the social context does not support basic psychological needs. Such contexts might be described as thwarting basic needs and driving need frustration and, ultimately, making people prone to negative behaviors (Vansteenkiste and Ryan, 2013).

Goals Contents Theory

Scholars in the SDT community have sought to identify the content of different goals and how that content is associated with individual well-being. Kasser and Ryan (1996) argue for two broad classifications of goals—intrinsic and extrinsic. The authors define *extrinsic goals* as those that 'typically depend on the contingent reaction of others. Further they are usually engaged as means to some other end' (p. 280). Such goals are commonly operationalized as money or some type of social recognition. In contrast, *intrinsic goals* are described as ones inherently rewarding to pursue and allow us to meet our innate psychological needs for competence, relatedness and autonomy (Sheldon et al., 2004, p. 475).

Goals Contents Theory (GCT) posits that while extrinsic goals can be important for some levels of satisfaction of basic needs, if extrinsic goals become particularly strong and become weighted more heavily as to be significantly imbalanced with intrinsic goals, then the consequence is going to negatively affect well-being (Sheldon et al., 2004). Some authors have contended that the content of the goals (extrinsic or intrinsic) was not important and what mattered were the motives (autonomous versus controlled). However, Carver and Baird (1998) present evidence suggesting that goal content (extrinsic and intrinsic) does explain variation in well-being beyond what is accounted for by the motivation to pursue the goal (autonomous versus controlled).

The SDT framework is broad and has been used to develop many streams of research on human motivation. SDT has also been incorporated into the public management and public administration literature. The following section will provide an overview of how scholars have used SDT to advance our understanding of public employee motivation.

SDT IN PUBLIC EMPLOYEE MOTIVATION RESEARCH

SDT is no stranger to public administration and management research. While the framework often is applied in the context of its mini-theories, its application spans the issues of formation of job preferences and hiring (Asseburg et al., 2020; Linos, 2018), empowerment and innovation (Fernandez and Moldogaziev, 2015; Park and Hassan, 2018) and accountability (Ossege, 2012). A search of the term 'self-determination theory' in December 2019 of the *Journal of Public Administration Research and Theory*, *Public Administration Review*, *Review of Public Personnel Administration*, *Public Administration*, *International Public Management Journal* and *Public Management Review* reveals that since 2007, 87 published research articles make reference to SDT. While a systematic literature review is not the goal of this chapter, a glance at the literature quickly demonstrates SDT's prevalence in public management and administration research.

One topic has adopted insights from SDT far more than any other in public management research: motivation. Motivation research in public management has utilized insights from SDT and its subcomponents when grappling with vexing questions, such as: Is there a unique public service motivation and, if so, what kind of motivation is it? How do public service workers' motivations change over time? Why do some factors in the environment cultivate (or 'crowd in') motivation when others destroy ('crowd out') it?

Following OIT, public management scholars have embraced the idea that public service professionals have motivational profiles composed of a mixed set of more or less autonomous and controlled types of motivation (Wise, 2004). Scholars have thus inquired into the role of intrinsic or fully autonomous types of motivation as well as more extrinsic or controlled motivational factors (Bellé, 2015; Bellé and Cantarelli, 2014; Mergel, Bellé, and Nasi, 2021; Weske and Schott, 2018). However, more disagreement exists around the conceptual basis of public service motivation. While often considered as an 'intrinsic motivation' in early research, scholars have drawn on OIT's more complex and nuanced continuum to suggest that public service motivation (PSM) involves an instrumentality between actions and the desired external effects on the well-being of other people and communities.

As noted by Jensen and Bro (2018), 'PSM has both autonomous and extrinsic characteristics. When public service motivated activities are based on the expected outcome of the activity (to do good), they may involve efforts directed at tasks that are not seen as inherently interesting' (p. 537). However, the expected outcomes of public service motivated actions are not exclusively driven by external demands, but rather emerge as a product of an alignment between the individual's self-concept and the values of the institutional and organizational context. While scholars can split hairs over labeling PSM as an 'identified regulated' or 'integrated regulated' motivation, this development showcases the utility of SDT's OIT in pushing the conceptual frontiers of PSM towards a theory with a clear institutional basis that emphasizes the role of socialization and internalization of social norms and values (Vandenabeele, 2007), rather than casting it as a mere application of intrinsic motivation theory to public service organizations.

A second key proposition in OIT that has received much less attention is the notion that motivation for a task can change over time as part of an internalization process—for instance, by developing more self-determined regulation of those behaviors. An institutional theory on PSM, and adjacent theories that provide inspiration such as social identity theory, is inherently dynamic in nature, suggesting that values are transmitted by an institutional or social logic. However, neither theories on PSM nor empirical evidence have adopted this key insight from OIT or subjected it to scrutiny in the field. Despite recent attempts to start tracking PSM over time (Brænder and Andersen, 2013; Jensen, Kjeldsen, and Vestergaard, 2020; Kjeldsen and Jacobsen, 2013; Vogel and Kroll, 2016) and value alignment and internalization (Jensen, 2018), these efforts have been limited in scope to changes in the intensity of motivation rather than any transitory effects on the type of motivation as a result of an internalization process. This points to an important blind spot of PSM theory that could benefit from further integration of insights from OIT, but that would also require very ambitious empirical research designs with experimental and longitudinal features to isolate motivation for specific tasks while observing dynamic changes in the type of motivation over time.

In addition to the application of OIT for 'labeling' PSM as a specific type of extrinsic autonomous motivation, public administration and management scholars have drawn on CET and BPNT for understanding how organizational leadership and governance initiatives cultivate or erode individuals' work motivation. The studies predominantly follow an assumption of negative effects on—or 'crowding out' of—worker motivation in response to stimuli in the environment such as command and control systems or pay-for-performance incentive structures (Andersen, Kristensen, and Pedersen, 2015; Bellé, 2015; Georgellis, Iossa, and Tabvuma, 2011; Weibel, Rost, and Osterloh, 2010). These studies adopt the notion from CET that individuals' intrinsic motivation can diminish in response to extrinsic rewards if the 'locus of causality' for an activity shifts from a state of self-determination to one where individuals feel pressured to behave in a certain way.

At the same time, public management scholars have drawn on BPNT to help understand why motivation is sometimes reinforced—or crowded in (Pedersen et al., 2018)—and why it is sometimes diminished—or crowded out (Andersen, Kristensen, and Pedersen, 2015; Weibel, Rost, and Osterloh, 2010). BPNT asserts that the factors in social environments influence the satisfaction of individuals' basic psychological needs, which in turn provide the foundation for autonomous types of work motivation, including PSM and intrinsic motivation. As such, public management scholars have followed 'motivation crowding theory' to argue and demonstrate that factors in the social environment like leadership or the implementation of policies can play a role in shaping individuals' basic needs satisfaction (Jensen and Bro, 2018), the perception of external interventions as supportive or controlling of one's work (Mikkelsen, Jacobsen, and Andersen, 2017) and how such perceptions, in turn, correlate with service professionals' autonomous motivations. In an example of the latter, Jacobsen and Andersen (2014) report a negative correlation between Danish school teachers' perceptions of a policy to adopt mandatory student plans for documenting learning goals and outcomes as controlling of their work and their intrinsic motivation as well as PSM.

These results offer a cautionary note to public management scholars and practitioners that external interventions such as documentation requirements and monetary incentives not only produce a positive price/disciplining effect, but also risk crowding out autonomous types of motivations; individuals' perceptions of such instruments critically hinge on how factors in the social environment support or thwart the satisfaction of workers' basic psychological needs for feeling autonomous, competent and related in one's work. Questions of how public managers can cultivate autonomous work motivation—or avoid diminishing it—are critical to high-performing public organizations. By integrating insights from SDT's mini-theories of CET and BPNT, public management scholars continue to advance theoretical frontiers of motivation research in the public sector as well as generating propositions and recommendations with real implications and value for public managers.

CONCLUSION

While this chapter provides an overview of the SDT framework and its application in public management and administration scholarship, like most social science theories, SDT has received its share of critiques and criticism over the years (e.g., Butler, 1989; Calder and Staw, 1975; Carver and Scheier, 2000; Gunnell et al., 2012; Locke and Latham, 1990; Rudy et al., 2007; Wasserkamf, Kleinert, and Chermette, 2018). For example, measurement concerns have long persisted regarding the operationalization of key constructs within the mini-theories. For instance, in OIT, Wasserkampf, Kleinert, and Chermette (2018) argue that the 'variable-centered approaches' in measurement and analysis as a way to analyze the impact of different autonomous and controlled motives on an individual may not fully accept 'OIT's central assumption of co-existing regulations when regulating behaviour' (pp. 31–2). Others have noted that an overreliance on single-item measures to operationalize constructs within BPNT and modifications of measures have led to unreliable and inaccurate reports of needs in research (Gunnel et al., 2012). While issues of measurement persist, we must note that similar concerns are common in many areas of social science research.

Perhaps more fundamental are the concerns about conceptual issues that have been raised regarding SDT. For example, Carver and Scheier (2000) argue that many concepts central to SDT lack clarity and question whether the concepts of autonomy, relatedness and competence are as distinct as those who operate within the SDT framework claim. In addition, researchers have raised questions about the validity of the continuum of external regulation that is central to OIT (Wasserkampf, Kleinert, and Chermette, 2018).

The issue of culture is one that also raises conceptual issues for SDT. Rudy et al. (2007) note that autonomy tends to only focus on the individual, which may not be the most important item in the culture. Jang et al. (2009) point to the need to consider how different cultures have different beliefs about what constitutes autonomy, motivation and the basic needs to be addressed. To be clear, the challenge of considering cultural differences has also been a common critique of positive psychology more generally (see Fineman, 2006). While a full review of the criticism leveled against the SDT framework is beyond our scope, these concerns are important to consider as the field of public management continues to integrate SDT into its research agenda.

As we demonstrate, SDT and its mini-theories have been prominently featured in studies of motivation and human performance. SDT has been used in studies of performance in education (Reeve, 2002), athletics and physical competition (Hagger and Chatzisarantis, 2007), mental health and behavioral change (Wild, Cunningham, and Ryan, 2006), as well as studies of workplace motivation (Gagné and Deci, 2005). In the field of public management, the framework has been particularly instructive for advancing beyond a simple intrinsic/extrinsic conceptualization of motivation. SDT offers a perspective that suggests a mixed set of motives—some more or less autonomous and controlled—affect attitudes and behavior (Brænder and Andersen, 2013; Jensen, Kjeldsen, and Vestergaard, 2020; Kjeldsen and Jacobsen, 2013; Vogel and Kroll, 2016). SDT also offers insights into how the social environments influence the satisfaction of individuals' basic psychological needs, which in turn provide the foundation for autonomous types of work motivation, including PSM and intrinsic motivation (Andersen, Kristensen, and Pedersen, 2015; Pedersen et al., 2018; Weibel, Rost, and Osterloh, 2010). Moving forward, the SDT framework and its associated mini-theories are likely to continue to contribute to our conceptual and theoretical understanding of public employee motivation and behavior in the workplace.

NOTE

1. Recently, a sixth 'mini-theory' has emerged, Relationships Motivation Theory. However, we have decided to focus on the first five given that their workplace implications have received more extensive consideration in the literature.

REFERENCES

Andersen, L.B., Kristensen, N., and Pedersen, L.H. (2015). Documentation requirements, intrinsic motivation, and worker absence, *International Public Management Journal*, *18*, 483–513.

Asseburg, J., Hattke, J., Hensel, D., Homberg, F., and Vogel, R. (2020). The tacit dimension of public sector attraction in multi-incentive settings, *Journal of Public Administration Research and Theory*, *30*, 41–59.

Bellé, N. (2015). Performance-related pay and the crowding out of motivation in the public sector: A randomized field experiment, *Public Administration Review*, *75*, 230–241.

Bellé, N., and Cantarelli, P. (2014). Monetary incentives, motivation, and job effort in the public sector: An experimental study with Italian government executives, *Review of Public Personnel Administration*, *35*, 99–123.

Brænder, M., and Andersen, L.B. (2013). Does deployment to war affect public service motivation? A panel study of soldiers before and after their service in Afghanistan, *Public Administration Review*, *73*, 466–477.

Butler, R. (1989). On the psychological meaning of information about competence: A reply to Ryan and Deci's comment on Butler (1987), *Journal of Educational Psychology*, *81*, 269–272.

Calder, B.J., and Staw, B.M. (1975). Interaction of intrinsic and extrinsic motivation: Some methodological notes, *Journal of Personality and Social Psychology*, *31*, 76–80.

Carver, C.S., and Baird, E. (1998). The American dream revisited: Is it what you want or why you want it that matters?, *Psychological Science*, *9*, 289–292.

Carver, C.S., and Scheier, M.F. (2000). Autonomy and self-regulation, *Psychological Inquiry*, *11*, 284–291.

Chen, C., and Bozeman, B. (2013). Understanding public and nonprofit managers' motivation through the lens of self-determination theory, *Public Management Review*, *15*, 584–607.

Deci, E.L. (1971). Effects of externally mediated rewards on intrinsic motivation, *Journal of Personality and Social Psychology*, *18*, 105–115.
Deci, E.L. (1975). *Intrinsic Motivation*, New York, NY: Plenum Press.
Deci, E.L., and Ryan, R.M. (1985a). The general causality orientations scale: Self-determination in personality, *Journal of Research in Personality*, *19*, 109–134.
Deci, E.L., and Ryan, R.M. (1985b). *Motivation and Self-Determination in Human Behavior*, New York, NY: Plenum Publishing.
Deci, E.L., and Ryan, R.M. (1991). A motivational approach to self: Integration in personality. In Richard Dienstbar (ed.), *Nebraska Symposium on Motivation*, Lincoln, NE: University of Nebraska Press, pp. 237–288.
Deci, E.L., and Ryan, R.M. (2004). *Handbook of Self-Determination Research*, Rochester, NY: University of Rochester Press.
Deci, E.L., and Ryan, R.M. (2008). Self-determination theory: A macrotheory of human motivation, development, and health, *Canadian Psychology/Psychologie Canadienne*, *49*, 182–185.
Deci, E.L., and Ryan, R.M. (2012). Self-determination theory. In P.A.M. Van Lange, A.W. Krunglanski, and E.T. Higgins (eds), *Handbook of Theories on Social Psychology*, London: Sage, pp. 416–437.
Fernandez, S., and Moldogaziev, T. (2015). Employee empowerment and job satisfaction in the US Federal Bureaucracy: A self-determination theory perspective, *The American Review of Public Administration*, *45*, 375–401.
Fineman, S. (2006). On being positive: Concerns and counter points, *Academy of Management Review*, *31*, 270–291.
Gagné, M. (2014). *The Oxford Handbook of Work Engagement, Motivation, and Self-Determination Theory*, New York, NY: Oxford University Press.
Gagné, M., and Deci, E.L. (2005). Self-determination theory and work motivation, *Journal of Organizational Behavior*, *26*, 331–362.
Gagné, M., and Vansteenkiste, M. (2013). Self-determination theory's contribution to positive organizational psychology. In Arnold B. Bakker (ed.), *Advances in Positive Organizational Psychology*, Bingley, UK: Emerald Group Publishing, pp. 61–82.
Georgellis, Y., Iossa, E., and Tabvuma, V. (2011), Crowding out intrinsic motivation in the public sector, *Journal of Public Administration Research and Theory*, *21*, 473–493.
Gunnell, K.E., Wilson, P.M., Zumbo, B.D., Mack, D.E., and Crocker, P.R.E. (2012). Assessing psychological need satisfaction in exercise contexts: Issues of score invariance, item modification, and context, *Measurement in Physical Education and Exercise Science*, *16*, 219–236.
Hagger, M.S., and Chatzisarantis, N.L.D. (2007). *Intrinsic Motivation and Self-Determination in Exercise and Sport*, Champaign, IL: Human Kinetics.
Hagger, M.S., and Chatzisarantis, N.L.D. (2011). Causality orientations moderate the undermining effect of rewards on intrinsic motivation, *Journal of Experimental Social Psychology*, *47*, 485–489.
Jacobsen, C.B., and Andersen, L.B. (2014). Performance management for academic researchers: How publication command systems affect individual behavior, *Review of Public Personnel Administration*, *34*, 84–107.
Jang, H., Reeve, J., Ryan, R.M., and Kim, A. (2009). Can self-determination theory explain what underlies the productive, satisfying learning experiences of collectivistically oriented Korean students?, *Journal of Educational Psychology*, *101*, 644–661.
Jensen, U.T. (2018). Does perceived societal impact moderate the effect of transformational leadership on value congruence? Evidence from a field experiment, *Public Administration Review*, *78*, 48–57.
Jensen, U.T., and Bro, L.L. (2018). How transformational leadership supports intrinsic motivation and public service motivation: The mediating role of basic need satisfaction, *The American Review of Public Administration*, *48*, 535–549.
Jensen, U.T., Kjeldsen, A.M., and Vestergaard, C.F. (2020). How is public service motivation affected by regulatory policy changes?, *International Public Management Journal*, *23*, 465u–495.
Kasser, T., and Ryan, R.M. (1996). Further examining the American dream: Differential correlates of intrinsic and extrinsic goals, *Personality and Social Psychology Bulletin*, *22*, 280–287.
Kjeldsen, A.M., and Jacobsen, C.B. (2013). Public service motivation and employment sector: Attraction or socialization?, *Journal of Public Administration Research and Theory*, *23*, 899–926.

Knee, C.R., and Zuckerman, M. (1996). Causality orientations and the disappearance of the self-serving bias, *Journal of Research in Personality*, *30*, 76–87.

Koestner, R., and Zuckerman, M. (1994). Causality orientations, failure, and achievement, *Journal of Personality*, *62*, 321–346.

Koestner, R., Ryan, R.M., Bernieri, F., and Holt, K. (1984). Setting limits on children's behavior: The differential effects of controlling vs. informational styles on intrinsic motivation and creativity, *Journal of Personality*, *52*, 233–248.

Linos, E. (2018). More than public service: A field experiment on job advertisements and diversity in the police, *Journal of Public Administration Research and Theory*, *28*, 67–85.

Locke, E.A., and Latham, G.P. (1990). *A Theory of Goal Setting and Task Performance*, Englewood Cliffs, NJ: Prentice-Hall.

Mergel, I., Bellé, N., and Nasi, G. (2021). Prosocial motivation of private sector IT professionals joining government, *Review of Public Personnel Administration*, *41*, 338–357.

Mikkelsen, M.F., Jacobsen, C.B., and Andersen, L.B. (2017). Managing employee motivation: Exploring the connections between managers' enforcement actions, employee perceptions, and employee intrinsic motivation, *International Public Management Journal*, *20*, 183–205.

Ossege, C. (2012). Accountability—are we better off without it? An empirical study on the effects of accountability on public managers' work behaviour, *Public Management Review*, *14*, 585–607.

Park, J., and Hassan, S. (2018). Does the influence of empowering leadership trickle down? Evidence from law enforcement organizations, *Journal of Public Administration Research and Theory*, *28*, 212–225.

Patterson, T.G., and Joseph, S. (2007). Person-centered personality theory: Support from self-determination theory and positive psychology, *Journal of Humanistic Psychology*, *47*, 117–139.

Pedersen, L.B., Andersen, M.K.K., Jensen, U.T., Waldorff, F.B., and Jacobsen, C.B. (2018), Can external interventions crowd in intrinsic motivation? A cluster randomised field experiment on mandatory accreditation of general practice in Denmark, *Social Science and Medicine*, *211*, 224–233.

Pedersen, M.J. (2015). Activating the forces of public service motivation: Evidence from a low-intensity randomized survey experiment, *Public Administration Review*, *75*, 734–746.

Porter, L.W., and Lawler III, E.E. (1968). *Managerial Attitudes and Performance*, Homewood, IL: R.D. Irwin.

Reeve, J.M. (2002). Self-determination theory applied to educational settings. In E.L. Deci and R.M. Ryan (eds), *Handbook of Self-Determination Research*, Rochester, NY: University of Rochester Press, pp. 183–203.

Rudy, D., Sheldon, K.M., Awong, T. and Tan, H.H. (2007), Autonomy, culture, and well-being: The benefits of inclusive autonomy, *Journal of Research in Personality*, *41*(5), 983–1007.

Rummel, A., and Feinberg, R.A. (1988), Cognitive evaluation theory: A meta-analytic review of the literature, *Social Behavior and Personality: An International Journal*, *16*(2), 147–164.

Ryan, R.M. (1982). Control and information in the intrapersonal sphere: An extension of cognitive evaluation theory, *Journal of Personality and Social Psychology*, *43*, 450–461.

Ryan, R.M., and Connell, J.P. (1989). Perceived locus of causality and internalization: Examining reasons for acting in two domains, *Journal of Personality and Social Psychology*, *57*, 749–761.

Ryan, R.M., and Deci, E.L. (2000). Self-determination theory and the facilitation of intrinsic motivation, social development, and well-being, *American Psychologist*, *55*, 68–78.

Ryan, R.M., Kuhl, J., and Deci, E.L. (1997). Nature and autonomy: An organizational view of social and neurobiological aspects of self-regulation in behavior and development, *Development and Psychopathology*, *9*, 701–728.

Scherhorn, G., and Grunert, S.C. (1988). Using the causality orientations concept on consumer behavior research, *Journal of Consumer Psychology*, *13*, 33–39.

Sheldon, K.M., and Ryan, R.M. (2011). Positive psychology and self-determination theory: A natural interface. In *Human Autonomy in Cross-cultural Context*, New York, NY: Springer, pp. 33–44.

Sheldon, K.M., Ryan, R.M., Deci, E.L., and Kasser, T. (2004). The independent effects of goal contents and motives on well-being: It's both what you pursue and why you pursue it, *Personality and Social Psychology Bulletin*, *30*, 475–486.

Van den Broeck, A., Ferris, L.D., Chang, C., and Rosen, C.C. (2016). A review of self-determination theory's basic psychological needs at work, *Journal of Management*, *42*, 1195–1229.

Vandenabeele, W. (2007). Toward a public administration theory of public service motivation: An institutional approach, *Public Management Review*, *9*, 545–556.

Vansteenkiste, M., and Ryan, R.M. (2013). On psychological growth and vulnerability: Basic psychological need satisfaction and need frustration as a unifying principle, *Journal of Psychotherapy Integration*, *23*, 263–280.

Vansteenkiste, M., Niemiec, C.P., and Soenens, B. (2010). The development of the five mini-theories of self-determination theory: An historical overview, emerging trends, and future directions, *Advances in Motivation and Achievement*, *16*, 105–165.

Vogel, D., and Kroll, A. (2016). The stability and change of PSM-related values across time: Testing theoretical expectations against panel data, *International Public Management Journal*, *19*, 53–77.

Vroom, V.H. (1964), *Work and Motivation*, New York, NY: Wiley.

Wasserkampf, A., Kleinert, J., and Chermette, C. (2018). Becoming active post-hospitalisation discharge—an exploration of motivational profiles during exercise change in obese patients, *Health Psychology and Behavioral Medicine*, *6*, 30–48.

Weibel, A., Rost, K., and Osterloh, M. (2010). Pay for performance in the public sector—benefits and (hidden) costs, *Journal of Public Administration Research and Theory*, *20*, 387–412.

Weske, U., and Schott, C. (2018). What motivates different groups of public employees working for Dutch municipalities? Combining autonomous and controlled types of motivation, *Review of Public Personnel Administration*, *38*, 415–430.

Wild, T.C., Cunningham, J.A., and Ryan, R.M. (2006). Social pressure, coercion, and client engagement at treatment entry: A self-determination theory perspective, *Addictive Behaviors*, *31*, 1858–1872.

Wise, L.R. (2004). Bureaucratic posture: On the need for a composite theory of bureaucratic behaviour, *Public Administration Review*, *64*(6), 669–680.

6. Goals as a driver of public sector motivation
Edmund C. Stazyk and Jisang Kim

INTRODUCTION

As the contributions in this *Handbook* demonstrate, scholars and practitioners have long grappled with the motives and motivations of workers in the hopes that, through a deeper understanding of human behavior, we can improve the performance of organizations and, in some cases, the plight of workers themselves. Much of what we now know about public and nonprofit sector workers has its roots, either directly or indirectly, in other social science disciplines, including sociology, business administration, and psychology. Yet, in our efforts to apply knowledge from these other disciplines, public and nonprofit management scholars have often found that the theories originating in other fields only partially characterize the institutional environments of public and nonprofit organizations. As a consequence, public and nonprofit management scholars often adopt and then adapt work motivation theories to the public sector context.

Our understanding of the importance of goals as a motivational force in the public and nonprofit sectors can certainly be said to fit this mold. Admittedly, public administration scholars have viewed organizational goals as significant since the field's earliest days (see, e.g., Barnard, 1938; Goodnow, 1900). However, it was not until Locke and Latham's (see, e.g., Latham and Locke, 1975) work on goal-setting theory that public administration and management scholars began to think seriously about the *motivational* force that goals might have on public and nonprofit employees and, in turn, on employee and organizational performance.

As with other work motivation theories, public management scholars applying and studying goal-setting theory have accepted the fundamental premise upon which the theory has been grounded: clear, challenging, but doable goals are more likely to motivate workers than unclear, too simple, or impossible goals. However, public management scholars have also noted that the inherently political environment of public organizations, coupled with significant constraints around the use of extrinsic incentives in public and nonprofit organizations, sets important checks and boundaries around core components of the theory; this, in turn, suggests it can be harder to rely on goals as a motivational device in the public sector. Because of this, public management scholars have devoted considerably more time and intellectual energy to unpacking the precise conditions and circumstances under which goals can and cannot be clarified for public sector workers. Meanwhile, goal-setting theorists in other social science disciplines have explored how best to set goals with and for workers as well as how goal-directed behaviors are shaped by environmental, situational, and individual factors and characteristics.

In this chapter, we review the history of goal-setting theory, its adoption and adaptation to the field of public management, and its current status in the field. Next, we consider how the discussion and debate around goals as a motivational tool have evolved in the public sector setting as well as in the broader social sciences. Finally, we turn to a discussion of the key issues and questions that, in our opinion, warrant additional study and consideration if we hope to capitalize on the benefits of goals as a motivational device capable of enhancing employee and organizational outcomes. Our aim is to both summarize where we stand and chart a course for future research in this space.

THE IMPORTANCE OF GOALS TO ORGANIZATIONS

As any true student of organization theory and behavior can attest, efforts to define 'organizations' are commonplace among scholars and practitioners. In fact, it has been said that there are almost as many definitions of organizations as there are theorists, highlighting the fact that organization theorists attach varying degrees of weight to different concepts, ideas, and explanations of what matters most in organizational settings. Yet, despite the surfeit of definitions, one of the most widely agreed-upon perspectives is that organizations are best understood as purposive, goal-directed entities (Locke and Latham, 1990, 2002; Ryan, 2012).

This perspective starts by considering what is implied in the term 'organization.' Organizations reflect the collective, shared efforts of *organized* individuals. Individuals organize (e.g., into organizations, societies, communities) to accomplish a shared goal or set of goals that cannot be achieved (or achieved as easily) by a single, given individual. Implied in this perspective are several important ideas: (1) that people have goals, (2) that certain goals are attainable only through the combined and coordinated effort of multiple individuals, (3) that organizations are one of the most common formal instruments used to secure simultaneous, coordinated effort from groups of individuals, and (4) that how goals are established and set also affects individuals' willingness to work toward the realization of goals. In simpler terms, there would be no need for organizations whatsoever without the existence of complex goals requiring the joint, purposive coordination of individuals to attain (Locke and Latham, 1990, 2002, 2019; Ryan, 2012).

Based on these assumptions, many organization theorists assume that purposive, goal-directed action is a—if not *the*—central characteristic of human behavior and, consequently, all organizations as well. In fact, Edwin Locke and Gary Latham, the progenitors of goal-setting theory, have long argued that goal-directed behavior is a fundamental biological imperative of humans, frequently noting

> Life is a conditional process; it requires action that sustains survival. If no action is taken or the wrong actions are taken, the organism does not survive and cannot reproduce. At the level of lower animals, actions guided by sensory perception and perceptual level learning are needed. At the human level, there is the need for conceptual thought (reason), volitional goal choices (Locke, 2018), and long-range thinking. (Locke and Latham, 2019, p. 101)

In other words, all life is goal-directed, but only human beings are capable of the development and pursuit of more profound, intentional goals, and organizations constitute our best effort to jointly pursue and accomplish complex, multifaceted goals. Therefore, how we determine which goals to pursue and how we pursue them—both generally and in an organizational context specifically—takes on tremendous importance.

Although these ideas are commonly held among most organization theorists, it is worth highlighting their importance to the field of public administration and management. In the wake of the Second Industrial Revolution and, in the US context, the Pendleton Act during the late 1800s and early 1900s, management scholars increasingly turned their attention toward developing new administrative systems and structures capable of addressing the needs of a changing economic environment—one characterized by improved communication systems and a rapid shift toward the mass production of goods and services (Chandler, 1977; Frederickson and Stazyk, 2010).

As these economic shifts occurred, the study of management became more common and increasingly important as an area of research. Among this new and burgeoning class of scholars and practitioners interested in the management of organizations, it became apparent that new gains in economy, efficiency, and effectiveness required the careful development of administrative systems capable of coordinating the actions and activities of increasingly large numbers of workers who were themselves engaged in increasingly complex tasks. Because of this, many of the earliest management scholars and practitioners increasingly considered organizational goals—directly and indirectly—to be an organizing principle for the development of new administrative systems and structures. Furthermore, many of these early management scholars were either primarily interested in public organizations (as in the case of Frank Goodnow and Luther Gulick) or were largely indifferent to and about sectoral differences (as in the case of Frederick Taylor and Charles Barnard).

Examples of the critical role goals played in shaping these new administrative systems are teeming. Consider, for example, the Scientific Management Movement. In this instance, Taylor (1911) suggested sound management was built around a division of labor with different offices or units responsible for managing and coordinating various work tasks. Take the tool shop as an example, which was responsible for the maintenance, care, and assignment of tools to workers. In this case, the tool shop is organized with the goal of better managing the upkeep and distribution of tools, while other work units are organized to tackle different core tasks and aims of the same organization, such as hiring and payroll. Put simply, Taylor and Fayol recognized that organizations can, and should, be organized around different sub-goals and tasks in order to improve organizational outcomes.

Likewise, consider public administration's most famous acronym, Luther Gulick's (1937) POSDCORB (see also Fayol, 1949). As students of public administration are sure to know, Gulick is widely considered one of the 'fathers' of public administration, and the 'P' in POSDCORB stands for 'planning.' For Gulick, the primary responsibility of good executives was (a) to set organizational goals, (b) to set these goals in the right manner, and then (c) to plan how organizational workforce and effort will be directed to reach these pre-determined goals. In other words, goals become the organizing principle around which executives engage in the act of Planning first and foremost; once goals have been established, and a plan is in place, executives then engage in the closely related tasks of Organizing, Staffing, Directing, COordinating, Reporting, and Budgeting (or POSDCORB)—all of which should dovetail with the executive's initial goals and planning efforts.

As these examples illustrate, public administration—like business administration—has long viewed goals as a central feature of management and administration. Furthermore, since the 1980s, public administration scholars have increasingly suggested that particular aspects of goals are especially critical to public organizations, who often find themselves more tightly constrained with respect to the kinds and levels of extrinsic incentives organizations can provide to workers (see, e.g., Nalbandian and Edwards, 1983; Perry and Rainey, 1988). These constraints have led to some significant divergences between public administration and other management traditions in terms of goal research; we will take up these differences shortly.

Next, we turn to the basic tenets of goal-setting theory, the dominant stream of research on goals, and more broadly, work motivation.

GOAL-SETTING THEORY: A BRIEF HISTORY AND BACKGROUND

The roots leading to the genesis of goal-setting theory and its eventual prominence are traced back to the early work of Edwin A. Locke during the 1960s. Locke entered graduate school in 1960 when the field of psychology was guided by the then-dominant philosophy of behaviorism (for a more detailed history, see Locke and Latham, 2019; Watson, 1924). Philosophically, behaviorism 'argued that because consciousness can be neither weighed nor measured as with physical entities, it should not be considered as part of science. Only observable behavior should be studied. Behaviorists denied free will and asserted that psychology should embrace environmental determinism' (Locke and Latham, 2019, p. 94). At the time, leading theories, such as B.F. Skinner's (1953) work on operant conditioning, offered compelling support for the fundamental assertions of behaviorism.

However, Locke and several of his contemporaries found the core tenets of behaviorism wanting. They believed behaviorists failed to fully consider the importance of human consciousness as one of the core building blocks of all human knowledge and perception (Locke, 1971, 1977; Locke and Latham, 2019). For Locke and his colleagues, this lapse was a significant one—an oversight that leads behaviorists to produce inadequate and, at best, partial explanations of human behavior. In response, scholars like Locke turned to the work of Murray (1938), Lewin (1939), Likert (1967), and Ryan (1970) for a broader understanding of human behavior that treated human consciousness more seriously.

Efforts to push back against behaviorism during the 1950s–1970s led to the gradual development of several fundamental motivation theories that inform our modern understanding of work motivation. Included in this list are McClelland's (McClelland et al., 1953) achievement motivation theory, Herzberg's motivation-hygiene theory (Herzberg, Mausner, and Snyderman, 1959) and Vroom's (1964) expectancy theory. It was in this context and environment that Edwin Locke commenced his work on goals, eventually leading to the development of a formal goal-setting theory with his long-time colleague and co-author Gary Latham.

Locke's earliest efforts in this space focused concomitantly on pushing back against the core assumptions of behaviorism (see, e.g., Locke, 1968, 1971, 1976, 1977) and, through careful applications of the earlier work of Mace (1935) and Ryan (1970), on exploring how tasks and goals might influence employee action and behavior (Locke and Latham, 2019). Ryan's (1970) work, in particular, convinced Locke that consciousness, tasks, and 'situationally specific intentions' were the strongest and 'most direct regulators of an individual's actions' (Locke and Latham, 2019, p. 94). Consequently, in his earliest research, he began focusing on exploring whether and how goals and tasks might guide and motivate workers, with an aim to produce empirical and statistical evidence that verified his assertions and supporting his conclusions.

These early efforts were incredibly successful, particularly in generating supportive statistical evidence, which, in turn, encouraged a growing number of scholars to quickly explore other ways in which goals and tasks might shape individual, on-the-job behavior. Eventually, this growth in research led to Locke and Latham's partnership.

Latham, for his part, started his doctoral studies when Locke's work on goals was slowly gaining traction. At the time, Latham was a student of Gary Yukl's, which informed his own thinking on goals. Many of Latham and Yukl's ideas on goals dovetailed neatly with Locke's findings. As a consequence, Latham—both independently and with Yukl—drew on Locke's research to begin exploring how various goal conditions (e.g., goal difficulty, participatively set goals, and monetary incentives) affected employee job performance (see, e.g., Latham and Yukl, 1975). Their early findings also echoed those in Locke's work (Locke and Latham, 2019).

In 1974, Latham and Locke met, for the first time, while attending the annual meeting of the American Psychological Association. They co-authored their first paper shortly thereafter, commencing the start of their decades-long collaboration as well as the creation of a formal goal-setting theory (Locke and Latham, 2019).

Within a few short years of their partnership, Locke and Latham had redefined entirely how management scholars thought about goals and motivation. In fact, by 1984, a notable organization theorist, Craig Pinder, noted the following about goal-setting theory in his review of work motivation approaches, concepts, and research:

> Goal-setting theory has demonstrated more scientific validity to date than any other theory or approach to work motivation ... Moreover, the evidence thus far indicates that it probably holds more promise as an applied motivational tool for managers than does any other approach. (Pinder, 1984, p. 169)

This reflection is unique and highly atypical when one considers the fact that Locke and Latham's joint work on goal-setting commenced in 1974, only a decade before. Today, more than 1000 studies have been published on goal-setting theory, with research cutting across numerous fields and disciplines; likewise, the basic tenets of goal-setting theory have been used to develop a number of practical organizational and managerial systems and structures. For example, the State of Virginia relies on the core assumptions of goal-setting theory in public education settings, where principals and teachers work together to create year-long teacher goals that align with best practices developed from Locke and Latham's work. In the next section of this chapter, we turn to a review of the core principles and findings of goal-setting theory.

DESIGNING GOALS TO MOTIVATE WORKERS

In their efforts to respond to behaviorism and begin developing a new perspective on the motivational force of goals, Locke and Latham started by applying an evolutionary and biological perspective to their work (Locke and Latham, 2013). These perspectives, in their minds, immediately lead to the conclusion that all life—human and otherwise—is motivated, at a minimum, by survival goals (e.g., food, safety, and reproduction). Put another way, for Locke and Latham, goals are an essential component of all life; to live means one must have and meet survival goals (e.g., to find food).

However, as Locke and Latham (2013) point out, humans are unique from all other forms of life in terms of our relationship to and with goals. We are exceptional because we are distinctly capable of volition or the exercise of will. Volition distinguishes us from other forms of life for three core reasons. First, that humans are capable of volition means we can consciously and intentionally derive goals that go well beyond mere efforts to survive. In other words, we can conceive of and pursue complex, multifaceted aims. Second and perhaps even more importantly, humans are the only species on Earth capable of using goals as a yardstick against which we can evaluate our successes and failures. Third and finally, humans are uniquely capable of pursuing other people's goals (Locke and Latham, 2013).

Based on these factors and contrary to behaviorism, Locke and Latham concluded that (1) goals are *the* central motivating force for humans, and (2) a deeper understanding of how goals enhance and inhibit motivation could be used to understand the conduct and behavior of individuals in organizations. If we could understand more fully how best to design goals and implement systems and structures that encouraged their pursuit, Locke and Latham were convinced we could improve individual and organizational performance.

From here, Locke and Latham set out to craft the basic foundations of goal-setting theory. They defined goals as the 'object or aim of an action' (Locke and Latham, 2002, p. 705). Next, they began the process of carefully measuring and testing the generality of their assumptions in organizations. To do so, they evaluated whether their fundamental assumptions held across different types of (1) organizational tasks, (2) participants (individuals and groups), (3) organizational contexts (e.g., small vs. large organizations), (4) goal sources (e.g., assigned goals, self-set goals), (5) countries, (6) outcomes, (7) time spans, and (8) research designs/settings (e.g., laboratory, simulations) (Locke and Latham, 2019, p. 98; see also Porter and Latham, 2013; Pritchard et al., 2013). Their efforts were aided by growing interest among other scholars, resulting in approximately 400 studies by 1990 (Locke and Latham, 1990).

The accumulation of findings across their own work and that of other researchers allowed Locke and Latham to begin inductively crafting a formal theory of goal-setting. This theory set forth the foundational principles of goal-setting. It asserted that goals could and would motivate workers if organizations (1) established goals that were specific, (2) challenging but attainable, (3) communicated to workers, (4) viewed as legitimate by employees, and (5) supported by managers (e.g., resources, credibility) (Locke and Latham, 1990, 2002).

Locke and Latham, across a number of studies, also considered the key attributes that affected the efficacy of goals as a motivational tool. Here, they assumed that (1) goal content (or *what* is being pursued) and (2) intensity mattered significantly. Among factors, goal content encompasses goal specificity, difficulty, time span, and the number of sheer goals pursued, while intensity refers primarily to the effort necessary or taken to set a goal, its relative importance, and organizational/worker commitment to attaining it (Locke and Latham, 2013).

They also considered—both in their own research and in their efforts to summarize the work of others—how various mediators, moderators, situational factors, affect, expectancies, self-efficacy, and goal types (e.g., learning goals, performance goals, primed goals) might shape employee motivation. In the case of mediators, they concluded that choice/attention, effort, persistence, and self-set goals could mediate the results of various motivators on performance (e.g., job design, incentives) (Locke, 2001; Locke and Latham, 2002, 2019).

With respect to moderators and situational factors, Locke and Latham argued that goal performance was shaped, in part, by (1) the quality and nature of the feedback employees received on their work, (2) goal commitment, (3) an employee's knowledge, skills, and abilities, and (4) various situational factors, such as resource availability (Locke and Latham, 2019). Equally important were a set of findings that led to the conclusion that goals should be challenging but attainable (whether assigned, self-set, or participatively established). Essentially, Locke and Latham concluded that overly simplistic or complex goals were unlikely to motivate workers; instead, goals needed to be challenging but not impossible or nearly impossible to achieve. This set of findings suggested to Locke and Latham that an employee's affect, sense of self-efficacy, and expectancies played an important role in motivating workers to strive toward goal attainment.

Many of these key findings have been supported time and time again in extant research, leading to Pinder's assessment (above) about the strength and merits of goal-setting theory relative to other work motivation theories. Moreover, as noted previously, the core takeaways from goal-setting theory have found their way into practice, both generally and more narrowly. Consider, for example, so-called SMART goals. This term draws on Locke and Latham's summary to encourage managers and organizations to develop goals that are Specific, Measurable, Attainable, Realistic, and Time-bound. Likewise, goal-setting tenets have been used to design incentive systems (see, e.g., Milkovich and Wigdor, 1991; Stazyk, 2013) to improve student performance in K-12 educational environments and a wide range of other fields. Next, we turn to how the field of public administration and public management has thought about goals and goal-setting theory.

GOAL-SETTING IN THE PUBLIC SECTOR: THE IMPORTANCE OF RECOGNIZING INSTITUTIONAL CONSTRAINTS

The significance of Locke and Latham's work on goal-setting theory has not been lost on that body of scholars and practitioners whose interest rests more fully in the public sector setting and in the management and performance of public and nonprofit organizations specifically. In fact, one would be on a relatively safe footing in arguing that most public management scholars accept the general thrust of goal-setting theory as both valuable and an important motivational tool for employees.

That being said, public management scholars have tended to assume that public and non-profit organizations function in an environment quite different than the typical private sector firm/agency. This assertion is a long-standing concern of public administration scholars, stretching back at least to the days of the Ashton Studies in the 1950s–1960s and subsequent claims from business administration scholars that all organizations—regardless of their sector—are more similar than dissimilar (see, e.g., Pugh and Hickson, 1976; Simon, 2000).

Many, though certainly not all, US public administration and management scholars have tended to take a dim view of this claim (see, e.g., Allison, 1980; Mosher, 1982). In fact, a substantial body of research has been produced by public administration scholars attempting to demonstrate just how different the institutional context of public organizations may be. These efforts have focused on value differences across sectors (e.g., with public organizations placing a higher premium on values like equity, fairness, and transparency), ownership (e.g., shareholders vs. the public), the role of politics and electoral bodies in constraining public organizations (e.g., with respect to decision-making, hiring, firing, and incentive systems), and laws among others (see, e.g., Bozeman, 2007; Meier and O'Toole, 2011; Perry and Rainey, 1988; Rosenbloom, 1983).

Although a great many public adminstrationists have participated in efforts to more fully demarcate the differences between public and private organizations, a narrower, more direct focus on what these differences might mean with respect to goals—both generally and as motivational tools—can be traced back to the early work of Hal Rainey.

Rainey, a contemporary of Locke and Latham, earned undergraduate and master's degrees in psychology, before joining Ohio State University (OSU) as a doctoral student in public administration. At the time, OSU was widely viewed as a leader among higher education institutions focused on psychology, organizations, and organizational behavior. Practically, this meant Rainey was fully aware of the behavioral debate occurring in psychology, as well as Locke and Latham's efforts to develop goal-setting theory.

As he was completing his doctoral studies and in his early years as a young junior scholar, Rainey joined the debate about public/private sector differences, arguing alongside other public management researchers that significant sectoral differences existed. He continued to return to this debate at various points throughout his subsequent career (see, e.g., Perry and Rainey, 1988; Rainey, 1979, 1982; Rainey and Bozeman, 2000; Rainey and Steinbauer, 1999; Rainey, Backoff, and Levine, 1976).

While Rainey was not unique in arguing that important differences exist across sectors, he was atypical, at the time, for his efforts to empirically test many of the ideas/claims levied as evidence of meaningful sector differences. Even more importantly, for the purposes of this chapter, he was the first to explore in-depth whether and how goals might matter in public organizations (Rainey, 1982, 1983). In short, Rainey treated seriously the importance of goals as well as Locke and Latham's work in this space. But he did so by contextualizing how, when, and why goal-setting strategies were more challenging in the public sector sphere.

Like many public administrationists, he pointed to value and ownership differences, legal environments, and so on, as critical distinguishing factors that checked what public organizations could do to motivate workers and improve organizational performance. However, chief among his critiques was the then long-standing assertion (see, e.g., Moe, 1980) that the inherently political environment within which public organizations operate often acts as a substantial foil that, in turn, limits the efficacy of goal-setting strategies and approaches.

Throughout his career, Rainey has argued—individually and jointly with colleagues and co-authors—that public employees are much more frequently subject to vague, ambiguous, and conflicting goals (as short-hand, we will refer to this point as goal ambiguity or goal clarity moving forward in this chapter). Goal ambiguity and conflict stem directly from the inherently confrontational and conflictual nature of politics and political decision-making. Simply, politicians often disagree over policy preferences, which leads, both intentionally and unintentionally, to poorly defined and constructed goals. Likewise, elected officials with different political preferences actively look for ways to limit organizational decision-making autonomy and/or may make equally legitimate but competing and conflicting requests of agencies (e.g., directing the US EPA to limit pollution from timber harvesting operations on the one hand and expanding permitting and logging opportunities on the other) (see, e.g., Moe, 1980). Further complicating this dynamic is the fact that interest groups and citizens themselves have their own preferences and expectations of public organizations.

When taken together, these factors suggested to Rainey and later public administration goal scholars that the efficacy and benefits of goal-setting strategies were less likely to be (easily) found and duplicated in the public sector setting. In short, Rainey suggested that the institutional context of public organizations mattered when we think about the importance of goals as a motivational tool.

GOALS AND MOTIVATION IN PUBLIC ORGANIZATIONS

Having argued that goals often look and function differently in the public sector setting, Rainey then turned his attention to supporting his assertion that public sector goals are more ambiguous and to exploring how and when goals could be clarified for workers.

In some cases, efforts on this front supported the assertion that goals can and are more ambiguous in the public sector; in others, evidence has failed to support this claim. For example, in a 1995 piece with Sanjay Pandey and Barry Bozeman, Rainey explored whether perceptions of red tape (unhealthy, burdensome rules and regulations) varied across public and private sector managers. In it, the authors explored three central hypotheses, including one that sought to determine whether public managers create more red tape in the face of high levels of goal ambiguity. They found that public and private sector managers did not meaningfully (statistically) differ with respect to how they responded to uncertainty.

At the same time, scholars such as George Boyne, Ken Meier, Brad Wright, and Sanjay Pandey also began exploring these themes, albeit sometimes less directly than Rainey and his collaborators. Many of these studies also produced mixed support for the notion that public sector goals are more ambiguous than those found in private sector organizations. For instance, Pandey and Wright (2006) found that certain forms of political influence impact goal ambiguity and, in turn, employee's understanding of their own individual organizational roles. Others, like Boyne (2002), demonstrated that there is little solid empirical evidence upon which to conclude that goals are more ambiguous and problematic among public organizations.

There are several potential explanations for the lack of convergence across research findings. For example, public administration scholars have tended to rely on subjective survey measures of organizational goal ambiguity. At a minimum, there are two potentially significant problems with this approach. First, it is possible that public and private sector employees have different levels of tolerance for ambiguity, conflict, and uncertainty generally. In such cases, public employees may be more tolerant of uncertainty but nonetheless report similar levels of ambiguity as private sector employees. Second, it may be the case that employees at different levels or in different types of organizations experience ambiguity and conflict quite differently (e.g., resource-constrained street-level bureaucrats vs. managers who may, due to their roles, have a greater goal clarity). The survey measures public management scholars typically employ may be unlikely to capture these differences, nor are surveys limited to managers likely to pick up on hierarchical differences within a given organization, for instance.

Based on these inconsistencies, Chun and Rainey (2005a, 2005b) undertook an effort to construct objective measures of goal ambiguity that could, in theory, be used to better determine when goals are viewed as vague or conflictual. For all intents and purposes, such an effort would generate a stronger basis for assertions that goals are (or are not) ambiguous, vague, and conflicting generally, but could also be used to make more precise comparisons across sectors, organizations, and classes of employees.

Although an important development in the field, Chun and Rainey's efforts to generate objective measures have also met with some resistance and problems. In this case, there are at least three overarching concerns that have stalled significant further work. First, as Locke and Latham's own scholarship on goal-setting has demonstrated, how people interpret goals and goal conditions is at least as important, if not more so, than whether a particular goal is, in fact, ambiguous or conflicting. Second, as scholars like Gene Brewer (2006) have suggested, researchers themselves introduce subjectivity into the evaluation process when they choose to focus on one particular goal or even a particular set of goals. In other words, how do we know that we have selected the right or most important goal(s) to emphasize in our analysis? Likewise, there may be a considerable gulf between the verbatim—the textual content of a goal (or set of goals)—and how employees interpret or are directed by management to respond to and prioritize goals. Finally, the process of establishing the objective basis upon which we deem a goal as ambiguous or not is time- and labor-intensive and may also limit generalizability as researchers attempt to make comparisons across sectors, groups, and individuals. Because of these factors, most public management scholars interested in goal ambiguity have tended to continue using survey items developed by Rainey in the early 1980s or closely related proxies.

Over the last 15–20 years, another batch of scholars have built on Rainey's work in several ways, often using his original subjective survey items (or closely related proxies) to consider three core questions: (1) what are the effects of ambiguous goals on the performance of public organizations and the motivation and performance of public employees, (2) what steps can public managers and organizations take to clarify goals for workers, and (3) how should we think about the nature of ambiguity itself? Scholarship produced in this space differs from what came before. It either tends to set aside questions of sectoral differences altogether or, alternatively, takes sectoral differences as given in favor of focusing on how organizations and individuals respond to complex, uncertain environments and goals instead.

Those scholars interested in understanding how goal ambiguity affects organizational and individual performance have tended to consider how employees experience and respond to uncertainty. Normally, researchers working in this space examine whether and how goal ambiguity is associated with changes in employee fit, job satisfaction, organizational commitment, turnover intention, and actual employee turnover. Pandey and Wright's (2006) efforts to evaluate how political influence shapes goal ambiguity and, in turn, employees' efforts to make sense of their own individual organizational roles clearly fit within this vein of research. In a subsequent piece, Stazyk, Pandey, and Wright (2011) confirmed these earlier results using a different sample of public employees; they also found that higher levels of perceived goal ambiguity and role ambiguity were associated with lower levels of organizational commitment. Sun, Peng, and Pandey (2014) demonstrated that employees who believe they 'fit' well with their organizations (higher person-environment fit) tend to report lower levels of goal ambiguity and role ambiguity as well as increased levels of public service motivation and organizational commitment.

Within this subset of goal research, several things stand out. First and perhaps foremost, many researchers working on these topics assume that employee performance and motivation drive organizational performance. In other words, tests of the direct impact of subjective perceptions of goal ambiguity on actual organizational performance or performance indicators are rare. One notable exception rests in the work of Hayes and Stazyk (2019), who explored whether differences in how school principals and teachers perceive goals and goal clarity had any bearing on actual teacher turnover. They found that greater divergence in perceptions of goal clarity was associated with increased turnover, with teachers leaving the field of education altogether or moving to new school districts. Turnover is typically associated with lower levels of organizational performance (except in cases of 'healthy' levels of turnover).

Second, the range of topics considered by scholars working in this area has been relatively narrow in scope. In some ways, this consistency has aided public sector goal research insofar as many study results and findings demonstrate a high degree of consistency across federal, state, and local government employees and in agencies and departments with distinct missions and goals. However, the clear downside is that goal researchers are able to shed little insight into the ways goal ambiguity affects or interacts with other important individual and organizational constructs frequently considered by public management scholars.

Finally, it is also worth highlighting that many of the findings produced in this space coincide with Rainey and colleagues' efforts to develop and test objective measures of goal ambiguity; for instance, Jung (2014) found that higher objective levels of goal ambiguity were associated with lower job satisfaction among public employees. In this sense, results tend toward some degree of triangulation and support the general idea that goal ambiguity harms individual performance.

Next, we turn to the second overarching question goal researchers have attempted to tackle over the past two decades: what steps can public managers and organizations take to clarify goals for workers? Because public sector goal ambiguity research developed partially as a response to concerns that the institutional context of public organizations limited the efficacy of Locke and Latham's goal-setting strategies, there has been a pronounced tendency to emphasize how ambiguous goals hamper public organizations and public employees. While important, the downside of this approach has been that it fails to consider how public organizations and managers can tap their own internal resources to combat ambiguity. When put another way, it has not fully considered those strategies and tools managers can tap to help clarify goals for workers.

In response to this, Davis and Stazyk—both separately and jointly—have produced a number of pieces that attempt to shed light on how organizations and managers might respond to heightened levels of ambiguity. For example, Stazyk and Goerdel (2011) applied a contingency theory perspective to examine whether and how organizational leaders could adapt an organization's hierarchical structure when confronted with high levels of uncertainty to help clarify goals for workers. Stazyk (2016) then evaluated whether and how the application of certain reinvention strategies could improve goal clarity for workers. In two subsequent pieces, Stazyk and Davis (2020, 2021) considered how organizational leadership could be tapped to improve decision-making and limit goal ambiguity for workers. These studies reinforce Hayes and Stazyk's earlier research and clearly demonstrate that the quality of an organization's leadership and leaders' efforts to proactively clarify goals for workers matter significantly.

Here, it is worth noting that some of Rainey's earliest research on goals and other scholars' subsequent efforts to unpack how goal ambiguity affects individual and organizational performance also produce 'actionable' strategies. For instance, Sun and colleagues' research on goal ambiguity and employee fit naturally leads to the conclusion that organizational leaders should pursue efforts to clarify goals for workers and to take steps to improve an employee's sense of fit specifically. That being said, Stazyk and Davis's research in this space has been explicitly directed toward identifying specific management strategies that can improve goal clarity, differentiating it from other efforts.

The third and final overarching question motivating goal ambiguity research involves how we should think about the nature of ambiguity itself. Research on this topic has, again, been limited but traces back to some of Rainey's earliest observations about goals and ambiguity. Over a series of articles and in his notable book (1991), *Understanding and Managing Public Organizations*, Rainey offered a number of specific insights that have become central in efforts to think more carefully and critically about the goal ambiguity concept. For example,

Rainey (1991) went to great lengths to distinguish between various goal types (e.g., official vs. operative goals) as well as remind scholars that organizations possess multiple goals.

The former point is significant because it highlights the fact that some goals, such as official mission or value statements, are inherently difficult to operationalize. What, for instance, does success in the Wars on Terror, Homelessness, or Drugs look like? How do we know we are making progress? The US Army's focus on body counts—the number of enemy dead—during the Vietnam War serves as a good example. Body counts, it turns out, are not a suitable metric for measuring progress toward the goal of winning the Vietnam War.

The latter point is itself important because, as Rainey noted, goals within a single organization may conflict or compete with one another. Likewise, the weight or significance attached to a particular goal will vary over time, based on shifting political preferences and public sentiment, and so on. Additionally, progress on one goal is often contingent on making progress on other goals.

As Rainey's work demonstrates, goals and goals contexts are complex and highly nuanced. At a minimum, this suggests that researchers need to approach their evaluation of goals and the implications of ambiguity carefully. Not all forms of ambiguity are the same, nor are they likely to have the same ramifications for organizational and individual performance. In fact, Rainey went so far as to suggest that there may be some cases in which ambiguity might be beneficial to organizations.

Interestingly, many of these points have largely been ignored in subsequent research. However, in 2015, Davis and Stazyk presented a new goal taxonomy that was deeply informed by Rainey's early observations. Essentially, Davis and Stazyk asserted and demonstrated that—consistent with the general thrust of public management research—there are certain circumstances in which ambiguity is likely to be harmful and damaging to individual and organizational performance. Yet, contrary to mainstream goal ambiguity scholarship, they also argued that ambiguity could actually be beneficial to organizations and employees in other circumstances (e.g., because it provides space for innovation, the exercise of discretion, and expertise). The key rests in determining when and why ambiguity is likely to be helpful or harmful.

There are many possible factors that determine whether and when ambiguity is healthy or harmful, though Davis and Stazyk originally focused on political factors (e.g., do politicians have a strong, shared perspective about how an issue should be addressed or are they deeply conflicted; do politicians trust an organization and its leadership?). For instance, they also have considered whether public sentiment shapes employees' understanding of the level of ambiguity present in different cases and whether this ambiguity is generally viewed as positive or negative by employees. In this subsequent work, Davis and Stazyk (2021) report results confirming their original assertions that goal ambiguity is highly nuanced and that it would be a mistake to presume all goal ambiguity is harmful to organizations.

Picking up on Rainey's points about the nested nature of goals in organizations, Davis and Stazyk (2016) have also considered how senior managers weigh competing goals. In this particular case, they sought to explore how managers navigate situations in which they confront potentially conflicting organizational goals and network goals. In cases such as these, it is reasonable to assume that conflicting organizational and network goals introduce greater ambiguity for managers; however, an alternative perspective is that managers can use network goals to further refine organizational goals, which may, in turn, improve both organizational and network performance. Although more research is necessary, Davis and Stazyk's results provide support for the latter rather than the former perspective.

Ultimately, the takeaway from research on this third core issue/question is that simplistic, dichotomous approaches to goals and goal ambiguity offer an incomplete or, even worse, inaccurate perspective on ambiguity. On its face, this may seem like an especially minor or trite point. However, there is a case to be made that Davis and Stazyk's approach feeds, more naturally, into the core tenets of Locke and Latham's goal-setting theory. As discussed above, Locke and Latham's research demonstrates that overly simplistic and overly difficult goals are unlikely to motivate workers. Instead, workers are most likely to be motivated by, and to find value in, goals that are simultaneously complex yet attainable. In this sense, public administration's efforts to focus on clarifying goals at all costs (or, alternatively, noting that they cannot be adequately clarified because of the institutional context of public organizations) misses the boat. As Locke and Latham have shown us, the motivational aspects of goals occur not when goals are clarified at all costs but rather when employees perceive goals as difficult but attainable. Simply, Davis and Stazyk's more nuanced presentation of ambiguity dovetails with generalist perspectives that the precise nature of ambiguity matters considerably.

FUTURE DIRECTIONS AND CONSIDERATIONS

As our discussion illustrates, research on goals—inside and outside of the field of public administration—is robust and has generally converged around a set of core findings and concerns. For instance, research clearly demonstrates that high levels of ambiguity can harm the commitment, satisfaction, and, in some circumstances, altruistic motives and motivations of public sector employees. Likewise, the design and content of goals and how they are set for and with employees clearly matter. We can also say with some surety that organizations and managers have tools at their disposal that can be used to help clarify goals for workers, even in the face of heightened environmental uncertainty.

Where, though, should scholars and practitioners interested in the motivational aspects of goals turn their attention? What next steps are necessary to advance and expand our understanding of goals and their impact on public employees and organizations?

On these questions, we posit several suggestions. First and foremost, we would encourage scholars to follow Davis and Stazyk's lead by focusing on the nature of ambiguity and its implications for employees and organizations. In particular, two overarching issues in this space seem particularly pressing and worthy of attention. First, significantly more intellectual energy should be directed toward distilling when and how ambiguity is either advantageous or harmful to organizations and workers. While Davis and Stazyk's taxonomy and subsequent replication move research in this direction, there are a great many other possible instances where ambiguous goals are actually beneficial. For instance, one could explore whether ambiguous goals afford teachers greater discretion and autonomy in the classroom and, in turn, when this discretion either improves or hampers student performance. Second, as described above, considerably more effort is needed to determine how nested and contingent goals interact to shape goals and goal ambiguity; what is particularly important here would also be to explore how employees prioritize goals.

Second, as debates on the relative merits of objective and subjective study measures demonstrate, concept measurement remains a considerable challenge in the field. The process of establishing objective measures is time-intensive, may be less generalizable across various organizations and contexts, and such measures may downplay the importance of employees' subjective interpretations (which clearly shape how workers respond and behave regardless of whether these employees are objectively correct in their interpretations) of goals and goal environments. Conversely, our subjective measures of goal ambiguity are dated, fail to meaningfully capture the nuanced nature of ambiguity, and generally make it difficult to produce actionable recommendations for managers. Efforts to refine both objective and subjective measures are, in our opinion, the key to advancing public sector goal research.

Third, scholars should grapple, more fully, with the ways in which employees intellectually process goal information and then prioritize competing or conflicting goals. Likewise, researchers should more fully explore the various situational and dispositional factors that make it more or less likely workers will have the capacity and personal resources necessary to interpret goals and goal content in the most favorable light possible. One possible approach would be to apply appraisal theory or 'conservation of resources' perspectives to begin unpacking how employees act and behave as ambiguity shifts (for a more detailed discussion, see Davis and Stazyk, 2021), although many other possible, equally legitimate approaches exist. Further, such efforts would seem valuable regardless of whether researchers draw on subjective or objective survey measures and may even enhance the confidence we can place on objective measurement efforts in a marked way.

Fourth, efforts to demonstrate that goal ambiguity meaningfully influence employee and organizational performance are desperately needed. As described above, this is a clear hole in extant scholarship, with most researchers using employee-level behaviors or outcomes as proxies for actual performance. While many of these proxies have been shown to affect performance in other scenarios, we should be cautious in assuming, absent further research on these links, that ambiguity is uniformly harmful to employees and organizations (again, see Davis and Stazyk's taxonomy, which produces some compelling evidence to the contrary).

Finally, researchers would do well to explore other goal correlates and contextual factors. As discussed previously, researchers have tended to focus on a small number of correlates (e.g., job satisfaction, organizational commitment, and red tape) in public sector goal scholarship. The upside of this approach is that we have a substantial degree of convergence across research findings so far (e.g., that deleterious levels of ambiguity reduce job satisfaction and organizational commitment). However, the downside is that our understanding of the significance of the goal ambiguity concept remains in a largely nascent state. A shortlist of potential correlates might include (1) the various ways in which goal ambiguity and discretion are related, (2) how intra-organizational communication systems and structures shape ambiguity, (3) the nature of different tasks (e.g., political vs. technical, rational vs. unstructured, complexity), (4) the extensiveness and deployment of organizational resources, (5) how goal structures and other incentive and motivational (e.g., compensation, performance-related pay, public service motivation) schemes interact, and (6) how individuals navigate ambiguity when working in groups and teams. Additionally, more work should examine how the socio-demographic profile of workers affects interpretations of ambiguity (e.g., education level) and whether similar findings are present in the nonprofit sector as the lion's-share of goal ambiguity research has been conducted on public organizations.

CONCLUDING REMARKS

Over the past 70 years, the importance of goals as a motivational tool has gained more and more attention, with many of the key findings from extant research supporting Locke and Latham's early assertions. The significance of Locke and Latham's work has remained in the public sector settings, and public administration and management scholars have strived to grasp a better understanding of organizational goals and their implication as a motivational tool in public and nonprofit sectors for managing organizations and motivating employees.

While the importance of goals to organizations is widely acknowledged, regardless of the sector difference, constraints inherent in the public sector have led public administration goal researchers to more carefully consider how institutional context may challenge core goal-setting strategies and approaches. As the current chapter has illustrated, although public sector goal research has reached a high degree of convergence across empirical findings, showing that goals matter to public organizations, there exist gaps, especially around goal ambiguity stemming from the institutional context of the public sector.

Much of what we have learned suggests the primary issues at play revolve around the concept of goal clarity and ambiguity, particularly the subjectivity of goals, the nature of goal ambiguity, and how goal ambiguity is managed. As these are issues that may be, at least partly, unique to public and nonprofit organizations, tackling them may necessitate moving beyond the core tenets of Locke and Latham's goal-setting theory in order to fill knowledge gaps. Nevertheless, as Pinder noted, goal-setting theory carries promise with its strength and merits. A careful application of Locke and Latham's work, coupled with public administration knowledge, presents opportunities to further our understanding of goals and their implications for public organizations and employees.

REFERENCES

Allison, G.T. (1980). *Public and private management: Are they fundamentally alike in all unimportant respects?* Cambridge, MA: Harvard University Press.
Barnard, C.I. (1938). *The functions of the executive.* Cambridge, MA: Harvard University Press.
Boyne, G.A. (2002). Public and private management: What's the difference? *Journal of Management Studies, 39,* 97–122.
Bozeman, B. (2007). *Public values and public interest: Counterbalancing economic individualism.* Washington, DC: Georgetown University Press.
Brewer, G.A. (2006). All measures of performance are subjective: More evidence on U.S. federal agencies. In G.A. Boyne, K.J. Meier, L.J. O'Toole, Jr, and R.M. Walker (eds), *Public services performance: Perspectives on measurement and management.* Cambridge: Cambridge University Press, pp. 35–54.
Chandler, A.D., Jr (1977). *The visible hand: The managerial revolution in American business.* Cambridge, MA: Belknap Press.
Chun, Y.H., and Rainey, H.G. (2005a). Goal ambiguity and performance in U.S. federal agencies. *Journal of Public Administration Research and Theory, 15,* 529–557.
Chun, Y.H., and Rainey, H.G. (2005b). Goal ambiguity in U.S. federal agencies. *Journal of Public Administration Research and Theory, 15,* 1–30.
Davis, R.S., and Stazyk, E.C. (2015). Developing and testing a new goal taxonomy: Accounting for the complexity of ambiguity and political support. *Journal of Public Administration Research and Theory, 25,* 751–775.

Davis, R.S., and Stazyk, E.C. (2016). Examining the links between senior managers' engagement in networked environments and goal and role ambiguity. *Journal of Public Administration Research and Theory, 26*, 3 433–447.

Davis, R.S., and Stazyk, E.C. (2021). Ambiguity, appraisal, and affect: Examining the connections between goal perceptions, emotional labor, and exhaustion. *Public Management Review*, first published online on April 6, 2021 at https://doi.org/10.1080/14719037.2021.1909348.

Fayol, H. (1949). *General and industrial management* (trans. C. Storrs). London: Sir Isaac Pitman & Sons.

Frederickson, H.G., and Stazyk, E.C. (2010). Myths, markets, and the 'visible hand' of American bureaucracy. In R.F. Durant (ed.), *The Oxford handbook of American bureaucracy*. New York, NY: Oxford University Press, pp. 349–371.

Goodnow, F.J. (1900). *Politics and administration: A study in government*. New York, NY: The Macmillan Co.

Gulick, L. (1937). Notes on the theory of organization. In L. Gulick and L. Urwick (eds), *Papers on the science of administration*. New York, NY: Institute of Public Administration, pp. 191–195.

Hayes, M., and Stazyk, E.C. (2019). Mission congruence: To agree or not to agree, and its implications for public employee turnover. *Public Personnel Management, 48*, 513–534.

Herzberg, F., Mausner, B., and Snyderman, B.B. (1959). *The motivation to work*. New York, NY: Wiley.

Jung, C.S. (2014). Organizational goal ambiguity and job satisfaction in the public sector. *Journal of Public Administration Research and Theory, 24*, 955–981.

Latham, G.P., and Locke, E.A. (1975). Increasing productivity with decreasing time limits: A field replication of Parkinson's Law. *Journal of Applied Psychology, 60*, 524–526.

Latham, G. P., and Yukl, G. A. (1975). Assigned versus participative goal setting with educated and uneducated woods workers. *Journal of Applied Psychology, 60*, 299–302.

Lewin, K. (1939). Field theory and experiment in social psychology. *American Journal of Sociology, 44*, 868–897.

Likert, R. (1967). *The human organization: Its management and values*. New York, NY: McGraw-Hill.

Locke, E.A. (1968). Toward a theory of task motivation and incentives. *Organizational Behavior and Human Performance, 3*, 157–189.

Locke, E.A. (1971). Is 'behavior therapy' behavioristic? (An analysis of Wolpe's psychotherapeutic methods). *Psychological Bulletin, 76*, 318–327.

Locke, E.A. (1976). The nature and causes of job satisfaction. In D. Dunnette (ed.), *Handbook of industrial and organizational psychology*. Chicago, IL: Rand McNally, pp. 1297–1349.

Locke, E.A. (1977). The myths of behavior mod in organizations. *Academy of Management Review, 2*, 543–553.

Locke, E.A. (2001). Self-set goals and self-efficacy as mediators of incentives and personality. In M. Erez, U. Kleinbeck, and H. Thierry (eds), *Work motivation in the context of a globalizing economy*. Mahwah, NJ: Erlbaum, pp. 13–26.

Locke, E.A. (2018). Long-range thinking and goal directed action. In G. Oettingen, A.T. Servincer, and P.M. Gollwitzer (ed.), *The psychology of thinking about the future*. New York, NY: Guilford Press, pp. 377–391.

Locke, E.A., and Latham, G.P. (1990). *A theory of goal setting and task performance*. Englewood Cliffs, NJ: Prentice Hall.

Locke, E. A., and Latham, G. P. (2002). Building a practically useful theory of goal setting and task performance. *American Psychologist, 57*, 705–717.

Locke, E.A., and Latham, G.P. (2013). *New developments in goal setting and task performance*. New York, NY: Routledge.

Locke, E.A., and Latham, G.P. (2019). The development of goal setting theory: A half century retrospective. *Motivation Science, 5*, 93–105.

Mace, C.A. (1935). *Incentives: Some experimental studies* (Report No. 72). Industrial Health Research Board (Great Britain).

McClelland, D.C., Atkinson, J.W., Clark, R.A., and Lowell, E.L. (1953). *The achievement motive*. New York, NY: Appleton-Century-Crofts.

Meier, K.J., and O'Toole, L.J. (2011). Comparing public and private management: Theoretical expectations. *Journal of Public Administration Research and Theory, 22*, i283–i299.

Milkovich, G.T., and Wigdor, A.K. (1991). *Pay for performance: Evaluating performance appraisal and merit pay*. Washington, DC: National Academy Press.
Moe, T.M. (1980). *The organization of interests: Incentives and the internal dynamics of political interest groups*. Chicago, IL: University of Chicago Press.
Mosher, F.C. (1982). *Democracy and the public service* (2nd edn). New York, NY: Oxford University Press.
Murray, H. (1938). *Explorations in personality*. New York, NY: Oxford University Press.
Nalbandian, J., and Edwards, J.T. (1983). The values of public administrators: A comparison with lawyers, social workers, and business administrators. *Review of Public Personnel Administration, 4*, 114–127.
Pandey, S.K., and Wright, B.E. (2006). Connecting the dots in public management: Political environment, organizational goal ambiguity, and the public manager's role ambiguity. *Journal of Public Administration Research and Theory, 16*, 511–532.
Perry, J.L., and Rainey, H.G. (1988). The public-private distinction in organization theory: A critique and research strategy. *Academy of Management Review, 13*, 182–201.
Pinder, C.C. (1984). *Work motivation in organizational behavior*. New York, NY: Psychology Press.
Porter, R.L., and Latham, G.P. (2013). The effect of employee learning goals and goal commitment on departmental performance. *Journal of Leadership & Organizational Studies, 20*, 62–68.
Pritchard, R.D., Young, B.L., Koenig, N., Schmerling, D., and Dixon, N.W. (2013). Long-term effects of goal setting on performance with the productivity measurement and enhancement system (ProMES). In E.A. Locke and G.P. Latham (eds), *New developments in goal setting and task performance*. New York, NY: Routledge, pp. 233–245.
Pugh, D.S., and Hickson, D.J. (1976). *Organizational structure in its context: The Aston programme one*. Lexington, KY: Lexington Books.
Rainey, H.G. (1979). Perceptions of incentives in business and government: Implications for civil service reform. *Public Administration Review, 39*, 440–448.
Rainey, H.G. (1982). Reward preferences among public and private managers: In search of the service ethic. *American Review of Public Administration, 16*, 288–302.
Rainey, H.G. (1983). Public agencies and private firms: Incentive structures, goals, and individual roles. *Administration & Society, 15*, 207–242.
Rainey, H.G. (1991). *Understanding and managing public organizations*. New York, NY: Wiley.
Rainey, H.G., and Bozeman, B. (2000). Comparing public and private organizations: Empirical research and the power of the a priori. *Journal of Public Administration Research and Theory, 10*, 447–470.
Rainey, H.G., and Steinbauer, P. (1999). Galloping elephants: Developing elements of a theory of effective government organizations. *Journal of Public Administration Research and Theory, 9*, 1–32.
Rainey, H.G., Backoff, R.W., and Levine, C.H. (1976). Comparing public and private organizations. *Public Administration Review, 36*, 233–244.
Rainey, H.G., Pandey, S.K., and Bozeman, B. (1995). Public and private managers' perceptions of red tape. *Public Administration Review, 55*, 567–574.
Rosenbloom, D. (1983). Public administrative theory and the separation of powers. *Public Administration Review, 43*, 219–227.
Ryan, R.M. (2012). Motivation and the organization of human behavior: Three reasons for the reemergence of a field. In R.M. Ryan (ed.), *The Oxford handbook of human motivation* (1st edn), pp. 3–10.
Ryan, T.A. (1970). *Intentional behavior*. New York, NY: Ronald.
Simon, H. (2000). Public administration in today's world of organizations and markets. *PS: Political Science & Politics, 33*, 749–756.
Skinner, B.F. (1953). *Science and human behavior*. New York, NY: Macmillan.
Stazyk, E.C. (2013). Crowding out public service motivation? Comparing theoretical expectations with empirical findings on the influence of performance-related pay. *Review of Public Personnel Administration, 33*, 252–274.
Stazyk, E.C. (2016). The prevalence of reinvention reforms in local governments and their relationship with organizational goal clarity and employee job satisfaction. *Public Performance & Management Review, 39*, 701–727.
Stazyk, E.C., and Davis, R.S. (2020). Transformational leaders: Bridging the gap between goal ambiguity and public value involvement. *Public Management Review, 22*, 364–385.

Stazyk, E.C., and Davis, R.S. (2021). Birds of a feather: How manager-subordinate disagreement on goal clarity influences value congruence and organizational commitment. *International Review of Administrative Sciences*, *87*, 39–59.

Stazyk, E.C., and Goerdel, H.T. (2011). The benefits of bureaucracy: Public managers' perceptions of political support, goal ambiguity, and organizational effectiveness. *Journal of Public Administration Research and Theory*, *21*, 645–672.

Stazyk, E.C., Pandey, S.K., and Wright, B.E. (2011). Understanding affective organizational commitment: The importance of institutional context. *American Review of Public Administration*, *41*, 603–624.

Sun, R., Peng, S., and Pandey, S.K. (2014). Testing the effect of person-environment fit on employee perceptions of organizational goal ambiguity. *Public Performance & Management Review*, *37*, 465–495.

Taylor, F.W. (1911). *The principles of scientific management*. New York, NY: Harper & Brothers.

Vroom, V. (1964). *Work and motivation*. New York, NY: Wiley.

Watson, J.B. (1924). *Behaviorism*. Chicago, IL: University of Chicago Press.

7. What do we know yet about public service motivation in Latin America? A review of the evolution of empirical research
Pablo Sanabria-Pulido and Cristian Pliscoff

INTRODUCTION

This chapter aims to explore the current state of research regarding Public Service Motivation (PSM) (Perry, 1996; Perry and Wise, 1990) in the public sector in Latin America. This region comprises more than 30 countries, which share key cultural, historical, and institutional development traits, but still show particularities in terms of the degree of development of their public administrations and their subsequent institutional capacity levels (OECD, 2020). Likewise, the public sector organizations in the continent show very mixed results within each country in terms of government effectiveness, as well as evident disparities in terms of the capacity of national and subnational governments. Different authors have found corruption levels in Latin America higher than most other regions globally, and their civil services still far from achieving the ideal of merit, professionalism, and autonomy (Langbein and Sanabria-Pulido, 2017). Moreover, the levels of people's satisfaction with government, and especially the Latin American citizens' perceptions about public servants, are amongst the lowest in the world (Sanabria-Pulido and Bello-Gómez, 2020).

Furthermore, one key trait that makes this region an exciting place to study is the *sui generis* combination of reforms that the Latin American governments have conducted in their public sectors. Due to international institutions' influence, policy transfer, fiscal pressures, and other local dynamics, Latin America is a region where significant reforms have occurred in the last decades. This antecedent eventually led to a combination of different public administration models, ranging from political patronage, the traditional Weberian bureaucracy, New Public Management (NPM)-like practices, and open government initiatives (Pliscoff, 2017; Ramos Larraburu, 2019; Sanabria-Pulido, forthcoming). By and large, this almost unique mixture of factors makes the Latin American case an exciting subject of organizational behavior analysis, particularly in terms of the attitudes and behaviors of public servants, in an organizational sphere that combines such dissimilar approaches to public administration. Accordingly, we aim to analyze the research that has explored public service motivation in this region's context. To do so, we will review recent empirical research that has applied the PSM construct in different Latin American countries and a group of comparative and cross-country works that have included Latin American countries in their analysis. We will also compare how the research from this region differs or looks like other regions of the world.

SOME BACKGROUND ABOUT LATIN AMERICA'S PUBLIC ADMINISTRATION

Latin America is a large region, part of the American continent. It comprises nearly 30 countries (including Mexico, Central and South America, and the Caribbean basin) with approximately 650 million inhabitants. Its public administration resembles a particular mixture of models and approaches that share a common background, in terms of State functioning, from their principal Iberian colonizers, the Spaniard and Portuguese empires. The continent has strived for decades with rampant poverty, unplanned urbanization, precarious economic development, violence, and other prominent social tensions. The State in this part of the world, following the tradition from the colonial past, has developed its institutional capacity very slowly, and several countries in the region still deal with wicked policy problems that appear to go beyond their capacity like social inequality, violence, drug trafficking, insecurity, inadequate coverage in the provision of goods and services, among other challenges. There is heterogeneity in State capacity in the region, ranging from Chile with high institutional capacity to countries like Haiti with deep social and collective troubles. Accordingly, public administration in Latin America is seen consistently as an issue still in progress.

When discussing public management and organizational behavior aspects such as PSM in Latin America, it is relevant to begin with some background to place the topic within a broader discussion. Since the early days of the public administration discussion, Latin American scholars have predominantly focused their attention on the normative and legal dimensions of public administration, rather than their actual administrative and managerial functioning, even less in studying the people inside the organizations. It is perhaps linked to the colonial and the subsequent independence process that most of the region's countries had in the 19th and early 20th centuries. Hence, although there might be many studies in different countries regarding the functioning of the nascent States, the future will show how most Latin American countries appear to resemble the prismatic societies depicted by Fred Riggs, very sophisticated legal frameworks with little attention to the practicalities of their implementation.

Yet, the discussion among public administration scholars about the ethos of public service and public servants' motivation started early in this region. One of the topics that one can identify in those early works was improving and fostering the notion of the common good and public service among State employees. Even before the work of Wilson (1887) and his claim for separating politics and public administration, Latin American scholars, such as Florentino González wrote his first book in 1854 in today's Colombia (Gonzalez, 1994), whereas, before the end of the 19th century, Pérez de Arce, as well as Valentín Letelier in Chile, wrote similar pieces on the key definitions for public administration in the new countries (Letelier, n.d.; Pérez de Arce, 1884). In those early pieces, the authors equally anticipated the need for differentiating the political domain with the administration of public affairs and the necessity to draw the architecture of a new public administration apparatus. In their writings, it is possible to find the notion that public employees should be motivated to help fellow citizens and promote society's well-being.

In the first part of the 20th century, public administration scholars in different countries aimed to address critical organizational issues such as the State apparatus's structure and functions. Nonetheless, the issues and problems at stake varied across countries, according to their institutionalization level (Kurtz, 2013). After the emergence of the 'social problem' in many countries of the region in the 1920s and 1930s, the discussion moved to the State's role and the creation of State-owned-enterprises. The imports substitution model (ISI) model was dominant in the region (Cardoso and Faletto, 1979), which had a particular public administration model, similar to the welfare state.

During the 1970s and 1980s, the region was affected by dictatorships and states of exception, amid a profound economic crisis. The intense concern about fiscal troubles diverted the conversation from key institutional aspects and opened the avenue for managerial reforms. The academic discussion regarding public administration was not relevant or even present. It was only in the early 1990s when the academic inquiry regarding civil servants regained attention. Public and private universities began creating academic programs in public administration and public policy (Sanabria-Pulido, Rubaii, and Purón, 2016) and different outlets for research and publication on public affairs. The fiscal pressures brought strong influence from multilateral organizations such as the World Bank, the Inter-American Development Bank, and the Organisation for Economic Co-operation and Development (OECD), which became some of the primary sources of inspiration for public management policies for the region's governments.

Public Employees Motivation and PSM in Latin America

Broadly speaking, the topic of public employees' motivation, before the emergence of PSM, had two approaches. The first one refers to a normative conception of public employment. It was thought that public employees committed to public values only because they were part of the State. The literature in this sense was more of an intention rather than verification. Scholars and senior public employees wanted to have a group of civil servants committed to public values and public interest. However, there was a second approach. Politicians used public employment as a place for rewarding those helping them in winning an election. Thus, civil servants' motivation was oriented to fulfill their duties according to the desires of their political bosses. The 20th century in Latin America was the time of politicization, political patronage, cronyism, clientelism, and other practices that were thought of as means for using public positions for political intentions. These two approaches engender a contradictory administrative culture characterized by formalism and autonomy.

> The former becomes a mechanism for avoiding responsibility, or for justifying dynamic immobilism and aloofness. The flip side of this contradiction is that it transforms the role of the civil servant into one of dispensing personal favors as well as facilitating exceptions from existing norms. Such exceptionalism gives rise to recurrent nepotism, corruption, patronage and abuse. (Nef, 2012, p. 647)

Nevertheless, the reform processes have modified this dominant administrative culture since the mid-1990s. The combination of patrimonialism, Weberian and neo-Weberian reforms, NPM-style policies, and the latest wave of open government and governance initiatives have modified public administration's type and configuration in Latin America. However, these reforms, usually conducted due to policy transfer from multilateral donors, were not always supported by an adequate characterization of public employees and public organizations in the region. A strong tendency for normative and mimetic isomorphism (Ramio, 2001), mainly explained by international institutions' recommendations, yielded some administrative doctrines that were decoupled with the reality of public administration in Latin America.[1] The limited number of public affairs schools, scholars, and research centers working in the region did not help in having a deep understanding of the main challenges of public administrations in the subcontinent (Gomes et al., n.d.).

Thus, the common background that characterizes most countries in the region, coming from rents-extracting models of colonial State presence, the subsequent slow development of institutional capacity, and defiant social and public challenges, shows a region that still has vital gaps in the understanding of their public administrations and policies. The absence of a robust academic community in public management and policy for most of the 20th century, as well as the hasty adoption of policy prescription from multilateral donors, in response to severe fiscal and economic pressures, brought most Latin American countries to the beginning of the 21st century without an adequate understanding of the challenges that public servants and public organizations face. The combination of political patronage, bureaucratic approaches, NPM, and more recently, the new public governance (following the models by Pollit and Bouckaert, 2017) shows a region that still needs to improve the cumulation of public management knowledge in topics as necessary as organizational behavior, human resources management and within the public service motivation.

STATE OF THE ART OF PSM RESEARCH IN LATIN AMERICA

Public Service Motivation (PSM) emerged as a concept around 1983 through Rainey and Perry's pioneering works about the factors that differentiate public sector employees from their private counterparts. Since then, this line of research has skyrocketed and developed in manifold latitudes. Nonetheless, according to Professor James Perry of Indiana University Bloomington's website https://psm.indiana.edu, there are only ten referenced works on PSM from Latin America. It illustrates how PSM scholarship from developing countries is still scarce and remarkably absent in the Latin American case. This line of research, however, although very initial, shows some new developments in this region.

Recently, different review articles have aimed to analyze the international trends in PSM research and scholarship, particularly in countries outside the US/Canada and Europe. This trend helps expand PSM empirical research since, as Van der Wal (2015) argues, the most visible research on PSM might not be representative of other contexts. Moreover, those works from less represented countries could add valuable elements to the global discussion and to the understanding of factors that affect organizational behaviors and perceptions about public service, and which can range from highly trusted services in China to those with shallow levels of trust in Latin America (Sanabria-Pulido and Bello-Gomez, 2020).

Thus, generating better knowledge about public service motivation in underrepresented settings can be helpful not only for those same countries but for the general field of public administration itself. Having evidence from a more significant number of countries will help check issues of convergent validity and improve the comprehensiveness of theories and approaches to motivation in the public sector. Nonetheless, a review of the number of empirical works that aim to explore PSM in Latin America is still very scarce. A search within the essential multidisciplinary databases and some of the main journals in our field indicates that the number of studies regarding PSM from Latin American countries is still low. That number is even lower when checking which of those published works are conducted by native Latin American authors.

Our search allowed us to identify two main groups of scholarship regarding PSM in Latin America. The first group, which shows a growing trend in recent years, comprises single-country studies from different Latin American countries, either authored or co-authored by Latin American authors. On the other hand, we found a few international comparative studies, which using data from international surveys such as the International Social Survey Program (ISSP) or the World Value Survey, compare approaches and views on public service motivation across different countries' samples. This second group of works makes some subtle references about Latin American countries, but they appear to be marginal compared to the references made about other countries. The low number in both groups does not allow us to make richer comparisons of the existing works in each of them. In the following two subsections, we explore the single-country studies from Latin America and the cross-country studies that include Latin American countries.

Country-based Studies

The first group of reviewed scholarship on PSM from Latin America and the Caribbean collects diverse countries such as Brazil, Mexico, Chile, Colombia, Jamaica, and Honduras. Most of these 11 identified studies followed a quantitative methodological approach. Some of them include research designs with mixed methods, however. The works pursue different research questions but focus principally on different aspects of organizational behavior (employment choice, organizational citizenship, job satisfaction, retention, turnover, among others). Next, we will present a description of the different works concentrating on their research questions, the methods used, and the conclusions.

A work by Contreras-Pacheco (2020), explores the relationship between prosocial behavior and affective commitment in Colombia. Although it does not use data from public officials or public sector employees, it uses some of the concepts related to PSM and altruistic behaviors inside organizations. Employing quantitative methods, the authors eventually find that in a sample of for-profit sector employees from different industries in this country, the two concepts appear to be related, but only when they are mediated by the intervention of meaningfulness at work.

Zarychta, Grillos, and Andersson (2020) drew on a field experiment with Honduran public officials to explore how what they call governance reforms influence motivation among cadres of public servants in this Central American country. According to their results, a decentralized governance model allows higher levels of self-sacrifice, one of the components of the PSM construct of James Perry. They did not find statistically significant differences between municipal and centrally administered systems. In their account, selection and attraction, instead of socialization, play a crucial role in attracting more motivated workers.

Sanabria-Pulido (2018) analyzes the job sector decisions of highly skilled professionals in Colombia across four different sectors (public, private, nonprofit, and academia), focusing on the role that public service motivation plays in that employment choice. Using a pooled time series of individual antecedents, preferences, salary, and other job traits, the author finds evidence that PSM exhibits a positive significant relationship with public sector employment and an inverse relationship with nonprofit and for-profit jobs. The study provides some policy recommendations to the Colombian government regarding the attraction of people with higher PSM levels.

Moloney and Chu (2016) explored the levels of PSM among Jamaican civil servants and students. The authors find quantitative evidence of the existence of PSM in Jamaica, but also explore, from a theoretical point of view, the presence of these high levels of PSM within a challenged context for public service ethics. For the authors, the existence of corruption, clientelism, and other undesired practices in public service limits the complete fulfilment of PSM in the Jamaican public sector. In their perspective, the strong incidence of evident institutional weaknesses lessens the benefits from having public servants with strong motivation to serve the public good.

Bottomley et al. (2016) explore the relationship between transformational leadership and organizational citizenship behaviors in Mexico. The authors find that such relation appears to be mediated by the role of PSM. In their account, the influence of transformational leadership on the motivation levels of a group of civil servants was lower for public sector employees with higher levels of PSM. According to Bottomley and colleagues, by comparing with a sample of private sector employees, their study allowed them to confirm extant scholarship that states that PSM is better aligned to the goals and values of public sector agencies as opposed to those of private sector organizations.

Klein and Mascarenhas (2016) explore for Brazil the motivational factors that explain job satisfaction and retention among 'gestores governamentais/publicos,' members of the senior executive service in its Brazilian version, at the State (subnational) level. Although they do not specifically explore PSM, they analyze intrinsic motivation's role on different outcomes such as job satisfaction. Their results show that intrinsic motivation is a crucial determinant for public officials' retention and satisfaction in this Senior Public Service in Brazil.

In her master's dissertation, Brito (2016) aims to define a theory of PSM for Brazil. She develops a mixed-methods approach in a case study of the Brazilian National Agency of Petroleum, Natural Gas and Biofuels (ANP). The author claims to assess the applicability of Perry's instrument to the context of a Brazilian public organization from a sample of roughly 1000 public officials (no mention about the representativeness of the sample was made). Although the study does not follow an empirical research design, and the results appear to be based on descriptive analysis, the author argued from the analysis that the PSM construct does not apply to Brazil's context in terms of attraction and entry to the public sector.

Also, in a quantitative study, Mostafa and Leon-Cazares (2015) analyze a sample of Mexican public sector employees to explore the relationship between public service motivation and perceived organizational performance. The authors find no direct effect of PSM but instead find an indirect effect through a positive influence on public servants' organizational citizenship behaviors. All in all, the authors conclude that their study confirms that PSM is an important factor in public employees' behavior.

One article by Dal Bó et al. (2013) analyzed the results of an experiment with a recruitment drive for public sector jobs in the Mexican public sector, whereby different job ads and salaries were randomized across different recruitment sites. They conducted various tests on the applicants, including testing motivational aspects at the individual level. The authors found no evidence of damage in employees' vocational profiles due to raising wages, namely, no better salaries on PSM levels. On the other hand, they found a positive correlation between the individual's PSM and the likelihood of engaging in prosocial behavior (charity, volunteering, and political party membership) and exhibiting altruistic behaviors in experimental games.

Pliscoff (2009), in his doctoral dissertation, conducted a survey of PSM among 767 public officials in Chile. In his work, the author explored how NPM practices affected public service ethics and values in Chile, a country characterized by substantial managerialist-type reforms even compared to other Latin American countries. He found that the PSM scores obtained through his survey show an above-average level of PSM across the sample of public officials surveyed. In this way, despite the progress in the incorporation of NPM practices in this Latin American country, it did not inflict an erosion of 'public service values' among Chilean public servants.

Finally, a master's-level dissertation from Brazil in 2007 by Carolina Buiatti mentioned the lack of studies outside the US, Europe, and Korea and aimed to validate Perry's PSM instrument in the context of this Latin American country. Using factor analysis, correlations, and structural equation modeling, the author finds preliminary evidence that PSM and organizational commitment are correlated. Moreover, she argues that according to their results, PSM as a construct was validated for its use in Brazil. However, Buiatti claims that such an instrument/scale needs adjustment before its application in this country's context.

Thus, all the single-country studies appear to have followed quantitative approaches. Most of them are empirical studies with a statistical inference strategy, use surveys from public officials and, in some cases, employees from other sectors such as nonprofit and for-profit. The reviewed studies share some similar conclusions regarding effects from PSM on a myriad of organizational outcomes such as, inter alia, job sector membership, perceived performance, prosocial behaviors, retention, and socialization. These studies have opened the avenue to further studies exploring PSM from a quantitative perspective, but their low number is far from allowing general conclusions about PSM in the region. Most single-case studies from a more significant number of Latin American countries are needed.

Cross-country Studies

On the other hand, we find the second group of international cross-country/longitudinal studies which have used data from multi-country surveys or databases, including data from some Latin American countries. A recent work by Mikkelsen, Schuster, and Meyer-Sahling (2020) includes data from around 5700 Chilean civil servants and 2830 from Brazil. The authors draw attention to the fact that many extant comparative studies on PSM primarily include data from developed countries but little data from countries in the global South, particularly Latin America. From their comparative analysis of ten countries, the authors conclude that there is a cross-cultural basis for PSM research and cross-country accumulation of knowledge. Nevertheless, they do not make specific mention of results from Brazil and Chile, whose civil services, worthy of mentioning, are not necessarily representative of Latin America as a whole.

In a similar study, Ritz et al. (2016) explored the evolution of international PSM scholarship. They claimed to include ten studies from (South) Latin America, but they do not include any Latin American authors. The article reports to include studies from Brazil (three studies), Mexico (three studies), Chile (two studies) Uruguay (two studies), but indeed, those studies cannot be easily identified from the titles included in the supplement of the article. Our intuition is that they count among these the studies that use international surveys (ISSP, for instance) as works from those countries. Although they do not make specific regional comparisons or comments about PSM in this region, they argue that research from Latin America (they refer to it as South America) is highly underrepresented.

In a similar vein, Van de Walle, Steijn, and Jilke (2015) conduct a comparative analysis of the determinants of public sector choice across a sample of 26 countries, focusing on the European Union members or the OECD. The authors also use data from the ISSP and in their sample include data only from one Latin American country, Mexico. The fact that there is only one Latin American country perhaps explains why their analysis omits specific references or conclusions regarding this world's region.

Vandenabeele and Van de Walle, in their chapter for the Perry and Hondeghem (2008) book, explore the international differences in PSM. They use data from the ISSP for 2004, including data from 38 countries, including five Latin American countries, namely, Chile, Brazil, Venezuela, Mexico, and Uruguay. In their comparative regional analysis, the authors find that the Latin American countries share with the US/Canada the higher levels of reported PSM scores in the survey. However, when the authors analyze the PSM construct's subdimensions, they find that the Latin American countries rank in the middle of the sample in terms of politics and policies, whereas the compassion subdimension and the general PSM are among the highest scores. However, when it comes to self-sacrifice, the scores from Latin American countries rank low. They claim that the trends that characterize countries from this region respond to the strong Roman Catholic heritage, even though they do not provide empirical evidence. The authors also explore the relationship of PSM with public sector employment, but Latin America results do not appear to be explained at large.

Finally, the early work by Snyder, Osland, and Hunter (1996), which can be considered a pioneering study of PSM in the region, conducts a comparative analysis of reward preferences in a group of 207 Latin American students from MPA (Masters of Public Administration) and MBA (Masters of Business Administration) programs in Costa Rica and Nicaragua. The sample appears to be biased towards Nicaraguan, Costa Rican, and other Central America students for obvious location reasons. However, it also includes 31 students from ten other Latin American countries. The authors conducted a test of means between the public sector and private sector participants in their sample. Accordingly, they argue that PSM appears to play a critical role, particularly when considering the purpose of contributing to national development. They claim that their results contradict the idea of Perlman (1989), which denied the existence of public service ethics among Latin American public workers. They also show a positive difference in public servants' public service motivation levels compared to their private sector counterparts.

To sum up, a few cross-country studies have included data in their sample from limited Latin American countries. The comparative studies usually explore cross-country convergence regarding results, issues about construct validity and measurement, and other conceptual and methodological issues. Hence, this perhaps explains why most of those studies do not show in-depth analysis about Latin America. Also, because the number of countries included is usually low or not necessarily representative across the samples. The evidence from those works does not allow general conclusions about the role of PSM in the public sector in Latin America. The lack of knowledge about Latin America starts from the very geography. Different works have nomenclature problems when referring to Latin America. For example, they usually refer to South America as all those countries other than the US and Canada in the American continent. This term is imprecise since Latin America is made up of a North American country (Mexico), the countries of Central and South America, and, in their extended versions, the Caribbean basin countries. This appreciation is vital to avoid misclassifications of the empirical research of these countries.

WHAT WE KNOW ABOUT PSM IN LATIN AMERICA: ACHIEVEMENTS AND LINES OF SCHOLARSHIP

The analysis of the different works on PSM in Latin America, made in the previous section, shows that, although there is a growing trend, the number of empirical works on PSM is still deficient in the region, even in comparison to other comparable areas with a significant number of emerging countries like the Middle East, Central and East Europe, South and Southeast Asia. Thus, we conclude that the embryonic research on public service motivation in Latin America is still far from generating a solid ground for knowledge about organizational behavior in our region's public sector.

Nevertheless, we can make some general observations from the different works analyzed. The first point is that there is convergence in terms of the existence of PSM in Latin American public sector organizations. Although one work in the late 1980s questioned the existence of an ethics of public service in the countries of our region, like the one of countries with fully developed, independent, and professionalized civil services (Perlman, 1989), the available evidence of empirical works from the last decade in this region confirms the applicability and evidence of PSM in different organizations and sectors across a group of Latin American countries.

In terms of research lines and topics of interest, since most studies are meager, most topics are isolated. Each work appears to have a particular research question, making it difficult to make generalized observations from the research and conclusions of convergence/divergence in findings. It also makes it difficult to see that clear research lines on PSM are being consolidated in Latin America. The 15 reviewed works provide evidence about a positive relationship between public service motivation and key organizational outcomes such as public sector employment, job satisfaction, retention, and organizational citizenship. The evidence is consistent across countries and different samples of public officials and organizations. On the contrary, there is no conclusive evidence in some studies regarding organizational commitment, but most studies tend to confirm the importance of PSM in affecting person-organization fit and performance.

The reviewed works, particularly those from single-country studies, show increasing use of more sophisticated analytical, quantitative approaches, ranging from initial two-group ANOVA and test means to more recently multivariate and multilevel models. In terms of samples, one interesting trait is that most studies are done with actual public officials or employees from other sectors instead of the systematic studies with MPA/MPP (Master of Public Policy) students usually conducted in other regions of the world. The samples are usually purposive, and sometimes their representativeness and their external validity are not clarified. The reviewed works tend to use the full or abridged versions of Perry's instrument, although the cross-country studies from international samples tend to rely more on proxy variables for PSM.

Most of the single-country works are conducted and either authored or co-authored by Latin American authors, who are usually native from the same countries, whereas European authors mostly run the cross-country studies. Nonetheless, the number of Latin American countries with devoted PSM works is deficient, with only five countries of 16 Spanish-Portuguese speaking countries from the continental part. There are various studies from Brazil, Mexico, and Chile, and single studies from Colombia and Honduras. This shows that other populous countries like Argentina, Perú, Guatemala, Costa Rica, and Venezuela are undoubtedly underrepresented.

These elements bring important lines for future research. First, Latin America is one of the regions with crucial remaining challenges in the configuration of independent civil services (OECD, 2020). Most countries still have *sui generis* combinations of political patronage practices, which coexist with ill-defined bureaucratic structures and NPM practices and, more recently, governance and open government traits. This unusual combination makes this region of the world a particular laboratory for research on organizational behavior and public employment. PSM is, without doubt, one of the topics that needs to be enhanced in the research agenda in the region if we want to join the global dialogue, but also if international research wants to improve the generalizability of findings and the cumulation of knowledge.

Conducting more research on PSM in Latin America would allow exploring issues like its relationship with corruption (objective and perception measures), which is one of the hot topics in a region that usually ranks high on the perception of corruption rankings. Also, more research on PSM is needed in relationship to trust and social capital. As mentioned above, Latin American countries exhibit some of the lowest trust levels in public officials and the State in the whole world. Thus, understanding the interaction with prosocial behaviors and PSM would allow us to understand better what are the variations that explain the low prestige of the public sector in our countries and how it affects the pool of people that join it and the subsequent quality of public policies and the performance of government itself.

Finally, knowing more about countries that share key historical traits but still portray variation in size, economic power, institutional capacity, or wicked problems that affect them allows an exciting set of comparable countries. Latin America's strong unity by language, culture, and history brings a natural research lab, hard to find in other regions of the world. These elements might help improve the understanding of PSM forms and shapes in less studied settings, leading to enhancing the cumulation knowledge about PSM by bringing more evidence from the global South. All in all, there is a fresh breeding ground for more significant research from the region. As we show in the conclusions, there are different actions from the international and Latin American research community that can help achieve the purpose of improving scholarship on these issues in this part of the world.

WHAT WE DO NOT KNOW: THE GAPS IN PSM SCHOLARSHIP IN LATIN AMERICA

According to the works already presented, the scope and breadth of PSM academic inquiry in Latin America are limited. In the present section, we cover the gaps in PSM theory and present an agenda of future topics that need to be addressed to add to the already vast and diverse literature of PSM in the world. In this context, the first topic that needs to be developed is how pertinent the notion of PSM is in Latin American culture. The majority of works on the applicability of PSM have been undertaken in Europe, the US/Canada, and Asia. In this way, more research is needed to link the cultural traits of Latin America with the construct of PSM. The outstanding work by Hofstede, Hofstede, and Minkov (2005) shows the similarities the countries of this region share in terms of collectivism and individualism, and other traits usually related to NPM practices (Stazyk et al., 2013) which appear to be entrenched in Latin America's public management such as personnel temporary contracting (Sanabria-Pulido,

Gonzalez, and Becerra, 2019). Bearing in mind these similarities, one can claim that these values can influence the very notion of PSM, similar to what has been studied in other regions (Lee et al., 2020; Parola et al., 2019).

Another topic that researchers in Latin America could address is the link between PSM and performance. PSM researchers have shown one of the critical findings of this line of research, the connection between those with a higher level of PSM and higher levels of performance Warren and Chen, 2013). Except for Alvarez (2016), this connection has not been studied thoroughly. Thus, more studies are required, mainly because there are contextual factors of public organizations (Lynggaard, Pederden, and Andersen, 2016) and organizational characteristics (Im, Campbell, and Jeong, 2013) that affect the relationship between performance and PSM. It is highly relevant in a continent with similarities, but with many differences in public sector performance and conditions (Cortázar Velarde et al., 2014; OECD, 2020).

The third area of future research that needs to be addressed in Latin America is the connection between PSM and ethics (Ripoll, 2019; Stazyk and Davis, 2015). So far, there is only one article regarding the topic with data from an experiment in Chile (Meyer-Sahling, Mikkelsen, and Schuster, 2019). This lack of interest in connecting PSM and ethics or corruption is counterintuitive in a region where corruption scandals have mushroomed in the last 20 years or so. There are some particularities of this phenomenon in the region (Arellano-Gault, 2019; Pliscoff, 2019). Thus, more research is needed to address topics as crucial as the potential link between high levels of PSM and ethics or the potential link between PSM and whistleblowers (Cho and Song, 2015).

Fourth, Human Resources Management (HRM) or Public Personnel policies have improved significantly in the region (OECD, 2020). PSM can be a valuable concept for fostering this process even more. Piatak et al. (2020) claim that PSM can improve two areas of HRM policies: job design and recruitment. In the latter, only Sanabria-Pulido (2018) has tested the issue for the case of a Latin American country. Thus, more research is required to improve the selection of future public servants that could have a better commitment to public duties and help the adoption of strategic HRM in public organizations in the region (Sanabria-Pulido, 2015).

Finally, public administration in Latin America has some negative traits, such as high senior civil servants' turnover, limited capabilities for performance measurement, scarce resources, corruption, clientelism, and constant conflicts between public employees' unions and political appointees. It is essential to test whether these problems affect diminishing PSM scores or not. In so doing, PSM research could help improve and make HRM policies in the State more valuable and purposeful for a better and more meaningful public administration oriented to address public problems and deliver services for society's betterment.

CONCLUSIONS AND RECOMMENDATIONS

Our review of the existing literature on public service motivation in Latin America reveals the empty glass or the full glass, depending on the perspective of whoever looks. On the one hand, the existing empirical literature is still scarce and limited to a few topics and isolated research questions. Although the works we review focus on the leading international journals on public affairs, other works on motivation (not necessarily adopting the conceptual framework of PSM) written in Spanish (not included in our analysis) are usually descriptive and generally weak in the approximations and methodologies used.

Furthermore, of the reviewed papers, those exploring specific country cases are still very few and limited in terms of countries (they cover only six countries). This evidences the need to encourage further works from a more comprehensive sample of countries in the region. On the other hand, the comparative international papers covering, among others, Latin American countries usually include a few or small samples of them and do not delve in-depth into elements that explain regional characteristics or particularities of PSM in the region. In turn, this shows the need for comparative works that explore PSM across Latin American countries.

On the positive side, the reviewed empirical works show increasing quality in terms of identification strategies and empirical approaches. Most are quantitative studies that have taken advantage of administrative databases and surveys of multi-sector officials and employees. Said works have also been inserted into a global conversation, as they are written in English and published in many of our discipline's most prestigious journals. Most of them are written by local authors in collaboration with international authors, showing a greater integration of Latin American scholars with public administration's global academic networks.

Different aspects can explain the small but promising offer of empirical research in the Latin American subcontinent. First, the capacity of the universities. As different studies in the region have shown, training and research in public affairs (public administration and public policies) is a relatively recent phenomenon in the region. Most of the programs have been created in the last three decades and remain concentrated in a few countries. The academic offer in smaller countries, and at the regional level, is still limited in most countries and poorly connected with global issues and state of the art in public affairs education and research at the international level. It somehow has limited the creation of research and academic teams, whose training and bilingualism may help connect them with international academic networks. Thus, the task of strengthening doctoral training in the region on public administration and public policy issues persists, and its insertion in global networks where cutting-edge issues in the discipline of public affairs are explored and studied.

Second, international networks and the way the research and publishing 'market' works may not facilitate underrepresented regions' participation. From the international review articles that we explored (e.g., Ritz et al., 2016; Vandenabeele and Van de Walle, 2008), we can infer that the flagship journals appear to be less interested in scholarship from countries other than US/Canada, Europe and some of Asia. A review of the articles from developing countries by Mussagulova and Van der Wal (2021) indicates that those pieces have found more straightforward publication in journals such as the *International Journal of Public Administration*. In contrast, according to their review, other flagship journals appear to be less oriented towards publication from countries other than the US/Canada, Australia, Europe, South Korea.

The fact that aspects such as the potential for citation and the audiences (academic community) of these countries on these issues are broader is possibly fostering a vicious circle whereby articles outside the primary circuit of countries are less attractive for the prominent journals. This negatively affects our discipline by limiting the global dialogue and the accumulation of knowledge that is representative and urgently needs to include in the conversation the multiple variations of models and approaches to public administration found in countries outside the global North. As Mussagulova and van der Wal (2021) argue, there is a real need to establish a global dialogue by bringing scholarship from non-Western countries that enriches our understanding of public service motivation, but scholarship that is properly rooted in their own contexts rather than replicating approaches from the 'Western tradition.'

Our analysis starts from the idea that there is already a nascent movement with better and more extensive literature and research on PSM in Latin America. However, for such efforts to find fertile ground, there is a need for support from the global community of researchers in public administration. From the demand side, several approaches can stimulate the greater participation of jobs from underrepresented countries, for example, by inviting a more significant number of researchers from those countries to be part of the most critical journals' editorial boards. On the other hand, forming research teams that include researchers from the countries on which research is being carried out and incorporating them into the decision-making and collegial spaces of the leading international networks and associations in our discipline.

The task also falls on the Latin American countries, from the supply side, to strengthen their academic and research networks to stimulate comparative and collaborative work with scholars from Latin America and other parts of the world, reinforcing their doctoral programs, supporting bilingualism, and bringing more solid training on methodological aspects both in quantitative and qualitative methods. Likewise, the universities and think tanks can help facilitate the exchange of academics and the connection of their research activities with international networks and teams. Also, from the State itself, some actions can help improve the quality of research in our countries by generating better databases, encouraging more outstanding joint university-State endeavors, and facilitating more significant financial resources for research on public administration issues.

Finally, we think it is the Latin American community of researchers' responsibility to provide a perspective about the usability and appropriateness of public management concepts such as PSM. In doing so, we should be more active in becoming part of the global discussion by pursuing further scholarship that enriches the global public administration dialogue. It is common in our region to accept foreign ideas and models that are successful in other continents. As this chapter shows, a pioneer group of scholars has already used this construct to characterize our civil servants. That is a good starting point. Nevertheless, future works should explore issues such as: Is the notion of public service motivation genuinely applicable in our region? Can it be another foreign idea that we are using without testing its real applicability? Our responsibility is to bring our identity to the fore and provide elements for enriching the global discussion. Making PSM more 'Latin American' should be our ultimate contribution.

NOTE

1. An excellent example of this is the implementation of performance-based incentives in Chile (Pliscoff, 2005).

REFERENCES

Alvarez, Á. (2016). La motivación y su incidencia en el desempeño del empleado de carrera. Medición e implicaciones para la administración pública colombiana. *Diálogos de saberes: investigaciones y ciencias sociales, 45*, 127–143.

Arellano-Gault, D. (2019). *Corruption in Latin America*. New York, NY: Routledge.

Bottomley, P., Mostafa, A.M.S., Gould-Williams, J.S., and León-Cázares, F. (2016). The impact of transformational leadership on organizational citizenship behaviours: The contingent role of public service motivation. *British Journal of Management, 27*, 390–405.

Brito, D.T.D. (2016). Towards a public service motivation theory for Brazil. Master's dissertation, Fundação Getulio Vargas.
Cardoso, F.H., and Faletto, E. (1979). *Dependency and development in Latin America*. Berkely, CA: University of California Press.
Cho, Y. J., and Song, H.J. (2015). Determinants of whistleblowing within government agencies. *Public Personnel Management*, 44, 450–472.
Contreras-Pacheco, O.E. (2020). Increasing affective commitment through prosocial behavior: Does perceived meaningfulness at work matter? *Cuadernos De Administración*, 36, 112–125.
Cortázar Velarde, J.C., Lafuente, M., Sanginés, M., Schuster, C., Echebarría, K., Longo, F., and Iacoviello, M. (2014). Al servicio del ciudadano: una década de reformas del servicio civil en América Latina (2004–13). Inter-American Development Bank.
Dal Bó, E., Finan, F., and Rossi, M.A. (2013). Strengthening state capabilities: The role of financial incentives in the call to public service. *The Quarterly Journal of Economics*, 128(3), 1169–1218.
Gomes, R., Sanabria, P., Pliscoff, C., and Teixeira, M. (n.d.). Public affairs education in Latin America and the shape of the State: The cases of Brazil, Chile, and Colombia.
Gonzalez, F. (1994). *Elementos de Ciencia Administrativa*. Bogotá: Escuela Superior de Administración Pública.
Hofstede, G., Hofstede, G.J., and Minkov, M. (2005). *Cultures and organizations: Software of the Mind*. New York, NY: Mcgraw-Hill.
Im, T., Campbell, J.W., and Jeong, J. (2013). Commitment Intensity in public organizations: Performance, innovation, leadership, and PSM. *Review of Public Personnel Administration*, 36, 219–239.
Klein, F.A., and Mascarenhas, A.O. (2016). Motivação, satisfação profissional e evasão no serviço público: o caso da carreira de especialistas em Políticas Públicas e Gestão Governamental. *Revista de Administração Pública*, 50, 17–39.
Kurtz, M.J. (2013). *Latin American state building in comparative perspective: Social foundations of institutional order*. Cambridge: Cambridge University Press.
Langbein L., and Sanabria-Pulido, P. (2017). Independent Professional bureaucracies and street-level bribery: Comparing changes in civil service law and implementation in Latin America. *Journal of Comparative Policy Analysis: Research and Practice*, 19, 435–451.
Lee, H.J., Kim, M.Y., Park, S.M., and Robertson, P J. (2020). Public Service motivation and innovation in the Korean and Chinese public sectors: Exploring the role of Confucian values and social capital. *International Public Management Journal*, 23, 496–534.
Letelier, V. (n.d.). Génesis del estado y de sus instituciones fundamentales: introducción al estudio del Derecho Público. Retrieved November 11, 2021 from http://www.memoriachilena.gob.cl/602/w3-article-8839.html.
Lynggaard, M., Pedersen, M.J., and Andersen, L.B. (2016). Exploring the context dependency of the psm–performance relationship. *Review of Public Personnel Administration*, 38, 332–354.
Meyer-Sahling, J.H., Mikkelsen, K.S., and Schuster, C. (2019). The causal effect of public service motivation on ethical behavior in the public sector: Evidence from a large-scale survey experiment. *Journal of Public Administration Research and Theory*, 29, 445–459.
Mikkelsen, K.S., Schuster, C., and Meyer-Sahling, J.H. (2020). A cross-cultural basis for public service? Public service motivation measurement invariance in an original survey of 23,000 public servants in ten countries and four world regions. *International Public Management Journal*, first published online on October 15, 2020 at https://doi.org/10.1080/10967494.2020.1809580.
Moloney, K., and Chu, H.Y. (2016). Linking Jamaica's public service motivations and ethical climate. *The American Review of Public Administration*, 46, 436–458.
Mostafa, A.M.S., and Leon-Cazares, F. (2016). Public service motivation and organizational performance in Mexico: Testing the mediating effects of organizational citizenship behaviors. *International Journal of Public Administration*, 39, 40–48.
Mussagulova, A., and Van der Wal, Z. (2021). 'All still quiet on the non-Western front?' Non-Western public service motivation scholarship: 2015–2020. *Asia Pacific Journal of Public Administration*, 43, 23–46.
Nef, J. (2012). Public administration and public sector reform in Latin America. In B.G. Peters and J. Pierre (eds), *The SAGE handbook of public administration*, 2nd edn. London: Sage, pp. 642–658.

OECD. (2020). Panorama de las Administraciones Públicas: América Latina y el Caribe 2020. Panorama de las Administraciones Públicas: América Latina y el Caribe 2020. https://doi.org/10.18235/0002232.

Parola, H.R., Harari, M.B., Herst, D.E.L., and Prysmakova, P. (2019). Demographic determinants of public service motivation: A meta-analysis of PSM-age and -gender relationships. *Public Management Review*, *21*, 1397–1419.

Pérez de Arce, H. (1884). El administrador público: o sea, Estudios sobre principios jenerales de administracion. Imprenta Victoria, de H. Izquidero.

Perlman, E.J. (1989). Modernizing the public service in Latin America: Paradoxes of Latin American public administration. *International Journal of Public Administration*, *12*, 671–704.

Perry, J.L., and Hondeghem, A. (eds) (2008*). Motivation in public management: The call of public service*. Oxford: Oxford University Press.

Perry, J. (1996). Measuring public service motivation: An assessment of construct reliability and validity. *Journal of Public Administration Research and Theory*, *6*, 5–22.

Perry, J., and Wise, L. (1990). The motivational bases of public service. *Public Administration Review*, *50*, 367–373.

Piatak, J.S., Sowa, J.E., Jacobson, W.S., and McGinnis Johnson, J. (2020). Infusing public service motivation (PSM) throughout the employment relationship: A review of PSM and the human resource management process. *International Public Management Journal*, *24*(1), 86–105.

Pliscoff, C. (2005). Sistema de Incentivos Monetarios y Reforma del Estado: Elementos para una discusión necesaria. Documentos de Apoyo Docente. Escuela de Gobierno y Gestión Pública.

Pliscoff, C. (2009). New Public Management in Chile (1990–2008): Exploring its impact on public employees. Dissertation, School of Policy, Planning and Development, University of Southern California.

Pliscoff, C. (2017). Implementando la nueva gestión pública: Problemas y desafíos a la ética pública. *El caso chileno. Convergencia*, *24*, 141–164.

Pliscoff, C. (2019). Ethics and public administration in Latin America. In A. Farazmand (ed.), *Global encyclopedia of public administration, public policy, and governance*. New York, NY: Springer, pp. 1–12.

Pollitt, C., and Bouckaert, G. (2017). *Public management reform: A comparative analysis—into the age of austerity*. New York, NY: Oxford University Press.

Ramio, C. (2001). Los problemas de la implementación de la nueva gestión pública en las administraciones públicas latinas: modelo de Estado y cultura institucional. *Reforma y Democracia (CLAD)*, 21, 16.

Ramos Larraburu, C. (2019). The politics of bureaucracy: A view from Latin America, *The British Journal of Politics and International Relations*, *21*, 513–521.

Ripoll, G. (2019). Disentangling the relationship between public service motivation and ethics: An interdisciplinary approach. *Perspectives on Public Management and Governance*, *2*, 21–37.

Ritz, A., Brewer, G.A., and Neumann, O. (2016). Public service motivation: A systematic literature review and outlook. *Public Administration Review*, *76*(3), 414–426.

Sanabria-Pulido, P. (2015). *Gestión Estratégica del Talento Humano en el Sector Público: Estado del Arte, Diagnóstico y Recomendaciones para el Caso Colombiano*. Colombia: Ediciones Uniandes. (ISBN 978-958-774-160-5).

Sanabria-Pulido, P. (2018). Public service motivation and job sector choice: Evidence from a developing country. *International Journal of Public Administration*, *41*, 1107–1118.

Sanabria-Pulido, P. (Forthcoming). Análisis de la Evolución de la Administración Pública Colombiana: Crisis y Turbulencias para la Construcción de Capacidad Institucional. In P. Sanabria-Pulido and S. Leyva (eds), *El Estado del Estado*. Bogotá: Ediciones Uniandes/Editorial EAFIT/Departamento Administrativo de la Función Pública.

Sanabria-Pulido, P., and Bello-Gómez, R.A. (2020). Public sector reform and perceptions of public servants: An international longitudinal review. In H. Sullivan, H. Dickinson, and H. Henderson (eds), *The Palgrave handbook of the public servant*, New York, NY: Springer, pp. 1–19.

Sanabria-Pulido, P., Rubaii, N., and Purón, G. (2016). Public affairs graduate education in Latin America: Emulation or identity? *Policy and Society*, *35*, 315–331.

Sanabria-Pulido, P., Gonzalez, M., and Becerra, O. (2019) Cómo mejorar y racionalizar la contratación por prestación de servicios en el sector público en Colombia? Una mirada desde la calidad del empleo. Colombia.

Snyder, M.M., Osland, J., and Hunter, L. (1996). Public and private organizations in Latin America: A comparison of reward preferences. *International Journal of Public Sector Management*, *9*, 15–27.

Stazyk, E.C., and Davis, R.S. (2015). Taking the 'high road': Does public service motivation alter ethical decision making processes? *Public Administration*, *93*, 627–645.

Stazyk, E.C., Davis, R.S., Sanabria, P., and Pettijohn, S. (2013). Working in the hollow state: Exploring the link between public service motivation and interlocal collaboration. In Y.K. Dwivedi, M.A. Shareef, S.K. Pandey, and V. Kumar (eds), *Public administration reformation: Market demand from public organizations*. New York, NY: Routledge, pp. 124–143.

Van de Walle, S., Steijn, B., and Jilke, S. (2015). Extrinsic motivation, PSM and labour market characteristics: A multilevel model of public sector employment preference in 26 countries. *International Review of Administrative Sciences*, *81*, 833–855.

Van der Wal, Z. (2015). 'All quiet on the non-Western front?' A review of public service motivation scholarship in non-Western contexts. *Asia Pacific Journal of Public Administration*, *37*, 69–86.

Vandenabeele, W., and Van de Walle, S. (2008). International differences in public service motivation: Comparing regions across the world. In J. Perry and A. Hondeghem (eds), *Motivation in public management: The call of public service*. New York, NY: Oxford University Press, pp. 223–244.

Warren, D.C., and Chen, L.T. (2013). The relationship between public service motivation and performance. *Meta-analysis for Public Management and Policy*, 442–473.

Wilson, W. (1887). The study of administration. *Political Science Quarterly*, *2*, 197–222.

Zarychta, A., Grillos, T., and Andersson, K.P. (2020). Public sector governance reform and the motivation of street-level bureaucrats in developing countries. *Public Administration Review*, *80*, 75–91.

8. Experiments and qualitative methods: towards a methodological framework
Kai Xiang Kwa

INTRODUCTION

Often touted by scholars and practitioners as a methodologically novel approach to pursuing innovative research of motivation in public administration, recent experiment driven motivation research in public administration has appeared in top public administration journals (e.g., Chen, Hsieh and Chen, 2019; Christensen and Wright, 2018). Generally, experimental research involves treatment and control groups.[1] Two broad camps under the experimental research category are notable. The first involves 'pure' experiments in which the participants are *randomly* assigned to the treatment and control groups. The second involves quasi-experiments in which the participants are *not* randomly assigned to the treatment and control groups. In the past few years, a body of motivation in public administration research using 'pure' experimental designs has been growing (e.g., Hattke and Kalucza, 2018; Kroll and Porumbescu, 2019). By randomly assigning participants to the treatment and control groups, many potential variables that can confound the causal nature of studied variables are accounted for and isolated. Hence, such research has strongly demonstrated the advantages of using experimental designs (e.g., greater methodological ability to establish causality and minimizing endogeneity[2]).

Endogeneity is a methodological problem that undermines research findings, which assert a causal relationship between variables *a* and *b*. Using variables *a* and *b*, the basic definition of the problem of endogeneity can be demonstrated as follows. Specifically, if in a hypothetical study, variable *a* is asserted to cause variable *b* when in fact, variables *a* and *b* are found to correlate to variables *b*, *c* and *d* that are not accounted for in the study, then variable *a* is deemed to be endogenous. Therefore, the study is deemed to suffer from the problem of endogeneity. Pertaining to public organizations' recruitment of their public employees, policies based on motivation in public administration research findings that do *not* account for and/or adequately correct endogeneity risk the critical failure of not recruiting the targeted or suitable candidate for the public sector job. If this failure is left unrectified in the long term, the capacity of the above-mentioned public organizations to deliver their respective public services efficiently can decline. In this regard, evidently, the problem of endogeneity in motivation in public administration research merits swift attention and redress by the scholarly community.[3] However, a potentially overlooked but significant weakness of experimental research merits greater attention here.

Specifically, experimental designs lack the methodological capacity to account for the deeper contextual factors (e.g., social and cultural norms) that can influence its results. By extension, experimental motivation research in public administration lacks the capacity to account for the motivation topic under investigation; and thereby limiting its capacity to practically apply its findings in its empirical context (i.e., external validity threat). On the contrary, qualitative methods (e.g., field observations, interviews), by accounting for the social and cultural con-

106 *Research handbook on motivation in public administration*

texts relevant to the topic under study, provide a more contextually grounded explanation of observed empirical phenomena. Importantly, qualitative methods can do likewise for results/ findings of an experiment. Having a more contextually grounded explanation of experiment results is extremely crucial as it enhances the results' external validity. Therefore, experiment results that are corroborated by qualitative findings are more usable especially to practitioners of public administration, including those handling portfolios covering motivation.

Yet, there is insufficient research that combines experimental and qualitative methods in the field of public administration, including the sub-field of motivation. This could be mainly attributable to an absence of a more systematic methodological framework that combines the two above-mentioned methods. In response, this chapter is structured as follows. All the reviewed articles are taken from the *Sage* journal database as it is arguably the leading academic platform for all the top-tiered public administration journals (see Clarivate Analytics, 2020). First, an updated brief overview of papers dating from 2000 to 2019 (n = 30), which investigate the notion of motivation is warranted; given that it is one of this chapter's central, albeit not the main, topical focuses. Second, to provide an updated review of key methodological elements of qualitative research of motivation in public administration, papers covering this research within the above-mentioned time period (n = 16), are studied closely. Third, by the same token, papers covering experimental research on motivation in public administration (n = 7) are examined deeply. Based on the findings of these three reviews, a methodological framework that combines both experimental and qualitative designs more systematically to study motivation in public administration is subsequently presented.

MOTIVATION

According to Ryan and Deci (2017, p. 6), motivation refers to forces that push or pull an individual to perform an action. Motivation in public administration pertains not only to the commonly cited notion of Public Service Motivation (PSM) (see Perry, 1996; Perry and Wise, 1990) but also to a wide variety of other elements. These elements include, but are not limited to, family history, social influences from friends, school, colleagues and teachers, cultural influences on the value of work and employment, organizational culture and policies, and so on. Indeed, recent scholarly efforts to merge different facets of motivation together (e.g., psychological, social, material) conceptually have been made (e.g., Forbes, 2011; Köpetz et al., 2013; Parker, Bindl and Strauss, 2010). Motivation itself is also not static; it can evolve and change. From a systemic perspective on motivation, Delton and Sell's (2014) study of the evolution of motivation through their investigations of cooperation and conflict cases revealed that:

> there is no motivation without representation: To generate adaptive behavior, motivational systems must be interwoven with the concepts required to support them ... (p. 115)

Notably, Ryan and Deci's (2017) Self-Determination Theory (SDT) outlines a typology of six categories of motivation.[4] SDT is used to theoretically frame this review section for the following reason. Specifically, its motivation typology is arguably the most generally and comprehensively crafted motivation landscape. This greatly allows for a systematic and clear classification of a myriad of motivation forces. Therefore, such a classification enables a clear presentation of the dominant types of motivation found in empirical public administration research dating from 2000 to 2019. By using the search phrases 'public service' and 'motivation' in the *Sage* journals database and by focusing on papers published from 2000 to 2019 that relate thematically and directly or indirectly (e.g., public service motivation and public sector decision-making) to these search terms, the 'results' and 'discussion' sections of 30 papers were selected for review. These papers covered a wide range of national contexts, such as the United States, Europe, China and India, and over a series of sectors (e.g., from the military to public education). For ease of reference, the *dominant* motivation findings from these papers are classified in Figure 8.1[5] accordingly.

External Extrinsic	Introjected Extrinsic	Identified Extrinsic	Integrated Extrinsic	Intrinsic
a) Organizational values/culture/ethics b) Field of study c) Job stability d) Job salary e) National culture f) Service-learning courses g) Collaborative team atmosphere h) Institutional support i) Organizational influences j) Professional environment	a) Patriotism b) Career development c) Procedural fairness d) Communal self-ego e) Transformational leadership f) Autonomy, capability and relation needs g) Family history	a) Adventure b) Testing one's self c) Meeting new people in foreign cultures d) Value on professional status e) Political loyalty f) Public value	a) Professional identity b) Public service motivation	a) Job satisfaction b) Job interest

Figure 8.1　　Summary of motivation themes

From Figure 8.1, it is evident that the majority of the *dominant* empirical findings reviewed point to external forces as drivers of motivation in public administration. Nonetheless, it must be noted that, in reality, public employees very often experience more than one form of motivation in any capacity. For example, a public employee may be motivated by both performance bonuses (i.e., extrinsic forces) *and* job passion (i.e., intrinsic forces) to pursue innovative job practices in his or her organization. Caveating this observation is a potential scenario. Specifically, a public school teacher is motivated primarily by a love of teaching itself (i.e., intrinsic forces) and secondarily by professional rules (i.e., extrinsic forces) to think of creative pedagogical methods to engage his or her students. In short, many motivation forms can operate together, with some potentially being more significant than the other forms, to collectively compel a public employee to perform a particular action.

Furthermore, a myriad of theoretical/conceptual perspectives to conceiving the motivation construct in public administration has been advanced. These perspectives include emotional

108 *Research handbook on motivation in public administration*

intelligence; public and nonprofit leadership (e.g., Levitats and Vigoda-Gadot, 2019; van Sylke and Alexander, 2006). With these perspectives, the knowledge stock of motivation constructs in public administration can be enhanced by providing it with multidisciplinary perspectives (e.g., psychological, economic, cultural) and delineating its multidimensional facets (e.g., self-belief, societal/cultural pressure). On this note, research on these motivation via qualitative approaches will now be reviewed in-depth in the following section.

QUALITATIVE RESEARCH ON MOTIVATION IN PUBLIC ADMINISTRATION

Generally, such qualitative research is *especially* geared towards making sense of the potential social and cultural forces that underpin individuals' motivations in public administration. Evidently, the terms 'social' and 'cultural' are generic; they can refer to a wide range of forces depending on the context of the study under focus. For instance, when studying whether or not gender norms influence the motivations of female public employees to rise to senior leadership in their respective organizations in a certain country, the social forces of interest here would pertain to social norms on 'acceptable' female behavior and ambitions; and their presumed professional capabilities for certain job roles (e.g., managerial positions, director positions). Turning to another scenario, when investigating whether or not culture motivates master of public administration students to join the public sector in a certain society, the cultural forces of interest here would relate to the cultural norms surrounding the public sector (e.g., is a public sector job traditionally regarded as a prestigious or a poorly esteemed/'back-up option' profession?).

Pertaining to the selection criteria of the qualitative papers on motivation in public administration to be reviewed here, the following steps were executed. First, from the *Sage* journals database, the search terms 'public service' and 'motivation' were keyed. Second, papers that adhered to these themes and adopted qualitative methods (i.e., non-statistical methods like interviews, observations, personal accounts and case studies) were shortlisted. Third, for an updated review, such papers (published from 2000 to 2019 (n = 16) were selected for an in-depth review. Fourth, as this chapter partly aims to review the methodological elements of qualitative research on motivation in public administration research, this review section focuses on the research design/method/methodology of the reviewed qualitative papers. The themes emerging from this focused reading are presented below.

Small Sample Size and Convenience Sampling Method

Importantly, qualitative inquiries on motivation in public administration are not looking to determine statistical correlation between an independent variable (e.g., job stability) and a dependent variable (e.g., innovative public sector practices). As such, these inquiries employ a convenient sampling method to select their sample population from a target population to collect data about their topic.[6] Also, their ultimate aim is not to determine the generalizability of their findings to their respective target populations. Following from this, their sample size is usually relatively small compared to quantitative studies on motivations in public administration. Overall, absolute sample sizes for qualitative research on motivation in public administration range from 20 to 150 individuals (e.g., Andersen, 2009; Balisi, 2014; Driver,

2017; Hondeghem and van Dorpe, 2012; van Bochove and Oldenhof, 2020). A commonly used qualitative methodology that supports the above-mentioned qualitative research objectives and is methodologically appropriate for relatively small sample size motivation in public administration studies is in-depth interviews.

In-depth Interviews

Broadly speaking, research interviews are typically composed of either in-person one-to-one interviews (e.g., researcher to one interviewee) or in-person group interviews (e.g., researcher to several interviewees). There is no arbitrary standard on the number of interviewees to be included in a group interview setting. However, around five to eight interviewees are likely to be included in a group interview setting. Having more than eight interviewees reduces the amount of time the researcher has to engage each interviewee individually in the group interview. Consequently, the ability of the researcher to gain in-depth insights from all of the interviewees present during the interview is compromised.

On the issue of data integrity, the in-person interview method situates the researcher to the interviewee(s) or research participant(s). This gives rise to a much-discussed methodological problem plaguing this method: social desirability bias/effect. This bias/effect refers to the tendency of research participants to furnish answers to questions in a research study that they deem socially more acceptable or desirable rather than 'choosing responses that are reflective of their true thoughts or feelings' (Grimm, 2010).[7] The problems concerning data integrity that arise from this bias/effect are severe. Indeed, interview data that are biased by social desirability is useless in shedding new light on the research topic under study because they are inaccurate or false (i.e., they do not reflect the 'actual' opinions or thoughts of the respective interviewees). Proposals to combat the social desirability effect/bias in interviews can range from building rapport with the interviewee prior to commencing the interview itself, providing adequate information to the interviewee on their anonymity rights and assuring them that these rights will be strictly upheld under stringent ethical and legal provisions.

Berg and Lune (2017) outlined a typology of the three major types of in-depth research interviews: standardized, semi-standardized, unstandardized.[8] Contributing to these three major interview types are a series of interview conducting approaches: neo-positivist, romantic, constructionist, postmodern and transformative (Brinkmann, 2014).[9] Despite the potential problems of social desirability, perhaps the most commonly used interview method in motivation in public administration research is the semi-standardized or semi-structured interview (e.g., Andersen, 2009; Andersen et al., 2018; Ferrucci, 2017; Jacobson, 2011; Tomlinson, O'Reilly and Wallace, 2013; Yung, 2014). However, some interview studies do not specify the interview type being used (e.g., Desmarais and Gamassou, 2014; Hondeghem and Van Dorpe, 2012; Nkyabonaki, 2019). Nonetheless, these interviews, given that they are meant to generate in-depth insights into their respective research topics, usually last at least about 20 minutes to an hour or so.

Generating these insights requires rapport (i.e., a professional relationship between the researcher and the interviewee to feel comfortable with voicing his or her actual views on the research topic to the researcher) (see Berg and Lune, 2017). As the objective of the interviews is for the researcher to get the interviewee to provide deep insights into the research topic under investigation, the initial responsibility of building this rapport therefore lies with the researcher. In this regard, rapport-building begins *before* the interview questions that directly concern the investigated research topic are posed. Still, this does not suggest that the rapport-building is a 'one-way' exercise; indeed, the interviewee can also respond to the rapport-building initiated by the researcher by leading the rapport-building after the researcher. Rapport-building in such settings involves a variety of strategies, including but not limited to asking questions about the interviewee's professional background that relates to the research topic under study. For instance, if the interview research topic is on motivations to become a public school teacher, a possible rapport-building question concerns the academic background of the interviewee.

Yet, despite the above-mentioned strategies to reduce the social desirability bias/effect, another methodological challenge facing interviews that cannot be eliminated is self-reporting bias. Simply put, the self-reporting bias can denote a phenomenon under which the interviewee's own responses are not necessarily supported by their actual actions.[10] A scenario to demonstrate this is as follows. In response to an interview question on whether or not innovative job practices in the public sector are carried out (e.g., use of big data), a public employee may report that such practices are used when, in fact, he or she might not have engaged in them at all during the course of his or her professional duties. Mitigating this bias hence requires the researcher to *physically* observe whether or not the public employee *actually* engages in the innovative practices in the workplace (i.e., natural setting). This brings to the fore the next used qualitative method in motivation in public administration research: observational studies.

Observational Studies

A heavily utilized methodology in Sociology, Anthropology and Culture, observational studies have recently gained usage, albeit limited, as a methodology to study motivation in the public administration sphere. Most generally, observational studies are:

> the systematic collection and examination of verbal and nonverbal behaviors as they occur in a variety of contexts. This method of data collection is particularly important when there are difficulties in obtaining relevant information through self-report because subjects are unable to communicate (e.g., with infants or confused adults) or provide sufficiently detailed information (e.g., about complex interaction patterns). Observations also are used to validate or extend data obtained using other data collection methods. (Bottorff, 2004)

Indeed, observational studies have been used to validate or corroborate other qualitative methods (e.g., interviews) in motivation in public administration research (e.g., Andersen et al., 2018). In a recent study on the relationship between transformational leadership and PSM in the childcare sector, Andersen and colleagues (2018) utilized systematic observations to identify interaction types and patterns as well as the occasional unconscious behavior of individuals in childcare centers. These observations are then used to 'strengthen [data] validity and provide information regarding different aspects of leadership and motivation' (p. 681). However, a key disadvantage of observational studies is that the researcher's ability to conduct them heavily relies on his or her accessibility to the 'natural settings' that he or she wishes to observe. Very often, such accessibility is difficult to obtain without social connections with individuals who can provide the researcher with access. These individuals are usually part of the 'natural settings' that the researcher wishes to enter. For example, if a researcher seeks to observe the teaching behavior of school teachers in a public school, he or she would need to get permission from the head teacher of this public school. Getting this permission necessitates the researcher being socially connected with the head teacher in the first instance, which may be difficult to establish. On this account, other qualitative methods that are more commonly used in motivation in public administration research are collectively known as document analysis.

Document Analysis

This methodology comprises a series of methodologies that include the analysis of personal/ official narratives; textual policy and administrative documents. As a form of analysis, it constitutes discourse and content/thematic analytical approaches.[11] Like observational studies, these methodologies are often used to validate or corroborate other qualitative data findings (e.g., interview responses). Indeed, such usage has been widely seen in motivation in public administration research (e.g., Andersen, 2009; Balisi, 2014; Driver, 2017; Hondeghem and Van Dorpe, 2012; Mellifont, 2018; Raimondo and Newcomer, 2017). Notably, approaches to analyzing the above-mentioned textual sources can be rooted in a variety of theoretical-methodological traditions. Towards this end, Driver's (2017) study is insightful; narrative inquiry paired with the Lacanian theories of the self were used to analyze the interview responses on PSM. Like observational studies before, the feasibility of document analysis relies on the researcher's access to them, although arguably not as difficult or challenging to establish as for observational studies. Yet, an equally important aspect of qualitative research rests in its ability to advance theory by providing deeper insight into the ways motivation can be constructed. These constructs can then be used to either empirically test or validate the theories/concepts in future motivation studies. Turning now to a novel and growing empirical approach to motivation in public administration research, the use of experiments has yet to be given a detailed review of its methodological strands. In response, this gap will be addressed in the next review section.

EXPERIMENTAL RESEARCH ON MOTIVATION IN PUBLIC ADMINISTRATION

By accessing the *Sage* journals database, the following keywords were used to facilitate the search for experimental motivation in public administration papers: public service, motivation, and experiment. Then, like the qualitative review section before, to provide an updated and methodologically focused review of experimental motivation in public administration papers, the 'research design/method/methodology' sections of such papers published from 2000 to 2019 (n = 7) were ultimately chosen for review. Key methodological elements emerging from this review are presented below.

Small to Large Sample Size and Random Sampling Method

Evidently, the paramount aim of experimental studies on motivation in public administration is to test for or determine correlation and causality between motivation and any variables examined (e.g., individual personality and beliefs), most preferably by means of having treatment and control groups. In order to enhance the testing for correlation and causality in such inquiries, confounding variables (i.e., rival variables) that can threaten the validity of the results need to be minimized.

An important strategy to minimize such variables is to randomly assign participants to the treatment and control groups (see Chen, Hsieh and Chen, 2019; Christensen and Wright, 2018; Hattke and Kalucza, 2019; Kroll and Porumbescu, 2019). Generally, as experimental studies require participants to be physically present to take part in an activity, the sample size can range from small to large size (i.e., usually from around 100 to above 1000 participants) (see Bromberg and Charbonneau, 2020; Chen, Hsieh and Chen, 2019) depending on two factors.

Specifically, the two factors are logistical limitations and access to sample populations. The former limitations usually pertain to clashes between the potential participant's schedule and the experiment schedule. The latter access usually refers to the researcher's ability to contact the sample populations and extend participatory invitation to them for the experiment. Two types of experimental designs stand out in public administration motivation research: pretest-posttest and vignette designs, thereby warranting further investigation below.

Pretest-posttest Design

While there are many strategies to execute such a design depending on its societal context, its key elements are presented in a concise and generic definition below:

> [It is] obtaining a pretest measure of the outcome of interest prior to administering some treatment, followed by a posttest on the same measure after treatment occurs. Pretest–posttest designs are employed in both experimental and quasi-experimental research and can be used with or without control groups. For example, quasi-experimental pretest–posttest designs may or may not include control groups, whereas experimental pretest–posttest designs must include control groups. (Bell, 2010)

In the case of quasi-experimental pretest-posttest research on motivation in public administration, causality between the identified independent variable(s) and the motivation variable can be more difficult to ascertain in the absence of control groups. On this note, Chen and colleagues' (2019) study of the relationship between training and PSM in the Taiwanese public sector is instructive. Specifically, in the absence of a control group due to ethical and legal concerns, the researchers applied the training treatment procedure to four waves of public employee trainees in Taiwan to determine if this training has an effect on the pretest and posttest groups (p. 11). Nonetheless, it seems that a more common experimental method used in motivation in public administration research is vignette designs.

Vignette Designs

At its core, experimental vignette designs[12] are 'realistic scenarios to assess dependent variables including intentions, attitudes, and behaviors' (Aguinis and Bradley, 2014, p. 352). These scenarios can be presented to participants in the form of games, real-life based questions to answer under certain treatment conditions (e.g., time pressure). Depending on the nature of the research objectives, vignettes can be part of a multi-step experimental study. In the context of motivation in public administration, several multi-step experimental studies provide useful insights.

For instance, Bromberg and Charbonneau's (2020) study on the relationship between PSM, personality and public managers' hiring decisions required participants to rank three vignettes; answer the PSM survey; and then the Big 5 personality survey. Similarly, in Kroll and Porumbescu's (2019) study on intrinsic motivation and PSM in public administration students in the United States, two sets of vignette questions were presented to the students before their annual Master of Public Administration program evaluation survey. In the European context, in Hattke and Kalucza's (2019) study on citizens' willingness to co-produce public services, 210 university students were first assigned to one of eight groups, with each group featuring three vignettes; following which a co-production initiative survey was administered to them. Turning back to the United States, Christensen and Wright's (2018) work on PSM and ethical behavior conducted three experiments. The first required students to complete four vignette exercises before completing a survey incorporating PSM and greed items (pp. 2–3). The second required students to first roll a six-sided die three times on a computer and were informed that the higher their total reported roll score, the more participating entries they would get for a draw for a 100 USD gift card; after which the students completed the PSM and greedy survey as in the first experiment[13] (p. 4). The third experiment is largely similar to the second experiment with some differences (i.e., sample size and certain procedures[14]) (pp. 4–5). With these descriptions of vignette designs in motivation in public administration research, a key question still persists on the strategies that researchers of motivation in public administration can adopt to maximize the methodological capacities of their studies to improve causality between their identified variables as well as highlight the social and cultural specificity of these variables to enhance their external validity.

In addressing this question, this chapter aims to combine all the motivation, qualitative and experimental insights from the reviews above to propose a more systematic experimental-qualitative methodological framework. This framework is designed as an aid for future motivation in public administration scholars to conduct such studies with more causality power and contextual sensitivity. Thus, the findings from these studies will not only further enrich the academic field of motivation in public administration as a whole, but also be more applicable to public policy practitioners seeking to enhance public service delivery and employee performance.

AN EXPERIMENTAL QUALITATIVE METHODOLOGICAL FRAMEWORK

Yet, perhaps unsurprisingly, such a framework is not absent from the research community in general. Indeed, the field of communication studies has already presented it primarily for communication scholars to utilize. Specifically, Robinson and Mendelson's (2012) study proposed a methodological framework merging in-depth interviews with experimental procedures.[15] However, this framework is too generic in its design components and therefore not adequately suited to the public administration context. As such, this chapter proposes its experimental-qualitative framework in Figure 8.2. Importantly, while this framework aims to be generic *enough* to be applicable to as much motivation in public administration studies as possible, it concurrently aims to incorporate motivation in public administration-specific research conditions (e.g., ethical, social, cultural and religious norms for certain sample groups).

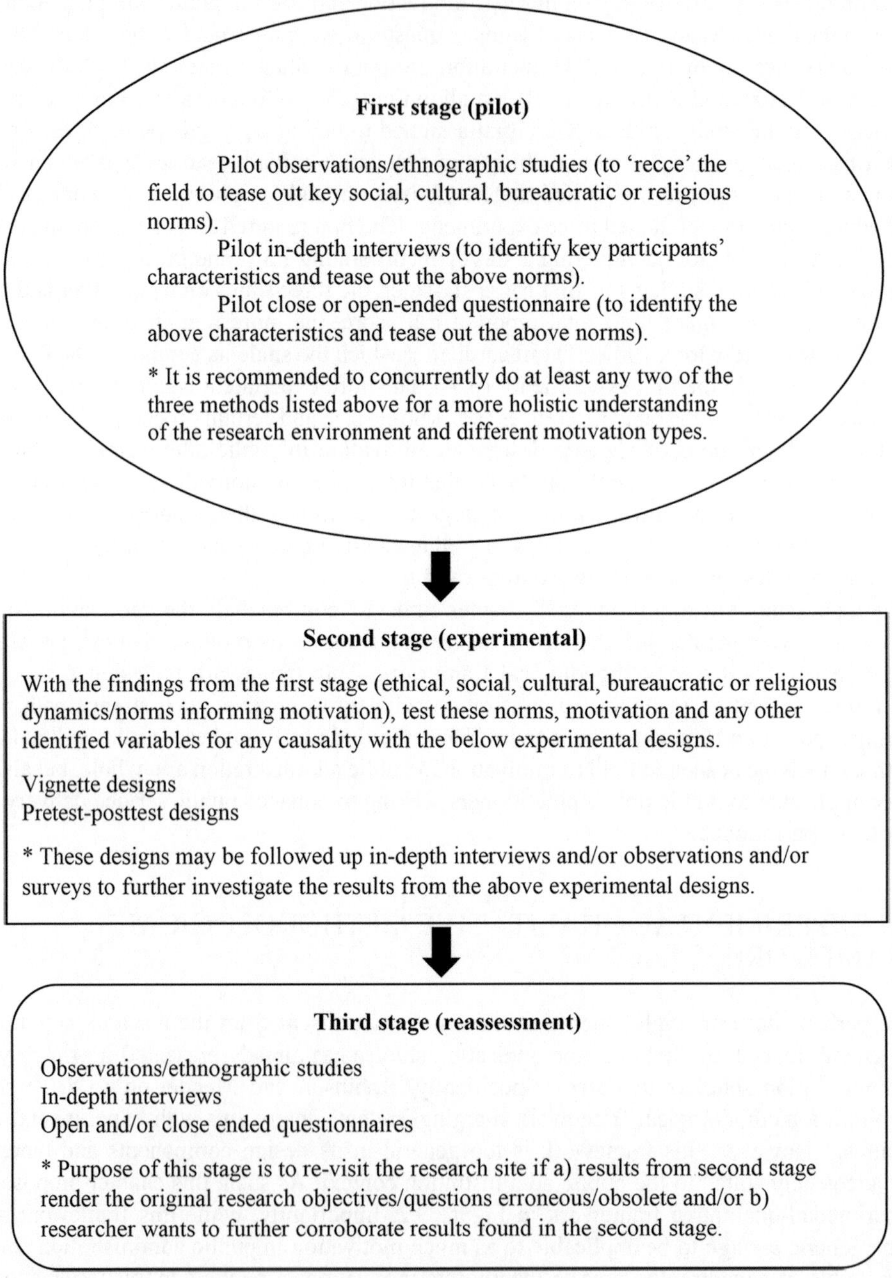

First stage (pilot)

Pilot observations/ethnographic studies (to 'recce' the field to tease out key social, cultural, bureaucratic or religious norms).

Pilot in-depth interviews (to identify key participants' characteristics and tease out the above norms).

Pilot close or open-ended questionnaire (to identify the above characteristics and tease out the above norms).

* It is recommended to concurrently do at least any two of the three methods listed above for a more holistic understanding of the research environment and different motivation types.

Second stage (experimental)

With the findings from the first stage (ethical, social, cultural, bureaucratic or religious dynamics/norms informing motivation), test these norms, motivation and any other identified variables for any causality with the below experimental designs.

Vignette designs
Pretest-posttest designs

* These designs may be followed up in-depth interviews and/or observations and/or surveys to further investigate the results from the above experimental designs.

Third stage (reassessment)

Observations/ethnographic studies
In-depth interviews
Open and/or close ended questionnaires

* Purpose of this stage is to re-visit the research site if a) results from second stage render the original research objectives/questions erroneous/obsolete and/or b) researcher wants to further corroborate results found in the second stage.

Figure 8.2   Proposed experimental-qualitative methodological framework

CONCLUSION

This framework contributes to the growing number of mixed methods (i.e., qualitative plus quantitative/experimental) driven motivation in public administration research (e.g., Andersen, 2009; Balisi, 2014; Desmarais and Gamassou, 2014; Hondeghem and Van Dorpe, 2012; Jacobson, 2011; Raimondo and Newcomer, 2017). While the above framework seeks to be helpful in pursuing qualitative research with experimental research on motivation in public administration, it does not claim to be a fully exhaustive one. Indeed, the framework can be adjusted per researchers' demands and/or research objectives accordingly.

Another final point pertains to the selection of the articles in this review chapter. Admittedly, the articles are all taken from the *Sage* journals database. The author is aware that many other platforms hosting motivation in public administration research are available (e.g., *Taylor and Francis online*; *Elsevier*; *Wiley*; *Science Direct*). Therefore, future research reviewing the state of qualitative and experimental motivation in public administration research should expand its article selections from a wider source.

ACKNOWLEDGMENTS

This work was supported by the Ministry of Education of the Republic of Korea and the National Research Foundation of Korea (NRF-2018S1A3A2075609).

NOTES

1. Experiments are aiming to investigate whether or not a group of individuals respond to a particular treatment. In the motivation in the public administration research arena, this treatment can take the form of researchers investigating whether or not public administration students indicate higher motivation levels to join the public service in a survey in the *presence* of financial rewards for doing so (i.e., treatment). Under this scenario, to test whether this treatment has an effect on the student's motivation levels, another group of similar students will form a control group in which the same group of researchers investigate whether or not these students indicate higher or lower or negligible change in motivation levels to join the public service in the *absence* of the above-mentioned treatment.
2. Antonakis et al.'s (2014) extensive and formative review of the problems of endogeneity provides a detailed outline of several causality errors (i.e., common methods variance; inconsistent inference; measurement error; model misspecification; omitted selection; omitted variables; simultaneity). For more information on these errors, see also Antonakis et al. (2010).
3. Nevertheless, several proposals to combat endogeneity have been made by the scholarly community in social science research. For more details on these proposals, see Antonakis et al. (2014), Bascle (2008), Ebbes, Papies and van Heerde (2016) and Menaldo (2011).
4. The most controlled form of motivation (i.e., controlled by external forces) is *external* extrinsic motivations (e.g., job salary, job stability). The second most controlled motivation is *introjected* extrinsic motivation. Examples of this motivation include personal guilt, shame or ego that compels an individual to perform an action whether or not external incentives are present. The third most controlled motivation is *identified* extrinsic motivation. Examples of this motivation type pertain to individuals being motivated to perform an action because it creates value that is acceptable to and identifiable with these individuals. The fourth most controlled motivation is *integrated* extrinsic motivation. Examples of this concern individuals who are motivated to perform an action not only because the value it brings is acceptable to and identifiable with them, but that this value is

integrated with the individual's personal values. The autonomous motivation type is intrinsic motivation. Individuals are intrinsically motivated to perform an action because they derive satisfaction from the action itself. For more details on this motivation typology, see Ryan and Deci (2017, pp. 13–15).

5. *External extrinsic:* themes adapted from Battaglio and French (2016); Bhatia and Purohit (2014); Blaum and Tobin (2019); Bright (2016); Kim and Kim (2016); Ko and Han (2013); Moloney and Chu (2016); Muñoz and Ramirez (2015); Oberfield (2014); Vandenabeele (2011); Zhu, Gardner and Chen (2018). *Introjected extrinsic:* themes adapted from Evans and Evans (2019); Fennimore (2020); Jensen and Bro (2018); Quratulain, Khan and Sabharwal (2019); Woodruff, Kelty and Segal (2006). *Identified extrinsic:* themes adapted from Andersen et al. (2012); Ballart and Riba (2017); Finnigan and Gross (2007); Hedlund (2011). *Integrated extrinsic:* themes adapted from Kim (2009); Liu (2009); Liu and Perry (2016); Liu, Yang and Yu (2015); Ngaruiya et al. (2014); Naff and Crum (1999); Schott, van Kleef and Steen (2018). *Intrinsic:* themes adapted from Katz and Shahar (2015); Weske and Schott (2018); Word and Carpenter (2013).

6. Convenient sampling methods are ways of non-randomly selecting a sample population from whom to collect data. Such methods often involve snowball sampling. Simply put, snowball sampling pertains to a researcher gaining access to the sample population through a series of personal contacts (e.g., social networks like friends, colleagues etc.). For a detailed review of the snowball sampling method, see Babbie (2008), Berg and Lune (2017) and Naderifar, Goli and Ghaljaie (2017).

7. Apart from Grimm (2010), see Callegaro (2008) and Holden and Passey (2009) for more extensive investigations into the social desirability effect/bias. Interestingly, see Furnham, Petrides and Spencer-Bowdage (2002) for the effects of different types of social desirability bias.

8. According to Berg and Lune (2017), standardized interviews consist of predetermined questions and the interview is conducted based on the question order, the questions being asked exactly as worded and the interviewee is required to answer the questions in this order. Semi-standardized interviews, in contrast, while consisting of predetermined questions, allow the interviewer to digress from the predetermined question order by probing deeper into the interviewee's answers with follow-up questions. Unstandardized questions, on the other hand, while having a predetermined set of research topics to inquire deeper into, do not have a predetermined set of interview questions per se. This means that the predetermined research topics act as a guide for the conversation but the interviewee is expected to initiate the interview flow. This flow then influences the types of questions asked by the interviewer.

9. According to Brinkmann (2014), *neo-positivist* approaches seek to uncover the actual/true essence of the interviewee's thoughts on the question being asked by an interviewer who does not interfere with the interview question flow. Somewhat similarly, *romantic* approaches seek to uncover the actual/true thoughts of the interviewee on the question being asked by an interviewer who builds rapport and intimacy with the interviewee. In contrast, *constructionist*, *postmodern* and *transformative* approaches call for the interviewer and interviewee to co-construct the interview conversation flow.

10. For more information on self-reporting bias, see West (2014) and Donaldson and Grant-Vallone (2002).

11. Herrera and Braumoeller (2004) provide a clear distinction between discourse and content analysis. Specifically, discourse analysis identifies the themes from the analyzed text *and* the context underlying these themes. On the contrary, content analysis in a strict sense refers to the identification of themes from the analyzed text. See Herrera and Braumoeller (2004) for a more detailed treatment of these two analyses and their differences.

12. Virtually all experimental methods, including vignette designs, face the risk of external validity threat (i.e., the ability of its results to reflect real-life characteristics of its target populations). However, some proposals have been made to combat this threat (e.g., Aguinis and Bradley, 2014; Eifler and Petzold, 2019). For more detailed strategies to conduct vignette designs in behavioral and social sciences, see Atzmüller and Steiner (2010).

13. For more details on the procedures of the second exercise, see Christensen and Wright (2018, p. 4).

14. For more details on the procedures of the third exercise, see Christensen and Wright (2018, pp. 4–5).

15. See Robinson and Mendelson (2012, p. 337) for a diagrammatic illustration of this framework. Due to copyright concerns, this diagram will not be reproduced or adapted in this chapter.

REFERENCES

Aguinis, H., and Bradley, K.J. (2014). Best practice recommendations for designing and implementing experimental vignette methodology studies. *Organizational Research Methods, 17*, 351–371.

Andersen, L.B. (2009). What determines the behaviour and performance of health professionals? Public Service Motivation, professional norms and/or economic incentives. *International Review of Administrative Sciences, 75*, 79–97.

Andersen, L.B., Jørgensen, T.B., Kjeldsen, A.M., Pedersen, L.H., and Vrangbæk, K. (2012). Public values and public service motivation: Conceptual and empirical relationships. *American Review of Public Administration, 43*, 292–311.

Andersen, L.B., Bjornholt, B., Bro, L, and Petersen-Holm, C. (2018). Leadership and motivation: A qualitative study of transformational leadership and Public Service Motivation. *International Review of Administrative Sciences, 84*, 675–691.

Antonakis, J., Bendahan, S., Jacquart, P., and Lalive, R. (2010). On making causal claims: A review and recommendations. *The Leadership Quarterly, 21*, 1086–1120.

Antonakis, J., Bendahan, S., Jacquart, P., and Lalive, R. (2014). Causality and endogeneity: Problems and solutions. In D.V. Day (ed.), *The Oxford Handbook of Leadership and Organizations*, New York, NY: Oxford University Press, pp. 93p–117.

Atzmüller, C., and Steiner, P.M. (2010). Experimental vignette studies in survey research: Methodology. *European Journal of Research Methods for the Behavioral and Social Sciences, 6*, 128–138.

Babbie, E.R. (2008). *The Basics of Social Research*. Boston, MA: Cengage.

Balisi, S. (2014). Training needs assessment in the Botswana public service: A case study of five state sector ministries. *Teaching Public Administration, 32*, 127–143.

Ballart, X., and Riba, C. (2017). Contextualized measures of public service motivation: The case of Spain. *International Review of Administrative Sciences, 83*, 43–62.

Bascle, G. (2008). Controlling for endogeneity with instrumental variables in strategic management research. *Strategic Organization, 6*, 285–327.

Battaglio, P.R., and French, E.P. (2016). Public service motivation, public management reform, and organizational socialization: Testing the effects of employment at-will and agency on PSM among municipal employees. *Public Personnel Management, 45*, 123–147.

Bell, A.B. (2010). Pretest–posttest design. In J.N. Salkind (ed.), *Encyclopedia of Research Design*. Thousand Oaks, CA: Sage, published online on December 27, 2012 at https://dx.doi.org/10.4135/9781412961288.n331.

Berg, L.B., and Lune, H. (2017). A dramaturgical look at interviewing. In L.B Berg, and H. Lune, *Qualitative Research Methods for the Social Sciences* (9th edn). New York, NY: Pearson, pp. 65–93.

Bhatia, S., and Purohit, B. (2014). What motivates government doctors in India to perform better in their job? *Journal of Health Management, 16*, 149–159.

Blaum, B., and Tobin, K. (2019). Motivating the motivators: An examination of high school principals' drive to succeed. *NASSP Bulletin, 103*, 253–267.

Bottorff, L.J. (2004). Observation. In S. Lewis-Beck, S. Michael, A. Bryman, and T.F. Liao (eds), *The SAGE Encyclopedia of Social Science Research Methods*. Thousand Oaks, CA, published online on January 1, 2011 at https://dx.doi.org/10.4135/9781412950589.

Brewer, B. (2003). The impact of differentiation and differential on Hong Kong's career public service. *International Review of Administrative Sciences, 69*, 219–233.

Bright, L. (2016). Public Service Motivation and socialization in graduate education. *Teaching Public Administration, 34*, 284–306.

Brinkmann, S. (2014). Unstructured and semi-structured unterviewing. In P. Leavy (ed.), *The Oxford Handbook of Qualitative Research*, New York, NY: Oxford University Press, pp. 277–299.

Bromberg, D.E., and Charbonneau, É. (2020). Public Service Motivation, personality, and the hiring decisions of public managers: An experimental study. *Public Personnel Management, 49*, 193–217.

Callegaro, Mario. (2008). Social desirability. In P.J. Lavrakas (ed.), *Encyclopedia of Survey Research Methods (Volume 2)*,Thousand Oaks, CA: Sage, pp. 825–826.

Chen, C., Hsieh, C., and Chen, D. (2019). Can training enhance public employees' Public Service Motivation? A pretest-posttest design. *Review of Public Personnel Administration*, first published online on September 5, 2019 at https://doi.org/10.1177/0734371X19872244.

Christensen, R.K., and Wright, B.E. (2018). Public Service Motivation and ethical behavior: Evidence from three experiments. *Journal of Behavioral Public Administration*, 1, 1–8.

Clarivate Analytics. (2020). Master Journal List. Retrieved from https://mjl.clarivate.com/home?PC=SS on March 20, 2020.

Delton, A.W., and Sell, A. (2014). The co-evolution of concepts and motivation. *Current Directions in Psychological Science*, 23, 115–120.

Desmarais, C., and Gamassou, C.E. (2014). All motivated by public service? The links between hierarchical position and Public Service Motivation. *International Review of Administrative Sciences*, 80, 131–150.

Donaldson, S.I., and Grant-Vallone, E.J. (2002). Understanding self-report bias in organizational behavior research. *Journal of Business and Psychology*, 17, 245–260.

Driver, M. (2017). Motivation and identity: A psychoanalytic perspective on the turn to identity in motivation research. *Human Relations*, 70, 617–637.

Ebbes P., Papies D., and van Heerde H.J. (2016). Dealing with endogeneity: A nontechnical guide for marketing researchers. In C. Homburg, M. Klarmann, and A. Vomberg (eds), *Handbook of Market Research*, Champaign, IL: Springer, pp. 1–37.

Eifler, S., and Petzold, K. (2019). Validity aspects of vignette experiments: expected 'what-if' differences between reports of behavioral intentions and actual behavior. In P.J. Lavrakas, M.W. Traugott, C. Kennedy, A.L. Holbrook, E.D. de Leeuw, and B.T. West (eds), *Experimental Methods in Survey Research: Techniques That Combine Random Sampling with Random Assignment*, Hoboken, NJ: John Wiley and Sons, pp. 393–413.

Evans, C., and Evans, G.R. (2019). Adverse childhood experiences as a determinant of Public Service Motivation. *Public Personnel Management*, 48, 123–146.

Fennimore, A.K. (2020). Duplicitous me: Communal narcissists and Public Service Motivation. *Public Personnel Management*, first published online on January 23, 2020 at doi: https://doi.org/10.1177/0091026019900355.

Ferrucci, P. (2017). Exploring public service journalism: Digitally native news nonprofits and engagement. *Journalism and Mass Communication Quarterly*, 94, 355–370.

Finnigan K.S., and Gross, B. (2007). Do accountability policy sanctions influence teacher motivation? Lessons from Chicago's low-performing schools. *American Educational Research Journal*, 44, 594–629.

Forbes, D.L. (2011). Toward a unified model of human motivation. *Review of General Psychology*, 15, 85–98.

Furnham, A., Petrides, K.V., and Spencer-Bowdage, S. (2002). The effects of different types of social desirability on the identification of repressors. *Personality and Individual Differences*, 33, 119–130.

Grimm, P. (2010). Social desirability bias. Retrieved from http://onlinelibrary.wiley.com.remotexs.ntu.edu.sg/doi/pdf/10.1002/9781444316568.wiem02057 on March 20, 2020.

Hattke, F., and Kalucza, J. (2019). What influences the willingness of citizens to coproduce public services? Results from a vignette experiment. *Journal of Behavioral Public Administration*, 2, 1–14.

Hedlund, E. (2011). What motivates Swedish Soldiers to participate in peacekeeping missions: Research note. *Armed Forces and Society*, 37, 180–190.

Herrera, Y.M., and Braumoeller, B.F. (2004). Symposium: Discourse and content analysis. *Qualitative Methods, Spring 2004*, 15–19, retrieved from https://wcfia.harvard.edu/files/wcfia/files/870_symposium.pdf on November, 17, 2021.

Holden, R.R., and Passey, J. (2009). Social desirability. In M.R. Leary and R.H. Hoyle (eds), *Handbook of Individual Difference in Social Behavior*, New York, NY: Guilford Press, pp. 441–454.

Hondeghem, A., and Van Dorpe, K. (2012). Performance management systems for senior civil servants: How strong is the managerial public service bargain? *International Review of Administrative Sciences*, 79, 9–27.

Jacobson, W.S. (2011). Creating a motivated workforce: How organizations can enhance and develop Public Service Motivation (PSM). *Public Personnel Management*, 40, 215–238.

Jensen, U.T., and Bro, L.L. (2018). How transformational leadership supports intrinsic motivation and Public Service Motivation: The mediating role of basic need satisfaction. *American Review of Public Administration*, 48, 535–549.

Katz, I., and Shahar, B. (2015). What makes a motivating teacher? Teachers' motivation and beliefs as predictors of their autonomy-supportive style. *School Psychology International*, *36*, 575–588.

Kim, S. (2009). Revising Perry's measurement scale of Public Service Motivation. *American Review of Public Administration*, *39*, 149–163.

Kim, S H., and Kim, S. (2016). National culture and social desirability bias in measuring Public Service Motivation. *Administration and Society*, *48*, 444–476.

Ko, K., and Han, L. (2013). An Empirical study on public service motivation of the next generation civil servants in China. *Public Personnel Management*, *42*, 191–222.

Kopetz, C.E., Lejuez, C.W., Wiers, R.W., and Kruglanski, A.W. (2013). Motivation and Self-regulation in addiction: A call for convergence. *Perspectives on Psychological Science*, *8*, 3–24.

Kroll, A., and Porumbescu, G.A. (2019). When extrinsic rewards become 'sour grapes': An experimental study of adjustments in intrinsic and prosocial motivation. *Review of Public Personnel Administration*, *39*, 467–486.

Levitats, Z., and Vigoda-Gadot, E. (2019). Emotionally engaged civil servants: tToward a multilevel theory and multisource analysis in public administration. *Review of Public Personnel Administration*, first published online on January 13, 2019 at https://doi.org/10.1177/0734371X18820938.

Liu, B. (2009). Evidence of public service motivation of social workers in China. *International Review of Administrative Sciences*, *75*, 349–366.

Liu, B., and Perry, J.L. (2016). The psychological mechanisms of public service motivation: A two-wave examination. *Review of Public Personnel Administration*, *36*, 4–30.

Liu, B., Yang, K., and Yu, W. (2015). Work-Related stressors and health-related outcomes in public service: Examining the role of Public Service Motivation. *American Review of Public Administration*, *45*, 653–673.

Mellifont, D. (2018). Soft affirmative action lacking traction? An early qualitative exploration of the Recruit Ability Scheme performance within the Australian Public Service. *Australian Journal of Career Development*, *27*, 20–28.

Menaldo, V. (2011). What is endogeneity bias and how can we address it? Retrieved from https://faculty.washington.edu/vmenaldo/Stuff%20for%20Students/Endogeneity%20Bias.pdf on March 15, 2020.

Moloney, K., and Chu, H. (2016). Linking Jamaica's public service motivations and ethical climate. *American Review of Public Administration*, *46*, 436–458.

Muñoz, A., and Ramirez, M. (2015). Teachers' conceptions of motivation and motivating practices in second-language learning: A self-determination theory perspective. *Theory and Research in Education*, *13*, 198–220.

Naderifar, M., Goli, H., and Ghaljaie, F. (2017). Snowball sampling: A purposeful method of sampling in qualitative research. *Strides in Development of Medical Education*, *14*.

Naff, K.C., and Crum, J. (1999). Working for America: Does public service motivation make a difference? *Review of Public Personnel Administration*, *19*, 5–16.

Ngaruiya, K.M., Velez, A.K., Clerkin, R.M., and Taylor, J.K. (2014). Public Service Motivation and institutional-occupational motivations among undergraduate students and ROTC cadets. *Public Personnel Management*, *43*, 442–458.

Nkyabonaki, J. (2019). Effectiveness of the public service code of ethics in controlling corrupt behaviour in the public service: Opinion from the grassroots at Toangoma WardTemeke Municipal Council, *Journal of Asian and African Studies*, *54*(8), 1195–1212.

Oberfield, Z. (2014). Motivation, change, and stability: Findings from an urban police department. *American Review of Public Administration*, *44*, 210–232.

Parker, S.K., Bindl, U.K., and Strauss, K. (2010). Making things happen: A model of proactive motivation. *Journal of Management*, *36*, 827–856.

Perry, L. James (1996). Measuring public service motivation: an assessment of construct reliability and validity. *Journal of Public Administration Research and Theory*, *6*(1), 5–22.

Perry, L.J, and Wise, R.L. (1990). The motivational bases of public service. *Public Administration Review*, *50*(3), 367–373.

Quratulain, S., Khan, A.K., and Sabharwal, M. (2019). Procedural fairness, public service motives, and employee work outcomes: Evidence from Pakistani public service organizations. *Review of Public Personnel Administration*, *39*, 276–299.

Raimondo, E., and Newcomer, K.E. (2017). Mixed-methods inquiry in public administration: The interaction of theory, methodology, and praxis. *Review of Public Personnel Administration, 37*, 183–201.

Robinson, S., and Mendelson, A.L. (2012). A qualitative experiment: Research on mediated meaning construction using a hybrid approach. *Journal of Mixed Methods Research, 6*, 332–347.

Ryan, R.M., and Deci, E.L. (2017). Self-determination theory: An introduction and overview. In R.M. Ryan and E.L. Deci, *Self-Determination Theory: Basic Psychological Needs in Motivation, Development, and Wellness*. New York, NY: The Guilford Press, pp. 3–25.

Schott, C., van Kleef, D.D., and Steen, T. (2018). The combined impact of professional role identity and public service motivation on decision-making in dilemma situations. *International Review of Administrative Sciences, 84*, 21–41.

Tomlinson, M., O'Reilly, D., and Wallace, M. (2013). Developing leaders as symbolic violence: Reproducing public service leadership through the (misrecognized) development of leaders' capitals. *Management Learning, 44*, 81–97.

Van Bochove, M., and Oldenhof, L. (2020). institutional work in changing public service organizations: The interplay between professionalization strategies of non-elite actors. *Administration & Society, 52*(1), 111–137.

Van Slyke, D.M., and Alexander, R.W. (2006). Public service leadership: Opportunities for clarity and coherence. *American Review of Public Administration, 36*, 362–374.

Vandenabeele, W. (2011). Who wants to deliver public service? Do institutional antecedents of Public Service Motivation provide an answer? *Review of Public Personnel Administration, 31*, 87–107.

Weske, U., and Schott, C. (2018). What motivates different groups of public employees working for Dutch municipalities? Combining autonomous and controlled types of motivation. *Review of Public Personnel Administration, 38*, 415–430.

West, M.R. (2014). The limitations of self-report measures of non-cognitive skills. Retrieved from https://www.brookings.edu/research/the-limitations-of-self-report-measures-of-non-cognitive-skills/ on March 20, 2020.

Woodruff, T., Kelty, R., and Segal, D.R. (2006). Propensity to serve and motivation to enlist among American combat soldiers. *Armed Forces and Society, 32*, 353–366.

Word, J., and Carpenter, H. (2013). The new public service? Applying the Public Service Motivation model to nonprofit employees. *Public Personnel Management, 42*, 315–336.

Yung, B. (2014). Differential public service motivation among Hong Kong public officials: A qualitative study. *Public Personnel Management, 43*(4), 415–441.

Zhu, Y., Gardner, D.G., and Chen, H. (2018). Relationships between work team climate, individual motivation, and creativity. *Journal of Management, 44*, 2094–2115.

PART II

MOTIVATION AS A DRIVER OF SECTOR DECISIONS

9. Employee motivation across job sectors
Jaclyn Piatak

INTRODUCTION

Understanding motivation is vital for managers to recruit, engage, and retain employees. However, certain job sector characteristics may attract or shape the motivation of employees. This chapter addresses the following questions:

- How does public service motivation (PSM) relate to job sector motives?
- How does the blurring of sectoral bounds influence motivation to work in a specific job sector?
- What motivates individuals to join the government, nonprofit, and for-profit sectors?
- How can government and nonprofit managers recruit and retain future generations?

JOB SECTOR DISTINCTIONS AND PUBLIC SERVICE MOTIVATION

Scholars have long examined differences between public and private organizations (e.g., Boyne, 2002; Perry and Rainey, 1988; Rainey, 2014; Rainey and Bozeman, 2000; Rainey, Backoff, and Levine, 1976), giving rise to examinations of what motivates people to join the public sector (e.g. Rainey, 1982) and the conceptualization of PSM as 'an individual's predisposition to respond to motives grounded primarily or uniquely in public institutions and organizations' (Perry and Wise, 1990, p. 368). Motivation and job sector matter, but two ongoing debates in PSM research warrant acknowledgement. First, whether public service motivation or public sector motivation better characterizes employee motivation, and second, whether attraction or socialization better explains employee motivation.

A Matter of Definition: Public *Service* Motivation or Public *Sector* Motivation?

One of the major critiques of PSM is the lack of clear conceptual boundaries (Bozeman and Su, 2015; Perry and Vandenabeele, 2015; Ritz, Brewer, and Neumann, 2016; Vandenabeele, Brewer, and Ritz, 2014). Scholars have begun to differentiate PSM from concepts in other disciplines (Boyd et al., 2018; Breaugh, Ritz, and Alfes, 2018; Nowell et al., 2016; Piatak and Holt, 2020a, 2020b, 2021), but questions concerning whether the motives of PSM are grounded in public service or, instead, in the public sector setting and context remain. In the original conception of PSM and more recent definitions, PSM is defined as being primarily grounded in public institutions (e.g., Perry and Hondeghem, 2008; Perry, Hondeghem, and Wise, 2010). However, putting the theoretical issue of the conceptual basis of PSM aside, the bounds of PSM, in terms of influence, extend beyond the public sector to public service.

First, PSM corresponds to prosocial behaviors outside of the workplace. Certain dimensions of PSM (Clerkin, Paynter, and Taylor, 2009) and overall PSM increases the likelihood people will volunteer (Christensen et al., 2015; Clerkin and Fotheringham, 2017; Clerkin, Paynter, and Taylor, 2009; Piatak, 2016; Piatak and Holt, 2020a; Walton et al., 2017). In a representative sample of the US, Piatak and Holt (2020a) find the influence of PSM is strongest on formal volunteering, but also extends to informal volunteering in the community. In a study of undergraduate students, Clerkin and Fotheringham (2017) find different dimensions of PSM correspond to formal and informal volunteering. In a public goods game, Esteve et al. (2016) find high PSM students act prosocially when group members are also prosocial. PSM corresponds to prosocial behaviors outside of the work context, but job sector also corresponds to prosocial behaviors.

Both government and nonprofit sector employees are more likely to volunteer compared to those working in the for-profit sector. Using the General Social Survey, Houston (2006) finds both government and nonprofit employees are more likely to volunteer, but later finds only government employees are significantly more likely to volunteer compared to the for-profit sector (Houston, 2008). Others find nonprofit employees are most likely to volunteer followed by government (Rotolo and Wilson, 2006) or compared to government (Chen and Lee, 2015). Government employees are more likely to volunteer than employees in the for-profit sector (Ertas, 2014), but this varies by level of government. Both Piatak (2015) and Holt (2020) find higher levels of volunteering among nonprofit employees and local government employees compared to those in the for-profit sector. Work is needed to disentangle how job sector and PSM relate to prosocial behaviors.

Second, PSM has been found to have positive job and organizational outcomes regardless of job sector. PSM has been linked to a number of positive outcomes, including job satisfaction (for a meta-analysis, see Homberg, McCarthy, and Tabvuma (2015)), citizen participation in decision-making (Huang and Feeney, 2016), reduced turnover (Naff and Crum, 1999), job performance (Bellé, 2013), and organizational citizenship behavior (Boyd et al., 2018; Gould-Williams, Mostafa and Bottomley, 2015; Ritz et al., 2014; Shim and Faerman, 2017). While PSM positively influences organizational citizenship behavior across job sectors (Ingrams, 2020; Piatak and Holt, 2020b), Kjeldsen and Hansen (2018) find the positive association between PSM and job satisfaction is mediated by job sector. Relatedly, Andersen and colleagues (2011) find no difference in levels of PSM in a given occupation—physiotherapists—in government and for-profit organizations, but find a difference in orientations whereby those in government are oriented towards serving the public interest. More work is needed to examine how PSM and job sector shape employee perspectives and engagement as well as job and organizational outcomes.

Third, PSM applies to public service broadly defined to include the government and nonprofit sectors. While Piatak (2016) finds PSM only corresponds to career ambitions for graduate students to pursue government careers and not nonprofits, Bright (2008) finds those with high PSM prefer nonprofit careers over government careers and Clerkin and Coggburn (2012) find PSM relates to both a government and nonprofit sector preference. As a result, PSM has been applied to the nonprofit sector (e.g., Word and Carpenter, 2013) and corresponds to calls to public service more broadly. With the growing role of the nonprofit sector both in society and in providing public services, research has largely moved from examining public-private distinctions to examining all three job sectors—government, nonprofit, and for-profit—and some (e.g., Holt, 2018; Lewis, Pathak, and Galloway, 2018a; Lewis, Boyd, and Pathak, 2018b; Piatak, 2015, 2017, 2019) have begun to examine motivation and management differences across levels of government: federal, state, and local.

The influence of PSM extends beyond the public sector. PSM corresponds to people working in public service, broadly defined, as well as positive outcomes within and outside of the workplace. However, how PSM and job sector relate to such outcomes is unclear.

Stable Trait or Dynamic State? The Attraction vs. Socialization Debate

Another major debate in PSM research is whether PSM is a stable trait where certain individuals are attracted to public service or a dynamic state where employees are socialized into public service. Some find support for job sector socialization (Becker and Connor, 2005; Piatak, Douglas, and Raudla, 2020) where PSM appears malleable (Battaglio and French, 2016; Vandenabeele, 2011; Ward, 2014), while others find support for PSM being a more stable trait that attracts certain individuals to public service (Holt, 2018; Wright, Hassan, and Christensen, 2017). Whether PSM is a trait or state is beyond the scope of this chapter, but determines how motivation relates to job sector.

PSM tends to relate to choosing a public sector job (Ritz, Brewer, and Neumann, 2016). However, this may be more nuanced, especially as the lines between the sectors become increasingly blurred. For example, among social work students, Kjeldsen (2014) finds PSM predicts work tasks rather than job sector and finds later shifts in both tasks and sector. As a result, a meta-analysis finds support for the relationship between PSM and job sector attraction, but occupational context may play a role (Asseburg and Homberg, 2020). This circles back to whether PSM corresponds to a motivation towards the public sector or public service.

With the blurring of the boundaries between job sectors and the debate over public service versus public sector motivation, scholars have increasingly examined career paths and sector switching. The lines have become increasingly blurred not only with the rise of government contracting with for-profit and nonprofit organizations to deliver public goods and services (e.g., Salamon, 1981; Smith and Lipsky, 1993), but also with the growth of the nonprofit sector (e.g., McKeever, Dietz, and Fyffe, 2016; Salamon, 1994) and the issue of publicness (e.g., Bozeman, 1987) as for-profits organizations focus on corporate social responsibility (Campbell, 2007) and with the rise of social enterprise and marketization of nonprofits (Eikenberry, 2009). No wonder Light (1999) argued people will pursue a career where they can make a difference regardless of sector.

Several have examined the job sector career choices of graduate students. In examining lawyers, Wright and Christensen (2010) find intrinsic motivation unrelated to one's first job but that it increases the likelihood of future jobs being in the public sector, and later that people with high PSM pursue jobs with an emphasis on service regardless of sector (Christensen and Wright, 2011). Meanwhile, Tschirhart et al. (2008) find MBA and MPA students change job sectors if they are not in their preferred job sector upon graduation, but tend to remain in their preferred sector. Similarly, Van der Wal and Oosterbaan (2013) find MPA students have higher levels of PSM and a more positive perception of the public sector, compared to MBA students. Research on sector switching reveals insights into the career paths in public service and across job sectors (Bozeman and Ponomariov, 2009; Georgellis, Iossa, and Tabvuma, 2011; Hansen, 2014; McGinnis Johnson and Ng, 2016; Piatak, 2017; Su and Bozeman, 2009). As the values and priorities of individuals shift and the fit between employees and their job, position, and sector change, employees may pursue a career in a different job sector, particularly as the lines blur and in occupations where the lines are less apparent.

The next section takes stock of job sector characteristics that seem to attract certain individuals to the government, nonprofit, and for-profit sectors. Putting the debates within PSM research aside, people tend to have different reasons for joining different job sectors and for pursuing certain career paths.

JOB SECTOR VALUES

People work in a given job in a given organization in a given job sector for a variety of reasons. The attraction-selection-attrition model puts forth that people apply for jobs that interest them, organizations select individuals that fit, and employees leave organizations that no longer fit (Schneider, 1987). While person-job and person-organizational fit influence career decisions, certain job sector characteristics have been found to attract, engage, and retain employees in government, nonprofit, and for-profit organizations.

Government

People may work in the government sector for a variety of reasons. Even PSM was originally conceptualized to capture rational, normative, and affective motives (Perry and Wise, 1990) and later to encapsulate six dimensions: commitment to the public interest, civic duty, social justice, attraction to policymaking, compassion, and self-sacrifice (Perry, 1996). However, some trends can be found in reviewing the literature on public-private distinctions and job sector differences.

The most common driver to work in the government sector is to serve the public interest. Both PSM and a general drive to serve the public correspond to choosing government careers or aspirations to work in the government sector (e.g., Boyne, 2002; Nalbanian and Edwards, 1983; Posner and Schmidt, 1996; Rainey, 1982). In a meta-analysis, the only clear pattern across studies was that public sector employees have a higher sense of community service (Baarspul and Wilderom, 2011). Moves from the for-profit sector to government also tend to be in pursuit of greater intrinsic rewards (Georgellis, Iossa, and Tabvuma, 2011). This aligns with PSM work (Ritz, Brewer, and Neumann, 2016) and the idea that people interested in serving the public interest pursue public service careers in government.

However, government employees' desire to serve the public is often coupled with placing less emphasis on financial rewards, especially in earlier public versus private studies (e.g., Boyne, 2002; Wittmer, 1991). Yet, as early as Rainey's (1982) article identifying the primary drive to government work being the 'fulfillment of service motives,' he cautioned not to overgeneralize the relative importance of financial rewards arguing that while government employees 'do not place overriding value on monetary incentives ... extrinsic rewards are highly valued by many public sector employees' (p. 297). Instead, government employees place a 'lower value on money and high income as *ultimate ends* in work and in life' (Rainey and Bozeman, 2000, p. 460, emphasis added). Indeed, research increasingly finds extrinsic motivators such as pay and benefits do matter (Choi and Chung, 2017; Ko and Jun, 2015; Lee and Wilkins, 2011; Stazyk, 2013). Recent work also finds that how performance pay systems are designed influence the effect on employee motivation (Wenzel, Krause, and Vogel, 2019). In addition, some countries have wage efficiency between the government and for-profit sectors (Taylor and Taylor, 2011). Yes, public service and contributing to society tends to be the primary motivator of government employees, but not at the expense of a fair compensation package, both salary and benefits.

Another extrinsic factor that plays a role is job security. In examining job sector changes, Hansen (2014) finds both serving society and job security to be negatively related to leaving government work. Others have found government employees value job security (e.g., Choi and Chung, 2017; Lee and Choi, 2016), which may be at risk with movements to at-will employment and other reforms at the state and local level (Battaglio and Condrey, 2006; Battaglio and French, 2016). Economic conditions and cutback management decisions shape employment dynamics (Piatak, 2017, 2019). Additional work is needed on how removing merit system protections influence government motivation.

In addition to serving the public interest, government employees value work that is important and provides a sense of accomplishment (Houston, 2000), intellectually stimulating and challenging (Frank and Lewis, 2004; Karl and Sutton, 1998; Lyons, Duxbury, and Higgins, 2006), gives opportunity for advancement (Lee and Wilkins, 2011; Su and Bozeman, 2009), recognition (Khojasteh, 1993), affiliation with politics and policy (Vandenabeele et al., 2004), and prestige (Cho and Lee, 2001). However, there is little consistency across studies as each examines different values and work characteristics.

Motivation is complex and every individual may have a unique drive to public service, but government employees tend to value serving the public interest followed by an appreciation for job security. However, managers can help foster the drive to serve by ensuring employees feel like they are making a difference, recognizing employee efforts, and providing opportunities to excel and have a greater impact. By emphasizing the importance of the organization's mission, managers can increase the work motivation of public employees (Wright, 2007) and hopefully retain public service-driven employees.

Nonprofit

Individuals tend to be drawn to the nonprofit sector for meaningful work to make a difference in society. Nonprofit employees value work that contributes to society (Lyons, Duxbury, and Higgins, 2006; Tschirhart et al., 2008) and are attracted to nonprofit organizations in order to serve the nonprofit's mission (Brown and Yoshioka, 2003; Kim and Lee, 2007; Word and Carpenter, 2013). While government employees are drawn to serve the public, nonprofit employees are drawn to serve society by working towards a cause.

Donative labor theory, whereby nonprofit employees are willing to 'donate' a portion of their salary for the benefit of satisfying their passion towards the mission, originated to explain why people chose to work in the nonprofit sector. Leete (2001) describes how 'nonprofit workers derive utility from the nature of the good produced and are thus willing to accept a lower (compensating) wage' (p. 137). Scholars have long found nonprofit employees value the nature of the work more than their salary (Handy and Katz, 1998; Lee and Wilkins, 2011; Leete, 2001, 2006; Mirvis and Hackett, 1983). Much like government employees were historically found to value serving the public over higher salaries, nonprofit employees are also thought to value the work over the pay.

While the social expectations of nonprofits shape the low-paying practices of nonprofits in the eyes of nonprofit executives (Kim and Charbonneau, 2020), reliance on donative labor from nonprofit employees is not sufficient for today's professionalized nonprofit sector. Nonprofits, much like government, are tasked to do more with less, but are also pressured by funders and the public to reduce administrative costs and overhead. This creates tensions between volunteers and employees as volunteers are asked to do more tasks that are critical to the mission (Bittschi, Pennerstorfer, and Schneider, 2019; Rimes et al., 2017; Russell, Mook, and Handy, 2017; Thomsen and Jensen, 2019). Many nonprofit employees also leave the sector for higher wages (AbouAssi, McGinnis Johnson, and Holt, 2021; Faulk et al., 2012; McGinnis Johnson, and Ng, 2016; Piatak, 2017). Mission attachment is not enough to overcome dissatisfaction with pay to retain employees in the nonprofit sector (Brown and Yoshioka, 2003; Kim and Lee, 2007). Chen (2014) finds nonprofit managers place the highest value on organizational quality and reputation, but this is directly followed by salary. Nonprofits can no longer rely on a wage donation from their employees.

In addition to the mission and serving society, the work environment plays a key role in the nonprofit sector. Nonprofit employees appreciate the work-life balance and family friendly policies (Lee and Wilkins, 2011; Leete, 2006; Park and Word, 2012). However, this may be an indication of the deeper connection between employee and employer in the nonprofit sector. Knapp and colleagues (2017) find that higher levels of perceived organizational support increase job satisfaction and reduce turnover intentions. Similarly, Stater and Stater (2019) find nonprofit employees who are proud of their employer and view their coworkers as helpful, report higher levels of job satisfaction. Nonprofit employees are satisfied in their positions when their work environment is supportive.

Scholars have also found that the nature of the work attracts and retains nonprofit employees. Those in the nonprofit sector prefer work that is personally challenging (Leete, 2006) and value responsibility (Lee and Wilkins, 2011), autonomy (Knapp, Smith, and Sprinkle, 2017), and opportunities for advancement (Kim and Lee, 2007; Park and Word, 2012). Nonprofit employees are driven to serve the mission and seem to want the flexibility and responsibility to do so.

The motivation to work in the nonprofit sector is more nuanced than just wanting to serve society and advance an organizational mission. Turnover is often a challenge in the nonprofit sector, especially among younger generations (Ng and McGinnis Johnson, 2016; McGinnis Johnson, Piatak, and Ng, 2017). Much like in the government sector, the motives to serve others should not be at the expense of fair pay. Nonprofit sector employees value the supportive work environment and challenging work. For nonprofit organizations to be truly supportive of their employees, the pay philosophy needs to move beyond donative labor to one that values the professional and large role of the nonprofit sector today.

For-profit

Opposite of employees in the government and nonprofit sectors, for-profit employees tend to be motivated by extrinsic rewards like pay. Cross-sector studies have found for-profit employees are more likely to value financial rewards (Houston, 2000; Karl and Sutton, 1998; Khojasteh, 1993; Rainey, 1982; Tschirhart et al., 2008), shorter hours (Houston, 2000), and the ability to be entrepreneurial (Tschirhart et al., 2008). In examining values, Stackman, Connor, and Becker (2006) find the private sector ethos has a competence, personal, and family security orientation compared to conscious, social, and societal. Related to competence, Fowler and Birdsall (2020) examine the influence of academic qualifications on job sector preferences, where they find the top law school graduates with high GPAs (grade point averages) are more likely to work in the for-profit or nonprofit sector rather than government. Employees in the for-profit sector value personal and family security and pay, but also value the nature of work, such as competence and the ability to be entrepreneurial.

However, employees in the for-profit sector sometimes move into the government or nonprofit sector. While for-profit employees may move to the government sector in pursuit of intrinsic rewards (Georgellis, Iossa, and Tabvuma, 2011), the likelihood of moving decreases with the number of subordinates (Su and Bozeman, 2009). However, for those that move, government employees with for-profit sector experience are more likely to be recently promoted and supervise more employees, but these benefits decrease with time (Bozeman and Ponomariov, 2009). In pursuit of a promotion, for-profit employees are more likely to move to the nonprofit sector rather than government (Su and Bozeman, 2009). Whether for a promotion to apply their for-profit sector experience or in pursuit of serving the public or a specific mission, people often change positions, employers, and even job sectors over the course of their careers.

RECRUITING AND RETAINING FUTURE GENERATIONS IN PUBLIC SERVICE

Government agencies and nonprofit organizations may need to appeal to a broader range of work values when recruiting, engaging, and working to retain future generations of employees. Employees are no longer willing to sacrifice salary in order to serve a public purpose or mission in society, particularly as the lines become increasingly blurred across job sectors. Government and nonprofit employees are also driven by the nature of the work and work environment in addition to the public or mission purpose of the work where managers should shape management and human resource management practices accordingly.

In examining Millennials, the latest generation to enter the workforce, employers are seeing a rise in employee expectations and higher rates of turnover when those expectations are not met (Ng, Schweitzer, and Lyons, 2010). Millennials indicate work-life balance, furthering their education, and contributing to society are their top career goals (Ng and Gossett, 2013). In deciding which job to take, Millennials also consider whether colleagues are diverse and whether the work environment is inclusive (Ng and Gossett, 2013). A few workplace areas that may help government and nonprofit managers recruit, engage, and retain the next generation of public servants are discussed below.

- Relate to the Mission. With serving the public (e.g., Boyne, 2002; Perry and Wise, 1990; Rainey, 1982) and mission attachment (Brown and Yoshioka, 2003; Kim and Lee, 2007; Lyons, Duxbury, and Higgins, 2006; Tschirhart et al., 2008; Word and Carpenter, 2013) being the primary drivers for work in the government and nonprofit sectors, managers should ensure employees see the impact of their work and help make a connection between their work and the mission of the organization.
- Recognition and Rewards. Government and nonprofit organizations must ensure adequate compensation and recognition of employees. Both government and nonprofit employees are mission-driven, but not at the expense of fair compensation as a growing number of studies have shown in both government (Choi and Chung, 2017; Ko and Jun, 2015; Lee and Wilkins, 2011; Stazyk, 2013) and nonprofits (AbouAssi, McGinnis Johnson, and Holt, 2021; Faulk et al., 2012; McGinnis Johnson and Ng, 2016; Piatak, 2017).

- Organizational Support. With the appreciation for organizational support (Knapp, Smith, and Sprinkle, 2017; Stater and Stater, 2019), government and nonprofit managers may want to consider the range of benefits provided to ensure each employee feels fully supported in their workplace and know that their employer cares about them as a person. High demands and low resources reduce PSM (Bakker, 2015). Employees each come with their own unique set of motivations and needs. Government and nonprofit sector organizations can compete with the for-profit sector by offering employees benefits to meet those needs. With the interest in furthering one's education (Ng and Gossett, 2013), this can range from tuition reimbursement to volunteer time to dress down days.
- Employer Compassion. While organizational support is valued, so too is employer compassion that has been found to reduce burnout and increase employee outcomes like organizational citizenship behavior, knowledge sharing, and service to citizens (Eldor, 2018). Overreliance on those driven by PSM and to serve the public or a specific mission can result in several negative personnel outcomes, such as burnout, turnover, and presenteeism (Jensen, Anderson, and Holten, 2019; Kim, 2015; Oelberger, 2016).
- Telework. Research has demonstrated that flexibility is important to those in public service (Lee and Wilkins, 2011) and Millennials have different ideas about work-life balance than previous generations (e.g., McGinnis Johnson, Piatak, and Ng, 2017). With the Telework Enhancement Act of 2010, a government-wide framework was put in place for federal government employees to telework. Management support is often a key factor for telework programs to have positive employee outcomes like job satisfaction (e.g., Kwon and Jeon, 2020; Lee and Kim, 2018), but may be an option to help employees manage their work-life balance.
- Diversity, Equity, and Inclusion. Social equity is a key value in public administration that extends to the workforce. In Executive Order 13583, President Obama stated: 'As the Nation's largest employer, the Federal Government has a special obligation to lead by example. Attaining a diverse, qualified workforce is one of the cornerstones of the merit-based civil service' (Federal Register, 2011). The federal government (US Government Accountability Office, 2005) and many state and local governments also have diversity, equity, and inclusion efforts underway (Gooden, 2017). While governments continue to pursue representative bureaucracies to face the communities they serve, governments across the federal, state, and local levels tend to have greater pay equity than the for-profit sector (Lewis, Pathak, and Galloway, 2018a; Lewis, Boyd, and Pathak, 2018b; US Government Accountability Office, 2020). In addition to Millennials considering diversity and inclusion in their employment decisions (Ng and Gossett, 2013), those with high PSM are more likely to leave when they perceive heightened workforce conflict (Davis et al., 2020). People come to work as whole people. Nelson and Piatak (2021) find women and women from historically underrepresented groups have varying perceptions of inclusion in the federal government. Government and nonprofit organizations, human resources, and managers should focus on diversity, equity, and inclusion efforts to ensure diverse and representative workforces with equitable and inclusive cultures.

Future research should address each of these areas to examine the direct influence of these management strategies on PSM and employee motivation and values across job sectors.

MOVING FORWARD

Public administration scholars have long examined public/private distinctions (e.g., Rainey, 1982; Rainey, Backoff, and Levine, 1976). Correspondingly, research on PSM has rapidly grown since Perry and Wise (1990) coined the term. At the same time, scholars have increasingly examined job sector differences in motivation, values, and job satisfaction across all three job sectors: government, for-profit, and nonprofit (e.g., Stater and Stater, 2019; Tschirhart et al., 2008). As a result, scholarship on both PSM and job sector distinctions have grown.

However, PSM research and job sector research rarely intertwine. While job sector is sometimes used as a proxy for PSM, little is known about how PSM and job sector relate aside from those with higher levels of PSM self-selecting into public service to satisfy their motivation. However, more work is needed to address the public service motivation versus public sector motivation debate as well as whether PSM is a trait, state, or both to understand the potential role of management and organizational cultures in shaping PSM.

In addition, research on job sector characteristics and values raise questions for future research. For example, Holt (2020) and Piatak (2015) find nonprofit and local government employees are most likely to volunteer and devote the most time, but we know little about how government employees vary across levels of government. Do employees at the federal, state, and local level have different levels of PSM? Might government employees across levels of government be motivated by different job sector characteristics and values? Additionally, AbouAssi, McGinnis Johnson, and Holt (2021) find government and nonprofit sector employees are less likely to change job sectors if they volunteer. Could opportunities for service, even outside the workplace, help retain Millennials in public service?

Many questions remain, but we have substantial evidence that government employees value serving the public and nonprofit employees value serving a societal mission. Organizations, human resources, and managers should ensure government and nonprofit employees see the connection of the sector to these values in order to recruit, engage, and retain those dedicated to public service.

REFERENCES

AbouAssi, K., McGinnis Johnson, J., and Holt, S. B. (2021). Job mobility among millennials: Do they stay or do they go? *Review of Public Personnel Administration, 41*, 219–249.

Andersen, L.B., Pallesen, T., and Holm Pedersen, L. (2011). Does ownership matter? Public service motivation among physiotherapists in the private and public sectors in Denmark. *Review of Public Personnel Administration, 31*, 10–27.

Asseburg, J., and Homberg, F. (2020). Public service motivation or sector rewards? Two studies on the determinants of sector attraction. *Review of Public Personnel Administration, 40*, 82–111.

Baarspul, H.C., and Wilderom, C.P. (2011). Do employees behave differently in public-vs private-sector organizations? A state-of-the-art review. *Public Management Review, 13*, 967–1002.

Bakker, A.B. (2015). A job demands–resources approach to public service motivation. *Public Administration Review, 75*, 723–732.

Battaglio, Jr, R.P., and Condrey, S.E. (2006). Civil service reform: Examining state and local government cases. *Review of Public Personnel Administration, 26*, 118–138.

Battaglio, Jr, R.P., and French, P.E. (2016). Public service motivation, public management reform, and organizational socialization: Testing the effects of employment at-will and agency on PSM among municipal employees. *Public Personnel Management, 45*, 123–147.

Becker, B.W., and Connor, P.E. (2005). Self-selection or socialization of public-and private-sector managers? A cross-cultural values analysis. *Journal of Business Research*, *58*, 111–113.

Bellé, N. (2013). Experimental evidence on the relationship between public service motivation and job performance. *Public Administration Review*, *73*, 143–153.

Bittschi, B., Pennerstorfer, A., and Schneider, U. (2019). The effect of volunteers on paid workers excess turnover in nonprofit and public organizations. *Review of Public Personnel Administration*, *39*, 256–275.

Boyd, N., Nowell, B., Yang, Z., and Hano, M.C. (2018). Sense of community, sense of community responsibility, and public service motivation as predictors of employee well-being and engagement in public service organizations. *American Review of Public Administration*, *48*, 428–443.

Boyne, G.A. (2002). Public and private management: What's the difference? *Journal of Management Studies*, *39*, 97–122.

Bozeman, B. (1987). *All organizations are public: Bridging public and private organizational theories.* San Francisco, CA: Jossey-Bass.

Bozeman, B., and Ponomariov, B. (2009). Sector switching from a business to a government job: Fast-track career or fast track to nowhere? *Public Administration Review*, *69*, 77–91.

Bozeman, B., and Su, X. (2015). Public service motivation concepts and theory: A critique. *Public Administration Review*, *75*, 700–710.

Breaugh, J., Ritz, A., and Alfes, K. (2018). Work motivation and public service motivation: Disentangling varieties of motivation and job satisfaction. *Public Management Review*, *20*, 1423–1443.

Bright, L. (2008). Does public service motivation really make a difference on the job satisfaction and turnover intentions of public employees? *American Review of Public Administration*, *38*, 149–166.

Brown, W.A., and Yoshioka, C.F. (2003). Mission attachment and satisfaction as factors in employee retention. *Nonprofit Management and Leadership*, *14*, 5–18.

Campbell, J.L. (2007). Why would corporations behave in socially responsible ways? An institutional theory of corporate social responsibility. *Academy of Management Review*, *32*, 946–967.

Chen, C.A. (2014). Nonprofit managers' motivational styles: A view beyond the intrinsic-extrinsic dichotomy. *Nonprofit and Voluntary Sector Quarterly*, *43*, 737–758.

Chen, C.A., and Lee, Y.J. (2015). A closer look at the difference between public and nonprofit employees' volunteering. *International Public Management Journal*, *18*, 108–129.

Cho, K., and Lee, S. (2001). Another look at public-private distinction and organizational commitment: A cultural explanation. *The International Journal of Organizational Analysis*, *9*(1), 84–102.

Choi, Y., and Chung, I.H. (2017). Attraction-selection and socialization of work values: Evidence from longitudinal survey. *Public Personnel Management*, *46*, 66–88.

Christensen, R.K., and Wright, B.E. (2011). The effects of public service motivation on job choice decisions: Disentangling the contributions of person-organization fit and person-job fit. *Journal of Public Administration Research and Theory*, *21*, 723–743.

Christensen, R.K., Stritch, J.M., Kellough, J.E., and Brewer, G.A. (2015). Identifying student traits and motives to service-learn: Public service orientation among new college freshmen. *Journal of Higher Education Outreach and Engagement*, *19*(4), 39–62.

Clerkin, R.M., and Coggburn, J.D. (2012). The dimensions of public service motivation and sector work preferences. *Review of Public Personnel Administration*, *32*(3), 209–235.

Clerkin, R.M., and Fotheringham, E. (2017). Exploring the relationship between public service motivation and formal and informal volunteering. *Journal of Public and Nonprofit Affairs*, *3*, 23–39.

Clerkin, R.M., Paynter, S.R., and Taylor, J.K. (2009). Public service motivation in undergraduate giving and volunteering decisions. *American Review of Public Administration*, *39*, 675–698.

Davis, R.S., Stazyk, E.C., Kochenour, A., and Neuhoff, E. (2020). Coping with conflict: Examining the influence of PSM on perceptions of workplace stressors. *Review of Public Personnel Administration*, *40*, 405–425.

Eikenberry, A.M. (2009). Refusing the market: A democratic discourse for voluntary and nonprofit organizations. *Nonprofit and Voluntary Sector Quarterly*, *38*, 582–596.

Eldor, L. (2018). Public service sector: The compassionate workplace—the effect of compassion and stress on employee engagement, burnout, and performance. *Journal of Public Administration Research and Theory*, *28*(1), 86–103.

Ertas, N. (2014). Public service motivation theory and voluntary organizations: Do government employees volunteer more? *Nonprofit and Voluntary Sector Quarterly*, *43*, 254–271.

Esteve, M., Urbig, D., Van Witteloostuijn, A., and Boyne, G. (2016). Prosocial behavior and public service motivation. *Public Administration Review*, *76*, 177–187.

Faulk, L., Edwards, L.H., Lewis, G.B., and McGinnis, J. (2012). An analysis of gender pay disparity in the nonprofit sector: An outcome of labor motivation or gendered jobs? *Nonprofit and Voluntary Sector Quarterly*, *42*, 1268–1287.

Federal Register. (2011, August 23). Establishing a coordinated government-wide initiative to promote diversity and inclusion in the federal workforce (Vol. 76, No. 163, 52847).

Fowler, L., and Birdsall, C. (2020). Are the best and brightest joining the public service? *Review of Public Personnel Administration*, *40*, 532–554.

Frank, S.A., and Lewis, G.B. (2004). Government employees: Working hard or hardly working? *American Review of Public Administration*, *34*(1), 36–51.

Georgellis, Y., Iossa, E., and Tabvuma, V. (2011). Crowding out intrinsic motivation in the public sector. *Journal of Public Administration Research and Theory*, *21*, 473–493.

Gooden, S.T. (2017). Social equity and evidence: Insights from local government. *Public Administration Review*, *77*, 822–828.

Gould-Williams, J.S., Mostafa, A.M.S., and Bottomley, P. (2015). Public service motivation and employee outcomes in the Egyptian public sector: Testing the mediating effect of person organization fit. *Journal of Public Administration Research and Theory*, *25*, 597–622.

Handy, F., and Katz, E. (1998). The wage differential between nonprofit institutions and corporations: Getting more by paying less? *Journal of Comparative Economics*, *26*, 246–261.

Hansen, J.R. (2014). From public to private sector: Motives and explanations for sector switching. *Public Management Review*, *16*, 590–607.

Holt, S.B. (2018). For those who care: The effect of public service motivation on sector selection. *Public Administration Review*, *78*, 457–471.

Holt, S.B. (2020). Giving time: Examining sector differences in volunteering intensity. *Journal of Public Administration Research and Theory*, *30*, 22–40.

Homberg, F., McCarthy, D., and Tabvuma, V. (2015). A meta-analysis of the relationship between public service motivation and job satisfaction. *Public Administration Review*, *75*, 711–722.

Houston, D.J. (2000). Public-service motivation: A multivariate test. *Journal of Public Administration Research and Theory*, *10*, 713–728.

Houston, D.J. (2006). 'Walking the walk' of public service motivation: Public employees and charitable gifts of time, blood, and money. *Journal of Public Administration Research and Theory*, *16*, 67–86.

Houston, D.J. (2008). Behavior in the public square. In J.L. Perry and A. Hondeghem (eds), *Motivation in public management: The call of public service*. New York, NY: Oxford University Press, pp. 177–199.

Huang, W.L., and Feeney, M.K. (2016). Citizen participation in local government decision making: The role of manager motivation. *Review of Public Personnel Administration*, *36*, 188–209.

Ingrams, A. (2020). Organizational citizenship behavior in the public and private sectors: A multilevel test of public service motivation and traditional antecedents. *Review of Public Personnel Administration*, *40*, 222–244.

Jensen, U.T., Andersen, L.B., and Holten, A.L. (2019). Explaining a dark side: Public service motivation, presenteeism, and absenteeism. *Review of Public Personnel Administration*, *39*, 487–510.

Karl, K.A., and Sutton, C.L. (1998). Job values in today's workforce: A comparison of public and private sector employees. *Public Personnel Management*, *27*, 515–527.

Khojasteh, M. (1993). Motivating the private vs. public sector managers. *Public Personnel Management*, *22*, 391–401.

Kim, J. (2015). What increases public employees' turnover intention? *Public Personnel Management*, *44*, 496–519.

Kim, M., and Charbonneau, É. (2020). Caught between volunteerism and professionalism: Support by nonprofit leaders for the donative labor hypothesis. *Review of Public Personnel Administration*, *40*, 327–349.

Kim, S.E., and Lee, J.W. (2007). Is mission attachment an effective management tool for employee retention? An empirical analysis of a nonprofit human services agency. *Review of Public Personnel Administration*, 27, 227–248.

Kjeldsen, A.M. (2014). Dynamics of public service motivation: Attraction–selection and socialization in the production and regulation of social services. *Public Administration Review*, 74, 101–112.

Kjeldsen, A.M., and Hansen, J.R. (2018). Sector differences in the public service motivation–job satisfaction relationship: exploring the role of organizational characteristics. *Review of Public Personnel Administration*, 38, 24–48.

Knapp, J.R., Smith, B.R., and Sprinkle, T.A. (2017). Is it the job or the support? Examining structural and relational predictors of job satisfaction and turnover intention for nonprofit employees. *Nonprofit and Voluntary Sector Quarterly*, 46, 652–671.

Ko, K., and Jun, K.N. (2015). A comparative analysis of job motivation and career preference of Asian undergraduate students. *Public Personnel Management*, 44, 192–213.

Kwon, M., and Jeon, S.H. (2020). Do leadership commitment and performance-oriented culture matter for federal teleworker satisfaction with telework programs? *Review of Public Personnel Administration*, 40, 36–55.

Lee, G., and Choi, D.L. (2016). Does public service motivation influence the college students' intention to work in the public sector? Evidence from Korea. *Review of Public Personnel Administration*, 36, 145–163.

Lee, D., and Kim, S.Y. (2018). A quasi-experimental examination of telework eligibility and participation in the US federal government. *Review of Public Personnel Administration*, 38, 451–471.

Lee, Y.J., and Wilkins, V.M. (2011). More similarities or more differences? Comparing public and nonprofit managers' job motivations. *Public Administration Review*, 71, 45–56.

Leete, L. (2001). Whither the nonprofit wage differential? Estimates from the 1990 census. *Journal of Labor Economics*, 19, 136–170.

Leete, L. (2006). Work in the nonprofit sector. In W.W. Powell and R. Steinburg (eds), *The Nonprofit sector: A research handbook*. New Haven, CT: Yale University Press, pp. 159–179.

Lewis, G.B., Pathak, R., and Galloway, C.S. (2018a). Trends in public–private pay parity in state and local governments. *Review of Public Personnel Administration*, 38, 303–331.

Lewis, G.B., Boyd, J., and Pathak, R. (2018b). Progress toward pay equity in state governments? *Public Administration Review*, 78, 386–397.

Light, P.C. (1999). *The true size of government*. Washington, DC: Brookings Institution Press.

Lyons, S.T., Duxbury, L.E., and Higgins, C.A. (2006). A comparison of the values and commitment of private sector, public sector, and parapublic sector employees. *Public Administration Review*, 66, 605–618.

McGinnis Johnson, J., and Ng, E.S. (2016). Money talks or millennials walk: The effect of compensation on nonprofit millennial workers sector-switching intentions. *Review of Public Personnel Administration*, 36(3), 283–305.

McGinnis Johnson, J., Piatak, J.S., and Ng, E. (2017). Managing generational differences in nonprofit organizations. In J.K.A. Word and J. Sowa (eds), *The nonprofit human resource management handbook*. New York, NY: Routledge, pp. 304–322.

McKeever, B.S., Dietz, N.E., and Fyffe, S.D. (2016). *The nonprofit almanac: The essential facts and figures for managers, researchers, and volunteers*. Lanham, MD: Rowman and Littlefield.

Mirvis, P.H., and Hackett, E.J. (1983). Work and work force characteristics in the nonprofit sector. *Monthly Labor Review*, 106, 3–12.

Naff, K.C., and Crum, J. (1999). Working for America: Does public service motivation make a difference? *Review of Public Personnel Administration*, 19, 5–16.

Nalbandian, J., and Edwards, J.T. (1983). The values of public administrators: A comparison with lawyers, social workers, and business administrators. *Review of Public Personnel Administration*, 4, 114–127.

Nelson, A., and Piatak, J. (2021). Intersectionality, leadership, and inclusion: How do racially underrepresented women fare in the federal government? *Review of Public Personnel Administration*, 41, 294–318.

Ng, E.S., and Gossett, C.W. (2013). Career choice in Canadian public service: An exploration of fit with the millennial generation. *Public Personnel Management*, 42, 337–358.

Ng, E.S., Schweitzer, L., and Lyons, S.T. (2010). New generation, great expectations: A field study of the millennial generation. *Journal of Business and Psychology, 25*, 281–292.

Nowell, B., Izod, A.M., Ngaruiya, K.M., and Boyd, N.M. (2016). Public service motivation and sense of community responsibility: Comparing two motivational constructs in understanding leadership within community collaboratives. *Journal of Public Administration Research and Theory, 26*, 663–676.

Oelberger, C.R. (2019). The dark side of deeply meaningful work: Work–relationship turmoil and the moderating role of occupational value homophily. *Journal of Management Studies, 56*, 558–588.

Park, S.M., and Word, J. (2012). Driven to service: Intrinsic and extrinsic motivation for public and nonprofit managers. *Public Personnel Management, 41*, 705–734.

Perry, J.L. (1996). Measuring public service motivation: An assessment of construct reliability and validity. *Journal of Public Administration Research and Theory, 6*, 5–22.

Perry, J.L., and Hondeghem, A. (2008). *Motivation in public management: The call of public service.* New York, NY: Oxford University Press.

Perry, J.L., and Rainey, H.G. (1988). The public-private distinction in organization theory: A critique and research strategy. *Academy of Management Review, 13*, 182–201.

Perry, J.L., and Vandenabeele, W. (2015). Public service motivation research: Achievements, challenges, and future directions. *Public Administration Review, 75*, 692–699.

Perry, J.L., and Wise, L.R. (1990). The motivational bases of public service. *Public Administration Review, 50*, 367–373.

Perry, J.L., Hondeghem, A., and Wise, L.R. (2010). Revisiting the motivational bases of public service: Twenty years of research and an agenda for the future. *Public Administration Review, 70*, 681–690.

Piatak, J.S. (2015). Altruism by job sector: Can Public sector employees lead the way in rebuilding social capital? *Journal of Public Administration Research and Theory, 25*, 877–900.

Piatak, J.S. (2016). Public service motivation, prosocial behaviours, and career ambitions. *International Journal of Manpower, 37*, 804–821.

Piatak, J.S. (2017). Sector Switching in good times and in bad: Are public sector employees less likely to change sectors? *Public Personnel Management, 46*, 327–341.

Piatak, J. (2019). Weathering the storm: The impact of cutbacks on public employees. *Public Personnel Management, 48*, 97–119.

Piatak, J.S., and Holt, S.B. (2020a). Prosocial behaviors: A matter of altruism or public service motivation? *Journal of Public Administration Research and Theory, 30*, 504–518.

Piatak, J.S., and Holt, S.B. (2020b). Disentangling altruism and public service motivation: Who exhibits organizational citizenship behaviour? *Public Management Review, 22*, 949–973.

Piatak, J.S., and Holt, S.B. (2021). *Public service motivation and public opinion: Examining antecedents and attitudes.* Cambridge, MA: Cambridge University Press.

Piatak, J.S., Douglas, J.W., and Raudla, R. (2020). The role perceptions of government professionals: The effects of gender, educational field, and prior job sector. *Public Management Review, 22*, 949–973.

Posner, B.Z., and Schmidt, W.H. (1996). The values of business and federal government executives: More different than alike. *Public Personnel Management, 25*, 277–289.

Rainey, H.G. (1982). Reward preferences among public and private managers: In search of the service ethic. *American Review of Public Administration, 16*, 288–302.

Rainey, H.G. (2014). *Understanding and managing public organizations* (5th edn). San Francisco, CA: John Wiley and Sons.

Rainey, H.G., and Bozeman, B. (2000). Comparing public and private organizations: Empirical research and the power of the a priori. *Journal of Public Administration Research and Theory, 10*, 447–470.

Rainey, H.G., Backoff, R.W., and Levine, C.H. (1976). Comparing public and private organizations. *Public Administration Review, 36*, 233–244.

Rimes, H., Nesbit, R., Christensen, R.K., and Brudney, J.L. (2017). Exploring the dynamics of volunteer and staff interactions: From satisfaction to conflict. *Nonprofit Management and Leadership, 28*, 195–213.

Ritz, A., Giauque, D., Varone, F., and Anderfuhren-Biget, S. (2014). From leadership to citizenship behavior in public organizations: When values matter. *Review of Public Personnel Administration, 34*, 128–152.

Ritz, A., Brewer, G.A., and Neumann, O. (2016). Public service motivation: A systematic literature review and outlook. *Public Administration Review, 76*, 414–426.

Rotolo, T., and Wilson, J. (2006). Employment sector and volunteering: The contribution of nonprofit and public sector workers to the volunteer labor force. *The Sociological Quarterly, 47*, 21–40.

Russell, A.R., Mook, L., and Handy, F. (2017). Interchangeability of labor: Managing a mixed paid and volunteer workforce. In J.K.A. Word and J.E. Sowa (eds), *The nonprofit human resource management handbook: From theory to practice*. New York, NY: Routledge, pp. 271–284.

Salamon, L.M. (1981). Rethinking public management: Third-party government and the changing forms of government action. *Public Policy, 29*, 255–275.

Salamon, L.M. (1994). The rise of the nonprofit sector. *Foreign Affairs, 73*, 109–122.

Schneider, B. (1987). The people make the place. *Personnel Psychology, 40*, 437–453.

Shim, D.C., and Faerman, S. (2017). Government employees' organizational citizenship behavior: The impacts of public service motivation, organizational identification, and subjective OCB norms. *International Public Management Journal, 20*, 531–559.

Smith, S.R., and Lipsky, M. (1993). *Nonprofits for hire: The welfare state in the age of contracting*. Cambridge, MA: Harvard University Press.

Stackman, R.W., Connor, P.E., and Becker, B.W. (2005). Sectoral ethos: An investigation of the personal values systems of female and male managers in the public and private sectors. *Journal of Public Administration Research and Theory, 16*, 577–597.

Stater, K.J., and Stater, M. (2019). Is it 'just work'? The impact of work rewards on job satisfaction and turnover intent in the nonprofit, for-profit, and public sectors. *American Review of Public Administration, 49*, 495–511.

Stazyk, E.C. (2013). Crowding out public service motivation? Comparing theoretical expectations with empirical findings on the influence of performance-related pay. *Review of Public Personnel Administration, 33*, 252–274.

Su, X., and Bozeman, B. (2009). Dynamics of sector switching: Hazard models predicting changes from private sector jobs to public and nonprofit sector jobs. *Public Administration Review, 69*, 1106–1114.

Taylor, J., and Taylor, R. (2011). Working hard for more money or working hard to make a difference? Efficiency wages, public service motivation, and effort. *Review of Public Personnel Administration, 31*, 67–86.

Thomsen, M.K., and Jensen, U.T. (2019). Service professionals' response to volunteer involvement in service production. *Journal of Public Administration Research and Theory*, first published online on October 15, 2019 at https://doi.org/10.1093/jopart/muz028.

Tschirhart, M., Reed, K.K., Freeman, S.J., and Anker, A.L. (2008). Is the grass greener? Sector shifting and choice of sector by MPA and MBA graduates. *Nonprofit and Voluntary Sector Quarterly, 37*, 668–688.

US Government Accountability Office. (2005). Diversity management: Expert-identified leading practices and agency examples (U.S. GAO-05-90). Washington, DC: Author.

US Government Accountability Office. (2020). Gender pay differences: The pay gap for federal workers has continued to narrow, but better quality data on promotions are needed (U.S. GAO-21-67). Washington, DC: Author.

Van der Wal, Z., and Oosterbaan, A. (2013). Government or business? Identifying determinants of MPA and MBA students' career preferences. *Public Personnel Management, 42*, 239–258.

Vandenabeele, W. (2011). Who wants to deliver public service? Do institutional antecedents of public service motivation provide an answer? *Review of Public Personnel Administration, 31*, 87–107.

Vandenabeele, W., Hondeghem, A., and Steen, T. (2004). The civil service as an employer of choice in Belgium: How work orientations influence the attractiveness of public employment. *Review of Public Personnel Administration, 24*, 319–333.

Vandenabeele, W., Brewer, G.A., and Ritz, A. (2014). Past, present, and future of public service motivation research. *Public Administration, 92*, 779–789.

Walton, M.A., Clerkin, R.M., Christensen, R.K., Paarlberg, L.E., Nesbit, R., and Tschirhart, M. (2017). Means, motive and opportunity: Exploring board volunteering. *Personnel Review, 46*, 115–135.

Ward, K.D. (2014). Cultivating public service motivation through AmeriCorps service: A longitudinal study. *Public Administration Review, 74*, 114–125.

Wenzel, A.K., Krause, T.A., and Vogel, D. (2019). Making performance pay work: The impact of transparency, participation, and fairness on controlling perception and intrinsic motivation. *Review of Public Personnel Administration, 39*, 232–255.

Wittmer, D. (1991). Serving the people or serving for pay: Reward preferences among government, hybrid sector, and business managers. *Public Productivity and Management Review, 14*, 369–383.

Word, J., and Carpenter, H. (2013). The new public service? Applying the public service motivation model to nonprofit employees. *Public Personnel Management, 42*, 315–336.

Wright, B.E. (2007). Public service and motivation: Does mission matter? *Public Administration Review, 67*, 54–64.

Wright, B.E., and Christensen, R.K. (2010). Public service motivation: A test of the job attraction–selection–attrition model. *International Public Management Journal, 13*, 155–176.

Wright, B.E., Hassan, S., and Christensen, R.K. (2017). Job choice and performance: Revisiting core assumptions about public service motivation. *International Public Management Journal, 20*, 108–131.

10. Monetary and non-monetary compensation in for-profit, nonprofit, and public organizations: comparison and competition
Laura Langbein and Fei W. Roberts

INTRODUCTION

Regardless of the source of revenues, virtually all managers seek to improve organizational performance by recruiting and retaining the most productive employees. The means to accomplish this task depends, in part, on improving employees' work motivation. Motivation is a critical concept with both theoretical and practical implications in public and business administration, as well as in other fields such as economics and psychology (Deci et al., 1991; Ryan and Deci, 2000).

Motivation plays a large role in determining whether employees will choose to work in one organization rather than another, as well as whether they will work to enhance not only their own but also the organization's productivity. Both public and private organizations have undertaken numerous efforts to augment employee motivation. In private for-profit companies, for example, monetary incentive structures including short- and long-term mechanisms, such as raises, cash bonuses, profit sharing, and stock purchasing, are often utilized as a means to reinforce productive work (WorldatWork and Deloitte, 2014). By contrast, both public and private nonprofit organizations, and the employees who work there, face weaker connections between tangible rewards and employee or organizational performance. In these organizations, partly because productivity is hard to measure, earnings cannot legally be retained, and 'customers' usually provide only some or none of the revenues. In the face of this problem, unique to public and nonprofit organizations, top managers in these organizations borrowed monetary incentive mechanisms used in the private sector. Although highly controversial, examples such as the pay for performance system in governmental agencies were copied from the business sector as a means to enhance employee work motivation (Perry and Wise, 1990; Ingraham, 1993).

This chapter discusses the role of both monetary and non-monetary compensation in enhancing employee work motivation. We begin by discussing one of the most important forms of controlling incentives: money. We focus on the theory of wage determination and the likely reasons for differences in monetary compensation of employees between and within each sector. Compensation reflects agreement on the monetary value of what employees are willing to accept in wages and other monetizable benefits (e.g., health and retirement benefits), and what the employer is willing to pay. The second part of this chapter reviews literature regarding non-monetary aspects of compensation including intrinsic incentives and public service motivation (PSM). The chapter concludes with a discussion about the implications of these studies of employee motivation for future research on organizational performance and employee motivation.

WAGE DETERMINATION: THEORY

In the theoretical model of a competitive private sector, employees work to earn money to buy goods and services. Profit-seeking employers buy labor to produce goods and services that consumers are willing to pay for; they seek to make sure that the revenues from consumers exceed their costs of production. When there is competition between firms, the producers from one firm cannot control the market price that consumers pay: they cannot charge more than the competition for comparable output. Producers need labor; their demand for labor curve represents what employers are willing to pay for a particular amount of the labor. The supply of labor curve that employers face represents what employees are willing to accept for the purchase of the particular type of labor they provide. In a reasonably competitive market, the intersection of those two curves determines wages (Guell, 2007). The buyers of a particular type of labor may include private, profit-seeking businesses, as well as private nonprofit organizations seeking donations in order to provide goods or services to clients at costs that do not exceed revenues; even public organizations provide services to selected groups at costs that do not exceed a budget provided by taxpayers. Often, but not always, these different types of firms compete to hire similar types of labor.

In the private sector, each supplier tries to maximize profit, but competition among them means that none of them are actually able to do that. Some suppliers make a lot, some lose money, most make a little, but no one makes maximum profit, because no single supplier controls the market price of the good or service. That price affects the price that each supplier pays to labor. Each supplier can, however, control its own costs, including the number of and compensation paid to employees. Employees will prefer to work for employers who offer more; employers prefer employees who will work for less. The price will be a compromise. However, if there is just one buyer of labor (i.e., one employer), the buyer controls the price of labor. In this case, called a monopsony, that price will be lower than a competitive price.

Employee pay is a measure of productivity, meaning the employee's ability either to reduce costs or add to sales. In a competitive market, employers have an incentive to pay more to productive employees, and productive employees will prefer to work for employers who offer higher wages. In the private sector, each employer seeks buyers (demanders, or consumers) of their goods or services; the buyers provide revenues for the suppliers. Each consumer chooses whether and how much of the good or service to buy, at the price offered by the supplier. The market price is determined by the next, marginal, buyer, whose willingness to pay for the next item (e.g., the first, or maybe the second, or maybe yet another, slice of pizza), matches the marginal provider's willingness to sell. Note that, in this example, the first slice is probably worth more to the buyer than the third slice: if the buyer has already consumed two slices, benefits at the next margin drop, and the third slice of pizza may not be worth the price. The price that the supplier is willing to accept is partly determined by how much the employee in the kitchen is willing to accept for his/her labor, and partly determined by what the buyer is willing to pay.

This simple story of a competitive private market is driven by money: the buyer (the pizza consumer) wants the lowest price and the seller (who needs to match the employee pay, or willingness to work, with consumer willingness to pay) wants the highest price. But the buyer will not pay if the price exceeds how much he/she values the additional good or service, and the seller won't sell if the revenue is less than his/her production cost. In this world of a competitive private sector, given the preferences of the consumer and seller, money is all that matters; both sides of the exchange measure 'value' and 'cost' by money.

In the private market, the consumer can judge the value of a slice of pizza; additionally, consumption is immediate, and the consumer pays the cost, or walks away. By contrast, in the nonprofit and public sectors, neither the consumer nor the seller is entirely able to judge the value of the good or service. Further, the consumer of the good or service may not pay for the good or service at all, or the consumer pays only a portion of the cost. Consequently, the market does not reveal the monetary value of the good or service.

Further, the supplier of funds for most or all of the goods or services provided in the nonprofit sectors usually does not directly confront the consumer: the money suppliers (e.g., the taxpayers, the donors, or a third-party, like a health insurer) are not the direct suppliers (who govern the employees). Rather, the supplier of the good or service is in the middle. The supplier has to match the preferences of those who supply the money (e.g., taxpayers or donors) for the goods or services produced by the supplier with the costs of paying employees to provide those goods or services to the consumers, who pay only some or none of the costs of supply. There is no direct contact between the consumers of the good or service and the supplier of the money to cover the supply cost. Clearly, such a market is not likely to operate without losses to some party.

The next question is clear: why bother to provide these goods or services? Clearly, the services in the public and nonprofit sectors are usually provided because the competitive private market cannot provide them at all, or cannot provide them to satisfy both the buyer and the funder/taxpayer, or over- or under-provides the good or service at a cost to one side or the other. In other words, the goods and services in the public and nonprofit sector exist because they are expected to reduce 'failures' in the private market (Guell, 2007).

Among the most common reasons is that private markets are likely to 'fail' when the complete cost or value of goods and services is not readily apparent to either or both the buyers and sellers. One property of both public and nonprofit providers is that it is difficult to measure the value of the good or service that are consumed, which also makes it difficult to monetize the value of the labor that is employed in those sectors. Yet consumers often can choose to buy these goods or services (e.g., education, health, transportation, housing, even the arts) in any sector (private for-profit, public, nonprofit), and employees can choose to work for an employer in any one sector service (e.g., transportation, in any one of the three sectors). Consequently, the sector services are competitive and hence interdependent: consumers compare the visible price of goods and services supplied in each sector (e.g., education) and employees (e.g., teachers) compare the wages and other benefits of employment in each sector.

In many fields of employment, private for-profit, nonprofit, and public employers compete for the same employees. We discuss whether the market wage reflects a competitive monetary equilibrium among the three sectors, and also when non-monetary values affect the demand of employers for employees, or employees' willingness-to-accept an employer's wage offer, in the different sectors. While the good or service that public and nonprofit producers provide to users may differ from the goods or services in the private for-profit market, the public and nonprofit employers cannot ignore the for-profit market: all of the producers buy goods, services, and labor from the same private market. Because employees (labor) can choose employers, employers cannot ignore the competition: when the employees have choice, public and nonprofit employers cannot ignore the wages offered by private for-profit employers for the same comparable employees.

However, public and nonprofit providers provide a good that is rarely produced, or, more commonly, is produced for different reasons, by the for-profit market. Consequently, they face different conditions and costs of production, including wages, when compared to private producers. But no producer can ignore the competition from the other two sectors: the labor they hire can choose to work in other jobs or the same type of job in different sectors. More generally, when goods and services are produced in different sectors, neither the employers, employees, nor consumers ignore the other sectors. Those who study wage determination should not ignore that interdependence either.

DETERMINANTS OF WAGES: SECTOR DIFFERENCES

A substantial body of research in economics and public administration compares wages as well as differences in the determinants of wage differentials across sectors. (See, for example: Smith, 1976a, 1976b; Lewis, 1986; Langbein and Lewis, 1998; Llorens, Wenger, and Kellough, 2007.) Langbein and Lewis (1998) noted that the economists' approach to studying wage comparisons starts by comparing workers with equivalent characteristics such as age, experience, and educational attainment, whereas the government's approach compares seemingly equivalent jobs. But the jobs, even if they look similar, may not be equivalent. For instance, since they do not seek profit, jobs (e.g., preschool teaching; electrical engineering; law; nursing) in the public and nonprofit sectors have a different purpose than a similarly labeled job in the private for-profit sector. Moreover, jobs in the government provide quasi or pure public goods; competitive private profit-seeking employers will not normally supply these jobs (e.g., many types of lawyers or police). The relative absence of private suppliers in jobs that commonly provide public or quasi-public goods or services (e.g., the military) makes it difficult to compare pay across sectors. Nonetheless, pay comparisons may be appropriate in occupations where there are many employers (and hence, many employees) in each of the public, private for-profit, and nonprofit sectors (e.g., nurses; doctors; teachers; lawyers; accountants; engineers; clerical staff; personnel specialists). More narrow pay comparisons may suffice in jobs largely provided in one sector. However, it is important to note that even largely public jobs (e.g., police, military) are also provided by employers in the private and nonprofit sectors, so wage competition across sectors cannot be assumed to be nonexistent even in those jobs.

It is common to assume that employees in the public and nonprofit sectors are distinctively motivated by the personal satisfaction of doing the work or providing the service, likely to be inadequately provided in the profit-seeking part of the private sector. Nonetheless, even in the public and nonprofit sectors, money matters to employees, especially to those at lower ends of the wage scale. Employees at lower organizational levels focus more on extrinsic rewards including wages and job security compared to those at higher levels (Rainey, 2014). Of course, other aspects of employment choice, besides money, affect wages. These include amenities in the local area, the specific occupational sector (e.g., the type of nurse and supply of that type relative to competitive opportunities nearby), numerous personal characteristics besides education and experience, and other factors as well.

The next section examines previous research on the relative importance of factors that appear to affect wages. We also consider other factors that may have a less clear relation to productivity, which is a clear determinant of wages in the private sector. We point to areas where more research is warranted, but the overall theme is that the story of wage determination can ignore neither the big picture (e.g., the industry and comparable jobs, and wages, in other sectors) nor the details of the particular employee-employer match.

WAGE DETERMINATION: FROM SIMPLICITY TO DETAIL AND COMPLEXITY

Wage determination models in economics began with the simple model proposed by Mincer (1974). The model included only two variables: education and, in diminishing returns, years of experience. That model is now regarded as both woefully incomplete and maybe even causally incorrect (Das and Polachek, 2019). First, education and experience may both be endogenous to wages: they may affect wages, but wages also directly affect the incentive and ability to acquire education and experience. Further, the relation between wages and these variables reveals large differences both cross-sectionally and over time. Adding to the complexity, both education and experience are incomplete measures of the fundamental underlying concept of human capital and ability. They may be biased indicators as well: they may be better measures for some occupations and tasks (e.g., complex but repetitive) than others. Further, evidence suggests that the two variables are not separable: the impact of education and experience are jointly dependent. In other words, they interact (and their effects are probably not linear) (Heckman, Lochner, and Todd, 2003).

Nearly all common models examine the impact of variables like education and experience, as well as other properties that employees can deliberately change, on the compensation of employees with different characteristics at a single point in time. Yet, because causes precede effects, temporal models provide a more complete identification of causal effects of variables that can change over time for each unit of analysis. While the equation form is probably log linear, models that estimate the compensation returns to human capital need not only account for time, but also must account for numerous other variables. In addition to education and experience, that list might include: age; occupation; industry; gender; race/color; family structure;[1] immigrant status; early childhood/preschool interventions; an indicator for the year of the measurement, and another for the specific firm or organization; firm or organization size in the year of measurement; location of the employment (an indicator for many unobservables, including amenities valued by the employee that may confer monopsony power on the employer) (Bruekner and Newmark, 2014); market structure within the relevant industry and occupation sector; laws in the governing area (e.g., minimum wage; union regulations); type of payment arrangement between employee and employer, including arrangements for wage increases; and, last but not least important, employee personality, or 'soft skills' (Heckman, Stixrud, and Urzua, 2006; Heckman and Kautz, 2012).

Many of these variables may be endogenous to wages, including education, experience, 'ability,' arrangements for wage increases and other job-related amenities, and even soft skills. Collectively, with respect to their possible impact on employee compensation, these are all indicators of 'human capital,' raising at least two additional research questions: is human capital homogeneous and are there interactions among all these variables?

Previous research indicates the presence of many of these complexities (Heckman, Lochner, and Todd, 2003). For example, while most models show that formal schooling raises productivity, the causal direction, and even the sign, of the link is not clear. While additional compensation raises the recipient's demand for schooling, it may also raise the wages foregone while in school, reducing the demand for more education relative to work. Additionally, the meaning of 'schooling' is not clear. Compared to years of schooling, there is evidence that finishing a degree on time (the 'sheepskin effect') signals persistence (Hungerford and Solon, 1987), which employers also value, but they probably value it differently than years of school. With respect to interactions, it is likely that the production function (the monetary return to the employer of an employee's indicators of human capital) varies by occupation and job function.

Moreover, selection into occupations and particular types of jobs reflects aspects of human capital that are difficult to measure, including both ability (hard skills) and personality (soft skills). For example, some persons appear to be able to create new human capital from previous human capital, which is a type of ability that is likely to matter for earnings. This is a temporal change that reflects many unmeasurable properties. Thus, the determinants of compensation should account not only for numerous differences between employees, but also how they change over time (Heckman, Lochner, and Todd, 2003). Overall, findings from previous research suggest that, while formal years of schooling are relevant for earnings differences, they actually play a limited role in explaining those differences. Concepts like the 'ability to learn and retain knowledge' are arguably more important (Griliches, 1977; Card, 1994), but largely unobservable. In conclusion, with respect to wage determinants, the Mincer model may no longer produce even roughly valid and generalizable estimates of rates of return to schooling or experience.

The properties of the local market describing the employer-employee pair also affect employee wages. For example, while many of these pairs, depending on their location, face competition from other employers and jobseekers in the public, nonprofit, and for-profit sectors, others show properties of monopsony or monopoly. For example, health is an area with providers in all three sectors, and so is higher education. By contrast, police/corrections and kindergarten through 12th grade education (K-12) are dominated by public providers. The implication is that, while public providers may compete among themselves, the large size of many local governance districts limits employee mobility (especially for married women) and may confer some wage price control on some public providers (e.g., police and K-12 education). This is a monopsony advantage of being a single buyer of the skill. It follows that salaries may be 'too low,' with the consequence of low employee quality (Mukherjee, 2011). On the other side, monopoly public services, such as regulated utilities, may have pricing power relative to their customers, and may overpay employees with competing opportunities. Alternatively, regardless of monopoly or monopsony power, the sector of employment may not matter at all with respect to jobs (like engineering) that have alternatives in many industries, competitive or not (Bysted and Hansen, 2015).

EMPIRICAL EVIDENCE: WAGE DETERMINATION IN THE PUBLIC SECTOR

Compensation of the public workforce is an area of controversy among both policymakers and the public. Voters and politicians almost universally think that public employees are overpaid (Mettler, 2014; Bysted and Hansen, 2015; Lucia, 2020). On the other side, scholars tend to worry about the likely result of that judgment: underpayment and consequential poor quality in the public sector.

This section examines previous research regarding the determinants of wages in the public sector, with a focus on whether and how the private for-profit, nonprofit, and the public labor markets influence each other in determining wages, as well as the direction of the differences.

Literature assessing the determinants of wage differentials in the three market sectors is particularly significant in labor economics (Smith, 1976a, 1976b; Ruhm and Borkoski, 2003). There is also complementary literature in public management on public-private differences that also provides information about factors that contribute to wage gaps between sectors. While demographic characteristics such as experience, age, educational attainment, gender, marital status, race, and many other factors (Blinder, 1973; Mincer, 1974; Smith, 1976a, 1976b; Lewis, 1986) are always relevant, they may operate differently in the public than in the private sectors. Moreover, factors such as perceived sexual and racial discrimination that relate to wage differences can also contribute to an individual's preference for work in one sector rather than another (Bergmann, 1971; Llorens, Wenger, and Kellough, 2007). Further, the organizational and institutional setting of the public organization is very different from private organizations. For example, private sector employment is at will, so that continued employment in both private for-profit and nonprofit sectors is less secure than public employment, where job security may be more protected. The competitive market, dominated by for-profit organizations, adjusts by offering higher pay for riskier, including at-will, jobs (Ramoni-Perazzi and Bellante, 2007).

More importantly, unlike private for-profit companies whose primary goal is to seek to maximize profit in a competitive environment, governmental (and nonprofit) agencies have different goals than private sector organizations and usually operate in a less competitive environment. Specifically, public and nonprofit goals are both difficult to measure, and pursuing them may not contribute to profit in a competitive environment (Meier and Bohte, 2007; Mettler, 2014). For example, a commonly held expectation is that governmental agencies serve as a role model for private firms by offering equal opportunities and compensation to people of different backgrounds (Melly, 2005; Riccucci and Van Ryzin, 2017), which may be more costly than compensation in similar profit-seeking organizations. Public agencies are also expected to provide safety net programs and serve clients who not only cannot pay but also may be especially costly to treat. Similarly, another common expectation is that the public sector may also lack incentives to reduce their costs due to a lack of competition (Langbein and Lewis, 1998).

Public ownership and goal ambiguity lead to other likely differences between public and private for-profit organizations including political influence and conflicting preferences among government (or governing) principals with oversight authority (Appleby, 1945; Allison, 1980; Bozeman, 1987; Scott and Falcone, 1998; Rainey and Bozeman, 2000; Campw and Gaes, 2002; Goodsell, 2007; Amirkhanyan, Kim, and Lambright, 2008; Meier and O'Toole, 2011). In terms of employee compensation, employees in private for-profit organizations are likely to face fewer politically motivated or other administrative constraints and consequently have more discretion compared to their public counterparts (Feeney and Rainey, 2009; Meier and O'Toole, 2011). In this regard, because for-profit organizations may have higher levels of flexibility in personnel management, they may be able to offer higher (efficiency) wages to retain particularly qualified job candidates (Rainey, 2014). Some state and local governments also conduct pay comparability studies to keep pace with wages offered by the private sector to remain competitive (Smith, 1976b; Langbein and Lewis, 1998; Rainey, 2014). However, because the goals of public organizations compared to either type of private organization are so disparate, seemingly similar job classifications may require different competencies. Overall, there appears to be consensus that wage determination in the public sector is distinctively different from the other two sectors, but there is no consensus about the magnitude of a wage difference (Ramoni-Perazzi and Bellante, 2006).

THE DISTRIBUTION OF WAGES BETWEEN SECTORS AND WITHIN THE WORKPLACE

Wage competition between the sectors depends, at least in part, on the particular skill level of the task the employer seeks. Automation in the private sector may explain why, in relatively recent years, wages at the top in the private sector have increased more than at the bottom. Nonetheless, since 1970, there has been a significant relative compression of the wage distribution in the public sector (Katz and Krueger, 1991; Borjas, 2002). Accordingly, the distribution of wages in the private sector (the difference between the top and bottom) exceeds that in the public sector, and that distance is driven by the larger wages at the top of the private sector rather than smaller wages at the bottom. As a result, it is increasingly more difficult to attract and retain high-skill workers in the public sector. Consequently, private sector workers who belong to highly skilled groups (such as some college graduates), or who have relatively high earnings within a particular skill group, have reduced incentives to enter the public workforce. Additionally, similar public sector workers who belong to highly skilled groups, or with relatively high incomes within a particular skill group, will have increased incentives to leave the public sector and enter private sector jobs. In short, the relative changes in the wage structure influence labor supply decisions, implying competition between the sectors to the detriment of the public sector employee at the local, state, and federal level, with the result of sorting the top quality into the private sector.[2]

Some studies examine wage competition at the local level, comparing private wages to the wages of state and local government workers in the same area. For example, Munnell et al. (2011) examine whether wages in the state-local sector, particularly when adjusted for the higher educational attainment of public sector workers, are lower than those in the nearby private sector. State and local employees, overall, have more education than private sector workers, since they are more likely to have white collar jobs: 52 percent have a college degree, compared to 35 percent in the private sector. Fringe benefits (pensions, retiree health insurance, and other amenities) might also offset the expected lower public wages. Another implicit fringe benefit is job security, usually assumed to be higher in the public sector, also implying a downward pressure on public wages. But, during the recession, public employment dropped more than in the private sector, so the overall effect of job security may not be clear. Putting aside job security, empirical results show that compensation overall in the public sector is about 4 percent less than in the comparable private sector, implying that state-local public employee wages, overall, are about equal to comparable private sector compensation. The implication is that the state/local compensation benefits may offset the seemingly apparent private sector wage premium.

But there is another source of wage differences: there are wage differences within an organization. Comparing for-profit to nonprofit organizations, Leete (2000) hypothesizes that nonprofit organizations rely on intrinsically motivated employees. While for-profit organizations produce goods that carry a visible monetary value, nonprofit organizations are likely to be more oriented to customer service rather than personal and company monetary return, carrying less or invisible monetary value. Consequently, public and nonprofit organizations are more likely to hire white collar employees whose relatively high salaries (compared to blue collar jobs more likely to be found in the for-profit sector) allow them to be intrinsically motivated to public service rather than require extra compensation at each salary margin. Thus, because nonprofit organizations (public and private) are more likely to deliver skilled white collar services rather than goods or routine services, wage differences between the highest and lowest paid workers may be less in nonprofit than for-profit organizations.

Using a time series cross-section regression with numerous controls,[3] Leete (2000) found that wage differences within a competitive for-profit enterprise are in fact larger than wage differences within a comparable nonprofit sector business. Nonprofit organizations are also supposed to be more oriented to 'fairness.' Accordingly, Leete (2000) also found that race and gender wage differences were smaller in the nonprofit sector as compared to salary differences within comparable organizations in the for-profit sector. Yet, from the perspective of competitive employment markets based on wages, wage levels and wage differences within comparable for- and nonprofit organizations should be the same.

Continuing with the issue of wage differences that appear not to reflect productivity differences, wage raises sometimes seem too high to be consistent with encouraging greater supply: the high salary at the top does not necessarily reflect personal productivity. While this seems strange using the logic of economics, it is comprehensible from the perspective of psychology, where both relative difference and absolute value matter (James, 2005; Kuvaas et al., 2017). High salaries at the top are chosen because the allure of the president's salary makes the workers below the top more productive over their careers as they compete for the next promotion. In other words, the larger the spread between the winner's and loser's prize raises the effort of both. If the prize money is split evenly between winner and loser, there is little incentive to win. However, if the president earns significantly more than the vice president, the VPs will work hard to win the president's job. Consistent with the idea of the attractiveness of relative pay differences, managers at all levels are compensated in part based on the deviation of their own firm's performance from industry performance. This is also what one would observe in any relative compensation 'game,' similar to the scheme that one normally observes in tournaments.

But psychology also predicts that wage inequality may induce wasteful effort by employees. Personnel departments often argue that wages must tend toward equality, because a salary structure that is too closely related to differences in individual productivity creates morale problems and destroys the team spirit of an organization. The implication is that firms that rely on cooperation may find that a more equal wage distribution enhances cooperative effort and increases productivity. In addition, if firms cannot monitor the output of workers perfectly, which is more likely in the nonprofit and public sectors, then workers have an incentive to exaggerate their output and lobby for higher wages. Ignoring some worker claims might be an optimal response to this problem, since it reduces the time wasted on internal politics (Milgrom, 1988). But, when output is hard to monitor, unequal pay is not always optimal, but nor is equal pay: it may reduce individual productivity more than it enhances cooperation. Overall, it is not empirically or theoretically clear whether or how wage inequality within an organization affects productivity. It is likely that the effect may be different in for-profit than other organizations, but that too is unanswered at this point.

THE PUZZLE OF THE PUBLIC SECTOR: PAY FROM NON-USERS WHILE COMPETING WITH THE PRIVATE SECTOR

Unlike wages in the private sector, wage determination in the public sector is not mostly driven by revenues from consumers, but by mandatory revenues from taxpayers, most of whom are not consumers of the specific good funded by the budget in question. Governments alter overall wage levels in response to economic conditions that are likely to affect government budgets and the tax base (Katz and Krueger, 1991). In sectors and jobs where money is an important motivator for employees, the likely consequence is higher quit rates for skilled public employees (e.g., engineers), and declining indicators of quality (e.g., students' math SAT scores) for public relative to private employers of workers (e.g., teachers) in the same industry.

Many other factors make wage determination in the public sector fundamentally different from wage determination in the private sector (Bullock, Stritch, and Rainey, 2015). The public (and nonprofit) sector provides goods and services that cannot or will not be distributed by markets. As we noted above, these usually are goods and services that are hard for both consumers and producers to value, often because the value is often not apparent at all or not until many years after the exchange. These conditions lead to distinctive behaviors, structures, and processes in public and nonprofit organizations (e.g., Dahl and Lindblom, 1953; Downs, 1967; Wamsley and Zald, 1973; Warwick, 1975) suggesting that public and nonprofit employees may have goals that differ from private sector workers, especially when the output is particularly difficult to measure. Consequently, public and nonprofit sector employees may place less importance on high income from their work than private for-profit sector employees. The expectation is that, compared to their private sector counterparts, they will have higher levels of public service-oriented motives and identify their work as being socially important (Bullock, Stritch, and Rainey, 2015).

Considerable evidence supports this conjecture, but much of that evidence looks at wage or job satisfaction rather than actual compensation. For example, Bullock, Stritch, and Rainey (2015), Lee and Whitford (2008), Kuvaas et al. (2017), and Wang, Yang, and Wang (2012) find that normative values (PSM, social importance, organizational commitment, importance of money income) appear to increase satisfaction with pay or just overall job satisfaction, using many statistical controls. Yet none of these papers examines actual pay. Further, the relation between satisfaction and intrinsic motives may well be endogenous, especially since these variables are both subjective survey responses from the same respondent.

It is also important to remember that for-profit, nonprofit, and public sectors are not independent. In most cases, they compete for the same workers, and also provide comparable services. Thus, what goes on in one sector of a service provided in multiple sectors (e.g., health, education, public safety, research, automation, etc.) is not independent of what goes on in other sectors. Even at relatively high levels of pay in the nonprofit sector, and with controls for standard Mincer and other variables, including indicators for geographic location and the specific field of the organizational service, McGinnis Johnson and Ng (2016) provide evidence that, among experienced (older) managers, lower current pay levels by their current nonprofit employer appear to induce 'sector switching intentions' toward the for-profit and public sectors. The implication is that academic comparisons of actual and perceived levels of compensation between sectors must account for the interaction not only within but between sectors.

THE PUZZLE OF NON-MONETARY INCENTIVES: COMPLEMENT OR SUBSTITUTE FOR MONEY?

A growing literature in economics and public administration focuses on the role of non-monetary incentives in employment, particularly in public and nonprofit employment (Lazear, 1991; Leete, 2000). The field of psychology initially identified two types of incentives that motivate individual behavior: basic human needs as well as extrinsic incentives (Sansone and Harackiewicz, 2000). Extrinsic incentives refer to the use of external rewards or punishments to induce certain behaviors (Lawler, 1971; Ryan and Deci, 2000; Rainey, 2014). Rewards such as salary and bonuses, promotions, enhanced working conditions, employee benefits, as well as more coercive approaches, such as deadlines, directions from supervisors, and punishments, can all be classified into this category. In real life, we can find a wide variety of examples using extrinsic rewards to induce behavioral changes, such as granting citizenship to non-citizens in exchange for military service and giving gifts and monetary rewards to voters who showed up in an election in the early history of the US (Panagopoulos, 2013).

However, scholars later found that these two types of incentives offer an incomplete explanation of human behavior: people are also motivated by intrinsic incentives, which refers to 'doing an activity for the inherent satisfaction of the activity itself' (Ryan and Deci, 2000, p. 71). The importance of intrinsic motivation is supported by a large number of theories of motivation. For instance, among the numerous taxonomies of individual needs, Maslow's seminal work (1954) classified different needs into five hierarchies: physiological, safety, social, esteem, and self-actualization. He argued the highest level is self-actualization, which was defined as fulfilling one's potential and becoming a person that they strive to be. Self-actualization goes beyond simply doing things for individual content but also includes dedication to missions in order to serve the interests of the society (Rainey, 2014).

Influenced by Maslow's work, McGregor (1960) proposed Theory Y as a new management theory focusing on employee self-fulfillment and motivation through management strategies such as decentralization, employee participation, and implementation of performance appraisal. Even public choice theory, which portrays bureaucrats as self-interested utility maximizers interested in extrinsic rewards such as prestige, power, and budget, consider that bureaucrats may also be driven by a desire to advocate for certain policy issues or to serve the interests of the general public (Tullock, 1965; Downs, 1967; Niskanen, 1971; Langbein, 1982).

Intrinsic motivation is particularly relevant in public administration as there is a substantial body of work that suggests people choosing to work in the public sector are motivated by different factors compared to those entering the private workforce. Moreover, people in certain professions or at higher organizational levels in the public sector earn less income than their private counterparts (Langbein and Lewis, 1998; Donahue, 2008; Delfgaauw and Dur, 2010; Rainey, 2014; Congressional Budget Office, 2017), yet lower earnings do not discourage them from working in the public sector. While money is important, its marginal value may decrease relative to other values. Public employees may place more emphasis on intrinsic goals such as the willingness to serve the public interest, making a positive impact on society, and helping people in need, compared to people entering the private, especially for-profit, sector (Feeney and Rainey, 2009; Rainey, 2014; Bullock, Stritch, and Rainey, 2015).

Another important factor that contributes to people's decision to enter the public workforce is PSM, defined as 'an individual's predisposition to respond to motives grounded primarily or uniquely in public institutions and organizations' (Perry and Wise, 1990, p. 368). It can be divided into three categories: instrumental, norm based, and affective motives (Perry and Wise, 1990). More specifically, PSM includes instrumental motives when individuals are attracted to public employment that enables them to participate in policy formulation and implementation processes for the purpose of pursuing special interests or self-identification (Perry and Wise, 1990). PSM also includes norm-based motives when some individuals working in public organizations have a desire to serve the interest of society as a whole as well as the interests of minority groups to enhance social equity, and 'loyalty to duty and to the government' (Perry and Wise, 1990, p. 369). Finally, PSM consists of affective motives including patriotism, benevolence, and a strong belief of the social importance of a program (Perry and Wise, 1990). Perry, Hondeghem, and Wise (2010) further distinguish among altruism, prosocial motivation, intrinsic motivation, and PSM. Altruism and prosocial motivation are more broadly and generally constructed. By contrast, intrinsic motivation, as mentioned earlier, includes attaining personal pleasure from certain behaviors. The difference is that obtaining personal pleasure is not a major component of PSM (Perry, Hondeghem, and Wise, 2010).

Since the publication of the seminal work by Perry and Wise (1990), PSM theory has generated immense scholarly interest and has become a subject of considerable theoretical and empirical investigation across countries in the past three decades. This stream of literature generally suggests that PSM is associated with a greater preference for public employment, higher employee satisfaction, and lower turnover rates (see Perry, Hondeghem, and Wise (2010) and the literature cited therein).

These non-monetary incentives, in theory, can be a substitute for money: for example, employees may accept lower pay for more job discretion. However, some non-monetary incentives, like PSM to serve the people most in need, may complement pay, making them costly to the employer, but may also increase employee productivity.

Some argue that motivation entirely through pay is ineffective and even counterproductive because it causes workers to lose interest in their intrinsically interesting job. In fact, a considerable body of scholarship in public administration and psychology suggests crowding-out effects of extrinsic incentives on both intrinsic motivation as well as PSM (see Deci, 1971; Deci and Porac, 1978; Frey, 1994; Deci, Koestner, and Ryan, 1999; Ryan and Deci, 2000; Frey and Jegen, 2001; James, 2005; Georgellis, Iossa, and Tabvuma, 2010).

For example, Frey (2017), Lazear (1991), and Carpenter and Gong (2016) have argued that there is an economic logic to the notion that extrinsic rewards can actually have a negative effect on effort. They explain that people who decide about incentives overestimate the role of money as a motivator, especially in white collar jobs where output is hard to measure. Pay for performance intends to raise performance by making compensation dependent on performance measured in a predetermined way and rewarded by a predetermined monetary amount. While this may work for training the family dog, empirical evidence demonstrates that pay for performance, especially when quality counts but is hard to measure, leads to undesired worker performance: quantity is substituted for quality.

As a policy consequence, the government, as well as nonprofit charitable and humanitarian organizations, should be very careful before they institute pay for performance schemes due to the risk of crowding-out better performance (Georg, Kube, and Zultan, 2010). Frey (2017) and Lazear (1991) also argue that an inappropriately designed compensation scheme can even be counterproductive. For example, a piece rate that is tied to quantity and ignores quality will induce the worker to produce lower quality items. Thus, when output is not easily observable, exclusive reliance on monetary motivation may actually be counterproductive.

In addition, higher salaries may not always attract more productive employees, especially when quality is hard to measure. Using a formal model, Barigozzi, Burani, and Raggia (2018) show that, when workers are heterogeneous with respect to characteristics (productivity and motivation) that are not observable to their employers, higher salaries may actually attract less productive workers. They also point to empirical evidence from many sources and countries (field experiments, and quasi-experimental studies of teachers and other bureaucrats) that support the formal model. The conclusion is that, under circumstances common in the public and nonprofit sector, a wage increase as a policy to overcome a labor shortage may trigger a decrease in the average ability of the workforce together with a decrease in average motivation.

IMPLICATIONS FOR PUBLIC ADMINISTRATION SCHOLARS AND PRACTITIONERS

In this chapter, we reviewed major theories of motivation and discussed extrinsic, intrinsic, and PSM. But after all, why should we spend so much time studying different types of motivation in public administration? The answer is obvious: motivation can improve performance. Therefore, it is critical for scholars and practitioners in public administration to examine approaches to improve employee motivation for the purpose of augmenting performance.

However, there are several caveats that scholars and practitioners need to be aware of. First, motivation alone does not improve productivity (Rainey, 2014), and nor does money. Other factors, such as ability, interact with motivation and thus they should also be considered. Second, a vast array of arguments and evidence suggests that extrinsic incentives can depress intrinsic motivation under certain conditions. Thus, it is important that public managers take into consideration the complex relationship between these two types of incentives when designing incentive structures. Finally, as a large number of public administration scholars have already cautioned, we need to account for the differences between public and private organizations when learning and applying theories and practices from economics and business administration (Waldo, 1948; Ingraham, 1993; Rainey, 2014).

NOTES

1. Such as marital status, number of children, amount of parent time spent with children, etc.
2. A more recent analysis suggests that, compared to (large) private firms, there is, overall, a public wage premium of about 14 percent. However, that premium does not exist at the state and local level. Further, among workers in the federal government, the premium is largest among workers with the lowest education, and it disappears among the most recent workers with graduate education. While the overall findings are different, the results also imply likely current retention problems among the highest skill federal workers. (See Biggs and Richwine, 2011.)
3. Experience, gender, ESL, hours worked, race, education (detailed dummies); occupation (white collar (executive vs not)/blue collar); industry (finance/real estate/entertainment/professional services).

REFERENCES

Allison, G.T. (1980). *Public and private management: Are they fundamentally alike in all unimportant respects?* Cambridge, MA: John F. Kennedy School of Government, Harvard University, pp. 283–298.

Amirkhanyan, A.A., Kim, H.J., and Lambright, K.T. (2008). Does the public sector outperform the nonprofit and for-profit sectors? Evidence from a national panel study on nursing home quality and access. *Journal of Policy Analysis and Management: The Journal of the Association for Public Policy Analysis and Management, 27*, 326–353.

Appleby, P.H. (1945). Government is different. In J.M. Shafritz, A.C. Hyde, and S.J. Parkes (eds), *Classics of public administration* (5th edn). Belmont, CA: Thomson/Wadsworth, 2004, pp. 131–135.

Barigozzi, F., Burani, N., and Raggi, D. (2018). Productivity crowding-out in labor markets with motivated workers. *Journal of Economic Behavior and Organization, 151*, 199–218.

Bergmann, B.R. (1971). The effect on white incomes of discrimination in employment. *Journal of Political Economy, 79*, 294–313.

Biggs, A.G., and Richwine, J. (2011). Comparing federal and private sector compensation. *American Enterprise Institute Working Paper*, 2011-02.

Blinder, A.S. (1973). Wage discrimination: Reduced form and structural estimates. *Journal of Human resources, 8*, 436–455.

Borjas, G.J. (2002). *The wage structure and the sorting of workers into the public sector* (No. w9313). National Bureau of Economic Research.

Bozeman, B. (1987). *All organizations are public: Bridging public and private organizational theories.* San Francisco, CA: Jossey-Bass.

Brueckner, J.K., and Neumark, D. (2014). Beaches, sunshine, and public sector pay theory and evidence on amenities and rent extraction by government workers. *American Economic Journal: Economic Policy, 6*, 198–230.

Bullock, J.B., Stritch, J.M., and Rainey, H.G. (2015). International comparison of public and private employees' work motives, attitudes, and perceived rewards. *Public Administration Review, 75*, 479–489.

Bysted, R., and Hansen, J.R. (2015). Comparing public and private sector employees' innovative behaviour: Understanding the role of job and organizational characteristics, job types, and subsectors. *Public Management Review, 17*, 698–717.

Camp, S.D., and Gaes, G.G. (2002). Growth and quality of US private prisons: Evidence from a national survey. *Criminology and Public Policy, 1*, 427–450.

Card, D. (1994). *Earnings, schooling, and ability revisited* (No. w4832). National Bureau of Economic Research.

Carpenter, J., and Gong, E. (2016). Motivating agents: How much does the mission matter? *Journal of Labor Economics, 34*, 211–236.

Congressional Budget Office. (2017). Comparing the compensation of federal and private-sector employees, 2011 to 2015. Retrieved on June 20, 2020 from https://www.cbo.gov/publication/52637.

Dahl, R.A., and Lindblom, C.E. (1953). *Politics, economics and welfare: planning and politico-economic systems, resolved into basic processes.* New York, NY: Harper and Brothers.

Das, T., and Polachek, S.W. (2019). Microfoundations of earnings differences. In T. Raa and W. H. Greene (eds), *The Palgrave handbook of economic performance analysis.* Cham, Switzerland: Palgrave Macmillan, pp. 9–76.

Deci, E.L. (1971). Effects of externally mediated rewards on intrinsic motivation. *Journal of Personality and Social Psychology, 18*, 105–115.

Deci, E.L., and Porac, J. (1978). Cognitive evaluation theory and the study of human motivation. In M.R. Lepper and D. Greene (eds), *The hidden costs of reward: New perspectives on the psychology of human motivation.* New York, NY: Psychology Press, pp. 149–176.

Deci, E.L., Vallerand, R.J., Pelletier, L.G., and Ryan, R.M. (1991). Motivation and education: The self-determination perspective. *Educational Psychologist, 26*, 325–346.

Deci, E.L., Koestner, R., and Ryan, R.M. (1999). A meta-analytic review of experiments examining the effects of extrinsic rewards on intrinsic motivation. *Psychological Bulletin, 125*, 627–668.

Delfgaauw, J., and Dur, R. (2010). Managerial talent, motivation, and self-selection into public management. *Journal of Public Economics, 94*, 654–660.

Donahue, J.D. (2008). *The warping of government work*. Cambridge, MA: Harvard University Press.
Downs, A. (1967). *Inside bureaucracy*. New York, NY: Little, Brown.
Feeney, M.K., and Rainey, H.G. (2009). Personnel flexibility and red tape in public and nonprofit organizations: Distinctions due to institutional and political accountability. *Journal of Public Administration Research and Theory*, 20, 801–826.
Frey, B.S. (1994). How intrinsic motivation is crowded out and in. *Rationality and Society*, 6, 334–352.
Frey, B. (2017). Policy consequences of pay-for-performance and crowding-out. *Journal of Behavioral Economics for Policy*, 1, 55–59.
Frey, B.S., and Jegen, R. (2001). Motivation crowding theory. *Journal of Economic Surveys*, 15, 589–611.
Georgellis, Y., Iossa, E., and Tabvuma, V. (2010). Crowding out intrinsic motivation in the public sector. *Journal of Public Administration Research and Theory*, 21, 473–493.
Goerg, S.J., Kube, S., and Zultan, R.I. (2010). Treating equals unequally: Incentives in teams, workers' motivation, and production technology. *Journal of Labor Economics*, 28, 747–772.
Goodsell, C.T. (2007). Six normative principles for the contracting-out debate. *Administration and Society*, 38, 669–688.
Griliches, Z. (1977). Estimating the returns to schooling: Some econometric problems. *Econometrica: Journal of the Econometric Society*, 45, 1–22.
Guell, R.C. (2007). *Issues in economics today* (4th edn). New York, NY: McGraw-Hill-Irwin.
Heckman, J.J., and Kautz, T. (2012). Hard evidence on soft skills. *Labor Economics*, 19, 451–464.
Heckman, J.J., Lochner, L.J., and Todd, P.E. (2003). *Fifty years of Mincer earnings regressions* (No. w9732). National Bureau of Economic Research.
Heckman, J.J., Stixrud, J., and Urzua, S. (2006). The effects of cognitive and noncognitive abilities on labor market outcomes and social behavior. *Journal of Labor economics*, 24, 411–482.
Hungerford, T., and Solon, G. (1987). Sheepskin effects in the returns to education. *The Review of Economics and Statistics*, 69, 175–177.
Ingraham, P.W. (1993). Of pigs in pokes and policy diffusion: Another look at pay-for-performance. *Public Administration Review*, 53, 348–356.
James, Jr, H.S. (2005). Why did you do that? An economic examination of the effect of extrinsic compensation on intrinsic motivation and performance. *Journal of Economic Psychology*, 26, 549–566.
Katz, L.F., and Krueger, A.B. (1991). *Changes in the structure of wages in the public and private sectors* (No. w3667). National Bureau of Economic Research.
Kuvaas, B., Buch, R., Weibel, A., Dysvik, A., and Nerstad, C.G. (2017). Do intrinsic and extrinsic motivation relate differently to employee outcomes? *Journal of Economic Psychology*, 61, 244–258.
Langbein, L.I. (1982). The Section 8-Existing Housing program's administrative fee structure: A formal model of bureau behavior with empirical evidence. *Public Choice*, 39, 371–386.
Langbein, L., and Lewis, G. (1998). Pay, productivity, and the public sector: The case of electrical engineers. *Journal of Public Administration Research and Theory*, 8, 391–412.
Lawler, E.L. (1971). *Pay and organization effectiveness: A psychological view*. New York, NY: McGraw-Hill.
Lazear, E.P. (1991). Labor economics and the psychology of organizations. *Journal of Economic Perspectives*, 5, 89–110.
Lee, S.Y., and Whitford, A.B. (2008). Exit, voice, loyalty, and pay: Evidence from the public workforce. *Journal of Public Administration Research and Theory*, 18, 647–671.
Leete, L. (2000). Wage equity and employee motivation in nonprofit and for-profit organizations. *Journal of Economic Behavior and Organization*, 43, 423–446.
Lewis, H.G. (1986). Union relative wage effects. *Handbook of labor economics*, 2, 1139–1181.
Llorens, J.J., Wenger, J.B., and Kellough, J.E. (2007). Choosing public sector employment: The impact of wages on the representation of women and minorities in state bureaucracies. *Journal of Public Administration Research and Theory*, 18, 397–413.
Lucia, Bill (2020). Cut the bureaucracy taxpayers vs. clients 'a safety net that's ripped' problems plague state unemployment systems. July 11. Retrieved on June 11, 2020 from https://www.routefifty.com/management/2020/07/unemployment-states-problems-coronavirus-delays-benefits/166817/.
Maslow, A.H. (1954). *Motivation and personality*. New York, NY: Harper and Row.

McGinnis Johnson, J., and Ng, E.S. (2016). Money talks or millennials walk: The effect of compensation on nonprofit millennial workers sector-switching intentions. *Review of Public Personnel Administration*, *36*, 283–305.

McGregor, D. (1960). *The human side of enterprise*. New York, NY: McGraw-Hill.

Meier, K.J., and Bohte, J. (2007). *Politics and the bureaucracy: Policymaking in the fourth branch of government*. Belmont, CA: Wadsworth.

Meier, K.J., and O'Toole Jr, L.J. (2011). Comparing public and private management: Theoretical expectations. *Journal of Public Administration Research and Theory*, *21*, i283–i299.

Melly, B. (2005). Public-private sector wage differentials in Germany: Evidence from quantile regression. *Empirical Economics*, *30*, 505–520.

Mettler, S. (2014). *Degrees of inequality: How the politics of higher education sabotaged the American dream*. New York, NY: Basic Books.

Milgrom, P.R. (1988). Employment contracts, influence activities, and efficient organization design. *Journal of Political Economy*, *96*, 42–60.

Mincer, J. (1974). Schooling, experience and earnings. *Human Behavior and Social Institutions*, *2*. New York, NY: National Bureau of Economic Research.

Mukherjee, D. (2011). 'Monopsony' in the market for nurses? A semiparametric note. *Regional and Sectoral Economic Studies*, *11*, 31–36.

Munnell, A.H., Aubry, J.P., Hurwitz, J., and Quinby, L. (2011). Comparing compensation: State-local versus private sector workers. *State and Local Pension Plans*, *20*, 1–19.

Niskanen, W.A. (1971). *Bureaucracy and representative government*. New Brunswick, NJ: AldineTransaction.

Panagopoulos, C. (2013). Extrinsic rewards, intrinsic motivation and voting. *The Journal of Politics*, *75*, 266–280.

Perry, J.L., and Wise, L.R. (1990). The motivational bases of public service. *Public Administration Review*, *50*, 367–373.

Perry, J.L., Hondeghem, A., and Wise, L.R. (2010). Revisiting the motivational bases of public service: Twenty years of research and an agenda for the future. *Public Administration Review*, *70*, 681–690.

Rainey, H.G. (2014). *Understanding and managing public organizations* (5th edn). San Francisco, CA: Jossey-Bass.

Rainey, H.G., and Bozeman, B. (2000). Comparing public and private organizations: Empirical research and the power of the a priori. *Journal of Public Administration Research and Theory*, *10*, 447–470.

Ramoni-Perazzi, J., and Bellante, D. (2006). Wage differentials between the public and the private sector: How comparable are the workers? *Journal of Business and Economics Research*, *4*, 43–57.

Ramoni-Perazzi, J., and Bellante, D. (2007). Do truly comparable public and private sector workers show any compensation differential? *Journal of Labor Research*, *28*, 117–133.

Riccucci, N.M., and Van Ryzin, G.G. (2017). Representative bureaucracy: A lever to enhance social equity, coproduction, and democracy. *Public Administration Review*, *77*, 21–30.

Ruhm, C.J., and Borkoski (2003). Compensation in the nonprofit sector. *Journal of Human Resources*, *38*(4), 992–1021.

Ryan, R.M., and Deci, E.L. (2000). Self-determination theory and the facilitation of intrinsic motivation, social development, and well-being. *American Psychologist*, *55*, 68–78.

Sansone, C., and Harackiewicz, J.M. (2000). *Intrinsic and extrinsic motivation: The search for optimal motivation and performance*. San Diego, CA: Academic Press.

Scott, P.G., and Falcone, S. (1998). Comparing public and private organizations: An exploratory analysis of three frameworks. *American Review of Public Administration*, *28*, 126–145.

Smith, S. (1976a). Government wage differentials by sex. *Journal of Human Resources*, *11*, 185–199.

Smith, S. (1976b). Pay differentials between federal government and private sector workers. *Industrial and Labor Relations Review*, *29*, 179–197.

Tullock, G. (1965). *The politics of bureaucracy*. New York, NY: Public Affairs Press.

Waldo, D. (1948). *The administrative state*. New York, NY: Ronald Press.

Wamsley, G.L., and Zald, M.N. (1973). The political economy of public organizations. *Public Administration Review*, *33*, 62–73.

Wang, Y.D., Yang, C., and Wang, K.Y. (2012). Comparing public and private employees' job satisfaction and turnover. *Public Personnel Management*, *41*, 557–573.

Warwick, D.P. (1975). *A theory of public bureaucracy*. Cambridge, MA: Harvard University Press.
WorldatWork and Deloitte Consulting. (2014). Incentive Pay Practices Survey. Retrieved on June 13, 2020 from
https://www2.deloitte.com/us/en/pages/center-for-board-effectiveness/articles/incentive-pay-practices-survey-public-companies-corporate-governance.html.

11. Unionization and the motivational context in public management
Randall S. Davis and Warefta Rahman

INTRODUCTION

Public administration scholars have devoted volumes of research toward examining the motivational processes that govern human behavior at work (Behn, 1995; Perry, 2000; Perry and Wise, 1990; Rainey and Steinbauer, 1999; Wright, 2001, 2004; Wright and Pandey, 2008). Although multiple theoretical perspectives characterize this domain of research many public management scholars treat work motivation as a broad concept that evaluates how individual dispositional factors, organizational context, and external environmental demands coalesce to shape one's desire to invest mental and/or physical effort to attain organizationally established work goals (e.g., Boyne and Meier, 2009; Davis and Stazyk, 2015; Davis, Stazyk, and Klingeman, 2020; Kim, 2012; Perry, 2000; Rainey and Steinbauer, 1999; Taylor, 2008; Wright, 2001, 2004). In this chapter we adopt Wright's (2001) characterization of work motivation as an examination of, at a minimum, three broad categories of factors (i.e., individual, organizational/structural, and environmental/external) that create the incentive structures influencing organizationally desirable work behaviors.

Research conducted by Davis, Stazyk, and multiple colleagues illustrates that variables within each of these three categories often intersect to shape motivational processes and behavior, sometimes in surprising ways (Davis and Stazyk, 2021; Davis, Stazyk, and Dickman, 2020; Davis, Stazyk, and Klingeman, 2020; Davis, Stazyk, Kochenour, and Neuhoff, 2020: see also other notable examples such as Bright, 2020; Giauque, Anderfuhren-Biget, and Varone, 2013; Van Loon, Vandenabeele, and Leisink, 2015). These models add to our understanding of motivation in public organizations because they recognize that motivation and behavior are embedded within complex systems, and illustrate that a shift in a single variable within any category, even when holding all else constant, can contribute to unanticipated behavioral consequences. Given the complexity of human motivation, scholars examining public sector work motivation must attend to at least two interrelated challenges.

First, the simplified categorization of organizations based on sector of ownership serves as an imperfect proxy to examine motivational differences across organizations and employees (Boyne, 2002; Bozeman and Bretschneider, 1994; Rainey, 2014; Rainey and Bozeman, 2000). While different factors appear to govern public employee motivation under certain conditions (e.g., Buelens and Van den Broeck, 2007; Jurkiewicz, Massey, and Brown, 1998; Lee and Wilkins, 2011), adopting a binary (or tripartite depending on how one views non-profit organizations) categorization of organizations tends to obscure within group variation while accentuating between group variation. As such, one could inadvertently commit an ecological fallacy by making inferences about the nature of specific employees' motives and performance based on characteristics of the category to which their respective organization belongs. Second, although an organization's sector of ownership serves as a weak proxy for specific contextual features, some exogenous constraints appear to more heavily influence governmental organizations (Boyne, 2002; Rainey and Bozeman, 2000). Those interested in examining public sector work motivation must endeavor to identify specific exogenous factors with the capacity to shape public employees' motivational processes, account for those differences by adopting validated measures, and assess subsequent patterns of employee behavior based on sound theoretical expectations (Boyne, 2002).

Developing a fully specified model of public sector work motivation is beyond the scope of our chapter. Instead, we pursue a narrower purpose. Specifically, we seek to integrate the public management research examining work motivation and performance with the interdisciplinary literature on unionization. While one can ground an examination of motivation in public organizations in multiple contexts, we argue that unionization represents one specific exogenous factor more salient in public organizations with the capacity to influence factors that shape employee motivation. Moreover, the framework we build in this chapter illustrates that unionization shapes the environmental constraints public organizations face, elements of organizational structure, and individual attitudes, all of which influence a public organization's motivational landscape. It is critical to note from the outset that we do not argue that unionization is uniformly favorable for public organizations, nor do we make the claim unionization unequivocally diminishes employee motivation. Instead, we seek to develop a framework that describes how the effects of unionization, even within a single organization, can result in outcomes across the categories of factors with contradictory influences on motivation.

Given this aim, our chapter proceeds in four sections. First, we discuss unionization as a salient contextual feature in many public organizations. In this section we present evidence illustrating staunch differences in public and private union membership rates in many countries around the world. We also make the claim that examining public sector work motivation in the absence of union variables paints an incomplete explanatory picture of employee behavior. After discussing why unionization represents a critical aspect of the motivational process for many public organizations, we develop a series of expectations by situating aspects of unionization within streams of public management literature that explore motivation and behavior. We will also articulate theoretical arguments for how union variables likely influence specific individual, organizational, and environmental components of motivation. Finally, we will conclude with how future research might profit from the framework developed in this chapter.

UNIONIZATION IN PUBLIC ORGANIZATIONS

In the United States (US), a series of legislative and economic changes during the middle twentieth century shifted union organization efforts dramatically toward government employment (Freeman, 1986; Kearney, 2010; Klingner, Nalbandian, and Llorens, 2010; Reder, 1988). One of the central factors preempting this shift was President Kennedy's Executive Order 10988, issued in 1962, which legally established federal employees' rights to collectively bargain (see Kearney and Mareschal, 2014 for a detailed discussion). While Executive Order 10988 addressed bargaining rights for US federal employees only, unionization levels in US state and local government kept pace with increasing federal trends from the 1970s onward (e.g., Farber, 2005). Moreover, favorable changes in legislation for public employees coupled with shifting economic, legal, and political conditions for unions representing employees in the private sector, which manifested as wide discrepancies between public and private union-

Table 11.1   Union density statistics by country

	2015			2016			2017		
	Public	Private	Diff.	Public	Private	Diff.	Public	Private	Diff.
Australia	–	–	–	38.5	10.4	28.1	–	–	–
Brazil	28.9	15.3	13.6	27.5	14.2	13.3	27.3	14.1	13.2
Canada	72.4	13.6	58.8	73	13.2	59.8	72	13.4	58.6
Colombia	35.3	2.8	32.5	36.3	2.5	33.8	36.4	2.1	34.3
Estonia	11.3	1.8	9.5	11.8	2.4	9.4	11.6	2.1	9.5
Finland	80.8	54.5	26.3	79.8	51.6	28.2	77.9	50.2	27.7
Hungary	16.5	5.4	11.1	–	–	–	–	–	–
France	–	–	–	18.7	8.3	10.4	–	–	–
Luxembourg	54.4	28.6	25.8	60.3	27.2	33.1	55.0	26.2	28.8
Mexico	43.9	6.4	37.5	43.8	6.3	37.5	43.5	6.2	37.3
Norway	–	–	–	80.0	38.0	42.0	80.0	38.0	42.0
South Africa	64.0	17.7	46.3	64.8	18.7	46.1	64.9	19.3	45.6
Sweden	79.2	61.5	17.7	77.8	61.8	16.0	77.4	60.8	16.6
United Kingdom	54.9	13.9	41.0	52.8	13.4	39.4	51.9	13.5	38.4
United States	35.1	6.4	28.7	34.5	6.1	28.4	34.6	6.2	28.4

Source: OECD/AIAS ICTWSS database (https://www.oecd.org/employment/ictwss-database.htm).

ization rates in the US (Farber, 2005; Kearney and Mareschal, 2014). For example, according to the Bureau of Labor Statistics (2021), in 2020, 34.8 percent of the public sector workforce in the US was unionized compared to only 6.3 percent of private workers.

Labor statistics illustrate the salience of the union context for US public organizations given large disparities in the volume of unionized employees in public organizations relative to those in the private sector. However, one might question the extent to which similar patterns hold in countries outside of the US. Based on publicly available data provided by the Organisation for Economic Co-operation and Development (OECD), public-private differences in union membership hold across multiple countries (OECD, 2021). The OECD has expanded on earlier efforts by Visser (2019) to maintain a database detailing union membership statistics across multiple OECD and European Union (EU) member countries. Table 11.1 provides public and private unionization statistics, computed as the proportion of employees in a given sector who are members of a labor union, in 17 OECD and EU member countries.

Admittedly, these data represent only a snapshot with certain limitations. Perhaps most importantly, the information presented here describes unionization rates for only 17 countries. While unionization data were readily available for these countries, the lack of available data for other regions of the world limits generalizability beyond these specific countries. Additionally, while rates of unionization indicate discrepancies between public and private organizations, they fail to account for legal and cultural differences across countries. Finally, data on unionization rates are far from comprehensive, even among the 17 countries listed here. Most of the countries on this list are characterized by missing information for one or more years since 2015. Nevertheless, these data do indicate that among the 17 countries with at least one year of available data since 2015, public sector unionization outstrips the private sector in every instance. Within these 17 countries from 2015 to 2020, public sector unionization is, on average, 31.05 percentage points higher as compared to unionization in private organizations. Despite the limitations of these data, evidence indicates that unionization is

Table 11.1   (continued)

	2018 Public	2018 Private	2018 Diff.	2019 Public	2019 Private	2019 Diff.	2020 Public	2020 Private	2020 Diff.
Australia	37.3	9.7	27.6	–	–	–	–	–	–
Brazil	–	–	–	22.5	10.5	12.0	–	–	–
Canada	71.8	12.9	58.9	72.6	13.0	59.6	74.4	12.9	61.5
Colombia	35.6	2.1	33.5	37.7	2.0	35.7	–	–	–
Estonia	13.6	3.0	10.6	13.7	2.7	11.0	–	–	–
Finland	77.2	48.8	28.4	75.5	46.6	28.9	–	–	–
Hungary	–	–	–	–	–	–	14.0	4.4	9.6
France	–	–	–	–	–	–	–	–	–
Luxembourg	51.7	23.1	28.6	51.2	22.6	28.6	–	–	–
Mexico	42.2	6.1	36.1	43.3	6.3	37.0	42.7	6.3	36.4
Norway	–	–	–	–	–	–	–	–	–
South Africa	65.7	19.8	45.9	65.7	19.6	46.1	–	–	–
Sweden	77.2	60.1	17.1	76.6	60.1	16.5	–	–	–
United Kingdom	52.5	13.2	39.3	52.3	13.3	39.0	–	–	–
United States	34.2	6.1	28.1	33.7	5.9	27.8	34.8	6.0	28.8

a central feature of the institutional landscape for government organizations in many countries around the world.

While comparatively large proportions of public employees are unionized in several countries, public management scholars have not developed sustained research agendas examining the causes and consequences of unionization for members (e.g., Davis, 2013b; Kearney, 2010; Riccucci, 2011). In many instances when public management scholars examine unionization, union variables are included for the purposes of controlling for alternative explanations in broader models of organizational behavior and performance. These efforts are useful, and provide valuable insights into how public employees behave. However, few have sought to specifically theorize about why unions influence public organizations and members (but see, e.g., Davis, 2011, 2013a, 2013b; Oberfield, 2019; Riccucci, 1988, 1990).

To the extent that unionization represents a central contextual feature for many government organizations, it is valuable to assess the role unions might play in shaping the psychological processes that govern organizational behavior (Barling, Fullagar, and Kelloway, 1992; Davis, 2018). Broadly speaking, labor unions represent social institutions within the government workplace that shape individual motives, influence aspects of organizational structure, and adjust the environmental demands levied on public organizations (e.g., Barling, Fullagar, and Kelloway, 1992; Davis, 2018; Hammer and Avgar, 2005; Methé and Perry, 1980; Moe, 2006, 2009). While empirical evidence suggests that unions alter, sometimes drastically, the constituent factors that influence employee behavior, public management research would profit from developing a robust framework articulating the role unions play in employee motivation across the environmental, organizational, and individual levels of analysis (Kearney, 2010; Riccucci, 2011). Models of public sector work motivation that fail to account for the union context paint an incomplete picture of how and why government employees behave as they do. In the following section we attempt to address this shortcoming by developing a series of expectations regarding the influence unions exert on employee motivation, and explicating the causal logic for how unionization is likely to influence the individual, organizational, and environmental determinants of public employee behavior.

HOW UNIONIZATION INFLUENCES MOTIVATION IN PUBLIC ORGANIZATIONS

The American Psychological Association defines general motivation as 'the impetus that gives purpose or direction to behavior and operates in humans at a conscious or unconscious level,' and work motivation more specifically as 'the desire or willingness to make an effort in one's work' (American Psychological Association, 2020). As Wright (2001) points out, however, the breadth of these definitions has encouraged some public management researchers to treat productivity as an approximate measure of a given employee's motivation levels. Unfortunately, under some circumstances this proclivity causes research to ignore 'other determinants of performance such as employee (e.g., ability or task comprehension) and environmental (e.g., situational constraints or task demands) characteristics' (p. 560).

As such, Wright (2001, citing Mitchell, 1997) argues that motivation research should be broadly construed to include the myriad factors that influence 'such aspects as the direction, intensity, and persistence of work-related behaviors desired by the organization or its representatives' (p. 560). As a result of this concept expansion, questions related to employee motivation have become one of the most extensively studied subjects in the public management literature (e.g., Moynihan and Pandey, 2007a, 2007b; Perry, 2000; Perry and Wise, 1990; Piatak et al., 2020; Rainey and Steinbauer, 1999; Stazyk and Davis, 2015; Wright, 2001, 2004; Wright and Davis, 2003). Based on public management studies examining motivation and employee performance, one can group the factors that influence organizationally desirable behaviors into broad categories across three levels of analysis.

First, several individual-level factors, including dispositional proclivities and ability, influence an employee's drive to perform work-related tasks. Second, elements of bureaucratic structure, such as rules, hierarchy, and span of control, provide meaning to the expectations placed on any given employee. Finally, environmental exigencies such as patterns of resource dependence and external stakeholder support provide necessary conditions required for organizations to transform raw materials into goods and services (e.g., Davis and Stazyk, 2015; Garnett, Marlowe, and Pandey, 2008; Pandey and Wright, 2006; Rainey and Steinbauer, 1999; Wright, 2001, 2004).

Given that unionization appears to serve as one contextual feature more prominent for government organizations across the world, researchers believe that the motivational outcomes associated with unionization occur across multiple levels of analysis. The interdisciplinary literature examining organized labor has evaluated the outcomes of unionization across environmental, organizational, and individual levels of analysis. When approached holistically these studies offer insights regarding how a multi-level perspective on unionization factors into patterns of employee motivation and performance. In keeping with the purpose of this study, we describe a select set of findings across all three levels, and articulate the logical connections between individual, organizational, and environmental predictors of motivation. Importantly, we do not claim to include an exhaustive list of all relevant studies of unionization. Instead, our purpose is illustrative and designed to develop a multi-level perspective on unionization. Future research may uncover other important factors that govern the connections between unionization, motivation, and performance.

UNION INFLUENCE AND THE EXTERNAL ENVIRONMENT

Union density within a given organization represents a reasonable origin to begin examining the motivational byproducts of unionization, because it represents a largely exogenous, environmental feature largely beyond the direct control of any given public organization. Union density refers to the percentage of employees within a given organization who belong to a labor union (e.g., Oberfield, 2019). Union density, however, is only important for motivational processes insofar as it indicates the relative power of a given union. Union power logically flows from union density because, as Barling, Fullagar, and Kelloway (1992) note, the ability of unions to exert influence over employing organizations 'is largely dependent on the ability of the union to achieve monopoly power within an industry' (p. 169). Given this observation it is reasonable to expect that unions will exhibit greater power in union dense environments. Union power, as we use the term here, refers to the ability of the union to exert control over member attitudes, organizational expectations placed on employees, and environmental demands levied on public organizations by external stakeholders.

However, even in those industries where union density is highest, legal prohibitions on certain union activities can condition their power to influence aspects of the work environment. Legal prohibitions on certain union negotiation tactics are particularly germane for some public sector organizations where, for example, the right to strike is prohibited (see Kearney and Mareschal, 2014 for a comprehensive discussion on public union members' right to strike). Given that conditions in the legal environment can limit union power even in union dense environments, it stands to reason that the political activities of unions seek to influence the external demands levied on public organizations within their broader political environments. Moe (2006, 2009) has persuasively illustrated how public sector unions design political action, particularly through support for specific political parties and voter mobilization efforts, to exert control over their organizations by altering the legal and political demands levied on public bureaucracy. Moreover, many politicians, particularly those in the Democratic Party, willingly structure policy based on union demands because it creates favorable political climates for future election cycles (Anzia and Moe, 2016). This research generally indicates that greater degrees of union density increase the leverage unions possess to influence the relationships between public organizations and the environmental constraints they face.

In summary, the logic articulated above suggests that public sector unions are likely to be more powerful when the degree of union density approaches a perfect monopoly within a given industry. The power of the union, understood as the ability to exert control over organizations and individuals, increases for two interconnected reasons. First, increased density enables the union to exert greater political control over elected officials and other attentive publics through, for example, increased donations to political parties, greater voter mobilization, and enhanced capacity to influence favorable media coverage. Increased union power in union dense environments affords organized labor greater control to influence the internal characteristics of the organizations in which they are embedded.

UNION INFLUENCE AND PUBLIC ORGANIZATIONS' INTERNAL STRUCTURE

Union density is likely to afford unions a greater degree of power over employing organizations via enhanced political control and a more permissive legal environment (Moe, 2006, 2009). Importantly, though, unions are likely to wield the political and legal power accrued via union density to also influence the motivational factors embedded in public organizations' internal structure. Perhaps the most obvious internal motivational factors over which unions have control include elements of the work environment (Davis, 2013a, 2013b). The work environment includes two broad categories of variables, which include job characteristics and contextual features of work. First, according to Perry and Porter (1982), job characteristics refer to 'the collection of tasks that comprise the job' (p. 90). Moreover, in their discussion of job characteristics, Perry and Porter (1982) go on to argue that the nature of the tasks that define the job shape the motivational landscape for employees. Second, the work context consists of structural features of an organization that describe, in part, the formal rules and goals that shape incentive structures designed to encourage employees to engage in organizationally desirable behavior.

Collective bargaining represents a system of human resources management favored by unions and their members (Klingner, Nalbandian, and Llorens, 2010), which tends to emphasize the necessity of protecting employee and individual rights from arbitrary managerial discretion (see also Donahue, Selden, and Ingraham, 2000). Union attempts to limit managerial discretion are frequently codified in formalized rules and the requirement that labor and management negotiate the collection of tasks that define jobs within the organization (Ingraham, 2006; Klingner, Nalbandian, and Llorens, 2010). Some research indicates that union dense work environments are characterized by increased frequency of work rules and enhanced precision expectations embedded in goals (Freeman and Medoff, 1984; Gallagher, 1983; Jackson, Schuler, and Carlos Rivero, 1989), as well as decreased autonomy for human resources managers to make personnel decisions based on these aspects of structure (Donahue, Selden, and Ingraham, 2000). Kochan (1980; see also Kochan and Helfman, 1981) refers to the internal, structural adjustments due to union action as the primary outcomes of collective bargaining.

These structural features likely result in contradictory motivational outcomes. On the one hand, as Wright (2001) illustrates, increased goal clarity and task specificity enhance work motivation. Research consistently illustrates that clear goals that are specific, but attainable enhance goal commitment and persistence (Locke and Latham, 2002, 2006). Moreover, clarity and specificity encourage one to exhibit some degree of self-efficacy, which leads to their ability to connect work effort to goal achievement and believe they can adequately accomplish task expectations (Bandura, 1977; House and Rizzo, 1972; Locke and Latham, 1990). On the other hand, the role unions play in the human resources management process likely increases the rule sum for a given organization. Bozeman (1993) used the term rule sum to describe 'the total number of written rules, procedures, and regulations in force for a given organization' (p. 280). Increased rule sum does not pose an inherent problem for employee motivation. However, the greater the rule sum in a given organization, the greater the probability that task demands or goal expectations conflict, and employees are less likely to understand how their work effort contributes to simultaneously attaining the multiple, contradictory expectations levied on them by the organization.

Overall, the influence unions exert on internal organizational structure is a logical outgrowth of the power they accumulate by interacting in the external environment of the employing organization. Increased union density enhances the monopoly power of a union within a given industry, which contributes to the accumulation of power through political and legal action. Unions subsequently leverage this power to influence the collection of tasks that define a job as well as the rule sum, rule content, and goal expectations within the organization through the collective bargaining process. These union negotiated rules and tasks are designed to limit managerial discretion in personnel matters that the union views as arbitrary and capricious. While research consistently indicates that unions, particularly those unions characterized by high degrees of density, influence motivational factors in an organization's external environment and internal structure, a comprehensive evaluation requires an examination of how unions influence the attitudes of individual members.

UNION DENSITY AND INDIVIDUAL ATTITUDES

The multi-level nature of union influence is incomplete in the absence of examining their ability to exert influence over members. While the power unions exert over organizations grows from their capacity to wield political authority, the mechanisms used to shape member attitudes is more subtle. Specifically, as unions interact with members they engage in socialization practices designed to encourage members to express favorable attitudes toward the labor organization (Barling, Fullagar, and Kelloway, 1992). The socialization practices levied by unions are varied and multifaceted, but can largely be grouped into two broad categories.

First, Fullagar and colleagues define institutional socialization as the formalized practices unions employ to integrate individuals into union membership (Fullagar et al., 1995). Such practices involve attendance at union sanctioned meetings and other mechanisms of formal participation such as a strike. These formal processes are intended to provide 'newcomers with a common set of experiences that are likely to elicit standardized responses' (Fullagar et al., 1995, p 147). Second, unions also engage in socialization practices outside of formal meetings. Individual socialization refers to interacting with other union members in ways that are more 'idiosyncratic and informal' (Fullagar et al., 1995, p. 147).

Importantly, it stands to reason that members within union dense environments are increasingly subjected to informal union socialization experiences. As an extreme example, if a given union has fully monopolized a given industry (i.e., 100 percent of employees belong to the union), then every informal interaction between employees offers the opportunity for individualized socialization. As the industry deviates from perfect monopoly exposure to socialization decreases. Yet, socialization practices are only valuable for the union insofar as they encourage members to commit to union espoused values.

A significant amount of research examining labor unions indicates that increased participation in socialization experiences also increases the extent to which members are committed to the values of the union and are willing to engage in more work on the union's behalf (Gordon et al., 1980). As such, union socialization shapes member attitudes and behaviors toward work including productivity, turnover intent, job satisfaction, and absenteeism (Barling, Fullagar, and Kelloway, 1992; Davis, 2011, 2013a, 2013b). Given these findings, it is also likely that union socialization activities and commitment to the union exhibit a reciprocal relationship. As union socialization activities increase, members are more likely to exhibit an increased willingness to work on the union's behalf. The increased willingness to work will, in subsequent time periods, result in the union's ability to schedule a greater number of formal socialization experiences. Ultimately, this creates more committed union members as the cycle continues. It is important to note, however, that union socialization practices do not exert a uniform force homogenizing members. As Newton and Shore (1992) point out, while some members fully internalize union values as a result of socialization, others express a feeling of alienation from the union. As such, union socialization experiences cannot serve as a proxy for the internalization of values.

The above sections seek to describe the multi-level role unions play in the motivational factors that shape employee behavior in public organizations. However, to fully articulate the role of unions in work motivation, these elements of unionization must be situated in broader theories of work motivation. In the subsequent section we describe the psychological process of appraisal to illustrate that the motivational outcomes of unionization are not uniformly favorable for employees and organizations. Specifically, the union initiated changes described above will elicit emotional responses from members and non-members alike. Subsequent behaviors will be structured to sustain positive, but eliminate negative emotions. The net balance of behavior resulting from employees' responses to emotions is likely to be favorable under some circumstances and unfavorable in others.

THE PSYCHOLOGICAL PROCESSES THAT GOVERN MOTIVATION: APPRAISAL AND AFFECT

Although few in public management recognize theories of stress as explicitly motivational, given Wright's (2001) characterization of motivation as an umbrella concept that theorizes about 'such aspects as the direction, intensity, and persistence of work-related behaviors desired by the organization or its representatives' (p. 560), theories of stress certainly fit within this mold. In fact, recent research in public management has sought to situate the relationship between unions and employing organizations within the psychological research on work stress and the public management literature on public service motivation (Davis, Stazyk, Kochenour, and Neuhoff, 2020). Specifically, Davis and colleagues (2020) illustrate that intra-individual dispositions interact with union-management conflict to shape one's emotional experiences at work, which subsequently shapes intent to separate from the organization.

They develop their argument based primarily on the work of Lazarus (1999, 2000, 2001) and Matteson and Ivancevich (1987) to define work stress as

> an adaptive [emotional] response, moderated by individual differences, that is a consequence of [appraising] any action, situation, or event that places [physical or psychological] demands upon a person. (Davis, Stazyk, Kochenour, and Neuhoff, 2020, p. 408)

Based on this definition, and the foundational work of Lazarus (1999, 2000, 2001), the psychological process of appraisal generates emotional responses to work demands, which influence the probability and persistence of work behavior. More specifically, Lazarus and Smith (1988) describe how the appraisal process unfolds in two stages. The first stage is labeled primary appraisal. During this phase of appraisal an individual must determine the extent to which the demands levied upon them constitute an immediate threat to personal welfare. In the second phase, labeled secondary appraisal, an individual assesses relative levels of personal resource availability to cope with perceived threats. To the extent that one determines that a given demand, or set of demands, threatens them they can leverage personal resources to offset the more damaging aspects of organizational demands. In states of relative resource deficiency the individual will express negative emotions, and respond with behaviors that, from the organization's perspective, serve counterproductive ends. In states of resource surplus one will respond with favorable emotions and behave in ways the organization deems productive.

Appraisal theory offers some distinct advantages for understanding the motivational byproducts of unionized environments. First, appraisal theory allows for behavioral variation among union members. There is no reason to expect uniformity of behavior across members. Moreover, accounting for these differences will allow researchers to adequately examine the relative benefits and drawbacks of unions in the public workplace on apolitical grounds. Second, this perspective explicitly factors emotion into the workplace behavior equation. As Davis and colleagues (2020) illustrate, holistic examinations of employee behavior must include the emotional intermediary that connects work demands to observable behavior. Finally, as Wright (2001) argues, a significant proportion of motivation research treats productivity and performance as a proxy for levels of motivation. Such a perspective assumes that motivation is only present when the behavioral outcome is favorable for the organization. The application of appraisal theory makes no such assumption. Instead, it acknowledges that all behavior is motivated by external demands, even those that work against the wishes of the organization.

The application of appraisal theory, when taken in conjunction with the influence unions exert over the environmental, organizational, and individual motivational factors, offers a comprehensive perspective connecting unionization and employee behavior. In summary, increased union density allows the union to accumulate power through political and legal action. The increase in power affords the union the capacity to exert control over the work organizations in which they are embedded. Given their power, the union plays a large part in establishing work rules, job tasks, and goal demands the organization imposes on employees. However, the employee must appraise these demands to determine the extent to which they pose a direct threat to personal welfare.

Unions likely communicate the demands inherent in elements of organizational structure established through collective bargaining as non-threatening to employees, whereas those demands not negotiated during bargaining are more likely to be presented as a threat to employee rights. Unions then communicate the relative degree of threat inherent in work demands to members through formal and informal socialization experiences. The committed member will likely embrace the union's position on the degree of personal threat embodied in work demands. Alternatively, the alienated member will oppose the threat level described by the union. Finally, those members that fully internalize union values are more likely to express anger, frustration, or resentment when the union characterizes a given demand as threatening, which reinforces counterproductive work behaviors. On the other hand, alienated members will likely appraise work demands without considering the union's assessment of threat levels.

CONCLUSION

This chapter sought to achieve three overarching purposes. First, we sought to make the claim that unionization is a salient contextual feature in government organizations around the world.

We amassed data from the U.S. Bureau of Labor Statistics and the OECD to illustrate that public sector organizations were comparatively union dense relative to those in the private sector. This same trend has held for 17 countries since 2015. Second, we drew from research across several social scientific disciplines to show that unions do have the capacity to shape the environmental, organizational, and individual factors that influence work motivation and behavior. Finally, we made the argument that the psychological process of appraisal is integral for connecting the multi-level influence of unionization on the public workplace. While we fully acknowledge that alternative theoretical approaches may be valuable for examining the role of unions, we believe this perspective can stimulate future research while offering a theoretical rationale for developing testable hypotheses. Although this represents a first step toward a motivational theory of public sector unions, we believe that incorporating these perspectives in public management research paints a more accurate picture of employee behavior.

REFERENCES

Anzia, S.F., and Moe, T.M. (2016). Do politicians use policy to make politics? The case of public-sector labor laws. *American Political Science Review, 110*, 763–777.

APA (American Psychological Association) Dictionary of Psychology. (2020). Retrieved June 22, 2021 from https://dictionary.apa.org/.

Bandura, Albert. 1977. Self-efficacy: Toward a unifying theory of behavioral change. *Psychological Review, 84*, 191–215.

Barling, J., Fullagar, C.J.A., and Kelloway, E.K. (1992). *The Union and Its Members: A Psychological Approach.* New York, NY: Oxford University Press.

Behn, R.D. (1995). The big questions of public management. *Public Administration Review, 55*, 313–324.

Boyne, G.A. (2002). Public and private management: What's the difference? *Journal of Management Studies, 39*, 97–122.

Boyne, G.A., and Meier, K.J. (2009). Environmental turbulence, organizational stability, and public service performance. *Administration & Society, 40*, 799–824.

Bozeman, B. (1993). A theory of government 'red tape'. *Journal of Public Administration Research and Theory, 3*, 273–304.

Bozeman, B., and Bretschneider, S. (1994). The 'publicness puzzle' in organization theory: A test of alternative explanations of differences between public and private organizations. *Journal of Public Administration Research and Theory, 4*, 197–224.

Bright, L. (2020). Does perceptions of organizational prestige mediate the relationship between public service motivation, job satisfaction, and the turnover intentions of federal employees? *Public Personnel Management*, first published online on August 28, 2020 at https://doi.org/10.1177/0091026020952818.

Buelens, M., and Van den Broeck, H. (2007). An analysis of differences in work motivation between public and private sector organizations. *Public Administration Review, 67*, 65–74.

Bureau of Labor Statistics (2021). Union members summary. Retrieved from https://www.bls.gov/news.release/union2.nr0.htm on November 11, 2021.

Davis, R.S. (2011). Blue-collar public servants: How union membership influences public service motivation. *American Review of Public Administration, 41*, 705–723.

Davis, R.S. (2013a). Union commitment and stakeholder red tape: How union values shape perceptions of organizational rules. *Review of Public Personnel Administration, 33*, 365–383.

Davis, R.S. (2013b). Unionization and work attitudes: How union commitment influences public sector job satisfaction. *Public Administration Review, 73*, 74–84.

Davis, R.S. (2018). Unions in the public sector. In N. Riccucci (ed.), *Public Personnel Management: Current Concerns, Future Challenges* (6th edn). New York, NY: Routledge, pp. 97–109.

Davis, R.S., and Stazyk, E.C. (2015). Developing and testing a new goal taxonomy: Accounting for the complexity of ambiguity and political support. *Journal of Public Administration Research and Theory, 25*, 751–775.

Davis, R.S., and Stazyk, E.C. (2021). Ambiguity, appraisal, and affect: Examining the connections between goal perceptions, emotional labour, and exhaustion. *Public Management Review*, first published online on April 6, 2021 at https://doi.org/10.1080/14719037.2021.1909348.

Davis, R.S., Stazyk, E.C., and Dickman, Z.T. (2020). Advantages of feeling appreciated: An examination of how receipt of gratitude influences the linkages between PSM and behaviour. *Public Administration*, first published online on November 8, 2020 at https://doi.org/10.1111/padm.12707.

Davis, R.S., Stazyk, E.C., and Klingeman, C.M. (2020). Accounting for personal disposition and organizational context: Connecting role ambiguity, public service motivation, and whistle-blowing in federal agencies. *The International Journal of Human Resource Management, 31*, 1313–1332.

Davis, R.S., Stazyk, E.C., Kochenour, A., and Neuhoff, E. (2020). Coping with conflict: Examining the influence of PSM on perceptions of workplace stressors. *Review of Public Personnel Administration, 40*, 405–425.

Donahue, A.K., Selden, S.C., and Ingraham, P.W. (2000). Measuring government management capacity: A comparative analysis of city human resources systems. *Journal of Public Administration Research and Theory, 10*, 381–412.

Farber, H.S. (2005, September 19). Union membership in the United States: The divergence between the public and private sectors. *DataSpace*. Retrieved from http://arks.princeton.edu/ark:/88435/dsp015999n338s on November 11, 2021.

Freeman, R.B. (1986). Unionism comes to the public sector. *Journal of Economic Literature, 24*, 41–86.

Freeman, R.B., and Medoff, J. (1984). *What Do Unions Do?* New York, NY: Basic.

Fullagar, C.J.A., Gallagher, D.G., Gordon, M.E., and Clark, P.F. (1995). Impact of Early socialization on union commitment and participation: A longitudinal study. *Journal of Applied Psychology, 80*, 147–157.

Gallagher, D.G. (1983). Integrating collective bargaining and human resources management research. In G.R. Ferris and K.M. Rowland (eds), *Research in Personnel and Human Resources Management: A Research Annual* (Vol. 1). Greenwich, CT: JAI Press, pp. 235–268.

Garnett, J.L., Marlowe, J., and Pandey, S.K. (2008). Penetrating the performance predicament: Communication as a mediator or moderator of organizational culture's impact on public organizational performance. *Public Administration Review, 68*, 266–281.

Giauque, D., Anderfuhren-Biget, S., and Varone, F. (2013). Stress perception in public organisations: Expanding the job demands–job resources model by including public service motivation. *Review of Public Personnel Administration, 33*, 58–83.

Gordon, M.E., Philpot, JW., Burt, R.E., Thompson, C.A., and Spiller, W.E. (1980). Commitment to the union: Development of a measure and an examination of its correlates. *Journal of Applied Psychology, 65*, 479–499.

Hammer, T.H., and Avgar, A. (2005). The impact of unions on job satisfaction, organizational commitment, and turnover. *Journal of Labor Research, 26*, 241–266.

House, R.J., and Rizzo, J.R. (1972). Role conflict and ambiguity as critical variables in a model of organizational behavior. *Journal of Organizational Behavior and Performance, 7*, 467–505.

Ingraham, P.W. (2006). Building Bridges over troubled waters: Merit as a guide. *Public Administration Review, 66*, 486–495.

Jackson, S.E., Schuler, R.S., and Carlos Rivero, J. (1989). Organizational characteristics as predictors of personnel practices. *Personnel Psychology, 42*, 727–786.

Jurkiewicz, C.L., Massey Jr, T.K., and Brown, R.G. (1998). Motivation in public and private organizations: A comparative study. *Public Productivity & Management Review, 21*, 230–250.

Kearney, R.C. (2010). Public sector labor-management relations: Change or status quo? *Review of Public Personnel Administration, 30*, 89–111.

Kearney, R.C., and Mareschal, P.M. (2014). *Labor Relations in the Public Sector* (5th edn). Boca Raton, FL: CRC Press.

Kim, S. (2012). Does person-organization fit matter in the public-sector? Testing the mediating effect of person-organization fit in the relationship between public service motivation and work attitudes. *Public Administration Review, 72*, 830–840.

Klingner, D.E., Nalbandian, J., and Llorens, J. (2010). *Public Personnel Management: Contexts and Strategies* (6th edn). New York, NY: Longman.

Kochan, T.A. (1980). *Collective Bargaining and Industrial Relations: From Theory to Policy and Practice.* Homewood, IL: Richard D. Irwin.

Kochan, T.A., and Helfman, D.E. (1981). The effects of collective bargaining on economic and behavioral job outcomes. In R.C. Ehrenberg (ed.), *Research in Labor Economics* (Vol. 4). Greenwich, CT: JAI Press, pp. 321–365.

Lazarus, R.S. (1999). *Stress and Emotion: A New Synthesis.* London: Free Association.

Lazarus, R.S. (2000). Toward better research on stress and coping. *American Psychologist,* 55, 665–673.

Lazarus, R.S. (2001). Relational meaning and discrete emotions. In K. Scherer, A. Schorr, and T. Johnstone (eds), *Appraisal Processes in Emotion: Theory, Methods, Research.* New York, NY: Oxford University Press, pp. 37–67.

Lazarus, R.S., and Smith, C.A. (1988). Knowledge and appraisal in the emotion-cognition relationship. *Cognition and Emotion,* 2, 281–300.

Lee, Y.J., and Wilkins, V.M. (2011). More similarities or more differences? Comparing public and nonprofit managers' job motivations. *Public Administration Review,* 71, 45–56.

Locke, E.A., and Latham, G.P. (1990). *A Theory of Goal Setting and Task Performance.* Englewood Cliffs, NJ: Prentice Hall.

Locke, E.A., and Latham, G.P. (2002). Building a practically useful theory of goal setting and task motivation: A 35-year odyssey. *American Psychologist,* 57, 705–717.

Locke, E.A., and Latham, G.P. (2006). New directions in goal-setting theory. *Current Directions in Psychological Science,* 15, 265–268.

Matteson, M.T., and Ivancevich, J.M. (1987). *Controlling Work Stress: Effective Human Resource and Management Strategies.* San Francisco, CA: Jossey-Bass.

Methé, D.T., and Perry, J.L. (1980). The impacts of collective bargaining on local government services: A review of research. *Public Administration Review,* 40, 359–371.

Mitchell, T.R. (1997). Matching motivation strategies with organizational contexts. In L.L. Cummings and B.M. Staw (eds), *Research in Organizational Behavior.* Greenwich, CT: JAI, pp. 57–150.

Moe, T.M. (2006). Political control and the power of the agent. *Journal of Law, Economics, & Organization,* 22, 1–29.

Moe, T.M. (2009). Collective bargaining and the performance of the public schools. *American Journal of Political Science,* 53, 156–174.

Moynihan, D.P., and Pandey, S.K. (2007a). Finding workable levers over work motivation: Comparing job satisfaction, job involvement, and organizational commitment. *Administration & Society,* 39, 803–832.

Moynihan, D.P., and Pandey, S.K. (2007b). The role of organizations in fostering public service motivation. *Public Administration Review,* 67, 40–53.

Newton, L.A., and Shore, L.M. (1992). A model of union membership: Instrumentality, commitment, and opposition. *The Academy of Management Review,* 17, 275–298.

Oberfield, Z. (2019). Unionization and street-level bureaucracy: An examination of public school teachers in the United States. *Review of Public Personnel Administration,* first published online on December 31, 2019 at https://doi.org/10.1177/0734371X19894376.

OECD (Organisation for Economic Co-operation and Development) (2021). OECD/AIAS ICTWSS Database. Retrieved from https://www.oecd.org/employment/ictwss-database.htm.

Pandey, S.K., and Wright, B.E. (2006). Connecting the dots in public management: Political environment, organizational goal ambiguity, and the public manager's role ambiguity. *Journal of Public Administration Research and Theory,* 16, 511–532.

Perry, J.L. (2000). Bringing society in: Toward a theory of public-service motivation. *Journal of Public Administration Research and Theory,* 10, 471–488.

Perry, J.L., and Porter, L.W. (1982). Factors affecting the context for motivation in public organizations. *Academy of Management Review,* 7, 89–98.

Perry, J.L., and Wise, L.R. (1990), The motivational basis of public service. *Public Administration Review,* 50, 367–373.

Piatak, J.S., Sowa, J.rE., Jacobson, W.S., and McGinnis Johnson, J. (2020). Infusing public service motivation (PSM) throughout the employment relationship: A review of PSM and the human resource management process. *International Public Management Journal*, first published online on February 20, 2020 at https://doi.org/10.1080/10967494.2020.1805381.

Rainey, H.G. (2014). *Understanding and Managing Public Organizations*. (5th edn). Hoboken, NJ: Wiley.

Rainey, H.G., and Bozeman, B. (2000). Comparing public and private organizations: Empirical research and the power of the a priori. *Journal of Public Administration Research and Theory*, *10*, 447–470.

Rainey, H.G., and Steinbauer, P. (1999). Galloping elephants: Developing elements of a theory of effective government organizations. *Journal of Public Administration Research and Theory*, *9*, 1–32.

Reder, M.W. (1988). The rise and fall of unions: The public sector and the private. *The Journal of Economic Perspectives*, *2*, 89–110.

Riccucci, N.M. (1988). A Typology for union discrimination: A public sector perspective. *Public Personnel Management*, *17*, 41–51.

Riccucci, N.M. (1990). *Women, Minorities, and Unions in the Public Sector*. New York, NY: Greenwood Press.

Riccucci, N.M. (2011). Public sector labor relations scholarship: Is there a 'there,' there? *Public Administration Review*, *71*, 203–209.

Stazyk, E.C., and Davis, R.S. (2015). Taking the 'high road': Does public service motivation alter ethical decision making processes? *Public Administration*, *93*, 627–645.

Taylor, J. (2008). Organizational influences, public service motivation and work outcomes: An Australian study. *International Public Management Journal*, *11*, 67–88.

Van Loon, N.M., Vandenabeele, W., and Leisink, P. (2015). On the bright and dark side of public service motivation: The relationship between PSM and employee wellbeing. *Public Money & Management*, *35*, 349–356.

Visser, J. (2019). ICTWSS Database. Version 6.1. Amsterdam: Amsterdam Institute for Advanced Labour Studies (AIAS), University of Amsterdam. Retrieved from uva-aias.net/en/ictwss.

Wright, B.E. (2001). Public-sector work motivation: A review of the current literature and a revised conceptual model. *Journal of Public Administration Research and Theory*, *11*, 559–586.

Wright, B.E. (2004). The role of work context in work motivation: A public sector application of goal and social cognitive theories. *Journal of Public Administration Research and Theory*, *14*, 59–78.

Wright, B.E., and Davis, B.S. (2003). Job satisfaction in the public sector: The role of the work environment. *American Review of Public Administration*, *33*, 70–90.

Wright, B.E., and Pandey, S.K. (2008). Public Service motivation and the assumption of person=organization fit testing the mediating effect of value congruence. *Administration and Society*, *40*, 502–521.

12. Public pensions and employment in the public sector

Gang Chen and Hyewon Kang

INTRODUCTION

In the recent decade, many state and local governments in the United States (US) have experienced difficulties in funding the liabilities accumulated in their employees' retirement systems (The Pew Charitable Trust 2019). State pension systems' average funded ratio, which measures how much assets have been accumulated to cover the accumulated liabilities, has dropped to near 69 percent in 2017 (The Pew Charitable Trust 2019). Many state and local pension systems have made changes in their pension systems to reduce fiscal risks and lower financial costs.

To date, most discussion on public pensions and reforms is focused on the financial management side of the issue. What is lacking in the literature is the discussion about how the changes in public pension systems influence public employees. Benefits from public pension systems account for a major portion of retirement income for public employees, especially for those who are not covered by the Social Security system. It is reasonable to expect that changes in benefits, contributions, and plan types in state and local pension systems would affect public employees' motivations, job satisfaction, and their decisions to join, stay, and exit the public workforce.

State governments in the US contribute near 7.4 percent of their own-source revenue to fund their retirement systems (The Pew Charitable Trust 2019). Public pensions provide more generous benefits and are more costly to maintain than private pensions (Biggs 2018; Foster 1997; Munnell et al. 2011). As an important human resource management strategy, the effectiveness of these systems to recruit and retain a high-quality public workforce has not been fully understood in the Public Administration literature.

To address this gap, some recent research has started to associate public pensions with public employees' motivations and behaviors. In this chapter, we summarize what factors have been examined in these studies, what empirical findings are discovered, and what remains to be found. This chapter aims to make two contributions. First, we provide theoretical explanations of why pensions would or would not affect public employees' motivations and decisions. We also describe the key pension benefit rules and plan design features that would affect employees' decisions. Second, we conduct a comprehensive literature review and summarize the empirical findings on the impact of pensions on employees' decisions. The empirical findings show how pension plan design, benefit changes, and plan types affect turnover rates, retirement decisions, and composition of the public workforce, as well as how employees' involvement in plan governance affects pension decisions.

ARE PUBLIC PENSIONS IMPORTANT FOR PUBLIC EMPLOYEES?

It seems easy to assert that pensions are essential for employees because most public employees rely on government-sponsored pensions as their primary income in their retirement years. However, when we delve into the literature on how pensions affect employees' motivations and decisions, we see that some studies show pensions are important, but some others suggest that employees might not fully understand the pension benefits or only view pensions as a low priority in their compensation package.

For most public employees, pensions are the most important income source among the three major sources in their retirement years: Social Security, employer-sponsored pensions, and personal savings. The sufficiency of retirement income is usually measured by the replacement ratio, which compares the pre-retirement salary with the retirement income. An 85 percent replacement ratio (i.e., the post-retirement income can 'replace' 85 percent of the pre-retirement income) is regarded as a sufficient level of retirement income (Peng 2009). For public employees, the first source, Social Security benefits, can provide around 30 percent of the pre-retirement income (Peng 2009). Assuming 30 years of service in the public sector, most pension systems provide generous benefits (assuming a 2 percent benefit factor) that can cover around 60 percent of the pre-retirement income, which, combined with Social Security benefits, can exceed the 85 percent replacement ratio benchmark. For those public employees who are not covered by the Social Security system, pension benefits are even higher. In comparison, private sector pensions are less generous on average, providing replacement rates that are around 15 to 20 percentage points lower than public pensions (Foster 1997).

Besides being an important retirement income source, public pensions are also highly secure because, in most states, public pensions are protected by laws and/or labor contracts (Monahan 2010). Most public employees' pension benefits are defined in advance by a benefit formula, which is why these plans are called 'defined benefit' (DB) plans. In DB plans, retirees always get the guaranteed benefits regardless of the investment performance. This is in contrast with defined contribution (DC) plans, which are primarily used in the private sector. In DC plans, only the contributions that go into the individual pension accounts are guaranteed. Because of the generous DB plans and legal protection, public pensions provide more financial security than private pensions.

These widely used DB plans in the public sector create a common perception that since the public sector provides higher and more secure retirement income than the private sector, the public sector can attract employees who prefer such job features when they make their career decisions. Indeed, high pension benefits are known as an important factor to attract employees to the public sector. According to a survey of education majors (Kimball et al. 2005), pensions and health benefits are the two most important job attributes in choosing a career in education. The certainty of guaranteed income of a pension plan is found to be one of the most important features for job seekers (Kimball et al. 2005).

Another factor to explain why pensions matter for employees' decisions is the 'quit cost,' which is the opportunity cost associated with the loss of accumulated pension benefits when an employee makes the decision to quit the job (Nyce 2007). Compared with the overall pension benefits, the 'quit cost' might play a more important role in employees' decision-making. Employees might not be fully aware of their overall pension benefits while working. However, when they are making the decision to leave their positions, the cost of losing the accumulated benefits might become significant. As will be discussed in the next section, the 'quit cost' might be used as a tool to retain public employees.

Despite the obvious importance of pension benefits to the employees, there are two reasons to explain that pensions might not have a substantial impact on employees' decisions. The first reason is that pensions are future income, while employees prefer income that they immediately have access to. Future income such as pension benefits is often discounted in employees' decision-making. The 'discounting effect' is more considerable if there are risks and uncertainties associated with the level of future pension benefits. Studies repeatedly find that pensions are less important than salary in determining job satisfaction (Kimball et al. 2005).

The second reason is that employees might not have full knowledge of their pension plans. Information about pension benefits and plan options is not necessarily delivered to employees in a way that they can understand. Pension plans are often designed in a sophisticated way. Plan types, eligibility rules, benefit formula, and post-retirement benefit adjustments are among many plan design features that create challenges for ordinary employees to understand the overall level of their pension benefits. Research shows that pension plan participants do not understand the basic features of their pension plans, including their pension options, employer's match, and retirement eligibility rules (Beshears et al. 2011; Chan and Stevens 2008; Gustman, Steinmeier, and Tabatabai 2007). DeArmond and Goldhaber (2010) show that many pension plan participants cannot correctly identify their pension plan type. Although pension systems have sought to provide information to employees through seminars and documents, the complexity of pension systems still makes it difficult for employees to grasp the information. Therefore, certain changes in the pension plans might not catch employees' attention and may not have affected their decisions.

HOW DO PENSION SYSTEMS AFFECT PUBLIC EMPLOYEES?

After highlighting the importance of public pensions to employees, in this section, we identify the key elements in public pension plan design and governance that would affect public employees' motivations and decisions. We describe three key factors: pension benefits, the difference between DB and DC plans, and plan governance.

Pension Benefits

As mentioned above, most public employees are covered by DB plans. In DB plans, the core pension benefits are typically determined by a benefit formula as follows:

Retirement benefit = Final average salary × Benefit factor × Years of service

In this formula, the final average salary is the average salary in the last several years (usually 3–5 years) before retirement. The benefit factor is the percentage of the final average salary per year of service. Most public pension plans also provide post-retirement benefit increases, called cost-of-living adjustments (or COLAs). COLAs decide the rate of benefit increase after retirement to protect the purchasing power of pension benefits. In the public sector, benefit reductions are usually done by creating a new tier with a new benefit formula or creating new

COLAs rules. If employees are fully informed about their pension benefits, the change of benefits should factor in their employment decisions.

In DB plans, benefits accrue (i.e., accumulate) in a nonlinear way. There are several points in a participant's career when the accumulated benefits substantially increase. In particular, the vesting period and the retirement age affect benefit accumulation and might influence employees' decisions.

The vesting period is a period of time an employee has to stay in the same pension system in order to fully claim their pension benefits. Employees who have completed the vesting period are entitled to 100 percent of the pension benefits even if they leave their jobs. Employees who quit before the vesting period would receive less or no pension benefits. Most public pension plans have a vesting period ranging from three to five years. The vesting period penalizes those who frequently change jobs but rewards those who stay with the same employer for a longer period.

The normal retirement age is the age when employees can receive full pension benefits. Some plans combine the employee's age with their years of service to decide eligibility for full retirement benefits. For example, the 'rule of 80' means if the employee's age plus the years of service equal to 80, they are eligible for full pension benefits. Many pension plans also have an 'early retirement age' for employees to retire with reduced benefits. Depending on the eligibility rules, by design, pension benefits jump to a higher level when a certain age is reached—when workers meet the vesting period or reach a certain retirement age. The age threshold is an important factor for employees' retirement decisions, according to a study of federal employees (Lewis and Pitts 2018).

The Differences between DB and DC Plans

Compared to DB plans, DC plans provide benefits based on a different benefit structure. DC plan benefits are based on individual accounts, which receive funding from employer contributions, employee contributions, and investment returns. The employers (i.e., the governments) only guarantee the contributions to the individual accounts. This key difference shapes how pensions influence employees in three ways.

First, there is little or even no 'quit cost' associated with DC plans. DC plans usually have a very short (i.e., one year) or no vesting period, while DB plans usually have a vesting period of three to five years. DC plan benefits are 'portable' because participants can transfer their balance in their individual accounts to other pension plans when they change jobs. The absence of the 'quit cost' also means there is no motivation for employees to stay at one job to secure retirement benefits.

Second, DC plan participants accumulate their benefits in a linear way. This is different from the DB plans because DB plan participants accumulate benefits slower in their earlier years and faster in the later years. In the DB benefit formula, two factors—years of service and final average salary—increase as employees stay longer with the same employer. Thus, in terms of benefit accumulation, DB plans would reward those employees with a longer tenure. This motivation structure is absent in DC plans in which the accumulation of pension benefits is just a fixed percentage of their salaries.

Third, DC plans are widely used in the private sector and are transferable between the private and public sectors. Therefore, DC plans might be more attractive to employees who prefer mobility and flexibility in employment. Studies show that DC plans are attractive to the younger population with higher education (e.g., Chingos and West 2015; Clark, Hanson, and Mitchell 2016; Goldhaber and Grout 2016). From the human resource management perspective, the introduction of DC plans might serve the purpose of attracting younger workers or workers from the private sector.

In recent years, many state and local pension systems have introduced DC plans either as the primary plan or a supplemental plan (Chen et al. 2013; Munnell, Aubry, and Cafarelli 2014). Many scholars and practitioners also advocate for more transition from DB to DC plans in the public sector for the purpose of sharing costs and risks with employees. The transition from DB to DC plans will likely affect employment decisions because of the three reasons mentioned above.

Pension Plan Governance

While benefit levels and plan types are critical factors to influence employees' motivation and decisions, plan governance can also affect employees' perception, involvement, and understanding of their pension plans, which in turn would influence their decisions regarding pensions or employment. The assumption is that if employees are involved in making difficult decisions regarding their pension benefits, the negative impact of those benefit changes might be reduced because they understand the tradeoffs.

A public pension plan's governance structure is important for employees to gain knowledge and exert their influence over pension plans. Public pension plans are usually governed by a board of trustees. Trustees can be elected by plan members or can be appointed by politicians. Unions can also have their representatives on the pension board. Unions may also participate in the negotiation over pension benefit changes. Employees' representatives on the pension board and the employees' unions provide important channels for employees to receive information, which would affect how they are influenced by pension decisions.

Public pension systems deliver information to employees through new employee training sections, public information on websites and brochures, and financial reports. Also, many pension systems provide education opportunities to improve employees' overall financial literacy, so they are more aware of the importance of their pensions. These information channels could increase employees' awareness of their pension benefits, which could be used to achieve the goal of using pensions as motivations. On the other hand, the lack of transparency might be used as a way to hide the pension changes that are not favorable to employees in order to reduce the negative impact of pension benefit reductions.

EMPIRICAL EVIDENCE FROM PRIOR STUDIES

In this section, we summarize the empirical evidence that shows how pensions affect public employees. The scope of our review includes a wide range of studies that examine public sector pension plans, including federal, state, and local general employees' plans, as well as teachers' plans. In the areas that we cannot find evidence from the public sector, we also show findings from studies that are based on private pension plans.

How Does the Benefit Accumulation Path Affect Employees' Decisions?

Prior studies have empirically tested how the accumulation path of pension benefits affects an employee's decision to exit the workforce. Most early studies are based on Social Security and private sector pensions. Several theories have been developed to explain the incentive effect created by pension benefit rules. Stock and Wise's (1988) 'option value' model assumes that individuals would assign a discount factor to future income streams and calculate the present value of retirement benefits. Their utility function consists of their wage earnings and discounted pension benefits. An individual's decision to retire will be determined by whether 'the value of the option to retire later exceeds the value of retiring today' (Stock and Wise 1988). Built on the 'option value' model, Coile and Gruber (2007) use forward-looking measures to calculate the future accumulation of pension benefits and develop a 'peak value' model. They argue that employees are most likely to retire when their pension benefits reach the 'peak value.' Therefore, the benefit rules of a pension plan would influence employees' decisions to exit the workforce, which might further shape the age structure of the workforce.

After examining federal civil service workers (Department of Defense), Asch, Haider, and Zissimopoulos (2002) find that public sector employees behave in the manner of 'retirement incentive' driven by typical DB plans (e.g., Civil Service Retirement System, CSRS)—1 percent increase of pension peak value decreases retirement by 0.1 percent. Employees being responsive to pension peak values are also examined at the state and local government pension systems and teacher's pension systems (e.g., Costrell and McGee 2010; Costrell and Podgursky 2007; Johnson et al. 2014). Based on the analysis of 612 traditional public pension plans administered at the state level, Johnson et al. (2014) find that a one-year spike of pension benefits accounts for 'nearly half of the expected lifetime benefits that employees have accumulated to that point' and often happens at age 55 for employees hired at age 25. Hence, state and local officials at their mid-career have strong incentives to remain in the job until they can realize the pension benefit peak. The study questions the implication of locking in the mid-career employees on workforce quality because years of service cannot always be translated into higher productivity.

Costrell and Podgursky (2007) examined teacher pension plans in four states (Arkansas, California, Massachusetts, and Missouri) and confirmed that DB pension plans form strong incentives for teachers to retire when pension wealth peaks. Although with some variations, all pension plans exhibit sharp spikes in the growth of pension wealth from additional years of work at specific points in a teacher's career, and negative returns afterward. These features create powerful incentives to retire at ages around mid-to-early 50s when they fulfill the retirement eligibility. Incentivizing teachers to retire at a certain point under DB plans is called the 'pushing and pulling' effect—pulling teachers to retire when they reach the pension spike and pushing them to retire right after the pension peak value turns negative because working past the pension wealth peak lowers the expected pension wealth (Costrell and Podgursky 2010).

The repercussion of such pushing and pulling retirement incentives is the high attrition rate among late-career teachers. Kim et al. (2017) simulated the effect of late-career salary bonuses and deferred retirement option plans (DROP) which can help retain experienced teachers in the STEM field (science, technology, engineering, and math) in Missouri. The study finds that the DROP plan can yield additional teaching years by senior teachers for as little as $1269 per year (50 percent DROP). Retention bonuses are costlier, at $35,000–38,000 per incremental year. Whether such policy cost is worth it depends on whether senior teachers are more effective or whether policy can target only the most effective senior teachers.

The retirement incentive structure also prevents teachers' mobility across pension systems. Costrell and Podgursky (2010) compare six state pension plans (Ohio, Arkansas, California, Massachusetts, Missouri, Texas) to examine the net pension redistribution between long-term teachers and short-term teachers and find that DB plans penalize teachers' cross-state mobility. Compared to fiscally equivalent cash balance plans (i.e., a DC plan with guaranteed returns), DB plans redistribute about half of the entering cohort's net pension wealth to those retiring at their 50s from early retiring teachers. The study also simulates that compared to a teacher staying in one system, a mobile teacher experiences losses of net pension wealth by 40 percent to 75 percent depending on the state when separated at the age of 55. Koedel et al. (2012) also find that DB plans hinder interschool leadership mobility.

Overall, studies of this strand confirm that pension wealth accrual of DB plans follow a nonlinear path and create strong incentives for the employees to retire when the expected value of pension wealth reaches its peak. Studies also investigate the repercussions of the retirement incentive structure and explain the implications on workforce quality in two aspects: incentivizing mid-career employees to stay and penalizing mobile employees compared to residing employees.

How Do Pension Benefit Changes Affect Recruitment, Retention, and Turnover?

Studies have also investigated the effects of benefit changes—either benefit cuts or enhancements—on employees' motivations and decisions. Most studies find consistent evidence that reduced pension benefits negatively affect the recruitment and retention of a quality workforce in the public sector.

Pension benefits affect public workforce recruitment. Munnell, Aubry, and Sanzenbacher (2015) examine the effect of reduced deferred benefits on workforce quality. The generosity of each state and local government's pension system is measured by pension normal costs. The workforce quality is defined as the quality gap—the wage difference between workers entering the public sector from the private sector and leaving the public sector for the private sector. From a plan-level analysis, Munnell, Aubry, and Sanzenbacher (2015) find that plans with higher normal costs (i.e., more generous plan) have smaller quality gaps but the relationship is nonlinear. The most generous plans have the smallest quality gaps between the public and private workforce, and such a relationship is weak for moderately generous plans. The study runs individual-level analysis as well, and finds that a one percentage point increase in the normal cost decreases the quality gap by 0.5 percentage points, indicating that more generous public pension plans are effective in recruiting and retaining high-paid private sector workers. The relationship between pension generosity and higher wage of new hires from the private sector is consistent when pension generosity is measured in terms of pension benefit cuts entailed by altering vesting period and retiring age, final average salary period, COLAs, or benefit multiplier (Quinby, Sanzenbacher, and Aubry 2018). Moreover, the authors' follow-up study finds that high employee contribution rates can offset the positive effects of generous pension benefits on recruiting high-quality workers (Quinby and Sanzenbacher 2020). Based on such offsetting relationships, the study concludes that 'many state and local governments currently ask their employees to pay too much for their pension benefits to reap a positive effect on recruitment' (p. 9).

Pension benefit changes affect public employees' decisions on exiting as well as entering the public sector. Gorina and Hoang (2020) constructed an index to quantify the degree of state and local governments' pension reforms. The explicit reform (lower benefit) category includes reducing benefit factors, reducing COLAs, introducing DC plans, or increasing employee contributions. The implicit reform (tighter eligibility rules) includes changes in retirement age, increase in total years of service for full-benefit eligibility, or increase in final years of service. Lastly, the benefit-neutral reform indicates a longer vesting period or higher employer contribution rate. The study finds that the state and local governments that enacted pension reforms have higher turnover rates than the plans without any pension reforms. Also, the relationship is only significant for the explicit reforms (lower benefits) than the implicit reforms (tighter eligibility rules). The study suggests that employees are less responsive to pension reforms when the changes are more difficult to comprehend and evaluate the repercussion. Moreover, the positive effect of pension reforms on the turnover rate is stronger for the pension systems that have a higher share of college-educated workers, raising the possible conflict between transparency and efficiency of pension reforms.

Studies have also found the relative importance of benefit factors on retirement decisions. For example, in the case of the California State Teachers Retirement System (CalSTRS), Brown (2013) finds that pension enhancement leads to delayed retirement. In 1998, the CalSTRS underwent two pension enhancements which were done by increasing the benefit factor. The first reform increased the maximum benefit factor from 2 percent to 2.4 percent. Prior to the reform, the benefit factor was 1.4 percent at age 55 and increased at an annual rate of 0.12 percentage points up to the maximum of 2.0 percent at age 60. After the reform, the benefit factor continues to increase at an annual rate of 0.133 percentage points after age 60, reaching the new maximum of 2.4 percent at age 63. The second reform provided a one-time increase of 0.2 percentage point increase in the benefit factors when reaching 30 years of service. The study shows such pension enhancements effectively delayed retirements at the age of 60, suggesting that the strong preference for retiring at age 60 is driven by financial incentives than other non-pension coincident incentives (e.g., social norms).

Kim (2020) also investigates two pension enhancement reforms imposed in Missouri in 2000 and 2002. The pension benefit changes included easing the milestone in collecting the full benefits and increasing benefit factors from 2.5 percent to 2.55 percent for some participants. Findings show that the change in eligibility age increased the probability of retirement by 6.1 percentage points and the benefit factor enhancement increased the probability of retirement by 13.9 percentage points. In the case of the St. Louis School District pension system, however, a study failed to find strong evidence that pension benefits increase via benefit factor change (from 1.25 percent to 2.00 percent retroactively) leads to a higher retention rate (Koedel and Xiang 2017). This suggests that the effect of pension benefits change is complicated because not only the benefit factor itself but also the way it is designed affects employees' behaviors.

In sum, the empirical studies on pension benefits change and its effect on employees' behaviors suggest that giving less benefits with tighter eligibility rules results in attrition of relatively young teachers while delaying the retirement for those who have higher motives and commitment in teaching. Moreover, each pension policy change (e.g., benefit factor) can have very different effects on employees' behaviors depending on how policies are combined under which policy goals.

How Does the Difference Between DB to DC Plans Affect the Workforce?

In the private sector, many firms changed from DB plans to DC plans, allowing scholars to compare employees' behaviors between the two types of pension plans. The findings are mixed. Gustman and Steinmeier (1993) find similar mobility rates for workers with DB and DC plans. Friedberg and Owyang (2004), however, find that workers with DB pensions have significantly longer tenure than workers without pensions or workers with DC pensions. Haverstick et al. (2010) find that workers in 5–10 years of tenure and covered by a DC plan are 22 percent more likely to shift jobs than workers covered by a DB plan. Workers with more than 20 years of tenure and under a DB plan are significantly more likely to retire than workers under a DC plan. The findings confirm the conventional argument that DB plans generate a unique incentive structure in retirement.

The incentive structure embedded in DB plans, in comparison with the DC plans, is empirically tested in the public sector as well. Ippolito (1987) investigated why federal workers have low turnover rates compared to private sector workers. Using 1979 Current Population Survey data, the study concludes that the DB plan, which is the pension plan for the federal workers (CSRS), increases the potential loss of quitting before reaching retirement eligibility, thus incentivizing workers to delay quitting until they meet the retirement eligibility. The explanation, however, fails to account for the prior findings that pension workers (either DB or DC plans) have longer tenure than non-pension workers (Gustman and Steinmeier 1993; Munnell, Aubry, and Sanzenbacher 2015).

The selection effect of pensions has been developed as an alternative explanation. Offering deferred compensation, regardless of the pension structure, attracts workers who value such benefits. Ippolito (2002) examines federal workers' quitting behaviors by comparing CSRS (traditional DB plan) and FERS (Federal Employee Retirement System; a less-generous DC plan which significantly reduces the quitting loss). The study finds that the quit rate among the new hires covered by the FERS is significantly higher in the early years of tenure than the CSRS employees, but the quit rate gradually converges to the CSRS quit rate after several years of tenure. Based on the finding, the author argues that deferred wage systems have a selection effect—the pension plan attracts more 'stayers' than 'quitters.' The study goes further to confirm the characteristics of the stayers and found that stayers are more likely to be 'savers' (more likely to participate in voluntary 40l(k) plan) and 'savers' are more likely to have higher performance ratings, be promoted, and less likely to have disciplinary actions.

The introduction of DC plans in the public sector allowed a quasi-experimental setting where scholars can investigate the effect of pension structures on employees' behaviors. Clark, Hanson, and Mitchell (2016) examine the effect of pension structure reform (DB vs. hybrid) in Utah to understand state employee's separation behaviors. Utah implemented a pension reform effective in 2011. The reform includes closing the DB plans to new hires and establishing the two-option replacement plan. New hires get to choose a DC plan or a hybrid pension plan (less generous than pre-reform DB plan). The study finds that more than 87 percent of those hired prior to the reform were still employed two years later, while fewer than 83 percent of those hired after the reform remained at the two-year mark. The finding confirms the conventional argument that the separation rate is higher under the DC plan than the DB plan.

Chalmers, Johnson, and Reuter (2014) investigate the Oregon Public Employee Retirement System (PERS). Oregon PERS had evolved into a complex pension plan with both DB and DC elements, serving almost all non-federal public employees in Oregon. Using individual-level administrative data, the study finds that retirement decisions are dependent upon the types of pension plans. As predicted from prior studies, the study finds that retirees under DB and hybrid plans are five to seven times more likely to retire at age 58 than they are at age 55. However, retirees under DC plans are more likely to retire at age 55 than at age 58. Such finding corresponds with prior knowledge that under DB plans, the decision to retire is sensitive to attaining the normal retirement age and that DC plans enable early retirement than DB plans.

The different attrition rate between a DB plan and a DC plan is also evidenced in the public teacher's pension system. Chingos and West (2015) find that teachers who opted in DC plans are more likely to leave the Florida public schools than teachers under DB plans, with a difference growing larger as the years of service increase—one percentage point in the second year to nine percentage points in the sixth year. Furthermore, the difference in attrition rate between the two pension plan groups is larger among teachers who are less than 30 years old at the time of selecting the plan type. From the findings, the study concludes that DC plans are more attractive to new (and hence younger) teachers who are less confident about whether they will remain in the career for a substantial amount of time.

However, a study examining the case of Washington State public school teachers' pension did not find significant evidence of higher turnover rates under a DC-DB hybrid plan than a DB plan (Goldhaber, Grout, and Holden 2017). In Washington, teachers hired between 1977 and 1996 are covered under the Teacher Retirement System: TRS2, which is a traditional DB plan. Teachers hired between 1996 and 2007 are covered under TRS3, a hybrid DB-DC plan, and existing TRS2 employees were given the option to transfer into TRS3. By comparing the turnover rates between the two cohorts, the study finds that the turnover rate of employees hired just before the reform compared with those hired just after the reform does not differ. Among the new hires since 2008 who can choose between TRS2 and TRS3, employees who chose TRS3 (hybrid) are slightly less likely to quit within one year than employees who chose TRS2. Furthermore, contrary to conventional wisdom, teachers who chose to transfer to hybrid plans from a DB plan have significantly lower turnover rates than those who chose to stay in the DB plan. Overall, the study finds little evidence to support the conventional wisdom that transformation to a DC pension structure will increase employee turnover.

By design, DC plans generate less opportunity costs for quitting than DB plans. Therefore, it is a widely accepted notion that DC plans are less effective in retaining employees. The empirical evidence, however, is inconsistent. Understanding the consequences of transforming a DB plan to a DC plan is becoming more critical in the public pension systems because many pension systems regard the DC plan as an effective way to ease the state governments' burden of pension costs. By examining more pension reform cases, researchers will then be able to provide better policy implications in transforming pension structures.

How Can Public Employees Get Involved and Informed about Pension Plans?

A body of literature also shows how employees can get involved in pension plan governance and how employees' involvement in governance affects pension decisions and pension systems' performance.

State and local pension systems are usually administered by a board of trustees. Although there are great variations in different states, pension boards are usually responsible for setting important policies such as investment decisions, contribution rates, actuarial assumptions, reporting, and monitoring. According to Chen, Kriz, and Ebdon (2015), on average public plan pension boards consist of ten trustees with almost half (49.67 percent) of the board trustees elected by public employees to represent their interests. The other trustees are government officials or political appointees. Employees on the governing boards are found to be effective in reducing political influence in pension policies (Hsin and Mitchell 1994; Wang and Peng 2018). When there are more employee representatives on the governing board, pension plans tend to make more responsible decisions and take less risk. Chen, Kriz, and Ebdon (2015) and Harper (2008) find that the percentage of elected members on the board is positively related to the level of plan funding. However, the findings are inconclusive because other research settings show mixed results (Mitchell and Hsin 1997; Yang and Mitchell 2005; Munnell, Aubry, and Haverstick 2008; Munnell, Aubry, and Quinby 2011).

Employees can also influence pension governance through their unions. Public employees' unions play a vital role in influencing pension policies. Prior studies have examined how public employees' unions affect pension plan benefits, contributions, and funding status. Most studies measure the strength of unions by the percent of public employees that are covered by unions. The impact of unions on public pension systems is complicated. On the one hand, unions tend to push for high benefits (Chen 2018). High benefits might increase pension liabilities to a level that governments cannot afford. On the other side, unions can also advocate for decisions that require governments to increase funding. Peng and Wang (2017) show that higher union coverage is positively related to higher contributions from the governments. Chaney, Copely, and Stone (2002) find that unionization of state employees significantly increases their pension plan funding status because unions serve as a watchdog group to protect employee pensions and restrict state discretion on funding decisions. However, other studies have shown mixed findings. Mitchell and Smith (1994) suggest that the degree of unionization negatively affects the funding ratio. They argue that employees' unions might assume that workers care more about their wages and allow inadequate pension funding in exchange for high wages. Johnson (1997) also finds that the employee unionization level is negatively related to pension funding. Munnell et al. (2011) find that unions significantly affect wage levels, but not pension plan generosity or the rate of growth in pension benefits. They explain that unions might have more influence on wages than pension benefits.

Many studies also find that individual employees lack the sophisticated financial knowledge to make rational decisions about participation, contribution, and investment in their pension plans, and therefore a workplace financial literacy program is necessary and effective (Fore 2001; Holland, Goodman, and Stich 2008). Without proper financial knowledge, average employees tend to remain as 'reluctant' or 'disengaged' investors (Byrne, Harrison, and Blake 2008). Studies show that when individual employees make decisions on pension plans, they tend to have low participation rates and use naive strategies in investments (Benartzi and Thaler 2001; Cranch and Notto 2008; Huberman 2001; Rugh 2003). This low participation rate and poor investment decisions will significantly reduce the potential benefits for the employees.

CONCLUSIONS AND FUTURE RESEARCH

In this chapter, we conduct a review of the existing literature on how public pension systems influence public employees' motivations and decisions. We also explain how public pensions affect employees' decisions to enter, stay, and exit employment in the public sector. Although there are many mixed findings in the prior literature, the review can give us some general understanding of the relationship between public pensions and employment in the public sector. Finally, we summarize the common themes and provide some directions for future inquiry along these lines.

First, public pension plan design features, especially the benefit eligibility rules, affect employees' motivations and decisions. Research demonstrates that DB plans accrue benefits in a nonlinear way, which creates incentives for employees to exit the workforce at certain ages. Thus, it is reasonable to expect that the incentive structure created by pension plans can be used to shape the quality of the workforce. For example, Urban Institute (n.d.) develops a grading system for state pension plans based on their benefit rules that favor 'younger workers,' 'short-term employees,' 'older ages,' and 'long-term employees.' Retaining quality public employees and reducing the turnover rate are important topics for public human resource management. How pension plans can be designed to achieve these human resource management goals can be further studied.

Second, research shows that public pension benefits are important for recruiting and retaining a quality workforce. Pension benefits affect the quality gap between the public sector and the private sector. Generous pension benefits are effective in recruiting workers from the private sector. Pension benefits reductions, whether they are done through altering COLAs, benefit factors, contribution rates, or benefit rules, reduce the attractiveness of public sector job positions. Therefore, we argue that reforms of pension systems should balance the tradeoff between reducing pension costs for governments and retaining quality employees. How can governments balance the goals of pension system reforms? Or, in other words, how can governments reduce pension costs without affecting employees' motivations and job satisfaction? These questions should be considered in future discussions on public pension reforms.

Third, most public pension plans are DB-based and most private pension plans are DC-based—this is the major difference between public and private pensions. A recent trend shows that many public plans follow private plans to introduce more DC features into their pension systems. How would this change affect public employees? On the one hand, when public pensions are more like private pensions, it provides flexibility for mobile and young employees and facilitates the transition of workers between sectors. On the other side, the competitive advantages of the traditional public DB plan, such as the certainty of income and the rewarding mechanism for a longer tenure, would be lost. Whether the transition from DB to DC plans in the public sector is good for the public workforce is a complicated issue. We argue that both the pros and cons of DC plans should be considered when governments consider introducing more DC plans into their pension systems.

Finally, there are opportunities to better inform employees about their pension plans and ways to further involve employees in plan governance. Informing employees about their pensions is important if pensions are used as a human resource management tool to motivate employees. Transparency of information to employees helps reveal employees' preferences toward benefit levels, risk levels, and plan designs, which could improve the quality of decision-making. If employees are better involved in plan governance through their representatives on the governing board or through their unions, they could better understand the difficult decisions pension systems have to make. Employees are key stakeholders of the pension systems. More involved and informed stakeholders can help integrate multiple interests in making financially responsible decisions. Future research can examine how pension systems can better communicate with employees and incorporate their preferences in making key decisions in public pension systems.

REFERENCES

Asch, B., Haider, S.J., and Zissimopoulos, J.M. (2002). The retirement behavior of federal civil service workers. Michigan Retirement Research Center Research Paper No. WP2002-026.

Benartzi, S., and Thaler, R.H. (2001). Naive diversification strategies in defined contribution saving plans. *American Economic Review*, 91, 79–98.

Beshears, J., Choi, J.J., Laibson, D., and Madrian, B.C. (2011). Behavioral economics perspectives on public sector pension plans. *Journal of Pension Economics and Finance*, 10, 315–336.

Biggs, A. (2018). Have public employee pensions become more generous, or less? Retrieved November 15, 2021 from https://www.forbes.com/sites/andrewbiggs/2018/08/14/have-public-employee-pensions-become-more-generous-or-less/#4957ab9a1e20.

Brown, K.M. (2013). The link between pensions and retirement timing: Lessons from California teachers. *Journal of Public Economics*, 98, 1–14.

Byrne, A., Harrison, D., and Blake, D. (2008). Defined contribution pensions: Dealing with the reluctant investor. *Journal of Financial Regulation and Compliance*, 16, 206–219.

Chalmers, J., Johnson, W.T., and Reuter, J. (2014). The effect of pension design on employer costs and employee retirement choices: Evidence from Oregon. *Journal of Public Economics*, 116, 17–34.

Chan, S., and Stevens, A.H. (2008). What you don't know can't help you: Pension knowledge and retirement decision-making. *The Review of Economics and Statistics*, 90, 253–266.

Chaney, B.A., Copley, P.A., and Stone, M.S. (2002). The effect of fiscal stress and balanced budget requirements on the funding and measurement of state pension obligations. *Journal of Accounting and Public Policy*, 21, 287–313.

Chen, G. (2018). Understanding decisions in state pension systems: A system framework. *American Review of Public Administration*, 48, 260–273.

Chen, G., Ebdon, C., Kriz, K., and Maisondieu-Laforge, O. (2013). The management of defined contribution pension plans in local governments. *Public Budgeting and Finance*, 33, 75–95.

Chen, G., Kriz, K., and Ebdon, C. (2015). The effect of board composition on public pension plan funding. *Journal of Public Budgeting, Accounting, and Financial Management*, 27, 352–376.

Chingos, M.M., and West, M.R. (2015). Which teachers choose a defined contribution pension plan? Evidence from the Florida retirement system. *Education Finance and Policy*, 10, 193–222.

Clark, R.L., Hanson, E., and Mitchell, O.S. (2016). Lessons for public pensions from Utah's move to pension choice. *Journal of Pension Economics and Finance*, 15, 285–310.

Coile, C., and Gruber, J. (2007). Future social security entitlements and the retirement decision. *The review of Economics and Statistics*, 89, 234–246.

Costrell, R.M., and McGee, J.B. (2010). Teacher pension incentives, retirement behavior, and potential for reform in Arkansas. *Education Finance and Policy*, 5, 492–518.

Costrell, R.M., and Podgursky, M. (2007). *Efficiency and equity in the time pattern of teacher pension benefits*. Working Paper 2007-01. National Center on Performance Incentives.

Costrell, R.M., and Podgursky, M. (2010). Distribution of benefits in teacher retirement systems and their implications for mobility. *Education Finance and Policy*, 5, 519–557.

Cranch, L.E., and Notto, D.A. (2008). Evolving fiduciary duty standards for defined contribution plan sponsors: The impact of new thinking about employee participation and investment selection. *Journal of Deferred Compensation*, 13, 19–35.

DeArmond, M., and Goldhaber, D. (2010). Scrambling the nest egg: How well do teachers understand their pensions, and what do they think about alternative pension structures? *Education Finance and Policy*, 5, 558–586.

Fore, D. (2001). Going private in the public sector: The transition from defined benefit to defined contribution pension plans. In O.S. Mitchell and E.C. Hustead (eds), *Pension in the public sector*. Philadelphia, PA: University of Pennsylvania Press, pp. 267–287.

Foster, A. (1997). Public and private sector defined benefit pensions: A comparison. Retrieved November 15, 2021 from https://www.bls.gov/opub/mlr/1997/article/public-and-private-sector-defined-benefit-pensions-a-comparison.htm.

Friedberg, L., and Owyang, M. (2004). *Explaining the evolution of pension structure and job tenure* (No. w10714). National Bureau of Economic Research.

Goldhaber, D., and Grout, C. (2016). Which plan to choose? The determinants of pension system choice for public school teachers. *Journal of Pension Economics and Finance, 15*, 30–54.

Goldhaber, D., Grout, C., and Holden, K.L. (2017). Pension structure and employee turnover: Evidence from a large public pension system. *ILR Review, 70*, 976–1007.

Gorina, E., and Hoang, T. (2020). Pension reforms and public sector turnover. *Journal of Public Administration Research and Theory, 30*, 96–112.

Gustman, A.L., and Steinmeier, T.L. (1993). Pension portability and labor mobility: Evidence from the survey of income and program participation. *Journal of Public Economics, 50*, 299–323.

Gustman, A.L., Steinmeier, T., and Tabatabai, N. (2007). *Imperfect knowledge of pension plan type* (No. w13379). National Bureau of Economic Research.

Harper, J. (2008). *Board of Trustee composition and investment performance of US public pension plans.* Retrieved November 15, 2021 from https://icpm.in1touch.org/document/4313/Joel_Harper_Board_of_Trustee_Composition_and_Investment_Performance_of_US_Public_Pension_Plans_February_2008.pdf.

Haverstick, K., Munnell, A.H., Sanzenbacher, G., and Soto, M. (2010). Pension type, tenure, and job mobility. *Journal of Pension Economics and Finance, 9*, 609–625.

Holland, J.H., Goodman, D., and Stich, B. (2008). Defined contribution plans emerging in the public sector: The manifestation of defined contributions and the effects of workplace financial literacy education. *Review of Public Personnel Administration, 28*, 367–384.

Hsin, P., and Mitchell, O.S. (1994). The political economy of public pensions: Pension funding, governance, and fiscal stress. *Revista de Análisis Económico–Economic Analysis Review, 9*, 151–168.

Huberman, G. (2001). Familiarity breeds investment. *Review of Financial Studies, 14*, 659–680.

Ippolito, R.A. (1987). Why federal workers don't quit. *Journal of Human Resources, 22*, 281–299.

Ippolito, R.A. (2002). Stayers as 'workers' and 'savers': Toward reconciling the pension-quit literature. *Journal of Human Resources, 37*, 275–308.

Johnson, R W. (1997). Pension underfunding and liberal retirement benefits among state and local government workers. *National Tax Journal, 50*, 113–142.

Johnson, R.W., Butrica, B.A., Haaga, O., and Southgate, B.G. (2014). Do state and local pensions lock in mid-career employees? Public Pension Project Brief 3, Urban Institute.

Kim, D. (2020). Worker retirement responses to pension incentives: Do they respond to pension wealth? *Journal of Economic Behavior and Organization, 173*, 365–385.

Kim, D., Koedel, C., Kong, W., Ni, S., Podgursky, M., and Wu, W. (2017). Pensions and late-career teacher retention. *Education Finance and Policy, 16*, 42–65.

Kimball, S.M., Heneman, H.G., and Kellor, E.M. (2005). Can pensions help attract teachers? *Journal of Education Finance, 30*(4), 399–411.

Koedel, C., and Xiang, P.B. (2017). Pension enhancements and the retention of public employees. *ILR Review, 70*, 519–551.

Koedel, C., Grissom, J.A., Ni, S., and Podgursky, M. (2012). *Pension-induced rigidities in the labor market for school leaders.* Working Paper 67. National Center for Analysis of Longitudinal Data in Education Research.

Lewis, G.B., and Pitts, D. (2018). Deciding to retire from the federal service. *Review of Public Personnel Administration, 38*, 49–82.

Mitchell, O., and Hsin, P. (1997). Public pension governance and performance. In S. Valdes-Prieto (ed.), *The economics of pensions: Principles, policies and international experience.* Cambridge, MA: Cambridge University Press.

Mitchell, O.S. and Smith, R.S. (1994). Pension funding in the public sector. *The Review of Economics and Statistics, 76*, 278–290.

Monahan, A.B. (2010). Public pension plan reform: The legal framework. *Education Finance and Policy, 5*, 617–646.

Munnell, A.H., Aubry, J.P., and Haverstick, K. (2008). The funding status of locally administered pension plans. Retrieved November 15, 2021 from http://crr.bc.edu/briefs/the-funding-status-of-locally-adminis tered-pension-plans/.

Munnell, A.H., Aubry, J.P., Hurwitz, J., and Quinby L. (2011). *Unions and public pension benefits*. Center for Retirement Research at Boston College. Retrieved November 15, 2021 from https://crr.bc.edu/wp-content/uploads/2011/07/slp_19.pdf.

Munnell, A.H., Aubry, J.P., and Cafarelli, M. (2014). Defined contribution plans in the public sector: An update. Center for Retirement Research at Boston College. Retrieved November 15, 2021 from https://www.nasra.org/files/Topical%20Reports/Plan%20Design/Defined_Contribution_Plans_An_Update.pdf.

Munnell, A.H., Aubry, J.P., and Sanzenbacher, G. (2015). *Recruiting and retaining high-quality state and local workers: Do pensions matter?* Working Paper 2015-1. Center for Retirement Research at Boston College.

Nyce, S.A. (2007). Behavioral effects of employer-sponsored retirement plans. *Journal of Pension Economics and Finance*, 6, 251–285.

Peng, J. (2009). *State and local pension fund management*. Boca Raton, FL: CRC Press.

Peng, J., and Wang, Q. (2017). Affordability of public pension benefit: A historical and empirical analysis of US state and local government pension contributions. *Journal of Pension Economics and Finance*, 16, 21–42.

Quinby, L.D., and Sanzenbacher, G.T. (2020). Do pensions matter for recruiting state and local workers? *State and Local Government Review*, 52, 6–17.

Quinby, L.D., Sanzenbacher, G.T., and Aubry, J. (2018). How have pension cuts affected public sector competitiveness? Center for Retirement Research at Boston College. Retrieved November 15, 2021 from https://crr.bc.edu/wp-content/uploads/2018/04/slp_59.pdf.

Rugh, J. (2003). Participant contribution and asset allocations during the recent bull and bear market: Evidence from TIAA-CREF. *Benefits Quarterly*, 19, 55–67.

Stock, J., and Wise, D. (1988). *The pension inducement to retire: an option value analysis* (No. w2660; p. w2660). National Bureau of Economic Research. https://doi.org/10.3386/w2660.

Stock, J.H., and Wise, D.A. (1990). Pensions, the option value of work, and retirement. *Econometrica*, 58, 1151–1180.

The Pew Charitable Trust (2019). The state pension funding gap: 2017. Retrieved November 15, 2021 from https://www.pewtrusts.org/en/research-and-analysis/issue-briefs/2019/06/the-state-pension-funding-gap-2017.

Urban Institute (n.d.). The state of retirement: Grading America's public pension plans. Retrieved November 15, 2021 from https://apps.urban.org/features/SLEPP/index.html.

Wang, Q., and Peng, J. (2018). Political embeddedness of public pension governance: An event history analysis of discount rate changes. *Public Administration Review*, 78, 785–794.

Yang, T., and Mitchell, O.S. (2005). *Public pension governance, funding, and performance: A longitudinal appraisal*. Working Papers 376. Wharton Pension Research Council.

13. Unreserved fund balance management practices in US counties
John A. Hamman, LaShonda M. Stewart, Brian C. Chapman and Jeremy N. Phillips

INTRODUCTION

It is often misleading to think of government agencies as unified, rational actors. Factors internal and external to an agency motivate administrators. How public agencies are structured and managed affects how they behave and perform (Thompson 1967; Wilson 1989). In this more intricate view of public agencies and their environments, managing uncertainty becomes a principal challenge (Thompson 1967). Agency decisions reflect the interaction of the operators responsible with those higher up in the organization and external to it which may set agency goals as well as the goals set by those who legislate or lobby over it (Wilson 1989; Dilulio et al. 1991). This gives rise to circumstances in which politics and ambiguous goals complicate agency decision making (Davis and Stazyk 2015). We then may observe agency behavior other than what best-practice conscious decision makers, or reason alone, might lead us to expect. This is not necessarily because officials are corrupt or inept, but because officials must cope with environmental uncertainties while reconciling goals for making good public policy with their agency's need to maintain political and public support (Rourke 1969; Arnold 1979; Hamman 1993).

In the case of county government budget decisions, professional norms and best practices dictate that local officials transparently maintain slack resources to contend with shortfalls in revenue that will inevitably arise out of dependence on revenue sources sensitive to business cycles. Revenue shortfalls, particularly likely during economic downswings, further stress government finances. Slack resources oftentimes thought of as government savings can help to temper revenue volatility.[1] They can enable governments to spend counter-cyclically to provide important local services through good and bad economic times. They may help to finance planned capital expenditures and reduce the need to borrow and incur interest expenses. On-hand reserves also help to demonstrate creditworthiness. Thus, slack resources represent an important hedge against uncertain future expenditures (Lucas and Stokey 1983; Massey and Tyer 1990; Tyer 1993; Wagner 2004; Marlowe 2005, 2013; Hendrick 2006; Finkler 2010; Stewart, Hamman, and Pink-Harper 2018). The National Association of State Budget Officers, the National Conference of State Legislatures, and the Government Finance Officers Association (GFOA) condone government developing budgetary slack in this way and recommend that state and local governments maintain moderately sized unreserved fund balances of up to 5 percent for state governments and as much as 15 percent, or two months' operating expenses for local governments (Gauthier 2002).

However, a lack of public support and the political incentives of other government officials to draw down these funds for other purposes complicate the straightforward implementation of these policies. For one thing, decision makers must contend with a lack of public support.

As far back as the passage of California's proposition 13, the lack of public and political support for governmental reserves is clear. Calls for shrinking government and lowering taxes continue to resonate with businesses and taxpayers, who complain that too much profit and personal income goes to the government, which stifles economic growth and/or simply wastes money. Businesses and taxpayers also push back against deteriorating infrastructure and service cutbacks that ultimately result from tax reductions. This creates strong incentives for redirecting any existing slack resources for these purposes. There can be considerable pressure to spend reserves on popular initiatives.

Lacking sufficient legal authority and/or a political mandate, a prudent strategy for coping with these conflicting uncertainties may be for local budget officials to reduce the transparency surrounding the establishment and administration of slack resources. Such a proposition is consistent with the widespread inability of local government budgeting studies to systematically explain the origins of widely varying slack resource levels (Marlowe 2005; Hendrick 2006; Stewart 2009, 2011) or to identify for what purposes the funds are ultimately drawn down (Marlowe 2005; Gianakis and Snow 2007; Wang and Hou 2012; Stewart, Hamman, and Pink-Harper 2018). Some research suggests that local governments use larger reserves to replace capital equipment, for self-insurance, or for the construction of major facilities (Hembree, Shelton, and Tyer 1999).

While the lack of transparency surrounding the management of unreserved fund balances is problematic from a public accountability perspective, it is not necessarily unexpected. There is accountability if one knows where to look for it. Auditing documents like comprehensive annual financial reports (CAFRs) commonly track fund balances. But budget documents or other sources, such as accompanying policy that elected officials may view, typically do not report fund balances. CAFRs also may not be readily available or intelligible to lay people (Marsh, Montondon, and Daniels 2004; Walters 2012; Funkhouser 2013b; Marlowe 2014). But reducing transparency in this way may make a lot more sense from the perspective of those managing local finances with uncertainty in mind.

This chapter assesses the implementation of GFOA recommended policy provisions for improving accountability in unreserved fund balance management practices. Specifically, it analyzes established county government fund balance policies in terms of whether they specify fund size, purpose, and replenishment. The chapter first reviews current knowledge of unreserved fund management practices which are typically limited to a single government jurisdiction. It then undertakes a nationwide analysis of county budgeting and whether they adopt policies governing the administration and use of unreserved funds. The chapter concludes by contemplating actions that could help local government fund balance management to be effective and accountable.

UNCERTAINTY AND SLACK RESOURCES IN LOCAL GOVERNMENT BUDGETING DECISIONS

Common sense suggests that local officials would maintain slack resources to contend with economic and political uncertainty. How much slack likely depends on unique local factors and contexts (Wolkoff 1987, p. 53). Although Hembree, Shelton, and Tyer (1999) concluded that the ideal fund size depends on each government's unique situation, the reserves some local governments hold likely exceed the community's contingency needs, and in such exceptional cases can result in unnecessary tax burdens (Massey and Tyer 1990). But this is difficult to determine when the purpose(s) for which governments hold unreserved fund balances are unclear. Economic conditions and financial, demographic, and institutional factors can only explain part of the variance in unreserved fund balance levels (Massey and Tyer 1990; Marlowe 2005; Hendrick 2006; Gianakis and Snow 2007; Stewart 2009, 2011; Wang and Hou 2012), and the relevant factors vary by study. For instance, Wang and Hou (2012) tested whether revenue volatility in North Carolina counties affected the creation and use of slack resources in local government finance. They found that property and sales tax effort as well as capital outlays related positively to the size of budgetary slack. They related negatively to population size and unemployment. Analyses of Minnesota and Michigan municipalities found that government perceptions of and responses to the fiscal environment were important determinants. Marlowe (2004) found that property tax revenues, rates of home ownership, and the burden of debt service mattered most. Similarly, Gianakis and Snow (2007), who also focused on municipalities, found that wealthier communities were more likely to hold unreserved fund balances, and that municipalities usually instituted these funds after experiencing a deep recession. In addition, municipalities often used the funds more to stabilize budgets when state aid decreased, rather than during economic downturns alone.

Stewart (2011) found that fund balances for slack resources in Mississippi counties varied from negative balances to over 100 percent of annual expenditures. Property taxes, other revenues, and county per-capita income contributed positively to the size of unreserved fund balances during times of economic prosperity. Counties with more debt per capita and larger minority populations, as well as faster growing counties, had smaller unreserved fund balances. County government form also affected unreserved fund balance levels. The most professional form of government institutionally separates political and administrative responsibilities by requiring that an elected board of supervisors appoint a county administrator to execute policy decisions, holding fewer unreserved funds (Stewart 2009, 2011).

Studies in Illinois found similar variability in local government slack resource levels. For instance, Stewart, Hamman, and Pink-Harper (2018) found that counties' savings generally exceeded recommended levels. Numerous factors seem to account for the overall variability in saving levels. Counties with professional administrators tended to save less in prosperous years. Assessing revenue diversification effects, intergovernmental revenue dependence, debt per capita, population change, and political ideology, Hendrick (2006) found that the fiscal performance of Chicago suburban municipalities (i.e., operating surplus or deficit) most affected fund balances. She argued that increased risk recognition and inadequate 'fiscal flexibility' (p. 42) resulted in more unreserved resources. Hendrick concluded that unreserved fund balances are most important during fiscal downturns.

Evidence that unreserved fund balance levels help local governments to tame revenue volatility and to stabilize expenditures is mixed (Marlowe 2005; Wang and Hou 2012; Stewart, Hamman, and Pink-Harper 2018). In a study of North Carolina counties, Wang and Hou (2012) found no evidence that North Carolina counties use funds counter-cyclically to stabilize expenditures over business cycles. However, in a panel study of Minnesota cities, Marlowe (2005) found that unreserved general funds bolstered expenditures during economic downturns. Likewise, in a recent panel study of Illinois counties, Stewart, Hamman, and Pink-Harper (2018) found that Illinois counties use unrestricted fund balances in governmental activity funds counter-cyclically. These results are consistent with Hendrick's work, which finds that slack is most significant in downturns.

So, studies of local governments in several states have found that various factors and circumstances may affect the size and use of unreserved fund balances, but the results are somewhat inconsistent and the purposes for the funds often remain elusive. This makes it difficult to assess whether slack resources are excessive or not (Marlowe 2005; Hendrick 2006; Stewart 2009, 2011; Wang and Hou 2012; Stewart, Hamman, and Pink-Harper 2018). These findings show varying degrees of obscurity in how local governments reveal how much slack resources to maintain and when and what to expend them on.

BEST PRACTICES IN UNRESERVED FUND BALANCE MANAGEMENT

To fully access transparency in fund balance management practices, it is important to closely examine auditing documents like CAFRs since that is often the only place these resources are reported. These documents are often the only place the public, even elected officials, have access to unreserved fund balances. The GFOA recommends that local governments maintain and report an unreserved fund balance in their CAFRs or annual audit reports rather than a formal reserve such as a rainy-day fund (GFOA 2016). CAFRs help to hold local governments fiscally responsible. They provide a uniform financial reporting standard for county governments, which includes information about the fiscal policies driving counties' financial practices. CAFRs include important information for government decision makers and the public, and they can be important tools in holding local governments fiscally accountable (Funkhouser 2013c). Over the years, the GFOA has refined and clarified standards, as well as taking steps to improve understanding of local government finances. The CAFR has been the primary means for accomplishing this. Still, the public is not likely to recognize practices and procedures officials put in place to mask current and future fund balances (Benito and Bastida 2009, p. 404). For years there has been push back from affected interests that has led local governments to fail to recognize important relationships between the cost of capital and infrastructure deficits, or to realize that they should report pensions as debt. Omissions such as these contribute to large unfunded liabilities for many local governments (Funkhouser 2013a). Funkhouser (2013b) concluded that citizen-centric reporting is a way to make local government fund balance management practices more transparent. The GFOA recommends that local governments follow measures to improve CAFR intelligibility, timeliness, accessibility, and a published policy.

INTELLIGIBILITY

Decision makers and citizens alike need numbers that they can understand (Funkhouser 2013b). CAFRs are notoriously difficult to understand or even to locate (Walters 2006; Marlowe 2014). A typical local government CAFR is hundreds of pages in length, and its different parts follow different accounting assumptions (Marlowe 2014). Even when they follow national accounting standards and guidelines, financial reports are difficult for citizens, media, and elected officials to understand fully (Marsh, Montondon, and Daniels 2004). CAFRs generally focus too much on tracking money in and out at the expense of incorporating the context necessary to understand whether expenditures are effective and local finances are healthy (Walters 2006, 2012). Shueh (2016) argued that even more progress is necessary to clarify definitions, unclear analyses connecting income with expenditures and overwhelming numbers of lists and spreadsheets typifying CAFRs.

Periodically, the Government Accounting Standards Board (GASB) issues statements to clarify and improve the effectiveness of generally accepted accounting principles (GAAP) and the way annual audits and CAFRs report fund balances. The GASB released statement no. 54 in February 2009. The statement spelled out new government fund type definitions. The new fund balance classifications eliminated an older twofold classification scheme of reserved and unreserved funds, and they replaced it with a five-category scheme of non-spendable, restricted, committed, assigned, and unassigned funds (GASB 2009). Generally, funds categorized further down in the classification scheme are less restricted, in the sense that municipalities can redirect them for alternative purposes or simply not spend them at all (Kelly 2013, p. 728). Moreover, the new scheme requires governments to disclose information about policies that regulate distribution of funds between categories, constraints that apply to the amounts, as well as a designation within the fund, in the notes to the financial reports (GASB 2009).

TIMELINESS AND ACCESSIBILITY

CAFRs sometimes face criticism for inaccessibility and being released too late to fend off scandals and financial meltdowns, which can go unnoticed, until well past the time for addressing them (Walters 2012). To fulfill their potential as participation and accountability instruments, financial reporting documents must be ready and accessible for constituents. Timely posting reports either on the county's or a centralized state website provides an opportunity to hold local governmental decision makers accountable. Recognizing the futility of overly late reports, such as CAFRs published as late as a year or more, Barrett and Greene (2015) commended governments that take measures to ensure more timely completion. However, intelligible, fund balance information must be ready in time to help inform important decisions.

The GFOA takes other measures to motivate local government financial reporting. For instance, the Popular Annual Financial Reporting Award program helps governments to distill essential information from their CAFRs for consumption by the public and by other interested parties that typically do not have a background in public finance. Local governments may submit these reports to the GFOA for award consideration each fiscal year. This program is in addition to the long-standing Certificate of Achievement of Excellence in Financial Reporting Program that the GFOA has run since 1945. That program awards governments whose financial statements conform well to GAAP such that it is easy to assess government finances (GFOA 2019).

UNRESERVED FUND BALANCE POLICIES

The GFOA further recommends that governments have fund balance policy statements as a stand-alone component of their CAFRs, as an independently available document, or included in the budget document. These best practices are in contrast to the long-standing practice of making statements about unrestricted funds within annual audit reports or other financial statements such as CAFRs. The intention of policy statements on how municipalities should manage funds is to temper the vulnerability of more visible government savings to political interests, improve citizens' acceptance of savings, and relieve pressure for tax reductions (Tyer 1993). Adopting a fund balance policy is likely to have the greatest impact if the funds' purpose and use are evident to an audience broader than just those managing the accounts (Funkhouser 2013a, 2013b; Stewart, Hildreth, and Antwi-Boasiako 2013). Proper planning and reserves can ultimately help to mitigate any adverse impacts borrowing money to meet unexpected expenses may have on the government's bond ratings and the cost of borrowing for commitments the government already has. Formalizing unreserved fund balance policies, in part, helps to stave off potential swings in tax rates caused by lack of planning (GFOA 2018).

To promote the adoption of these policies, the GFOA has developed a model fund balance policy that local governments can tailor to their own unique political and financial circumstances. The model policy recommends that governments anticipate how much reserve will be sufficient to mitigate financial risks, revenue shortfalls, severe budget cuts, and sizable expenditures for unanticipated emergencies. Municipalities need to create reserves large enough to cope with revenues and/or expenditure volatility. There needs to be provision for substantial one-time outlays due to disasters, immediate capital needs, and/or state budget cuts. In setting unreserved fund levels, it is important for local governments to consider covering the potential drain upon general fund resources from other funds as well as the availability of resources that may be available in other funds. The GFOA notes that governments may wish to maintain higher levels of unreserved fund balances to compensate for any portion of an unreserved fund balance the government has already committed or assigned for a specific purpose. Proper planning and reserves can ultimately help to mitigate the adverse impacts borrowing money to meet unexpected expenses may have on the government's bond ratings and the cost of borrowing for commitments the government already has. Formalizing unreserved fund balance policies, in part, helps to stave off potential swings in tax rates due to lack of planning (GFOA 2016).

GFOA standards suggest that unreserved fund balance policies should incorporate the following criteria:[2]

- explanation of the need for an unreserved reserve fund
- requirements for an unreserved fund level of at least two months of operations
- statement of the purposes for and/or how the municipality may spend the unreserved funds
- provisions for how the municipality must replenish the unreserved funds and
- the establishment of a minimum and maximum unreserved fund balance level.

Adopting a fund balance policy really only matters if the overall process of fund management is evident enough that the funds' purpose and use are evident to an audience broader than just those managing the accounts (Funkhouser 2013a, 2013b; Stewart, Hildreth, and Antwi-Boasiako 2013). Public accountability further requires, in part, the provision of:

- a definitive, declarative statement of what the municipality is saving money for and how much it is saving
- a separate policy or autonomous policy statement in the CAFR posted online
- GAAP compliant accounting placed in context and

- completed documents in time to assess financial decisions.

COUNTY GOVERNMENT FUND BALANCE MANAGEMENT PRACTICES: A NATIONAL ASSESSMENT

The analysis of national fund balance management practices is based on a random sample of 341 US counties. The sample had an error margin of plus or minus 5 percent. The analysis tested whether sample variable means were statistically significantly different from the population mean to ensure the data were representative and the random sample was not somehow biased. Tests showed no statistically significant differences between the sample and population means for the variables for which there are available population means. *T* tests for ideology, median family income, the natural log of county population, whether a county's state legally requires compliance with GAAP, and whether the county had a county manager in 2009 and/or 2015 all failed to reject their null hypotheses that there was no difference between means. The test results are in Table 13.1.

Table 13.1   Sample/population mean equivalencies (probability means are significantly different)

Variable	N	t	Sig.
Ideology	341	1.04	0.30
Median Family Income	341	0.41	0.68
Population Logged (Ln)	341	0.07	0.95
GAAP Compliance State Mandated	341	0.93	0.35
Appointed County Administrator 2009	341	0.75	0.35
Appointed County Administrator 2015	341	1.22	0.41

The analysis focuses on two practices that speak to the transparency of fund balance management practices in each county—making the county's CAFR publicly available and/or adopting a policy for the management of government savings. CAFRs are distinguishable from normative annual audits, and they include fiscal policies (www.gfoa.org/print/403). Many, but not all counties post CAFRs and other financial statements. The analysis then tests several contextual and institutional factors that might affect the transparency of fund balance management practices including county population and median family income from the US Census Bureau, Department of Commerce. There is a proxy variable for county ideology, liberal, which is the percentage in the last presidential election in favor of the Democratic Party candidate. There are also variables indicating whether the state government by statute requires counties to comply with GAAP (Istrate, Mills, and Brookmyer 2016), and whether the county has an appointed administrator (Murphy 2009). Variable descriptions and their sources are in the Appendix.

Table 13.2 presents frequencies for several important indicators of openness and professionalism in county government saving practices. The frequencies in Table 13.2 show that just under half of the counties had FY 2016 CAFRs readily available for the time under study—September 1, 2017 to October 31, 2017. Of these, only about a third adopted an unreserved/unassigned general fund policy or fiscal practice to guide them in their general fund balance management. It seems highly unlikely that counties that do not have and/or file a CAFR will

Table 13.2   Accountability and fund balance management

County Characteristic	Frequency	Percentage	N
State Law Mandates GAAP Compliance	228	67	341
CAFR Available on Website	152	44	341
Policy in CAFR	46	13	341
Professional County Administrator	31	62	49
Policy Set Out Separately on Website	18	37	49
GFOA Award	32	65	49

have a policy, so it seems plausible there is also a lack of 'openness' overall as well (although admittedly the design does not directly test for openness). Focusing on just the 49 counties with fund balance policies, the analysis shows that 31 (62 percent) employ a professional administrator. While over half have received a GFOA award for their policy, just 18 (37 percent) set the policy out separately on their website.

COUNTIES MOST LIKELY TO MAKE CAFRS PUBLICLY AVAILABLE

To understand better why only some counties had CAFRs accessible to the public, the analysis estimated whether different county characteristics affected availability. Specifically, it tested whether population size, family income, ideology, the appointment of a county manager, and state laws requiring compliance with GAAP helped to predict having CAFRs. The findings from past research predicted that populous, in effect, more urban counties will have CAFRs. It is similarly likely that more liberal and wealthy counties will too. A sizable body of research suggests that the form of government affects local government financial administration (Desantis and Renner 1994; Marlowe 2005; Stewart 2011). Svara (1998), Marlowe (2004), and Stewart (2011) cautioned that reformed local government impacts may be difficult to disentangle, as reform structures generally exhibit hybrid characteristics, tempering progressivism with political accountability. While professional administrators may be on point where policymaking is concerned, elected officials tend to affect the implementation of policy and its administration, regardless of the type of structure. Greater accountability is likely among more progressive, professional government forms that employ professional administrative assistance (Banovetz and Peters 2006). Finally, the analysis anticipated that counties in states that legally require GAAP compliance would be more likely to complete CAFRs.

The results of the equation predicting making CAFRs publicly available are in the left-hand column of Table 13.3. The model performs satisfactorily. The chi-squared is statistically significant at 0.000 and the Pseudo R^2 is just under 0.11. Larger counties, counties with higher median family incomes, and counties in states with laws requiring local government finances to comply with GAAP are more likely to have CAFRs. Ideology and having a county administrator did not affect the likelihood of having one.

The marginal effects depicted in Figures 13.1 and 13.2 show the impact the variables have on the probability of making a CAFR available. The population of the county has the largest impact on the availability of a CAFR. The probability of different sized counties adopting CAFRs is in Figure 13.1. There is a substantial difference between the smallest and largest counties and the probability of providing a public CAFR. Holding all other variables at their

Table 13.3 Logged odds predicting county filing of CAFR and adoption of government savings policy

Variable	CAFR	Policy Adoption
Natural Log County Population	0.40***	0.45***
Median Family Income	0.00002**	0.00004**
Ideology	0.06	−2.09
Appointed Administrator	−0.15	1.10**
State Requires GAAP	0.81**	0.88*
CAFR	–	2.84***
Constant	−6.078***	−11.56***
N	340	340
LR Chi-Squared (5) (6)	49.98	103.25
Probability > 0.000	0.000	0.000
Pseudo R^2	0.1070	0.3782
Log Likelihood	−208.5545	−88.5820

Note: * $p > 0.10$; ** $p > 0.05$; *** $p > 0.001$.

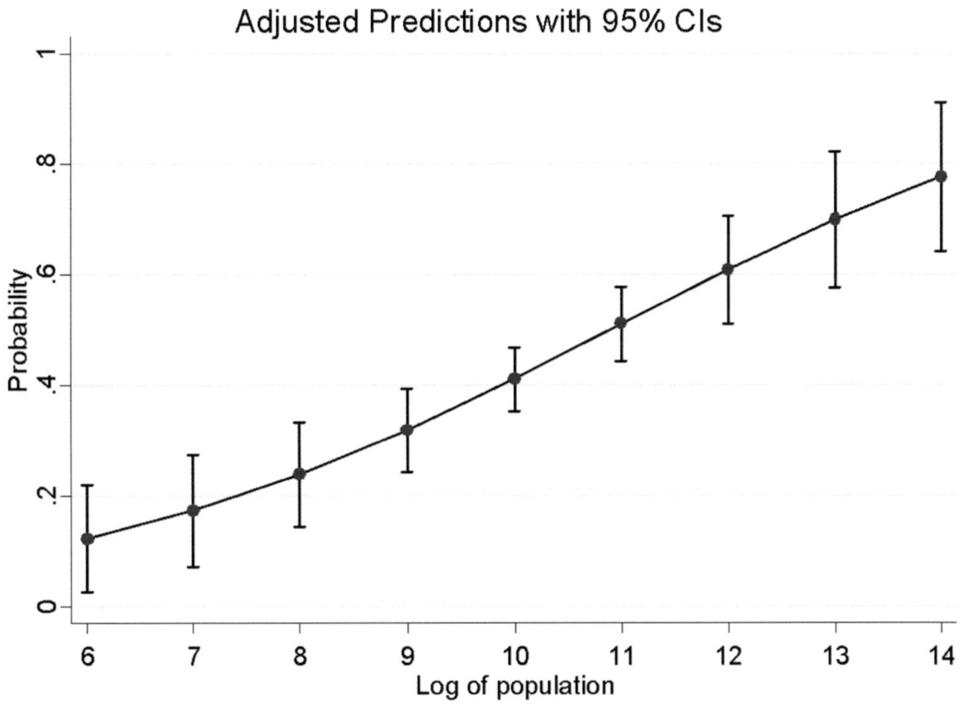

Figure 13.1 Probability of different sized counties making CAFRs publicly available

mean values, a one standard deviation increase in population above the mean increases the probability of making a CAFR available by 15 percent. The other statistically significant variables have less of an impact. For instance, there is a 7 percent increase in the probability of having a CAFR with a one standard deviation shift in median family income (not shown).

192 *Research handbook on motivation in public administration*

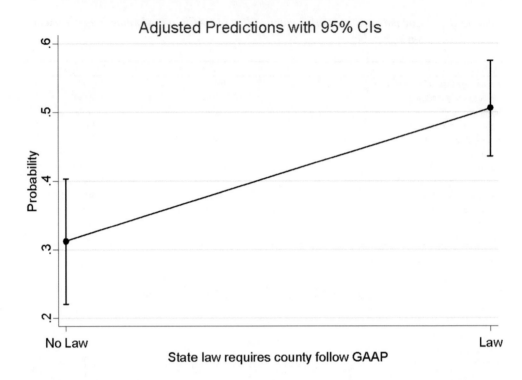

Figure 13.2   Probability of counties in states with statutes requiring GAAP compliance making CAFRs publicly available

Table 13.4   Conformity with GFOA policy characteristics

County Characteristics	Frequency	Percentage
Explains Need for Funds	39	79
Specifies Minimum Fund Level	47	96
Specifies Maximum Fund Level	16	33
Requires 2 or More Months Operating Revenue	28	57
Regulates Expenditures	16	33
Specifies Replenishment of Funds	11	22

Of the variables in the model, requiring local governments to comply with GAAP has the largest impact on whether a county makes a CAFR available. As Figure 13.2 highlights, the probability of a publicly available CAFR in states without laws requiring counties to conform to GAAP is 31 percent. In comparison, counties in states that require compliance with GAAP have a 50 percent chance of making a CAFR available.

COUNTIES MOST LIKELY TO HAVE ADOPTED UNRESERVED GENERAL FUND BALANCE POLICIES

The GFOA guidelines recommend that local governments maintain policies that explain the need for saving revenues. Of the 49 counties with a policy or fiscal practice, 39 do exactly that (Table 13.4). Common purposes for county savings include maintaining contingency funds for natural disasters, building working capital, and seeking protection against unexpected economic downturns. Less frequent rationales include preserving the counties' creditworthiness or foregoing the need to increase taxes to cover unexpected events and reductions in service. All but two of the policies set a minimum fund level. The minimum balance levels range from 5 to 40 percent of annual operations. About a third of the policies limit the size of the fund capping balances from 10 percent to 35 percent of annual expenditures. One exception is a cap at a fixed level of $10 million. A couple of the policies give provisions for how to spend down the reserve should the fund exceed its maximum level. One states that anything above its cap must go into the Capital Reserve Fund, Hospitalization Fund, Liability Fund, or Worker's Compensation Fund. Another stipulates that any balance over 21 percent at the end of the fiscal year will go to capital projects.

Just California and Utah mandate that counties establish an unreserved fund policy. For instance, the California code provides that: '[t]he budget for each fund may contain non-spendable, restricted, committed, or assigned fund balance classifications in such amounts as the board deems sufficient. General reserves and stabilization arrangements may also be included as part of the restricted, committed, assigned, and unassigned fund balance' (California Code—GOV § 29085). Utah also authorizes counties to spend unreserved general funds, and it prohibits counties from allowing expenditures to go below 5 percent of general fund revenues. Finally, about two-thirds of the counties in the study submitted their CAFRs to the GFOA and received awards for sound budget practices and sound financial reporting. Of the counties with policies, only one county had not adopted a formal policy, but instead, its auditor recognized it as having a fiscal practice that acts as a guiding fiscal policy.

The GFOA recommends that counties maintain an unreserved general fund level of two months or more of operating reserves. So, just under 30 percent fully comply with the GFOA guidelines, while the rest of the counties hold just 2.5 to five weeks of operation expenses. The GFOA also advises counties to be clear about how they can use unreserved general funds, and it suggests that expenditures relate directly to the funds' general purpose. About a third of the county policies restrict the possible uses of the money in this way. Also important to ensuring counties have the appropriate amount of funds is ensuring the replenishment of funds that draw down fund balances. Nearly a fifth of the policies explicitly spell out sources and timelines for replenishing funds. A few do not specify the source of the funds, but they require replenishment of the fund within one year. Five additional counties require that payback take place within one year, even if it means cutting government operations and services or raising taxes. Other counties allow up to two years with a reduction in expenditures if necessary. Another county allows up to three years, and it charged the county administrator to develop a replenishment plan. A few others allow up to five years, while one county policy just stipulates that the county must replenish the money.

To begin to understand the characteristics of counties that adopt unreserved fund balance policies, the analysis included a second logistic regression equation. The dependent variable this time is whether a county has a general unreserved fund policy. The independent variables are county population, median family income, ideology (percentage of the vote for Clinton in 2016), appointed county manager, being in a state legally requiring local governments to comply with GAAP, and whether the county complied with and completed the CAFR. Results from the analysis so far suggest that population will affect policy adoption positively and that wealthier, more liberal counties will have a policy. The results are in the right-hand column of Table 13.2.

The overall model fits adequately with chi-squared = 0.0000 and pseudo R^2 = 0.23. Five of the variables are positive and statistically significant. As expected, larger, more professional counties are more likely to have policies. The signs of the variables measuring whether there is a professional administrator are both positive and statistically significant. More specifically, holding all other variables at their mean value, a one standard deviation shift above the mean for both median income and population results in a 3 percent increase in the probability of adopting a formal savings policy. Requiring counties to follow GAAP has a similar impact. Counties with a professional administrator have a 5 percent greater probability of adopting a formal policy than counties without a professional administrator. Counties that provide transparency through publicly available financial reports (CAFRs) are much more likely to adopt a formal policy around savings (Figure 13.3). Counties without a publicly available CAFR have less than a 1 percent chance of having a formal savings policy. Having CAFRs available meant a probability score 16 percentage points higher. The findings for the most part confirm our initial expectations. Larger, wealthier, professional counties are more transparent,

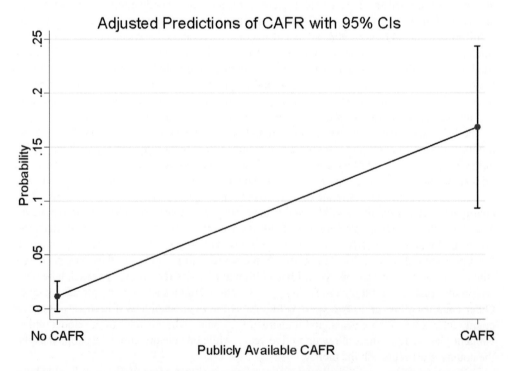

Figure 13.3   *Probability of counties with publicly available CAFRs adopting fund balance policies*

in that they are most likely to have a policy, particularly if their financial records are more visible to the public.

DISCUSSION AND CONCLUSION

The primary theme that emerges from the data is that county government unreserved fund balance management practices minimize visibility, accessibility, lay-person intelligibility, and timeliness. Few counties are open about why they accumulate slack resources, what they intend for the money they do save, or whether they will replenish that money if they spend it. Indeed, while almost two-thirds of the counties are legally required to follow GAAP standards, less than half post CAFRs in a timely fashion on their websites. Of the counties that do, just over a third have savings policies, which translates into only about 5 percent of counties nationally maintaining a policy on their websites in a timely fashion. For those counties that have policies, just under 5 percent meet all five of the GFOA criteria. Most commonly, policies explained the needs for accumulating slack resources and the minimum amount that the county can hold in reserve. Even counties with policies most often do not set maximum fund levels, specify how to spend the money, or explain how counties should replenish savings when they draw them down. Just two states either insist or mandate that county governments adopt policies. California and Utah both have laws authorizing and mandating counties to establish such policies, and all the counties in this study from both states posted CAFRs and policies on their websites.

There likely will always be a need to balance budgetary discretion with transparency and considerations to mitigate misuse of public monies while still allowing professional administrators the flexibility they need to manage over budget cycles. Such initiative inevitably will create tension and it is not clear where the balancing points may lie. Drawing on earlier scholarship (Fung, Graham, and Weil 2007), Stewart, Hildreth, and Antwi-Boasiakio (2013) argue that the optimal balance lies closer to the transparency, that visibility to the public should be the primary, but not the only goal. Determining such an ideal tradeoff is beyond the scope of this study, and the analysis is not capable of revealing unethical or incompetent uses of public monies. What the findings do show is that local government management of slack resources in terms of the accessibility of their CAFRs and the implementation of GFOA's recommended policy is not very transparent. One contribution of administrative theory to this conversation is the recognition that transparency for its own sake is not desirable and risks inhibiting local government's potential to deal effectively with economic uncertainties. The guidelines should take both accountability and managerial discretion into account.

The study finds that US counties underutilize policies and practices, which represents the current balance between the need to constrain pressures to divert funds and/or reduce revenues and the need to fortify county finances to meet longer term needs and uncertainties. These observations may represent the sentiments of county officials and/or administrators who do not want to bind themselves to debating the size, use, and replenishment of reserves in public or to placing too much in focus for special interest demands. The GFOA may wish to establish a training program for counties, addressing the need specifically to address the replenishment of reserves. Moreover, further research should pursue the study of how contextual factors such as state laws that require the public filing of CAFRs with deadlines and state laws that either encourage the passage of such fiscal policies or create barriers to doing so affect county fiscal policies. These relationships need further study, and this may help associations such as the GFOA and bonding agencies to design and develop legislation to assist county governments in meeting CAFR mandates and with adopting unreserved general fund reserve policies.

This seems to be the first attempt to study county government saving policy and how transparent counties are in managing unreserved fund balances from a national perspective. This analysis, then, serves as a first cut analysis of county adoption of government fund balance policy, and it raises important implications for organizations like the GFOA for improving public accountability as well as for bonding agencies as they seek dedicated revenue sources. As this research progresses, the findings will be helpful to Master of Public Administration programs, so that they can develop more effective training and courses addressing the need for reserve fund policies and how to develop and implement them.

NOTES

1. The chapter points out below that over the years, the GASB has revised its standards (e.g., Statements #34 and #54 on categories pertaining to uncommitted funds). This chapter adopts Statement #34's term 'unreserved' to refer to counties still following Statement #34. The chapter uses the assigned/unassigned funds designation for counties now following the Statement #54 protocol.
2. The importance of these criteria is all too evident from reports such as one issued by GFOA in 1990, which acknowledged a lack of research and literature in this area; in part, because public officials did not disclose this information to citizens (http://www.gfoa.org/main/about.shtml).

REFERENCES

Arnold, D.R. (1979). *Congress and the Bureaucracy*. Newhaven, CT: Yale University Press.
Banovetz, J.M., and Peters, D.S. (2006). The county administrator form: A modern approach to Illinois county government. *Policy Profiles*, 6, 1–8.
Barrett, K., and Greene, R. (2015). Financial reports: Better late than never? *Governing: The States and Localities*. http://www.governing.com/columns/smart-mgmt/gov-comprehensive-annual-financial-report.html (accessed February 15, 2018).
Benito, B., and Bastida, F. (2009). Budget transparency, fiscal performance, and political turnout: An international approach. *Public Administration Review*, 69, 403–417.
California Code, Government Code—GOV § 29085 on Westlaw. https://codes.findlaw.com/ca/government-code/gov-sect-29085.html (accessed February 15, 2018).
Davis, R.S., and Stazyk, E.C. (2015). Developing and testing a new goal taxonomy: Accounting for the complexity of ambiguity and political support. *Journal of Public Administration Research and Theory*, 25(3), 751–775.
Desantis, V.S., and Renner, T. (1994). The impact of political structures on public policies in American counties. *Public Administration Review*, 54, 291–295.
Dilulio, J.J., Kelman, S., Foreman, Jr, C.H., Katzmann, R.A., and Nivola, P.S. (1991). The public administration of James Q. Wilson: A symposium on bureaucracy. *Public Administration Review*, 51, 193–201.
Finkler, S.A. (2010). *Financial Management for Public, Health, and Not-for-Profit Organizations*. Upper Saddle River, NJ: Prentice Hall.
Fung, A., Graham, M., and Weil, D. (2007). *Full Disclosure: The Perils and Promise of Transparency*. Cambridge: Cambridge University Press.
Funkhouser, M. (2013a). Accountability, transparency and the uncertain future of GASB. *Governing: The States and Localities*. http://www.governing.com/gov-institute/on-leadership/col-accountability-transparency-uncertain-future-gasb-governmental-accounting-standards-board.html (accessed February 15, 2018).

Funkhouser, M. (2013b). Giving citizens numbers they can understand. *Governing: The States and Localities.* http://www.governing.com/gov-institute/on-leadership/col-citizen-centric-financial-reporting-accountability-transparency.html (accessed February 15, 2018).

Funkhouser, M. (2013c). Learning to love the numbers of government. *Governing: The States and Localities.* http://www.governing.com/gov-institute/on-leadership/col-how-read-government-audited-financial-statement.html (accessed February 15, 2018).

Gauthier, S. (2002). Reserve fund balance policy promulgated. *American City and County, 117,* 6.

Gianakis, G.J., and Snow, D. (2007). The implementation and utilization of stabilization funds by local governments in Massachusetts. *Public Budgeting and Finance, 27,* 86–103.

GASB (Government Accounting Standards Board). (2009). Statement No. 54: Fund Balance Reporting and Government Fund Type Definitions. http://www.gasb.org/jsp/GASB/Document_C/GASBDocumentPage?cid=1176159972156andacceptedDisclaimer=true (accessed February 10, 2018).

GFOA (Government Finance Officers Association). (2016). Periodic disclosure and the comprehensive annual financial report. http://www.gfoa.org/periodic-disclosure-and-comprehensive-annual-financial-report (accessed March 1, 2018).

GFOA (Government Finance Officers Association). (2018). Fund Balance Guidelines for the General Fund). http://www.gfoa.org/fund-balance-guidelines-general-fund (accessed March 30, 2018).

GFOA (Government Finance Officers Association). (2019). Popular annual financial reporting award program. January 15, 2019. http://www.gfoa.org/popular-annual-financial-reporting-awards-program-pafr-program-0 (accessed February 2, 2019).

Hamman, J.A. (1993). Bureaucratic accommodation of congress and the president: Elections and the distribution of federal assistance. *Political Research Quarterly, 46,* 863–879.

Hembree, H., Shelton, M., and Tyer, C.B. (1999). Benchmarking and local government reserve funds: Theory versus practice. *Public Management, 81,* 16–21.

Hendrick, R. (2006). The role of slack in local government finances. *Public Budgeting and Finance, 26,* 14–46.

Istrate, E., Mills, C., and Brookmyer, D. (2016). *Counting Money: State and GASB Standards for County Financial Reporting* (Vol. 4). Washington, DC: National Association of Counties.

Kelly, J.M. (2013). Fund balance for budget stabilization: Does the new accounting presentation matter? *Journal of Public Budgeting, Accounting and Financial Management, 25,* 719.

Lucas, Jr, R., and Stokey, N.L. (1983). Optimal fiscal and monetary policy in an economy without capital. *Journal of Monetary Economics, 12,* 55–93.

Marlowe, J. (2005). Fiscal slack and counter-cyclical expenditure stabilization: A first look at the local level. *Public Budgeting and Finance, 25,* 48–72.

Marlowe, J. (2013). Fiscal slack, reserves, and rainy day funds. In H. Levine, J.B. Justice, and E.A. Scorsone (eds), *Handbook of Local Government Fiscal Health.* Burlington, MA: Jones and Bartlett Learning, pp. 321–342.

Marlowe, J. (2014). This annual financial report says? *Governing: The States and Localities.* http://www.governing.com/columns/public-money/gov-whats-in-your-cafr.html (accessed February 15, 2018).

Marsh, T.L., Montondon, L.G., and Daniels. J. (2004). Readability of award-winning popular annual financial reports. *Journal of Accounting and Finance Research, 1,* 32–39.

Massey, J., and Tyer, C.B. (1990). Local government fund balances: How much is enough? *South Carolina Forum: A Review of Public Affairs in South Carolina, 1,* 40–46.

Murphy, K. (2009). *County Government Structure: A State By State Report.* Washington, DC: National Association of Counties. https://www.pfw.edu/dotAsset/98216b7d-e66c-4da6- a78b-1871b6c1f439.pdf (accessed February 15, 2018).

Rourke, F.E. (1969). *Bureaucracy, Politics, and Public Policy* (3rd edn). Boston, MA: Little, Brown.

Shueh, J. (2016). *Financial Transparency—Platform Works to Demystify City Budgets.* http://www.govtech.com/products/Financial-Transparency-Platform-Works-to-Demystify-City-Budgets.html (accessed March 1, 2018).

Stewart, L.M. (2009). Examining factors that impact Mississippi counties' unreserved fund balance during relative resource abundance and relative resource scarcity. *Public Budgeting and Finance, 29,* 45–73.

Stewart, L.M. (2011). Governmental influence on the unreserved fund balances for Mississippi counties. *Journal of Public Budgeting, Accounting and Financial Management*, *23*, 478–506.

Stewart, L.M., Hildreth, R.W., and Antwi-Boasiako, K.B. (2013). The fund balance conundrum: An ethical perspective. *Administration and Society*, *47*, 915–942.

Stewart, L.M., Hamman, J.A., and Pink-Harper, S.A. (2018). The stabilization effect of local government savings: The case of Illinois counties. *Public Budgeting and Finance*, *38*, 23–39.

Svara, J.H. (1998). The politics-administration dichotomy model as aberration. *Public Administration Review*, *58*, 51–58.

Thompson, J.D. (1967). *Organizations in Action: Social Science Bases of Administrative Theory*. New York, NY: McGraw-Hill.

Tyer, C.B. (1993). Local government reserve funds: Policy alternatives and political strategies. *Public Budgeting and Finance*, *13*, 75–84.

Wagner, G.A. (2004). The bond market and fiscal institutions: Have budget stabilization funds reduced state borrowing costs? *National Tax Journal*, *58*, 785–804.

Walters, J. (2006). Reporting results. *Governing: The States and Localities*. http://www.governing.com/topics/finance/Reporting-Results.html (accessed February 15, 2018).

Walters, J. (2012). Are comprehensive annual financial reports useless? *Governing: The States and Localities*. http://www.governing.com/topics/finance/gov-are-annual-financial-reports-useless.html (accessed February 15, 2018).

Wang, W., and Hou, Y. (2012). Do local governments save and spend across budget cycles? *American Review of Public Administration*, *42*, 152–169.

Wolkoff, M. (1987). An evaluation of municipal rainy day funds. *Public Budgeting and Finance*, *7*, 52–63.

Wilson, J.Q. (1989). *Bureaucracy: What Government Agencies Do and Why They Do It*. New York, NY: Basic Books.

APPENDIX

Table 13A.1   Variable coding and sources

Variable	N	Description
CAFR is Available on County Webpage	341	Variable equals 1 if it appeared on a county website in the sample, zero otherwise
Policy Adoption (Fund Balance Management Policy Elements in CAFR)	341	Variable equals 1 if some form of a fund balance management policy appeared in a CAFR posted on the county website, zero otherwise
Policy Adoption (Fund Balance Management Policy Elements Posted Separately on Website)	341	Variable equals 1 if some form of a fund balance management policy appeared separately on the county website, zero otherwise
Ideology	341	Variable is a proxy for county ideology measured as the percentage of vote for the Democratic Party candidate in the previous presidential election
Median Family Income	341	Provided by the US Census Bureau, Department of Commerce
Appointed Administrator	341	Variable equals 1 if the county has an appointed administrator, zero otherwise. Data publicly available from the National Association of Counties (NAoC)
GAAP Compliance Legally Required by the State	341	Variable equals 1 if state legislates counties comply with GAAP, zero otherwise. Data publicly available from NAoC
Policy Explains Needs for Funds	49	Variable equals 1 if policy explains a purpose for fund balance, zero otherwise. Source: county policies obtained in national survey
Policy Specifies Minimum Fund Balance Level	49	Variable equals 1 if policy sets a minimum balance for the fund balance, zero otherwise. Source: county policies obtained in national survey
Policy Specifies Maximum Fund Balance Level	49	Variable equals 1 if policy sets a maximum balance for the fund balance, zero otherwise. Source: county policies obtained in national survey
Policy Requires Two or More Months of Operating Revenue	49	Variable equals 1 if policy requires 2 or more months of operating revenue in the fund balance, zero otherwise. Source: county policies obtained in national survey
Policy Regulates What Fund Balance can be Spent On	49	Variable equals 1 if policy regulates what fund balance can be used for, zero otherwise. Source: county policies obtained in national survey
Policy Requires Fund Balance Replenishment	49	Variable equals 1 if policy regulates what fund balance can be used for, zero otherwise. Source: county policies obtained in national survey

PART III

FACTORS AFFECTING RECRUITMENT, SELECTION, AND RETENTION

14. Responsibility toward others is vital in public and non-profit organizations: can we recruit, hire, and cultivate it?
Neil M. Boyd and Branda Nowell

INTRODUCTION

Employee motivation has been a central issue in the field of public management for many years. Researchers have explored employee motivation, in part, because of the benefits it can produce for oneself and others including the likelihood of engaging in organizational citizenship behaviors as well as worker satisfaction, happiness, and psychological well-being (Bright, 2008; Locke and Latham, 1990; Malka and Chatman, 2003). Moreover, scholars have often attempted to determine if motivation relates to organizational outcomes like efficiency, effectiveness, and responsiveness (Brewer and Selden, 2000; Kim, 2005; Ritz, 2009).

In public management research, Public Service Motivation (PSM) has clearly been the most studied motivation concept and has received enormous attention as a construct to explain other-regarding behavior of public officials (Ritz, Brewer, and Neumann, 2016). Perry and Wise (1990) originally defined PSM as 'an individual's predisposition to respond to motives grounded primarily or uniquely in public institutions and organizations' (p. 368). A more recent definition highlights its 'other-regarding' nature by claiming it to be 'an individual's orientation to delivering services to people with a purpose to do good for others and society' (Perry and Hondeghem, 2008, p. 7). Scholars suggest that PSM can guide individuals toward public service careers (Christensen and Wright, 2011; Perry and Wise, 1990), and generate impacts on motivated activity within public service organizations (Alonso and Lewis, 2001; Andersen and Kjeldsen, 2013; Bright, 2008; Homberg, McCarthey, and Tabvuma, 2015; Naff and Crum, 1999; Perry and Hondeghem, 2008; Petrovsky and Ritz, 2014; van Loon, Vandenabeele, and Leisink, 2015).

More recently, spurred in part by research revealing limitations of PSM for explaining many aspects of organizational behavior within public settings, scholars have branched out to consider a diverse array of 'other-regarding' concepts that could change how we think about motivation toward the delivery of vital public and non-profit services.

The landscape includes concepts like altruism, prosocial motivation, and a sense of community responsibility, and evolving research is showing that these variables have utility in public and non-profit settings.

For example, Batson (2011, p. 20) defines altruism as 'a motivational state with the ultimate goal of increasing another's welfare.' And, while some scholars have stated that altruism and PSM are more or less interchangeable (Rainey and Steinbauer, 1999), others believe that altruism is a more global disposition that is not necessarily grounded primarily in public institutions. As Piatak and Holt (2020) note, PSM focuses on 'where' the call to serve is oriented, and altruism focuses on 'why' an individual is motivated to help others (out of concern for oneself or others). Like PSM, empirical studies bear out that altruism is a unique form of motivation rooted in a mechanism of self-sacrifice. For example, when individuals high in altruism experience extrinsic rewards such as salary increase which nullify the personal sacrifice associated with helping behavior, altruistic individuals experience lower motivation (e.g., Le Grand, 2003).

Prosocial motivation is another other-regarding concept, which has been defined as 'the desire to expend effort to benefit other people' (Grant, 2008, p. 48). Some view prosocial motivation as equivalent to public service motivation (Jensen and Andersen, 2015; Wright, Christensen, and Pandey, 2013), while others see public service motivation as a specific type of prosocial motivation (Andersen, Pedersen, and Petersen, 2018). Schott et al. (2019) argue the two concepts are both theoretically and empirically distinct, suggesting that prosocially motivated actors are motivated by the consequences of their actions on individuals they have personal contact with whereas PSM motivation is rooted in more global aims for improving society at large.

Nowell and Boyd (2010) propose that a sense of community responsibility is born as individuals develop personal values, norms, ideals, and beliefs when they are embedded in various institutions (e.g., families, churches, schools, neighborhoods, social groups). As individuals enter into institutions, the specific organizational context will evoke sentiments of duty and obligation for some people as they seek to reconcile who they perceive they are in a given setting and their normative beliefs about what a person like them 'should' do in such a setting. Once invoked, sense of community responsibility (SOC-R) perceptions are theorized to stimulate community engagement behaviors that are not based solely out of an expectation for direct personal gain (see Boyd and Nowell, 2014; Nowell and Boyd, 2010, 2014). Like PSM, recent empirical studies show that a SOC-R leads non-profit and public servants to engage in leadership and organizational citizenship behaviors (Boyd and Nowell, 2017, 2020; Boyd et al., 2018; Nowell and Boyd, 2014; Nowell et al., 2016).

Given the continued vigor by which scholars focus attention on PSM, and fervent views of its legitimacy as one of the most prominent concepts in public management, it is important to study and evaluate PSM within the milieu of a broader conceptual and theoretical landscape across related disciplines (i.e., primarily management and the social sciences). This chapter will help us understand the similarities and differences between concepts in a crowded landscape and will propose ways in which these concepts can help us understand how to hire, train, and cultivate cultures of responsibility toward others.

CONCEPTUAL CLARITY AND APPLICABILITY IN HIRING, TRAINING, AND FURTHER CULTIVATION

The crowded landscape of other-regarding constructs in public management at this moment in time requires scholars to clarify, disentangle, and propose theoretically robust arguments for their choice of motivational constructs within appropriate organizational systems. Human motivation can apply to virtually any system within an organization including strategic and structural design, and process issues in operational areas like public relations/marketing, citizen/client interaction, managerial finance and accounting, and human resource management. In this chapter, we focus on human resource management systems because scholars have shown consistent interest in a desire to understand how to attract motivated individuals to public service, and how to dualistically improve an individual's psychological experience while striving to achieve the mission of the organization. It also makes sense to focus on human resource management systems because they would be the primary way to bring individuals into the organization and cultivate motivated states that could then be enacted within the many organizational systems at work.

We have several aims in the following pages. First, we will attempt to clarify the definition and scope of each other-regarding construct, and briefly highlight the main theoretical lens(es) by which scholars understand them. Next, we discuss how each construct might be employed as a measure of attraction to public service as part of the hiring process, and how the construct might be cultivated via training processes and other human resource functions. We start with public service motivation because it has gained the most attention in public management scholarship in the past 30 years. We then turn our attention to prosocial motivation, altruism, and a sense of community responsibility. Finally, we will offer ideas to help guide future directions for research.

PUBLIC SERVICE MOTIVATION

PSM has long been a topic of scholarly interest and is believed to play an important role in distinguishing the field of public administration from similar fields such as business administration (Perry and Hondeghem, 2008; Perry and Vandenabeele, 2015; Wright and Pandey, 2008). Originally defined by Perry and Wise (1990) as 'an individual's predisposition to respond to motives grounded primarily or uniquely in public institutions and organizations' (p. 368), PSM is a concept 'native' to the discipline of public administration (Perry and Vandenbeele, 2015, p. 693).

A variety of theoretical lenses have been applied to PSM. Perry (1997) argued that PSM emerges due to socialization in the family, religious organizations, and as a consequence of life events, and as such becomes part of the identity of an individual. In line with an identity lens, Ritz et al. (2020) suggest that institutional theory is applicable to PSM because values, norms, and beliefs within public institutions are the origin of public service motivation (Perry and Vandenabeele, 2008; Perry and Wise, 1990). When individuals are exposed to public institutions, a public service identity can develop, and that can later manifest as a public service motivation (Breaugh, Ritz, and Alfes, 2017). An institutional lens highlights that public service motivation can be a context and culturally dependent concept. Andrews (2016) suggests that self-determination theory (SDT) applies to PSM, even though scholars rarely mention it (Wright and Grant, 2010). One exception is Perry and Vandenabeele (2015) who acknowledge that SDT could be useful for understanding how PSM activates within public settings. SDT posits that humans need to satisfy three basic psychological needs: autonomy, competence, and relatedness (Ryan and Deci, 2000), regardless of where they work. Moreover, humans need to perceive themselves as autonomous and competent to enjoy fulfilling relationships. SDT assumes that humans are naturally motivated, but that motivation will be attenuated when the organizational context cannot satisfy autonomy, competence, and relatedness needs. The lack of a singular theory of PSM is perhaps why Bozeman and Su (2015) proposed that the PSM concept is difficult to grasp, and that it does not provide good cues as to the cause of it, or in some cases, permit valid research into what would cause it. And while the concept might be fuzzy, if one were to assimilate the variety of theoretical lenses of PSM, it likely derives

Table 14.1   Analysis of other-regarding constructs

Analysis Component	Public Service Motivation	Prosocial Motivation/Altruism	Sense of Community Responsibility
Definition	A predisposition to respond to motives grounded primarily or uniquely in public institutions and organizations	The desire to expend effort to benefit other people. Behaviors that an actor engages in, with personal costs, in order to provide benefits for a recipient	A feeling of duty to advance the individual and collective well-being of a community of people that is not directly rooted in an expectation of personal gain
Theory Lens(es)	Identification, Institutional, Self-Determination	Egoism and Altruism	Identification; Cognitive Dissonance; Self-Determination
Referent	Public Service/Society	People	Any Collective Entity
Hiring	Might have utility for public service-oriented positions	Used in personality tests as a hiring tool; has limited utility	Good potential for use
Training	n/a	n/a; maybe altruism applicable as a behavioral measure	Good potential for cultivation
Further Cultivation	Creating conceptual linkages between work activities and larger societal impact would be crucial for potential cultivation	Creating conceptual linkages between work activities and larger societal impact would be crucial for potential cultivation	Good potential for cultivation

from identification (with previously developed values and exposure to public institutions), and as a form of intrinsic motivation rooted in a desire to serve and have a positive impact on society. To the extent an organization or task environment is perceived as an effective vehicle to fulfill these needs for societal impact, a moderated linkage between PSM and work-related outcomes such as job satisfaction and performance may emerge (e.g., Bright, 2007; Ryu, 2017; Table 14.1).

HIRING FOR PSM

To date, considerable evidence has converged in support of the proposition that higher levels of PSM are associated with an increased likelihood to seek out public service-oriented careers (Ballart and Rico, 2018; Bright, 2009, 2016; Clerkin and Coggburn, 2012; Holt, 2018; Piatak, 2016; Steijn, 2008; Vandenabeele, 2008; Wright and Christensen, 2010; Wright and Grant, 2010; Wright, Hassan, and Christensen, 2017). By contrast, scholars continue to debate if the nature of the position matters (Kjeldsen, 2014; Kjeldsen and Jacobsen, 2012; Taylor, 2014), if institutional and individual variations matter (e.g., Vogel and Kroll, 2016), and if self-selection (e.g., Pandey and Stazyk, 2008) or socialization (e.g., Moynihan and Pandey, 2007) drives interest in public service careers. One study (Linos, 2018) showed PSM to be an ineffective means to attract applicants, however, because research in this area is scant, Jacobson et al. (2019) suggest recruiting for PSM within job advertisements and include PSM components in a variety of hiring methods (e.g., survey screens, resumes, work samples, situational exercises). On the other hand, questions remain about PSM efficacy in hiring as evidenced by Bromberg and Charbonneau (2019) who found that HR managers did not rate cover letters emphasizing PSM better than those without. In short, we do not have enough evidence to clearly articulate that we should screen for high PSM or to use it as an exclusionary measure in hiring. Moreover, we have no evidence of the need for PSM recruiting and screening in the organizations that do not claim missions directed toward public service. Bozeman and Su (2015) note that 'PSM is not just a public sector phenomenon but pertains to all work sectors' (p. 702), and Liu et al. (2015) support this notion by stating that corporate social responsibility and organizational citizenship behavior in private sector organizations can be interpreted as the fulfillment of PSM-related needs. At this point, we do not know if PSM can be applied across all sectors and organizational forms. As Jacobson and colleagues (2019) lament, there are a lot of unanswered questions about the appropriateness of the use of PSM in recruiting and hiring strategies (see Table 14.1).

CULTIVATING PSM

Once an applicant is hired, PSM has been theorized to be an important variable for public and non-profit employees and organizations (Petrovsky and Ritz, 2014), however, empirical support of PSM as a driver of 'other-regarding' behavior has been mixed (Alonso and Lewis, 2001; Bright, 2008; Petrovsky and Ritz, 2014; Wright and Pandey, 2008). Some scholars have shown positive relationships between PSM and employee behavior (Brewer and Selden, 1998; Cerase and Farinella, 2006; Crewson, 1997; Gould-Williams, Mostafa, and Bottomley, 2013; Kim, 2006, 2012; Jensen and Andersen, 2015; Naff and Crum, 1999; Pandey, Wright, and Moynihan, 2008; van Loon, Vandenabeele, and Leisink, 2015), while others have demonstrated non-significant or more complicated relationships (Alonso and Lewis, 2001; Boyd et al., 2018; Bright, 2007, 2008; Gabris and Simo, 1995; Homberg, McCarthy, and Tabvuma, 2015; Nowell et al., 2016; Wright and Pandy, 2008). As the above research highlights, a great deal is still unknown regarding when, and to what extent, PSM relates to employee attitudes and behavior once on the job (Bright, 2008; Wright and Grant, 2010; Wright and Pandey, 2008), however, there is strong evidence emerging for the moderating influence of person-environment fit (Homberg, McCarthy, and Tabvuma, 2015). This suggests that motivation rooted in the desire to serve the public and positively impact society will likely interact strongly with one's workplace task environment and the nature of opportunities available therein.

If PSM serves as a basis of motivation for action, then it would be reasonable to assume agencies would want to harness it to advance organizational goals. Some findings suggest that PSM may be malleable and therefore can change within individuals over time (Jensen and Vestergaard, 2017). If this is true, onboarding programs and further training may be able to help stimulate PSM awareness, insight, and action. In addition, compensation and rewards might be used to enhance PSM. While public service human resource management research on compensation and rewards exists (e.g., Bellé and Cantarelli, 2015; Lewis, Pathak, and Galloway, 2018; McGinnis Johnston, Piatak, and Ng, 2016; Wenzel, Krause, and Vogel, 2019), most of it has not been specifically tied to enhancing and cultivating PSM. One exception is the work on a 'crowding out effect' that suggests PSM is an intrinsically motivated construct and therefore external rewards are apt to crowd out intrinsic-oriented efficacy (Georgellis, Iossa, and Tabvuma, 2011). However, growing research shows that extrinsic motivators do matter for public service employees (Chen, 2014; Kim and Lee, 2007; McGinnis Johnson, Piatak, and Ng, 2016; Stazyk, 2013; Stringer, Didham, and Theivananthampillai, 2011). Jacobson and colleagues (2019) note that those with high PSM want to serve the public and make a difference, but they do also want to be paid appropriately and rewarded for that work.

Another way to cultivate PSM may be through the performance management process, which includes employee performance appraisal methods and processes (Pynes, 2013; Selden and Sowa, 2011; Walk and Kennedy, 2017).

However, even though research has focused on the importance and challenges of performance management in public service contexts, virtually nothing is known about how one might incorporate PSM into performance appraisal methods and processes. Ultimately, while the theorized antecedents of PSM are argued to be rooted in exposure to institutionalized contexts, more research is needed to understand the relationship of past work experiences as the basis for one's motivational orientation toward or away from public service (see Table 14.1).

PROSOCIAL MOTIVATION

A third type of other-regarding motivation increasingly discussed and studied in public management is the concept of prosocial motivation (Grant, 2008; Steijn and Van der Voet, 2019). Grant (2008, p. 48) defines prosocial motivation as 'the desire to expend effort to benefit other people,' and it is often conceptualized as a disposition of empathy, helpfulness, and concern for others (Wright, Christensen, and Pandy, 2013). Some view prosocial motivation as interchangeable with PSM or even as subtypes of each other (Andersen, Pedersen, and Petersen, 2018; Jensen and Andersen, 2015; Wright, Christensen, and Pandey, 2013). In a recent study, Schott et al. (2019) demonstrate that PSM and prosocial motivation are theoretically and empirically distinct. They highlight that PSM is a general motivation directed at society-at-large with a long-term focus, and that prosocial motivation is directed toward individuals, groups, or an organization with a near-term focus. They also distinguish that prosocial motivation is different from altruism, which is behaviorally oriented, and not a form of motivation per se (see Table 14.1).

The scholarship on prosocial motivation is theoretically rooted in Kurt Lewin's (1951) seminal work. Lewin viewed behavior as goal-directed and, as such, argued that to understand why one might be motivated to act for the benefit of someone else, one needed to first understand the goal the actor was seeking to achieve. Further, Lewin argued that while the different types of goals one might have for helping someone else were both varied, multifaceted, and endless in the potential foci, all motivations for helping could be linked back to one of four root goals. The first plausible goal is the pursuit of self-benefit which is referred to as egoism; the second is the desire to help someone else which is referred to as altruism, the third is the desire to help a group which is collectivism, and the fourth is to uphold a principle which is referred to as principlism. Accordingly, the focus for prosocial motivation theorists is to identify/distinguish between the root goals underlying helping behavior with the implication being that behavior rooted in egoism, for example, is going to operate on a different mechanism than an altruistic goal (for further discussion, see Batson, 1994; Batson et al., 2008) (see Table 14.1).

ALTRUISM

While Lewin (1951) posited four root goals underlying helping behavior, arguably altruism has received the greatest scholarly attention. Altruism was first defined by the French philosopher Comte (1851/1875) (Pickering, 1993) as a genuine concern for others that could be contrasted with helping behaviors with egoistic self-interest benefits. Altruism consists of behaviors that an actor (an individual, group, or organization) engages in, with personal costs, in order to provide benefits for a recipient (Oda et al., 2014). Altruism has roots in many areas, including the diverse fields of evolutionary psychology, economics, developmental psychology, social psychology, sociology, political science, and philosophy.

In organizational settings, Hemingway and Maclagan (2004) argue that ethical decisions are guided by personal values and beliefs. Individuals exhibit these values through the exercise of personal discretion and decision-making. Within the field of public management, altruism and PSM have often been presented as overlapping or interchangeable. For example, Perry and Hondeghem (2008) define PSM as 'individual motives that are largely, but not exclusively, altruistic and are grounded in public institutions' (p. 6). Further, some scholars define PSM as general altruism (e.g., Rainey and Steinbauer, 1999; Bright, 2008; Pandey, Wright, and Moynihan, 2008), while others suggest that specific PSM dimensions of self-sacrifice are akin to altruism (Perry, 1996). For most public management scholars, PSM has altruistic features that are specifically grounded in public institutions.

The main theoretical debate with altruism centers on the dialectic that Comte originally defined, which is to question the genesis of helping behavior from a self-interested or other-interested perspective (see Table 14.1). On the one hand, altruism can be defined as the selfless exhibition of trading one's personal resources to benefit another. Yet, philosophical debates persist as to whether human conduct can ever be genuinely altruistic and indeed whether it is always desirable. Like many of the constructs above, scholars differ in their conception of altruism. Altruism has been variably conceptualized as the motivation not rooted in expectation of personal gain, to a general desire to help others regardless of personal gain, to actions requiring self-sacrifice for the good of others whether intended or not. Collectively, these works suggest that self-sacrifice, desire to help others, and willingness to subordinate purely individual interests for collective interests are all key elements of altruism. For example, Clavien and Chapuisat (2013) define a preference as altruistic if it results from preferences for improving others' interests and welfare at some cost to oneself.

Moreover, scholars suggest that the altruist is always receiving some form of reciprocal reward for their action or having certain needs fulfilled (Batson, 2011; Honeycutt, 1981; Krebs, 1991; Trivers, 1971), which is akin to notions of social exchange and self-determination theory that pervade public management organizational behavior scholarship.

However, as a point of departure from Lewin's (1951) theory, much of the organizational science literature has looked at extra role behaviors and organizational citizenship behavior as the behavioral manifestations of altruism (e.g., Li, Kirkman, and Porter, 2014), further emphasizing key differences in behavioral versus goal perspectives on altruism. Altruistic action such as extra role and organizational citizenship behavior (OCB), regardless of the motivation, is more akin to Lewin's (1951) concept of prosocial action. Some theorists posit an egoism mechanism for OCB that draws heavily from social exchange theory, viewing altruism as a version of egoism that is based on establishing norms of reciprocity (Hoffman et al., 2007). However, an alternative explanation for prosocial action lies with the empathy-altruism hypothesis, which argues that altruism emerges as a result of emotional empathy (Batson et al., 1988). Emotional empathy is a state of arousal in which one perceives another in need of help coupled with a concern for other's welfare. This arousal is hypothesized to generate motivation to help the other person, independent of any benefit to self. Support for this hypothesis in experimental designs has been found, even controlling for alternative egoistic mechanisms

(Batson and Shaw, 1991; Batson et al., 1988; Dovidio, Allen, and Schroeder, 1990; Schroeder et al., 1988).

HIRING FOR ALTRUISM

Early on, personality researchers sought to establish an 'altruistic personality' that was associated with a general proclivity for altruistic action and thus organizational citizenship behaviors (OCB). However, inconsistencies in this research led attention to be diverted principally to consideration of the five-factor theory of personality and its relationship to organizational citizenship behaviors (Organ, 1994). In particular, agreeableness and conscientiousness have been found as dispositional antecedents to OCBs (e.g., Spitzmuller, Van Dyne, and Ilies, 2008). Collectively, this research suggests that, consistent with Lewin's ideas, altruism may not be a trait characteristic so much as a situationally dependent motivation that varies over time and is associated with different personality traits (Oda et al., 2014). As such, while altruism scales are not uncommon in personality inventories used in making hiring decisions, there remain important questions about whether it is appropriate to conceptualize altruism as a personality trait that should be tested for in hiring (see Table 14.1).

CULTIVATING ALTRUISM

In juxtaposition to the personality-oriented program of research on altruism, more recently scholars have begun to view behavioral altruism as a cultural trait that is embedded within, and invoked by, organizational settings (e.g., Grant, 2013; Li, Kirkman, and Porter, 2014). The thrust of this work makes a compelling argument for the importance of culture and leadership for invoking altruistic motivations and subsequent action. Further, to the extent we view OCBs as the behavioral manifestation of altruism, research has shown that perceptions of organizational support, fairness, and positive relationships with leadership are positively related to OCBs (Hoffman et al., 2007; Organ and Ryan, 1995; Organ, Podsakoff, and MacKenzie, 2005). Further, task characteristics such as degree of task interdependence and how intrinsically rewarding the tasks have also been shown to have a positive relationship to OCBs (Bachrach et al., 2006; Podsakoff et al., 2000).

In sum, this body of work suggests that altruism—behaviorally defined as actions taken for the benefit of the organization or work team that go above and beyond role expectations—can be cultivated individually and collectively through job design, team design, and leadership support (see Table 14.1).

SENSE OF COMMUNITY RESPONSIBILITY

The most recent entry into the public management literature is the concept sense of community responsibility (SOC-R), which was first discovered while asking respondents to express how they experience community at work in a qualitative study that served as a platform for further theoretical work (Boyd and Nowell, 2014; Nowell and Boyd, 2010, 2014). In short, employees noted that they experienced community in instances when they provided benefits for others, the organization, and its clients that were not grounded in cognitive perceptions of receiving anything in return. The discovery of a SOC-R led to the creation of a theoretical model called the Community Experience Framework (Nowell and Boyd, 2014), which posits that community experiences can be organized under two overarching and complementary dimensions. The first dimension, a sense of community, is born when physiological and psychological needs of inclusion, membership, influence, and identity are met (McMillan and Chavis, 1986). The second dimension, a sense of community responsibility, is born when one's a priori normative values and beliefs about responsibility interact with the community context at work. For example, if an individual enters an organization with strong beliefs and values of responsibility, and the organizational culture expresses strong values of responsibility, the work culture will validate and enhance a social identity of community responsibility in the individual. Nowell and Boyd (2014) theorized that a SOC-R is created through a mechanism of cognitive dissonance such that actors who experience a strong sense of community responsibility are going to be motivated to take action to facilitate alignment between their social identity and their behavior. As such, SOC-R was theorized to be more strongly associated with behavioral action within organizations compared to a SOC. SOC-R development is also consistent with Self-Determination Theory (Ryan and Deci, 2017) in that an individual is intrinsically motivated to enact on values that are at the center of their autonomous self. In short, when an individual joins an organization with intrinsic motivation toward a sense of responsibility they will act on that responsibility unless there are significant contextual barriers that thwart their ability to act (see Table 14.1).

Recent empirical work (Boyd and Nowell, 2017; Nowell and Boyd, 2014; Nowell et al., 2016) has supported the propositions of the community experience model. Nowell and Boyd (2014) showed SOC to be a stronger predictor of one's satisfaction with a statewide healthcare work collaborative while SOC-R was shown to be the stronger predictor of higher-order leadership behaviors within the collaborative. Boyd and Nowell (2017) demonstrated in a large US hospital system that SOC was the strongest predictor of psychological well-being, while SOC-R best predicted behavioral engagement via organizational citizenship behaviors toward individuals (OCBIs) and toward organizations (OCBOs). Recent work has also sought to understand the construct distinctions between SOC, SOC-R, public service motivation (PSM), organizational identity (OI), and affective organizational commitment (AOC). In a study by Boyd and Nowell (2020) in another large US healthcare system, the findings supported PSM, SOC, SOC-R, organizational identity, and organizational commitment to reflect related but unique constructs. Further, SOC was found to be the strongest predictor of psychological well-being outcomes (thriving and job satisfaction), and SOC-R was shown to be the strongest predictor of organizational citizenship behaviors and job engagement. Other researchers (Pedersen and Andersen, 2020) recently conducted a study with local councilors in a Denmark public management setting and showed that councilors with high SOC-R are less likely to voluntarily retire compared to PSM. Further, consistent with Nowell et al. (2016), SOC-R was a stronger predictor of visionary leadership behavior compared to PSM. Consistent across all of these studies is the notion that certain concepts may be global dispositions (e.g., PSM) or aligned to distal referents (e.g., organizational identity) from where individuals are situated in organizations, and that responsibility toward others, an organization, or its clients may be primarily driven by proximal human relationships.

HIRING FOR SOC-R

Scholarly activity around SOC-R has grown significantly over the past decade, from conceptual development, to theory and model building, and to empirical work that has shown it to be an important motivational construct in organizational behavior. However, very little is currently known about SOC-R in the context of hiring. The Community Experience Model posits that individuals enter organizations with values, norms, and beliefs about how one should act in regard to responsibility toward others. However, because a SOC-R is activated by interactions with a specific community, a SOC-R toward such an entity cannot develop prior to engagement with the community. Instead, new employees would bring knowledge of their sense of community responsibility toward others from previous community contexts, and that might shape initial perceptions and actions of responsibility toward others in their new role, however, ultimate SOC-R development would occur over time as one engages in the new community. If SOC-R measures were to be used (see Nowell and Boyd, 2014), they might need to be oriented toward perceptions of responsibility associated with the geographic community within which organizations are nested or that were present in previous communities (i.e., a past job or communal context). Alternatively, measures could be oriented toward expectations of responsibility toward their new setting.

To date, only one known study has investigated SOC-R in the context of attraction to public service (Brincker and Pedersen, 2020). The study sought to determine if PSM, SOC-R, SOC, and excitement motivation (EM) are relevant to the attraction and attrition of employees who work in challenging work environments. The study was situated in an extremely challenging work environment in the Eastern Greenland town of Tasiilaq and focused on teachers at a state-run school (many of whom are Danish expats). The school experienced shortage of staff, and the town of Tasiilaq struggles with socio-economic problems as well as severe issues stemming from substance abuse and sexual abuse. The school is also located in a geographically remote area, partially isolated by sea ice, and during the winter months, the community can only be reached by helicopter or dog sled. Findings from the in-depth case study showed that EM is particularly relevant to attract employees from abroad who seek adventure in the indigenous nature and culture. Moreover, they found that SOC-R to the geographic community within which one works serves as a source of attraction for East-Greenlanders who are drawn to return home, and who have been living in other parts of Greenland for quite some time. The power of SOC-R in this instance may be enhanced because of previous embedded connections with the community. By contrast, although noted by some respondents, SOC was much less pronounced as an attractor, yet it should be noted that some participants expressed aspirations, longing, and hope to become part of a community. Finally, PSM did not attract anyone. The authors argued that PSM was not an attractor in this context because if you want to do good for others in the form of a general, unidentified referent, there is no need to go all the way to Tasiilaq.

The findings of this study highlight that SOC-R could be conceptualized as a factor to consider in recruiting and hiring, but it is clear that development of SOC-R in such contexts is nascent. Because we lack consistent empirical evidence that SOC-R measurement has utility in hiring situations, it is difficult to gauge if and how SOC-R measures would predict attraction to public and non-profit organizations. Yet, this is an empirical question that certainly can be tested in future research studies (see Table 14.1).

CULTIVATING SOC-R

After an individual enters public service, we have plenty of evidence to believe that a SOC-R can be developed and cultivated. The Community Experience Model posits that a SOC-R grows when one's identity toward responsibility is congruent with the community culture toward responsibility. As the culture of an organization supports responsibility toward others, the organization, and its clients via a variety of manifestations, an individual's social identity of responsibility can grow in that fertile landscape. Therefore, the organizational context of responsibility is crucial for SOC-R development. As noted earlier, we have ample evidence to suggest that SOC-R is a robust predictor of a variety of behavioral outcomes for employees, however, data on antecedent factors that stimulate SOC-R development is also just budding. The best example of such scholarship is a study by Boyd, Larson, and Nowell (in process) that explored the cultural factors that lead to SOC-R development. The study was conducted in a large healthcare system in the United States in two waves. The first wave investigated organizational culture antecedents via qualitative interviews with C-suite members and a series of focus groups with upper- and mid-level leadership across the healthcare system. A number of antecedents were discovered and organized into groups including (1) CEO/top leadership support of the organization as a community, (2) broad organizational context features, (3) organizational structure, (4) human resource issues, (5) the work unit, and (6) job and individual characteristics. In relation to human resource issues, a number of contextual features were mentioned including the need to develop an onboarding program that focuses on community and becoming a member of it, training about community to current employees, and training and mentoring managers on aspects of community so they can develop it in their work units. Moreover, respondents felt that leadership should develop career counseling, mentoring, continuing education programs on community experiences, creating incentive programs for employees that align to responsibility toward others, and building community experience metrics into employee engagement surveys, performance evaluations, and in decisions for promotion.

The second wave of the study investigated the relationship between market-based, hierarchical adhocracy, and clan cultural types (Cameron and Quinn, 1999) with other-regarding constructs of PSM, prosocial motivation, SOC-R, and a sense of community. The findings demonstrated that clan cultures are important in predicting multiple other-regarding constructs, but they are especially important in predicting SOC-R and SOC. In short, these findings show that cultivating clan cultures (i.e., a very friendly working environment where people have a lot in common and which strongly resembles a large family) are not only important for enhancing a sense of community, but also for enhancing a sense of community responsibility toward others. An additional finding of interest that was captured in both waves of the study is the importance of SOC-R and SOC development within one's proximal work unit as powerful psychological experiences for individuals. This was the first study to investigate if the proximity of the referent matters in the development of community experiences, and the findings showed that SOC and SOC-R are more important for individuals within their work unit as opposed to the organization as an entity. Such findings help us understand that community experiences can be cultivated, and the need to especially cultivate them within our proximal communities of practice at work (see Table 14.1).

CONCLUSIONS

This chapter attempted to help us understand the similarities and differences between 'other-regarding' constructs and propose ways in which these concepts have utility in hiring, training, and in cultivating cultures of responsibility toward others. These goals are important for helping to create a workforce that delivers the intentions of public and non-profit organizations, and for helping to realize positive employee and organizational outcomes.

In terms of hiring, it seems that PSM is a dispositional construct that works as an attractor toward public service, and as such, it might have utility for HR professionals as a screen for individuals who show a predisposition for public and non-profit settings. However, concurrent and predictive validity studies that show PSM to be an excellent predictor of public service mission delivery, and other-regarding behavioral action toward citizens and clients within public and non-profit work settings do not exist. This is especially true when we consider comparative hiring battery studies that would 'cage match' several tests against each other on current or prospective employees. This logic holds for prosocial motivation, its sub-construct of altruism, and a sense of community responsibility. Future public service HR scholarship should be designed to test the validity of these 'other-regarding' constructs on outcome measures of interest (e.g., mission delivery, work performance, and others), to determine if other-regarding measures matter in a hiring process.

In the absence of such studies, on the surface, some of the constructs appear more suitable as hiring measures compared to others. PSM seems like a logical choice because it is grounded primarily or uniquely in public institutions and organizations. Yet, it could also show promise as a dispositional factor that aligns to private sector organizations that have 'cause missions.' Adam Grant's (2008) measure of prosocial motivation at work also has potential as a hiring test across sectors, because similar to PSM, it appears to be conceived as a dispositional factor. Interestingly, altruism, and its parent construct of prosocial motivation in psychology, may not be as suitable given that they are conceived as behavioral manifestations of other-regarding qualities, and that altruism in personality testing studies has not necessarily fared well in hiring research to date. Sense of community responsibility measures could be a candidate in a hiring process, but because SOC-R is created by interactions with a specific community, they would need to be oriented toward anticipated perceptions of responsibility associated with the new organization or aligned to a previous organization where their sense of responsibility was activated.

In terms of cultivation through training, rewards, and other HR mechanisms, PSM and prosocial motivation do not appear to be as suitable as measures of altruism or a sense of community responsibility. Because PSM and Grant's conception of prosocial motivation at work are dispositional constructs, training interventions, rewards, and inclusion in performance appraisal systems are unlikely to modify them. On the other hand, behavioral notions of altruism (e.g., OCBs) have potential to be invoked by organizational contexts. There is plenty of scholarship to suggest that altruism—behaviorally defined as actions taken for the benefit of the organization or work team that go above and beyond role expectations—can be cultivated individually and collectively through job design, team design, and leadership support. A sense of community responsibility is also a strong candidate for cultivation because as the Community Experience Model posits, a SOC-R can grow or recede as a function of the organizational context.

In short, a SOC-R needs a community context at work for it to activate and impact employee and organizational outcomes. Therefore, training about responsibility to co-workers, the organization, and its clients, in that specific organizational community context, seem likely to be effective. In addition, it seems reasonable that a SOC-R could be activated by independent reward structures or accountabilities that are included in performance review systems. Of course, the ability of 'other-regarding' constructs to have utility in hiring, training, and other HR systems are empirical questions that, to date, we have not answered. Perhaps this chapter serves as a way forward for scholars to consider these empirical questions in future HR studies in public management and in the field of management.

REFERENCES

Alonso, P., and Lewis, G.B. (2001). Public service motivation and job performance evidence from the federal sector. *American Review of Public Administration, 31*, 363–380.

Andersen, L.B., and Kjeldsen, A.M. (2013). Public service motivation, user orientation, and job satisfaction: A question of employment sector? *International Public Management Journal, 16*, 252–274.

Andersen, L.B., Pedersen, L.H., and Petersen, O.H. (2018). Motivational foundations of public service provision: Towards a theoretical synthesis. *Perspectives on Public Management and Governance, 1*, 283–298.

Andrews, C. (2016). Integrating public service motivation and self-determination theory: A framework. *International Journal of Public Sector Management, 29*, 238–254.

Bachrach, D.G., Powell, B.C., Collins, B.J., and Richey, R.G. (2006). Effects of task interdependence on the relationship between helping behavior and group performance. *Journal of Applied Psychology, 91*, 1396–1405.

Ballart, X., and Rico, G. (2018). Public or nonprofit? Career preferences and dimensions of public service motivation. *Public Administration, 96*, 404–420.

Batson, C.D. (1994). Why act for the public good? Four answers. *Personality and Social Psychology Bulletin, 20*, 603–610.

Batson, C.D. (2011). *Altruism in humans*. New York, NY: Oxford University Press.

Batson, C.D., and Shaw, L.L. (1991). Evidence for altruism: Toward a pluralism of prosocial motives. *Psychological Inquiry, 2*(2), 107–122.

Batson, C.D., Dyck, J.L., Brandt, J.R., Batson, J.G., Powell, A.L., McMaster, M.R., and Griffitt, C. (1988). Five studies testing two new egoistic alternatives to the empathy-altruism hypothesis. *Journal Of Personality and Social Psychology, 55*, 52–77.

Batson, C.D., Ahmad, N., Powell, A.A., and Stocks, E.L. (2008). Prosocial motivation. In J.Y. Shah and W.L. Gardner (eds), *Handbook of motivation science*. New York: Guilford Press, pp. 135–149.

Bellé, N., and Cantarelli, P. (2015). Monetary incentives, motivation, and job effort in the public sector: An experimental study with Italian government executives. *Review of Public Personnel Administration, 35*, 99–123.

Boyd, N., and Nowell, B. (2014). Psychological sense of community: A new construct for the field of management. *Journal of Management Inquiry, 23*, 107–122.

Boyd, N., and Nowell, B. (2017). Testing a theory of sense of community and community responsibility in organizations: An empirical assessment of predictive capacity on employee well-being and organizational citizenship. *Journal of Community Psychology, 45*, 210–229.

Boyd, N., and Nowell, B. (2020). Sense of community, sense of community responsibility, organizational commitment and identification, and public service motivation: A simultaneous test of affective states on employee well-being and engagement in a public service work context. *Public Management Review, 22*, 1024–1050.

Boyd, N., Nowell, B., Yang, Z., and Hano, M. (2018). Sense of community, sense of community responsibility, and public service motivation as predictors of employee well-being and engagement in public sector organizations. *American Review of Public Administration, 48*, 428–443.

Boyd, N., and Larson, S. (in process). Cultural antecedents that help build community experiences at work: A two-phase mixed methods study in a large healthcare institution.

Bozeman, B., and Su, X. 2015. Public service motivation concepts and theory: A critique. *Public Administration Review*, 75, 700–710.

Breaugh, J., Ritz, A., and Alfes, K. (2017). Work motivation and public service motivation: Disentangling varieties of motivation and job satisfaction. *Public Management Review*, 20, 1423–1443.

Brewer, G.A., and Selden, S.C. (1998). Whistle blowers in the federal civil service: New evidence of the public service ethic. *Journal of Public Administration Research and Theory*, 8, 413–439.

Brewer, G.A., and Selden, S.C. (2000). Why elephants gallop: Assessing and predicting organizational performance in federal agencies. *Journal of Public Administration Research and Theory*, 10, 685–711.

Bright, L. (2007). Does person-organization fit mediate the relationship between public service motivation and the job performance of public employees? *Review of Public Personnel Administration*, 27, 361–379.

Bright, L. (2008). Does public service motivation really make a difference on the job satisfaction and turnover intentions of public employees? *American Review of Public Administration*, 38, 149–166.

Bright, L. (2009). Why do public employees desire intrinsic non-monetary workplace opportunities? *Public Personnel Management*, 38, 15–37.

Bright, L. (2016). Is public service motivation a better explanation of nonprofit career preferences than government career preferences? *Public Personnel Management*, 45, 405–424.

Brincker, B., and Pedersen, L.H. (2020). Attraction and attrition under extreme conditions: Integrating insights on PSM, SOC-R, SOC and excitement motivation. *Public Management Review*, 22, 1051–1069.

Bromberg, D.E., and Charbonneau, É. (2019). Public service motivation, personality, and the hiring decisions of public managers: An experimental study. *Public Personnel Management*, 49, 193–217.

Cameron, K.S., and Quinn, R.E. (1999). *Diagnosing and changing organizational culture*. Reading, PA: Addison-Wesley.

Cerase, F.P., and Farinella, D. (2006). Explorations in public service motivation: The case of the Italian Revenue Agency. Paper presented at the *A*nnual Conference of the European Group of Public Administration, Milan, Italy.

Chen, C.A. (2014). Nonprofit managers' motivational styles: A view beyond the intrinsic-extrinsic dichotomy. *Nonprofit and Voluntary Sector Quarterly*, 43, 737–758.

Christensen, R.K., and Wright, B.E. (2011). The effects of public service motivation on job choice decisions: Disentangling the contributions of person-organization fit and person-job fit. *Journal of Public Administration Research and Theory*, 21, 723–743.

Clavien, C., and Chapuisat M. (2013). Altruism across disciplines: One word, multiple meanings. *Biology and Philosophy*, 28, 125–140.

Clerkin, R.M., and Coggburn, J D. (2012). The dimensions of public service motivation and sector work preferences. *Review of Public Personnel Administration*, 32, 209–235.

Crewson, P.E. (1997). Public service motivation: Building empirical evidence of incidence and effect. *Journal of Public Administration Research and Theory*, 4, 499–518.

Dovidio, J.F., Allen, J.L., and Schroeder, D.A. (1990). Specificity of empathy-induced helping: Evidence for altruistic motivation. *Journal of Personality and Social Psychology*, 59, 249–260.

Gabris, G.T., and Simo, G. (1995). Public sector motivation as an independent variable affecting career decisions. *Public Personnel Management*, 24, 33–51.

Georgellis, Y., Iossa, E., and Tabvuma, V. (2011). Crowding out intrinsic motivation in the public sector. *Journal of Public Administration Research and Theory*, 21, 473–493.

Gould-Williams, J.S., Mostafa, A.M.S., and Bottomley, P. (2013). Public service motivation and employee outcomes in the Egyptian public sector: Testing the mediating effect of person-organization fit. *Journal of Public Administration Research and Theory*, 25, 597–622.

Grant, A. M. (2008). Employees without a cause: The motivational effects of prosocial impact in public service. *International Public Management Journal*, 11, 48–66.

Grant, A. M. (2013). Givers take all: The hidden dimensions of corporate culture. *McKinsey Quarterly*, 2, 52–65.

Hemingway, C., and Maclagan, P. (2004). Managers' personal values as drivers or corporate social responsibility. *Journal of Business Ethics*, 50, 33–44.

Hoffman, B.J., Blair, C.A., Meriac, J.P., and Woehr, D.J. (2007). Expanding the criterion domain? A quantitative review of the OCB literature. *Journal of Applied Psychology*, *92*, 555–566.

Holt, S.B. (2018). For those who care: The effect of public service motivation on sector selection. *Public Administration Review*, *78*(3), 457–471.

Homberg, F., McCarthy, D., and Tabvuma, V. (2015). A meta-analysis of the relationship between public service motivation and job satisfaction. *Public Administration Review*, *75*, 711–722.

Honeycutt, J.M. (1981). Altruism and social exchange theory: The vicarious rewards of the altruist. *Mid-American Review of Sociology*, *6*, 93–99.

Jacobson, W.S., McGinnis Johnson, J.M., Piatak, J.S., and Sowa, J.E. (2019). Infusing public service motivation (PSM) throughout the employment relationship: A review of PSM and the human resource management process. Paper presented at the PSM Aspen Grove Conference. Aspen Grove, Utah.

Jensen, U.T., and Andersen, L.B. (2015). Public service motivation, user orientation, and prescription behaviour: Doing good for society or for the individual user? *Public Administration*, *93*, 753–768.

Jensen, U.T., and Vestergaard, C.F. (2017). Public service motivation and public service behaviors: Testing the moderating effect of tenure. *Journal of Public Administration Research and Theory*, *27*, 52–67,

Kim, S. (2005). Individual-level factors and organizational performance in government organizations. *Journal of Public Administration Research and Theory*, *15*, 245–261.

Kim, S. (2006). Public service motivation and organizational citizenship behavior in Korea. *International Journal of Manpower*, *27*, 722–740.

Kim, S. (2012). Does person-organization fit matter in the public-sector? Testing the mediating effect of person-organization fit in the relationship between public service motivation and work attitudes. *Public Administration Review*, *72*, 830–840.

Kim, S.E., and Lee, J.W. (2007). Is mission attachment an effective management tool for employee retention? An empirical analysis of a nonprofit human services agency. *Review of Public Personnel Administration*, *27*, 227–248.

Kjeldsen, A.M. (2014). Dynamics of public service motivation: Attraction–selection and socialization in the production and regulation of social services. *Public Administration Review*, *74*, 101–112.

Kjeldsen, A.M., and Jacobsen, C.B. (2012). Public service motivation and employment sector: Attraction or socialization? *Journal of Public Administration Research and Theory*, *23*, 899–926.

Krebs, D.L. (1991). Altruism and egoism: A false dichotomy? *Psychological Inquiry*, *2*, 137–139.

Le Grand, J. (2003). Knights and knaves return: Public service motivation and the delivery of public services. *International Public Management Journal*, *13*, 56–71.

Lewin, K. (1951). *Field theory in social science*. New York, NY: Harper.

Lewis, G.B., Pathak, R., and Galloway, C.S. (2018). Trends in public–private pay parity in state and local governments. *Review of Public Personnel Administration*, *38*, 303–331.

Li, N., Kirkman, B.L., and Porter, C.O. (2014). Toward a model of work team altruism. *Academy of Management Review*, *39*, 541–565.

Linos, E. (2018). More than public service: A field experiment on job advertisements and diversity in the police. *Journal of Public Administration Research and Theory*, *28*, 67–85.

Liu, B.C., Zhang, X., Du, L., and Hu, Q. (2015). Validating the construct of public service motivation in for-profit organizations: A preliminary study. *Public Management Review*, *17*, 262–287.

Locke, E.A., and Latham, G.P. (1990). Work motivation and satisfaction: Light at the end of the tunnel. *Psychological Science*, *1*, 240–246.

Malka, A., and Chatman, J.A. (2003). Intrinsic and extrinsic work orientations as moderators of the effect of annual income on subjective well-being: A longitudinal study. *Personality and Social Psychology Bulletin*, *29*, 737–746.

McGinnis Johnson, J., Piatak, J.S., and Ng, E. (2017). Managing generational differences in nonprofit organizations. In J.K.A. Word and J.E. Sowa (eds), *The nonprofit human resource management handbook: From theory to practice*. New York, NY: Routledge, pp. 304–322.

McMillan, D.W., and Chavis, D.M. (1986). Sense of community: A definition and theory. *Journal of Community Psychology*, *14*, 6–23.

Moynihan, D.P., and Pandey, S.K. (2007). The role of organizations in fostering public service motivation. *Public Administration Review*, *67*, 40–53.

Naff, K.C., and Crum, J. (1999). Working for America: Does public service motivation make a difference? *Review of Public Personnel Administration, 19*, 5–16.
Nowell, B., and Boyd, N. (2010). Viewing community as responsibility as well as resource: Deconstructing the theoretical roots of psychological sense of community. *Journal of Community Psychology, 38*, 828–841.
Nowell, B., and Boyd, N. (2014). Sense of community responsibility in community collaboratives: Advancing a theory of community as resource and responsibility. *American Journal of Community Psychology, 54*, 229–242.
Nowell, B., Izod, A., Ngaruiya, K., and Boyd, N. (2016). Public service motivation and sense of community responsibility: Comparing two motivational constructs in understanding leadership within community collaboratives. *Journal of Public Administration Research and Theory, 26*, 663–676.
Oda, R., Machii, W., Takagi, S., Kato, Y., Takeda, M., Kiyonari, T., Fukukawa, Y., and Hiraishi, K. (2014). Personality and altruism in daily life. *Personality and Individual Differences, 56*, 206–209.
Organ, D.W. (1994). Personality and organizational citizenship behavior. *Journal of Management, 20*, 465–478.
Organ, D.W., and Ryan, K. (1995). A meta-analytic review of attitudinal and dispositional predictors of organizational citizenship behavior. *Personnel Psychology, 48*, 775–802.
Organ, D.W., Podsakoff, P.M., and MacKenzie, S.B. (2005). *Organizational citizenship behavior: Its nature, antecedents, and consequences*. Thousand Oaks, CA: Sage.
Pandey, S.K., and Stazyk, E.C. (2008). Antecedents and correlates of public service motivation. In J.L. Perry and A. Hondeghem (eds), *Motivation in public management: The call of public service*. New York, NY: Oxford University Press, pp. 101–117.
Pandey, S.K., Wright, B.E., and Moynihan, D.P. (2008). Public service motivation and interpersonal citizenship behavior in public organizations: Testing a preliminary model. *International Public Management Journal, 11*, 89–108.
Pedersen, L.H., and Andersen, L. (2020). Motivated to take responsibility? Integrating insights from community psychology in psm research. *Public Management Review, 22*, 1051–1069.
Perry, J.L. (1996). Measuring public service motivation: An assessment of construct reliability and validity. *Journal of Public Administration Research and Theory, 6*, 5–22.
Perry, J.L. (1997). Antecedents of public service motivation. *Journal of Public Administration Research and Theory, 7*, 181–197.
Perry, J.L., and Hondeghem, A. (2008). Editors' introduction. In J.L. Perry and A. Hodeghem (eds), *Motivation in public management: The call of public service*. Oxford: Oxford University Press, pp. 1–14.
Perry, J.L., and Vandenabeele, W. (2008). Behavioral dynamics: Institutions, identities, and self-regulation. In J.L. Perry and A. Hondeghem (eds), *Motivation in public management: The call of public service*. New York, NY: Oxford University Press, pp. 56–79.
Perry, J.L., and Vandenabeele, W. (2015). Public service motivation research: Achievements, challenges, and future directions. *Public Administration Review, 75*, 692–699.
Perry, J.L., and Wise, L.R. (1990). The motivational basis of public service. *Public Administration Review, 50*, 367–373.
Petrovsky, N., and Ritz, A. (2014). Public service motivation and performance: A critical perspective. *Evidence-based HRM: A Global Forum for Empirical Scholarship, 2*, 57–79.
Piatak, J.S. (2016). Public service motivation, prosocial behaviours, and career ambitions. *International Journal of Manpower, 37*, 804–821.
Piatak, J.S., and Holt, S.B. (2020). Disentangling altruism and public service motivation: Who exhibits organizational citizenship behaviour? *Public Management Review, 22*, 949–973.
Pickering, M. (1993). *Auguste Comte: An intellectual biography*. Cambridge: Cambridge University Press.
Podsakoff, P.M., MacKenzie, S.B., Paine, J.B., and Bachrach, D.G. (2000). Organizational citizenship behaviors: A critical review of the theoretical and empirical literature and suggestions for future research. *Journal of Management, 26*, 513–563.
Pynes, J.E. (2013). *Human resources management for public and nonprofit organizations* (4th edn). San Francisco, CA: Jossey-Bass.

Rainey, H.G., and Steinbauer, P. (1999). Galloping elephants: Developing elements of a theory of effective government organizations. *Journal of Public Administration Research and Theory*, 9, 1–32.

Ritz, A. (2009). Public service motivation and organizational performance in Swiss federal government. *International Review of Administrative Sciences*, 75, 53–78.

Ritz, A., Brewer, G.A., and Newmann, O. (2016). Public service motivation: A systematic literature review and outlook. *Public Administration Review*, 76, 414–426.

Ritz, A., Schott, C., Nitzl, C., and Alfes, K. (2020). Public service motivation and prosocial motivation: Two sides of the same coin? *Public Management Review*, 22, 974–998.

Ryan, R.M., and Deci, E.L. (2000). Intrinsic and extrinsic motivations: Classic definitions and new directions. *Contemporary Educational Psychology*, 25, 54–67.

Ryan, R.M., and Deci, E.L. (2017). *Self-determination theory: Basic psychological needs in motivation, development, and wellness*. New York, NY: Guilford Press.

Ryu, G. (2017). Rethinking public service motivation from the perspective of person–environment fit: Complementary or supplementary relationship? *Review of Public Personnel Administration*, 37, 351–368.

Schott, C., Neumann, O., Baertschi, M., and Ritz. A. (2019). Public service motivation, prosocial motivation and altruism: Towards disentanglement and conceptual clarity. *International Journal of Public Administration*, 42, 1200–1211.

Schroeder, D.A., Dovidio, J.F., Sibicky, M.E., Matthews, L.L., and Allen, J.L. (1988). Empathic concern and helping behavior: Egoism or altruism? *Journal of Experimental Social Psychology*, 24, 333–353.

Selden, S., and Sowa, J.E. (2011). Performance management and appraisal in human service organizations: Management and staff perspectives. *Public Personnel Management*, 40, 251–264.

Spitzmuller, M., Van Dyne, L., and Ilies, R. (2008). Organizational citizenship behavior: A review and extension of its nomological network. In J. Barling and C.L. Cooper (eds), *The SAGE handbook of organizational behavior*. Los Angeles, CA: Sage, pp. 106–123.

Stazyk, E.C. (2013). Crowding out public service motivation? Comparing theoretical expectations with empirical findings on the influence of performance-related pay. *Review of Public Personnel Administration*, 33, 252–274.

Steijn, B. (2008). Person-environment fit and public service motivation. *International Public Management Journal*, 11, 13–27.

Steijn, B., and Van der Voet, J. (2019). Relational job characteristics and job satisfaction of public sector employees: When prosocial motivation and red tape collide. *Public Administration*, 97, 64–80.

Stringer, C., Didham, J., and Theivananthampillai, P. (2011). Motivation, pay satisfaction, and job satisfaction of front-line employees. *Qualitative Research in Accounting and Management*, 8, 161–179.

Taylor, J. (2014). Public service motivation, relational job design, and job satisfaction in local government. *Public Administration*, 92, 902–918.

Trivers, R.L. (1971). The evolution of reciprocal altruism. *Quarterly Review of Biology*, 46, 35–57.

Van Loon, N.M., Vandenabeele, W., and Leisink, P. (2015). On the bright and dark side of public service motivation: The relationship between PSM and employee wellbeing. *Public Money and Management*, 35, 349–356.

Vandenabeele, W. (2008). Government calling: Public service motivation as an element in selecting government as an employer of choice. *Public Administration*, 86, 1089–1105.

Vogel, D., and Kroll, A. (2016). The stability and change of PSM-related values across time: Testing theoretical expectations against panel data. *International Public Management Journal*, 19, 53–77.

Walk, M., and Kennedy, T. (2017). Making nonprofits more effective: Performance management and performance appraisals. In J.K.A. Word and J.E. Sowa (eds), *The nonprofit human resource management handbook: From theory to practice*. New York, NY: Routledge, pp. 250–268.

Wenzel, A.K., Krause, T.A., and Vogel, D. (2019). Making performance pay work: The impact of transparency, participation, and fairness on controlling perception and intrinsic motivation. *Review of Public Personnel Administration*, 39, 232–255.

Wright, B.E., and Christensen, R.K. (2010). Public service motivation: A test of the job attraction–selection–attrition model. *International Public Management Journal*, 13, 155–176.

Wright, B.E., and Grant, A.M. (2010). Unanswered questions about public service motivation: Designing research to address key issues of emergence and effects. *Public Administration Review*, 70, 691–700.

Wright, B.E., and Pandey, S.K. (2008). Public service motivation and the assumption of person-organization fit: Testing the mediating effect of value congruence. *Administration and Society*, *40*, 502–521.

Wright, B.E., Christensen, R.K., and Pandey, S.K. (2013). Measuring public service motivation: Exploring the equivalence of existing global measures. *International Public Management Journal*, *16*, 197–223.

Wright, B.E., Hassan, S., and Christensen, R.K. (2017). Job choice and performance: Revisiting core assumptions about public service motivation. *International Public Management Journal*, *20*, 108–131.

15. Merit system integrity and public service motivation in the US federal civil service: evidence on the importance of merit principles
Gene A. Brewer, J. Edward Kellough and Hal G. Rainey

INTRODUCTION

Civil service reforms designed to increase managerial flexibility and executive authority have been pursued with vigor for more than 40 years. The accompanying reduction of employee rights achieved through strategies such as expanding at-will employment, limiting appeal rights, and extending probationary periods have eroded protections public employees historically enjoyed within merit systems (Brewer and Kellough, 2016; Kearney and Coggburn, 2016; Rainey, 2014; Selden and Brewer, 2011). The administration of George W. Bush pursued this strategy at the federal level by seeking substantial management flexibility and reductions in employee rights within new personnel systems established at the departments of Homeland Security and Defense, but those reforms did not survive court challenges and opposition by the Obama administration (Brewer and Kellough, 2016). More recently, however, the Trump administration revived this agenda by issuing a series of Executive Orders intended to make it easier to fire federal workers and restricting union activity and bargaining rights.[1] Central elements of those Orders were overturned by the United States District Court for the District of Columbia, but that ruling was vacated by the D.C. Court of Appeals, and federal agencies implemented those new restrictions during the Trump years. In addition, toward the end of the Trump term, on October 21, 2020, the President issued Executive Order 13957 creating a new category of federal employment with the excepted service known as Schedule F. Employees determined by their agency heads to have 'confidential, policy-determining, or policy-advocating responsibilities' were to be transferred into this Schedule where they would have no due process rights or union representation, and hiring was to be at the discretion of the political leaders of the agencies. All of these radical reforms by the Trump administration were overturned immediately by President Biden, but the question is whether these kinds of personnel management reforms, that have been occurring with regularity for more than 40 years, have undermined central principles of merit in the federal civil service. If merit principles and associated rights of public employees are diminished, what are the implications for employee motivation? These are the specific issues we address in this chapter.

Merit principles specifying employee selection, management, and removal procedures are the centerpiece of civil service systems in most developed countries. They provide the basis for claims of workforce professionalism and neutral competence, and they confer legitimacy to public administration (Kettl, 2015; US Merit Systems Protection Board, 2013). The civil service system, which enshrines merit principles, is one of the few institutional safeguards that insulate public employees from political turmoil and partisanship. These safeguards are designed to ensure a professional, neutrally competent public workforce.

MERIT PRINCIPLES AND THE NEGATIVE ORIENTATION OF CIVIL SERVICE REFORM

The most fundamental principles of merit encompass three basic ideas: (1) employee selection must be based on the results of an open and competitive examination process designed to measure job-related abilities, (2) employees are expected to behave in a politically neutral manner on the job, and (3) employees are to be protected from political abuse or manipulation (Brewer and Kellough, 2016; Van Riper, 1958). Traditional civil service systems based on these principles typically have central personnel agencies to establish regulations and review agency practices to ensure compliance. The unambiguous purpose is to restrict inappropriate actions by political executives and line managers.

But this characteristic of merit systems is the core aspect of those structures that reforms over the past few decades have sought to relax or reverse. At all levels of government, these reforms typically seek to reduce rules and regulations and ease constraints on managers (Brewer and Walker, 2013; Kellough and Nigro, 2006; Kellough, Nigro, and Brewer, 2010). The limitations on managerial discretion under traditional merit systems, and the additional layers of personnel system red tape they entail, can produce delays and inefficiencies in personnel processes, including employee recruitment, selection, motivation, development, and retention. The objective of reform is to roll back these aspects of traditional centralized personnel systems, while at the same time empowering public managers (Condrey and Maranto, 2001). The goal is to increase managers' ability to administer rewards and punishments, and thereby regulate employee performance (e.g., see Brewer and Kellough, 2016; Brewer and Walker, 2013; Rainey, 2006). The centralized nature of traditional civil service merit systems, relying on compliance-inducing rules and regulations, is widely believed to unduly limit the ability of managers to structure work, reward performance, and punish or terminate low performers.

As a result of various reform efforts, the centralized civil service system for the US federal workforce has evolved over time. The original system has splintered through a proliferation of more decentralized personnel sub-systems run by individual federal agencies or departments, which have gained increased autonomy. Agencies are now utilizing a staggering variety of ways to hire and pay federal employees—even though some other features of the personnel system remain largely centralized (e.g., the General Schedule Pay Plan and Hatch Act prohibitions). In addition, reforms have repeatedly emphasized employee performance appraisals and pay for performance on the one hand, while streamlining appeals' processes and eliminating whistleblower protections on the other. The common denominator in this double-edged approach is more deference to managers and less concern for individual employees.

Change is also occurring at the state and local levels (Battaglio and Condrey, 2006; Kellough and Nigro, 2006). For example, Selden and Brewer (2011) examined multiple changes to civil service coverage and employee job protections in US state civil service systems during the period 1999–2006. In some states, reform had occurred even earlier. In Texas, for example, all personnel functions except the state compensation and classification system were decentralized in 1985. In Georgia, the entire state civil service system was decentralized and at-will employment was dramatically expanded in 1996. Selden and Brewer (2011) found that many state personnel directors reported that state civil service coverage was shrinking; that employee job protections had decreased; and that these changes had likely increased employee turnover. Some states were also employing large numbers of non-classified workers to circumvent or limit the scope of merit system protections. Similar evidence has been reported at the local level in the US (Battaglio and Condrey, 2006; Getha-Taylor, 2006), at the national government level (Light, 1999), and internationally (e.g., Bekke, Toonen, and Perry, 1996; Bouckaert and Halligan, 2007; Brewer, 2000, 2001).

In recent decades, many civil service reforms have been implicitly or explicitly based upon the beliefs that pay is the most important reward for public service, and that the threat of being fired is the main reason employees work hard. Kettl (2015), for example, describes how the civil service reforms enacted during the Carter administration began with a sophisticated 'good government' emphasis. As the effort evolved, however, the reforms began to emphasize making it easier to fire federal employees, in part because the public image of safely ensconced federal bureaucrats drew more press coverage than other problems addressed in the proposal. The National Performance Review (NPR) 15 years later during the Clinton administration again proposed reforms aiming to make it easier to fire federal workers (Gore, 1993). As described above, some state and local governments enacted reforms designed to remove due process protections for public employees and to eliminate or reduce collective bargaining rights, thus increasing managerial authority over employee dismissal. The Trump administration and Republican politicians generally increased the tempo of these reform proposals, referring to government employees as 'the deep state' and pledging to 'drain the swamp' and 'deconstruct the administrative state.' An example of such efforts came in mid-2017, when the US Department of Veterans Affairs (VA) came under intense criticism in the news media and from elected officials for performance problems. While the VA did have problems, the causes were complex. Nonetheless, President Trump seized the moment and used the incident as justification for fulfilling a campaign promise to give agency leaders more power to discipline and fire employees. He promptly signed into law legislation giving VA leaders more power to do so. The President then revoked an Executive Order that established labor-management forums to improve the delivery of public services, which further marginalized federal employee rights.

These recurrent initiatives often emphasize weakening employee job protections by taking away their ability to advocate or bargain for improved working conditions and by implementing crude motivational tools such as poorly designed pay for performance reforms. Such reforms are consistent with a 'carrot and stick' approach, and they have remained popular among political leaders even though there is little evidence that they work, and much evidence that they are harmful (Bowman, 2010; Kellough and Lu, 1993; Park and Berry, 2014; Perry, Engbers, and Jun, 2009). In fact, researchers often puzzle over why weakening employee job protections and implementing pay for performance systems remain popular reforms.[2] These reforms focus on managing extrinsic rewards and imposing threatening, punitive measures that weaken employee job security and discount higher motives for public service. Such measures raise the specter of inequitable and unjust management practices that provide employees with no recourse for unfair treatment. These reforms can conflict with merit principles and dampen employee motivation. They also conflict with contemporary literature on the theory and practice of human resource management in business and government. That literature tends to emphasize the quality of working life, work enrichment, intrinsic incentives, employee development, greater work-life balance, and generally positive orientations toward people in organizations. These more positive emphases suggest that the negative emphasis of many contemporary civil service reforms will prove dysfunctional.

RESEARCH PROPOSITIONS

This study reports on how well federal employees believe their agencies are administering and preserving fundamental merit principles. Are these agencies working toward and ensuring the integrity of the merit system? The trend toward personnel system decentralization is allowing individual agencies to have more control over hiring, rewarding, and firing employees, and thus, those agencies form the battleground for the future of merit principles in the federal government. This study reports on the status of merit system integrity in the US civil service and individual agencies, and examines the association between employee perceptions of merit system integrity and employee motivation—specifically, their levels of public service motivation.

Evidence indicates that employee perceptions of merit system integrity in their agencies influence important employee attitudes and behaviors (Brewer, Kellough, and Rainey, 2021; US Merit System Protection Board, 2013).[3] Indeed, the US Merit Systems Protection Board has conducted numerous employee surveys through the years based upon this premise. In addition, Wright and Nishii (2006) note the importance of employee perceptions and their impact on human resource management (HRM) performance, concluding that employee perceptions are a key element in determining HRM's impact on performance. Most researchers acknowledge the importance of employee motivation and many contend that it can be undermined by 'bureaucrat bashing' and low regard for public employees by elected officials and citizens. Since civil service systems are designed to insulate public employees from political intrusion, give them enough autonomy to carry out their duties in a professional, neutrally competent manner, and ensure fairness and justice in the workplace, how employees perceive the integrity of the merit system may be integral to their motivation and performance.

Federal agencies differ widely in their missions, strategic approaches, core work processes, and management practices. They serve different clienteles, employ their own workforces, and develop distinctive organizational cultures. While most federal employees are federal civil servants, they are socialized by their organizations and tend to promote their 'agency's view' of the world (Rourke, 1969; Wilson, 1989). These agency differences strongly imply that centralized personnel practices are likely to be implemented differently, and are likely to produce varying results, across federal agencies.

Based on the foregoing, we anticipate that federal employee perceptions of merit system integrity will vary within the federal service and across the 24 largest agencies. Our second expectation is that levels of public service motivation will vary also across the federal workforce. Thirdly, we expect that lower levels of merit system integrity will be associated with lower levels of public service motivation, both as a unitary concept and on its three dimensions of commitment to the public interest, self-sacrifice, and compassion. Together, such results would support the contention that erosion of merit system integrity may negatively affect employee motivation and thus urge caution for civil service reformers who are bent on dismantling civil service systems and weakening merit principles.

DATA AND METHODS

Data for this study come from the 2010 Merit Principles Survey conducted by the US Merit Systems Protection Board (MSPB). The survey was taken midway through President Barack

Obama's first term in office and just before the midterm Congressional elections that autumn, closing on July 15, 2010. This survey is the most recent large-scale survey that asks federal employees to rate how well their supervisors and agencies are adhering to the legally mandated set of merit principles.[4] The MSPB included a battery of 25 merit system integrity questions in the survey (see Appendix) and factor analyzed the results (DeVellis, 2012). Three underlying themes or dimensions emerged and were labeled as follows:

1. Fairness—perceptions of the fairness of the organization's human resources practices and decisions, especially matters related to hiring and pay;
2. Protection—perceptions of the effectiveness of measures to protect employees from inappropriate influences and improper actions, including attributes such as openness, tolerance of criticism, and willingness to act to prevent or rectify such actions; and
3. Stewardship—perceptions of the proper utilization and development of employees and organizations, including matters such as leadership, alignment, support, and efficiency.

The first two dimensions of fairness and protection reflect themes in the Pendleton Civil Service Reform Act of 1883 (chapter 27, 22 Stat. 403), which established that federal positions would be awarded on the basis of merit rather than political affiliation or patronage. This legislation was revamped by the Civil Service Reform Act of 1978 (October 13, 1978, Pub.L. 95-454, 92 Stat. 1111), which broadened the scope of merit to reflect good management practices in the civil service, thus forming the third dimension referred to as stewardship.

We formed measurement indices for the three dimensions of merit at both the overall and agency levels of aggregation (see the Appendix for a list of the measurement items for each dimension). Cronbach's alphas (α) for the three indexes are: fairness 0.92; protection 0.93; and stewardship 0.95, which indicates excellent reliability and internal consistency.

The primary dependent variable in this study is public service motivation. This concept is measured using a 5-item version of Perry's (1996) scale, which has been widely used in earlier work (see Ritz, Brewer, and Neumann, 2016; Wright and Pandey, 2008; Wright, Moynihan, and Pandey, 2012). This scale includes three dimensions of public service motivation: commitment to the public interest, compassion, and self-sacrifice (see the Appendix).[5] Together, these items represent the normative and affective motives that relate closely to public sector values and the altruistic appeal of public service.[6] These measurement items allow us to compute both overall and dimensional scores. Together these items are good indicators of the core concept of public service motivation and its respective dimensions. The unitary scale achieves a Cronbach's alpha of 0.76. One caveat is that one item in the self-sacrifice dimension is slightly different from the widely used version. It states, 'I am prepared to make enormous sacrifices for the good of the agency,' rather than 'sacrifices for the good of society' as stated in Perry's original index. We contend that this does change the meaning of the item. We thus tried omitting the item, but the results were almost the same, so we retained it in the present study.[7]

Finally, we include a number of control variables such as supervisory status, tenure, race and ethnicity, and education. While the unit of analysis for this study is the individual federal employee (n = 25,000),[8] we also include agency dummy variables to control for agency fixed effects on management, culture, context, and other factors. The US Department of Labor is used as the reference category for the dummy variables because it had the median score on public service motivation. The other agencies are arrayed around the median score and their coefficients reflect change from the median. We use sample weights, provided by the survey, for the regression model, and the standard errors are clustered at the agency level. To assess the possibility of multicollinearity, we ran multiple variance inflation factor (VIF) tests for the regression models. The results indicate no serious multicollinearity problems. The highest VIF in any of the models is 3.6, a level well below cause for concern.

FINDINGS AND DISCUSSION

Federal employee perceptions of merit system fairness, protection, and stewardship are shown in Table 15.1. This table reports the means and standard deviations for the overall sample, which represents the federal workforce as a whole, and for the 24 largest federal agencies reported individually. Overall, fairness received the highest score from federal employees with an overall mean of 3.55 on a 5-point scale, followed by protection and stewardship—each at 3.35. The standard deviations for these means reveal that the range of individual scores share much common space on the measurement scale; this suggests the need for caution when interpreting differences. Even so, clearly there is room for improvement on all three elements. While employees rated each one above the mid-point of the 5-point Likert scale, this scoring indicates their agencies are only moderately successful in ensuring merit system fairness, protection, and stewardship.

Table 15.1 also shows variation in merit system integrity among the 24 largest federal civilian agencies. The results show that employees in several agencies report that their organizations are doing better than the overall workforce average on fairness. These agencies include the following ranked in descending order (from highest downwards): NASA, FDIC, and SSA. Conversely, some agencies received employee assessments below the total workforce mean, including the following ranked in ascending order (from lowest upwards): HUD, Interior, and Education. Beyond the overall scores, Table 15.1 shows that employees in some federal agencies report that their organizations are doing better than average on protection. The top three on this dimension, ranked in descending order (from highest downwards) are: NASA, FDIC, and VA. The agencies receiving employee assessments below the mean on Protection include the following ranked in ascending order (from lowest upwards): HUD, DHS, and Education (Interior scored nearly as low as Education). Finally, employees in some federal agencies report that their organizations are doing better than average on stewardship (see Table 15.1). The highest three include the following ranked in descending order (from highest downwards): FDIC, NASA, and SSA. The agencies receiving the three lowest employee assessments below the mean include the following ranked in ascending order (from lowest upwards): HUD, Education, and DHS (Interior had a score nearly as low as DHS).

One obvious conclusion is that the highest and lowest ranked agencies are fairly consistent in their performance across the dimensions of fairness, protection, and stewardship. However, we do not know why certain agencies fare better than others. Political and public support, administrative capacity, type of mission (e.g., scientific or technical versus routine service delivery) and degree of professionalization may affect how well agencies perform on merit system criteria. Nevertheless, the ensuing analysis takes variations among agencies into consideration. With agency fixed effects included in the model, the results show significant overall relationships between perceived merit system integrity, especially fairness and stewardship, and public service motivation and its three dimensions.

Table 15.1   Descriptive statistics for perceptions of fairness, stewardship and protection

	Fairness n = 25 532		Protection n = 25 122		Stewardship n = 24 871	
	Score	SD	Score	SD	Score	SD
Total Workforce	3.55	0.93	3.35	0.94	3.35	0.85
Air Force	3.56	0.92	3.38	0.96	3.40	0.83
Agriculture	3.51	0.87	3.29	0.88	3.23	0.77
Army	3.58	0.97	3.39	0.97	3.37	0.90
Commerce	3.68	0.88	3.45	0.92	3.44	0.79
Defense	3.54	0.95	3.38	0.93	3.37	0.83
Justice	3.54	0.92	3.31	0.94	3.36	0.85
Labor	3.46	0.99	3.30	0.98	3.30	0.88
Energy	3.47	0.97	3.29	0.98	3.27	0.80
Education	3.40	1.05	3.20	1.02	3.14	0.94
EPA	3.54	0.97	3.25	0.94	3.23	0.80
FDIC	3.83	0.82	3.56	0.88	3.68	0.70
GSA	3.65	0.96	3.44	0.95	3.53	0.84
HHS	3.54	0.97	3.31	0.96	3.36	0.88
DHS	3.43	0.95	3.18	0.96	3.17	0.88
HUD	3.30	1.00	3.14	0.97	3.06	0.91
Interior	3.38	0.91	3.21	0.93	3.18	0.82
NASA	3.86	0.86	3.64	0.91	3.61	0.75
Navy	3.64	0.94	3.45	0.93	3.42	0.85
OPM	3.56	0.89	3.38	0.85	3.45	0.82
State	3.65	0.92	3.43	0.93	3.50	0.84
SSA	3.72	0.93	3.51	0.91	3.60	0.79
Transportation	3.52	0.93	3.38	0.96	3.33	0.85
Treasury	3.60	0.89	3.41	0.91	3.46	0.80
VA	3.61	0.93	3.52	0.94	3.42	0.86

Table 15.2 shows mean scores for public service motivation in the US federal civil service overall and in the agencies examined. The overall mean for the unitary concept is relatively high, and so are the means for the three dimensions (commitment to public interest, self-sacrifice, and compassion), with commitment to the public interest being the highest. Agencies with the highest mean levels of public service motivation are the VA, Army, SSA, and State. The three lowest scoring agencies are Treasury, Commerce, and Energy, respectively. It is worth noting that the differences between agencies are quite small.

Table 15.3 reports the results from a set of ordinary least squares multiple regression equations estimating the impact of the three dimensions of merit system integrity on public service motivation and its three dimensions along with a set of control variables that include agency dummy variables. The R^2 estimates reveal that these models explain somewhere between 5 and 14 percent of the variance in public service motivation. Table 15.3 shows that the dimensions of fairness and stewardship are positively and significantly related to the unitary public service motivation concept, but the protection component does not achieve statistical significance. When we decompose public service motivation and examine its three dimensions separately, a slightly different picture emerges. Two of the three merit system components (fairness and stewardship) produce significant positive effects on the anchor dimension of public service motivation, commitment to public interest (CPI), while one (Protection) produces a significant

Table 15.2   Levels of public service motivation (PSM) in federal agencies

	PSM n = 25 373 Score	Std Dev.	PSM: CPI n = 25 437 Score	Std Dev.	PSM: COM n = 25 470 Score	Std Dev.	PSM: SS n = 25 470 Score	Std Dev.
Mean	3.97	0.60	4.32	0.69	3.82	0.88	3.89	0.69
Air Force	3.98	0.62	4.16	0.73	3.82	0.86	3.97	0.67
Agriculture	3.89	0.57	4.31	0.65	3.74	0.87	3.79	0.67
Army	4.05	0.62	4.28	0.71	3.85	0.92	4.05	0.67
Commerce	3.85	0.61	4.22	0.68	3.72	0.84	3.77	0.70
Defense	3.98	0.61	4.28	0.72	3.84	0.88	3.92	0.70
Justice	4.01	0.60	4.35	0.66	3.78	0.91	3.98	0.67
Labor	3.97	0.62	4.37	0.67	3.77	0.91	3.91	0.71
Energy	3.88	0.62	4.23	0.75	3.81	0.91	3.78	0.73
Education	4.00	0.60	4.44	0.67	3.78	0.91	3.92	0.72
EPA	3.94	0.61	4.38	0.72	3.78	0.83	3.85	0.68
FDIC	3.89	0.63	4.19	0.70	3.88	0.82	3.79	0.71
GSA	3.95	0.60	4.33	0.69	3.90	0.89	3.84	0.67
HHS	4.00	0.57	4.41	0.66	3.85	0.85	3.91	0.66
DHS	4.02	0.61	4.31	0.70	3.86	0.89	3.98	0.68
HUD	4.03	0.61	4.41	0.69	3.90	0.84	3.95	0.71
Interior	3.91	0.59	4.31	0.69	3.75	0.87	3.83	0.68
NASA	3.95	0.58	4.18	0.75	3.92	0.81	3.88	0.65
Navy	3.97	0.60	4.20	0.69	3.84	0.88	3.93	0.67
OPM	3.95	0.64	4.33	0.69	3.80	0.94	3.88	0.73
State	4.04	0.63	4.40	0.71	3.96	0.85	3.95	0.71
SSA	4.05	0.58	4.55	0.61	3.99	0.84	3.89	0.70
Transportation	3.95	0.60	4.36	0.68	3.76	0.88	3.87	0.68
Treasury	3.85	0.60	4.19	0.71	3.78	0.89	3.76	0.69
VA	4.07	0.60	4.43	0.67	3.98	0.87	3.98	0.69

Note: COM = Compassion; CPI = Commitment to the Public Interest; SS = Self-Sacrifice.

but negative effect. In the model with self-sacrifice (SS) as the dependent variable, fairness and stewardship have significant positive effects while protection has a negative, but insignificant, coefficient. Finally, in the model predicting compassion (COM), the third dimension of public service motivation, all merit system dimensions produce positive coefficients, but only fairness and stewardship are significant. Protection fails to achieve statistical significance.

Of the three components of merit system integrity, stewardship produces the largest effects, which are consistently positive. That is, stewardship seems to promote higher levels of public service motivation. We have omitted the very long list of results for agency dummy variables from Table 15.3 for brevity, but the results show that 22 of the 23 agency dummy variables produce statistically significant impacts on public service motivation as a unitary concept, although the effect is negative in some agencies and positive in others. This pattern suggests that agency management, culture, and context matter.

Results on the demographic variables indicate that supervisory and minority (i.e., Black and Latino) status produce positive and mostly statistically significant impacts on public service motivation. In addition, we find that employees with more years of federal service are less public service motivated. This result contrasts with findings that often show more tenured employees hold more positive attitudes in work satisfaction studies (Rainey, 2014). Perhaps these federal employees have keener and more accurate perceptions of eroding merit princi-

Table 15.3 Regression results with public service motivation (PSM) and its three dimensions as dependent variables

	(1) Model 1 PSM	(3) Model 2 CPI	(4) Model 3 SS	(5) Model 4 COM
Variables				
Fairness	0.04***	0.05***	0.03**	0.07***
	(0.01)	(0.01)	(0.01)	(0.01)
Stewardship	0.17***	0.13***	0.14***	0.29***
	(0.01)	(0.02)	(0.01)	(0.02)
Protection	−0.01	−0.03***	−0.02	0.02
	(0.01)	(0.01)	(0.01)	(0.01)
Supervisor	0.07***	0.04***	0.08***	0.08***
	(0.00)	(0.01)	(0.01)	(0.01)
Tenure	−0.01***	−0.00	−0.01***	−0.00
	(0.00)	(0.00)	(0.00)	(0.00)
Latino	0.08***	0.11***	0.10***	−0.01
	(0.01)	(0.02)	(0.02)	(0.02)
Black	0.10***	0.08***	0.11***	0.08***
	(0.01)	(0.01)	(0.02)	(0.02)
Education	−0.01*	0.02***	−0.02***	−0.00
	(0.00)	(0.00)	(0.00)	(0.00)
Agency Dummy Variables	§	§	§	§
Constant	3.92***	4.21***	3.91***	3.67***
	(0.02)	(0.02)	(0.03)	(0.02)
Observations	24 522	24 570	24 579	24 610
R-squared	0.11	0.05	0.07	0.14

Notes:
Unstandardized coefficients with robust standard errors in parentheses.
*** $p < 0.01$, ** $p < 0.05$, * $p < 0.1$.
§ Agency dummy variables are omitted for brevity as explained in the text.
COM = Compassion; CPI = Commitment to the Public Interest; SS = Self-Sacrifice.

ples because of their longer years of service, or maybe they have grown skeptical or healthily guarded after long careers. Unfortunately, the dataset did not contain a gender variable, so we were unable to explore this potentially important variable. Lastly, the respondents' education level produced mixed and sometimes insignificant results.

CONCLUSIONS

The evidence found in this study supports the conclusion that merit system integrity, including fairness, protection, and stewardship, may affect employees' level of public service motivation. Their perceptions of merit system integrity are positively associated with their levels of public service motivation, both as a unitary concept and dimensionally. This study examined these relationships in depth, exploring three components of merit system integrity (fairness, stewardship, and protection) and three dimensions of public service motivation (commitment to the public interest, self-sacrifice, and compassion), which provides a fine-grained understanding of the correlational relationship between these concepts.

We do, however, note that the results are not uniform or consistently strong. In fact, there are some contrarian findings on the protection dimension, which has no significant effect on public service motivation as a unitary concept or on the dimensions of self-sacrifice or compassion, but which does significantly and negatively relate to commitment to the public interest. On the other hand, stewardship is positively, significantly, and powerfully associated with the unitary measure of public service motivation and three of the dimensional measures. The compassion dimension of public service motivation shows the most response to changes in merit system integrity. Lower levels of fairness and stewardship are associated with significantly lower levels of compassion among federal employees. One interpretation is that erosion of merit system integrity affects employee compassion for needy clients more than it affects their ability to function as professional, neutrally competent public servants who serve the public interest. Another interpretation is that employees deprived of job security and due process rights are forced to spend more time worrying about themselves rather than their clients.

The main limitations of this study include its cross-sectional nature, which limits our ability to make causal attributions, and the fact that the survey was not designed for empirical research on the relationship between merit system integrity and employee motivation. We needed to rely on the questionnaire items in the survey to develop measures of key concepts for the analysis. These measures should be strengthened in future research and additional variables should be included to examine moderating and mediating effects. In addition, other issues should be examined to clarify our findings. Perhaps employees with high levels of public service motivation feel more vested in their jobs and are more sensitive to the possibility that merit principles are eroding. This interpretation does not, however, comport with our finding that employees with more experience tend to report lower levels of public service motivation. Rather, it suggests that veteran employees might actually report less concern about merit system erosion than their junior counterparts.

Large federal employee surveys provide important glimpses into the inner workings of the American federal bureaucracy. To a large extent, perceptions can be extremely important when it comes to merit principle adherence and protection of employees. What employees see becomes their reality. Equally important are perceptual measures of employee and organizational performance, partly because they are often the only available measures of these important concepts. Certainly, large federal employee surveys that have been conducted over the years affirm that policymakers and public managers deem employee perceptions important—even as they often contemplate and implement civil service reforms that are harmful to employees. These employees are correctly seen as important elements in the chains of accountability and performance. A litany of reports by organizations such as the Office of Management and Budget, the Government Accountability Office, and the US Merit Systems Protection Board make clear that overhead political authorities and regulatory bodies see employee perceptions of problems as indicators of deeper-seated troubles in government. Indeed, the erosion of important dimensions of merit system integrity (i.e., fairness, protection, and stewardship) can lower the reputation of the federal government as a place to work, lower employee perceptions of job satisfaction and organizational performance, and hasten the departure of many current civil servants, thus worsening the long dreaded 'quiet crisis' (Brewer et al., 2016; Brewer, Kellough, and Rainey, 2021). In addition, this study shows that loss of merit system integrity may lower employees' public service motivation, both when measured as a unitary concept and on several of its dimensions. Future research should follow up on this important set of findings because it is directly relevant to efforts to weaken merit principles and dismantle civil service systems. Our clarion call is for reformers to exercise greater caution and understanding when tinkering with public personnel systems.

NOTES

1. See Executive Orders 13836, 13837, and 13839 of May 25, 2018, published in the Federal Register and accessible at: https://www.federalregister.gov/presidential-documents/executive-orders/donald-trump/2018.
2. Pay-banding and group pay for performance schemes (i.e., 'gainsharing') have emerged as ways to factor performance into pay and there are scattered claims of success, even though scientific evidence of their efficacy is still lacking in government.
3. The report contends that MSPB research shows that actual or perceived failure to abide by merit system principles can lead to decreased individual and organizational performance, increased Equal Employment Opportunity complaints, and increased employee turnover intentions. The article demonstrates empirically that federal employees who perceive greater adherence to merit principles in their organizations report greater general satisfaction with their agencies as workplaces, higher level satisfaction with leadership and recognition received, lower turnover intentions, and better quality of work unit output.
4. The Pendleton Act of 1883 established the civil service system for civilian employees in the US federal government, and the subsequent Civil Service Reform Act of 1978 modified the system and took the extra step of codifying the underlying merit principles into law (5 USC § 2301). The survey questions in this study come from those legally mandated merit principles.
5. Kim (2011) found evidence that public service motivation is a second-order, formative concept, meaning that it has relatively independent dimensions that should be preserved when developing measurement models of the concept. Theory further suggests that these dimensions are of equal importance in forming the overall or unified construct. Practically, this means that measurement dimensions should first be formed and measured; then standardized scores for those dimensions should be aggregated to form an overall or unitary measure of the construct. We followed this set of assumptions when measuring public service motivation in this study.
6. Another dimension in Perry's original index, attraction to policymaking, is omitted because it represents a rational, self-interested motive that is less value or mission specific and has proven to be weakly correlated with the other five items (Wright, Moynihan, and Pandey, 2012).
7. The scores of all multi-dimensional concepts and their respective dimensions (including the merit system integrity construct and its dimensions of fairness, protection, and stewardship; and the public service motivation construct and its dimensions of commitment to the public interest, self-sacrifice, and compassion) are calculated by taking the average (mean) of the responses on the survey items comprising the respective concept, thus, they are reported on the same standardized 5-point Likert scale that was implemented in the survey. The scale ranges from 1 = Strongly Disagree to 5 = Strongly Agree.
8. The survey data originally contains more than 42,000 responses with a response rate of 58 percent. After data cleaning, about 25,000 respondents are included in the analysis. Data cleaning involved eliminating respondents who chose a 'do not know' response and those for whom responses on one or more items were missing. We found no evidence that these missing values are systematic and no evidence that these procedures influenced the results of the analysis.

REFERENCES

Battaglio, Jr, R.P, and Condrey, S.E. (2006). Civil service reform: Examining state and local government cases. *Review of Public Personnel Administration, 26*, 118–138.

Bekke, H.A., Toonen, T.A., and Perry, J.L. (eds) (1996). *Civil service systems in comparative perspective*. Bloomington, IN: Indiana University Press.

Bouckaert, G., and Halligan, J. (2007). *Managing Performance: International Comparisons*. New York, NY: Routledge.

Bowman, J.S. (2010). The success of failure: The paradox of performance pay. *Review of Public Personnel Administration*, 30, 70–88.

Brewer, G.A. (2000). Administrative reform and organizational change in the public sector. Paper presented at Democracy Project AP 24/2000, University of Copenhagen, Copenhagen, Denmark.

Brewer, G.A. (2001). The great transformation? Administrative and civil service reform in western democracies. In Stephen E. Condrey and Robert A. Maranto (eds), *Radical Reform of the Civil Service*. Lexington, MD: Lexington Books, pp. 43–68.

Brewer, G.A., and Kellough, J.E. 2016. Administrative values and public personnel management: Reflections on civil service reform. *Public Personnel Management*, 45(2), 171–189.

Brewer, G.A., and Walker, R.M. (2013). Personnel constraints in public organizations: The impact of reward and punishment on organizational performance. *Public Administration Review*, 73, 121–131.

Brewer, G.A., Kellough, J.E., Rainey, H.G., Jin, R., and Rubin, E.V. (2016). The merit principle under assault: Evidence from the frontlines of the U.S. federal government. Paper presented at the 2016 Public Management Research Conference (PMRC), Aarhus University, Denmark, June 22–24.

Brewer, G.A., Kellough, J.A., and Rainey, H.G. (2021). The Importance of merit principles for civil service systems: Evidence from the U.S. federal sector. *Review of Public Personnel Administration*, 26(2), 118–138.

Condrey, S.E., and Maranto, R.A. (2001), *Radical Reform of the Civil Service*. Lexington, MD: Lexington Books.

DeVellis, R.F. (2012). *Scale Development: Theory and Applications*. Thousand Oaks, CA: Sage.

Getha-Taylor, H. (2006). Preparing leaders for high-stakes collaborative action: Darrell Darnell and the Department of Homeland Security. *Public Administration Review*, 66, 159–160.

Gore, A. (1993). Reinventing human resource management. Accessed July 6, 2021 at https://babel.hathitrust.org/cgi/pt?id=umn.31951d00279451t;view=1up;seq=3.

Kearney, R.C., and Coggburn, J.D. (2016). The civil service under siege. In R.C. Kearney and J.D. Coggburn, (eds), *Public Human Resource Management: Problems and Prospects* (6th edn). Washington, DC: CQ Press, pp. 375–384.

Kellough, J.E., and Lu, H. (1993). The paradox of merit pay in the public sector: Persistence of a problematic procedure. *Review of Public Personnel Administration*, 13, 45–64.

Kellough, J.E., and Nigro, L.G. (2002). Pay for performance in Georgia state government: Employee perspectives on Georgia gain after 5 years. *Review of Public Personnel Administration*, 22, 146–166.

Kellough, J.E., Nigro, L.G., and Brewer, G.A. (2010). Civil service reform under George W. Bush: Ideology, politics, and public personnel administration. *Review of Public Personnel Administration*, 30, 404–422.

Kettl, D.F. (2015). *Politics of the Administrative Process* (6th edn). Washington, DC: Sage/CQ Press.

Kim, S. (2011). Testing a revised measure of public service motivation: Reflective versus formative specification. *Journal of Public Administration Research and Theory*, 21, 521–546.

Light, P. (1999). *The True Size of Government*. Washington, DC: Brookings Institution Press.

Park, S., and Berry, F. (2014). Successful diffusion of a failed policy: The case of pay-for-performance in the U.S. federal government. *Public Management Review*, 16(6), 763–781.

Perry, J.L. (1996). Measuring public service motivation: An assessment of construct reliability and validity. *Journal of Public Administration Research and Theory*, 6, 5–22.

Perry, J., Engbers, T., and Jun, S. (2009). Back to the future? Performance-related pay, empirical research, and the perils of persistence. *Public Administration Review*, 69, 39–51.

Rainey, H.G. (2006). Reform trends at the federal level with implications for the states: The pursuit of flexibility and the human capital movement. In J.E. Kellough and L.G. Nigro (eds), *Civil Service Reform in the States: Personnel Policies and Politics at the Subnational Level*. Albany, NY: State University of New York Press, pp. 33–58.

Rainey, H.G. (2014). *Understanding and Managing Public Organizations* (5th edn). San Francisco, CA: Jossey-Bass.

Ritz, A., Brewer, G.A., and Neumann, O. (2016). Public service motivation: A systematic literature review and outlook. *Public Administration Review*, *76*, 414–426.

Rourke, F.E. (1969). *Bureaucracy, Politics, and Public Policy*. Boston, MA: Little-Brown.

Selden, S.C., and Brewer, G.A. (2011). Rolling back state civil service systems: Assessing the erosion of employee rights and protections, and their impacts. *SSRN*, first published online on August 31, 2011 at http://dx.doi.org/10.2139/ssrn.1919624.

US Merit Systems Protection Board (2013). *Managing Public Employees in the Public Interest*. Washington, DC: US Merit Systems Protection Board.

Van Riper, P.P. (1958). *History of the United States Civil Service*. Evanston, IL: Row, Peterson and Company.

Wilson, J.Q. (1989). *Bureaucracy: What Government Agencies Do and Why They Do It*. New York, NY: Rand.

Wright, P.M., and Nishii, L. (2006). Strategic HRM and organizational behavior: Integrating multiple levels of analysis. Working paper 06-05. Ithaca, NY: CAHRS Cornell University.

Wright, B.E., and Pandey, S.K. (2008). Public service motivation and the assumption of person-organization fit: Testing the mediating effect of value congruence. *Administration and Society*, *40*, 502–521.

Wright, B.E., Moynihan, D.P., and Pandey, S.K. (2012). Pulling the levers: Transformational leadership, public service motivation, and mission valence. *Public Administration Review*, *72*, 206–215.

APPENDIX: CONSTRUCTION OF INDICES

Each survey item utilized was measured on a 5-point Likert-type scale ranging from 1 = strongly disagree to 5 = strongly agree. We constructed simple indices by taking the mean value of responses on the items comprising the following concepts:

Public Service Motivation (5-items)

Cronbach's alpha = 0.76, Eigenvalue = 2.57

Commitment to the Public Interest:

- Meaningful public service is important to me.

Compassion:

- I am often reminded by daily events about how dependent we are on one another.

Self-Sacrifice:

- I am prepared to make enormous sacrifices for the good of the agency.
- Making a difference in society means more to me than personal achievements.
- I am not afraid to go to bat for the rights of others even if it means I will be ridiculed.

Fairness Dimension of Merit System Principles (7-items)

Cronbach's alpha = 0.92, Eigenvalue = 4.74

My organization:

1. recruits a diverse pool of applicants for job vacancies
2. holds fair and open competition for job vacancies
3. selects the best-qualified candidates when filling jobs
4. treats employees fairly
5. takes steps to prevent prohibited discrimination
6. takes steps to rectify prohibited discrimination
7. pays employees fairly.

Protection Dimension of Merit System Principles (5-items)

Cronbach's alpha = 0.93, Eigenvalue = 3.96

My organization:

1. protects employees against reprisal for whistleblowing
2. protects employees against reprisal for exercising a grievance, complaint, or appeal right
3. protects employees against arbitrary action
4. does not engage in favoritism

5. protects employees from political coercion.

Stewardship Dimension of Merit System Principles (13-items)

Cronbach's alpha = 0.95, Eigenvalue = 7.92

My organization:

1. recognizes excellent performance
2. rewards excellent performance
3. holds employees to high standards of conduct
4. puts the public interest first
5. uses the workforce efficiently and effectively
6. eliminates unnecessary functions and positions
7. makes good use of employees' skills and talents
8. focuses employee attention and efforts on what is most important
9. provides employees with the resources needed to get the job done
10. addresses poor performers effectively
11. retains its best employees
12. provides employees with necessary training
13. provides employees with opportunities for growth and development.

16. Job design and motivation: crafting the work of the public sector
Alexander C. Henderson and Jessica E. Sowa

INTRODUCTION

Individual motivation in the workplace is influenced by several factors, one of the more important of which is the design of one's job. When individuals have a job that aligns with, reinforces, and allows them to practice and grow their skills, knowledge, and abilities, they are likely to be motivated to work hard for their organization. In the public service, individuals also want jobs that tap into the public values and goals they want to pursue. The question, then, is how to effectively design or build jobs in a way that harnesses this motivation.

The essence of job design—the methods through which work-related processes, tasks, autonomy, and responsibility are defined and packaged—serves as the foundation for how individuals consider and understand the concept of a job and whether they remain motivated to do that job. When combined with considerations of the work environment, job design becomes central to work life and influences effectiveness, efficiency, decision-making, and the health and wellness of employees. Public agencies challenged with enacting complex public service functions must be attentive to the nature of work design, which can be difficult given institutional inertia and the sometimes-inflexible nature of government work. That being said, the more public managers can design jobs that harness the motivation of their employees and match employees into the right job designs, the better the performance of these public agencies.

The benefits of a focus on work or job design are myriad. For example, Parker (2014) notes that 'work design can be a powerful vehicle for learning and development, for maintaining and enhancing employees' physical and mental health, and for achieving control and flexibility simultaneously' (p. 661).[1] Fit between individuals and the design of work can promote employee well-being, along with improved performance. Therefore, work or job design contributes to individual motivation in a substantive way (Herzberg, 1974; Latham and Pinder, 2005), making it critical for better understanding the relationship between individuals and performance. When public sector leaders want to create desirable work conditions and outcomes for public sector workers, job design factors, including the ways in which jobs and tasks are selected and packaged, interpersonal interactions, and working conditions, are important levers these leaders can influence to encourage highly motivated and high-performing workers.

While job design is central to the operation of public agencies, scholarly attention to considerations of work and job design has ebbed and flowed within related fields of management, industrial/organizational (I/O) psychology, and public administration. Humphrey, Nahrgang, and Morgeson (2007), in a meta-analysis of work design research, found that top management and I/O psychology journals have published fewer studies on work design over the last several decades, though other journals in related fields have continued this focus through the introduction of new ways of conceptualizing and developing work. In particular, a resurgence of attention to job design and the importance of relationships (Grant, 2007, 2008) is evident in general management journals, but also in public administration, health care, and other fields of inquiry where relationships inside organizations and with service recipients may be particularly essential. This growing focus on relational job design blends classic job design (in terms of understanding the component part of the job and how they fit together) with the recognition of the environment in which these jobs operate and, in particular, how the relational component of these jobs can be a powerful motivator for individuals (Steijn and van der Voet, 2019; van der Voet and Steijn, 2019).

Though much attention is devoted to describing and specifying the knowledge, skills, abilities, and other characteristics (KSAOCs) essential for jobs through human resources functions (Pynes, 2013), less attention is paid to carefully and purposefully developing and packaging the processes and relationships that make up the job itself (Grant, 2007, 2008). An improved focus on the integration of these components helps us understand the interconnectedness and complexity of the work public servants do on a day-to-day basis and ensures that employees view work as meaningful and fulfilling. Parker (2014) notes the importance of job design, stating that it 'has been linked to almost every end goal that is of concern in an organization—safety, performance, and innovation, to name a few. Work design also matters for individuals; it affects their sense of meaning, their health, and their development' (p. 662).

This chapter provides a synthesis of existing knowledge of job design, with a focus on linkages between core concepts in job design and motivation, and examines the future of job design and motivation in the public sector as fundamentally impacted by technology and societal change. As public organizations must adapt to rapidly changing environments at the same time that more workers expect meaningful work, understanding how well-designed jobs contribute to employee and organizational outcomes is essential for public administration research.

PERSPECTIVES OF JOB DESIGN

Definitions of work or job design have varied significantly over the past several decades, moving from early discussions of tasks to a more comprehensive perspective that incorporates the concrete activities of employees as situated in specific work settings and with varying types of interpersonal relationships. While the design of a job—the coherence of tasks fitting together and the clear specification of what is needed to successfully perform the components of the job—is important, that job does not exist in a vacuum. The environment in which it is situated, and the relationships associated with the job impact the efficacy of the design. Therefore, we adopt this more comprehensive definition of work design as 'the content and organization of one's work tasks, activities, relationships, and responsibilities' (Parker, 2014, p. 662). It is the relational aspect of this definition that builds on earlier work and provides a more accurate picture of both job design and the implications for motivation; these centrally important relationships include both those key linkages with other individuals, specifically peers, close collaborators, and direct supervisors, but also our individual relationships with our work environment and, importantly for the public sector, with clients and citizens.

Recognition of the importance of these relationships with respect to the work environment was not always present in work and job design. Most famously, work by Frederick Taylor

(1916 [2011]) shaped ideas about individuals, roles, and the very specific examination and understanding of tasks. Taylor focused on understanding the components that make up jobs and the most efficient way to do those components—his work advanced knowledge on the scientific, standards-based selection of workers and training as well as on the creation of work processes best able to accomplish the task with efficiency in mind. In this perspective, efficiency, while important, is not necessarily the only (or even primary value) of work, necessitating an approach to job and work design that is broader than Taylor's narrowed focus. The recognition of alternative public values, the inherent discretion involved in much public service work, the relational aspects of job design, and the connection of jobs to the environment need to be considered in work and job design in the public service. These components were not a major focus of his research, but Taylor's conceptualization of work is still influential in highlighting the managerial responsibilities for job design and the importance of careful attention to how work is allocated and grouped together in jobs (1916 [2011]).

The study of work design is fundamentally linked to our understanding of public service and administration. Waldo (1980) linked concepts of administration—and by extension the roles, functions, and design of work—to the advent of civilization, indicating that, though the formality of work design may be more recent, examinations of how work is completed are not new. Slightly more recently, the focus on job design was elevated to a key aspect of considerations of work. In a review of a century of job design scholarship, Parker, Morgeson, and Johns (2017) provide a comprehensive overview of the history of the field of work design through an analysis of several thousand articles in management and psychology. They identify, through bibliographic mapping, citations, and consensus from subject matter experts, the 35 most important articles on the topic. This analysis results in a clustering of core topics on work design, including:

- *Sociotechnical systems and autonomous work groups* (social and technical aspects of work, teams and adaptation, leadership, autonomy)
- *Job characteristics* (notably, the Job Characteristics Model: job characteristics, job perceptions, complexity, feedback, design, significance)
- *Job demands-control* (job demands and working conditions, decision-latitude, physical demands, risk factors, strain, stress, depression, and others)
- *Job demands-resources* (job demands and job resources, self-esteem, optimism, absorption, dedication, personal accomplishment, as well as burnout, exhaustion, cynicism)
- *Role theory* (role conflict, role ambiguity, role overload) (Parker, Morgeson, and Johns, 2017, pp. 406–8).

Research specifically focused on job design (cf, Grant, 2007, 2008; Parker, 2014) has worked to integrate core topics from these clusters in meaningful ways. Overall, when considering the design of jobs in the public sector and how those jobs influence individual behavior (and, in particular, motivation), it is important to think about the characteristics of jobs, the balance between job demands, resources, and autonomy, the clarity of one's place or role in the organization as embodied in the job design, and how the job is placed within a larger system of interpersonal, team, and authority relations.

More recent discussions have applied principles of design science in public administration, focusing on the importance of more deliberative activities related to the specification of administrative processes (Barzelay, 2019; Barzelay and Thompson, 2010). By extension, this includes narrowed concepts of job design to ensure that these jobs are, in fact, carefully designed. Barzelay and Thompson (2010) note, in a discussion of the future of the scholarly field of administration, that they 'take the view that if scholars of public administration want to offer practical, useful advice to practitioners, we need to give them a set of heuristics for designing practical interventions and a set of heuristics for the discovery of practically useful knowledge' (Barzelay and Thompson, 2010, p. S296). As such, public administration needs to better understand how jobs and work are designed to promote high motivation amongst employees and high performance at the organizational level.

Focusing specifically on the relationship between job and work design and motivation, the questions, then, are what are the connections between these—how do task design, consideration of roles, job impact and significance, the relational aspects of work, the work environment, and multiple aspects of individual fit affect motivation? Importantly, this chapter does not provide a full and complete summary and integration of the full body of job design and motivation literature. Rather, we examine contemporary research that informs our understanding of job design and link that research to individual motivation and other desirable organizational outcomes. The next section highlights this literature and unpacks relevant theory to work towards a better understanding of motivation in relation to jobs.

JOB DESIGN AND MOTIVATION

Many core aspects of job design directly connect to concepts of motivation, as the mechanisms through which an individual's experiences with people, processes, and culture impact their desires to work more intensely and persistently towards goals. These factors include job and task characteristics, the match with individual characteristics, relational job design, and the environment of work. Though presented here as separate topics, in reality this separation is artificial and there is significant conceptual overlap. Those considering the impact of job design on motivation should closely consider those overlaps and adopt a holistic and potentially flexible perspective of these areas of inquiry that fit with contextual needs. One challenge with our current knowledge of job design is that our attention to the outcomes of work design are not limited to a single concept; rather, much of the research in this realm of inquiry is focused on attitudinal factors (like job satisfaction), motivation, and performance. This creates difficulties in the processes of integrating knowledge in the service of crafting 'better' practices for work, and forces scholars and practitioners to carefully and purposefully discuss potentially overlapping and complementary aspects of organizational behavior. Regardless, discussion and integration of this work provides important insights into job design and motivation.

Job Characteristics, Resources, and Demands

The vast majority of existing knowledge on job design focuses on the characteristics of the specific tasks individuals must complete as part of their job, a key component of Hackman and Oldham's (1980) Job Characteristics Model (JCM). The JCM focuses on five core tenets of work design including skill variety, task identity, task significance, autonomy, and feedback (Hackman and Oldham, 1980, p. 90). This collection of job characteristics is related to an individual's attention to work and the impact of that attention on the types of behaviors managers consider important, beneficial to employee performance, or otherwise desirable, including motivation. Hackman (1980) notes that these concepts emerge from activation theory, which

> specifies that a person's level of activation or 'arousal' decreases when sensory input is unchanging or repetitive, leading to [undesirable work behaviors]. Varying or unexpected patterns of stimuli, on the other hand, keep an individual activated and more alert ... (Hackman, 1980, p. 446)

If managers want workers to be active, attention to a blend of different job characteristics, with variety, different levels of challenge, and different levels of autonomous action may be a way to encourage this and thereby motivate workers. The challenge lies in determining this mix—what is the 'best recipe' of job characteristics? As such, the JCM and related job design models are not without criticism, most notably that these models have 'demonstrated links between job characteristics (such as autonomy and skill variety) and employee affect, and yet they have been unable to consistently confirm hypothesized linkages between task motivation and work performance' (Burr and Cordery, 2001, p. 28).

The key tenets of JCM have been tested periodically, including a large-scale meta-analysis by Fried and Ferris (1987) and a more comprehensive and updated meta-analysis by Humphrey, Nahrgang, and Morgeson (2007). In an early integration of work on JCM, Fried and Ferris (1987) found moderate support for relationships between the five components of JCM and desirable psychological states and work performance to varying degrees. Similarly, work by Humphrey, Nahrgang, and Morgeson (2007) found an expanded model that included the components of JCM and additional motivational, social, and contextual factors impacted both job satisfaction and work performance. Grant (2008) also found task significance had a direct and significant impact on work performance.

While job characteristics may affect performance, there can be aspects of the working environment that may shape how these characteristics are experienced by employees and thereby shape their motivation and their performance. Shantz and colleagues (2013) examined employee engagement as a mediator for the relationship between job design and employee performance, finding employees with higher autonomy, task variety, task significance, and feedback are more engaged, and consequently perform better. Similarly, Wood and colleagues (2012) found jobs characterized by high enrichment and high involvement resulted in higher performance, which was mediated by job satisfaction. In their study, the concept of an 'enriched' job included 'discretion, variety and high levels of responsibility,' while highly involved jobs included 'teamworking, idea-capturing schemes and functional flexibility' (Wood et al., 2012, p. 420). A study by Park (2017) examined JCM in the context of work appraisal and rater accuracy, finding that the five core components of JCM are mediated by important psychological states of meaningfulness, responsibility, and knowledge of rating results, all of which impact the accuracy of ratings of subordinates. Reflecting on these findings, managers may want to think about how to engage individuals, both in the design process and through the execution of their tasks, to foster high motivation and high performance. Research on high involvement or high-performance work practices in the public sector aligns with the idea of giving employees the opportunity to be involved to encourage their performance (Mostafa, Gould-Williams, and Bottomley, 2015).

Mohr and Zoghi (2008) examined individual involvement in core work practices that include involvement in the workplace. Their findings suggest individuals enacting roles characterized by significant input and interaction, including project-focused teams, frequent discussions of performance and quality, and the use of formal and informal feedback mechanisms, are likely to be increasingly satisfied. Related to this, Burr and Cordery (2001) examined the mediating role of self-management efficacy—a measure that examines individual perceptions of abilities to complete core work tasks—between core job characteristics like skill utilization and work control (closely conceptually linked to autonomy) and affective and motivational outcomes. They found utilization of skills directly impacted both job satisfaction and motivation, and that self-management efficacy mediated the relationships between work method control (autonomy) and motivation (Burr and Cordery, 2001, p. 40). Interestingly, Burr and Cordery (2001) note that challenging jobs may impact how individuals see themselves in those positions, which suggests that purposeful job design that encourages individual development may pay dividends in terms of supporting and enhancing individual capacity.

Along with the JCM, the fundamental nature of our individual roles in the workplace creates perhaps the clearest connection between job design and motivation. Biddle (1986) noted that role theory is characterized by 'patterned and characteristic social behaviors, parts or identities that are assumed by social participants, and scripts or expectations for behavior that are understood …' (p. 68). Roles may encompass a number of different perspectives of behavior, individual views of identity, and expectations for work, each of which may impact motivation. The question, then, is what kinds of roles can be built into job designs to encourage motivated workers?

Chae and Choi (2018) identify creativity as a specific type of role-related prosocial behavior in the workplace and find that creativity mediates the relationship between task complexity and job performance. Information-seeking behaviors are important as well; individuals who engaged in informal field-based learning as a part of their enactment of a role (as compared to formal training offered by organizations) were more likely to demonstrate performance improvements (Wolfson et al., 2019). Interestingly, existing studies have also found that those with experience in work design are likely to design work in different ways; those with experience in industrial/organizational psychology were more likely to design jobs that are more focused on enrichment through task allocation and work strategy (Parker, Andrei, and Van den Broeck, 2019). A study by Scharp et al. (2019) found employees who engage in 'playful work design,' which purposefully includes designed fun and designed competition as a part of considering daily activities, were more likely to be engaged and creative in those roles. Overall, thinking about how to build into job designs the ability of workers to play with their roles, experiment, and find new ways of getting at tasks may be a way to keep people from feeling threatened in their roles (if there is an ambiguity, as is often the case in the public sector). If people feel comfortable to experiment and improve on their tasks (versus running the risk of being penalized), they may be more motivated and hopefully deliver high performance.

In addition to job characteristics and individual conceptions of roles, the demands of jobs and the resources provided to complete tasks associated with jobs—both of which are core components of designing work—have been linked to individual affective states and performance outcomes. In particular, employee well-being (including stress and burnout from a negative perspective and engagement and motivation from a positive perspective) is affected by how jobs are designed and what the individual experiences when filling that job. The Job Demands-Resources model is built on the assumption that occupations have 'specific risk factors' (demands and resources) built into them 'associated with job stress'—factors that either reduce stress or increase it (Bakker and Demerouti, 2007, p. 312; Bakker et al., 2003). When designing jobs, attention should be placed on whether or not the demands and resources are more or less balanced. This is not to say that jobs should have no or low demands—few jobs are without any stress. Public service workers indeed often welcome challenging jobs and these jobs in particular provide meaning for public employees, especially when they believe they have made a difference (Bauwens, Decramer, and Audenaert, 2019). However, if a job has high demands (e.g., emotionally charged or draining tasks, a high-pressure work environment and tight deadlines, high volume of work), managers designing those jobs and providing support to the employees filling those jobs should ensure these employees have sufficient job resources, as high demands and low resources together reduces the motivation of employees, impacts their well-being, and could lead to burnout (Bakker and Demerouti, 2007; Lizano and Mor Barak, 2012). The trick is identifying the right resources that will buffer the job demands and reduce the strain, burnout, and motivational decline that can result from mismanaged high job demands.

Some resources brought to the job are personal to the individual (Salanova, Llorens, and Schaufeli, 2011; Xanthopoulou et al., 2007); resources that impact how they process and experience job demands and can lead to a hopeful reduction of the stress and burnout of significant demands (e.g., resilience, emotional intelligence and control, overall motivation or, in the case of public service workers, public service motivation). Managers can hopefully screen for these or emphasize these resources when looking to fill positions. Some resources that impact employee motivation are at the organizational and interpersonal level, such as pay and job security, but many are at the job and work level. Supervisor-subordinate interactions are definitely within the control of managers; other resources associated with tasks and the working environment can be influenced by managers either through initial job design or through redesign over time.

Through job and work design, managers can examine the clarity of roles given to individuals and they can give attention to the blend of job characteristics discussed earlier to ensure enough significant tasks and enough task variety. This should improve employee outcomes, including well-being, motivation, and engagement. For example, though focused on private sector front-line employees, a study by Qi, Ellinger, and Franke (2018) sheds light on the importance of resources and engagement; they find job resources are important and operate to increase engagement through the influence of organizational support and customer orientation (p. 649). Public administration scholars have begun applying the JD-R model to study a number of employee and organizational outcomes, overall and specifically in relation to how employee motivation factors into the balance of job resources and demands (Bakker, 2015; Borst, Kruyen, and Lako, 2019; Cooke, Brant, and Woods, 2019; Giauque, Anderfuhren-Biget, and Varone, 2013) Drawing on the idea of high involvement work practices, managers can think about the work design and create opportunities for employees to be involved in the decision-making process and autonomy in carrying out particular tasks, which can be seen as a resource that can encourage and motivate employees (Borst, Kruyen, and Lako, 2019).

Taken together, our understanding of job design—the characteristics, the roles, and the resources and demands—has several implications for how we understand motivation in public sector agencies. Many of the central aspects of JCM (skill variety, task identity, task significance, autonomy, and feedback) are likely to be partially or wholly under the control of those in leadership positions. Developing an understanding of these factors and developing an appropriate mix of design characteristics on a position-by-position basis is likely to positively shape motivation. In addition, leaders can help workers make sense of their roles and also give them the opportunity to grow and experiment in their roles to improve on their task performance and hopefully remain highly motivated. Likewise, leaders must be attentive to the demands created by specific positions and the resources afforded to employees as they enact roles and cope with challenges. Scholars have begun to integrate many of these aspects together and, in particular, recent developments in examining the nature of work have focused intently on interpersonal relationships and the role relationships play in how we understand the importance of work, feelings of mutuality, and support.

Relational Job Design

Jobs are rarely enacted in isolation, and the nature and types of relationships in the workplace can substantively shape employees' feelings of engagement, satisfaction, and motivation (Freeney and Fellenz, 2013; Grant, 2006, 2008; Morgeson and Humphrey, 2006). Grant (2007), in a discussion of the 'relational architecture' of work, examines the impact of work context on individual motivations to make a prosocial difference. In doing so, he notes the centrality of interactions in shaping motivation, stating that 'interpersonal relationships both cultivate and result from the motivation to make a prosocial difference' (Grant, 2007, p. 394). In shaping his argument for these linkages, Grant notes that the underlying structure of jobs is intrinsically based on interaction, collaboration, and cooperation, and the emotional labor associated with coworker and service recipient requires attention to relationships (2007, p. 395). Likewise, Grant (2008) found that interpersonal relationships mediated the relationship between task significance and job performance, finding that 'employees process task significance as true social cognition …, experiencing their jobs as more strongly related to other people through heightened perceptions of social impact and social worth' (p. 119).

Taylor (2014), in a study of local government workers in Australia, found a component of relational job design—that of perceived impact on service recipients—mediates the relationship between public service motivation and job satisfaction. The relational component of this study points to the importance of a core relational aspect of work particularly front-line work, that 'the extent to which they perceived that their jobs provided avenues for worthwhile accomplishment through the frequency, magnitude, and scope of job impact' (Taylor, 2014, p. 912). Similarly, in a volunteer context, Alfes, Shantz, and Saksida (2015) found volunteers serving in organizations in which jobs are relationally designed hold lower intentions to leave and, at the same time, spend more time volunteering given the tangible impact of work on service recipients. Freeney and Fellenz (2013), in a study of midwives working in hospitals, found that several aspects of relational work—specifically supervisor and peer support, and perceived impact on service recipients—had a significant impact on worker engagement. Recent research on human service workers has reaffirmed the relationship between motivation and relational aspects of jobs (Steijn and van der Voet, 2019; van der Voet and Steijn, 2019).

The relational nature of work extends to the physical work environment, and individual relationships with their immediate physical space may matter in shaping individual motivation. Notably, the evidence here is much less developed than many of the areas of inquiry related to job design. Griffin and Neal (2000) found that the creation of a workplace safety climate, which includes leader behaviors and values, training, communication, and safe practices, encouraged workers to more closely engage with safety compliance and practices. A study by Bangwal, Tiwari, and Chamola (2017) found that both workplace design and departmental space in Leadership in Energy and Environmental Design (LEED)-certified 'green' buildings impacted organizational commitment via job satisfaction. Individuals working in these environmentally friendly buildings recognized and appreciated these characteristics, which contributed to feelings of job satisfaction and ultimately organizational commitment. It may be that the effort and resources that go into the creation and maintenance of physical workspaces perceived as increasingly healthy or sustainable may signal to employees that leaders are conscious of the short- and long-term physical wellness and mental health of employees, which may indicate increased care and stronger affiliations.

Much of the work in the public sector involves people and recognizing the importance of this in job designs and in motivation is important. This turn towards the relational aspects of work in job design scholarship will hopefully spur increased attention in practice, as the social aspects of work and perceptions of impact on service recipients is significant. However, this increased attention may be more challenging in practice than a focus on job characteristics, given that relationships are more ethereal and less tangible. This does not make it any less important, as research has demonstrated that the emotive component of work is equally as important as the technical aspects of a job (Guy, 2020). Similarly, the physical environment, and leader and employee perspectives of their relationships with that environment, may shape satisfaction, motivation, performance through socially constructed conscious and unconscious reflection on people, purpose, and place. Those in leadership roles should focus purposefully on crafting messages and meaning for public sector workers that stress the importance of work, the supportive nature of place, and creating a culture that is well aligned with core organizational functions.

Integrative Approaches

A number of approaches to job design explicitly work to integrate many of the above components of work to better understand the relationship between motivation and performance. The sociotechnical systems approach noted by Parker, Morgeson, and Johns (2017) is one such example, focusing on core activities and relationships. Hackman (1980) noted the sociotechnical systems approach 'emphasizes the importance of designing entire work systems, in which the social and technical aspects of the workplace are integrated and mutually supportive of one another' (p. 448). Designing jobs requires focused attention on the core processes of work as well as connections with coworkers, team effectiveness, leader-follower relationships, and the integration of these parts into a meaningful whole. Morgeson and Humphrey (2006), in developing their comprehensive Work Design Questionnaire (WDQ), sought to integrate the components of jobs and the working environment, focusing on task and knowledge characteristics (which have some overlap with the components of JCM), social characteristics (which include support, interdependence, interactions, and feedback), and work context (physical conditions, work equipment, and use). In a large-scale meta-analysis, Humphrey, Nahrgang, and Morgeson (2007) examined both the impact of motivational characteristics of jobs (i.e., an expanded and more comprehensive view of JCM) as well as social and physical aspects of jobs on a number of work outcomes that were behavioral and attitudinal in nature and also captured role perceptions and well-being. They found support for the impact of the components of JCM on work outcomes like job satisfaction, and both social and physical work characteristics were also found to be impactful. Notably, much of this effect occurred through an important mediator of 'experienced meaningfulness,' indicating that employee perspectives of the importance and value of work is essential in creating these relationships (Humphrey, Nahrgang, and Morgeson, 2007).

These integrated and more comprehensive approaches to job design, that emphasize both the characteristics of jobs but also how those jobs nest in relationships and the working environment, provide a firmer foundation for understanding the ways in which public leaders can shape jobs and spur motivation among public servants. Approaching jobs as more than titles, job descriptions, and job specifications is important in thinking about what creates engagement and motivation. And, importantly, the interactions of job characteristics, social connections, and work context may potentially impact motivation and performance in different ways on an individual or functional basis; the match or mismatch between individual needs, role conceptualizations, experiences, and expectations may vary significantly. Likewise, leaders must be clear in what they are seeking as they create or recreate jobs. Attitudinal, motivational, and performance outcomes may be of differing importance depending on functional area or even situational factors.

ENDURING CHALLENGES IN JOB DESIGN

Despite the significant body of research on job and work design, the nature of public sector work and continuing changes in technology require continued attention to these related areas of study. The factors that shape public service job design and motivation are closely linked to broader changes in society, including shifting demands for public work, the evolution of the networks of individuals and organizations providing services, the characteristics of individuals who self-select into critical public service positions, and the technologies, particularly digital technologies, that undergird these jobs. One is of particular importance here as we consider the nature of job design and motivation: that of the introduction and implementation of digital technologies in public services.

Societal and technological changes are ever-present, and public services must be responsive to both. At the intersection of these concepts is the introduction of technology, both in the natural evolution of jobs given the availability of technology and in the creation of new technologies in response to new, pressing public challenges. Public services are increasingly incorporating the use of digital technologies in the design of standard work practices, methods of communicating with constituents, information collection and processing, and other core government activities. The purposes of increasing use of technology range from improved understanding of performance, to achievement of core public service values like effectiveness, efficiency, and equity, and the extent to which current services meet organizational goals.

Given this, it is incumbent on those considering and reconsidering work design to incorporate discussions of digital and information and communication technologies (ICT). These discussions can range from the incorporation of existing and well-honed technologies in functional areas that previously did not rely on computers, to the creation and maintenance of data collection and performance reporting, to new, purpose-built applications to solve specific public problems, to more advanced examples like artificial intelligence and its subfields like machine learning (Anastasopoulos and Whitford, 2019), and others. Of note, though more advanced technologies have shown promise in public applications (Newcombe, 2018), many are still untested, and not without potential challenges for work design (Boyd and Wilson, 2020).

Richter et al. (2018) note that this attention to 'digital work design' (DWD) is an enduring challenge and, interestingly, rather than push people to the side through increasing automation, it is one that brings the worker back to the core of discussions. They note that

> Building on a thorough understanding of existing human work practices and the subsequent design and implementation of ICT artifacts, DWD reinstates the human worker at the core of information systems development efforts. This requires an integrated, interdisciplinary, participative, and agile approach, which allows identifying, analyzing, and supporting human work practices and their context in a predominantly digital environment. (p. 260)

Rather than simply provide another means of 'doing' the work of government, this attention to the integration of digital technologies and DWD fundamentally changes the work itself, and 'simultaneously demands and enhances different human capabilities, such as the ability to flexibly respond to unforeseen events, learn continuously, or solve novel problems collaboratively' (Richter et al., 2018, p. 260).

Of note, the design and integration of technology in the work of public servants requires close and sustained collaboration in crafting processes and software, considering the ways in which both are incorporated into practice, and in the deployment of these technologies. Those at the front lines of service provision—the individuals who will actively use software and hardware as they interact with constituents—should be deeply involved from the beginning; Richter et al. (2018) indicate this interaction does not begin with implementation, rather 'software should be designed in close interaction with the workers it is aimed for, starting with exploring their work practices and then developing appropriate solutions' (p. 261). Likewise, the ways in which we produce, process, and consume data in public service must include expert input, even in complex processes like the development of machine learning algorithms (Anastasopoulos and Whitford, 2019). These pose a number of management challenges beyond work design, including considerations of organizational and professional culture, translation of work practices to digital applications, and working closely with individuals to overcome learning challenges.

Creating ideal practices to include more digital tools in work design must consider a number of factors to ensure the fundamental nature of work is altered in a productive manner, that individuals are able to complete essential tasks, and that the categories of individuals served by those public agencies are not harmed in unintended ways. Attentiveness to these processes together ensures that job design and redesign incorporates technology in meaningful ways that will improve service provision substantively, will avoid unforeseen issues in related service areas, are flexible enough for continued development as service needs change and new technologies are developed and introduced, and aim for both efficiency and effectiveness.

As noted in previous discussion of job resources, the *absence* of appropriate or useful technology may also become a key consideration in the design of jobs and linkages to motivation. Public sector workers are increasingly comfortable with the integration of technology in the workplace, as well as in personal lives. This may create differing expectations for what public sector workers want to see in job processes and resources, especially if a common or low-cost type of hardware or software exists that may be easily applied and may have a positive impact on performance. Failure to adopt and implement these technologies effectively may harm motivation.

The development, integration, and continued use of new technologies into jobs can impact individual motivation substantively. Providing employees with input into decisions to adopt and modify new technologies can provide a sense of connection to tasks, underscore individual value in service provision, and increase general employee engagement. This comes with a caveat, though, namely that of genuine listening and attention to that input. Soliciting feedback on changes to digital tools in public service requires being attentive to details and ensuring that tools provide promised improvements, do not make jobs unnecessarily complex, and are not viewed as a wasteful use of resources; this guards against harm to individual motivation.

Related to the introduction of new technologies is a need to understand and improve our ways of studying job design and the resulting impacts on motivation. Improvements may come both through increased abilities to assess what employees are doing via the use of technology and in the acknowledgement that comprehensive, integrated assessments of job design discussed previously are essential. Though the rapidity of data collection and analysis has improved significantly with the mainstreaming of digital technologies, a complicating factor remains. Four decades ago, Hackman noted organizations are not good at 'holding still' until all factors are assessed (1980, p. 453). Capturing real time work design in the ever-changing world remains a vexing problem for researchers and practitioners.

The future of work design leaves both scholars and practitioners of public services with both daunting challenges and also significant promise. Rapid development in technology means new applications and the adaptation of existing technology are available to work towards solutions for enduring public problems. However, this requires focus on the part of managers to ensure that processes and technologies are appropriate, that those using those technologies are trained and capable of tackling new tasks, that systems are in place to assess the efficacy of those systems, and that evaluation and individual and organization learning are taking place. Though our abilities to understand and foster employee motivation in the workplace have improved, we have much work to do here given myriad continuous social and technological changes (Latham and Pinder, 2005).

CONCLUSION

The work of government requires careful attention to goals, values, and outcomes, but requires the necessary flexibility to ensure public servants are motivated and focused on effective service provision. That flexibility may come through the review and reconsideration of job design as a core motivational tool.

Though our abilities to understand and foster employee motivation in the workplace have improved, we have much work to do here given continuous social and technological changes (Latham and Pinder, 2005) and the complexity and interactions among job characteristics, relationships, and desired outcomes. Hackman (1980) noted the individual component of work redesign is challenging, and this remains the case now. He argued that

> there are important individual differences in readiness for enriched work and reactions to it seem indisputable; but it also is clear that existing theories and research methods have so far failed to provide satisfactory ways of conceptualizing and measuring whatever it is that accounts for the highly variegated reactions of people to their work. (Hackman, 1980, p. 451)

Four decades later we are left with as many questions as answers, which creates important and worthwhile challenges for public administration academics and practitioners. The results of additional attention to job design theory, motivation, and work outcomes are likely to be powerful and enduring—a more satisfied, healthy, and focused workforce is increasingly likely to embody core public service values and make strides moving us closer to meeting organizational goals.

NOTE

1. Of note, some scholars differentiate between concepts of 'work design' (which includes both the work and the job environment) and a narrower view of 'job design' (Parker and Wall, 1998). We use these terms interchangeably here to avoid repetitive language.

REFERENCES

Alfes, K., Shantz, A., and Saksida, T. (2015). Committed to whom? Unraveling how relational job design influences volunteers' turnover intentions and time spent volunteering. *VOLUNTAS: International Journal of Voluntary and Nonprofit Organizations*, 26, 2479–2499.

Anastasopoulos, L.J., and Whitford, A.B. (2019). Machine learning for public administration research, with application to organizational reputation. *Journal of Public Administration Research and Theory*, 29, 491–510.

Bakker, A.B. (2015). A job demands-resources approach to public service motivation. *Public Administration Review*, 75, 723–732.

Bakker, A.B., and Demerouti, E. (2007). The job demands-resources model: State of the art. *Journal of Managerial Psychology*, 22, 309–328.

Bakker, A.B., Demerouti, E., De Boer, E. and Schaufeli, W.B. (2003). Job demands and job resources as predictors of absence duration and frequency. *Journal of Vocational Behavior*, 62, 341–356.

Bangwal, D., Tiwari, P., and Chamola, P. (2017). Workplace design features, job satisfaction, and organization commitment. *SAGE Open*, 7, at https://doi.org/10.1177/2158244017716708.

Barzelay, M. (2019). *Public management as a design-oriented professional discipline*. Cheltenham, UK and Northampton, MA, USA: Edward Elgar.

Barzelay, M., and Thompson, F. (2010). Back to the future: Making public administration a design science. *Public Administration Review*, 70, S295–S297.

Bauwens, R., Decramer, A., and Audenaert M. (2019). Challenged by great expectations? Examining cross-level moderations and curvilinearity in the public sector job demands–resources model. *Review of Public Personnel Administration*, first published online on November 8, 2019 at https://doi.org/10.1177/0734371X19884102.

Biddle, B.J. (1986). Recent developments in role theory. *Annual Review of Sociology*, 12, 67–92.

Borst, R.T., Kruyen, P.M., and Lako, C.J. (2019). Exploring the job demands–resources model of work engagement in government: Bringing in a psychological perspective. *Review of Public Personnel Administration*, 39, 372–397.

Boyd, M., and Wilson, N. (2020). Catastrophic risk from rapid developments in artificial intelligence. *Policy Quarterly*, 16, 53–61.

Burr, R., and Cordery, J.L. (2001). Self-management efficacy as a mediator of the relation between job design and employee motivation. *Human Performance*, 14, 27–44.

Chae, H., and Choi, J.N. (2018). Contextualizing the effects of job complexity on creativity and task performance: Extending job design theory with social and contextual contingencies. *Journal of Occupational and Organizational Psychology*, 91, 316–339.

Cooke, D.K., Brant. K.K., and Woods, J.M. (2019) The role of public service motivation in employee work engagement: A test of the job demands-resources model. *International Journal of Public Administration*, 42, 765–775.

Freeney, Y., and Fellenz, M.R. (2013). Work engagement, job design and the role of the social context at work: Exploring antecedents from a relational perspective. *Human Relations*, 66, 1427–1445.

Fried, Y., and Ferris, G.R. (1987). The validity of the job characteristics model: A review and meta-analysis. *Personnel Psychology*, *40*, 287–322.

Giauque, D., Anderfuhren-Biget, S., and Varone, F. (2013). stress perception in public organisations: Expanding the job demands–job resources model by including public service motivation. *Review of Public Personnel Administration*, *33*, 58–83.

Grant, A.M. (2006). A relational perspective on job design and work motivation: How making a difference makes a difference. Doctoral dissertation, University of Michigan.

Grant, A.M. (2007). Relational job design and the motivation to make a prosocial difference. *Academy of Management Review*, *32*, 393–417.

Grant, A.M. (2008). The significance of task significance: Job performance effects, relational mechanisms, and boundary conditions. *Journal of Applied Psychology*, *93*, 108–124.

Griffin, M.A., and Neal, A. (2000). Perceptions of safety at work: A framework for linking safety climate to safety performance, knowledge, and motivation. *Journal of Occupational Health Psychology*, *5*, 347–358.

Guy, M.E. (2020). Emotive Skills are work skills. *Public Personnel Management*, *49*, 327–330.

Hackman, J.R. (1980). Work redesign and motivation. *Professional Psychology*, *11*, 445–455.

Hackman, J.R., and Oldham, G.R. (1980). *Work redesign*. Reading, MA: Addison-Wesley.

Herzberg, F. (1974). Motivation-hygiene profiles: Pinpointing what ails the organization. *Organizational Dynamics*, *3*, 18–29.

Humphrey, S.E., Nahrgang, J.D., and Morgeson, F.P. (2007). Integrating motivational, social, and contextual work design features: A meta-analytic summary and theoretical extension of the work design literature. *Journal of Applied Psychology*, *92*, 1332–1356.

Latham, G.P., and Pinder, C.C. (2005). Work motivation theory and research at the dawn of the twenty-first century. *Annual Review of Psychology*, *56*, 485–516.

Lizano, E.L., and Mor Barak, M.E. (2012). Workplace demands and resources as antecedents of job burnout among public child welfare workers: A longitudinal study. *Children and Youth Services Review*, *34*, 1769–1776.

Mohr, R.D., and Zoghi, C. (2008). High-involvement work design and job satisfaction. *ILR Review*, *61*, 275–296.

Morgeson, F.P., and Humphrey, S.E. (2006). The Work Design Questionnaire (WDQ): Developing and validating a comprehensive measure for assessing job design and the nature of work. *Journal of Applied Psychology*, *91*, 1321–1339.

Mostafa, A.M.S., Gould-Williams, J.S., and Bottomley, P. (2015), High-performance human resource practices and employee outcomes: The mediating role of public service motivation. *Public Administration Review*, *75*, 747–757.

Newcombe, T. (2018, July/August). Is government ready for AI? *Government Technology*, accessed 6 July 2021 at https://www.govtech.com/products/Is-Government-Ready-for-AI.html.

Park, S. (2017). Motivating raters through work design: Applying the job characteristics model to the performance appraisal context. *Cogent Psychology*, *4*, at https://doi.org/10.1080/23311908.2017.1287320.

Parker, S.K. (2014). Beyond motivation: Job and work design for development, health, ambidexterity, and more. *Annual Review of Psychology*, *65*, 661–691.

Parker, S.K., and Wall, T.D. (1998). *Job and work design: Organizing work to promote well-being and effectiveness*. Thousand Oaks, CA: Sage.

Parker, S.K., Morgeson, F.P., and Johns, G. (2017). One hundred years of work design research: Looking back and looking forward. *Journal of Applied Psychology*, *102*, 403–420.

Parker, S.K., Andrei, D.M., and Van den Broeck, A. (2019). Poor work design begets poor work design: Capacity and willingness antecedents of individual work design behavior. *Journal of Applied Psychology*, *104*, 907–928.

Pynes, J.E. (2013). *Human resources management for public and nonprofit organizations: A strategic approach* (4th edn). San Francisco, CA: Jossey-Bass.

Qi, J., Ellinger, A.E., and Franke, G.R. (2018). Work design and frontline employee engagement. *Journal of Service Theory and Practice*, *28*, 636–660.

Richter, A., Heinrich, P., Stocker, A., and Schwabe, G. (2018). Digital work design. *Business and Information Systems Engineering*, *60*, 259–264.

Salanova, M., Llorens, S., and Schaufeli, W.B. (2011), 'Yes, I can, I feel good, and I just do it!' On gain cycles and spirals of efficacy beliefs, affect, and engagement. *Applied Psychology, 60*, 255–285.

Scharp, Y.S., Breevaart, K., Bakker, A.B., and van der Linden, D. (2019). Daily playful work design: A trait activation perspective. *Journal of Research in Personality, 82*, at https://doi.org/10.1016/j.jrp.2019.103850.

Shantz, A., Alfes, K., Truss, C., and Soane, E. (2013). The role of employee engagement in the relationship between job design and task performance, citizenship and deviant behaviours. *The International Journal of Human Resource Management, 24*, 2608–2627.

Steijn, B., and van der Voet, J. (2019). Relational job characteristics and job satisfaction of public sector employees: When prosocial motivation and red tape collide. *Public Administration, 97*, 64–80.

Taylor, F.W. (1916). The principles of scientific management. In J.M. Shafritz, J.S. Ott, and Y.S. Jang (eds), *Classics of organization theory* (7th edn, 2011). Boston, MA: Wadsworth, pp. 65–76.

Taylor, J. (2014). Public service motivation, relational job design, and job satisfaction in local government. *Public Administration, 92*, 902–918.

van der Voet, J., and Steijn, B. (2019). Relational job characteristics and prosocial motivation: A longitudinal study of youth care professionals. *Review of Public Personnel Administration*, first published online on July 23, 2019 at https://doi.org/10.1177/0734371X19862852.

Waldo, D. (1980). *The enterprise of public administration: A summary view*. Novato, CA: Chandler and Sharpe Publishers.

Wolfson, M.A., Mathieu, J.E., Tannenbaum, S.I., and Maynard, M.T. (2019). Informal field-based learning and work design. *Journal of Applied Psychology, 104*, 1283–1295.

Wood, S., Van Veldhoven, M., Croon, M., and de Menezes, L.M. (2012). Enriched job design, high involvement management and organizational performance: The mediating roles of job satisfaction and well-being. *Human Relations, 65*, 419–445.

Xanthopoulou, D., Bakker, A.B., Demerouti, E., and Schaufeli, W.B. (2007). The role of personal resources in the job demands-resources model. *International Journal of Stress Management, 14*, 121–141.

17. Job design and public employee work motivation: towards an institutional reading
David Giauque and Rafaël Weissbrodt

INTRODUCTION

The literature on job design and work design is currently very abundant. This is probably because the theoretical model proposes a specific reading of the functioning of organizations and the workplace—one that has demonstrated a very high degree of reliability and scientific validity. Since the middle of the 20th century, studies have proven the importance of several characteristics linked to working conditions and the ways by which tasks are carried out by employees in explaining both their motivation (whether they work in the public or private sector) and their well-being or arduousness at work. Therefore, it is probably no exaggeration to say that job or work design is a theoretical point of view that has great importance in the field of management. This chapter is precisely dedicated to the study of this model of analysis, with the particularity of adopting an institutional reading, which allows us to account for the organizational specificities of the public sector. In other words, the aim here is to better understand the motivation of public employees on the basis of an institutional reading of the job design model. Therefore, in this chapter, we propose to discuss this job design model.

Indeed, a rich body of knowledge has been developed about the links between work characteristics and different outcomes, such as job satisfaction and motivation, quality, and performance. Identifying the factors that positively and negatively influence these dimensions seems to be useful in the implementation of policies and practices aimed at orienting strategies for regulating public employees in directions that are favorable to both organizational efficiency and their well-being and satisfaction.

We start by defining the notions of job design and work design. Based on a review by Parker et al. (2017), we then present five streams of research on this subject. We briefly review the relationships between work characteristics and work outcomes. After having stressed the importance of motivation in the public sector, the heart of the chapter is devoted to an institutional and cultural reading in which we highlight the specificities of public administrations in terms of job design. We focus on six elements: (1) the cultural and institutional context; (2) the organizational climate; (3) changes and reforms; (4) role ambiguity, political interference, and administrative constraints; (5) relational work; and (6) human resource management (HRM) in the public sector. The chapter concludes with proposals for possible research topics in future works.

JOB CHARACTERISTICS AND JOB DESIGN MODEL: DEFINITION, ORIGINS, AND WORK OUTCOMES

Definition and Origins

Job (or work) characteristics and design emerged as a research domain just before the middle of the 20th century. Confronted with the shortcomings of the scientific organization of work and its reliance on task simplification, researchers began to look for alternative work models that are suitable for enhancing both job performance and worker satisfaction. Hence, the relationships between the way work is organized and designed and a number of objective and subjective outcomes have become very popular.

According to Parker and colleagues (2017), the concept of *job design* refers to the content and organization of tasks. Yet, workers do not only perform the duties officially assigned to them: they also initiate tasks and craft their role in the course of their activities. The notion of *work design* is used to reflect this broader perspective. Parker (2014) defines it as 'the content and organization of one's work tasks, activities, relationships, and responsibilities' (p. 662). Meanwhile, Morgeson and Humphrey (2008) describe work design as 'the study, creation, and modification of the composition, content, structure, and environment within which jobs and roles are enacted' (p. 47).

Using a bibliographic mapping analysis, Parker and colleagues (2017) identified five research trends associated with the work design perspective: (1) sociotechnical systems and autonomous work groups; (2) the job characteristics model; (3) the job demands-control model; (4) the job demands-resources model; and (5) the role theory. First, since its initiation by the Tavistock Institute in the 1940s, the sociotechnical approach has aimed to optimize the social and technical components of an organization to improve productivity, quality, efficiency, and worker satisfaction. For instance, Cherns (1976) suggested the following nine principles in the design of a sociotechnical system: ensuring compatibility between the design process and its objectives; specifying no more than needed; identifying sources of variance and controlling them as near to their point of origin as possible; promoting multifunctionality rather than specialization; defining the boundary maintenance role of supervisors; providing information in the first place to the point where it is needed; supporting congruence between the system design and the management philosophy; providing a high quality of work based on human values; and designing reiteratively.

Parallel to the sociotechnical approach, North American researchers have also developed an influential stream of research on 'job characteristics' aimed at finding alternatives to mechanistic conceptions of work. The job characteristics model by Hackman and Oldham (1976) is one of the most cited models in the field of job design. These authors based their Job Design Survey instrument (Hackman and Oldham, 1975) on five central work characteristics: skill variety (the degree to which a job requires different activities, skills, and talents); task identity (doing a job from beginning to end with a visible outcome); task significance (the degree to which the job has a substantial impact); autonomy (independence and discretion in performing a task); and feedback from the job itself (obtaining direct information on the effectiveness of the performance).

The third research stream cited by Parker and colleagues (2017) is the job demands-control model originally proposed by Robert Karasek (1979) and further developed by Karasek and Theorell (1990). The recent model has been developed quite independently from the two previous ones. The emphasis of the model is on the impact of work design on the workers' physical and mental health. It highlights the effects of job demands on stress and the role of two protective factors, namely, decision latitude and social support. The model suggests four work combinations of job demands and decision latitude, which correspond to four types of work situations: 'passive jobs' with low demands and latitude, 'low-strain' jobs with low demands and high latitude, 'active jobs' with high demands and latitude, and 'high-strain' jobs with high demands and low latitude. This model is still very commonly used in studies focused on occupational stress and health at work.

The fourth set of studies refers to the job demands-resources model by Demerouti and colleagues (2001). These authors complement the job demands-control model on two levels. First, it indicates that dimensions of work design other than decision latitude and social support can serve as protective resources (e.g., rewards, security, and so on). Second, this model is based on a dual causal pathway. Work demands mainly have a negative impact on strain, and thus on health, while resources lead to increased commitment, and thus to better performance.

Finally, the last cluster emerging from the analysis by Parker and colleagues (2017) deals with role theory; it originates from the studies by Kahn et al. (1964) on role ambiguities and role conflicts as stress factors. This current version has evolved to include the consideration of how workers change their professional roles (e.g., through the notion of job crafting) (Wrzesniewski and Dutton, 2001). Finally, various authors have proposed an integrative perspective aimed at bringing together the contributions of these five streams of research. For example, Morgeson and Humphrey (2008), in their Work Design Questionnaire, included 21 work characteristics covering task, knowledge, relational aspects, and contextual dimensions.

Job/Work Design and Work Outcomes

Why does research on work design matter? According to Parker and colleagues (2017), work design is a key predictor of a variety of individual and organizational outcomes. Job and work design have been proven to greatly impact several important and central work outcomes in private and public organizations (e.g., positive attitudes or behaviors among employees, or even work performance). Studies of sociotechnical experiments in the US have been shown to improve productivity, quality, efficiency, and satisfaction (Pasmore et al., 1982). The job characteristics model by Hackman and Oldham (1976) hypothesizes that the core job dimensions induce three critical psychological states: experienced meaningfulness of the job, experienced responsibility for work outcomes, and knowledge of results. These states are conceptualized as mediators between job characteristics and work outcomes, including job satisfaction, motivation, performance quality, absenteeism, and turnover. Several hundred studies relied on this model to investigate the relationship between job characteristics and work outcomes. The job demands-control model (Karasek, 1979) has also been tested in a vast array of studies documenting the links between job demands, decision latitude, and social support, on the one hand, and various health outcomes, such as stress, burnout, or repetitive strain injuries, on the other hand.

Meanwhile, a meta-analysis of the job demands-resources model by Crawford and colleagues (2010) showed a positive association between demands and burnout, a negative association between resources and burnout, and a positive association between resources and engagement. The relationship between demands and engagement depended on whether the demands were appraised as hindrances or as challenges by the employees in their sample.

Finally, Parker and colleagues (2017) reported on several publications showing the influence of role ambiguities and role conflicts on turnover, commitment, and job strain.

JOB DESIGN RESEARCH AND MOTIVATION IN THE PUBLIC SECTOR: AN INSTITUTIONAL READING

In the public administration (PA) literature, the job characteristics model has been extensively used and the empirical evidence shows that the model is reliable when it comes to identifying antecedents of positive work outcomes, such as employees' motivation (Tsigilis and Koustelios, 2019). Therefore, as stated by van der Voet and Steijn, 'Job characteristics are a central point of attention in classic theories on employee motivation. The core of Hackman and Oldham's (1976) job characteristics theory is that the design of the job determines the motivational state of the worker' (2019, pp. 6–7). It is clearly beyond the scope of the present section to develop a complete and exhaustive literature review with respect to the relationships between job design and motivation in public settings. Nevertheless, the main aim is to identify variables that are typical of public sector organizations, which have been identified as characteristics related to public employees' motivation. In this vein, this section is specifically dedicated to a 'cultural' and 'institutional' reading of the job design literature, precisely according to the specific characteristics or features of public organizations.

Motivation in the Public Sector: Does Job Design Matter?

Plenty of empirical evidence has been presented with respect to the importance of job design so as to foster job satisfaction or motivation among public employees (Demirkol and Nalla, 2018; Jurkiewicz and Massey, 1997; Lesener, Gusy, and Wolter, 2019; Moynihan and Pandey, 2007; Noesgaard and Hansen, 2018; Van den Broeck et al., 2008; Vigan and Giauque, 2018). For instance, Kim (2016) showed that skill variety, task significance, and feedback are three components of the job characteristics model positively related to public service motivation (PSM). The same study demonstrated that PSM is related to work performance (Kim, 2016). Therefore, several studies already confirmed that the job design approach could bring important and central insights when it comes to studying work outcomes among public servants. For instance, among others, a paper published recently investigated whether several social and organizational factors are related to stress among a population of middle managers working in Swiss public hospitals. The results showed that perceived social support, autonomy in performing tasks, flexibility in the organization of working time, and the perceived degree of organizational conflict are significantly related to stress perception (Giauque, 2016). Another study, based on data gathered by the National Health Service in the UK during the 2011 Staff Survey, found that training, participation in decision making, opportunity for development, and communication are all positively associated with quality of care and safety, and that these relationships are mediated by work engagement (Shantz, Alfes, and Arevshatian, 2016).

In addition to this research demonstrating the importance of work design in shaping positive work outcomes in public organizations or mitigating negative ones, several recent studies highlighted specific PA work design features, which have been proven to greatly impact public employees' motivation. The rest of this section will be devoted to the presentation of some of these public specificities, which are considered as relevant for developing and improving motivation in the public sector. In other words, the rest of this chapter proposes an institutional reading of the job design model in public organizations in relation to motivation and other important work outcomes, whether positive or negative.

Cultural and Institutional Contexts

In the management and sociological literature, many authors stressed that employees' outcomes are dependent on cultural and/or institutional contexts (Alvesson, 2002; Dingwall and Strangleman, 2007), but few dealing with the job design model have really taken into consideration the cultural or institutional contingency factors. Rattrie, Kittler, and Paul (2020) explored this understudied issue related to the relationships among burnout, work engagement, and cultural differences. They started from the point of view that cultural differences have been largely ignored in studies that investigated the impacts of workplace characteristics on well-being or work engagement. Drawing on the seminal work of Hofstede, who defined countries with respect to different cultural dimensions (1980), Rattrie and colleagues found that, on the one hand, high job demands have specifically negative effects in countries with masculine and/or tightly knit cultural traits. On the other hand, countries exhibiting more feminine and/or loosely knit cultural traits demonstrate better resistance towards job demands and, therefore, show less pronounced negative effects. This specific study highlights the fact that work design must be adapted to national cultural differences. More importantly, this conclusion suggests that cultural characteristics should be better investigated in the future.

In the same order of ideas, institutional contexts may contribute to shaping public employees' perceptions as well. In PA journals, several authors have already investigated whether or not different public institutional contexts may impact employees' job outcomes. For instance, with respect to the PSM literature, it has been demonstrated that the levels and types of employees' PSM may differ not only according to the nature of the public organizations they work for, but also in relation to the public policies they are in charge of (Anderfuhren-Biget, Varone, and Giauque, 2014; van Loon, 2017; van Loon, Leisink, and Vandenabeele, 2013). Based on these considerations, Borst (2018) included specific elements of the public sector context (PSM, autonomy, and red tape) that may impact the work engagement of public servants. He hypothesized that the effects of those elements on work engagement might depend on various institutional contexts within the public sector. Hence, he included several new factors in his research model (i.e., bureaucratic structures, perceived red tape, PSM, and necessary discretionary space experienced by public employees). Furthermore, he investigated a diverse range of public sector organizations, specifically those displaying one of two opposing normative institutional logics: people-changing (mainly education and public health care) and people-processing (mainly police, local government, and the judicial sector) organizations. According to Borst (2018), the differences between the two kinds of organizations reside in the amount of contact they have with users/clients and the kinds of services provided to them. Relying on data from the Dutch Ministry of the Interior and Kingdom Relations (N = 24,334), he found that perceived red tape was negatively associated with work engagement. Furthermore, perceived autonomy had a significant positive impact on the work engagement, but this relationship was stronger in people-processing than in people-changing organizations. Two dimensions of PSM (commitment to public interest and compassion) also had a significant positive effect on work engagement, but the effect was higher in people-processing organizations. Finally, Borst (2018) pointed out that work engagement mediates the relationships between two specific work outcomes (job satisfaction and job performance) and PSM, red tape, and autonomy. His article aimed to highlight the notion that institutional logics related to the diversity of public organizations may greatly interact with job design when it comes to studying antecedents of public servants' work outcomes, be it positive or negative.

Job Design and Organizational Climate

Another stream of research deals with organizational climate—defined as shared perceptions of practices, procedures, policies, and events—as an important factor to consider when it comes to investigating job design in the public sector. Indeed, organizational climate has been recently rediscovered in strategic human resource management (HRM) literature and, more specifically, in scientific literature discussing the antecedents and outcomes of high-performance work practices (Ashkanasy, Bennett, and Martinko, 2016). Organizational climate, defined as the shared perceptions of practices, procedures, policies, and events in an organization, is increasingly being investigated in the management and organizational behavior literature (Clarke, 2006; Destler, 2017; Gould-Williams, 2007). For instance, Spector (2016) developed a model of the negative effects of high-performance work systems, thus underlining the importance of organizational climate in the process leading to negative work outcomes. Pecino et al. (2019) used the job demands-resources model to investigate the relationships between organizational climate, role stress, and employee well-being (in terms of burnout and job satisfaction) in public organizations. In their research, the authors defined organizational climate as the shared meanings attached by organizational members to events, policies, practices, procedures, and structures and then tried to capture how employees' shared perceptions were connected to their work environments. They found that positive organizational climate correlated negatively with role stress and burnout and positively with job satisfaction. Furthermore, they found that role stress was associated positively with burnout and negatively with job satisfaction (Pecino et al., 2019). Thus, organizational climate may greatly impact work outcomes and is worth considering in studies using the job design perspective.

In the same vein, Conway and colleagues (2016) investigated whether or not two HR practices (performance management and employee voice) have an impact on two elements of employee well-being (exhaustion and engagement). Based on a survey of Irish public servants (N = 2348), they found that performance management was related positively to emotional exhaustion and negatively to engagement. Moreover, experiences of employee voice were related negatively to emotional exhaustion and positively to employee engagement. Furthermore, the authors found support for the moderating effect of employee voice on the relationship between performance management and emotional exhaustion/employee engagement. They also demonstrated that employee voice can shape a positive organizational climate, which, in turn, may lead to the buffering effects and positive work outcomes. Other recent studies have highlighted the notion that organizational climate can be seen as a more powerful antecedent than external pressures on organizations. In this vein, Destler's (2016) study of a large urban school district underlines the idea that organizational climate can better explain members' adoption of performance values rather than external incentives. Therefore, while the job design matters, it also depends on organizational conditions that can provide more or less fertile ground for its effects.

Organizational Changes and Reforms

Another interesting avenue with respect to the application of the job design approach to the study of public organizations is related to employees' perception of reforms or changes. In this perspective, several researchers have demonstrated that perceptions about organizational changes are also important considerations. For instance, Nguyen and colleagues (2018) investigated whether or not organizational changes, which have occurred frequently in the public sector during the last 20–30 years, may impact workload and job control and, therefore, contribute to creating cynicism about organizational change (CAOC). They collected their data from 220 public sector nurses in Australia. With respect to empirical results, they identified a critical path: organizational changes were associated with high workloads and an increase in administrative stressors that led to an increase in nurses' CAOC. They also found that job control was clearly needed as it can help nurses deal with the increase in workload and, therefore, can decrease CAOC. Moreover, CAOC is a psychological mechanism that has been found to be directly and negatively related to nurses' engagement, which, in turn, has been found to be negatively related to job satisfaction.

Similarly, other studies have highlighted the importance of organizational context when it comes to studying motivation or de-motivation among public servants. One study demonstrated that public servants reporting higher levels of compassionate public service motivation are also more likely to report higher levels of resignation (in the sense of reduced personal involvement), specifically if they perceive high levels of red tape in their work environment (Giauque, Varone, and Anderfuhren-Biget, 2012). Moynihan, in a now well-known article, is also concerned about the perverse and harmful effects of the waves of New Public Management (NPM) reforms on the values of public officials. In particular, he believes that these reforms may lead to the development of cynicism in public organizations. In other words, NPM reforms can erode public service motivation and induce public officials to develop a form of disillusioned cynicism about their work and the recipients of public benefits (Moynihan, 2010). Once again, this type of research shows the importance of organizational context in studying the links between different job characteristics and motivation in public sector organizations.

Goal Ambiguity, the Importance of Political Interference, and Red Tape as Typical Public Work Characteristics

The impact of job design on the behaviors and attitudes of public servants can also strongly depend on another factor typical of public sector organizations: the vagueness and ambiguity of objectives and goals. Studies have shown, quite convincingly enough, that the absence of well-defined and specific organizational goals can have a negative influence on the job satisfaction of public servants, just as the presence of red tape—or administrative constraints or burdens—can (Kjeldsen and Hansen, 2018). Other research also highlighted the importance of the ambiguity of organizational goals on the de-motivation and dissatisfaction of public employees (Chan Su Jung and Rainey, 2011; Jung, 2014; Vakkuri, 2010). Here again, job characteristics may be insufficient to motivate public employees if the organizational context is not favorable. Furthermore, organizational ambiguity may lead to role conflicts, or role ambiguity, and can have a negative impact on work motivation (Wright, 2004).

In terms of motivation or, on the contrary, in order to understand public officials' intention to leave, another phenomenon can clearly have a strong impact: the perception of the political context (Ali, 2019). Even the incessant political interventions in administrative activities, which can lead to the politicization of public organizations, could have detrimental effects on public servants' motivation (Bach, Hammerschmid, and Löffler, 2020; Fuenzalida and Riccucci, 2019). In other words, the increased politicization of the administrative field and the ambiguity of organizational objectives and professional roles are factors that must be considered when analyzing the motivation of public agents from the perspective of a job design approach.

Finally, it is also important to note that a whole range of recent studies have demonstrated the often deleterious effects of red tape on the motivation of public servants (Borst, Kruyen, and Lako, 2019; Bozeman, 2000; Cooke, Brant, and Woods, 2019; Giauque and Anderfuhren-Biget, 2012; Giauque, Varone, and Anderfuhren-Biget, 2013a; Quratulain and Khan, 2015; Scott and Pandey, 2005). In other words, administrative constraints can be considered an organizational feature of public administrations, specific to Weberian administrations, which contribute to reducing the motivation or even increasing the stress and malaise of public employees. Research on job design in public organizations should, therefore, be extended to better understand the organizational and work-related sources of these administrative constraints in order to better highlight their importance.

The Importance of Relational Job Characteristics

Adopting the job design approach to better study motivational phenomena within the public sector naturally leads us to question the specificities of the work done by public agents. In this respect, a large number of studies have highlighted the characteristics of the respective jobs of street-level bureaucrats (Brodkin, 2012; Hupe and Hill, 2007; Nisar and Masood, 2019). As Lipsky (1980) already pointed out in his 1980 book, public officials in the field, also known as 'street-level bureaucrats,' benefit from working conditions, the characteristics of which greatly depend on the application and, above all, the adaptation of very general legal standards to concrete individual cases, which are as varied as they are numerous. In this sense, they have considerable room to navigate through the tasks of classifying and sorting out the potential beneficiaries of the public policies for which they are responsible and performing the necessary individualization of the handling of individual cases. This gives them considerable discretionary power and, to some extent, greater job autonomy. In terms of motivation, the specific job characteristics of these street-level bureaucrats are, therefore, deemed important.

For example, one study points out that the logic behind the activities of different public organizations can have an impact on the type of motivation developed among employees. Thus, working in organizations whose services are sought after by the population (education or health) is different from working in organizations whose services are not actively sought after by the population (police or prison) (van Loon, Leisink, and Vandenabeele, 2013). Several authors found that the type of organization matters (Borst, 2018; van Loon, Vandenabeele, and Leisink, 2015) when it comes to studying motivation or job satisfaction. For instance, drawing upon relational job design theory, van der Voet and Steijn (2019) tested whether or not several characteristics related to public sector jobs may contribute to the cultivation of prosocial motivation among youth care professionals. More specifically, they studied two relational job characteristics (job contact with beneficiaries and job impact on beneficiaries) and their relationships with prosocial motivation. The results of their longitudinal study revealed that job contact with beneficiaries and job impact are clearly related to prosocial motivation. In other words, these relational job characteristics can be considered as important job design factors, which could shape motivation. In another recent study, Stejin and van der Voet (2019) showed that, on the one hand, relational job characteristics (job impact on beneficiaries and job contact with beneficiaries) are positively related to job satisfaction. On the other hand, the presence of strong administrative constraints or red tape tends to interact in this relationship in the sense that red tape will reduce job impact and job contact, thus leading to a lower satisfaction at work.

Other surveys have shown that the relationship between PSM and the actual behavior of public servants depends on the context and the type of organization (van Loon, 2017). For example, in people-changing organizations, public servants' PSM is clearly linked to positive effects in terms of outputs, outcomes, and responsiveness, but this is not the case in people-processing organizations. Meanwhile, another paper pointed out that the relationship between the level of PSM and employees' well-being also depends on the potential societal impact of their work (van Loon, Vandenabeele, and Leisink, 2015). Thus, in people-changing organizations, high levels of PSM are related to a higher level of burnout and a lower level of job satisfaction, but only when the potential social impact is high. This can be explained by the fact that employees tend to sacrifice too much for their jobs in order to serve the beneficiaries of the public policies they are working for.

All these studies tend to demonstrate, in an increasingly objective manner, that the relational specificities of public sector jobs, their potential societal impacts, the frequency of contact with beneficiaries, and the perceived impact on the latter are important factors that must be considered in studying the motivation of public servants.

Do HRM Practices Matter as Well?

When it comes to job design, it is also interesting to look at scientific studies dealing with HRM practices in public sector organizations. In this respect, interesting developments have taken place, particularly regarding the concepts of high-performance HR practices (HPHRP) or high-commitment HR practices (HCHRP), or even high-involvement HR practices (Gould-Williams, 2016). Empirical studies have pointed out that several HRM practices may positively impact the attitudes and behaviors of public servants, thus facilitating beneficial effects at the organizational level.

For example, Mostafa, Gould-Williams, and Bottomley (2015) showed that HPHRP can positively influence the affective commitment and organizational citizenship behaviors (OCB) of public employees, but that this link is partially mediated by PSM. In other words, HPHRP has positive effects on PSM, and in turn, PSM influences affective commitment and OCB. Other scholars considered HRM practices, defined as work characteristics, as potential levers to increase public service motivation and perceived organizational performance. They demonstrated, based upon a quantitative research concerning Swiss public employees, that perceptions of fairness, job enrichment, individual appraisal or feedback, and professional development can be considered as practices enabling the development of either PSM or perceived organizational performance (Giauque, Anderfuhren-Biget, and Varone, 2013b). In another piece of work, Giauque and colleagues (2015) showed that intrinsic HRM practices (diversified work tasks, independency at work, flexible working hours, possibility of influencing important decisions, and the possibility of reconciling one's private and professional life) are positively related to PSM, whereas extrinsic ones (work security, high wages, performance-related pay, good career perspectives, and a prestigious job) are mostly negatively related to PSM, except work security. Furthermore, mediation tests showed that intrinsic HRM practices are mediated by person–organization (P–O) fit. This means that public servants who value intrinsic work incentives tend to maintain a high level of PSM, provided that congruence exists between their individual expectations and the values of their organization. Similar findings can be identified in other research (Homberg and Vogel, 2016).

In the same vein, Kloutsiniotis and Mihail (2017) examined the effects of high-performance work systems on health care employees' work engagement and job satisfaction as well as the mediating effects of these variables on employees' affective commitment and their intention to leave. Their findings support previous research demonstrating the importance of these innovative HR practices in strengthening the positive attitudes and behaviors of public employees and in mitigating negative outcomes (e.g., intention to leave) among their ranks.

Consequently, this literature on the links between HRM and motivation (more specifically PSM) clearly indicates that several practices, which can be seen as work opportunities offered by management, can have favorable impacts on employees' motivation, organizational commitment, and job satisfaction. Therefore, the job or work design approach would benefit from further integrating this HRM stream of research, in order to better identify recommendations for use by practitioners.

DISCUSSION AND FUTURE RESEARCH AVENUES

This chapter had several objectives. The first was to present a brief introduction to the theory of job design. The second was to present, without any ambition of exhaustiveness, the main results related to this theoretical model, that is, the main work outcomes, whether positive or negative. However, the most important part, and also the most interesting in the context of a *Handbook* dedicated to the study of public administrations, was to offer an institutional reading of the job design model, particularly by comparing it with the specific managerial, procedural, and organizational characteristics of public administrations. This gave us the opportunity to associate the literature with respect to the job design model with the literature on public administration and public management.

As already stated by previous studies, work design research and theory contribute greatly to academic research, management practices, and even management thinking. The scientific validity and the applied utility of the work design theory are strongly supported by scientific assessments.

Moreover, in an analysis of the value of various theories in organizational behavior (OB), Miner (2003) highlighted the usefulness of work design theory. He evaluated 73 OB theories using 95 expert judges (past presidents of the Academy of Management (AOM), past editors/board members of top-tier management journals) to assess each on a range of criteria. The Job Characteristics Model was one of just eight theories rated as simultaneously high on scientific validity and applied utility (Parker, Morgeson, and Johns, 2017, p. 413).

The importance of such a theoretical perspective is also reflected in the numerous practical publications inspired by the job characteristics model. In other words, the work design perspective does have huge impacts on management thinking as well. With that said, when it comes to studying PA issues, the work design perspective must be adapted to organizational features that are specific to public settings.

As we demonstrated earlier in this chapter, context matters when investigating public administrations. Therefore, a contextual and institutional reading is needed when it comes to studying job design in the world of PA. National cultural traits as well as institutional characteristics are probably worth studying in relation to work design (Kickert, 2011; Painter and Peters, 2010), and this would allow us to better understand administrative processes, outputs, and outcomes. In relation to this, further research is needed to better identify the interconnections between institutional, cultural, and organizational climate variables, on the one hand, and job characteristics, on the other hand, with the latter being largely impacted, of course, by the former ones. Nevertheless, the mechanisms through which these interactions occur remain probably understudied so far.

The work design models are also confronted with recent changes in the world of work due to the COVID-19 pandemic. Profound organizational changes and the massive development of telework, in record time, have had huge impacts on employees and on organizational procedures and operations. The characteristics of jobs obviously change a great deal during institutional or organizational crises or during profound reforms. Therefore, it would be interesting to conduct further research, particularly in the world of public administration in order to gain a better understanding of the effects of these crises—and of the many administrative reforms that have taken place in recent years—on the characteristics of public sector jobs. Similarly, it would be very useful to know more about the job characteristics that are most useful when dealing with periods of organizational turbulence. Few studies have already explored such questions (Giauque, 2015; Marinova et al., 2015; Suseno et al., 2020), but many questions with respect to these issues remain to be dealt with. For example, it would be interesting to study work design as a proactive strategy in dealing with changes in the workplace, or to consider work design in a broader sense, by integrating it into reflections currently under development, which are related to high-performance work practices, high-commitment work practices, and high-involvement work practices.

Furthermore, other factors influencing work design should be investigated more substantially. For example, the impact of leadership or managerial choices on job characteristics are clearly understudied issues to date. The question is related to the mechanisms and organizational practices that could favor the development of positive job characteristics. For instance, when it comes to job design, HRM probably matters as much as leadership. Further research is thus needed to better identify which management practices or bundle of practices might contribute best to the development of favorable characteristics, either for the organization as a whole or for employees' motivation.

Meanwhile, public administrations are very particular organizational universes. They are made up of equally specific jobs, some of which involve important, lasting, and sustained relationships with beneficiaries. Thus, studying work design according to the specificities of 'back office' or 'front office' jobs, the specificities of 'street-level bureaucracy,' and the types of organizations (whether they are 'people-processing' or 'people-changing') are new lines of research that may prove to be prolific. Similarly, it would be interesting to consider the literature on 'job crafting' (Oprea et al., 2019; Wingerden, Derks, and Bakker, 2017), that is, the ability of actors to adapt the characteristics of their jobs to the work situations they face in relation to the more general considerations related to street-level bureaucracy. Finally, future research should also focus on the importance of PSM in relation to job characteristics.

Certainly, the latter can have an impact on the PSM level of public agents, but it has also been shown that PSM can either moderate or mediate the relationship between job characteristics and work outcomes (e.g., motivation, job satisfaction, stress, or burnout). No doubt, this is a line of research that is worthy of further exploration.

Finally, it would also be useful to investigate the possible impacts of the political–administrative relationship on job characteristics in public administrations. Indeed, recent studies have shown that we can observe a slow but observable politicization of public administration (Bach, Hammerschmid, and Löffler, 2020; Fuenzalida and Riccucci, 2019). Does this phenomenon affect the characteristics of public jobs? And if so, in what way? Similarly, what are the effects of political strategies and, more generally, of the political orientations of leaders on organizational and job characteristics? In other words, can strategic significance play a role similar to that of task significance, which has already been investigated repeatedly? These are questions that certainly deserve to be considered in future studies.

These above considerations may probably be considered as the most interesting avenues to be pursued in future studies so as to complete the reflection on job design in the field of public administration. In any case, an institutional reading of the job design model is essential when it comes to applying it to the public sector, and this is what we have tried to show in our chapter.

REFERENCES

Ali, S.B. (2019). Politics, bureaucracy, and employee retention: Toward an integrated framework of turnover intent. *Administration and Society*, *51*, 1486–1516.

Alvesson, M. (2002). *Understanding organizational culture*. London: Sage.

Anderfuhren-Biget, S., Varone, F., and Giauque, D. (2014). Policy environment and public service motivation. *Public Administration*, *92*, 807–825.

Ashkanasy, N.M., Bennett, R., and Martinko, M.J. (2016). *Understanding the high performance workplace: The line between motivation and abuse*. New York, NY: Routledge.

Bach, T., Hammerschmid, G., and Löffler, L. (2020). More delegation, more political control? Politicization of senior-level appointments in 18 European countries. *Public Policy and Administration*, *35*, 3–23.

Borst, R.T. (2018). Comparing work engagement in people-changing and people-processing service providers: A mediation model with red tape, autonomy, dimensions of PSM, and performance. *Public Personnel Management*, *47*, 287–313.

Borst, R.T., Kruyen, P.M., and Lako, C.J. (2019). Exploring the job demands–resources model of work engagement in government: Bringing in a psychological perspective. *Review of Public Personnel Administration*, *39*, 372–397.

Bozeman, B. (2000). *Bureaucracy and red tape*. Upper Saddle River, NJ: Prentice Hall.

Brodkin, E.Z. (2012). Reflections on street-level bureaucracy: Past, present, and future. *Public Administration Review*, *72*, 940–949.

Chan Su Jung, and Rainey, H.G. (2011). Organizational goal characteristics and public duty motivation in U.S. federal agencies. *Review of Public Personnel Administration*, *31*, 28–47.

Cherns, A. (1976). The principles of sociotechnical design. *Human Relations*, *29*, 783–792.

Clarke, S.P. (2006). Organizational climate and culture factors. *Annual Review of Nursing Research*, *24*, 255–272.

Conway, E., Fu, N., Monks, K., Alfes, K., and Bailey, C. (2016). Demands or resources? The relationship between HR practices, employee engagement, and emotional exhaustion within a hybrid model of employment relations. *Human Resource Management*, *55*, 901–917.

Cooke, DK., Brant, K.K., and Woods, J.M. (2019). The role of public service motivation in employee work engagement: A test of the job demands-resources model. *International Journal of Public Administration*, *42*, 765–775.

Crawford, E.R., LePine, J.A., and Rich, B.L. (2010). Linking job demands and resources to employee engagement and burnout: A theoretical extension and meta-analytic test. *Journal of Applied Psychology*, *95*, 834–848.

Demerouti, E., Bakker, A.B., Nachreiner, F., and Schaufeli, W.B. (2001). The job demands-resources model of burnout. *Journal of Applied Psychology*, *86*, 499–512.

Demirkol, I.C., and Nalla, M.K. (2018). Predicting job satisfaction and motivation of aviation security personnel: A test of job characteristics theory. *Security Journal*, *31*, 901–923.

Destler, K.N. (2016). Creating a performance culture: Incentives, climate, and organizational change. *American Review of Public Administration*, *46*, 201–225.

Destler, K.N. (2017). A matter of trust: Street level bureaucrats, organizational climate and performance management reform. *Journal of Public Administration Research and Theory*, *27*, 517–534.

Dingwall, R., and Strangleman, T. (2007). Organizational cultures in the public services. In E. Ferlie, L.E. Lynn, and C. Pollitt (eds), *The Oxford handbook of public management*. Oxford: Oxford University Press, pp. 468–490.

Fuenzalida, J., and Riccucci, N.M. (2019). The effects of politicization on performance: The mediating role of HRM practices. *Review of Public Personnel Administration*, *39*, 544–569.

Giauque, D. (2015). Attitudes toward organizational change among public middle managers. *Public Personnel Management*, *44*, 70–98.

Giauque, D. (2016). Stress among public middle managers dealing with reforms. *Journal of Health Organization and Management*, *30*, 1259–1283.

Giauque, D., Ritz, A., Varone, F., and Anderfuhren-Biget, S. (2012). Resigned but satisfied: The negative impact of public service motivation and red tape on work satisfaction. *Public Administration*, *90*, 175–193.

Giauque, D., Anderfuhren-Biget, S., and Varone, F. (2013a). Stress perception in public organisations: Expanding the job demands–job resources model by including public service motivation. *Review of Public Personnel Administration*, *33*, 58–83.

Giauque, D., Anderfuhren-Biget, S., and Varone, F. (2013b). HRM practices, intrinsic motivators, and organizational performance in the public Sector. *Public Personnel Management*, *42*, 123–150.

Giauque, D., Anderfuhren-Biget, S., and Varone, F. (2015). HRM practices sustaining PSM: When values congruency matters. *International Journal of Public Sector Performance Management*, *2*, 202–220.

Gould-Williams, J. (2007). HR practices, organizational climate and employee outcomes: Evaluating social exchange relationships in local government. *International Journal of Human Resource Management*, *18*(9), 1627–1647.

Gould-Williams, J.S. (2016). Managers' motives for investing in HR practices and their implications for public service motivation: A theoretical perspective. *International Journal of Manpower*, *37*, 764–776.

Hackman, J.R., and Oldham, G.R. (1975). Development of the job diagnostic survey. *Journal of Applied Psychology*, *60*, 159–170.

Hackman, J.R., and Oldham, G.R. (1976). Motivation through the design of work: Test of a theory. *Organizational Behavior and Human Performance*, *16*, 250–279.

Hofstede, G.H. (1980). *Culture's consequences: International differences in work-related values*. Newbury Park, CA: Sage.

Homberg, F., and Vogel, R. (2016). Human resource management (HRM) and public service motivation (PSM): Where are we, and where do we go from here? *International Journal of Manpower*, *37*, 746–763.

Hupe, P., and Hill, M. (2007). Street-level bureaucracy and public accountability. *Public Administration*, *85*, 279–299.

Jung, C.S. (2014). Organizational goal ambiguity and job satisfaction in the public sector. *Journal of Public Administration Research and Theory*, *24*, 955–981.

Jurkiewicz, C.L., and Massey, T.K. (1997). What motivates municipal employees: A comparison study of supervisory vs. non-supervisory personnel. *Public Personnel Management*, *26*, 367–377.

Kahn, R.L., Wolfe, D.M., Quinn, R.P., and Snoek, J.D. (1964). *Organizational stress: Studies in role conflict and ambiguity*. New York, NY: Wiley.

Karasek, R.A. (1979). Job demands, job decision latitude, and mental strain: Implications for job redesign. *Administrative Science Quarterly*, 24, 285–308.

Karasek, R.A., and Theorell, T. (1990). *Healthy work: Stress, productivity and the reconstruction of working life*. New York, NY: Basic Books.

Kickert, W.J.M. (2011). Public management reform in continental Europe: National distinctiveness. In T. Christensen and P. Laegreid (eds), *The Ashgate research companion to new public management*. New York, NY: Routledge, pp. 97–112.

Kim, S. (2016). Job characteristics, public service motivation, and work performance in Korea. *Gestion et management public*, 5, 7–24.

Kjeldsen, A.M., and Hansen, J.R. (2018). Sector differences in the public service motivation-job satisfaction relationship: Exploring the role of organizational characteristics. *Review of Public Personnel Administration*, 38, 24–48.

Kloutsiniotis, P.V., and Mihail, D.M. (2017). Linking innovative human resource practices, employee attitudes and intention to leave in healthcare services. *Employee Relations*, 39, 34–53.

Lesener, T., Gusy, B., and Wolter, C. (2019). The job demands-resources model: A meta-analytic review of longitudinal studies. *Work and Stress*, 33, 76–103.

Lipsky, M. (1980). *Street-level bureaucracy: The dilemmas of individuals in public service*. New York, NY: Russel Sage Foundation.

van Loon, N.M. (2017). Does context matter for the type of performance-related behavior of public service motivated employees? *Review of Public Personnel Administration*, 37, 405–429.

van Loon, N.M., Leisink, P., and Vandenabeele, W. (2013). Talking the talk of public service motivation: How public organization logics matter for employees' expressions of PSM. *International Journal of Public Administration*, 36, 1007–1019.

van Loon, N.M., Vandenabeele, W., and Leisink, P. (2015). On the bright and dark side of public service motivation: The relationship between PSM and employee wellbeing. *Public Money and Management*, 35, 349–356.

Marinova, S.V., Peng, C., Lorinkova, N., Van Dyne, L., and Chiaburu, D. (2015). Change-oriented behavior: A meta-analysis of individual and job design predictors. *Journal of Vocational Behavior*, 88, 104–120.

Miner, J.B. (2003). The rated importance, scientific validity, and practical usefulness of organizational behavior theories: A quantitative review. *Academy of Management Learning & Education*, 2(3), 250–268.

Morgeson, F.P., and Humphrey, S.E. (2008). Job and team design: Toward a more integrative conceptualization of work design. *Research in Personnel and Human Resources Management*, 27, 39–91.

Mostafa, A.M.S., Gould-Williams, J.S., and Bottomley, P. (2015). High-performance human resource practices and employee outcomes: The mediating role of public service motivation. *Public Administration Review*, 75, 747–757.

Moynihan, D.P. (2010). A workforce of cynics? The effects of contemporary reforms on public service motivation. *International Public Management Journal*, 13, 24–34.

Moynihan, D.P., and Pandey, S.K. (2007). Finding workable levers over work motivation. *Administration and Society*, 39, 803–832.

Nguyen, D.T.N., Teo, S.T.T., Pick, D., and Jemai, M. (2018). Cynicism about change, work engagement, and job satisfaction of public sector nurses. *Australian Journal of Public Administration*, 77, 172–186.

Nisar, M.A., and Masood, A. (2019). Dealing with disgust: Street-level bureaucrats as agents of Kafkaesque bureaucracy. *Organization*, first published online on November 6, 2019 at https://doi.org/10.1177/1350508419883382.

Noesgaard, M.S., and Hansen, J.R. (2018). Work engagement in the public service context: The dual perceptions of job characteristics. *International Journal of Public Administration*, 41, 1047–1060.

Oprea, B.T., Barzin, L., Vîrgă, D., Iliescu, D., and Rusu, A. (2019). Effectiveness of job crafting interventions: A meta-analysis and utility analysis. *European Journal of Work and Organizational Psychology*, 28, 723–741.

Painter, M., and Peters, B.G. (2010). *Tradition and public administration*. New York, NY: Palgrave Macmillan.

Parker, S.K. (2014). Beyond motivation: Job and work design for development, health, ambidexterity, and more. *Annual Review of Psychology*, 65, 661–691.

Parker, S.K., Morgeson, F.P., and Johns, G. (2017). One hundred years of work design research: Looking back and looking forward. *Journal of Applied Psychology, 102*, 403–420.

Pasmore, W., Francis, C., Haldeman, J., and Shani, A. (1982). Sociotechnical systems: A North American reflection on empirical studies of the seventies. *Human Relations, 35*, 1179–1204.

Pecino, V., Mañas, M.A., Díaz-Fúnez, P.A., Aguilar-Parra, J.M., Padilla-Góngora, D., and López-Liria, R. (2019). Organisational climate, role stress, and public employees' job satisfaction. *International Journal of Environmental Research and Public Health, 16*, 1–12.

Quratulain, S., and Khan, A.K. (2015). Red tape, resigned satisfaction, public service motivation, and negative employee attitudes and behaviors: Testing a model of moderated mediation. *Review of Public Personnel Administration, 35*, 307–332.

Rattrie, L.T.B., Kittler, M.G., and Paul, K.I. (2020). Culture, burnout, and engagement: A meta-analysis on national cultural values as moderators in JD-R theory. *Applied Psychology, 69*, 176–220.

Scott, P.G., and Pandey, S.K. (2005). Red tape and public service motivation. *Review of Public Personnel Administration, 25*, 155–180.

Shantz, A., Alfes, K., and Arevshatian, L. (2016). HRM in healthcare: The role of work engagement. *Personnel Review, 45*, 274–295.

Spector, P.E. (2016). When more can become less: High performance work systems as a source of occupational stress. In N.M. Ashkanasy, R.J. Bennett, and M.J. Martinko (eds), *Understanding the high performance workplace: The line between motivation and abuse*. New York, NY: Routledge, pp. 148–169.

Steijn, B., and Voet, J. van der (2019). Relational job characteristics and job satisfaction of public sector employees: When prosocial motivation and red tape collide. *Public Administration, 97*, 64–80.

Suseno, Y., Standing, C., Gengatharen, D., and Nguyen, D. (2020). Innovative work behaviour in the public sector: The roles of task characteristics, social support, and proactivity. *Australian Journal of Public Administration, 79*, 41–59.

Tsigilis, N., and Koustelios, A. (2019). Development and validation of an instrument measuring core job characteristics. *International Journal of Educational Management, 34*, 373–385.

Vakkuri, J. (2010). Struggling with ambiguity: Public managers as users of NPM-oriented management instruments. *Public Administration, 88*, 999–1024.

Van den Broeck, A., Vansteenkiste, M., De Witte, H., and Lens, W. (2008). Explaining the relationships between job characteristics, burnout, and engagement: The role of basic psychological need satisfaction. *Work and Stress, 22*, 277–294.

Van der Voet, J., and Steijn, B. (2019). Relational job characteristics and prosocial motivation: A longitudinal study of youth care professionals. *Review of Public Personnel Administration*, first published online on July 23, 2019 at https://doi.org/10.1177/0734371X19862852.

Vigan, F.A., and Giauque, D. (2018). Job satisfaction in African public administrations: A systematic review. *International Review of Administrative Sciences, 84*, 596–610.

Wingerden, J.V., Derks, D., and Bakker, A.B. (2017). The impact of personal resources and job crafting interventions on work engagement and performance. *Human Resource Management, 56*, 51–67.

Wright, B.E. (2004). The role of work context in work motivation: A public sector application of goal and social cognitive theories. *Journal of Public Administration Research and Theory, 14*, 59–78.

Wrzesniewski, A., and Dutton, J.E. (2001). Crafting a job: Revisioning employees as active crafters of their work. *The Academy of Management Review, 26*, 179–201.

18. For the children? Teachers' motivation and systems for recruitment, retention, and evaluation
Stephen B. Holt

INTRODUCTION

Perhaps no public service profession exemplifies the administrative, management, and policymaking relevance of understanding motivation in the workforce more so than the teaching profession. In the United States (US), recent decades have seen waves of both state and federal efforts to implement school accountability systems and reform teacher salary schemes throughout the country. The reforms often adopt both implicit and explicit assumptions about what motivates teacher performance and has resulted in an abundance of research on the effects of policy-based changes in incentives facing teachers on a variety of outcomes. Beyond the energy and attention policymakers and administrators alike focus on education services, teachers serve as an informative subject for examining motivation and workplace behaviors because their jobs are relatively standardized across locales, stakeholders provide teachers with varied and competing priorities, and teachers inherently enjoy relative autonomy in their daily conduct. Moreover, while many current practices in hiring and retaining teachers use licensure, training, and development to ensure only those motivated to be teachers enter the classroom, recent policy and management interventions have experimented with a variety of evaluation and performance-pay systems to motivate teachers in new ways. In short, teachers present a class of frontline public sector workers from whom management scholars can learn a great deal about motivation and performance.

Beginning in the early 1990s and continuing into 2020, local, state, and federal policymakers in the US have pursued reforms aimed at better measuring teacher performance, sharing performance information with the public, and tying teacher pay and retention to measures of performance. Driven by increased attention to racial and class-based educational achievement gaps between students and concern about educational outcomes relative to the rest of the world, 30 states had passed educational accountability reforms in the lead-up to the bipartisan passage of the national No Child Left Behind Act (NCLB) in 2002. The NCLB, as with many education reforms before and since, set an ambitious policy target for schools and focused on mandating measures of student performance aligned with state curricula to be taken each year in order to track progress toward the broader policy target. Moreover, the NCLB attached stakes to meeting the performance benchmarks—teachers and principals could lose their jobs and schools could lose funds. In 2015, the NCLB was replaced by the Every Student Succeeds Act (ESSA) which unwound some of the punitive measures in NCLB and gave states more flexibility in determining their own accountability measures. Policymakers across the country continue to experiment with education policy reforms and accountability systems in the hopes of optimizing both school performance and the quality of the teaching workforce.

The logic of education reforms broadly follows the assumptions and prescriptions of principal-agent models of implementation. Such models diagnose the issue of achievement gaps and educational shortcomings as the result of agents benefiting from an information advantage over the public regarding student performance and policymakers lacking the tools for appropriately focusing agent behavior. That is, administrators and policymakers cannot readily observe what teachers are doing in their classrooms or systematically observe students' learning outcomes resulting from those actions. Consequently, many education reforms initially focused on developing measures of student achievement, creating systems for sharing performance measures with the public, and setting achievement targets for schools and teachers. The combined efforts of policymakers and researchers to construct measures of educational progress and models for estimating the impact of teachers on said measures (e.g., Chetty et al., 2014a, 2014b) greatly improved the information available for assessing students' outcomes and underscored the importance of access to good teachers (e.g., Hanushek, 2011; Hanushek and Rivkin, 2010).

The question administrators and policymakers alike face is what to do with the performance information now available to them? Two competing schools of thought have emerged, each drawing on different theoretical models of what motivates teachers, to design policy solutions for how to use measures of teacher performance to improve educational outcomes for students (Firestone, 2014). In this chapter, I review some of the recent policy changes in the education sector, relate those policies to their theoretical understanding of what motivates teachers, and review evidence of the effects of those policies on a variety of outcomes to highlight insights about teachers' motivation that can be gleaned from recent experience in this policy domain.[1] Finally, I present descriptive evidence regarding the motivational base of a set of high school seniors who go on to become teachers later in life.

BACKGROUND

Motivation and the Education Sector

What motivates workers has been a central topic of public management research for decades (Behn, 1995). Assumptions about the motivations of public sector workers informs the design of personnel selection policies to ensure the responsible administration of government authority (Bertelli and Lynn, 2006) and offers insight into how the performance of public programs can be optimized (Heinrich and Marschke, 2010; Perry et al., 2009). Generally, in the context of public management scholarship, questions of motivation involve the alignment between a factor valued by a public servant and a goal valued by the relevant authority (e.g., a manager, elected official, members of the public). Both sides of this simple definition contain complex theoretical elements and interactions for which the educational context can be illuminating. Regarding the factor valued by a public servant, Ryan and Deci (2000) provide a helpful theoretical distinction between extrinsic factors, such as remuneration or personal prestige, and intrinsic factors, such as a desire to help others or perform well in a meaningful task. In public management, public service motivation, pioneered by Perry and Wise (1990) and extensively examined by researchers (see Perry and Vandenabeele, 2015; Ritz et al., 2016 for reviews), argues the motivation to engage in public service contains both extrinsic and intrinsic dimensions distinct to public institutions. Applied to education, all three conceptualizations of motivation carry different implications for how to best hire, manage, and retain the public school teaching workforce.

A focus on incentives and other extrinsic factors remains among the most common approaches in contemporary education policy and administration. Administrative strategies focused on extrinsic factors implicitly draw on principal-agent models of teachers in relation to school administrators, policymakers, and the public at large. In the simplest iteration of these relationships, a principal (administrators, the public) desires an agent (teachers) to engage in a particular behavior or produce a particular outcome while the interests and incentives of the agent may or may not align with the goal of the principal. Moreover, principals cannot adequately monitor agents to ensure the agents produce the desired outcome.

In education, examples of common principal-agent arrangements abound. For instance, administrators may want teachers to engage in continuous professional development or the community may want students to learn at a higher rate or develop more skills. Both goals would require additional effort from teachers—effort that administrators or the community might have difficulty observing. Moreover, teachers in the US receive pay on a standard scale that adjusts salary for years of tenure and earned credentials (graduate degrees, licensure, etc.). The flat structure of teacher salaries creates the possibility that, if teachers are highly motivated by extrinsic factors, teachers may lack the incentive to put additional effort into uncompensated tasks. Policies informed by a principal-agent conceptualization of the problem facing educational progress focus on both aligning teachers' incentives with the goals of administrators and policymakers and improving monitoring capacity to ensure said goals are met (see Moynihan and Pandey, 2010 for a general discussion of performance management in government). Here, the emphasis on teachers' extrinsic motivations becomes clearer—purely extrinsically motivated teachers would pursue the objectives being awarded and the incentives would provide a clear signal of which objectives to pursue.

Two recent federal initiatives in the US, one from President George W. Bush's administration and one from President Barack Obama's, can aid in bringing the abstract world of theory into the illustrative concrete world of policy. In 2002, President George W. Bush signed into law the No Child Left Behind Act (NCLB). The NCLB, following state-level policies passed in several states during the preceding decades (Dee and Jacob, 2011), established the requirement that all states receiving federal education aid establish standardized math and reading tests for grades 3 through 8 and secondary school, use test scores to assess student proficiency rates in reading and math at the school-level, and report school performance publicly. Additionally, annual benchmarks were set for schools, based on the percent change in students at or above proficiency in math and reading, and failure to meet these standards would result in increasingly punitive measures, from teacher and principal layoffs to school closure. In NCLB, the creation of a standardized metric of learning in each state and the public reporting of these standards both aim to resolve the monitoring dilemma of principal-agent problems noted previously. Further, the attachment of stakes to these performance measures—the risk of job loss and school closure—aims to align the (assumed) incentives of teachers to the goal of policymakers.

A second example of education policy targeting extrinsic motivation, also begun by President George W. Bush in 2006 but expanded greatly by President Barack Obama in 2009, is the Teacher Incentive Fund (TIF). Under TIF, state governments and school districts could apply for grant funding to establish pay-for-performance systems for teachers and school administrators. Applicants designed pay bonuses tied to various metrics, such as teacher attendance, participation in professional development, and student growth on standardized tests. The program allowed grantees to devise reward systems to meet their needs; however, TIF required that at least 50 percent of the total bonuses made available to teachers and administrators related to growth in student scores on standardized tests. Similar to district- and state-level policies related to performance-based pay, TIF grants aim to use additional compensation to induce extra teacher effort toward both raising student test scores and pursuing other district goals. States commonly use pay incentives to drive teacher behaviors in a variety of directions, some reflective of supply issues and others targeting performance issues (Kolbe and Strunk, 2012). The logic underpinning pay-for-performance incentives and attaching stakes to performance measures, as in the TIF and NCLB approaches, is that teacher performance is a function primarily of effort and extrinsic incentives will properly motivate the additional effort needed to correct performance problems.

On the other hand, teachers may be drawn into their professional careers by factors intrinsic to their jobs, such as helping students learn their subject matter or service to the community. A theoretical model of public worker performance and behavior built around intrinsic motivation alters the management problem from one of directing the alignment between goals and effort to one of selection, ensuring self-efficacy, and creating an environment in which teachers believe their efforts will have the intended effect (Bandura, 1977; Pajares, 1996).

From the perspective of managing a teacher workforce, many standard practices in teacher selection and in-service training reflect the logic of focusing on intrinsic motivation. For instance, most districts in the US require teachers to earn specific certifications before working in public schools. Certification requirements often include completion of a four-year bachelor's degree in education or a master's degree in education and reaching a minimum threshold score on a professional skills test. The implicit logic of the policy is that only individuals with the strongest intrinsic motivation to become a teacher will navigate the certification process and the skills measured by the certificate will ensure teachers enter the classroom confident in their ability to perform. As Kolbe and Strunk (2012) note, many districts also offer incentives, such as tuition subsidies for completing an education program or salary enhancements for obtaining various certifications, aligning extrinsic and intrinsic factors by providing a reward for an activity aimed at improving self-efficacy in the classroom. Similarly, some TIF programs, such as the one in Ohio, provide bonuses for participating in a number of professional development sessions (Putman et al., 2011).

Administrative practices aimed primarily at extrinsic or intrinsic factors face potential tensions and trade-offs. Programs that emphasize tying extrinsic rewards to performance risk 'crowding out' intrinsic motivation to excel in teaching due to the intrinsic value of effective teaching (Heinrich and Marschke, 2010; Pandey and Stazyk, 2008; Perry et al., 2009). Attaching stakes to performance measures may also lead to gaming behaviors—such as teaching only items or content included in standardized tests (Jacob, 2005), manipulating tests directly (Jacob and Levitt, 2003), or removing students who might perform poorly from the test sample through suspensions (Figlio, 2006) or assignment to special education (Figlio and Getzler, 2002)—making measures of performance less reliable over time. Finally, management practices built around extrinsic motivators assume that agents know and understand how to produce the desired outcome. For instance, teachers may be underperforming not due to shirking or pursuit of different goals; instead, underperforming teachers might simply not know that their students are behind or the practices that can improve student learning (Jackson et al., 2014).

As previously noted, governments at all levels of education policymaking—federal, state, and school district—have adopted policies over time that attach extrinsic incentives to performance directly through public reporting of school performance, high-stakes consequences for school performance, and individual salary enhancement for individual performance. How do teachers respond to these interventions? Before NCLB, many states adopted accountability measures built around publicly reporting school performance and attaching consequences for persistent poor performance. States with such policies showed higher growth rates in math performance (Carnoy and Loeb, 2002). Evidence from the implementation of NLCB, which included public reporting of school ratings and severe consequences up to and including school closure for consecutive years of poor performance, showed that states with no state-level accountability policies prior to NCLB showed larger rate of growth in math scores than a control group of states with pre-existing state-level policies, which suggests that threat of severe consequences does induce performance improvement (Dee and Jacob, 2011). Further, at schools that fell below the performance threshold set by NCLB, thereby facing the risk of job loss or school closure, teacher attendance increased dramatically (Gershenson, 2016). Together with recent evidence that the release of individual teacher and school performance ratings in Los Angeles newspapers did not impact subsequent performance (Pope, 2019), the components of NCLB related to employment and fiscal consequences, rather than the public sharing of performance ratings, likely drove the effects of NCLB.

On pay-for-performance, experimental studies from Israel (Lavy, 2009), England (Atkinson et al., 2009), and India (Muralidharan and Sundararaman, 2011a, 2011b) show significant increases in student growth when instructed by teachers randomly assigned to eligibility for a performance bonus. However, in the US, the results are mixed and the efficacy is contingent on the unit-level of performance that is being rewarded (e.g., individual teachers, groups, or entire schools) and the design of the award (Brehm et al., 2017; Hill and Jones, 2020; Speroni et al., 2020). For instance, randomized trials of performance-based bonuses paid to teachers, again using math and reading test score growth at the team-level as the rewarded metric, show both small incentives in New York ($1500 to $3000 per teacher) and large incentives in Tennessee ($5000 to $15,000) did not significantly impact teacher performance (Fryer, 2013; Goodman and Turner, 2013; Springer et al., 2011).

That said, evidence from Minnesota (Sojourner et al., 2014) and Texas (Imberman and Lovenheim, 2015) shows positive impacts on teacher performance when rewards go to the performance outcomes of smaller groups of teachers, theoretically due to reducing the free-rider program of incentives provided at a larger unit-level. A randomized trial in Chicago Heights demonstrated that, beyond the unit-level of the incentive, providing a bonus upfront that would be rescinded if performance goals were not met led to large performance gains relative to a conventional award, highlighting that loss aversion rather than pursuit of a financial bonus provides a stronger motivation for teachers (Fryer et al., 2012). Similarly, Dee and Wyckoff (2015) find positive effects of Washington DC's IMPACT program—which paired possible dismissal for low performance with large bonus pay for high performance—on teacher performance, though effects have faded over time (James and Wyckoff, 2020). Finally, a high school program that provided cash incentives to both teachers *and* students for passing Advanced Placement (AP) end-of-course exams increased AP enrollment, student performance, educational attainment, and higher adult earnings (Jackson, 2010, 2014). Collectively, the results suggest that teachers do respond to some performance incentives; however, teachers seem less likely to respond to purely monetary incentives tied to test score results. Instead, teachers seem more responsive to punitive measures (e.g., job loss, bonus rescinding) or incentives paired with supports (e.g., training, incentives for students as well).

As with policies targeting primarily extrinsic factors in motivating teacher performance, practices that target intrinsic motivation also face a variety of potential challenges. First, certification requirements drive up the cost of entry to the profession and may present a barrier to entry for people of color or people from a lower socioeconomic status (Carter Andrews et al., 2019). Teaching has, for decades, been a predominantly white and female profession (Ingersoll and Merill, 2017) potentially due, in part, to pipeline issues driven by certification requirements and better outside options dissuading college students of color from entering education programs (Angrist and Guryan, 2008; Goldhaber and Hansen, 2010; Redding and Baker, 2019; Tyler, 2011). Indeed, evidence from North Carolina suggests that Black teachers who failed their certification test but received a provisional certification were as effective as certified white teachers who passed (Goldhaber and Hansen, 2010). Recent evidence examining the effect of charter schools—privately managed and publicly funded schools—on public school labor markets also suggests the lack of certification requirements at charter schools induces more people, including more people of color, to explore a teaching career before investing the resources into certification (Bruhn et al., 2020; Gershenson, 2019; Sorensen and Holt, 2021). More importantly, one trade-off of screening processes aimed at improving selection on intrinsic motivation is that the screening itself can become a barrier to achieving other important personnel goals (Angrist and Guryan, 2008).

Second, the usefulness of selection mechanisms like certification requirements hinges on their ability to identify teachers with requisite motivation to complete an education program *and* education programs producing teachers with skills needed to be effective in the classroom (Nunn, 2016). Unfortunately, the evidence suggests only a modest link between certification status, professional exam scores, or graduate degrees and teacher effectiveness (e.g., see Goldhaber, 2011; Staiger and Rockoff, 2010). Moreover, Cowan and Goldhaber (2016) show that scores on professional exams tied to certification requirements do not have a meaningful threshold in their relationship to effectiveness in the classroom; thus, score cutoffs for certification reflect a somewhat arbitrary threshold. While such indicators can be easily observed by administrators and can therefore be efficiently rewarded and might ensure a performance floor in the teaching workforce, they provide, at best, a noisy measure of teacher quality and a loose proximation of a candidate's intrinsic motivation to teach. That said, an analysis of linked survey and administrative data from New York teachers revealed that an index of teachers' cognitive skills, personality traits, content knowledge, professional exam scores for certification, and self-efficacy beliefs together predict teacher effectiveness (Rockoff et al., 2011).

Finally, given the centrality of self-efficacy to sustaining the intrinsic motivation to perform well, professional development of in-service teachers remains a common approach to increase teacher effectiveness (Parsad et al., 2001). However, again, the evidence on the efficacy of professional development varies widely (Jacob and Lefgren, 2004; Yoon et al., 2007), largely due to the wide range of attributes of professional development curricula in use. Generally, longer and more rigorous professional development programs tend to be successful at improving teacher effectiveness by providing teachers with intensive counseling, feedback, training on use of instructional aid time, and training on classroom time management (Angrist and Lavy, 2001; Pianta, 2011).

However, practices aimed at cultivating collaboration and mentorship among teachers provide an even more promising means of improving teacher effectiveness than in-service professional development classes. For instance, the quality of mentorship student teachers receive during the pre-service field training that accompanies education programs predicts in-service effectiveness (Goldhaber et al., 2020). Similarly, supportive school environments and effective peers enhance teachers' professional growth over time, particularly early in their careers (Jackson and Bruegman, 2009; Kraft and Papay, 2014), and some evidence indicates assignment to one-on-one coaching or mentor observation and feedback during teacher on-boarding or while in-service improves teacher performance and retention (Glazerman et al., 2010; Isenberg et al., 2009; Kraft et al., 2018; Rockoff, 2008). Moreover, randomized trials testing the effects of classroom observation and feedback on teacher performance show that students learn more when randomly assigned to a school using low-stakes teacher observations and feedback for evaluating teachers, and both the observer *and* observee improved in effectiveness (Burgess et al., 2019).

What can we learn from the wealth of research and analysis accrued by assessing policy changes in the education sector in recent decades? First, teachers do not seem particularly responsive to conventional performance-based pay measures, even when offered a large earnable bonus. A few mechanisms may explain this. Teachers may be intrinsically motivated to pursue a career and teaching and therefore may not find financial awards to be motivating enough for altering how they do their jobs. Relatedly, teachers may not buy into the outcome being rewarded as a meaningful measure of student success and learning. Recent evidence suggests teachers' impact on a variety of educationally, socially, and economically important outcomes—such as student attendance, behavioral issues, course grades, and failure to advance to the next grade—are only weakly related to teachers' effects on test scores (Jackson, 2018). If teachers are predominantly intrinsically motivated public servants who see the value in their jobs as largely unrelated to the performance metrics on which extrinsic rewards are determined, they will be unlikely to alter their behavior much in pursuit of the reward. In this regard, teachers would be quite similar to other public workers more commonly studied by scholars of public administration (e.g., Lee, 2019; Park, 2021). Finally, teachers may wish to improve, both generally or simply to receive the merit award, and simply not know how to improve student performance on measured outcomes (generally, test scores).

Second, teachers do respond to punitive incentives, likely driven by loss aversion rather than a strict response to an extrinsic motivator. Consider that, as noted previously, the threat of dismissal (in Washington DC under IMPACT or via NCLB) and the reverse performance incentive, whereby the incentive is given and only rescinded if teachers fail to meet targets, were the policies in which teacher performance, as measured by test score growth, measurably improved (Dee and Jacob, 2011; Dee and Wycoff, 2015; Fryer et al., 2012; Gershenson, 2016). Of course, such high stakes come at a cost. Teachers and schools may respond with cheating and other forms of gaming (Figlio and Getzler, 2002; Jacob, 2005; Jacob and Levitt, 2003) and such gaming can make the measures of performance less accurate, undermining teachers' confidence in the fairness of the evaluation system. Worse, given the detrimental effects of teacher turnover on schools (e.g., Ronfeldt et al., 2013; Sorensen and Ladd, 2020), dismissal of teachers on the basis of inaccurate or incomplete measures of performance may offset the potential gains from removing poorly performing teachers.

Finally, the efficacy of working with quality peers, mentoring, coaching, intensive professional development programs, and classroom observations with feedback aimed at improving teacher performance underscores that most teachers value teaching as an end in itself and are intrinsically motivated to perform well. A disproportionate focus on extrinsic factors, narrow performance measures, or punitive policies might be driven by a misdiagnosis of the problem as one of treating teachers as self-interested agents shirking in their responsibilities rather than one of well-intended agents in need of continued skill development. If public service motivation or other intrinsic aspects of teaching drives teachers, the administrative and policy problem of poor school performance is one of developing career ladders, providing mentorship, and using observations and perhaps more frequent testing as a means for evaluation and feedback rather than metric upon which carrots are attached or with which sticks are swung.

In the remainder of this chapter, I briefly examine a nationally representative sample of a cohort of teenagers to observe, descriptively, what motivates those who become teachers and whether and how their motivational base differs from their peers. First, I describe the data and provide a light summary of the method of analysis, then I present the results of a descriptive analysis of these adolescents as they age into the workforce.

DATA AND METHODS

I investigate the possibility that teachers simply differ systematically from non-teachers in the base of motivation they carry into the workplace using data from the Education Longitudinal Study of 2002 (ELS) conducted by the US National Center for Education Statistics (NCES). The NCES designed the ELS to collect data on secondary students' social, economic, and educational experiences in school and long-run outcomes in higher education and early adulthood. Beginning with a nationally representative sample of sophomores in high school in 2002, the ELS collects data during respondents' sophomore and senior years of high school, their 'on-time' sophomore year of college (2006), and four years after their 'on-time' college graduation year (2012).

One advantage of longitudinal data that cover an extended time horizon of individuals' lives is that researchers can account for a variety of alternative explanations for observed relationships over time. For instance, simply asking a sample of teachers to respond to survey items regarding their motivations leaves open the possibility that their responses are biased by knowing their responses are being recorded (social desirability bias) or that observed links between motivation and being a teacher are actually explained by education, demographics, or socialization effects (e.g., exposure to other teachers shapes their reported motivations rather than motivation driving their selection into teaching). In this case, since I can observe measures of motivational base years before respondents enter the workforce, I can identify the link between motivation and career choice unlikely to be explained by other factors.

Important for the purposes of studying motivation and the teaching workforce, the ELS asks students a set of items aimed at measuring the social values that may motivate their behavior. The items use a 3-point scale ('not all important,' 'somewhat important,' and 'very important') and students answer the items during their senior year of high school. Since students have little professional experience, the items capture respondents' motivational base before postsecondary education and the influence of professional experience. If motivation acts as a context contingent trait, rather than a more ephemeral state, we might observe a systematic association between the base of motivation reported by respondents in late adolescence and entering the teaching profession. Prior work shows that these items load reliably onto three latent factors: one that resembles items commonly used to measure public service motivation (PSM), one that corresponds with professional and career motivations, and one that corresponds with

Table 18.1   ELS provided dimensions of motivation

Index	Item	Weight
Public Service Motivation	Importance of helping others in community	0.65
	... working to correct inequalities	0.73
	... being an active/informed citizen	0.71
	... supporting environmental causes	0.78
	... being patriotic	0.42
Professional	... being successful in line work	0.67
	... being able to find steady work	0.64
	... being expert in field of work	0.49
	... getting good education	0.63
	... getting good job	0.76
Family	... marrying right person/having happy family	0.76
	... having strong friendships	0.58
	... giving children better opportunities	0.32
	... having children	0.73

family-oriented motivation.[2] Each factor has been standardized with a mean of zero and a standard deviation of one. Finally, indicators for each response category regarding the importance of money (a proxy measure for extrinsic motivation) are included in the analysis as potential motivators. Table 18.1 shows the items included in each measure and the weight each item contributes to its corresponding index.

Beyond a person's base of motivation, a variety of factors might influence their desire to enter a career in education. For instance, family life, parents' influence and involvement, academic talent, demographics, and religiosity may all impact both an individual's motivational base and their decision to enter teaching as a career. Consequently, in addition to descriptively comparing teachers and non-teachers along the dimensions of their motivation as adolescents, I run simple linear regression models to control for demographics (race and gender), GPA, math and reading ability, family status (single parent home, number of siblings), religious affiliation, parents' education, and parents' academic expectations (a proxy measure for involvement). Finally, all non-teachers potentially represent too broad a comparison group. A comparison group of students who went into other frontline public service jobs, particularly those also with predominantly women in the workforce, would provide an opportunity to see if what we observe about teachers' motivation is unique to teachers or generalizable to similar occupations. For the purposes of similar occupations, I include respondents who later become social workers, other teachers (adult learning or vocational teachers not in K through 12 schools), nurses, and librarians. In all, the analytic sample includes about 6810 respondents, 270 of whom enter teaching and 700 of whom enter similar occupations (referred to as comparison group from here on).

RESULTS

What motivates teachers? I begin with a simple descriptive comparison of the scores on the different dimensions of motivation described in the previous section between teachers, the full sample of respondents, and the comparison group of frontline public service workers. Recall that the dimensions of motivation are measured during the senior year of high school while

Table 18.2   Summary statistics of the analytic sample

	(1) All	(2) Teachers	(3) Elementary	(4) Middle	(5) Secondary	(6) Comparison
Motivational bases						
PSM	−0.03	0.12***	0.15**	0.14	0.06	0.09
	(0.98)	(0.96)	(0.91)	(1.09)	(0.97)	(0.96)
Professional	0.02	0.01	0.06	−0.11	0.01	0.01
	(1.00)	(1.00)	(0.89)	(1.09)	(1.09)	(1.01)
Family	0.07	0.37***	0.39***	0.43***	0.31**	0.13[a]
	(0.94)	(0.72)	(0.70)	(0.61)	(0.80)	(0.91)
Money unimportant	0.12	0.18***	0.20***	0.23**	0.13	0.14
Money very important	0.30	0.19***	0.20***	0.23	0.15***	0.23
Children's future unimportant	0.03	0.01	0.02	0.00	0.01	0.03
Children's future very important	0.81	0.81	0.82	0.81	0.78	0.80
Respondent characteristics						
Male	0.46	0.23***	0.17***	0.19***	0.35**	0.17[b]
White	0.64	0.75***	0.76***	0.73	0.76**	0.65[a]
Black	0.10	0.10	0.09	0.13	0.11	0.12
Hispanic	0.12	0.06***	0.08	0.06	0.03***	0.11[b]
HH income < $20 000	0.07	0.04**	0.01***	0.06	0.07	0.07[b]
HH income > $100 000	0.18	0.23**	0.25**	0.21	0.22	0.15[a]
Father teacher	0.02	0.03	0.04[+]	0.00	0.02	0.02
Mother teacher	0.09	0.16***	0.15***	0.21***	0.14**	0.08[a]
10th grade math score	53.14	56.13***	54.38	57.23***	58.07***	52.61[a]
	(9.46)	(7.84)	(7.47)	(8.36)	(7.60)	(8.88)
10th grade reading score	52.96	56.56***	54.98***	57.71***	58.21***	53.42[a]
	(9.56)	(7.93)	(7.98)	(6.96)	(7.96)	(8.82)
Observations	6810	270	130	50	90	700

Notes: Number of observations rounded to the nearest ten in accordance with NCES rules and regulations. Standard errors clustered at the school-level in parentheses.
[+] $p < 0.10$, ** $p < 0.05$, *** $p < 0.01$ for t-test of difference in means between teachers and all other students (columns 2 through 5 and column 1).
[a] $p < 0.10$, [b] $p < 0.05$, [c] $p < 0.01$ for t-test of difference in means between teachers and comparable occupations (columns 2 and 6).
Source: US Department of Education, National Center for Education Statistics, Education Longitudinal Study of 2002 First Follow-up and Second Follow-up (ELS:2004/06).

the occupation is measured four years after college graduation. Thus, the comparison provides some insight if people enter the teaching profession with systematically different motivations than others in their age cohort or those who go into similar service occupations.

Table 18.2 presents the characteristics of the sample overall (column 1), by those who become teachers (columns 2 through 5), and by those who enter comparison occupations (column 6). Regarding motivation, several patterns in the data suggest some stark differences between people who become teachers and the broader sample. First, as might be expected considering the documented link between PSM and entering public service (Holt, 2018), people who become teachers have much higher levels of PSM, on average. PSM is particularly high among elementary and middle school teachers, however, the difference for the middle school teacher subsample is less precise due to the smaller sample size. Notably, people who enter comparison occupations also have relatively high PSM on average—and the difference between teachers and comparison occupations is not statistically significant.

Second, relative to the full sample and comparison group occupations, teachers score high on the family dimension of motivation. The gap seems driven not by concern for giving children better opportunities, which is generally rated as very important by three groups, but instead by the items related to establishing a family of one's own. Here, people who become teachers stand out as particularly driven by family considerations, as they score significantly higher on this dimension relative to those who enter comparison occupations as well. A variety of factors could explain the link between being driven by family considerations and entering teaching. Perhaps the scheduling structure of teaching, with time off aligning with children's time out of school, carried a particular pull for those intent on having a family. Perhaps the desire to have children corresponds with a desire to work with young people more generally. Regardless, family considerations clearly motivate many of those who become teachers. Finally, relative to others of the same age, teachers are much more likely to view money as unimportant and much less likely to see making lots of money as very important. Those who enter other frontline public service occupations in the comparison group report similarly low rates of pecuniary motivation.

The characteristics of people who become teachers in the ELS resembles the teacher workforce more broadly: predominantly white women, more likely to be from upper income households, higher academic ability on average, and, consistent with recent evidence on the increasingly intergenerational nature of teaching (Jacinto and Gershenson, 2020), more likely to have mother who was a teacher. Notably, the characteristics of the comparison group occupations resemble the teachers on gender; however, those who enter comparison group occupations are slightly less likely to be from upper income households and have a racial and ethnic composition more representative of national demographics, perhaps attributable to the more costly certification process to enter teaching, as previously discussed.

Table 18.3 presents the results from linear regressions predicting whether a person majors in education in college, a precursor to certification and entering a teaching career. Note that after accounting for observable characteristics, school effects, and whether the respondent reported wanting to be a teacher in high school, people who major in education remain more likely to view money as unimportant and score higher on being motivated by family considerations. Relative to other motivational factors, PSM does not significantly predict majoring in education, perhaps due to the comparison outcome of non-education majors including other public sector career tracks that also attract high PSM students. Thus, though descriptively people who become teachers are higher PSM individuals, PSM does not uniquely explain sorting into teaching versus other public service occupations.

Finally, Table 18.4 examines the link between motivation, college major, and other controls on the likelihood of entering a teaching career. Column 1 uses the full analytic sample, column 2 restricts the sample to only respondents who graduated from college by 2012 to compare people with similar career options, and columns 3 and 4 restrict the analysis to only those who become teachers or enter comparison occupations (with and without a college degree restriction). First, unsurprisingly, college major is the strongest predictor of becoming a teacher and absorbs much of the effect of the motivation variables in the full sample as these dimensions affect becoming a teacher through selecting a major. Second, when I restrict the sample to the most direct comparison group—those who enter other frontline service occupations dominated by women—respondents who score 1 standard deviation above the mean on the family

Table 18.3   Motivational base associated with choosing an education major

	(1)	(2)	(3)	(4)	(5)	(6)
PSM-related values	0.00	−0.00	−0.00	−0.00	−0.00	−0.00
	(0.00)	(0.00)	(0.00)	(0.00)	(0.00)	(0.00)
Professional motivation	0.00	−0.00	−0.00	−0.00	−0.00	−0.00
	(0.00)	(0.00)	(0.00)	(0.00)	(0.00)	(0.00)
Family motivation	0.01***	0.01***	0.01***	0.01***	0.01***	0.01***
	(0.00)	(0.00)	(0.00)	(0.00)	(0.00)	(0.00)
Money not important	0.04***	0.04***	0.04***	0.04***	0.04***	0.03***
	(0.01)	(0.01)	(0.01)	(0.01)	(0.01)	(0.01)
Money very important	−0.02***	−0.01**	−0.01+	−0.01**	−0.01+	−0.00
	(0.01)	(0.01)	(0.01)	(0.01)	(0.01)	(0.01)
Children's future not important	−0.02	−0.02	−0.02	−0.02	−0.02	−0.02
	(0.01)	(0.01)	(0.01)	(0.01)	(0.01)	(0.01)
Children's future very important	0.00	0.01	0.01	0.01	0.01	0.01
	(0.01)	(0.01)	(0.01)	(0.01)	(0.01)	(0.01)
Father was teacher			0.04	0.04	0.03	0.03
			(0.03)	(0.03)	(0.03)	(0.03)
Mother was teacher			0.02	0.02	0.02	0.01
			(0.01)	(0.01)	(0.01)	(0.01)
Student wants to be a teacher						0.32***
						(0.03)
Control for demographics and family X	No	Yes	Yes	Yes	Yes	Yes
Control for parental modeling	No	No	Yes	Yes	Yes	Yes
Control for academic ability	No	No	No	Yes	Yes	Yes
Control for school FE	No	No	No	No	Yes	Yes
Control for student aspirations	No	No	No	No	No	Yes
Adjusted R^2	0.01	0.03	0.03	0.03	0.03	0.11
Observations	6240	6240	6240	6240	6240	6240

Notes: Number of observations rounded to the nearest ten in accordance with NCES rules and regulations. Standard errors clustered at the school-level in parentheses; FE = Fixed effects.
+ $p < 0.10$, ** $p < 0.05$, *** $p < 0.01$.
Source: US Department of Education, National Center for Education Statistics, Education Longitudinal Study of 2002 First Follow-up and Second Follow-up (ELS:2004/06).

dimension of motivation are about 3 or 4 percentage points more likely to be teachers relative to otherwise similar peers.

While the ELS provides a national sample and an opportunity to look at the early life predictors of career-related decisions, the data and analysis presented here carry some limitations that warrant caution and consideration. First, the design of the sample, stratified by high school to be nationally representative of the high school population, means that while the proportion of respondents who sort into particular occupations is representative of the population, the sample size of particular occupations is quite small and details about the schools at which respondents become teachers are unavailable. Second, as with all longitudinal studies that cover such a long time-period, attrition from the sample is high and may be non-random in ways that bias the sample. While the analysis presented here uses weights that aim to correct for attrition on observable information to mitigate attrition-related bias, there may be unobserved variables that systematically differ for non-respondents. Third, the relationships laid out in the regression analysis remain descriptive and not causal. Finally, the time frame only

Table 18.4 Motivational base associated with becoming a teacher

	(1) All	(2) College+	(3) Comparison Occupations	(4) Comparison Occ. – College+
PSM	0.00	0.01	−0.01	−0.01
	(0.00)	(0.00)	(0.02)	(0.02)
Professional	−0.00+	−0.01	0.00	0.00
	(0.00)	(0.01)	(0.01)	(0.02)
Family	0.00**	0.01	0.03**	0.04+
	(0.00)	(0.00)	(0.02)	(0.02)
Money unimportant	0.00	0.00	0.03	0.05
	(0.01)	(0.01)	(0.03)	(0.05)
Money very important	−0.00	−0.01	0.03	0.01
	(0.00)	(0.01)	(0.03)	(0.05)
Children's future unimportant	−0.00	−0.02	−0.09	−0.10
	(0.01)	(0.02)	(0.08)	(0.12)
Children's future very important	0.01	0.00	0.01	−0.01
	(0.01)	(0.01)	(0.03)	(0.05)
Father teacher	−0.02	−0.02	−0.04	−0.14+
	(0.02)	(0.02)	(0.08)	(0.08)
Mother teacher	0.02	0.02	0.09+	0.09
	(0.01)	(0.02)	(0.05)	(0.06)
Education major	0.36***	0.46***	0.46***	0.51***
	(0.03)	(0.03)	(0.05)	(0.05)
Social science major	0.03	0.04**	0.22***	0.23***
	(0.02)	(0.02)	(0.07)	(0.06)
STEM major	0.01	0.02+	0.16***	0.18***
	(0.01)	(0.01)	(0.06)	(0.06)
Married	0.01	0.01	0.01	0.01
	(0.00)	(0.01)	(0.02)	(0.03)
No. of dependents	−0.00**	−0.00	−0.01***	−0.01
	(0.00)	(0.00)	(0.00)	(0.01)
2011 earnings ($1000s)	0.00	0.00	0.00	0.00
	(0.00)	(0.00)	(0.00)	(0.00)
Teacher aspiration	0.07***	0.10**	0.13**	0.15**
	(0.02)	(0.04)	(0.05)	(0.07)
All controls	Yes	Yes	Yes	Yes
State FE	Yes	Yes	Yes	Yes
Adjusted R^2	0.20	0.23	0.31	0.23
Observations	6810	3120	970	620

Notes: Number of observations rounded to the nearest ten in accordance with NCES rules and regulations. Standard errors clustered at the school-level in parentheses. FE = Fixed effects.
+ $p<0.10$, ** $p<0.05$, *** $p<0.01$.
Source: US Department of Education, National Center for Education Statistics, Education Longitudinal Study of 2002 First Follow-up and Third Follow-up (ELS:2004/12).

allows for an examination of early career decisions and cannot speak to who remains a teacher in the long run.

Still, the results present a few important insights that shed some preliminary light on the patterns of effects of teacher evaluation, accountability, and pay policy interventions on teacher behaviors and performance. First, descriptively, people who later become teachers score much higher than the national average on a measure of PSM-related values (0.12 of a standard deviation) and are 6 percentage points more likely to view money as unimportant. Note that these differences in motivation appear in adolescence, long before the socialization processes of college, professional work experience, or experience teaching. Second, the motivation to start a family seems to be the motivational dimension that remains distinct to choosing a career in teaching relative to similar occupations. For instance, prior work examining public sector workers generally in the same sample finds little predictive power of family motivation and selecting into the public sector broadly (Holt, 2018). Here, family motivation predicts both selection into an education major and, relative to other similar service occupations, predicts becoming a teacher. Finally, even after accounting for ability, demographics, and household dynamics, adolescents who report that money is unimportant to them are more likely to enter the teaching pipeline.

DISCUSSION AND CONCLUSIONS

Teachers represent a large share of public sector workers operating on the frontlines of delivering a cornerstone public service—education—to families across the US. In the course of their jobs, they exercise discretion in conducting lessons, managing their classrooms, disciplining students, and communicating with families. As with other bureaucrats and frontline public workers, policymakers provide specific guidelines to teachers, from setting curricula to defining student learning targets. Moreover, as noted previously, the combination of the social importance of their service quality and the relatively standardized structure of their jobs (e.g., grade sequencing by student age, student assignment to classrooms, class schedules, etc.) has led to increased local, state, and federal attention to measuring and evaluating teacher performance and crafting incentives, rewards, and sanctions to optimize the teacher workforce. The policy and administrative attention directed at improving the public education system has yielded a wealth of knowledge about measuring student learning, modeling teacher performance, and documenting how teachers and students respond to a variety of management practices.

As noted at the outset of this chapter, many of the hiring, evaluating, pecuniary, and retention practices built into the education system follow a logic of how the motivation teachers bring to their jobs influences their performance. Some programs, such as pure pay-for-performance programs or punitive accountability measures, assume a generic motivation for personal gain and external validation drives teachers and diagnoses the performance problem as one of misaligned incentives or teachers investing insufficient effort. Others, such as mentoring, professional development, opportunities for advancement, and setting selection criteria to identify committed teachers, assume that those entering the teaching profession intrinsically value the aim of the job and diagnose performance problems as one of a skills or knowledge deficit.

Regarding programs adopting extrinsic motivators for teachers, the weight of the evidence suggests that while performance-based pay only modestly influences teacher performance, punitive measures—from school-level cuts or individual job loss to claw-back rewards—elicit additional teacher effort to avoid losses both large and small. A variety of potential mechanisms may explain these patterns. If teachers generally enter the profession because they intrinsically value the work and mission, avoiding the loss of employment or cuts to their schools provides a powerful alignment of intrinsic motivation and extrinsic incentives—an alignment missing when the incentive is tied to personal rewards for a single outcome. However, stakes as severe as the loss of employment or school closure, placed before an intrinsically motivated workforce that believes in their work and perceives the evaluation of their work as flawed, provides a motivation for gaming behavior that both evades accountability and undermines the accuracy of performance measures—such as the manipulation of tests or suspension of struggling students on test day discussed previously.

A variety of problems greet policymakers and school administrators when considering a system built around extrinsic motivators, particularly punitive measures. First, the success of the program requires measures of performance that correctly identify high performers and low performers in a timely fashion. More than most public services, the development of standardized tests in math and reading aligned to skills expected of students at various stages has provided a rich measure of performance. Yet even here, the measure of performance is incomplete—many states do not have standardized tests for all subjects (e.g., science, history, social studies, the arts). Moreover, teachers' effects on other academically and socially important outcomes do not strongly correlate with their effects on test scores (Jackson, 2018), suggesting teacher effects on scores may not perfectly identify good and bad teachers. Second and relatedly, while some evidence suggests removing the lowest performing teachers improves student outcomes (e.g., Chetty et al., 2014b), the benefit relies on accurately identifying the lowest performing teachers. If teachers adapt their behaviors in ways that game the high-stakes measures, value-added measures of teacher effectiveness, already noisy early in a teacher's career, become less precise over time. Given the large and lasting deleterious effects teacher turnover can have on a school's effectiveness and ability to attract good teachers in the future (Sorensen and Ladd, 2020), districts may face a small margin for error in identifying poor performers for removal without doing more harm than good. Finally, given the growth that teachers show over the course of their careers (e.g., Ladd and Sorensen, 2017; Wiswall, 2013), districts face a potentially large opportunity cost if they remove teachers early and are unable to replace them with better teachers immediately.

On the other hand, rigorous professional development programs, coaching, mentoring, and evaluation programs in which teachers receive low-stakes observation and assessment from peers show positive effects on teacher performance. I presented evidence in this chapter that people who become teachers tend to be high PSM people who find money less important than people who sort into other jobs—a set of traits they share with public sector workers more broadly. Further, they tend to be motivated by family considerations, perhaps drawn to teaching for a work schedule that aligns with the needs of parenting and the opportunity to work with other children from the community. The relatively inconsistent and small effects of incentive pay on teachers' behaviors and effectiveness observed in the studies outlined throughout this chapter might be attributable, in part, to the teaching workforce attracting people with a stronger intrinsic motivation to serve their communities and weaker concern for monetary rewards relative to the general public. While teachers do respond to incentives, the attenuated response to purely financial incentives, as in bonus-style reward schemes, may be explained by motivation of the average teacher differing from that of workers in profit-driven occupations.

Administrators of school systems would be wise to acknowledge the intrinsic motivation to teach that teachers carry into their workplaces. Implicitly, managing such a workforce for optimal performance means administrators should ensure broad trust and buy-in from teachers on the evaluation criteria used to gauge performance and provide frequent opportunities for teachers to learn from one another not just *if* they are performing poorly but *how* to perform well. Beyond building a collaborative environment for teachers to share best practices without competing for awards, a system in which younger teachers are assigned mentors or teaching coaches opens a new step in a teacher's career ladder—rewarding effectiveness and growth in one's teaching with not only additional money but an expanded role to contribute more to their school's mission. As with government workers more broadly, crafting policies and management practices for bringing the best out of teachers requires a clear and accurate understanding of what motivates them to teach in the first place.

Beyond education, scholars of public management should work with practitioners and foundations to identify salient measures of performance in other domains, such as public health, social work, policing, regulatory enforcement in a variety of areas, and devise similar natural experiments, field experiments, and randomized trials to explore the extent to which the documented differences in motivation between public servants and private sector workers creates similar patterns to what has been observed with teachers—a real but modest response to monetary incentives with stronger responses to punitive consequences and developmental resources. Elected officials and administrators in state and local governments could substantially advance knowledge by simply devising and implementing more systematic performance measures, collecting such information in an organized fashion, and making individual- and organization-level data available to researchers. Much of the research covered in this chapter was enabled by state and local governments adopting state-level standards, funding the creation of both measures of progress on those standards and administrative capacity to regularly collect and store data of those measures, and working in ongoing partnerships with the research community. Public management research and practice would benefit from a similar movement in other areas of government.

NOTES

1. For comprehensive reviews of policies and practices aimed at improving teacher effectiveness, including some that fall beyond the scope of this chapter's focus on motivation-related policies and interventions, please see Jackson et al. (2014) and Gershenson (2021).
2. Holt (2018) uses principal components factor analysis to investigate the reliability of these items for measuring their latent factors. He finds an alpha of 0.72 for the PSM measure, 0.66 for the professional motivations measure, and 0.57 for the family motivations measure. While the family measure is on the margin for reliability, he finds that it significantly correlates with family formation later in life, which supports the measure's construct validity. Further, the PSM measure (using 5 items or 3 items) significantly predicts sector selection.

REFERENCES

Angrist, J.D., and Guryan, J. (2008). Does teacher testing raise teacher quality? Evidence from state certification requirements. *Economics of Education Review*, *27*, 483–503.

Angrist, J.D., and Lavy, V. (2001). Does teacher training affect pupil learning? Evidence from matched comparisons in Jerusalem public schools. *Journal of Labor Economics*, *19*, 343–369.

Atkinson, A., Burgess, S., Croxson, B., Gregg, P., Propper, C., Slater, H., and Wilson, D. (2009). Evaluating the impact of performance-related pay for teachers in England. *Labour Economics*, *16*, 251–261.

Bandura, A. (1977). Self-efficacy: Toward a unifying theory of behavioral change. *Psychological Review*, *84*, 191215.
Behn, R. D. (1995). The big questions of public management. *Public Administration Review*, *55*, 313–324.
Bertelli, A.M., and Lynn Jr., L.E. (2006). Public management in the shadow of the constitution. *Administration and Society*, *38*, 31–57.
Brehm, M., Imberman, S.A., and Lovenheim, M.F. (2017). Achievement effects of individual performance incentives in a teacher merit pay tournament. *Labour Economics*, *44*, 133–150.
Bruhn, J.M., Imberman, S.A., and Winters, M.A. (2020). Regulatory arbitrage in teacher hiring and retention: Evidence from Massachusetts charter schools (No. w27607). National Bureau of Economic Research.
Burgess, S., Rawal, S., and Taylor, E.S. (2019). Teacher peer observation and student test scores: Evidence from a field experiment in English secondary schools. (EdWorkingPaper: 19-139). Annenberg Institute at Brown University.
Carnoy, M., and Loeb, S. (2002). Does external accountability affect student outcomes? A cross-state analysis. *Educational Evaluation and Policy Analysis*, *24*, 305–331.
Carter Andrews, D.J., Castro, E., Cho, C.L., Petchauer, E., Richmond, G., and Floden, R. (2019). Changing the narrative on diversifying the teaching workforce: A look at historical and contemporary factors that inform recruitment and retention of teachers of color. *Journal of Teacher Education*, *70*, 6–12.
Chetty, R., Friedman, J.N., and Rockoff, J.E. (2014a). Measuring the impacts of teachers I: Evaluating bias in teacher value-added estimates. *American Economic Review*, *104*, 2593–2632.
Chetty, R., Friedman, J.N., and Rockoff, J.E. (2014b). Measuring the impacts of teachers II: Teacher value-added and student outcomes in adulthood. *American Economic Review*, *104*, 2633–2679.
Cowan, J., and Goldhaber, D. (2016). National board certification and teacher effectiveness: Evidence from Washington State. *Journal of Research on Educational Effectiveness*, *9*, 233–258.
Dee, T.S., and Jacob, B. (2011). The impact of No Child Left Behind on student achievement. *Journal of Policy Analysis and Management*, *30*, 418–446.
Dee, T.S., and Wyckoff, J. (2015). Incentives, selection, and teacher performance: Evidence from IMPACT. *Journal of Policy Analysis and Management*, *34*, 267–297.
Figlio, D.N. (2006). Testing, crime and punishment. *Journal of Public Economics*, *90*, 837–851.
Figlio, D.N., and Getzler, L.S. (2002). Accountability, ability and disability: Gaming the system (No. w9307). National Bureau of Economic Research.
Firestone, W.A. (2014). Teacher evaluation policy and conflicting theories of motivation. *Educational Researcher*, *43*, 100–107.
Fryer, R.G. (2013). Teacher incentives and student achievement: Evidence from New York City public schools. *Journal of Labor Economics*, *31*, 373–407.
Fryer, Jr., R.G., Levitt, S.D., List, J., and Sadoff, S. (2012). Enhancing the efficacy of teacher incentives through loss aversion: A field experiment (No. w18237). National Bureau of Economic Research.
Gershenson, S. (2016). Performance standards and employee effort: Evidence from teacher absences. *Journal of Policy Analysis and Management*, *35*, 615–638.
Gershenson, S. (2019). Student-teacher race match in charter and traditional public schools. Thomas B. Fordham Institute.
Gershenson, S. (2021). Identifying and Producing effective teachers. (EdWorkingPaper: 21-351). Retrieved from Annenberg Institute at Brown University at https://doi.org/10.26300/rzsy-7158.
Glazerman, S., Isenberg, E., Dolfin, S., Bleeker, M., Johnson, A., Grider, M., and Jacobus, M. (2010). Impacts of comprehensive teacher induction: final results from a randomized controlled study. NCEE 2010-4027. National Center for Education Evaluation and Regional Assistance.
Goldhaber, D. (2011). Licensure: Exploring the value of this gateway to the teacher workforce. In E.A. Hanushek, S. Machin, and L. Woessmann (eds), *Handbook of the economics of education* (Vol. 3). San Diego, CA: Elsevier, pp. 315–339.
Goldhaber, D., and Hansen, M. (2010). Race, gender, and teacher testing: How informative a tool is teacher licensure testing? *American Educational Research Journal*, *47*, 218–251.

Goldhaber, D., Krieg, J., and Theobald, R. (2020). Effective like me? Does having a more productive mentor improve the productivity of mentees? *Labour Economics*, *63*, at https://doi.org/10.1016/j.labeco.2019.101792.

Goodman, S.F., and Turner, L.J. (2013). The design of teacher incentive pay and educational outcomes: Evidence from the New York City bonus program. *Journal of Labor Economics*, *31*, 409–420.

Hill, A.J., and Jones, D.B. (2020). The Impacts of performance pay on teacher effectiveness and retention: Does teacher gender matter? *Journal of Human Resources*, *55*, 349–385.

Hanushek, E.A. (2011). The economic value of higher teacher quality. *Economics of Education Review*, *30*, 466–479.

Hanushek, E.A., and Rivkin, S.G. (2010). Generalizations about using value-added measures of teacher quality. *American Economic Review*, *100*, 267–271.

Heinrich, C.J., and Marschke, G. (2010). Incentives and their dynamics in public sector performance management systems. *Journal of Policy Analysis and Management*, *29*, 183–208.

Holt, S.B. (2018). For those who care: The effect of public service motivation on sector selection. *Public Administration Review*, *78*, 457–471.

Imberman, S.A., and Lovenheim, M.F. (2015). Incentive strength and teacher productivity: Evidence from a group-based teacher incentive pay system. *Review of Economics and Statistics*, *97*, 364–386.

Ingersoll, R., and Merill, L. (2017). A quarter century of changes in the elementary and secondary teaching force: From 1987 to 2012. Washington, DC: National Center for Education Statistics.

Isenberg, E., Glazerman, S., Bleeker, M., Johnson, A., Lugo-Gil, J., Grider, M., Dolfin, S., and Britton, E. (2009). Impacts of comprehensive teacher induction: Results from the second year of a randomized controlled study. NCEE 2009-4072. National Center for Education Evaluation and Regional Assistance.

Jacinto, A., and Gershenson, S. (2020). The intergenerational transmission of teaching. *American Educational Research Journal*, first published online on October 14, 2020 at https://doi.org/10.3102/0002831220963874.

Jackson, C.K. (2010). A little now for a lot later: A look at a Texas advanced placement incentive program. *Journal of Human Resources*, *45*, 591–639.

Jackson, C.K. (2014). Do college-preparatory programs improve long-term outcomes? *Economic Inquiry*, *52*, 72–99.

Jackson, C.K. (2018). What do test scores miss? The importance of teacher effects on non–test score outcomes. *Journal of Political Economy*, *126*, 2072–2107.

Jackson, C.K., and Bruegmann, E. (2009). Teaching students and teaching each other: The importance of peer learning for teachers. *American Economic Journal: Applied Economics*, *1*, 85–108.

Jackson, C.K., Rockoff, J.E., and Staiger, D.O. (2014). Teacher effects and teacher-related policies. *Annual Review of Economics*, *6*, 801–825.

Jacob, B.A. (2005). Accountability, incentives and behavior: The impact of high-stakes testing in the Chicago public schools. *Journal of Public Economics*, *89*, 761–796.

Jacob, B.A., and Lefgren, L. (2004). The impact of teacher training on student achievement: Quasi-experimental evidence from school reform efforts in Chicago. *Journal of Human Resources*, *39*, 50–79.

Jacob, B.A., and Levitt, S.D. (2003). Rotten apples: An investigation of the prevalence and predictors of teacher cheating. *The Quarterly Journal of Economics*, *118*, 843–877.

James, J., and Wyckoff, J.H. (2020). Teacher evaluation and teacher turnover in equilibrium: Evidence from DC public schools. *AERA Open*, *6*, at https://doi.org/10.1177/2332858420932235.

Kolbe, T., and Strunk, K.O. (2012). Economic incentives as a strategy for responding to teacher staffing problems: A typology of policies and practices. *Educational Administration Quarterly*, *48*, 779–813.

Kraft, M.A., and Papay, J.P. (2014). Can professional environments in schools promote teacher development? Explaining heterogeneity in returns to teaching experience. *Educational Evaluation and Policy Analysis*, *36*, 476–500.

Kraft, M.A., Blazar, D., and Hogan, D. (2018). The effect of teacher coaching on instruction and achievement: A meta-analysis of the causal evidence. *Review of Educational Research*, *88*, 547–588.

Ladd, H.F., and Sorensen, L.C. (2017). Returns to teacher experience: Student achievement and motivation in middle school. *Education Finance and Policy*, *12*, 241–279.

Lavy, V. (2009). Performance pay and teachers' effort, productivity, and grading ethics. *American Economic Review, 99*, 1979–2011.
Lee, H.W. (2019). Performance-based human resource management and federal employee's motivation: Moderating roles of goal-clarifying intervention, appraisal fairness, and feedback satisfaction. *Review of Public Personnel Administration, 39*, 323–348.
Moynihan, D.P., and Pandey, S.K. (2010). The big question for performance management: Why do managers use performance information? *Journal of Public Administration Research and Theory, 20*, 849–866.
Muralidharan, K., and Sundararaman, V. (2011a). Teacher opinions on performance pay: Evidence from India. *Economics of Education Review, 30*, 394–403.
Muralidharan, K., and Sundararaman, V. (2011b, March). Teacher performance pay: Experimental evidence from India. *Journal of Political Economy, 119*, 39–77.
Nunn, J. (2016). The benefits to individual teachers, to schools and to the teaching profession of Masters level initial teacher education. UCET.
Pajares, F. (1996). Self-efficacy beliefs in academic settings. *Review of Educational Research, 66*, 543–578.
Pandey, S.K., and Stazyk, E.C. (2008). Antecedents and correlates of public service motivation. In J.L. Perry and A. Hondeghem (eds), *Motivation in public management: The call of public service.* New York, NY: Oxford University Press, pp. 101–117.
Park, J. (2021). What makes performance-related pay effective in the public sector? Target, pay design, and context. *Review of Public Personnel Administration*, first published online on January 29, 2021 at https://doi.org/10.1177/0734371X21990722.
Parsad, B., Lewis, L., and Farris, E. (2001). Teacher preparation and professional development, 2000. US Department of Education, Office of Educational Research and Improvement.
Perry, J. L., and Vandenabeele, W. (2015). Public service motivation research: Achievements, challenges, and future directions. *Public Administration Review, 75*, 692–699.
Perry, J.L., and Wise, L.R. (1990). The motivational bases of public service. *Public Administration Review, 50*, 367–373.
Perry, J.L., Engbers, T.A., and Jun, S.Y. (2009). Back to the future? Performance-related pay, empirical research, and the perils of persistence. *Public Administration Review, 69*, 39–51.
Pianta, R.C. (2011). Teaching children well: New evidence-based approaches to teacher professional development and training. Center for American Progress.
Pope, N.G. (2019). The effect of teacher ratings on teacher performance. *Journal of Public Economics, 172*, 84–110.
Putman, H., Ristow, L., and MacAllum, K. (2011). The Ohio Teacher Incentive Fund External Evaluation: Year 1 Literature Review. Westat. Rockville, MD.
Redding, C., and Baker, D.J. (2019). Understanding racial/ethnic diversity gaps among early career teachers. *AERA Open, 5*, 2332858419848440.
Ritz, A., Brewer, G.A., and Neumann, O. (2016). Public service motivation: A systematic literature review and outlook. *Public Administration Review, 76*, 414–426.
Rockoff, J.E. (2008). Does mentoring reduce turnover and improve skills of new employees? Evidence from teachers in New York City (No. w13868). National Bureau of Economic Research.
Rockoff, J.E., Jacob, B.A., Kane, T.J., and Staiger, D.O. (2011). Can you recognize an effective teacher when you recruit one? *Education Finance and Policy, 6*, 43–74.
Ronfeldt, M., Loeb, S., and Wyckoff, J. (2013). How teacher turnover harms student achievement. *American Educational Research Journal, 50*, 4–36.
Ryan, R.M., and Deci, E.L. (2000). Intrinsic and extrinsic motivations: Classic definitions and new directions. *Contemporary Educational Psychology, 25*, 54–67.
Sojourner, A.J., Mykerezi, E., and West, K.L. (2014). Teacher pay reform and productivity panel data evidence from adoptions of q-comp in Minnesota. *Journal of Human Resources, 49*, 945–981.
Sorensen, L.C., and Holt, S.B. (2021). Sorting it out: The effects of charter expansion on teacher and student composition at traditional public schools. *Economics of Education Review, 82*, at https://doi.org/10.1016/j.econedurev.2021.102095.
Sorensen, L.C., and Ladd, H.F. (2020). The hidden costs of teacher turnover. *AERA Open, 6*, at https://doi.org/10.1177/2332858420905812.

Speroni, C., Wellington, A., Burkander, P., Chiang, H., Herrmann, M., and Hallgren, K. (2020). Do educator performance incentives help students? Evidence from the Teacher Incentive Fund National evaluation. *Journal of Labor Economics*, *38*, 843–872.

Springer, M.G., Ballou, D., Hamilton, L., Le, V.N., Lockwood, J.R., McCaffrey, D.F., Pepper, M., and Stecher, B.M. (2011). Teacher pay for performance: Experimental evidence from the Project on Incentives in Teaching (POINT). Society for Research on Educational Effectiveness.

Staiger, D.O., and Rockoff, J.E. (2010). Searching for effective teachers with imperfect information. *Journal of Economic Perspectives*, *24*, 97–118.

Tyler, L. (2011). Toward increasing teacher diversity: Targeting support and intervention for teacher licensure candidates. Educational Testing Service.

Wiswall, M. (2013). The dynamics of teacher quality. *Journal of Public Economics*, *100*, 61–78.

Yoon, K.S., Duncan, T., Lee, S.W.Y., Scarloss, B., and Shapley, K.L. (2007). Reviewing the evidence on how teacher professional development affects student achievement. Issues and answers. rel 2007-no. 033. Regional Educational Laboratory Southwest (NJ1).

19. Public service motivation education and government career preferences: a teaching agenda
Leonard Bright

INTRODUCTION

One of the goals of a college degree is to prepare students for their chosen fields of employment. In the field of public administration, this goal is usually translated into the development of core technical competencies. Often public administration programs have focused less on developing students' interest in their 'chosen' careers or fostering an ethic for public service. Public service motivation (PSM) and career goals are often assumed to have been well developed in students before they enter their degree programs, especially at the graduate level. Students are believed to have self-selected into their graduate programs on the basis of well-developed motivations, and clear career goals. These assumptions are misguided in light of the evidence that graduate students with little to no formal work experience (i.e., pre-service) in public service make up the vast majority of students in most graduate programs; students are increasingly less interested in government work, even as they progress through their degree programs in public service; and students with high levels of PSM may be more interested in nonprofit careers when compared to government careers. This situation requires help from both faculty and researchers to explore new ways of teaching public administration that improve students' sense of fit in government. This chapter will contribute to this goal by providing a brief review of the research on the career interest of graduate students in public affairs programs and will conclude with a set of recommendations that can help guide the development of teaching pedagogy aimed at increasing graduate students' interest in government careers, especially students with high levels of PSM.

DECLINING INTEREST IN GOVERNMENT CAREERS

The ability of government organizations to attract individuals who are interested in its work is not very encouraging. There is evidence that interest in government careers is waning among the next generation of workers (Andersen et al., 2012; Kjeldsen and Jacobsen, 2013). In a survey of over 37,000 students conducted in 2013, the National Association of Colleges and Employers found that just 2 percent of students planned to work in any level of government.

Many students hold the viewpoint that government organizations are not satisfying places to work. This problem is graver when one considers the opinions of students entering and graduating from public administration programs. Research suggests that students enrolled in public service programs are not overwhelmingly interested in government careers either. There is some evidence that students' interest in government careers declines as they progress through their public service degree programs (Adams, 2000; Bright and Graham, 2015; Chetkovich, 2003; Infeld and Adams, 2011; Light, 1999; Liu et al., 2011). The reasons for this decline are not entirely clear, even though Fowler and Birdsall's (2020) recent finding that law school students' interest in nonprofit careers were driven by their perception that nonprofit organizations offered the strongest intrinsic incentives is noteworthy.

PREDICTORS OF CAREER INTEREST IN GOVERNMENT

There are many potential factors that drive students' career interest, such as the job market, salary considerations, and the political climate. These preferences may also be influenced by the fact that public service is no longer a government-centered enterprise and have expanded to include nongovernmental organizations (Osborne and Gaebler, 1992; Rhodes, 1994; Salamon, 1995). One sector that has become a major player in the delivery of public service goods is the nonprofit sector. Students' career interest may just be a reflection of these new opportunities to make a difference in society. However, one of the most important predictors of interest in government careers is years of work experience in government (Bright, 2018; Tschirhart et al., 2008). Students with few years of work experience in government were significantly less likely to prefer government careers. This finding may be due to the fact that students with work experience in government understand and accept the realities of the public sector. They have already invested time and resources into their careers. Hence, they are entering public service programs to gain advanced credentials that will help them advance to the next level of their jobs.

However, there are those that suggest that public administration degree programs themselves may be unknowingly inhibiting student interest in government work and are driving graduates toward other sectors (Henry et al., 2009). This is related to the apparent shifts made by some public administration programs from a traditional institutional orientation to the more analytical orientations of public management, public policy, and policy analysis, which all emphasize economic theory (Averch and Dluhy, 1992; Elmore, 1986; Roeder and Whitaker, 1993; Stokes, 1986). It is argued that these analytical orientations encourage students to be skeptical of government intervention, prioritize private market solutions to solve public problems, and thus lower their interest in government work (Chetkovich, 2003; Elmore, 1986; Schultze, 1977).

However, despite what some have theorized, most empirical studies had failed to find a meaningful connection between the curricular differences among public administration degree programs and students' preferences for government careers (Bright and Graham, 2015; De Soto, Opheim, and Tajalli, 1999; Hur and Hackbart, 2009; Infeld and Adams, 2011). Nevertheless, in a more recent study, Bright (2018) re-explored this issue to determine the extent to which students' perception of their fit in government was the missing link between the relationship that degree orientations had to students' government career preferences. If Elmore (1986) was correct, one would expect to find that degree programs that emphasize analytical/economic analysis would produce students who were more than likely to believe that government work environments were less congruent with their characteristics. Bright's (2018) findings confirmed this relationship. Programs that emphasized research and economic analysis were associated with graduate students who reported being significantly less fitting in government organizations, which was subsequently associated with significantly lower intentions to seek employment in a local, state, or federal government.

PUBLIC SERVICE MOTIVATION AND CAREER INTEREST

The strong connection between students' perceptions of fit in government and their interest in government careers suggests that PSM may be one of the keys to addressing the career interest of students, especially given its strong positive relationship with individuals' perception of organizational and job fit in government organizations (Bright, 2007, 2008, 2013; Christensen and Wright, 2011; Gould-Williams, Mostafa, and Bottomley, 2015; Hinna et al., 2021; Kim, 2012; Liu, Tang, and Yang, 2015; Quratulain and Khan, 2015). PSM has been defined in many different ways, such as an individual's predisposition to respond to motives uniquely grounded in government institutions (Perry and Wise, 1990), or as values that motivate individuals to act in the interest of a larger political entity (Vandenabeele, 2007).

Interestingly, the theory of PSM was originally developed to explain why individuals choose government employment, rather than other more lucrative career options. It was argued that PSM drew individuals to government employment because of the inherent opportunities to serve the public interest and community goals. As Perry and Wise (1990) once noted, the greater an individual's level of PSM, the more likely they will seek membership in a public organization. Research has been largely supportive of the notion that PSM is a distinguishing characteristic of public employees and a strong predictor of government career interest, especially when compared to employees in the business sector (Carpenter, Doverspike, and Miguel, 2012; Ko and Jun, 2015; Lee and Wilkins, 2011; Liu et al., 2011; Ritz and Waldner, 2011; Vandenabeele, 2008; Winter and Thaler, 2015).

However, few studies compare the association of PSM to the attractiveness of government careers and nonprofit career options. When comparative studies were conducted between government and nonprofit careers the results strongly suggest that PSM was a significantly better predictor of students' interest in nonprofit careers rather than those present in local, state, and federal levels of government (Bright and Graham, 2015; Clerkin and Coggburn, 2012; Rose, 2012). These findings appear to support the notion that PSM is not public sector specific (Perry and Hondeghem, 2008).

THE ROLE OF GRADUATE EDUCATION: CONNECTING PSM, FIT, AND GOVERNMENT CAREER INTEREST

The declining interest of graduate students for government careers and the strong association found between PSM and the attractiveness of nonprofit careers are significant barriers that must be addressed in public administration degree programs. However, these findings may be partially the result of how public administration is being taught to students. The ability of students to connect their academic coursework to the realities of public administration work environment will impact their perceptions of fit and competence within the field of public service (Bright, 2018; Tschirhart et al., 2008). There appears to be a growing gap between the needs and interests of students with high levels of PSM and their understanding of the benefits of government careers. Public administration educators have a role in teaching students in ways that close this gap.

The existing research suggests that the problem of low interest in government among public affairs students centers on pre-service students. As previously discussed, students with years of experience in government are significantly more likely to prefer government employment. Students without work experience in government often lack a clear understanding of the field of public service. Their understanding of the field needs to be developed, their interest in government careers needs to be nurtured, and their perceptions of their competence for public service needs to be built up. Public administration programs should focus not only on the development of competence and expertise, but also on fostering the interest of students for government careers. Pre-service students' career interests are not fully formed prior to entry nor are they stable over the course of their education. To make matters worse, when they enter degree programs, they are often faced with a cafeteria of degree choices from which they are expected to decide among intelligently. This is problematic for pre-service students who often lack a clear understanding of what public administration is, nor the benefits of careers in this sector. Instead, many of these students are looking to be convinced of which sector fits them best, and subsequently need help to counteract the heavy pressure to choose any career other than a government career, a problem that is unique to the field of government. Certainly, government careers may not fit every pre-service student in public administration programs. Some students will find that other public service sectors are a better match for their interest, such as the nonprofit sector. Nonetheless, public administration programs should do more than just sort students according to their undeveloped interest, but should actively promote the value of government careers in a matter that connects PSM, fit, and interest. Based on the literature, below are five strategies that may be helpful toward this end.

Require in Class Assignments that Focus on Government Agencies

First, public administration courses should integrate graded assignments that require students to conduct research on government agencies. Aguado (2017) describes a set of assignments he used in an undergraduate public administration course to improve students' public service career interests. The assignments required students to research specific jobs, duties, and qualifications, describe what an average day looks like, outline the job's real challenges, and explain how this job contributes to the public interest. Aguado (2017) noted the difficulty that many students have of even defining public administration. This is a problem that has been inherent in a field with over 1500 definitions of public administration. Nonetheless, these assignments helped students understand the complexities of government work and gain an improved appreciation of the field.

Foster Enhanced Engagement Opportunities between Students and Government Officials

Second, public administration degree programs should foster engagement between students and government practitioners. Research suggests that involvement of experienced practitioners, consultants, and adjuncts in public affairs degree programs has positive effects on students' learning and career interest (Bright and Graham, 2015; Cox III et al., 2007; Irvin, 2003; Letzmann, Nickels, and Stockdale, 2010). Some suggest that practitioners are better at advancing student learning beyond the textbook and provide a better picture of the real world of public administration, as well as offering enhanced networking opportunities as a result of their years of experience. Public administration programs can foster these interactions through guest lecturers in required courses, speakers at special events such as program luncheons or student meetings, and practitioners serving as internship or capstone partners and career mentors. Students should also be encouraged to participate in professional public service associations which give students an opportunity to comfortably interact with practitioners.

Improve Faculty Understanding of the Realities of Government Work

Third, efforts must be made to improve faculty members' understanding of the practical realities of government work environments. Most full-time faculty teach public administration from an academic standpoint focusing heavily on theories and academic research. Fewer faculty have formal experience working in government organizations. This situation can create disconnects between the academic requirements of public administration courses and the practical realities of government work environments. In response, there are calls in the field of public administration for degree programs to leverage partnerships and relationships with government officials to help faculty better prepare students for work in these environments (Gabris, Davis, and Nelson, 2010). Kinsella and Waite (2020) describe one such program offered by a local government in the State of Indiana for public administration faculty. This program gives the faculty an opportunity to shadow several highly experienced department heads over the course of their day. The faculty members were also expected to interview the department heads about the skills they were looking for in new hires, and use the information and experiences they gained from this program to better align their lesson plans with the needs and realities of local governments.

Focus on Career Development in Introductory Public Service Courses

Fourth, public administration degree programs should encourage the development of introductory courses that are specifically designed to improve not only students' understanding of the theories of public administration, but also enhance their awareness of the various career paths in government. Many pre-service students have a very limited understanding of the vastness of the public sector, what the federal government really does, and of the unique career options that are available at all levels of government. An introduction to public service courses could be used to address this issue. For example, the course could explore the foundation of public administration history, concepts, and theories using examples from a broad range of government agencies.

In a similar example, Mallinson and Burns (2019) describes a public service course that was developed in partnership with political science faculty and their college career center. The development of this course was driven by the need to better expose students to the career opportunities in public service and to provide them with the skills necessary for gaining these careers. They believe that such a course would help address the declining interest in public sector work. Their course focused on the skills that students needed for their chosen careers and included assignments that required them to develop resumes, create LinkedIn profiles, and conduct informal interviews with representatives from their targeted employers. The course lesson plan was delivered by both internal faculty who had significant public service work experience and by external community leaders. At the very least, all of the required textbooks emphasized the practical realities of government careers. Pretest and posttest analysis suggested that students' self-efficacy and career indecision improved over time in the class.

According to Mallinson and Burns (2019), degree programs that are interested in developing a similar course should find a reliable career center partner who can help enhance the skill building sessions of the course, foster an open and robust discussions and QandA environment during each class session, give class speakers the opportunity to deliver their lessons in the manner they believe is best, and leverage the wealth of experiences that internal speakers and adjuncts can bring to these courses.

Actively Promote the Field of Government and Public Service

Finally, public administration faculty should actively promote the field of public administration and government. Many public administration faculty members are uncomfortable with advocating for the field of public administration. Too much time is spent in classes driving home the negatives of government work environments and how hard it is to manage. There appears to be a belief that professors must teach the topic with as much indifference as possible. After all, public servants are supposed to be neutral competent experts! This approach has convinced many students that government is indeed not the place for them, even students with high levels of PSM. While at the same time, other fields such as the nonprofit and business sectors are singing a much more attractive song. These fields have benefited from our neglect.

All employment sectors have weaknesses and difficulties that must be overcome. Government organizations are no different. Yes, government work sometimes can be hard and slow. We are handling wicked problems! However, there is indeed room to be critical of government actions without dissuading students from the field. Yet, we have a responsibility to effectively counter the negative messaging that students received regarding the worth and characteristics of government organizations. We must avoid confirming students' worst suspicions and stereotypes about government employment, especially those with few years of work experience in the field (Chetkovich, 2003; Elmore, 1986). We must be willing to become the cheerleaders of our field.

REFERENCES

Adams, W.C. (2000). MPAs view federal employment: Incentives and impediments. *Public Administration and Management*, 3, 123–127.
Aguado, N.A. (2017). Assignments for studying frontline bureaucracy. *Journal of Public Affairs Education*, 23, 759–766.
Andersen, L.B., Jørgensen, T.B., Kjeldsen, A.M., Pedersen, L.H., and Vrangbæk, K. (2012). Public values and public service motivation: Conceptual and empirical relationships. *American Review of Public Administration*, 42, 292–311.
Averch, H., and Dluhy, M. (1992). Teaching public administration, public management, and policy analysis: Convergence or divergence in the masters core. *Journal of Policy Analysis and Management*, 11, 541–551.
Bright, L. (2007). Does person-organization fit mediate the relationship between public service motivation and the job performance of public employees? *Review of Public Personnel Administration*, 27, 361–379.
Bright, L. (2008). Does public service motivation really make a difference on the job satisfaction and turnover intentions of public employees? *American Review of Public Administration*, 38, 149–166.

Bright, L. (2013). Where does public service motivation count the most in government work environments? A preliminary empirical investigation and hypotheses. *Public Personnel Management, 42*, 5–26.

Bright, L. (2018). Government career interests, perceptions of fit, and degree orientations: Exploring their relationship in public administration graduate programs. *Teaching Public Administration, 36*, 63–80.

Bright, L., and Graham, B.C. (2015). Why does interest in government careers decline among public affairs graduate students? *Journal of Public Affairs Education, 21*, 575–594.

Carpenter, J., Doverspike, D., and Miguel, R.F. (2012). Public service motivation as a predictor of attraction to the public sector. *Journal of Vocational Behavior, 80*, 509.

Chetkovich, C. (2003). What's in a sector? The shifting career plans of public policy students. *Public Administration Review, 63*, 660–674.

Christensen, R.K., and Wright, B.E. (2011). The effects of public service motivation on job choice decisions: Disentangling the contributions of person-organization fit and person-job fit. *Journal of Public Administration Research and Theory, 21*, 723–743.

Clerkin, R.M., and Coggburn, J.D. (2012). The dimensions of public service motivation and sector work preferences. *Review of Public Personnel Administration, 32*, 209–235.

Cox III, R.W., Leven, M.M., Banovetz, J.M., and McDowell, M. (2007). *Managers as teachers: A practitioner's guide to teaching public administration*, accessed July 6, 2021 at https://icma.org/sites/default/files/308614_16-333%20Managers%20as%20Teachers-A%20Practitioners%20Guide_Final.pdf.

De Soto, W., Opheim, C., and Tajalli, H. (1999). Apples and oranges? Comparing the attitudes of public policy versus public administration students. *American Review of Public Administration, 29*, 77–91.

Elmore, R.F. (1986). Graduate education in public management: Working the seams of government. *Journal of Policy Analysis and Management, 6*, 69–83.

Fowler, L., and Birdsall, C. (2020). Are the best and brightest joining the public service? *Review of Public Personnel Administration, 40*, 532–554.

Gabris, G.T., Davis, T.J., and Nelson, K.L. (2010). Demand versus supply: Can MPA programs satisfy the need for professional management in local government? *Journal of Public Affairs Education, 16*, 379–400.

Gould-Williams, J.S., Mostafa, A.M.S., and Bottomley, P. (2015). Public service motivation and employee outcomes in the Egyptian public sector: Testing the mediating effect of person-organization fit. *Journal of Public Administration Research and Theory, 25*, 597–622.

Henry, N., Goodsell, C.T., Lynn, Jr, L.E., Stivers, C., and Wamsley, G.L. (2009). Understanding excellence in public administration: The report of the task force on educating for excellence in the master of public administration degree of the American Society for Public Administration. *Journal of Public Affairs Education, 15*, 117–133.

Hinna, A., Homberg, F., Scarozza, D., and Verdini, V. (2021). Public service motivation and public sector employment preference: Comparing Italian and British students. *Public Money and Management, 41*, 46–54.

Hur, Y., and Hackbart, M. (2009). MPA vs. MPP: A distinction without a difference? *Journal of Public Affairs Education, 15*, 397–424.

Infeld, D.L., and Adams, W.C. (2011). MPA and MPP students: Twins, siblings, or distant cousins? *Journal of Public Affairs Education, 17*, 277–303.

Irvin, R.A. (2003). Use of consultants as adjunct faculty in graduate nonprofit management programs. *Journal of Public Affairs Education, 9*, 181–192.

Kim, S. (2012). Does person-organization fit matter in the public-sector? Testing the mediating effect of person-organization fit in the relationship between public service motivation and work attitudes. *Public Administration Review, 72*, 830–840.

Kinsella, C., and Waite, B. (2020). Identifying and developing desirable soft skills for public service. *Teaching Public Administration*, first published online on June 17, 2020 at https://doi.org/10.1177/0144739420931552.

Kjeldsen, A.M., and Jacobsen, C.B. (2013). Public service motivation and employment sector: Attraction or socialization? *Journal of Public Administration Research and Theory, 23*, 899–926.

Ko, K., and Jun, K.-N. (2015). A comparative analysis of job motivation and career preference of Asian undergraduate students. *Public Personnel Management*, *44*, 192–213.

Lee, Y.-j., and Wilkins, V.M. (2011). More similarities or more differences? Comparing public and nonprofit managers' job motivations. *Public Administration Review*, *71*, 45–56.

Letzmann, P., Nickels, A., and Stockdale, J. (2010). Engaging students to connect beyond the text: A reflection on the value of professionals as adjuncts. *Journal of Public Affairs Education*, *16*, 67–76.

Light, P.C. (1999). *The new public service*. Washington, DC: Brookings Institution Press.

Liu, B., Hui, C., Hu, J., Yang, W., and Yu, X. (2011). How well can public service motivation connect with occupational intention? *International Review of Administrative Sciences*, *77*, 191–211.

Liu, B., Tang, T.L.-P., and Yang, K. (2015). When does public service motivation fuel the job satisfaction fire? The joint moderation of person-organization fit and needs-supplies fit. *Public Management Review*, *17*, 876–900.

Mallinson, D.J., and Burns, P. (2019). Increasing career confidence through a course in public service careers. *Journal of Political Science Education*, *15*, 161–178.

Osborne, D., and Gaebler, T. (1992). *Reinventing government: How the entrepreneurial spirit is transforming the public sector*. Reading, MA: Addison-Wesley.

Perry, J., and Hondeghem, A. (eds) (2008). *Motivation in public management: The call of public service*. New York, NY: Oxford University Press.

Perry, J., and Wise, L. (1990). The motivational bases of public service. *Public Administration Review*, *50*, 367–373.

Quratulain, S., and Khan, A.K. (2015). How does employees' public service motivation get affected? A conditional process analysis of the effects of person-job fit and work pressure. *Public Personnel Management*, *44*, 266–289.

Rhodes, R.A.pW. (1994). The hollowing out of the state: The changing nature of the public service in Britain. *The Political Quarterly*, *65*, 138–151.

Ritz, A., and Waldner, C. (2011). Competing for future leaders: A study of attractiveness of public sector organizations to potential job applicants. *Review of Public Personnel Administration*, *31*, 291–316.

Roeder, P.W., and Whitaker, G. (1993). Education for the public service: Policy analysis and administration in the MPA core curriculum. *Administration and Society*, *24*, 512–540.

Rose, R.P. (2012). Preferences for careers in public work: Examining the government-nonprofit divide among undergraduates through public service motivation. *American Review of Public Administration*, *43*, 416–437.

Salamon, L.M. (1995). *Partners in public service: Government-nonprofit relations in the modern welfare state*. Baltimore, MD: Johns Hopkins University Press.

Schultze, C.L. (1977). *The public use of private interest*. Washington, DC: Brookings Institution Press.

Stokes, D.E. (1986). Political and organizational analysis in the policy curriculum. *Journal of Policy Analysis and Management (1986–1998)*, *6*, 45–55.

Tschirhart, M., Reed, K.K., Freeman, S., and Anker, L.A. (2008). Is the grass greener? Sector shifting and choice of sector by MPA and MBA graduates. *Nonprofit and Voluntary Sector Quarterly*, *37*, 668–688.

Vandenabeele, W. (2007). Toward a public administration theory of public service motivation: An institutional approach. *Public Management Review*, *9*, 545–556.

Vandenabeele, W. (2008). Government calling: Public service motivation as an element in selecting government as an employer of choice. *Public Administration*, *86*, 1089–1105.

Winter, V., and Thaler, J. (2015). Does Motivation matter for employer choices? A discrete-choice analysis of medical students' decisions among public, nonprofit, and for-profit hospitals. *Nonprofit and Voluntary Sector Quarterly*, *45*, 762–786.

PART IV

MOTIVATION AND EMPLOYEE BEHAVIOR

20. Linking justice and employee performance in public organizations
Ellen V. Rubin and Minsung Michael Kang

INTRODUCTION

During the early years of the performance management movement in the US federal government in the 1990s, we often heard the phrase: 'what gets measured gets done.' This was applied to government agencies, public programs, and public employees. Many public management scholars worried that if Constitutional values like transparency, non-discrimination and inclusion, and due process, for example, were not easily measurable, then they would be devalued and ignored. Constitutional and procedural values are notoriously difficult to operationalize in a substantively meaningful way (Piotrowski and Rosenbloom, 2002). Radin (2006) was concerned about the difficulty of measuring concepts like equity and fairness because they are hard to define and may be ignored if included along with efficiency-driven measures. She went on to argue that leaving fairness out of performance regimes did not make sense, as many governmental services are designed to increase equity, fairness, and democracy. Even before the performance movement, Waldo (1948) was also concerned about 'the gospel of efficiency' in public organizations crowding out the core values of democratic public administration (p. 19).

Statutes and court decisions for managing public personnel reflect the core values of due process, non-discrimination, merit, freedom of speech and association, to name just a few. Writers on the history of the merit system have described non-discrimination and the right to unionize, for example, as 'add ons' to the core goal of running an efficient and effective civil service (Ingraham, 1995; Mosher, 1968) in part because public employees were not afforded these rights until many decades after the initial establishment of the merit system. It is time to ask the question: how does fair treatment in the workplace relate to employee performance, if at all? Organizational justice scholars, primarily in psychology, have spent five decades researching the implications of fair treatment in the workplace. While organizational justice is frequently considered to be a desired end in itself, a growing set of research in psychology indicates fair treatment is also good for performance.

In the public administration literature, a growing number of organizational justice studies find that higher justice perceptions contribute to employee behavior such as task performance (Potipiroon and Faerman, 2016), organizational citizenship behavior (Potipiroon and Rubin, 2018; Shim and Rohrbaugh, 2014), and complaint filing and dispute resolution (Nesbitt, Nabatchi, and Bingham, 2012; Rubin and Kellough, 2012). Other public sector studies replicate private sector findings that justice perceptions are related to job satisfaction (Choi, 2011; Ko and Hur, 2014; Rubin, 2009), job involvement (Hassan, 2013), and performance appraisal acceptance (Kim and Holzer, 2016). There is also preliminary evidence indicating employees in the public and private sectors hold different perceptions of procedural and distributive justice (Kurland and Egan, 1999) and that public service motivation and justice perceptions interact (Potipiroon and Faerman, 2016; Quratulain, Khan, and Sabharwal, 2019).

In this chapter, we organize the two dominant approaches to studying the justice-performance link and propose fruitful avenues for future research. The two competing explanations of why justice is linked to better performance include the social exchange approach and the relational approach. The *social exchange approach* is used the most frequently to explain the fair process effect. Fair treatment, typically from a manager, is said to create a feeling of social obligation to reciprocate with work effort (e.g., Masterson et al., 2000). In comparison, the *relational approach* argues that fair treatment leads people to identify with their work group or employer, and this self-identification in turn motivates people to cooperate to accomplish group goals (e.g., Blader and Tyler, 2009). Across the two approaches, the social exchange argument has been used the most frequently, but the relational model has received the most explicit empirical analysis.

In total, this body of empirical research demonstrates we can have both high fairness and good performance. They are not a trade-off; more fairness leads to better performance. Not only does the justice-performance scholarship give us tools for measuring fairness, it also provides empirical support from a variety of settings that performance is enhanced when fairness is enhanced. This is important for government employees and taxpayers alike. The chapter proceeds first by defining the ways in which organizational justice is measured by psychology scholars. The two theoretical arguments for linking justice and performance, the social exchange approach and the relational approach, are presented next. This is followed by propositions for future research.

FIVE FORMS OF ORGANIZATIONAL JUSTICE

Organizational justice perceptions are divided into five different types: (1) distributive, (2) procedural, (3) informational, (4) interpersonal, and (5) overall or global justice perceptions. First, distributive justice has its roots in equity theory, which argues that perceived inequity in outcomes, either positive or negative, results in psychological and/or behavioral consequences (Adams, 1965). The concept of distributive justice contends that social behavior is influenced by 'beliefs that the allocation of benefits and costs within a group should be equitable, that is, that outcomes should be proportional to the contribution of group members' (Lind and Tyler, 1988, p. 10).

Second, the concept of procedural justice perceptions developed from a realization that fairness judgements were based on more than outcomes alone. While studies of procedural justice initially focused instrumentally on how fair process led to beneficial outcomes, modern procedural justice scholarship has shown that people value fair process on its own, separately from outcome fairness. In the workplace, perceptions of procedural fairness derive from opportunities for voice, consistent treatment across individuals, the use of accurate information to make decisions, the absence of bias, the opportunity to correct mistakes, and whether the process reflects underlying ethical values (Lind and Tyler, 1988). Procedural justice has been consistently applied to evaluate personnel management systems (e.g., Nesbit, Nabatchi, and Bingham, 2012; Rubin, 2009).

Third and fourth, informational and interpersonal justice perceptions were developed as a way to add more precision in the evaluation of fairness reactions in the workplace. While an organization or manager may implement process fairly and consistently, and rules may seem fair on their face, an employee may be treated rudely or not given clear explanations for decisions. Scholars thus narrowed procedural justice perceptions to focus on perceptions of the rules for decision-making. In contrast, interpersonal justice captures the respect and sincerity shown to employees when decisions are being made, while informational justice reflects the extent to which employees are given clear explanations for the reasoning behind decisions (Colquitt, Greenberg, and Zapata-Phelan, 2005). Occasionally, scholars will not consider informational and interpersonal justice separately, and will instead refer to them jointly as interactional justice.

Finally, the concept of overall or global justice perceptions emerged as a way to capture the overall justice climate in an organization. Experiencing injustice of one form or another is likely to cloud one's view of the entire organization even if other forms of justice are not violated. Overall justice perceptions are not simply the sum of the four justice types. Rather, overall justice is seen as a distinct concept in its own right, as a mediator between the four more specific justice types (distributional, procedural, informational, and interpersonal) and work attitudes that are linked to performance. Specifically, overall justice represents both a macro-level assessment of personal experiences with an organization and fairness perceptions of the organization generally. It aims to capture both personal experience and observations of how others are treated (Ambrose, Wo, and Griffith, 2015).

TWO APPROACHES TO LINKING JUSTICE AND EMPLOYEE PERFORMANCE

Organizational justice scholars are increasingly interested in explaining *why* justice is related to workplace performance and behaviors after earlier research provided initial empirical support that they are connected. Under the social exchange approach, fair treatment can directly contribute to greater individual performance by enhancing trust and reducing job uncertainty (Colquitt et al., 2012). A significant amount of the empirical work on the social exchange approach employs the concept of trust, and scholars are further considering the interaction of social exchange concepts and affect. Next, under the relational approach, greater organizational justice ties employee self-identity and self-esteem to the organization or work group (Blader and Tyler, 2009). In theory, these positive cognitive responses are translated into cooperative behavior (Tyler and Blader, 2003).

Social Exchange

Social exchange focuses on the sharing of resources, broadly defined, between individuals who interact on a regular basis over time and differs from economic exchanges which are more clearly measurable through contracts (Blau, 1964). Through multiple interactions, benefits and favors are exchanged over time, developing into a reciprocal obligation to invest effort to maintain the relationship (Colquitt, Greenberg, and Zapata-Phelan, 2005; Colquitt et al., 2013). Fair treatment is one benefit exchanged in a stable social exchange relationship. In the justice literature, leader-member exchange, perceived organizational support, and various forms of trust are used to characterize whether the ongoing exchange is respectful. The outcome of this reciprocation is often measured as organizational citizenship behavior in addition to task and job performance. Figure 20.1 represents the social exchange view of the justice-performance linkage.

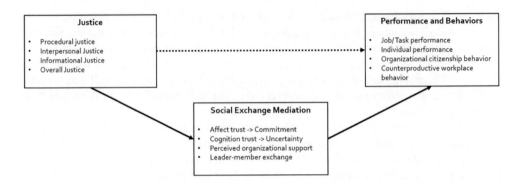

Figure 20.1   Summarizing the justice, social exchange, and performance relationship

Empirical evidence on the relationship between justice, social exchange, and workplace performance and behavior has been available at least since 2000. Masterson et al. (2000) presented the first empirical analysis to evaluate whether social exchange concepts mediate the relationship between forms of justice and performance. Leader-member exchange partially mediated the relationship between interactional justice and the outcomes of job performance, satisfaction, and supervisor-directed citizenship behaviors. Furthermore, perceived organizational support partially mediated the relationship between procedural justice and the outcomes of turnover intention and organization-focused citizenship behaviors. In addition to testing multiple forms of justice, and multiple forms of social exchange, this study stands out for its careful consideration of whether the perceptions/behaviors being measured were targeted towards supervisors or the organization. This entity focus is now a key consideration in justice research.

A meta-analysis conducted by Colquitt and colleagues (2013) confirms the findings of Masterson and colleagues (2000) have been replicated in other studies. Specifically, procedural justice continued exhibiting the largest correlations with organizational commitment and perceived organizational support, as compared to other forms of justice. Also consistent with the Masterson and colleagues' (2000) findings, the meta-analysis demonstrated interpersonal and informational justice exhibiting larger correlations with leader-member exchange than other forms of justice. Lastly, the meta-analysis demonstrated support for the mediating effects of social exchange variables between the justice types and task performance, citizenship behaviors, and counterproductive behaviors.

A recent study on the relationship between interactional justice, leader-member exchange, and task performance sought to understand whether the relationship between the concepts would be different if an individual noticed that colleagues were treated unfairly while they themselves were treated fairly (He et al., 2017). This builds on the deontic approach to justice which argues that justice reactions emerge after either a personal experience or the observation of how others are treated (Bobocel and Goss, 2015). He and colleagues (2017) hypothesized that inconsistent or differential treatment directed towards others in the workgroup would violate justice norms and thus have a dragging effect on performance. Findings from two vignette experiments supported the hypothesis. High differentiation, or inconsistent treatment between self and colleagues, weakens the moderation effect of leader-member exchange on the relationship between interactional justice and task performance.

Social exchange and trust

Research using social exchange to explain the justice-performance relationship has focused detailed attention on the mediating role of trust. As social exchange theory posits, trust is an essential lens to understand the organizational consequences of an individual's behavior because trust 'reduces uncertainty about a partner's reciprocation while fostering a sense of obligation' (Colquitt et al., 2012, p. 2: referencing Blau, 1964). When organizational members trust each other and consistent reciprocal relationships are present, individuals are more likely to behave to achieve the organizational goals and missions. In addition, high levels of trust reduce task uncertainty along with the function of high levels of justice (Bobocel and Gosse, 2015). Concerns about uncertainty are managed by high justice because fair treatment makes people more willing to be vulnerable—a key component to trust (Colquitt and Rodell, 2011). Furthermore, trust amplifies the positive effects of justice on task and job performance by enabling individuals to focus more on their tasks and by fostering commitment to their working unit.

Justice is consistently considered as a necessary antecedent to trust: fair and open processes by authorities enable individuals to perceive their working units and/or managers as trustworthy, thus encouraging them to participate in the decision-making processes. Multiple justice meta-analyses demonstrate the linkages between the various forms of justice and trust (Cohen-Charash and Spector, 2001; Colquitt, 2001; Colquitt et al., 2013). In particular, among the six components of procedural justice—consistency, accuracy, unbiasedness, correctability, and representativeness—consistency and accuracy are also the key determinants of cognition-based trust (Colquitt et al., 2012, p. 3: referencing Tyler and Lind, 1992). Furthermore, fair interpersonal rules are theoretically associated with affect-based trust, as these two concepts focus on communication quality among organizational members (Colquitt et al., 2012). Informational justice appears to have particularly strong associations with the willingness to be vulnerable (Colquitt and Rodell, 2011). Stated simply, if employees perceive that their working unit and/or supervisor treats them fairly, employees are more likely to trust their organization and supervisor.

Rather than focusing on a generic form of trust, affect- and cognition-based trust have been examined as social exchange mediators between fair treatment and employee performance (Colquitt et al., 2012). Affect-based trust is understood as respective and emotional sentiment directed towards colleagues, mainly concerning the workforce culture, and cognition-based trust is a perception of work-related professional competence of colleagues, mainly regarding work and job performance. This conceptual distinction between the two types of trust is important for the justice-performance link, as there are two separate mechanisms regarding how justice relates to performance. The 'exchange deepener mechanism' (Colquitt et al., 2012, p. 4) suggests high levels of justice and trust together deepen an individual's normative commitment to their work by instilling a sense of obligation. The 'uncertainty reducer mechanism' (Colquitt et al., 2012, p. 5) alternatively suggests employees are better able to cope with uncertainties; trust reduces the task and job complexity by minimizing certain dangers while highlighting possibilities for alternative actions that would otherwise have been impractical.

Social exchange and affect

Scholars using social exchange to explain the link between justice and performance are also using affect as a mediating concept. Affect can be defined as 'consciously accessible feelings' and the justice literature focuses most frequently on emotions felt in reaction to a particular event or person rather than a more general mood or trait of the respondent (Fortin et al., 2015, p. 420). The affect argument claims fair treatment inspires positive feelings about the workplace, supervisors, and/or coworkers, and this positive state encourages intrinsic motivation and increased work effort (e.g., Colquitt et al., 2013). Similarly unfair treatment can inspire negative emotional reactions to situations. It is important to acknowledge this description implies fair treatment determines affect. This causal direction is not fully agreed upon—some scholars model affect impacting justice perceptions, while others note this could be an iterative sequence, with affect leading to the formation of a justice perception, which then further informs a revised set of emotions (Barsky and Kaplan, 2007; Colquitt et al., 2013; Fortin et al., 2015). Colquitt and colleagues' (2013) meta-analysis served to focus scholarly attention on the role of affect in explaining justice effects, and in proposing how social exchange and affect may play a joint role. On the one hand, a specific event that creates negative emotions, such as a lay-off, could impact trust in management and depress performance. On the other hand, a well-functioning, productive, supportive social exchange could generate positive emotional responses which increases effort and attention, and thus performance.

Two studies demonstrate the importance of including affect in justice-performance explanations. Zapata-Phelan and colleagues (2009) evaluated whether intrinsic motivation partially mediated the relationship between procedural and interpersonal justice and task performance. They described intrinsic motivation as an affective trait in that higher intrinsic motivation indicates work is more enjoyable and inspires more concentration and persistence. The relationship between procedural justice and task performance was partially mediated by intrinsic motivation. In a public sector study, Potipiroon and Faerman (2016) evaluated whether public service motivation, a form of intrinsic motivation, moderated the relationship between ethical leadership, interpersonal justice, task performance, and citizenship behavior. The results from a sample of Thailand government employees provided similar findings to Zapata-Phelan and colleagues (2009), supporting the moderation hypothesis. Specifically, low public service motivation significantly mediated the effects of interpersonal justice on task performance and citizenship behaviors, whereas high public service motivation did not (Potipiroon and Faerman, 2016).

Empirical work incorporating both the social exchange and affect explanations for the justice-performance relationship identifies a number of interesting findings. Aryee and colleagues (2015) explicitly sought to respond to the findings of Zapata-Phelan and colleagues (2009) by evaluating the role of trust in the organization (a social exchange component) and need satisfaction (affect) on the relationship between overall justice, intrinsic motivation (an affect concept) and job performance. The relationship between overall justice and trust was mediated by need satisfaction, and then intrinsic motivation moderated the relationship between trust and job performance. In essence, justice impacted the nature of the social exchange relationship and this, in turn, inspired a positive emotional response in the form of intrinsic motivation, improving job performance. In comparison, Haynie and colleagues (2016) evaluated distributive and procedural justice, rather than overall justice. Specifically, Haynie and colleagues (2016) hypothesized that job engagement would mediate the relationship between distributive and procedural justice and task performance, describing engagement as a form of affect because it makes work more meaningful and intrinsically motivating. They further hypothesized that trust in senior management would enhance the effect of justice on job engagement. Results of the study found support for a mediated relationship between distributive justice, job engagement, and task performance, but not for procedural justice. However procedural justice did matter to task performance when accounting for both high levels of trust and job engagement.

Relational Approach

The relational approach to the justice-performance link pays more attention to the non-instrumental values that fair procedures are likely to convey to employees. Under the relational approach employees use fair or unfair treatment to evaluate their association with supervisors, teams, or organizations (Bobocel and Gosse, 2015). Positive justice perceptions can contribute to greater organizational performance as fairness inspires identification with the team or organization, which in turn enables cooperation or organizational citizenship behaviors (Blader and Tyler, 2015). In comparison, under the social exchange approach employees evaluate whether they should expend time and effort as a trade for someone else treating them fairly. Figure 20.2 represents the relational view of the justice-performance connection.

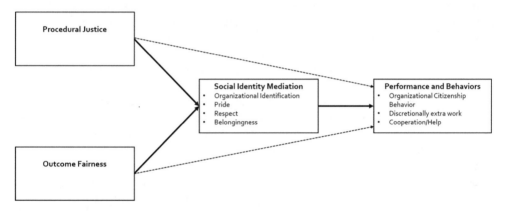

Source: Adapted from Blader and Tyler (2009).

Figure 20.2   Justice, social identity, and extra-role behavior

The concepts of social identity and the social self are key to the relational approach. In accordance with social identity theory, identity informs how much effort is contributed to collective endeavors (Tajfel and Turner, 2001). Employees want to be associated with groups that build or improve their own sense of self-worth; identification with the group will be stronger if the group is viewed as valuable (Tyler and Blader, 2003). Fair treatment informs the strength of that identification because the experience of fair procedures signals to the employee that she is a valued member of the team (Bobocel and Gosse, 2015). Conversely, disrespectful treatment can have an especially large impact on identity because the unfair treatment threatens one's personal identity (Blader and Tyler, 2015).

The relational approach similarly considers the functional effects of the social self on organizational behavior (Blader and Tyler, 2003), where the social self is defined as 'one's tendency to define the self in terms of relationships and group memberships' (Blader and Tyler, 2015, p. 360). Fair treatment by others strengthens identity when relationships are central to identity, and that identity is oriented more towards interdependence. The sense of social self, when aligned with pride for the group and a sense that the group respects you, shapes an employee's work behavior (Tyler and Blader, 2000).

Group engagement model
Among the different relational approaches, the group engagement model has been applied most frequently to examine the justice-performance link. In the group-engagement model, justice travels via an individual's social identity to change their work-related behaviors including counterproductive behavior, performance, and cooperation (Blader and Tyler, 2003, 2009, 2015; Tyler and Blader, 2003). According to the model, both fair procedures (formal) and fair interpersonal treatment (informal) influence how people define themselves. Under these justice conditions, individuals make decisions with respect to who they are and how they define themselves in relation to their organization, supervisor, and coworkers (Tyler, 1999). For instance, they have options for being more interdependent or independent, more collectivist or individualistic. This range of social categorizations then informs cooperation.

A collection of studies provides empirical evidence for the group engagement model's argument that identity mediates the justice-performance relationship. Blader and Tyler (2009) examined whether the strengthened social identity mediated the relationship between procedural justice and extra-role behavior. This study described two aspects of social identity: cognitive connection to the group and self-assessed pride/respect. Social identity fully mediated the relationship between procedural justice and extra-role behavior (Blader and Tyler, 2009). Ma, Liu, and Liu (2014) confirmed these findings of identity fully mediating the relationship between procedural justice perceptions and performance in a Chinese setting. In another private sector study in Australia, organizational identity fully mediated the relationships between (a) procedural and distributive justice and (b) discretionary work effort and coworker assistance (Frenkel, Restubog, and Bednall, 2012). In a public sector study, Hassan (2013) examined whether organizational identity mediated the relationship between procedural and distributive justice perceptions and turnover intention and job involvement. This study provided initial evidence that the insights of the group engagement model hold true for public employees.

Relational approach and leader roles
Another application of the relational approach in the context of the justice-performance relationship is the inclusion of the role or trait of leaders. While the social exchange approach operationalizes the role of leaders as a form of leader-member exchange or trust in supervisor, the relational approach tends to emphasize the social role of leaders grounded in the group engagement model (de Cremer, van Dijke, and Mayer, 2010; van Dijke et al., 2012). These studies contend that leaders play a critical role in inducing positive justice effects by paying attention to how employees are valued and respected within social settings. Under this view, leaders are viewed as a key person 'who enacts decision-making procedures in a fair manner [to] promote cooperative behaviors' (van Dijke et al., 2012, p. 235).

Two empirical studies examined the role of leaders grounded in the group engagement model. De Cremer and colleagues (2010) evaluated the effect of the leader displaying behavior viewed as consistent with group norms or inconsistent with group norms, combined with fair treatment received by the individual (first-person experience) and the fairness of treatment meted out to other members of the group (third-person observation). Across three studies presented in the paper, the results confirmed that leader consistency matters, as it significantly moderated the relationship between procedural justice perceptions, cooperative behavior, and citizenship behaviors (de Cremer, van Dijke, and Mayer, 2010). Furthermore, when the leader is viewed as highly consistent, both first-person and third-person fairness impacts cooperation and citizenship behaviors. Rather than focusing on how well the leader reflected group values, van Dijke and colleagues (2012) focused on the effort of leaders to empower colleagues, and considered whether empowerment mediated the relationship between the perceptions of the leader's procedural justice and citizenship behaviors. This study provided evidence that the form of empowering leadership can have a differential impact. To be specific, empowering leadership that encourages self-development positively mediates the justice-performance link, whereas encouraging independent action exhibits negative mediating effects (van Dijke et al., 2012). These two studies altogether provide practical implications regarding the role of leaders when it comes to the justice effects.

FUTURE RESEARCH DIRECTIONS

A key goal of undertaking this review was to identify areas where public management scholars can contribute to the growing research evaluating the justice-performance link. While scholars have found evidence that the two are linked, it is only in the last decade and a half that scholars have been developing sophisticated theoretical explanations for why the link is present. Much of this research has focused on key mediators. The social exchange approach focuses on perceived supervisory support, leader-member exchange, affect, and trust as key mediators. In comparison, the relational approach evaluates the degree to which one identifies with their group as the key mediator. In addition to testing these relationships further, there are also opportunities for public management scholars to add additional questions on sector differences.

Evaluate Social Exchange and Relational Explanations Jointly

Scholars using relational explanations and social exchange explanations provide competing hypotheses for determining the associations between fairness and employee performance in their separate studies. It is worth considering whether these approaches are entirely conflicting with each other or whether they are compatible. A social exchange is fundamentally a relationship, albeit for a different purpose than assumed under the relational approach. It would be useful to compare the effects of each explanation in the same study. Given the primacy of the desire to have high self-esteem, it is possible that the relational approach is the stronger explanation for the effects on performance, potentially crowding out exchange concerns. Alternatively, do trust or affect on the one hand, and identity on the other hand interact in some way to connect justice perceptions and performance?

Furthermore, do different forms of justice relate to performance through different mechanisms? It is worth noting all of the relational studies included procedural justice perceptions, only two included an assessment of distributive justice, and none considered interpersonal or informational justice perceptions. The social exchange studies, in comparison, included a mix of all five of the different forms of justice, but most frequently included procedural and interpersonal justice. It is a bit surprising that relational studies do not include interpersonal and informational justice since these explicitly evaluate the fairness of social interactions. Future studies could evaluate the hypotheses that (1) social exchange is the appropriate mediator between procedural justice and performance whereas (2) identity is the appropriate mediator between informational and interpersonal justice and performance.

Evaluate the Role of Affect More Thoroughly

Only a few studies include variables to represent affect within social exchange models. As noted above, it is not yet clear if it is more appropriate to represent affect as a determinant of justice perceptions or if it is a consequence of justice perceptions. Future studies should consider more carefully whether affect concepts are mediators or moderators with other social exchange variables. These studies should also carefully consider time (i.e., when information on different concepts is measured) so that causality is clear.

Furthermore, it is worth considering whether affect fits into the relational model. Affect is likely to be associated with identity because people prefer to identify with high status groups as a way to improve their own self-esteem. It is reasonable to assume that a high justice event would improve one's emotional response to a group, which could then increase identification. Conversely, a low justice event like discrimination or downsizing would likely decrease affect and thus negatively impact identity.

Two of the studies evaluating social exchange and affect variables focused on intrinsic motivation to operationalize affect. This opens a unique opportunity to consider whether and how public service motivation, or components of public service motivation, fit into the affect explanation. Potipiroon and Faerman (2016) found that interpersonal justice perceptions have a strong effect on task performance when public service motivation was low. It is worth replicating this study in other public sector settings to see if this moderation holds.

Consider Sector Differences

As public management scholars, we would be remiss if we did not also consider whether social exchange or relational explanations are more or less appropriate in the public versus private sector. For example, do relational explanations have a stronger impact on public sector employee performance than social exchange explanations? Identification with an agency mission, a group of service recipients, or a specific policy may enhance cooperative behaviors and overall effort. On the other hand, it is possible that social exchange, via trust and affect, plays a larger role for performance in the public sector than it does in the private sector. Since the public sector is not able to offer financial rewards like the private sector and due process is a key value within public sector work, it may be that the exchange relationship between fairness and trust is the more critical mediation. As noted previously, including intrinsic motivation as an indicator for affect would allow scholars to demonstrate any differences in motivation levels between sectors and then evaluate how that is related to performance and extra-role behaviors.

Public sector managers report different levels of red tape than do managers in the private sector, especially relating to personnel management and contracting (Rainey and Bozeman, 2000) and preliminary evidence suggests public and private employees may have different justice perceptions (Kurland and Egan, 1999). It is worth replicating Kurland and Egan's (1999) findings with a broader sample and the validated measures of organizational justice to see if these findings still hold today after decades of New Public Management reforms at all levels of government. Another avenue for future study could include assessments of red tape. This is likely to be consequential for procedural justice perceptions in particular since they focus on the fairness of the rules themselves and how they are implemented. High levels of red tape could depress the effects of procedural justice on performance, especially if the red tape interacts with perceived organizational support or leader-member exchange. An employee may perceive the organization cares more about the rules than employees, or may view a manager as being inflexible to unique needs.

It could also be interesting to evaluate how fair treatment is associated with the street-level bureaucratic behaviors of rule following, rule bending, or rule breaking (Tummers et al., 2015), which are strategies used to respond to stressful resource constraints. Social exchange would argue that stress and resource constraints are significant sources of uncertainty. As a result cognition-based trust could be a reasonable mediator connecting fairness perceptions to these behaviors (Colquitt et al., 2012). On the other hand, peer conceptions of what counts as acceptable reactions to resource constraints may provide a stronger explanation for which form of behavior is more likely to emerge (Sandfort, 2000). If the street-level bureaucrat values their peers, and perceives these peers as treating each other fairly, identification with those peers may be the stronger connector.

CONCLUSION

There is increasing empirical evidence that fair treatment impacts employee performance. The social exchange explanation for the justice-performance linkage argues that fair treatment inspires a sense of obligation to reciprocate in interpersonal relationships. In empirical research, social exchange evaluations are often embodied in the form of trust, with fair treatment inspiring confidence (Colquitt and Rodell, 2011), which in turn leads to performance (Colquitt et al., 2012). More recent efforts have found a complex interplay between social exchange and affect reactions to fair treatment. We clearly need additional research to more clearly identify causality and the moderating or mediating roles of affect and social exchange within a single model across multiple studies.

In comparison to the social exchange approach, the relational explanations for the justice-performance link consider how fair treatment is used by employees to evaluate their social standing in the workplace. Specifically, the group engagement model offers a set of testable propositions linking justice perceptions, social identity, and cooperative workplace behaviors. Empirical research informed by the relational approach consistently shows that justice can enhance performance via organizational identification processes (Blader and Tyler, 2009; Frenkel, Restubog, and Bednall, 2012; Hassan, 2013). In addition, leaders can enhance the justice and social identification process (de Cremer, van Dijke, and Mayer, 2010; van Dijke et al., 2012).

These different causal stories are important for managers to understand because they lead us to focus on different activities to improve performance. If the group engagement model is best, managers should work more intently on building connections between team members and building employees' identification with the organization. For managers, this may mean the hiring or project assignment process becomes even more critical to ensure that people are a good fit with the task, team, and agency mission. On the other hand, if the social exchange approach dominates the manager should focus on developing better interpersonal relationships between themselves and their employees.

Regardless of which approach is more accurate, it is important to emphasize this body of empirical research documents that we can have both high fairness and good performance. They are not a trade-off; better fairness leads to better performance. This is an important finding because early critics of the performance management movement in the United States worried that, because it is difficult to measure fairness, fairness would be ignored or devalued (Radin, 2006). Constitutional and procedural values are notoriously difficult to operationalize in a substantively meaningful way (Piotrowski and Rosenbloom, 2002). Not only does the justice-performance scholarship give us tools for measuring fairness, it also provides empirical support from a variety of settings that performance is enhanced when fairness is enhanced. This is important for government employees and taxpayers alike.

REFERENCES

Adams, J.S. (1965). Inequity in social exchange. In L. Berkowitz (ed.), *Advances in experimental social psychology* (Vol. 2). New York, NY: Academic Press, pp. 267–299.

Ambrose, M.L., Wo, D.X., and Griffith, M.D. (2015). Overall justice: Past, present, and future. In R. Cropanzano and M. Ambrose (eds), *The Oxford handbook of justice in the workplace*. Oxford: Oxford University Press, pp. 109–138.

Aryee, S., Walumbwa, F.O., Mondejar, R., and Chu, C.W. (2015). Accounting for the influence of overall justice on job performance: Integrating self-determination and social exchange theories. *Journal of Management Studies, 52,* 231–252.

Barsky, A., and Kaplan, S.A. (2007). If you feel bad, it's unfair: A quantitative synthesis of affect and organizational justice perceptions. *Journal of Applied Psychology, 92,* 286–295.

Blader, S.L., and Tyler, T.R. (2003). A four-component model of procedural justice: Defining the meaning of a 'fair' process. *Personality and Social Psychology Bulletin, 29,* 747–758.

Blader, S.L., and Tyler, T.R. (2009). Testing and extending the group engagement model: Linkages between social identity, procedural justice, economic outcomes, and extrarole behavior. *Journal of Applied Psychology, 94,* 445–464.

Blader, S.L., and Tyler, T.R. (2015). Relational models of procedural justice. In R. Cropanzano and M. Ambrose (eds), *The Oxford handbook of justice in the workplace*. Oxford: Oxford University Press, pp. 351–370.

Blau, P.M. (1964). *Exchange and power in social life*. New York, NY: Wiley.

Bobocel, D.R., and Gosse, L. (2015). Procedural justice: A historical review and critical analysis. In R. Cropanzano and M. Ambrose (eds), *The Oxford handbook of justice in the workplace*. Oxford: Oxford University Press, pp. 51–88.

Choi, S. (2011). Organizational justice and employee work attitudes: The federal case. *American Review of Public Administration, 41,* 185–204.

Cohen-Charash, Y., and Spector, P.E. (2001). The role of justice in organizations: A meta-analysis. *Organizational Behavior and Human Decision Processes, 86,* 278–321.

Colquitt, J.A. (2001). On the dimensionality of organizational justice: A construct validation of a measure. *Journal of Applied Psychology, 86,* 386–400.

Colquitt, J.A., and Rodell, J.B. (2011). Justice, trust, and trustworthiness: A longitudinal analysis integrating three theoretical perspectives. *Academy of Management Journal, 54,* 1183–1206.

Colquitt, J.A., Greenberg, J., and Zapata-Phelan, C.P. (2005). What is organizational justice? A historical overview. In J. Greenberg and J. A. Colquitt (eds), *Handbook of organizational justice*. Mahwah, NJ: Lawrence Erlbaum Associates, pp. 3–56.

Colquitt, J.A., LePine, J.A., Piccolo, R.F., Zapata, C.P., and Rich, B.L. (2012). Explaining the justice–performance relationship: Trust as exchange deepener or trust as uncertainty reducer? *Journal of Applied Psychology, 97,* 1–15.

Colquitt, J.A., Scott, B.A., Rodell, J.B., Long, DM., Zapata, C.P., Conlon, D.E., and Wesson, M.J. (2013). Justice at the millennium, a decade later: A meta-analytic test of social exchange and affect-based perspectives. *Journal of Applied Psychology*, *98*, 199–236.

De Cremer, D., Van Dijke, M., and Mayer, D.M. (2010). Cooperating when 'you' and 'I' are treated fairly: The moderating role of leader prototypicality. *Journal of Applied Psychology*, *95*, 1121–1133.

Fortin, M., Blader, S.L., Wiesenfeld, B.M., and Wheeler-Smith, S.L. (2015). Justice and affect: A dimensional. In R. Cropanzano and M. Ambrose (eds), *The Oxford handbook of justice in the workplace*. Oxford: Oxford University Press, pp. 419–440.

Frenkel, S., Restubog, S.L.D., and Bednall, T. (2012). How employee perceptions of HR policy and practice influence discretionary work effort and co-worker assistance: Evidence from two organizations. *The International Journal of Human Resource Management*, *23*, 4193–4210.

Hassan, S. (2013). Does fair treatment in the workplace matter? An assessment of organizational fairness and employee outcomes in government. *American Review of Public Administration*, *43*, 539–557.

Haynie, J.J., Mossholder, K.W., and Harris, S.G. (2016). Justice and job engagement: The role of senior management trust. *Journal of Organizational Behavior*, *37*, 889–910.

He, W., Fehr, R., Yam, K.C., Long, L.R., and Hao, P. (2017). Interactional justice, leader–member exchange, and employee performance: Examining the moderating role of justice differentiation. *Journal of Organizational Behavior*, *38*, 537–557.

Ingraham, P.W. (1995). *The foundation of merit: Public service in American democracy*. Baltimore, MD: Johns Hopkins University Press.

Kim, T., and Holzer, M. (2016). Public employees and performance appraisal: A study of antecedents to employees' perception of the process. *Review of Public Personnel Administration*, *36*, 31–56.

Ko, J., and Hur, S. (2014). The impacts of employee benefits, procedural justice, and managerial trustworthiness on work attitudes: Integrated understanding based on social exchange theory. *Public Administration Review*, *74*, 176–187.

Kurland, N.B., and Egan, T.D. (1999). Public v. private perceptions of formalization, outcomes, and justice. *Journal of Public Administration Research and Theory*, *9*, 437–458.

Lind, E.A., and Tyler, T.R. (1988). *The social psychology of procedural justice*. New York, NY: Plenum Press.

Ma, B., Liu, S., and Liu, D. (2014). The impact of organizational identification on the relationship between procedural justice and employee work outcomes. *Social Behavior and Personality: An International journal*, *42*, 437–444.

Masterson, S.S., Lewis, K., Goldman, B.M., and Taylor, M.S. (2000). Integrating justice and social exchange: The differing effects of fair procedures and treatment on work relationships. *Academy of Management Journal*, *43*, 738–748.

Mosher, F.C. (1968). *Democracy and the public service*. New York, NY: Oxford University Press.

Nesbit, R., Nabatchi, T., and Bingham, L.B. (2012). Employees, supervisors, and workplace mediation: Experiences of justice and settlement. *Review of Public Personnel Administration*, *32*, 260–287.

Piotrowski, S.J., and Rosenbloom, D.H. (2002). Nonmission–based values in results–oriented public management: The case of freedom of information. *Public Administration Review*, *62*, 643–657.

Potipiroon, W., and Faerman, S. (2016). What difference do ethical leaders make? Exploring the mediating role of interpersonal justice and the moderating role of public service motivation. *International Public Management Journal*, *19*, 171–207.

Potipiroon, W., and Rubin, E.V. (2018). Who is most influenced by justice perceptions? Assessing the role of occupational status. *Review of Public Personnel Administration*, *38*, 271–302.

Quratulain, S., Khan, A.K., and Sabharwal, M. (2019). Procedural fairness, public service motives, and employee work outcomes: Evidence from Pakistani public service organizations. *Review of Public Personnel Administration*, *39*, 276–299.

Radin, B.A. (2006). *Challenging the performance movement: Accountability, complexity, and democratic values*. Washington, DC: Georgetown University Press.

Rainey, H.G., and Bozeman, B. (2000). Comparing public and private organizations: Empirical research and the power of the a priori. *Journal of Public Administration Research and Theory*, *10*, 447–470.

Rubin, E.V. (2009). The role of procedural justice in public personnel management: Empirical results from the Department of Defense. *Journal of Public Administration Research and Theory*, *19*, 125–143.

Rubin, E.V., and Kellough, J.E. (2012). Does civil service reform affect behavior? Linking alternative personnel systems, perceptions of procedural justice, and complaints. *Journal of Public Administration Research and Theory*, *22*, 121–141.
Sandfort, J.R. (2000). Moving beyond discretion and outcomes: Examining public management from the front lines of the welfare system. *Journal of Public Administration Research and Theory*, *10*, 729–756.
Shim, D.C., and Rohrbaugh, J. (2014). An explanation of differences between government offices in employees' organizational citizenship behaviour. *Public Management Review*, *16*, 807–829.
Tajfel, H., and Turner, J.C. (2001). In M.A. Hogg and D. Abrams (eds), *Intergroup relations: Essential readings*. Philadelphia, PA: Psychology Press, pp. 94–109.
Tummers, L.L., Bekkers, V., Vink, E., and Musheno, M. (2015). Coping during public service delivery: A conceptualization and systematic review of the literature. *Journal of Public Administration Research and Theory*, *25*, 1099–1126.
Tyler, T.R. (1999). Why people cooperate with organizations: An identity-based perspective. In R.I. Sutton and B.M. Staw (eds), *Research in organizational behavior* (Vol. 21). Boston, MA: Elsevier Science/JAI Press, pp. 201–246.
Tyler, T.R., and Blader, S.L. (2000). *Cooperation in groups: Procedural justice, social identity, and behavioral engagement*. Philadelphia, PA: Psychology Press.
Tyler, T.R., and Blader, S.L. (2003). The group engagement model: Procedural justice, social identity, and cooperative behavior. *Personality and Social Psychology Review*, *7*, 349–361.
Tyler, T.R., and Lind, E.A. (1992). A relational model of authority in groups. In *Advances in experimental social psychology* (Vol. 25). New York, NY: Academic Press, pp. 115–191.
Van Dijke, M., De Cremer, D., Mayer, D.M., and van Quaquebeke, N. (2012). When does procedural fairness promote organizational citizenship behavior? Integrating empowering leadership types in relational justice models. *Organizational Behavior and Human Decision Processes*, *117*, 235–248.
Waldo, D. (1948). *The administrative state: A study of the political theory of American public administration*. New York: Ronald Press Co.
Zapata-Phelan, C.P., Colquitt, J.A., Scott, B.A., and Livingston, B. (2009). Procedural justice, interactional justice, and task performance: The mediating role of intrinsic motivation. *Organizational Behavior and Human Decision Processes*, *108*, 93–105.

21. Ethics, prosocial and public service motivation: disentangling their relationship and identifying the implications for the public and nonprofit sectors

Jessica Breaugh and Guillem Ripoll

INTRODUCTION

Motivation and ethics are two major areas of research in public management due to their importance for work environments, institutional values, and society in general. Over the last decade, there has been a steady increase in the number of studies examining the links between the two concepts (Leisink and Steijn 2009; Maesschalck, Van De Wal, and Huberts 2008; Ripoll 2019a; Ripoll and Breaugh 2019; Stazyk and Davis 2015; Wright, Hassan, and Park 2016). The reasoning behind this upsurge is because motivation requires individuals to draw upon personal values and motives in decision-making situations, and as a result, plays a role in shaping ethical behaviors and attitudes of public servants.

As many other concepts in social sciences, motivation is not a single clear-cut construct. Humans can be motivated by a variety of different things. One prominent area of motivation research is the concept of public service motivation (PSM), and the closely related concept of prosocial motivation. While some have argued that PSM is a form of prosocial motivation, others have made strides in formally distinguishing the two concepts (Ritz et al. 2020; Schott et al. 2019). Despite this, the differentiation between PSM and prosocial motivation in terms of ethical attitudes and behaviors is, however, negligent in the literature. Therefore, the first purpose of this chapter is to examine the two types of motivation and test their distinctiveness with respect to ethical attitudes and behaviors.

While research related to PSM is quite firmly established as a clear stream of research, more and more scholars have begun to examine PSM and prosocial motivation within the context of the nonprofit sector. This is particularly relevant as nonprofits begin to play a larger role in public service provision. While the work and sphere of influence of nonprofits is generally accepted by society, there is still the question of how the application of ethical principles may differ across sectors. This is particularly interesting because ethics in the public sector (in democratic countries) are regulated by strict laws, codes of ethics, accountability, best practices, clear guidelines regarding compensation, procurement and disclosure of financial assets for leaders and politicians. When ethical misconduct occurs (and is caught) in the public sector, it is handled in a systematic way. By contrast, the nonprofit sector does not have that level of scrutiny beyond tax declarations and the media. In general, financial transparency is not always legally obliged, nor do they necessarily follow specific rules or regulations regarding internal conduct. While ethical behaviour is generally guided by internal codes of conduct, there are very few actual legal repercussions (Choi and Mirabella 2020). This makes ethical misconduct harder to restrain. As a result of this, the second purpose of this chapter is to examine the implications of the studied relationships across public and nonprofit sectors.

The chapter is organized as follows. First, a theoretical framework will be presented as a means of understanding how prosocial motivations are linked to ethics. Second, we provide a systematic overview of the link between prosocial motivation, PSM and ethics, and how this may apply to both public and nonprofit sectors. Third, we explore the implications of the predicted relationships within the public and nonprofit sectors. Finally, we present potential avenues for further research.

A FRAMEWORK TO STUDY MOTIVATION AND ETHICS

Ethics are defined as a set of norms and values that function as standards used to assess the morality of certain attitudes, decisions and/or behaviors (Lasthuizen, Huberts, and Heres 2011). According to Huberts (2018), ethical outcomes can be separated into two parts: content and outcomes. Accordingly, the separation of the content of a particular outcome from the process that leads to this outcome is essential. The content component refers to the end goal achieved by a policy, or law or decision. By contrast, the process refers to a series of decisions and/or behaviors that occur during the process of arriving at the end goals, or what Huberts directly refers to as 'moral quality' (p. S19). Integrity violations (i.e., acting unethically) tend to occur more prominently in the process, rather than content of an outcome because this is where morality is most salient (Huberts 2018). For example, examining the morality of a restrictive migration policy in the European Union is done first by examining the morality of the policy itself (i.e., the content). The process in which this law developed is the second area in which morality can be examined. For example, it may generate discussions between conservatives and liberals because they must prioritize some crucial values over others (e.g., national security versus social justice). However, if a conservative or liberal leaks information to the media, violating secrecy rules, they have committed an integrity violation, or behaved unethically, in the process leading towards the intended policy outcome. In general, what is ethical in terms of content, or the end goal, may vary across cultures and institutions. However, integrity violations, or the process of arriving at an ethical outcome tend to be more universal. When applied to the public sphere, the distinction between content and process means that one can study whether or not integrity violations (i.e., the process component) occur that enhance or thwart ethical outcomes such as upholding public values or the public interest.

Alongside the dichotomy between content and process, it is also necessary to analyze potential determinants of ethical behaviors. Departing from the person-situation interactionist model envisaged by Treviño (1986), based on the results of a large-scale meta-analysis, Kish-Gephart, Harrison, and Treviño (2010) proposed that the antecedents of (un)ethical behavior can be grouped in three primary categories. First, personal characteristics make individuals potentially 'good or bad.' For example, the researchers found that cognitive moral development, moral identity, locus of control or other demographic variables such as gender or education level tend to predict (un)ethical behavior. Second, the ethical dilemmas themselves are contextual by nature and may vary over time. In this case, context may also include aspects such as conflicting values, and closeness to the victim within the context of a specific ethical or unethical occurrence. Finally, individuals are surrounded by broader institutional environments. For instance, ethical climate, organizational culture or codes of conduct influence (un)ethical behavior.

While Huberts (2018) offers a framework to study the morality of certain attitudes and behaviors from a governance perspective, Kish-Gephart, Harrison, and Treviño (2010) analyze the antecedents of ethical attitudes and behaviors from a more interactionist perspective, placing emphasis on individual determinants. Both approaches are needed to fully understand the link between ethics and motivation. In this chapter we investigate whether public service and prosocial motivations (characterized as two personal characteristics) shape the probability of behaving (un)ethically.

As suggested by Stazyk and Davis (2015), motivation enables individuals to use their values in decision-making situations. Therefore, to understand how motivation shapes ethical attitudes and behaviors, one needs to account for the internal processes involved in the ethical decision making. In other words, it is crucial to assess how individuals' values and norms may shape their response to ethics-related situations. There are two classic philosophical approaches to do so. These are quandary ethics and character ethics. Stemming from the works of Mill or Kant, quandary ethics (e.g., teleology or deontology) propose that ethical decisions and behaviors are derived following a set of rules. By contrast, character ethics such as Aristotle's notion of 'virtues' argue that if and when certain identity traits are cultivated, ethical outcomes naturally arise (Pincoffs 1986). The problem with these approaches is that they interpret social reality in an either/or fashion. As a result, they lack the universalism necessary to understand the link between motivation and ethics. In response to this, Arendt (1963, 1978) provides a broader analytical framework that can be applied. According to Arendt, identity traits (or virtues) promote ethical outcomes by deduction or reflection. Deduction tends to apply general rules to particular situations, while reflection (or induction) moves from particular situations and applies them to the general. It is the social environment surrounding individuals that influences particular deductive or reflective thinking. In taking the social environment into consideration, the framework allows one to understand how the institutional environment shapes ethical preferences (as a first step), and also how individuals apply ethical principles in these contexts (second step), helping one to accurately predict their ethical decisions and behaviors (Ripoll 2019a).

While Arendt's work focuses on the interplay between deduction, reflection and the social environment, it is necessary to introduce moral identity to reflect an identity that emerges from individual-institution interactions and is able to guide individuals' ethical outcomes. Moral identity is a self-concept that reflects personal sets of moral values that are attached to a social referent (Aquino and Reed 2002; Blasi 1984). The moral schemas and values embedded within this identity enable individuals to (self-consistently) interpret and respond to social situations (Gibbs 2013; Lapsley and Narvaez 2004). According to Ripoll (2019a), moral identity is able to connect motivation and ethics because it 'supplies a set of moral values, acquired from institutional logics, that provide the guidelines to obtaining ethical outcomes and the motivation to be adhered to these standards' (p. 25). Moreover, moral identity fits with Arendt's refined approach to ethics because it highlights the importance of 'being' (cultivate virtues or identity traits) in order to consistently apply the framework of the 'right' action ('doing').

We assume that prosocial and public service motivation represent two different (moral) identities, with diverse (moral) values. PSM reflects a broad focus on society, and prosocial motivation reflects a more focused approach towards individual beneficiaries (Ritz et al. 2020; Schott et al. 2019). These differences may lead to a contrasting understanding of the process and content dimensions of ethics (as per Huberts 2018) as well as emerge in different contextual and institutional situations (as per Kish-Gephart, Harrison, and Treviño 2010). Thus, although we expect that both high public service and prosocial motivated individuals display ethical attitudes and behaviors as personal characteristics, we also believe that these contributions will be markedly different due to different motivational basis and reference points (as outlined by Ritz et al. 2020 and Schott et al. 2019). How this may occur is outlined in the following subsections.

DEFINING PROSOCIAL AND PUBLIC SERVICE MOTIVATION

What is PSM?

Perry and Wise refer to the concept of PSM as 'an individual's predisposition to respond to motives grounded primarily or uniquely in public institutions and organizations' (Perry and Wise 1990, p. 368). In the years following this publication, the concept was further developed to better capture the specific meaning and importance of it in the literature (for a review, see Bozeman and Su 2015). In a recent review of PSM, Vandenabeele, Ritz, and Neumann (2018) identified two main commonalities among all conceptualizations of PSM. First, PSM arises in public institutions. Second, it can be understood as an other-oriented motivation connected to the abstract idea upholding the public interest[1] for society at large.

Although usually understood as a motivation, PSM is better interpreted as a social identity that is developed through the interaction between an individual and public institutions themselves (see, e.g., Meyer et al. 2013; Schott, van Kleef, and Steen 2015; Vandenabeele 2007). This public service identity can become the basis for PSM (Breaugh, Ritz, and Alfes 2018). Within the context of identity development, public institutions transmit their institutional logics through the process of socialization and social learning (see, e.g., Thornton and Ocasio 1999). Individuals integrate these institutional logics into their self-concepts and in doing so, develop a public service identity (Perry and Vandenabeele 2008). This identity is thus infused with public values and norms acquired from the institutional level. Because of the desire to maintain self-consistency and/or avoid cognitive dissonance, high PSM individuals are likely to display attitudes and behaviors protecting or promoting the internalized public values (Vandenabeele 2007).

What is Prosocial Motivation?

Prosocial motivation, or an other-oriented motivation, can be defined as the general desire to make a positive impact or benefit to others and is based on values related to benevolence and universalism (Bierhoff 2008; Grant 2007). Taking a psychological perspective, the origins of prosocial motivation are the combined effect of the 'perceived impact on beneficiaries (an awareness that one's actions affect other people) and affective commitment to beneficiaries (a concern for the welfare of these people)' (Grant 2007, p. 399). Perceived impact is subjective and relative (Grant 2007), which means it can vary from person to person because they do not conform to one specific moral framing (Folkes and Kamins 1999). Prosocial motives that revolve around a person's work are therefore directly linked to the job-related outcomes as well as organizational performance such as cooperative behaviors, a concern for others and thinking beyond individual outcomes towards team outcomes (Cardador and Wrzesniewski 2015; Meglino and Korsgaard 2004).

Prosocial motivation has received extensive research in organizational psychology and organization behavior primarily due to its link to organizational citizenship behavior (Grant and Mayer 2009). While the development of prosociality has an evolutionary origin, scholars have also shown that culturally specific social norms and behaviors are essential drivers of prosocial behaviors in adults that may go beyond personal norms (House et al. 2020). Similar to PSM, scholars have argued that prosocial motivations develop through an individual's interaction within institutional structures (Hansmann 1980; Rose-Ackerman 1996). Institutions promote specific values and ideas, in which individuals learn through social interactions/corrections of false behavior. In these interactions, they learn social rules application in specific social settings which can become internalized within the individual (Messick 2000). As a result of this, personal norms may develop that include the feelings of obligation or necessity to act in line with a specific set of values, beliefs and rules (Schwartz 1977). Because of the internalization of norms and values, we propose that prosocial motivation can be better interpreted as a prosocial identity.

COMPARISON OF PSM AND PROSOCIAL MOTIVATION

The differentiation of PSM with prosocial motivation is a large topic of interest and debate in the PSM literature (Bozeman and Su 2015). For some, PSM and prosocial motivation are one and the same (Wright, Christensen, and Pandey 2013), others have argued that PSM is a type of prosocial motivation (Andersen, Pedersen, and Petersen 2018), while others have attempted to distinguish the concept of PSM with prosocial motivation altogether (Schott et al. 2019). Schott et al. (2019) argue that the scope of beneficiaries, the temporal focus of PSM and 'changes in human action' (p. 3) distinguishes PSM from prosocial motivation. More specifically, the authors argue that PSM focuses on the abstract notion of 'society,' the public interest or 'man kind,' on indirect, longer term goals and on 'societal altruism.' By contrast, departing from the work of Grant (2009), Schott et al. (2019) indicate that prosocial motivation focuses on helping behaviors from individual to individual, on more direct, shorter-term goals, and on engaging in interpersonal altruism. On top of this theoretical distinction, the findings of subsequent research generally confirmed this distinction. For example, qualitative interviews with police officers yielded conscious differentiation between joining the police force to help people versus upholding social values related to justice and/or security (Schott et al. 2019). Moreover, in conducting a redundancy analysis, Ritz et al. (2020) found clear and distinct differences between PSM and prosocial motivations providing further support that PSM is a type of motivation with a future focused outcome with a more global or undefined beneficiary (Breaugh, Ritz, and Alfes 2018; Nowell et al. 2016), compared to prosocial motivation.

ETHICS, PUBLIC SERVICE AND PROSOCIAL MOTIVATION

When applied to ethics, PSM can be better interpreted as a public service moral identity, or 'a collection of virtues which are normatively oriented to further the public interest' (Ripoll 2019a, p. 27). The public interest, which is determined by the public institution in which PSM emerges, defines the morally right attitudes, decisions and behaviors of public service motivated individuals, and the tangibility of the underlying motives or virtues of PSM (self-sacrifice, rational, affective and normative). These motives also reflect different virtues (e.g., ethical heroism or self-discipline) which are oriented to safeguard the public interest (Ripoll and Breaugh 2019). These virtues can also vary by institutions and countries. According to Ritz et al. (2020), PSM is therefore based upon the motivation to uphold particular moral principles (Rawls 1971). According to Aquino and Reed (2002), moral identities are a type of social identity and become components of a person's sense of self. Like the work of Stryker and Burke (2000), key traits that form a person's identity become salient based on environmental cues, which allows for individuals to possess and utilize multiple identities.

To understand the ethical commitment of PSM, we return to the content and process distinction proposed by Huberts (2018). The end goal (i.e., content) guiding the decisions or behaviors of highly public service motivated individuals is to promote or protect the public interest (and public values). Thus, if an integrity violation (i.e., process) occurs that harms public values (understood here as content), then high PSM individuals will be less likely to commit it.

The conception of 'the public interest' is not universal (Bozeman 2007). Due to its abstract nature, if two individuals possess high levels of PSM, their ethical outcomes might differ because of being orientated to a different interpretation of the public interest or public values (Schott and Ritz 2018; Steen and Rutgers 2011). This resulted in scholars arguing that 'depending on the interpretation of the public interest (content), public service motivated individuals may differ in the justification of the same integrity violation (process)' (Ripoll 2019b, p. 6). Previous research accounts for the meaning of the public interest when studying the ethics-related consequences of PSM. For example, Ripoll and Schott (2020) found that individuals with high levels of PSM are more likely to justify an integrity violation (the process component) that advances efficiency (the content component) if they are highly identified with efficiency as a public value (see Bozeman 2007). By contrast, individuals with high PSM are less likely to justify unethical behaviors that advance efficiency when they do not identify with efficiency as a public value. While PSM's moral component is embedded in public institutions, the development of a prosocial moral identity is far broader. This will be explored in the following paragraphs.

As previously stated, prosocial motivation also emerges through individual-institutional interactions. This enables us to interpret it as a specific moral identity. In contrast to PSM, prosocial motivation moral benchmarks (or the content component of Huberts 2018) may not be found in the public values linked to public interest, but in the specific social environment of an individual. Prosocial motivation is therefore more focused on helping specific individuals or groups rather than the society at large. In other words, prosocial motivation focuses more strongly on individual actions, rather than actions for the collective (Ritz et al. 2020). This is key in differentiating it from PSM.

As a result of this, from a process perspective, ethical decisions and behaviors are likely to arise when prosocial motivated individuals protect or assist specific people or groups in a way they perceive as correct based on their own moral identity. Therefore, if an integrity violation (the process component) harms the individuals they wish to help (i.e., the content component), then high prosocial motivated individuals will be less likely to commit it. This argument implies that when having high levels of prosocial motivation, ethics-related decisions or behaviors are also based on a case-by-case basis, largely ignoring the notions of the public interest.

Using the same logical reasoning applied for PSM, we propose that depending on the nature of the individuals affected by an ethical outcome (content), prosocial motivated individuals may vary in their justification of a particular integrity violation (process). For example, a prosocial motivated individual who identifies with the rights of an ethnic minority in the US (United States) (content) will be less likely to show confidential information (integrity violation, process) that puts this group in danger. At the same time, this individual may be more likely to use illegal investigation methods (process) to safeguard the welfare of this group (content). This example underscores the important differentiation between the process in which ethical behaviors are undertaken, and the content (or goal) in which it seeks to achieve and how this may be applied within the context of prosocial motivation.

ETHICS IN THE PUBLIC SECTOR, PUBLIC SERVICE AND PROSOCIAL MOTIVATION

Politicians and public servants are the main actors within the public sector (Lane 2000). In modern democracies politicians are expected to identify the public interest and develop policies to further or protect it. These policies are then implemented by the bureaucracy. Given our interest on how ethical attitudes and behaviors arise in the public sector, we are particularly interested in the rules governing this process. To do so, we introduce an 'ideal-type' general public administration model (Lane 2000). According to Lane (2000), there are a set of maxims which constitute the ideal-type general public administration model.

Although every maxim revolves around different concepts and ideas, some of them have a direct link to ethics because they prescribe how public servants ought to behave, both from a content and process perspective. As suggested by Frederickson (1996), a certain amount of unselfishness is a prerequisite to behave ethically in the public sector. This links well with Lane's tenth maxim, which states that public servants should be able to go beyond their self-interests and act on behalf of the public interest. A common feature both in PSM and prosocial motivation is the ability to go beyond self-interest. However, their reference point differs. While PSM directs this self-sacrifice towards the public interest, prosocial motivation is mainly oriented towards specific individuals or groups. In fact, because PSM reflects the public interest and public institutions, it can be construed as an expression of this collective will.

As the classical bureaucratic ethic suggests, public servants behave ethically when complying with the norms regulating their day-to-day work (Chandler 2000). This closely mirrors Lane's third maxim: rules and procedures organize public service tasks or provision. Since the ideals and values reflected on the public interest are translated into specific rules that serve to further or protect it, public servants are expected to follow them. Hence, within the public sector, the public interest (and its related/more specific public values) sets the content dimension of ethics indicating what is desirable, good or morally justified, and what is not. Therefore, in this specific setting any action against the public interest will be unethical from a content perspective, and it may also be so from a process perspective (e.g., maxim 8). Public servants are supposed to adhere to this content and avoid integrity violations that might violate it. Because of simply balancing whether an act respects the public interest, ethical attitudes and behaviors in the public sector are therefore promoted by applying deductive thinking proposed by Arendt, or applying a general set of rules towards specific situations.

PSM and prosocial motivation also apply deductive thinking, but the major rules they follow are distinct. As previously stated, the public interest draws the moral benchmarks of PSM. Therefore, PSM motivates public servants to protect the public interest. In doing so, individuals display ethical attitudes and behaviors from a content dimension and avoid integrity violations (process dimension) that might put the public interest in danger. PSM also motivates them to protect or further the public interest. By contrast, prosocial motivation is not directly linked to the public interest as defined by public institutions. It is linked to specific individuals, or groups of individuals within society. Thus, high prosocial motivated public servants will only promote the public interest if by doing so the interests of these isolated individuals or groups are also advanced. If this is the case, we assume the same ethical strength as for PSM. However, in all other situations, their actions will be unethical from a content perspective because they are being guided by group-specific interests that may not reflect the public interest.

At the beginning of this chapter, we defined the public interest using the public values tradition (Bozeman 2007; Jørgensen and Bozeman 2007). This tradition assumes that the public interest is an institutional ideal guiding individual attitudes and actions. The above reasoning assumes a unified definition of the public interest. However, as an institutional ideal, the public interest may be too general to guide individuals. Therefore, the public values tradition also embraces the inherently pluralistic nature of the public interest suggesting that more specific public values are needed to realize the public interest (see, e.g., Andersen et al. 2013; Bozeman 2007; Long 1988). By adding diversity into its definition, we also add complexity into the relationship between PSM and prosocial motivation and ethics. Following Ripoll and Schott (2020), we argue that PSM might reflect different interpretations of the public interest, and that this might trigger different consequences in terms of ethical behavior (both from a content and process perspective). In other words, two different public servants with high levels of PSM might differ about what the public interest is and therefore develop different ethical attitudes and behaviors. When prosocial motivation matches the public interest, the same situation can be expected.

ETHICS IN THE NONPROFIT SECTOR, PUBLIC SERVICE AND PROSOCIAL MOTIVATION

In this section, we explore the main elements allowing us to link PSM and prosocial motivation to ethics in the nonprofit sector. The nonprofit sector, also referred to as 'the third sector' refers to organizations that are typically founded to serve a social purpose (DiMaggio and Anheier 1990). There are many different manifestations of what nonprofit organizations are (e.g., service provisions, religious organizations, lobbying, etc.), however, for the purpose of this chapter we retain a wider range definition that includes any organization that operates with a social purpose in mind. Nonprofits emerge because a particular need and these needs may differ quite substantially from one group to another. Like the public sector, the forces of marketization and market-based management approaches have infiltrated the ways in which nonprofits are managed, opening up questions regarding the role of ethics within these organizations (Ebrahim, Battilana, and Mair 2014). In this case, organizations' own codes of conduct dictate their boundaries of moral action (Choi and Mirabella 2020).

Although nonprofits are not guided by laws and statutes as public organizations are, their ethical beliefs are typically guided through codes of conduct within each organization that map the boundaries of what is right and what is wrong (Choi and Mirabella 2020). However, there is no unique principle setting the ethical benchmarks. Since nonprofits span across a variety of different subject and focus areas, their understanding of what is morally 'good' or 'bad' easily differs from one organization to another. It is on this notion that the differentiation between the public and the nonprofit resides. Within this differentiation, three key points arise. First, contrary to public sector organizations, nonprofits often derive their ethical standards from values and ideals that may not necessarily reflect the public interest as defined by the public sector. Second, the selected values and ideals to guide action are of an infinite variety, which implies that although being 'social' they do not necessarily require an amount of self-sacrifice or unselfishness to be pursued. And third, some organizations could be aligned with what the public interest means, but their focus remains on group-specific interest, rather than society.

Given these distinctions, the effects of PSM and prosocial motivation on ethical attitudes and behaviors within the nonprofit sector substantially differ from the ones identified in the public sector. The content dimension of ethics is now much more difficult to identify. In the nonprofit sector there are a vast number of ideals and values capable of defining what is right or wrong, and they are not necessarily linked to the notion of the public interest. Because of this, the ethical power of PSM in this context is quite limited, as it will only be played out when public values or the public interest are present. If this is the case, then we expect the same relationships as the ones we identified for the public sector. By contrast, prosocial motivation seems to be more suited to this new amalgam of content, regardless of whether the values are public-related or not. Since it is attached to the immediate social environment, it is capable of promoting ethical actions (content dimension) in favor of the foundational values of a nonprofit organization. On top of that, to protect or further these values and its related goals, prosocial motivation may also move individuals to commit integrity violations (process dimension).

Both PSM and prosocial motivation motivate people to consistently respond to ethics-related situations in which nonprofit organizations promote the public interest. Therefore, one must present the situations in which this might happen. As argued before, the public interest can take the form of more specific public values. A nonprofit organization attached to some of these public values can indeed be pursuing a specific interpretation of the public interest. If studied in isolation, PSM and prosocial motivation will promote consistent ethical attitudes and behaviors both from a content and process perspective. However, as in the case of the public sector, reality is far more complex, and competing visions of what is the public interest may arise. This implies that, also in the nonprofit sector, the ethical attitudes, decisions and behaviors (in terms of both content and process dimensions) of two nonprofit workers with high levels of PSM or prosocial motivation might differ depending on the preferred interpretation of the public interest. In particular, we argue that nonprofit workers with high levels of PSM and prosocial motivation can be attached to a variety of broad public goals identified in conflicting situations, and that they will therefore be ready to protect and defend them displaying ethical attitudes and behaviors both from a content and process dimension. Two archetypal cases have been identified in which these situations might occur.

First, two nonprofit organizations might defend conflicting interpretations of the public interest. For example, some nonprofit organizations like the National Rifle Association (NRA), a lobbying group for the freedom of firearms in the US, are diametrically opposed to others such as the Brady campaign who lobby for stronger gun controls. In both organizations, the content (or goals) that they work towards are both interpreted as being 'good for society,' and they can be linked to public values such as security, protection of rights of the individual and justice. Although being linked to public values, the basis in which their moral compass (content dimension) emerges differs because of using different public values or a distinct interpretation of one. Second, the interpretation of the public interest promoted by a nonprofit organization might differ from the one being pursued by the public sector (or/and its specific organizations). For example, because nonprofits in particular tend to be at the forefront of social justice, their ethical behaviors may actually be at odds with the public sector especially if they push the boundaries of pre-existing policies and laws. This might be indeed the case for nonprofit organizations who campaign for gender rights, a new form of government or an alternative educational system. In these cases, the broad goals can be linked to public values such as democracy or equity, and they might be in conflict with different interpretations of these very same values pursued by the government, or with different ones such as legality.

CONCLUSIONS AND AVENUES FOR FUTURE RESEARCH

The purpose of this chapter was to examine the concepts of public service motivation, prosocial motivation and ethics, and then apply this distinction to the public and nonprofit sector. Inspired by the work of Huberts (2018) and Kish-Gephart, Harrison, and Treviño (2010), it began by outlining a theoretical framework to understand how ethical intentions and behaviors can be conceptualized taking into consideration both the lifecycle of ethical behavior itself (the process and content) as well as individual characteristics that come into play. As argued, the interplay of individual characteristics in the form of a moral identity is where PSM and prosocial motivation became highly relevant in understanding ethical behaviors. This is explored in the second section of the chapter. It was argued that while PSM and prosocial motivation are indeed similar in their conceptualization, the focus on society (PSM) versus the individual (prosocial) provides an interesting distinction on ethical decision making, especially when ethical outcomes diverge in benefiting either society or groups of people.

Having provided this theoretical overview and its application to both PSM and prosocial motivation, the chapter then shifts towards applying the framework to the public and nonprofit sector. It was argued that the division in the ethical guidelines is a large demarcation between the core of the public versus nonprofit sector. In the case of the public sector, politicians and the government define what the public interest is, although differences do exist. However, it is the definition of the public interest that draws the boundaries of what is ethical and what is not. By contrast, within a liberal democratic country, nonprofits are typically established based on one particular issue that might or might not be related to the public interest as defined by the current government administration. Because of its orientation towards the public interest, PSM seems to better capture the ethical compromise required in the public sector, but it may also play a role in nonprofit organizations if they are also committed towards the public interest. In contrast, the plasticity of prosocial motivation makes it more suited to the ethical demands of the nonprofit sector, but also able to play a role in public sector organizations when the demands of a specific group match the public interest. Although being the two main propositions of this chapter, we want to highlight the importance of accounting for the differences in the moral benchmarks guiding both PSM and prosocial motivation in a specific situation, as conflicting ethical outcomes might be expected. For example, in the case of PSM, ethical responses of two high PSM individuals vary depending on their interpretation of the public interest.

This chapter attempted to provide an induction to how motivational and sector differences can be understood within the context of ethical behavior. Although being based on previous theoretical and empirical research, the arguments presented in this chapter need to be put to test. Hence, we encourage the inclusion of both PSM and prosocial motivation in future research studying (un)ethical behavior and attitudes in public and nonprofit sectors. Moreover, the approach presented here is only a single endeavor in trying to explain the relationships between our concepts of interest. Undoubtedly, biases or/and shortcomings exist, and therefore future research might challenge some of the propositions made in this theoretical framework.

Further research should also attempt to directly link the main arguments presented in this chapter. We offer three intertwined areas of future research that need to be considered to further enlarge the contributions of this chapter. First, we assume that there are differences in the interpretation of the public interest. These can occur between public and nonprofit institutions, but also within the public sector: across one level of government, or between different levels of government. For example, interpretation of the public interest may clash between different ministries and/or departments (e.g., the environmental protection agencies tasks with protecting wildlife may be at odds with urban development tasks concerned with approving large-scale urban development). These divergences may also exist between levels of government. For example, in the US, there are large divergences in climate policies at the federal versus state level, and these divergences directly reflect the different interpretations of the public interest. Related to this, cross-national applications of this framework need to be explored. One area in which this can be done is to examine the societal context of a country. For example, what happens to PSM in countries where there is high corruption? See for example Moloney and Chu's (2016) research regarding PSM in Jamaica. Future research should explore the implications of diverging public interests (also within the public sector) and PSM, especially with respect to ethical outcomes, when content components are at odds with one another.

Due to their academic value in public management, and its societal relevance, the clash between personal and public values, and the link between polarization of politics (i.e., differences in ideology), motivation and ethics need to be explored. For example, our framework would suggest that individuals who have high PSM would identify very strongly with public institutional values. However, how might a public worker behave if these public institutional values (suddenly) clash with their own personal or religious values. For example, for many, the adoption of a wider scope of gender identity and sexual orientation is a signal of adopting a progressive and inclusive society. For others, adopting these new forms of identity is at odds with their own social and religious beliefs. What would be the driving force of ethical behaviors in this situation: PSM, prosocial motivation, ideology or religious beliefs? If individuals possess, at the same time, several social identities, further research needs to explain how and why different (moral) identities are played out in specific situations like the one described above.

Finally, given the increased role that nonprofits now play in the provision of public services, future research should explore how public sector values may begin to mold the behaviors of nonprofits. For example, nonprofits may adopt different values and actions related to transparency if they are forced to report earnings and spending as a condition for receiving government funds. In doing so, there may be the beginnings of institutional isomorphism occurring across sectors (Powell and Dimaggio 1991), and this therefore might be especially relevant when assessing the potential of PSM and prosocial motivation in promoting ethical outcomes.

NOTE

1. The public interest is defined as 'in a particular context, the outcomes best serving the long-run survival and well-being of a social collective construed as a "public"' (Bozeman 2007, p. 12). This definition emerges from the public values tradition (Bozeman 2007; Jørgensen and Bozeman 2007), which aims to study how public managers, politicians, citizens and organizations define, identify and promote public values (Fukumoto and Bozeman 2019). The values of pluralism, inherent to this tradition, are particularly relevant for the scope of this chapter.

REFERENCES

Andersen, L.B., Jørgensen, T.B., Kjeldsen, A.M., Pedersen, L.H., and Vrangbæk, K. (2013). Public values and public service motivation: Conceptual and empirical relationships. *American Review of Public Administration, 43*, 292–311.
Andersen, L.B., Pedersen, L.H., and Petersen, O.H. (2018). Motivational foundations of public service provision: Towards a theoretical synthesis. *Perspectives on Public Management and Governance, 1*, 283–298.
Aquino, K., and Reed II, A. (2002). The self-importance of moral identity. *Journal of Personality and Social Psychology, 83*, 1423–1440.
Arendt, H. (1963). *Eichmann in Jerusalem: A report on the banality of evil.* New York, NY: Viking.
Arendt, H. (1978). *The life of the mind.* San Diego, CA: Harcourt.
Bierhoff, H. (2008). Prosocial behaviour. In M. Hewstone, W. Stroebe, and K. Jonas (eds), *Introduction to social psychology: European perspective.* Melden: Blackwell Publishing.
Blasi, A. (1984). Moral identity: Its role in moral functioning. In W.M. Kurtines and J.L. Gewirtz (eds), *Morality, moral behaviour, and moral development.* New York, NY: John Wiley and Sons, pp. 128–139.
Bozeman, B. (2007). *Public values and public interest: Counterbalancing economic individualism.* Washington, DC: Georgetown University Press.
Bozeman, B., and Su, X. (2015). Public service motivation concepts and theory: A critique. *Public Administration Review, 75*, 700–710.
Breaugh, J., Ritz, A., and Alfes, K. (2018). Work motivation and public service motivation: Disentangling varieties of motivation and job satisfaction. *Public Management Review, 20*, 1423–1443.
Cardador, M.T., and Wrzesniewski, A. (2015). Better to give and to compete? Prosocial and competitive motives as interactive predictors of citizenship behaviour. *The Journal of Social Psychology, 155*, 255–273.
Chandler, R. (2000). Deontological dimensions of administrative ethics revisited. in T. Cooper (ed.), *Handbook of administrative ethics.* New York, NY: CRC Press, pp. 179–194.
Choi, K., and Mirabella, R. (2020). Beyond codes: Values, virtues, and nonprofit ethics. In H. Anheier and S. Toepler (eds), *The Routledge companion to nonprofit management.* New York, NY: Routledge, ch. 12.
DiMaggio, P.J., and Anheier, H.K. (1990). The sociology of nonprofit organizations and sectors. *Annual Review of Sociology, 16*, 137–159.
Ebrahim, A., Battilana, J., and Mair, J. (2014). The governance of social enterprises: Mission drift and accountability challenges in hybrid organizations. *Research in Organizational Behaviour, 34*, 81–100.
Folkes, V.S., and Kamins, M.A. (1999). Effects of information about firms' ethical and unethical actions on consumers' attitudes. *Journal of Consumer Psychology, 8*, 243–259.

Frederickson, H.G. (1996). Comparing the reinventing government movement with the new public administration. *Public Administration Review*, *56*, 263–270.
Fukumoto, E., and Bozeman, B. (2019). Public values theory: What is missing? *American Review of Public Administration*, *49*, 635–648.
Gibbs, J. (2013). *Moral development and reality: Beyond the theories of Kohlberg, Hoffman, and Haidt*. Oxford: Oxford University Press.
Grant, A.M. (2007). Relational job design and the motivation to make a prosocial difference. *Academy of Management Review*, *32*, 393–417.
Grant, A.M. (2009). Putting self-interest out of business? Contributions and unanswered questions from use-inspired research on prosocial motivation. *Industrial and Organizational Psychology*, *2*, 94–98.
Grant, A.M., and Mayer, D.M. (2009). Good soldiers and good actors: Prosocial and impression management motives as interactive predictors of affiliative citizenship behaviours. *Journal of Applied Psychology*, *94*, 900–912.
Hansmann, H.B. (1980). The role of nonprofit enterprise. *The Yale Law Journal*, *89*, 835–902.
House, B.R., Kannegiesser, P., Barrett, H.C. et al. (2020). Universal norm psychology leads to societal diversity in prosocial behaviour and development. *Nature Human Behaviour*, *4*, 36–44.
Huberts, L.W. (2018). Integrity: What it is and why it is important. *Public Integrity*, *20*, S18–S32.
Jørgensen, T.B., and Bozeman, B. (2007). Public values. *Administration & Society*, *39*, 354–381.
Kish-Gephart, J.J., Harrison, D.A., and Treviño, L.K. (2010). Bad apples, bad cases, and bad barrels: Meta-analytic evidence about sources of unethical decisions at work. *Journal of Applied Psychology*, *95*(1), 1–31.
Lane, J. (2000). *The public sector: Concepts, models, and approaches*. Thousand Oaks, CA: Sage.
Lapsley, D., and Narvaez, D. (2004). A social-cognitive approach to the moral personality. In D. Lapsley and D. Narvaez (eds), *Moral development, self, and identity*. Mahwah, NJ: Lawrence Earlbaum, pp. 189–212.
Lasthuizen, K., Huberts, L., and Heres, L. (2011). How to measure integrity violations: Towards a validated typology of unethical behaviour. *Public Management Review*, *13*, 383–408.
Leisink, P., and Steijn, B. (2009). Public service motivation and job performance of public sector employees in the Netherlands. *International Review of Administrative Sciences*, *75*, 35–52.
Long, N.S. (1988). Public administration, cognitive competence, and the public interest. *Administration & Society*, *20*, 334–343.
Maesschalck, J., Van De Wal, Z., and Huberts, L. (2008). Public service motivation and ethical conduct. In J.L. Perry and A. Hondeghem (eds), *Motivation in public management: The call of public service*. New York, NY: Oxford University Press, pp. 157–176.
Meglino, B.M., and Korsgaard, A. (2004). Considering rational self-interest as a disposition: Organizational implications of other orientation. *Journal of Applied Psychology*, *89*, 946–959.
Messick, D. (2000). Context, norms, and cooperation in modern society. In M. Van Vugt, M. Snyder, R. Tyler, and A. Biel (eds), *Cooperation in modern society: Promoting the welfare of communities, states, and organizations*. New York, NY: Routledge, pp. 231–240.
Meyer, R.E., Egger-Peitler, I., Höllerer, M.A., and Hammerschmid, G. (2013). Of bureaucrats and passionate public managers: Institutional logics, executive identities, and public service motivation. *Public Administration*, *92*, 861–885.
Moloney, K., and Chu, H.Y. 2016. Linking Jamaica's public service motivations and ethical climate. *American Review of Public Administration*, *46*(4), 436–458.
Nowell, B., Izod, A.M., Ngaruiya, K.M., and Boyd, N.M. (2016). Public service motivation and sense of community responsibility: Comparing two motivational constructs in understanding leadership within community collaboratives. *Journal of Public Administration Research and Theory*, *26*, 663–676.
Perry, J.L., and Vandenabeele, W. (2008). Behavioral dynamics: Institutions, identities, and self-regulation. In J.L. Perry and A. Hondeghem (eds), *Motivation in public management: The call of public service*. New York, NY: Oxford University Press, pp. 56–79.
Perry, J.L., and Wise, L.R. (1990). The motivational bases of public service. *Public Administration Review*, *50*, 367–373.
Pincoffs, E. (1986). *Quandaries and virtues: Against reductivism in ethics*. Lawrence, KS: University of Kansas Press.

Powell, W., and Dimaggio, P. (1991). *The new institutionalism in organizational analysis*. Chicago, IL: University of Chicago Press.

Rawls, J. (1971). *A theory of justice*. Cambridge, MA: Harvard University Press.

Ripoll, G. (2019a). Disentangling the relationship between public service motivation and ethics: An interdisciplinary approach. *Perspectives on Public Management and Governance*, *2*, 21–37.

Ripoll, G. (2019b). In charge of safeguarding the public interest: The role of goal clarity in shaping public service motivation and the acceptance of unethical behaviours. *International Review of Administrative Sciences*, first published online on December 20, 2019 at https://doi.org/10.1177/0020852319878255.

Ripoll, G., and Breaugh, J. (2019). At their wits' end? Economic stress, motivation and unethical judgement of public servants. *Public Management Review*, *21*, 1516–1537.

Ripoll, G., and Schott, C. (2020). Does public service motivation foster justification of unethical behavior? Evidence from survey research among citizens. *International Public Management Journal*, first published online on October 12, 2020 at https://doi.org/10.1080/10967494.2020.1825576.

Ritz, A., Schott, C., Nitzl, C., and Alfes, K. (2020). Public service motivation and prosocial motivation: Two sides of the same coin? *Public Management Review*, *22*, 974–998.

Rose-Ackerman, S. (1996). Altruism, nonprofits, and economic theory. *Journal of Economic Literature*, *34*, 701–728.

Schott, C., and Ritz, A. (2018). The dark sides of public service motivation: A multi-level theoretical framework. *Perspectives on Public Management and Governance*, *1*, 29–42.

Schott, C., van Kleef, D., and Steen, T. (2015). What does it mean and imply to be public service motivated? *American Review of Public Administration*, *45*(6), 689–707.

Schott, C., Neumann, O., Baertschi, M., and Ritz, A. (2019). Public Service motivation, prosocial motivation, altruism and prosocial behavior: Towards disentanglement and conceptual clarity. *International Journal of Public Administration*, *42*(14), 1200–1211.

Schwartz, S.H. (1977). Normative influences on altruism. In *Advances in experimental social psychology* (Vol. 10). New York: Academic Press, pp. 221–279.

Stazyk, E.C., and Davis, R.S. (2015). Taking the 'high road': Does public service motivation alter ethical decision making processes? *Public Administration*, *93*, 627–645.

Steen, T.P., and Rutgers, M.R. (2011). The double-edged sword: Public service motivation, the oath of office and the backlash of an instrumental approach. *Public Management Review*, *13*, 343–361.

Stryker, S., and Burke, P.J. (2000). The past, present, and future of an identity theory. *Social Psychology Quarterly*, *63*, 284–297.

Thornton, P.H., and Ocasio, W. (1999). Institutional logics and the historical contingency of power in organizations: Executive succession in the higher education publishing industry, 1958–1990. *American Journal of Sociology*, *105*, 801–843.

Treviño, L.K. (1986). Ethical decision making in organizations: A person-situation interactionist model. *Academy of management Review*, *11*, 601–617.

Vandenabeele, W. (2007). Toward a public administration theory of public service motivation: An institutional approach. *Public Management Review*, *9*, 545–556.

Vandenabeele, W., Ritz, A., and Neumann, O. (2018). Public service motivation: State of the art and conceptual cleanup. In E. Ongaro and S. Thiel (eds), *The Palgrave handbook of public administration and management in Europe*. London: Plagrave Macmillan, pp. 261–278.

Wright, B.E., Christensen, R.K., and Pandey, S.K. (2013). Measuring public service motivation: Exploring the equivalence of existing global measures. *International Public Management Journal*, *16*, 197–223.

Wright, B.E., Hassan, S., and Park, J. (2016). Does a public service ethic encourage ethical behaviour? Public service motivation, ethical leadership and the willingness to report ethical problems. *Public Administration*, *94*, 647–663.

22. Organizational identity orientation: a public sector research agenda

Julie Langer and Mary K. Feeney

INTRODUCTION

Organizational Identity Orientation (OIO) refers to the 'nature of assumed relations between an organization and its stakeholders' (Brickson, 2005, p. 577). OIO asks, who are we as an organization vis-à-vis others? Do we see our organization primarily as individualistic (a distinct and separate entity), relational (a dyadic partner), or collectivistic (a member of a larger collective). OIO is a prominent feature of organizational identity, or the deepest values and commitments that organizations commit to across time and circumstances (Albert and Whetten, 1985; Whetten, 2006). OIO theory argues that how organizational members define and compare their organization to others, and the organization's primary motivations and values will differ depending on whether an organization espouses an individualistic, relational, or collectivistic identity orientation (Brickson, 2000, 2005). Public administration researchers can use OIO to investigate how motivations and values specific to public sector workers and organizations shape organizational identity and how public organizations orient their identity to a wider array of internal and external stakeholders as compared to for-profit and nonprofit organizations. Potential research questions emerge about how OIO aligns with employee motivation (public service motivation, prosocial motives) and values (accountability, equity, transparency, democracy), sector (government, for-profit, nonprofit), organizational mission (achievement of public outcomes), and orientation to stakeholders (collaborative governance, street-level bureaucracy). Are employees attracted to public, nonprofit, or for-profit jobs as a function of their own value set, the identity orientation of the organization, or both? Does OIO (individualistic, relational, and collectivistic) track along sectors (for-profit, nonprofit, public), and if so, what does that mean for motivating public and nonprofit employees?

While we cannot answer all of these questions in one research project or chapter, we have taken a first step in the development of reliable and valid quantitative measures for collecting cross-organization and cross-sector data about OIO. In this chapter, we describe the OIO framework. We then draw from qualitative OIO research to generate a set of questionnaire items capturing collectivistic, relational, and individualistic OIO. We report the results of three studies testing the OIO measures: (1) two pilot studies to develop the measures, (2) a test of the measures in the National Cross Sector Organizational Studies Project (NCSOSP), and (3) a national online survey administered to a sample of local government managers. We discuss how OIO and these measures can advance our understanding of identity and motivation in public organizations. We conclude with a discussion of opportunities for future research applying the OIO framework to public and nonprofit research.

ORGANIZATIONAL IDENTITY ORIENTATION

The attributes of an organization that reflect its highest values and deepest commitments across time and circumstances form the foundation of its identity (Albert and Whetten, 1985; Whetten, 2006). Organizational identity is defined by central, distinctive, and enduring attributes perceived and negotiated by both internal and external stakeholders (Gioia, 1998; Hatch and Schultz, 2002; Scott and Lane, 2000). OIO is how those attributes are understood in relation to other organizations. OIO is a stable feature of organizational identity as it is guided by fundamentally different perspectives on the nature of independence and interdependence (Brickson, 2007). OIO draws from multiple theoretical perspectives including individual identity orientation and organizational identity, more broadly.

Research on identity orientation at the individual level suggests that people view themselves in three ways: as distinct and separate (individualistic/personal), as dyadic partners (relational), and as members of a larger collective (collectivistic) (Brewer and Gardner, 1996; Brickson, 2005). Similar to individuals, an organization's identity orientation can be primarily individualistic (self-serving), relational (oriented toward a dyadic other), or collectivistic (community serving) (Bingham et al., 2011; Brickson, 2005; Korschun, 2015; Li, Tang and Chen, 2012). While the alignment of individual and organizational identity orientation may have implications for organizational identification and other organizational outcomes, the two are distinct constructs (Brewer and Garder, 1996; Brickson, 2005).

OIO theory bridges values and motivations to understand organizational identity at a fundamental level and in relation to other organizations. Stakeholders of individualistic organizations often refer to them as 'the best' and describe them as motivated to 'outshine other similar organizations.' Characteristics connecting an organization to close partners are more salient in relational organizations. Stakeholders might describe relational organizations as 'caring and compassionate partners.' In these organizations, the primary motivation is to maximize the well-being of particular others. Collectivistic organizations are identified in relation to a larger group or collective where the emphasis is on ensuring the welfare of a group, cause, or community. Each OIO is associated with the production of diverse forms of social value ranging from power and wealth generation to social capital creation and engendering dignity (Brickson, 2007).

OIO is comprised of four elements: (1) the locus of organizational self-definition, (2) salient traits and values, (3) primary motivations, and (4) comparison referents (Brickson, 2007). An organization's locus of self-definition is determined by organizational members, who define whether the organization is primarily an independent entity (individualistic), a close relationship partner (relational), or part of a larger collective (collectivistic) (Brickson, 2007). The organizational traits and values most salient to an organization's members inform the locus of self-definition. Salient organizational traits and values have powerful implications for whether or not the organization is *primarily* motivated to pursue its own interests (individualistic), the interests of particular others (relational), or the welfare of a group, cause, or community (collectivistic) (Brickson, 2007). The 'comparison referent' is the frame of reference organizational members use to evaluate how well the organization is doing. Individualistic organizations evaluate how well they are doing in comparison to other similar organizations. Relational organizations use dyadic role standards to assess their success and collectivistic organizations assess how well they are doing according to inter-group or in-group role standards.

While OIO draws on individual identity theory and is culturally embedded in organizations, OIO is different from organizational identity or culture. OIO is grounded in symbols, meaning, and values that are both internal and external to the organization (Hatch and Schultz, 1997) and a function of its orientation to the larger social system (e.g., other organizations). Similarly, while organizational identity is comprised of 'central and enduring attributes that distinguish it from other organizations' (Whetten, 2006, p. 220) and OIO is a prominent feature of identity, identity orientation is concerned more specifically with the nature of assumed relations between the organization as a whole and its stakeholders. In this way, OIO refers to the organization's entitativity or the meaning of the social system, rather than meaning within a social system, which is more closely aligned with constructs such as organizational culture.

Researchers have identified important antecedents and outcomes of OIO. Brickson's (2000, 2005) seminal work on OIO was the first to apply identity orientation at the organizational-level and to provide evidence of three distinct organizational identity orientations. Contrary to the common expectations that for-profit entities are solely individualistic, Brickson (2005) finds all three orientations are present among for-profit organizations in the legal services and non-alcoholic beverage industries. Brickson (2005) found that OIO variation was primarily the result of organizational-level factors such as structure and client type, rather than individual-level factors such as tenure and sex.

Langer (2017) replicated and extended Brickson's findings by showing all three orientations (individualistic, relational, collectivistic) are present in for-profit, nonprofit, and government organizations. Langer (2017) found that factors such as industry, client type and client centrality are important antecedents to OIO. For example, in the public and nonprofit sectors the frequency of providing services to non-paying clients was positively and significantly associated with relational OIO. Conversely, the frequency of providing goods and services to for-profit organizations was positively and significantly associated with an individualistic identity orientation in government organizations (Langer, 2017). Research indicates that each orientation is also associated with both positive and negative outcomes. For example, Brickson (2000) finds that when organizations activate relational identity orientations, they may be better able to promote the positive advantages associated with diversity. Further, Bingham et al. (2011) suggest that for-profit organizations espousing relational and collectivistic identity orientations may be more likely to engage in activities to improve social conditions. In the case of non-profit schools that adopt individualistic orientations, Bartlett, McDonald and Pini (2015) find that stakeholders are considered valuable if they bring resources, connections, and prestige, and there was less focus on child well-being and the inherent value of relationships with families, teachers, and communities. Taken together, these early studies indicate the importance of the contextual antecedents of OIO as reported by organizational members, as well as the attitudes and behaviors that can result from OIO.

OIO RESEARCH RELATED TO MOTIVATION AND PUBLIC ADMINISTRATION

OIO offers a framework to advance and expand public administration research on individual motivation, individual and group identity, public values, organizational culture, governance, and collaboration. Public and nonprofit organizations attract, recruit, and retain employees who are focused on public values and the achievement of public goods and services (Ritz,

Brewer and Neumann, 2016). Much of the motivation research in public administration, whether focused on intrinsic motivation in general, or prosocial or public service motivation (PSM) in particular, has struggled to align individual motivation with organizational values and culture more broadly. Individuals clearly have motivations, which are often focused on achievement of individual benefits, improved relationships, public outcomes, and the collective good. Yet, we know little about how those individual motivations align with the missions, values, and identity orientations of public-serving organizations.

According to identity theory, individuals come to view 'who they are' in part based on their comparisons with other individuals, groups, or role standards. To maintain a consistent identity, individuals often align themselves with organizations that reflect their values and motivational states (Dutton, Dukerich and Harquail, 1994). Thus, OIO can be related to or reinforced by individual identity orientation. An organization's primary aims or motivations can become identification targets for those seeking self-continuity; organizations can act as conduits through which an individual's identity can be actualized and, thus, when individual and organizational identity aligns OIO is reinforced (Brickson, 2013). OIO offers a framework for connecting research on individual identity, identification and motivation with organizational identification, fit and job attraction. Are public organizations more likely to attract and retain individuals whose identity orientation aligns with the organizational identity orientation?

While OIO research has taken a generic approach to organizations, it overlaps with public values research in public administration. Research on public values has generally sought to identify, list, compare, and contrast individual and organizational values (Bozeman, 2007; Bozeman and Moulton, 2011; Jørgensen and Bozeman, 2007; Van Der Wal, De Graaf and Lasthuizen, 2008; Witesman, 2016). This research has typically relied on individual reports of values to represent organizational values, rather than seeking to assess organizational identity through the values it embodies, the values organizational employees and leaders hold, and values exemplified in the production of goods and services. But values do not happen in a vacuum, they are negotiated and prioritized among individuals and within and across organizations. OIO offers a framework to advance public values research by tying values and motivations to the higher order social psychological fabric of an organization. OIO seeks to understand how organizational values and motivations interact and are prioritized to construct identity (e.g., a collective sense of who we are or are not). In this sense, OIO focuses not only on internal organizational values but how values shape an organization's identity in relation to the world. Scholars can use OIO to capture diverse public values ranging from superiority and uniqueness to compassion and community in order to better understand how to promote diverse public service outcomes in a more complex, interconnected organizational environment.

Public administration research tends to focus on organizational culture, values that are internal to the organization, for example missions and objectives that require employees to be focused on communities, collective outcomes, and other-oriented perspectives. Organizational identity orientation moves beyond the internal culture of the organization, to understanding the organization's identity (values, motives, traits) in relation to other stakeholders. Thus, OIO offers a framework for assessing the motivational assumptions underlying organizational independence and interdependence—and the prioritization of individual motivations, organizational culture, and values. OIO can bridge public administration research on organizational and individual-level values, interests, and motivations to characterize organizational identity in orientation to relevant stakeholders. In this way OIO ties organizational governance to stakeholder engagement.

Another important contribution that OIO brings to public administration research is the assessment of identity in orientation to others. OIO is fundamentally interested in how the organization's identity is understood in relation to stakeholders, including competitors, clients, suppliers, customers, or collaborators. Early definitions of sectoral differences in public administration were instrumental in nature, focusing on organizational ownership, funding, and control. As organizations have evolved to be more complex and the boundaries across organizations and sectors have become more permeable, scholars have shifted to accounting for differences based on the social-psychological fabric of organizations—including character, values, motivations, and interests—and investigating the ways in which contracting and collaborative governance have altered organizational priorities, values, and interests. OIO offers a framework for assessing organizational identity—distinctive, central, and enduring traits and motivations—within collaborative governance networks, across stakeholder arrangements, or in cross-sector collaborations.

There are numerous opportunities in public administration scholarship to connect research on individual motivation, individual and group identity, public values, organizational culture, and orientation to others. OIO bridges concepts and measures of individual motivation, organizational culture and values, and stakeholder perspectives enabling micro- and macro-level examination of important public administration questions. By investigating identity and values as oriented to others and as perceived by those within and outside of an organization, OIO assesses the prioritization of values in shaping identity.

MEASURING ORGANIZATIONAL IDENTITY ORIENTATION IN THE PUBLIC SECTOR

The OIO framework lends to the exploration and discovery of diverse motivations and values both within and across organizations and sectors, enabling a more comprehensive and systematic view of similarities and differences. We aim to advance the OIO literature and its application to public administration by translating the theoretical dimensions of OIO into empirical scales to assess OIO and offer a useful measure and framework for investigating organizational identity as it relates to individual motivation in the public sector.

To investigate questions of OIO across sectors and within the public sector, we developed quantitative measures to advance systematic, generalizable research on OIO. Drawing from extensive qualitative work in this area, we worked with a team of survey experts and Brickson to translate the theoretical OIO dimensions into empirical measures. This effort resulted in 36 questionnaire items representing collectivistic, relational, and individualistic OIO. We administered those 36 items in a pre-test to 300 respondents. Using data from that pre-test and in consultation with survey experts, we reworked the language and consolidated them into 12 items, four for each type of OIO.

To test the reliability and validity of the OIO index, we conducted three studies using the 12 questionnaire items: (1) two pilot studies to develop the measures, (2) a test of the measures in the National Cross Sector Organizational Studies Project, and (3) a national online survey administered to a representative sample of US local government managers. Below, we present the OIO items, factor analysis, scale reliability results, and comparisons of the OIO empirical measures within and across the three studies.

QUALITATIVE RESPONSES TO QUESTIONNAIRE ITEMS

In order to develop a quantitative measurement model of the OIO construct, we began with the qualitative work of OIO from 88 law firms and non-alcoholic beverage companies (Brickson, 2005). This research included 1126 individual survey responses from employees working in 88 organizations. The survey included four qualitative and one quantitative question, including adaptations of Kuhn and McPartland's (1954) Twenty Statements Test. Brickson (2005) developed a Ten Statements Test which asked individuals to complete the statement, 'My organization is ___,' ten times and questions about the organization as a whole, as a person, as it related to troubling events, and its motto.

Brickson developed a codebook from responses to the survey items, noting the terms and phrases used to describe the organization as a whole, as a person, as it relates to troubling events, and its motto. A team of coders organized responses based on question type and identity orientation (individualistic, relational, collectivistic). Example terms include: fighting competitors (individualistic); loyalty (relational); promoting community welfare (collectivistic); rugged individualism (individualistic); provide security for employees (relational); teamwork (collectivistic); loss of important client will be bad public relations (individualistic); internal relations issue threatens client well-being (relational); firm dedicated to principles of diversity (collectivistic).

Drawing from Brickson's codebook, we developed 36 identity statements to be tested as questionnaire items to approximate the OIO concepts. The questionnaire items were developed to meet the following criteria: (1) use key terms from Brickson's research that distinctly relate to individualistic, relational, and collectivistic OIO. Terms that might overlap categories were not used; (2) use terms that would be intuitive to an average respondent; (3) combine synonyms into a single questionnaire item.[1] The items presented statements about an organization and instructed respondents to indicate if the statement is not at all like my organization, not very much like my organization, somewhat like my organization, very much like my organization, or completely like my organization. The 36 questionnaire items were pre-tested to a set of 300 MTurkers from August 8, 2015 to August 12, 2015. The purpose of the pre-test was to explore the empirical relationship between the items and to reduce the number of scale items by removing or altering those that didn't meet psychometric criteria (Netemeyer, Bearden and Sharma, 2003). Based on data analysis focused on overlap and distinction across items and feedback from two expert survey researchers and Shelly Brickson, the items were revised. Table 22.1 shows a crosswalk of select qualitative terms, initial identity statements, draft questionnaire items, and the subsequent revisions to finalize 12 questionnaire items.

PILOT STUDIES

Pilot 1 and Pilot 2 tested the 12 OIO questionnaire items on Amazon's Mechanical Turk Platform (MTurk). Each pilot test sample consisted of 150 organizational members distributed across the for-profit, nonprofit, and public sectors. MTurk respondents that participated in the pilot studies lived and worked in the US and were over the age of 18. For full and accurate completion respondents received 0.50 cents. Pilot 1 was administered from August 10 to August 17, 2017. Pilot 2 was administered to a new sample of 150 individuals from August 29 to September 4, 2017. The purpose of Pilot 2 was to ensure replication of results from Pilot

Organizational identity orientation   327

Table 22.1 OIO items

OIO	Brickson Codebook (terms & phrases)	Identity Statements	Pilot 1 Item	Pilot 2 Item	Revision Reasoning
Individualistic	Unique; Values uniqueness/creativity	My organization is exceptional and rare	My organization can be described as unique and unlike any other	My organization can be described as unique and unlike any other	
	Rare/unique/distinctive/distinction/uniqueness from others	My organization emphasizes differences rather than similarities with other like organizations	My organization emphasizes how different it is from other similar organizations	My organization emphasizes how different it is from other similar organizations	
	Fighting competitors (fine line b/w this and perseverance)	My organization does not work hard to differentiate itself from competitors (Rev)	My organization considers itself to be 'doing well' when it maintains its distinctiveness from other similar organizations	My organization considers itself to be 'doing well' when it maintains its distinctiveness from other similar organizations	
	Wants to be the best; Encourage competitions among employees; Aggressive/ambitious	My organization is primarily motivated to maximize its own good fortune, prosperity, well-being, welfare	My organization is extremely motivated to outshine other similar organizations	My organization is extremely motivated to outshine other similar organizations	
Relational	Loyal, good relationships, generous, care about suppliers, tolerance, trust employees, open or accessible, they 'listen' to you	My organization mostly promotes relational values as sincerity, empathy, and compassion	My organization can be described as warm	My organization can be described as warm	
	People care about each other; We help each other out	My organization emphasizes the importance of forming strong interpersonal relationships	My organization emphasizes the importance of deep interpersonal relationships	My organization emphasizes the importance of deep interpersonal relationships	
	Investment in employees—promoting from within, training, seminars, etc.; Treats employees well, wants best for them, supportive; Wanting the best for customers; Loyalty to/dedication to/reliability with/appreciation of others	My organization is genuinely concerned with ensuring the success of others, especially those with whom it has close relationships	My organization defines success according to how well it treats individual clients, customers, stakeholders or citizens	My organization considers itself to be 'doing well' when it is able to maintain close relationships with individual clients, customers, citizens or stakeholders	Revised to match similar 'going well' items across OIO categories. Add reference to 'relations'
	Care about suppliers, producers, distributors. Treat them well; Company is defined relationally (e.g., we are a co-packer, we produce X for others, we deliver product to customers); Organization is accommodating, supportive, understanding, sensitive to people	My organization is primarily motivated to connect in a close and personal way with others	My organization is extremely motivated to connect with others in a close and personal way	My organization is extremely motivated to connect with others in a close and personal way	

OIO	Brickson Codebook (terms & phrases)	Identity Statements	Pilot 1 Item	Pilot 2 Item	Revision Reasoning
	Excellence/perfection (e.g., obsessive or compulsive, excellent attorneys, devoted to excellence, excellent quality, top notch, great quality, superior quality, premier, first rate, highest level or quality)	My organization is primarily motivated to pursue ideological objectives, values, or causes	My organization can be described as cause-driven	My organization can be described as cause-driven	
	People all united in their passion for the company/individual feels s/he represents company or likes being associated with it; People adhere to certain set of values or principles; Sense of membership; Identify with a particular location—city, town, area	My organization forms relationships based on a desire to make a joint contribution to a larger cause or collective agenda	My organization emphasizes the importance of its affiliation with a group, cause or broader community	My organization emphasizes the importance of its affiliation with a group, cause or broader community	
Collectivistic	Consensus building, values orientation; Promoting cause (e.g., healing, environmentalism, organic movement, herbal movement, etc.)/promoting a public service (e.g., knowledge, education, healthy product, place for public to come, etc.); ethical/charitable	My organization is focused on building consensus around a larger cause, ideological objective, or set of shared values	My organization considers itself to be 'doing well' when it advances a larger cause, ideological objective or set of shared values	My organization considers itself to be 'doing well' when it *contributes to the well-being of a broader group, cause or community*	Clearer description of the collective
	Humanistic (e.g. believing in principles of humanism, concern for welfare of human beings); In-group identification (e.g., Chinese herbal medicine, organics, woman owned a dying breed)	My organization is concerned with maximizing the welfare of a group, cause, or community it values	My organization is largely concerned with advancing the welfare of a broader community or cause	My organization is *extremely motivated* to advance the welfare of a broader community or cause	Revision aligns item with other OIO categories

Note: Response categories: not at all like my organization, not very much like my organization, somewhat like my organization, very much like my organization, or completely like my organization.

1, following slight item wording adjustments (see Langer, 2017 for a full review). Three of the questionnaire items were altered between Pilot 1 and Pilot 2 to ensure consistency across OIO categories and clear statements of relationships or a collective (Table 22.1). The factor analysis tests across the two pilot studies show the revised items have stronger loadings onto their conceptual grouping and are thus retained for subsequent studies.

NATIONAL CROSS SECTOR ORGANIZATIONAL STUDIES PROJECT

The 12 OIO questionnaire items from Pilot 2 were then tested as part of the National Cross Sector Organizational Studies Project (NCSOSP) administered to 600 MTurk respondents who lived and worked in the US and were over 18 years old. The online survey was open from September 8 through September 14, 2017. For full and accurate completion participants received 0.85 cents.

LOCAL GOVERNMENT MANAGER STUDY

The 12 OIO questionnaire items were administered in a national online survey conducted by the Center for Science, Technology and Environmental Policy Studies (CSTEPS) at Arizona State University. The online survey was conducted from April 18, 2018 to August 7, 2018, with an alert letter, a survey invitation, and multiple follow-ups by email, postcard, and phone. The sampling frame of 2500 was reduced by 54 due to retirements, open positions, and ineligibility. Of the 2476 surveyed, 243 were not contactable due to no or invalid email address or blocked emails, 23 refused to participate, and 621 completed the survey (see Feeney et al., 2018 for detailed response, cooperation, contact, and refusal rates).

RESULTS

For each dataset, we ran a principal component factor analysis with varimax rotation using Stata as the primary exploratory method for scale construction. Principal component factor (PCF) analysis is a useful tool for extracting linear composites and constructing scales of observed variables. PCF weights the responses and combines the questionnaire items into a single component for measuring the concept. Tabachnick and Fidell (2007) suggest that items be correlated at 0.30 or above to be included in a factor analysis. We took a more conservative approach and set it at 0.40 or above with at least one item within each of the three theoretical dimensions. We then reviewed the data for inter-item correlations and ran Bartlett's test of Sphericity and the Kaiser-Meyer-Olkin measure of Sampling Adequacy (KMO) on the data.

Overall, we find that the 12 OIO questionnaire items capture their intended concepts. The four items for individualistic OIO measure consistently load together (Table 22.2). In all four studies, the individualistic OIO items load together into a single factor with values higher than 0.542. They also have strong scale reliability scores, with Cronbach's alphas above 0.69. The four items capturing relational OIO items have factor loadings of 0.702 or higher and

Table 22.2 Factor analysis and scale reliability results for OIO measures

	Pilot 1	Pilot 2	NCSOSP	CSTEPS
Individualistic OIO Measures				
My organization can be described as unique and unlike any other	0.760	0.790	0.670	0.542
My organization emphasizes how different it is from other similar organizations	0.780	0.770	0.790	0.810
My organization considers itself to be 'doing well' when it maintains its distinctiveness from other similar organizations	0.840	0.830	0.840	0.770
My organization is extremely motivated to outshine other similar organizations	0.720	0.800	0.800	0.747
Initial Eigenvalues	2.41	2.56	2.41	2.10
% of variance explained	60.30	64.10	60.21	52.50
Cronbach's Alpha	0.78	0.82	0.78	0.69
Relational OIO Measures				
My organization can be described as warm	0.800	0.820	0.820	0.702
My organization emphasizes the importance of deep interpersonal relationships	0.830	0.860	0.850	0.804
My organization defines success according to how well it treats individual clients, customers, stakeholders or citizens	0.790	n/a	n/a	n/a
My organization is extremely motivated to connect with others in a close and personal way	0.910	0.870	0.790	0.790
My organization considers itself to be 'doing well' when it is able to maintain close relationships with individual clients, customers, citizens or stakeholders	n/a	0.830	0.880	0.748
Initial Eigenvalues	2.78	2.86	2.78	2.32
% of variance explained	69.50	71.53	69.61	58.08
Cronbach's Alpha	0.85	0.87	0.85	0.76
Collectivistic OIO Measures				
My organization can be described as cause-driven	0.780	0.790	0.710	0.697
My organization emphasizes the importance of its affiliation with a group, cause or broader community	0.840	0.760	0.800	0.759
My organization considers itself to be 'doing well' when it advances a larger cause, ideological objective or set of shared values	0.870	n/a	n/a	n/a
My organization is largely concerned with advancing the welfare of a broader community or cause	0.850	n/a	n/a	n/a
My organization considers itself to be 'doing well' when it contributes to the well-being of a broader group, cause or community	n/a	0.900	0.870	0.797
My organization is extremely motivated to advance the welfare of a broader community or cause	n/a	0.910	0.890	0.775
Initial Eigenvalues	2.80	2.84	2.69	2.30
% of variance explained	69.96	71.08	67.28	57.47
Cronbach's Alpha	0.85	0.86	0.83	0.75

Note: Response categories: not at all like my organization, not very much like my organization, somewhat like my organization, very much like my organization, or completely like my organization.

Cronbach's alphas over 0.76, indicating the items reliably capture the same concept. The collectivistic OIO items have factor loadings over 0.697 and Cronbach's alphas at more than 0.75.

Run as separate factor analyses and scale reliability tests, the measures for each OIO concept are reliable and stable (see Langer, 2017 for in-depth results). When run together in a single factor analysis as part of the NCSOSP, the 12 items load onto three distinct factors. However, when we run the 12 questionnaire items together in a single factor analysis in the fourth study, which was administered to a representative sample of local government managers, we find lower factor loadings and some conceptual overlap across the three orientations. The results of the factor analyses of all 12 items for each study are reported in Table 22.3. In the study of local government managers, three of the four individualistic OIO items load on a separate, distinct component with an Eigenvalue of 1.41. One item 'My organization can be described as unique and unlike any other' doesn't load to a single factor and a second item loads at 0.474, which is sufficient, but not strong. Similarly, one item fails to load on the collectivistic factor, 'My organization can be described as cause-driven.' Three of the expected relational items load to a single factor, but the fourth relational questionnaire item 'My organization considers itself to be "doing well" when it is able to maintain close relationships with individual clients, customers, citizens or stakeholders' loads with the collectivistic items. In sum, for the government sample, two items do not load cleanly to a factor and two items indicate some conceptual overlap across the relational and collectivistic factors. Thus, we find some conceptual overlap across the relational and collectivistic OIO questionnaire items in the study of local government managers.

To better understand the overlap across the OIO groupings in the local government dataset, we ran scale reliability tests of the collectivistic, individualistic, and relational items using the local government data. The 12 items combined have a Cronbach's alpha of 0.849 (n = 557). The Cronbach's alpha is not improved by removing a single item. We then ran separate scale reliability tests for the collectivistic, individualistic, and relational OIO items. The four collectivistic items load with a Cronbach's alpha of 0.693. Dropping the item that also did not load well in the factor analysis ('my organization can be described as unique and unlike any other') improves the Cronbach's alpha to 0.719.

The scale reliability test on the four relational items has a Cronbach's alpha of 0.757 (n = 562) and would not be improved by removing one of the four items. The four collectivistic OIO items have a Cronbach's alpha of 0.747 (n = 578) and would not be improved by removing an item. A scale reliability test with the relational and collectivistic items together has a Cronbach's alpha of 0.838 (n = 558), resulting in a higher scale reliability than two separate scales. The higher Cronbach's alpha when the eight items are scaled together may be the function of additional items in the scale or an indicator of conceptual overlap. Separate factor analyses and scale reliability tests show that the relational OIO items create a factor or scale and the collectivistic OIO items make a scale. But a factor analysis of the eight items results in the relational and collectivistic OIO items overlapping and a scale reliability test shows the eight items scale together.

There are multiple potential explanations for these results, which indicate a conceptual overlap (or lack of clear distinction) between the relational and collectivistic OIO items in the analysis of local government managers. This conceptual overlap could be theoretical, empirical, or contextual. The theoretical issue may be that there are not clear theoretical differences between the relational and collectivistic OIO. Are orientations to the relational other—dyadic—and orientation to the collective other—a group or community—theoretically distinct for public managers?

Empirical explanations might include errors in empirical coding of the qualitative data from Brickson's research or poor design from the qualitative language to the questionnaire items. Public and nonprofit sector research focused on testing concepts such as values and

Table 22.3   Factor analysis results for 12 OIO measures

OIO items	Pilot 1 C	Pilot 1 R	Pilot 1 I	Pilot 2 C	Pilot 2 R	Pilot 2 I	NCSOSP C	NCSOSP R	NCSOSP I	CSTEPS C	CSTEPS I	CSTEPS R
My organization can be described as unique and unlike any other	0.231	0.359	*0.543*	0.246	0.346	*0.591*	0.190	0.240	*0.460*	0.038	0.274	0.236
My organization emphasizes how different it is from other similar organizations	0.063	0.192	*0.642*	0.048	0.262	*0.618*	0.080	0.110	*0.650*	0.094	*0.694*	0.107
My organization considers itself to be 'doing well' when it maintains its distinctiveness from other similar organizations	0.274	0.213	*0.713*	0.195	0.151	*0.741*	0.130	0.190	*0.730*	0.293	*0.631*	0.066
My organization is extremely motivated to outshine other similar organizations	−0.101	−0.002	*0.675*	0.097	0.029	*0.729*	0.010	0.090	*0.720*	0.160	*0.474*	0.230
My organization can be described as warm	0.307	*0.612*	0.141	0.284	*0.644*	0.168	0.300	*0.660*	0.070	0.221	0.108	*0.484*
My organization emphasizes the importance of deep interpersonal relationships	0.311	*0.670*	0.162	0.297	*0.745*	0.148	0.270	*0.710*	0.170	*0.435*	0.236	*0.529*
My organization considers itself to be 'doing well' when it is able to maintain close relationships with individual clients, customers, citizens or stakeholders	n/a	n/a	n/a	0.386	*0.599*	0.234	0.370	*0.580*	0.190	*0.608*	0.118	*0.361*
My organization is extremely motivated to connect with others in a close and personal way	0.350	*0.777*	0.189	0.416	*0.719*	0.137	0.390	*0.720*	0.170	0.285	0.098	*0.587*
My organization defines success according to how well it treats individual clients, customers, stakeholders or citizens	0.312	*0.620*	0.131	n/a	n/a	n/a	n/a	n/a	n/a	n/a	n/a	n/a
My organization can be described as cause-driven	*0.621*	0.223	0.233	*0.648*	0.235	0.072	*0.520*	0.220	0.030	0.331	0.217	0.112
My organization emphasizes the importance of its affiliation with a group, cause or broader community	*0.672*	0.343	0.085	*0.565*	0.268	0.138	*0.620*	0.250	0.090	*0.558*	0.241	0.183
My organization considers itself to be 'doing well' when it contributes to the well-being of a broader group, cause or community	n/a	n/a	n/a	*0.817*	0.255	0.169	*0.770*	0.320	0.090	*0.707*	0.173	0.151
My organization is extremely motivated to advance the welfare of a broader community or cause	n/a	n/a	n/a	*0.832*	0.317	0.122	*0.800*	0.290	0.070	*0.430*	0.064	0.274
My organization considers itself to be 'doing well' when it advances a larger cause, ideological objective or set of shared values	*0.756*	0.288	0.119	n/a	n/a	n/a	n/a	n/a	n/a	n/a	n/a	n/a
My organization is largely concerned with advancing the welfare of a broader community or cause	*0.722*	0.365	0.012	n/a	n/a	n/a	n/a	n/a	n/a	n/a	n/a	n/a
Initial Eigenvalues	2.48	2.43	1.85	2.70	2.35	2.00	2.40	2.23	1.82	1.92	1.41	1.26
% of variance explained	39.32	38.49	29.24	36.66	34.52	29.41	40.60	37.64	30.87	40.49	29.78	26.55

Notes:
C = collectivistic, R = relational, I = individualistic.
Response categories: not at all like my organization, not very much like my organization, somewhat like my organization, very much like my organization, or completely like my organization.

identity orientation face common measurement challenges, including sorting overlapping concepts and terms, measuring dynamic concepts (e.g., values, public interest), distinguishing among other-oriented organizations (e.g., public versus nonprofit), and understanding how individual perceptions are related to organizational priorities. Assessing OIO, as with many measures of organizations, relies on individual-level perceptions and reporting. In an ideal world, measuring OIO would include assessments from multiple stakeholders including the organization's employees and leaders; partners, suppliers, and contractors; and consumers, clients, and community members. It is possible that the overlap seen in the local government sample is a function of the empirical limitations of single respondents reporting organizational identity orientation.

A third explanation for the lack of empirical distinction between relational and collectivistic OIO might be the context of local government. Government employees may view relational and collectivist OIO as intertwined. Given the public-serving nature of their work, the focus on both relationships with clients, citizens, constituents, politicians, other government officials, nonprofit service providers, and private sector businesses and collective or community outcomes, it's conceivable that government organizations and managers are less likely to separate relational and collectivistic identity orientation. A final explanation is that the third round of data collection presented here may have suffered from some unknown error related to sampling, measurement, or response bias. Despite these potential limitations, this research offers theoretically grounded, empirically tested questionnaire items that can be used to advance OIO research in public and nonprofit studies.

FUTURE DIRECTIONS FOR OIO RESEARCH AND PRACTICE IN PUBLIC ADMINISTRATION

This research developing 12 quantitative questionnaire items for measuring individualistic, relational, and collectivistic organizational identity orientation offers promise for applying OIO theory to public and nonprofit studies, bringing together individual and organizational-level concepts to understand OIO toward employees, clients, and the communities they serve. OIO can advance research on employee attraction, recruitment, and retention in public and nonprofit research by enabling researchers to align identity orientation across individuals and organizations. OIO can also enable researchers to begin to investigate the ways in which public and nonprofit employees may differ in their perceptions of the organization's identity orientation as compared to those outside of the organization—both taxpayers supporting the organization and clients receiving public goods and services from the organization.

Our research offers a reliable and valid set of questionnaire items that can be applied to varying organizations in the public and nonprofit sectors to investigate questions related to employee motivation, state-client interactions, sector comparisons, and collaborative governance. Future research should aim to further test and validate these measures, while investigating the antecedents and consequences of OIO. Are relational and collectivistic orientations distinct concepts in the public and nonprofit sectors? Do these concepts differentiate among for-profit organizations, but not within government organizations that have less autonomy to relate to stakeholders as they wish or that might prioritize and pursue the two orientations simultaneously? Or, do public and nonprofit organizations have hybrid other-orienting identities?

There are ample opportunities for mixed-methods research in this area. For example, applying Brickson's qualitative approaches inside an organization and the 12 OIO questionnaire items to stakeholders outside the organization. Offering an opportunity to assess OIO from multiple perspectives. Are there better mechanisms for measuring OIO outside of individual reports? Individual reports can be paired with objective coding of mission statements, documents, clientele served and other measures that serve as proxies for organizational identity. Do leaders' views of the organization's identity differ from employee views and how does that relate to performance and employee retention? Do internal assessments of OIO differ or align with stakeholder views of OIO? Are organizations that have stakeholder-aligned OIO more effective at motivating employees and achieving organizational goals? For organizations that have differing OIO assessments as compared to external stakeholders, how does that relate to employee motivation and performance? Because OIO moves beyond organizational culture to capture organizational identity in relation to other stakeholders, it offers an ideal frame for investigating key public administration research questions that center on understanding organizational identity and action that requires diverse stakeholder engagement to solve public problems. The OIO framework is a tool that public and nonprofit researchers can use to advance our understanding of how individual and organizational motivation and identity, public values, and stakeholder relations enhance collaborative governance and public outcomes, especially in times of uncertainty.

NOTE

1. The initial research used simultaneous collection of both qualitative and quantitative data through four questionnaire techniques: (1) an open-ended 10 Statement Test, (2) ranked responses to relational, individualistic, and collectivistic items, (3) Organization as a Person Questions, and (4) a Quantitative Adaptation of the Ten Statements Test. The analysis in this chapter focuses on quantitative adaption of the Ten Statements Test, though initial analysis of the reliability and validity of the items included statistical analysis in relation to the other items in the pilot tests, anchored items related to employee motivation and satisfaction, and demographic characteristics. Results from those analyses are available in Langer (2017).

REFERENCES

Albert, S., and Whetten, D.A. (1985). Organizational identity. *Research in Organizational Behavior, 7*, 263–295.

Bartlett, J., McDonald, P., and Pini, B. (2015). Identity orientation and stakeholder engagement—the corporatisation of elite schools. *Journal of Public Affairs, 15*, 201–209.

Bingham, J.B., Dyer, W.G., Smith, I., and Adams, G.L. (2011). A stakeholder identity orientation approach to corporate social performance in family firms. *Journal of Business Ethics, 99*, 565–585.

Bozeman, B. (2007). *Public values and public interest: Counterbalancing economic individualism*. Washington, DC: Georgetown University Press.

Bozeman, B., and Moulton, S. (2011). Integrative publicness: A framework for public management strategy and performance. *Journal of Public Administration Research and Theory, 21*, i363–i380.

Brewer, M.B., and Gardner, W. (1996). Who is this 'we'? Levels of collective identity and self representations. *Journal of Personality and Social Psychology, 71*, 83–93.

Brickson, S. (2000). The impact of identity orientation on individual and organizational outcomes in demographically diverse settings. *Academy of Management Review, 25*, 82–101.

Brickson, S.L. (2005). Organizational identity orientation: Forging a link between organizational identity and organizations' relations with stakeholders. *Administrative Science Quarterly, 50*, 576–609.

Brickson, S.L. (2007). Organizational identity orientation: The genesis of the role of the firm and distinct forms of social value. *Academy of Management Review, 32*, 864–888.

Brickson, S.L. (2013). Athletes, best friends, and social activists: An integrative model accounting for the role of identity in organizational identification. *Organization Science, 24*, 226–245.

Dutton, J.E., Dukerich, J.M., and Harquail, C.V. (1994). Organizational images and member identification. *Administrative Science Quarterly, 39*, 239–263.

Feeney, M.K., Welch, E., Leonor, C., and Fusi, F. (2018). Open data, participation, and technology use in local government agencies: Findings from a national survey (November 3). Accessed March 1, 2020 at SSRN: http://ssrn.com/abstract=3531275.

Gioia, D.A. (1998). From individual to organizational identity. In D.A. Whetten and P.C. Godfrey (eds), *Foundations for organizational science. Identity in organizations: Building theory through conversations*. Thousand Oaks, CA: Sage, pp. 17–31.

Hatch, M.J., and Schultz, M. (1997). Relations between organizational culture, identity and image. *European Journal of Marketing, 31*, 356–365.

Hatch, M.J., and Schultz, M. (2002). The dynamics of organizational identity. *Human Relations, 55*, 989–1018.

Jørgensen, T.B., and Bozeman, B. (2007). Public values an inventory. *Administration & Society, 39*, 354–381.

Korschun, D. (2015). Boundary-spanning employees and relationships with external stakeholders: A social identity approach. *Academy of Management Review, 40*, 611–629.

Kuhn, M.H., and T. McPortland (1954). An empirical investigation of self attitudes. *American Sociological Review, 19*, 58–76.

Langer, J.A. (2017). Organizational identity and the nature of stakeholder relationships in the blended age of organizing (Order No. 10956941). Available from ProQuest Dissertations and Theses Global (2086083157). Accessed March 12, 2020 at https://www.ulib.niu.edu:2661/docview/2086083157?accountid=12846.

Li, J., Tang, G., and Chen, Y. (2012). Firms' human resource in information system and sustainable performance: Does their organizational identity matter? *The International Journal of Human Resource Management, 23*, 3838–3855.

Netemeyer, R.G., Bearden, W.O., and Sharma, S. (2003). *Scaling procedures: Issues and applications*. Thousand Oaks, CA: Sage.

Ritz, A., Brewer, G.A., and Neumann, O. (2016). Public service motivation: A systematic literature review and outlook. *Public Administration Review, 76*, 414–426.

Scott, S.G., and Lane, V.R. (2000). A stakeholder approach to organizational identity. *Academy of Management Review, 25*, 43–62.

Tabachnick, B.G., and Fidell, L.S. (2007). *Using multivariate statistics* (5th edn). Boston: Allyn and Bacon.

Van der Wal, Z., De Graaf, G., and Lasthuizen, K. (2008). What's valued most? Similarities and differences between the organizational values of the public and private sector. *Public Administration, 86*, 465–482.

Whetten, D.A. (2006). Albert and Whetten revisited: Strengthening the concept of organizational identity. *Journal of Management Inquiry, 15*, 219–234.

Witesman, E. (2016) From public values to public value and back again. Public Values Workshop. Accessed March 4, 2020 at https://cord.asu.edu/sites/default/files/wp-content/uploads/2015/02/2015123001-Public-value-to-public-values-and-back-for-PVC1.pdf.

23. Change-oriented organizational citizenship behavior in public organizations: appropriateness, opportunity, risk, and public service motivation

Jesse W. Campbell

INTRODUCTION

Public service organizations must address performance pressure through a commitment to continuous process improvement. Without change, service performance will stagnate. Public servants are the foundation of public sector performance, and public service providers at all levels have detailed knowledge of the processes and context of public service delivery. Integrating this distributed and localized expertise into the design of public service processes can lead to process and efficiency improvements, and ultimately to more satisfied citizens. However, while organizations that are culturally and structurally conducive to employee proactive behavior can capitalize on employee knowledge, public sector organizations can be subject to powerful forces that limit employee autonomy and heighten the risks of independent initiatives for change. Consequently, even though every public employee has some level of unique insight into their own work situation, public organizations may fail to utilize this resource, and thereby fail to reach their potential.

This chapter focuses on change-oriented organizational citizenship behavior (OCB) in a public organizational setting. Change-oriented OCB denotes proactive and voluntary employee efforts to improve work processes and is vital to the long-term performance of organizations (Bettencourt, 2004; Morrison and Phelps, 1999). Change-oriented OCB has particular significance for public service organizations, however, which often have the reputation of being poor performers, especially compared to market-based organizations (Hvidman and Andersen, 2016; Marvel, 2015). Through improving service quality, change-oriented OCB can help public organizations more directly address the needs of citizens, build trust, and ultimately help them shed their image as indifferent to performance and unresponsive to citizens (Campbell, 2015; Vigoda-Gadot and Beeri, 2012).

Although change-oriented OCB is a critical factor in public service performance, cultivating a change-oriented workforce is a challenge. Importantly, unlike performance expectations that are written into a job description or public service contract, change-oriented OCB is discretionary and does not constitute a component of an employee's formal responsibilities (Morrison and Phelps, 1999). Although the organization may benefit substantially from change-oriented initiatives, their discretionary status entails that individual employees can have few positive incentives to engage in them. More than this, change-oriented OCB represents a challenge to the established way of doing things, and therefore its pursuit can involve non-trivial risks for the focal employee (Bergeron and Thompson, 2020; Van Dyne and LePine, 1998). Because of the discretionary, high-risk, and low benefit nature of change-oriented OCB, employees may pursue independent change-oriented initiatives only in specific conditions.

While a number of theoretical lenses have been adopted to study change-oriented OCB, many draw upon the original expectancy-based framework proposed by Morrison and Phelps (1999), who suggest that the decision to engage in change-oriented OCB is based on a rational calculation of costs, benefits, and consequences. In this chapter, I develop this perspective, arguing that an organization's culture, structure, and interpersonal dynamics each play a distinct role in determining whether change-oriented OCB occurs. Additionally, building on the enduring belief that change-oriented OCB is driven by both contextual and individual factors, I focus on the potential of public service motivation (PSM) (Perry and Wise, 1990) to act as a countervailing force for change in unfavorable organizational contexts. Studies on PSM have consistently linked the construct to important outcomes such as job satisfaction, commitment, and performance (Ritz, Brewer, and Neumann, 2016). However, PSM is also associated with resolute public service commitment in challenging conditions (Campbell and Im, 2016a; Coursey, Yang, and Pandey, 2012; Perry and Vandenabeele, 2008; Potipiroon and Faerman, 2020), and a few studies have now made the link between PSM and change-oriented behavior (Campbell and Im, 2016b; Hassan et al., 2020). I argue that employees driven by PSM may view change-oriented OCB in an instrumental manner, draw upon an internal attribution of organizational control to generate opportunities to engage in it, and discount the personal risks involved if they believe the public can benefit. In short, the greater degree to which the service values associated with PSM are involved in the decision to engage in change-oriented OCB, the more likely will the cost-benefit and risk-reward ratio encourage it.

The remainder of this chapter is organized as follows. First, I introduce the concept of change-oriented OCB, distinguishing it from both formal performance and affiliative types of citizenship behavior. I then provide an organizational model of change-oriented OCB, reviewing existing literature in order to isolate causal factors in the cultural, structural, and interpersonal makeup of the organization. In this section, I describe how certain features of the public organizational context can disincentivize change-oriented OCB. Next, I briefly introduce PSM and discuss how higher levels of PSM are likely to be linked to change-oriented OCB, particularly in unfavorable organizational contexts. I close by discussing the proposed model and suggesting a number of ways that change-oriented OCB may come to play a more important role in public sector research.

CHANGE-ORIENTED OCB: CONCEPT, CAUSES, AND IMPORTANCE IN PUBLIC ORGANIZATIONS

The Nature of Change-oriented OCB

Employees contribute to the performance of their organization in different ways (Katz and Kahn, 1978). Formal or 'in role' behaviors refer to those behaviors that are specified in a given employee's contract or job description. The written form of these expectations partly makes up the organization's formal structure and are a foundation of organizational performance. If employees imperfectly fulfill their job responsibilities and fail to meet performance standards, the performance of the organization will decline.

At the same time, formal employee performance does not exhaust the range of behaviors that are relevant to the organization. For all but the simplest jobs, and perhaps even in these cases, it is impossible for written contracts and job descriptions to capture the full range of relevant job behaviors required from employees, and all contracts are therefore necessarily incomplete. The behaviors necessary for organizational functioning and performance that are unspecified in contracts or job descriptions are referred to as informal, extra role, or, as I will refer to them in this chapter, organizational citizenship behaviors (OCB). Initiated by Dennis Organ and colleagues (Organ, 1988, 1997), there is now a substantial body of empirical research on OCB that details its ubiquity as well as its impact on organizational performance. Organ (1988, p. 4) defined OCB as having three components: it is discretionary, it is not recognized by the reward system, and it contributes (in aggregate) to organizational effectiveness. OCB has also received a good deal of attention from public sector researchers and has been linked with a number of concepts central to this area of study (de Geus et al., 2020).

There remains debate about the number and types of OCB, with the initial formulation of the construct containing behaviors related to sportsmanship, civic virtue, courtesy, and others (Organ, Podsakoff, and MacKenzie, 2005). Williams and Anderson (1991) provide a simplified taxonomy with OCB behaviors grouped based on whether they benefit the organization itself (such as when employees are willing to tolerate inconveniences or make efforts to stay informed about the organization beyond what is specifically necessary for their work) or its employees (voluntarily helping colleagues, providing informal training, etc.). Both types of OCB support existing operational forms and are sometimes referred to as 'affiliative' forms of OCB (Van Dyne and LePine, 1998). These behaviors contribute to the performance of the organization but, because they are not specified explicitly in job descriptions, often go unrewarded.

Change-oriented OCB denotes employee behaviors that aim to improve micro-level work processes through the introduction of productivity enhancing change (Morrison and Phelps, 1999). Like affiliative types of OCB, change-oriented OCB contributes to the performance of the organization. Not specified in the employment contract or job description, it is also discretionary and may go unrewarded. The critical difference between change-oriented OCB and its affiliative cousins is the essentially challenging nature of change-oriented behaviors. Rather than simply supporting current operational formats, change-oriented OCB seeks to modify them. Challenging the status quo, even when doing so will lead to performance improvement, can be a source of conflict for the challenger, and change-oriented OCB, unlike affiliative OCB, is primarily a disruptive force within the organization (Campbell, 2020b; Van Dyne and LePine, 1998). Nevertheless, much like affiliative OCB, without change-oriented initiatives on the part of employees, organizations may fail to adapt to changing circumstances, both within the organization and in the environment, and will ultimately face a decline in performance. Consequently, understanding the factors that facilitate change-oriented OCB may be critical for an organization's medium to long-term viability.

Figure 23.1 shows the relationships between formal job performance, classic OCB, and change-oriented OCB. Because change-oriented OCB is neither measured nor incentivized, and moreover because it is among the most high-risk organizational behaviors, its likelihood of enactment is lower than both classic, affiliative OCB or formal performance.

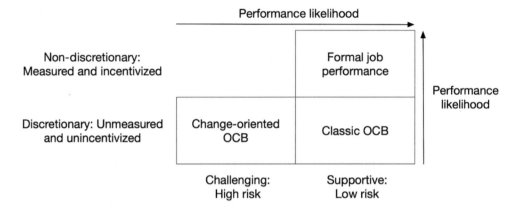

Figure 23.1   Formal performance, classic OCB, and change-oriented OCB

CHANGE-ORIENTED OCB IN PUBLIC ORGANIZATIONS

The context of public management is often characterized by both performance pressure and resource scarcity. Although some of the enthusiasm for the private sector-based reform initiatives typical of the New Public Management philosophy has evaporated, the imperative to continually improve the performance of public service delivery and other public sector processes remains. Improving the performance of public service provision through the implementation of change is fundamental to the managerial approach to public administration and is a key challenge for public organizations. By cultivating an organizational atmosphere and incentive system that motivates employees to engage in change-oriented OCB, public organizations can enhance citizen satisfaction and support (Vigoda-Gadot and Beeri, 2012).

Some performance improvement can be obtained through top-down reforms that impact the overall structure and operations of public sector organizations. However, due to their discretion, public employees at all levels have opportunities to frustrate change initiatives, and for many changes it is necessary to secure their participation in order to overcome resistance (Fernandez and Rainey, 2006). Moreover, real knowledge about the operations of public service organizations, and, therefore, how to improve operational effectiveness, is possessed by public employees, and sometimes those at relatively low positions in the organizational hierarchy. Public services are intangible and consumed at the point of production, and though the types of services that a given organization is mandated to provide are written into law, their objective character will vary greatly, even to the point that the same service is never provided identically twice (Osborne, 2013). This great variation entails that those implementing public services have knowledge about the performance of public service delivery that is of a different type than their managers or organization leaders, and also the discretion to act on it. On the other hand, while frontline worker and middle management-initiated change is not uncommon in the public sector (Borins, 2002), research on the change-oriented behavior of frontline public sector employees is not highly developed.

Change-oriented OCB contributes to the formal performance of the organization and performance improvement through change can be analyzed within a rational framework. In an idealized case, a change-oriented initiative may begin with the focal employee breaking down their work process into discrete steps and evaluating the efficiency of each relative to the overall task goal. If one of the steps in the process can be modified such that the overall efficiency of the process increases, the employee implements the change. As more employees go through this process over time, the efficiency of the entire organization enjoys incremental improvements.

Although the worn view of public service organizations as conservative, lacking in initiative, and generally out of touch with the needs of their clients provides at best an incomplete picture, public managers and their subordinates do face significant, structural disincentives inhibiting a fully results and change-driven approach (Behn, 2002). The clean description of the change-oriented OCB process above leaves out a distinctive lack of positive incentives for change, and glosses over the potentially significant disincentives that would-be change agents face in public organizations. It also says nothing about how the structural characteristics of public organizations, which can be more bureaucratic than those of private sector organizations, can eliminate opportunities for change-oriented OCB. If change-oriented OCB is deemed inappropriate, costly, or simply impossible by employees, it is unlikely to occur.

ORGANIZATIONAL CONTEXT AND CHANGE-ORIENTED OCB: CULTURE, STRUCTURE, AND INTERPERSONAL DYNAMICS

The empirical literature on change-oriented OCB in both the public and private sectors has focused on factors at the cultural, structural, and interpersonal levels of organizations. I review this literature below. To frame the discussion, I present the following model (Figure 23.2). In the figure, the culture, structure, and interpersonal dynamics of the organization interact

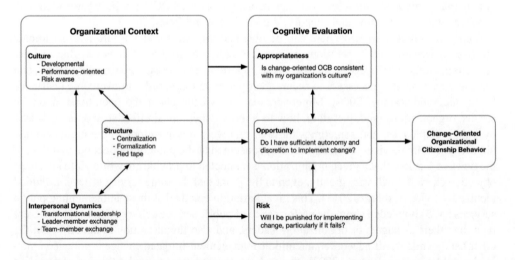

Figure 23.2   *An organizational model of change-oriented organizational citizenship behavior*

to determine the perceived appropriateness of, opportunity for, and risk associated with change-oriented OCB.

Organizational Culture

Organizational culture is a broad concept that captures the intersubjective understanding of an organization's practices, values, symbols, ideologies, and other intangible features (Alvesson, 2012). Culture is built on the assumption that organizational members, through exposure to the same phenomena over time, come to have a shared understanding of the organization (Ostroff, Kinicki, and Muhummad, 2012). Culture furnishes the normative context of the organization and thereby acts as a framework within which an employee can evaluate the appropriateness and legitimacy of potential behaviors. Cultures that place an emphasis on change, development, and results are likely to facilitate change-oriented OCB by communicating to employees that such actions are appropriate and valued by the organization. Cultures wherein adherence to established processes is prioritized communicates to employees that risk-taking and independent change-oriented initiatives will be viewed with disfavor.

A developmental culture is associated with employee beliefs that change is desirable and change-oriented initiatives are legitimate. Developmental cultures emphasize adaptability and growth and research suggests that employees working in organizations with developmental cultures take proactive actions to mitigate some of the performance undermining constraints of the public sector job context (Bozeman and Kingsley, 1998; Pandey, Coursey, and Moynihan, 2007). A developmental organizational culture tends to focus employee attention on results and facilitates risk-taking by organizational members (Langer and LeRoux, 2017; Moynihan and Pandey, 2010). When change and growth are emphasized by leaders, employees may be able to draw upon a logic of appropriateness to justify change-oriented initiatives.

A developmental culture is linked to an organization's performance orientation (Yang and Kassekert, 2010). A strong performance orientation promotes the intersubjective belief that the organization and its members will be held accountable and rewarded (or sanctioned) for their performance. In a performance-oriented organization, results, rather than the vigor with which employees adhere to organizational rules and standardized procedures, are the primary criteria by which behavior is evaluated. A strong performance orientation conveys to employees that results are relatively more important than procedural compliance. Channels of value communication may be informal, or they may be embedded in the organization's performance management and reward systems. Organization-level performance management processes help make salient and clarify organizational goals for employees, which in turn provides a framework in which potential change-oriented behavior can be evaluated. At the individual level, performance pay and other results-based incentives provide one of the few positive incentives for engaging in change-oriented OCB, as change-oriented initiatives that improve individual performance may indirectly result in rewards (Campbell, 2015).

Not all public organizations are change, development, and results oriented. The political context of public management can lead to conservative, process-oriented modes of decision making, which are necessary for survival (Behn, 2002). Risk averse cultures, which emphasize control and adherence to procedural rules (Bozeman and Kingsley, 1998), cannot tolerate change-oriented behavior by employees. Some evidence suggests that risk averse individuals sort into public sector jobs (Buurman et al., 2012) and, as Chen and Bozeman (2012) note, in the aggregate these risk averse individuals can influence an organization's overall level of risk aversion. Change-oriented OCB is inherently risky, a feature that will be more salient in risk averse organizational cultures. Consequently, whereas developmental, performance-oriented cultures may motivate change-oriented OCB, risk averse organizations will discourage it.

Organizational Structure

Organizational structure consists in the written rules, standardized procedures, and distribution of formal power within the organization. These formal elements are designed and used to coordinate the actions of organizational members towards the achievement of organizational goals. While all organizations have a formal dimension, the design, scope, and rigidity of a given organization's formal structure can be a key factor determining the frequency of change-oriented OCB by its members.

The degree of centralization is a core component of organizational structure (Andrews et al., 2009). In general, the degree of centralization is inversely correlated with the number and scope of decisions that are made at lower levels of the organizational hierarchy. Without sufficient discretion and autonomy, employees will lack the flexibility to try out new ideas (Cai et al., 2019; Cerit, 2017; Marinova et al., 2015; Marinova, Cao, and Park, 2019), and, consequently, more centralization will be related to less change-oriented OCB. Organizational leaders, because they are structurally isolated from operations at lower levels of the hierarchy while also being responsible for them, may seek to impose rules and procedures upon subordinates that constrain behavior (Bozeman and Rainey, 1998; Thompson, 1977). Public organizations can also operate in turbulent environments, where political factors induce goal ambiguity and encourage public managers to rely on centralized instruments of behavioral control (Stazyk and Goerdel, 2011). Even though lower-level employees may be able to clearly understand the inefficiencies associated with these controls and have ideas about how to improve them, they will lack the autonomy to do so. However, centralization can also have second order effects that may undermine the possibility of change-oriented OCB by creating ambiguity for employees about how their work is connected to organizational goals (Pandey and Wright, 2006), which will in turn make it more difficult to evaluate the potential productivity impact of a given change. These first and second order effects make change-oriented OCB less likely in centralized organizations.

Formalization and job routinization are additional aspects of organizational structure related to change-oriented OCB. Formalization, or the extent to which job behaviors are predetermined by written rules and other formal aspects of the organization (Marinova et al., 2015), can reduce the opportunities for individuals to engage in change-oriented behavior. Change-oriented OCB requires a certain degree of operational flexibility, and if processes and procedures are written down in minute detail (details which, in the public sector, often have their basis in law), employees will have little scope to implement change. High levels of formalization were long ago identified by Burns and Stalker (1961) as being characteristic of organizations with low levels of innovation (i.e., mechanistic organizations). Similarly, formalization is negatively correlated with leadership behaviors linked to subordinate change-oriented OCB (van der Voet, Kuipers, and Groeneveld, 2016). Employees are less likely to break formalized rules, even when doing so will be of direct benefit to clients (Piatak, Mohr, and McDonald, 2020), and we generally expect that formalization will be inversely associated with change-oriented OCB.

Particularly relevant to public organizations is the phenomenon of red tape, which refers to rules and processes that entail a compliance burden for the organization but contribute little to its legitimate goals (Bozeman, 1993). Red tape is associated with the formal structure of the organization, including levels of centralization and formalization (Bozeman and Scott, 1996; Kaufmann and Feeney, 2012; Kaufmann, Borry, and DeHart-Davis, 2019), and may be related to change-oriented behavior in different ways. On the one hand, an organization burdened by red tape has many opportunities to improve operations, and, therefore, many opportunities for employees to engage in change-oriented behavior. Overcoming red tape has also been proposed as one of the most important goals of change-oriented OCB in the public sector (Vigoda-Gadot and Beeri, 2012), and search and innovation can mitigate the impact of red tape on performance (Walker and Brewer, 2009). However, because the origins of red tape are often external to the organization (e.g., imposed upon it by a legislature seeking to exert control (Behn, 1995)), or, for lower-level employees, red tape may be imposed upon them by their superiors, employees may have little scope to make changes. Altogether, red tape can be understood to have both a 'push' and 'pull' relationship with change-oriented behavior (Moon and Bretschneider, 2002), and more research can help us understand the probable relationship between red tape and change-oriented OCB.

Interpersonal Dynamics: Leaders, Managers, Supervisors, and Coworkers

The social context of the organization is an important medium through which employees learn about the appropriateness and risks associated with change-oriented behaviors. Organizational communications flow along both vertical and horizontal channels and can travel both by formal and informal mediums (Campbell, 2020b; Williams and Bland, 2020). Although formal authority is vested in those situated at higher echelons of the organization, members of a given employee's workgroup, though lacking in formal power, can also affect organizational behavior. Like organizational culture, the interpersonal context of the organization can provide a powerful normative framework in which potential change efforts can be evaluated.

Leadership behavior has been the most studied interpersonal factor in empirical research on change-oriented OCB. Leaders at all levels of the organizational hierarchy represent the organization in some capacity and communicate (or fail to communicate) its goals and values. Leaders and supervisors can communicate the appropriateness of change-oriented behavior, provide (or withhold) appropriate feedback, and extend (or deny) the necessary levels of discretion to implement change (Ruck, Welch, and Menara, 2017; Townsend, Dundon, and Loudoun, 2015). Some changes introduced by employees will inevitably result in failure, and leaders may also act in ways that make subordinates believe they will be punished for (failed) change-oriented initiatives (Lebel and Patil, 2018; Zeng, Zhao, and Zhao, 2020). Leadership is also closely linked with organizational justice climate (Ehrhart, 2004), which encourages change-oriented OCB (Fuchs, 2011; Ha et al., 2020).

Leadership behavior varies greatly, and a variety of leadership behaviors have been linked to change-oriented OCB in both the public and private sector empirical literature. These include empowering (Fernandez and Moldogaziev, 2013; Qian et al., 2018; Zhang et al., 2020), inclusive (Li, Guo, and Wan, 2019; Zeng, Zhao, and Zhao, 2020), transformational (Campbell, 2018; do Nascimento, Porto, and Kwantes, 2018; Homberg, Vogel, and Weiherl, 2019; López-Domínguez et al., 2013), and ethical (Wang et al., 2020) leader behaviors. Additionally, leader-member exchange (LMX), which captures the quality and intensity of the superior-subordinate interpersonal relationship in the individual case, has been shown to be a consistent predictor of change-oriented OCB in both private (Bettencourt, 2004; Cerit, 2017; Van Dyne, Kamdar, and Joireman, 2008; Yang, 2017) and public organizations (Garg and Dhar, 2017; Ha et al., 2020; Park and Jun, 2018; Vigoda-Gadot and Beeri, 2011).

While the interpersonal dynamic of the organization can encourage change-oriented OCB, it can also heighten the risks associated with it. Organizational politics is an interpersonal phenomenon which captures the extent to which individuals use their influence in the organization to pursue their self-interests rather than organizational goals (Randall et al., 1999; Vigoda-Gadot, 2007), and the strength of this phenomenon can undermine change-oriented initiatives (Bergeron and Thompson, 2020; Yang, 2017). On the surface level, high levels of organizational politics likely heighten the risk of engaging in change-oriented behaviors, especially when such behaviors are more likely to fail. In highly politicized organizations, opportunities for punishment are seen as occasions to 'score points' and advance one's career at the expense of others. Such organizations lack any collectively felt obligation to improve performance. However, organizations with a culture characterized by high levels of politics also present to employees alternative means by which to advance their careers.

Rather than improving performance through change-oriented initiatives, what discretion and influence employees have in politicized organizations may be channeled towards initiatives that specifically benefit them, rather than the organization. Finally, information secured through vertical chains of communication tends to have a certain authority associated with it, and therefore is important in shaping whether employees will consider change-oriented OCB appropriate or too risky. However, in public organizations, employees seldom work in isolation, and workgroup culture as well as informal communication between workgroup members can be a powerful determinant of change-oriented OCB. Moreover, while leaders and supervisors can provide job-relevant feedback to subordinates, others in the same workgroup have tasks that are likely to be similar, and therefore other employees can be a valuable source of ideas (Campbell, 2016). At the same time, high levels of accord in a workgroup can also dissuade individuals from engaging in change-oriented OCB, as employees may be reluctant to behave in ways that can undermine personal relationships (Campbell, 2020b). In a more serious case, as change-oriented OCB is a challenge to the status quo, employees that engage in it can expose themselves to workplace aggression and bullying by their peers (Liang and Yeh, 2019).

A PUBLIC SERVICE MOTIVATION-BASED MODEL OF CHANGE-ORIENTED OCB FOR PUBLIC ORGANIZATIONS

Although contextual factors are an important driver of change-oriented OCB, such factors do not exhaust the causal basis for discretionary change initiatives, as even in the same organization, all employees do not engage in change-oriented OCB at the same rate. As such, models of change-oriented OCB often integrate individual-level direct and moderating factors including proactive personality (Marinova et al., 2015) and risk aversion (Li, Zhang, and Tian, 2016). Next, I discuss the potential importance of PSM as an individual-level trait relevant specifically to change-oriented OCB in public organizations. PSM has been linked directly with change-oriented OCB (Campbell and Im, 2016b; Homberg, Vogel, and Weiherl, 2019) and related constructs such as innovative behavior (Miao, 2018), acceptance of change (Wright,

Chritensen, and Isett, 2013), and felt responsibility for change (Campbell, 2020b). The private sector literature has also linked concepts related to PSM, including prosocial motivation (Cai et al., 2019; Lebel and Patil, 2018), to change-oriented OCB. I discuss both the direct relationship between PSM and change-oriented OCB as well as the possibility for PSM to act as a pro-change force in unfavorable contexts.

PSM and Change-oriented OCB

Since the 1990s, PSM has become the dominant framework for discussing motivation in the public sector. PSM captures an individual's proclivity to respond to the unique incentives associated with public sector organizations or public institutions more broadly (Perry and Wise, 1990; Ritz, Brewer, and Neumann, 2016). Generally, the PSM concept arose as a response to the public choice perspective that individuals are motivated predominantly by self-interest and will attempt in all instances to maximize their own utility. The PSM perspective does not deny rational self-interest, but rather also argues that some individuals have strong service motives and are concerned with whether and to what extent they can contribute to society. Working in public sector organizations can be understood as a means by which to satisfy this need (Perry and Wise, 1990; Ritz, 2011).

Theory suggests that PSM will be directly related to change-oriented OCB as it can specifically address the lack of incentives for engaging in change initiatives (Campbell and Im, 2016b). Due to its discretionary nature, change-oriented OCB generally goes unrewarded, even though it benefits the organization. PSM-driven employees, however, are concerned with the performance of their organization, and are willing to exert considerable effort on its behalf (even while receiving no individual reward) when they perceive the organization to have a public service efficacy (Bellé, 2013; van Loon et al., 2018). As cited above, in addition to being related to (effort-mediated) performance, PSM has also been linked to change-oriented behavior in various ways.

PSM and Change-oriented OCB in Unfavorable Organizational Contexts

While the empirical literature suggests that organizational context—culture, structure, and interpersonal dynamics—can shape change-oriented OCB in the average case, PSM may have the largest impact on change-oriented OCB precisely when the organizational context is unfavorable. Drawing on social cognitive theory (Bandura, 1991), Perry and Vandenabeele (2008) suggest that PSM can furnish individuals with an internal service-oriented standard against which potential behaviors can be judged. When public service identities become situationally activated, PSM values may become the dominant self-regulatory force, even at personal cost. Consistent with this, numerous studies have documented how PSM can insulate employees from organizational stressors (Bakker, 2015; Campbell, Im, and Jeong, 2014; Liu, Yang, and Yu, 2015; Shim, Park, and Eom, 2017; Sun, Wu, and Chen, 2019), and can also act as a buffer against the emotionally deleterious effect of sustained individual initiative (Potipiroon and Faerman, 2020). As such, while favorable organizational contexts do not require the activation of service-based values to produce change-oriented OCB, employees driven by PSM, drawing upon an alternative, internal, and autonomous public service standard, may choose to pursue them even when such conditions are lacking.

Table 23.1 The effect of PSM on change-oriented OCB in unfavorable organizational contexts

Unfavorable organizational context for change-oriented OCB	Self-regulatory effect of PSM
A risk averse culture frames change-oriented OCB as inappropriate	Framing of change-oriented OCB as instrumentally beneficial
A mechanistic organizational structure reduces the opportunities for change-oriented OCB	Perception of organizational autonomy as internally determined
A politicized interpersonal dynamic increases the personal risk of engaging in change-oriented OCB	Willingness to bear personal risk for the benefit of the public

Table 23.1 shows the framework I use for analyzing the effect of PSM on change-oriented OCB in unfavorable organizational contexts.

The appropriateness of engaging in change-oriented OCB is shaped by organizational culture. Cultures that frame change-oriented behaviors as appropriate and desirable make them more likely, whereas cultures that frame change-oriented OCB as undesirable make them less so. However, even when culture makes change-oriented OCB less likely for the average employee, employees with high levels of PSM may still engage in it.

Such employees understand their organizations as an instrument with which to benefit the public, which they in turn have a strong interest in doing. Even if a given organization has a culture that discourages change-oriented behavior, if a PSM-driven employee sees an opportunity to improve public service through change, they may draw upon a 'logic of consequence' rather than a logic of appropriateness and pursue it. Rational motives to engage in public service have been part of PSM theory since its inception (Perry and Wise, 1990), and, to the extent that employees with high levels of PSM understand public organizations as instruments of public service, this view will serve as a counterweight to a culture that discourages individual change-oriented OCB.

Second, organizational structure can determine whether or not the employee sees the opportunity to engage in change-oriented OCB. Organizations that have an organic structure, where employees are encouraged to contribute broadly to the mission of the organization, provide the autonomy necessary to enact change-oriented behaviors. In contrast, centralized organizations with high levels of formalization and red tape provide fewer opportunities for employees to engage in change-oriented OCB. However, Scott and Pandey (2005) argue that PSM will be associated with a tendency to understand organizational circumstances from a perspective of internal rather than external control. This internal attribution will be related to an understanding of structure as a legitimate phenomenon, but also as something over which the individual exercises a degree of control.

As a practical consequence, they suggest that PSM-driven employees will be better able to cope with the sometimes-restrictive structural realities of public organizations in order to pursue their goals. Individuals will react differently to aspects of organizational structure, and some research shows that structure can interact with PSM in order to determine levels of proactive work behaviors (Luu, 2018).

Third, as explained above, even though the organization benefits from change-oriented OCB, the employees engaging in it may not. As such, from an individual utility maximization perspective, there are few positive incentives to induce change-oriented OCB (Campbell, 2015). However, not only does change-oriented OCB generally go unrewarded, it also carries with it significant risks which are borne entirely by the potential change agent. As suggested above, the interpersonal context of the organization can be a major source of risk for the focal employee. Specifically, if the interpersonal context is highly politicized, and leaders, managers, and coworkers engage with one another in bad faith and seek to use any personal influence to further their individual interests, individual employees may perceive the personal risks of engaging in change-oriented behavior to be prohibitive. However, central to PSM theory is the notion that PSM-driven employees, when working in organizations that directly contribute to the public good, are willing to take on personal sacrifice in order to further the interests of the organization. Although politicized organizational contexts increase the personal risks of engaging in change-oriented OCB for individual employees, an employee motivated by PSM may be more willing to take on such risk as the benefits of doing so will ultimately benefit the organization and its clients.

DISCUSSION AND CONCLUSION

Change-oriented organizational citizenship behavior can help public organizations adapt to evolving environmental conditions, mitigate resource scarcity, assimilate promising technologies, and combat the perception of public servants as indifferent to the real needs of citizens (Vigoda-Gadot and Beeri, 2012). This chapter discussed the nature of change-oriented OCB and the factors that make such behavior more or less likely in the public organizational context. Despite its real and varied benefits, there are significant barriers to pursuing change-oriented OCB in the public sector. Factors related to the cultural, structural, and interpersonal levels of organizational experience together determine the appropriateness of, opportunities for, and risks associated with change-oriented OCB. However, even in organizational contexts that discourage change-oriented OCB, public employees with high levels of PSM may still engage in change-oriented behaviors due to their instrumental manner of understanding their organization, an internal attribution of behavioral control, and, finally, a willingness to take on personal sacrifice in order to further the ends of public service organizations. In this final section, I discuss a number of questions for future study relevant to change-oriented OCB in the public sector.

First, the importance of change-oriented OCB for public organizations has been recognized and its antecedents have been studied in public organizations. However, while some studies make connections between change-oriented OCB and the specific nature of organizational behavior in the public sector, there are many potential links for future research to pursue. For example, while there is much in common between the public and private sector managerial context, one of the main determinants of the peculiarities of public sector organizations is the specific environment in which these organizations operate (Boyne, 2002). Levels of political salience and support are related to the internal structure of public organizations (Pandey and Wright, 2006), and managers may adopt instruments of organizational control that stifle change-oriented behavior in the face of ambiguous goals (Stazyk and Goerdel, 2011). Better linking up the structure and culture of public organizations with their environment can help form the foundation of a middle range theory of change-oriented OCB for public organizations that is currently lacking in the literature.

Similarly, future studies on change-oriented OCB should grapple more with the complex nature of performance in public sector organizations. Unlike business organizations, which can optimize for profit generation, public sector organizations must consider not only efficiency but also effectiveness, equity, accountability, transparency, and other factors in the course of organizational decision making. Unfortunately, sometimes these values can come into conflict, with actions that improve performance in one area undermining it in another (Campbell, 2020a). These different values can be more or less salient in a given situation and it may be the case that public servants are willing to engage in change-oriented OCB in the service of certain values more than others. Or, perhaps more pertinently, value conflict may itself be a significant obstacle to the initiation of change-oriented initiatives in the public sector. Change-oriented OCB has until now generally been understood as a means by which to enhance the efficiency of organizations. However, accounting for the more complex nature of performance in public organizations can help ground the concept more authentically in the public sector setting.

One additional area of study relates to the broader societal context of public administration and how various aspects of culture, such as the expectations that citizens project onto public organizations, may be relevant. Like most topics in public administration, studies on change-oriented OCB and related constructs have been carried out primarily in the Western context. And, while some studies have used data from countries outside the Western cultural sphere, these have not explicitly explored the relationship between cultural institutions and change-oriented behavior. Moreover, the interpersonal dimension of public organizations is likewise shaped to an extent by culture (Perlow, Gittell, and Katz, 2004), and constructs such as power distance or collectivism may also shape the risks associated with change-oriented OCB and the perception that change-oriented initiatives are appropriate and legitimate. Future studies that incorporate broader cultural considerations will ultimately help integrate the change-oriented OCB concept better into a comparative framework.

Next, this study focused on the effect of organizational context, conceptualizing PSM as a countervailing force for change-oriented OCB in unfavorable conditions. However, although the model of change-oriented OCB in this study is explicitly aimed at *public* organizations, it is important to understand the nature of public in its relevance to the topic. Specifically, the theoretical assumption underlying the moderating force of PSM is not actually whether the organization is public or private, but whether or not the organization is perceived to contribute to the public good. Perry and Vandenabeele's (2008) position implies that it is not whether an organization is technically public that matters in whether PSM becomes an active force in decision making and behavior. Rather, it is the extent to which the employee believes that the organization is contributing to the public good. Non-government organizations also contribute to the public good, and PSM is not the exclusive right of public sector workers. As such, we would expect that PSM may act as a force for change-oriented OCB in any organization that is perceived to contribute to the public good, but not necessarily in every public organization.

Relatedly, just as PSM is not exclusive to public sector workers, neither will all public sector workers be driven by public values (Campbell and Im, 2019; Tang and Liu, 2011). Even though PSM has served as the foundation for motivational research in public organizations now for several decades, other relevant individual-level concepts should not be ignored if they are useful in understanding behavior in public organizations. One potentially fruitful research path relates to the extent to which a given employee identifies with the organization itself rather than its policies or mission. Organizational identification theory suggests that an individual's membership in a given organization can become part of their self-concept and, when it does, the employee will assess the successes of the organization as their own (Ashforth and Mael, 1989; Pratt, 1998). Like PSM, organizational identification provides a solution to the motivational puzzle of change-oriented OCB as identified employees are motivated to contribute to the success of the organization (Campbell, 2015), and the construct has been connected both to PSM and OCB in public organizations (Shim and Faerman, 2017). PSM is undoubtedly an important factor when public identities are salient. However, this is not always the case, and it is unwise to rely exclusively on PSM as a means to improve public sector performance through change.

Change-oriented OCB is a valuable but potentially rare species of organizational behavior in the public sector and understanding the contextual and individual factors that encourage or prevent change-oriented initiatives at all levels of the organization is a valid research goal. At the same time, due to the complex nature of values at play in public organizations, the desire for change and continuous improvement needs to be balanced against the need for transparency, accountability, inclusiveness, and other legitimate dimensions of public sector performance. Organizations are systems and the impact of any non-trivial change will seldom be limited to its immediate context of implementation. Rules and procedures that undermine efficiency may serve less salient but nevertheless valuable goals, and as such increasing efficiency in all cases will not necessarily result in a real performance gain. Consequently, integrating change-oriented OCB authentically into the public sector research agenda will require reconciling it with the multi-dimensional nature of performance in public organizations.

REFERENCES

Alvesson, M. (2012). *Understanding Organizational Culture*. Thousand Oaks, CA: Sage.

Andrews, R., Boyne, G.A., Law, J., and Walker, R.M. (2009). Centralization, organizational strategy, and public service performance. *Journal of Public Administration Research and Theory*, *19*(1), 57–80.

Ashforth, B.E., and Mael, F. (1989). Social identity theory and the organization. *Academy of Management Review*, *14*(1), 20–39.

Bakker, A.B. (2015). A Job Demands–Resources Approach to Public Service Motivation. *Public Administration Review*, *75*, 723–732.

Bandura, A. (1991). Social Cognitive Theory of Self-regulation. Organizational Behavior and Human Decision Processes. *Organizational Behavior and Human Decision Processes*, *50*, 248–287.

Behn, R.D. (1995). The Big Questions of Public Management. *Public Administration Review*, *55*, 313–324.

Behn, R.D. (2002). The Psychological Barriers to Performance Management: Or Why Isn't Everyone Jumping on the Performance-management Bandwagon? *Public Performance and Management Review*, *26*, 5–25.

Bellé, N. (2013). Experimental Evidence on the Relationship between Public Service Motivation and Job Performance. *Public Administration Review*, *73*, 143–153.

Bergeron, D.M., and Thompson, P.S. (2020). Speaking Up at Work: The Role of Perceived Organizational Support in Explaining the Relationship between Perceptions of Organizational Politics and Voice Behavior. *The Journal of Applied Behavioral Science*, *56*, 195–215.

Bettencourt, L.A. (2004). Change-oriented Organizational Citizenship Behaviors: The Direct and Moderating Influence of Goal Orientation. *Journal of Retailing*, *80*, 165–180.

Borins, S. (2002). Leadership and Innovation in the Public Sector. *Leadership and Organization Development Journal*, *23*, 467–476.

Boyne, G.A. (2002). Public and Private Management: What's the Difference? *Journal of Management Studies*, *39*, 97–122.

Bozeman, B. (1993). A Theory of Government 'Red Tape.' *Journal of Public Administration Research and Theory*, *3*, 273–304.

Bozeman, B., and Kingsley, G. (1998). Risk Culture in Public and Private Organizations. *Public Administration Review*, *58*, 109–118.

Bozeman, B., and Rainey, H.G. (1998). Organizational Rules and the 'Bureaucratic Personality.' *American Journal of Political Science, 42*(1), 163–189.
Bozeman, B., and Scott, P. (1996). Bureaucratic Red Tape and Formalization: Untangling Conceptual Knots. *American Review of Public Administration, 26,* 1–17.
Burns, T., and Stalker, G. M. (1961). *The Management of Innovation.* London: Tavistock.
Buurman, M., Delfgaauw, J., Dur, R., and Van den Bossche, S. (2012). Public Sector Employees: Risk Averse and Altruistic? *Journal of Economic Behavior and Organization, 83,* 279–291.
Cai, Z., Huo, Y., Lan, J., Chen, Z., and Lam, W. (2019). When Do Frontline Hospitality Employees Take Charge? Prosocial Motivation, Taking Charge, and Job Performance: The Moderating Role of Job Autonomy. *Cornell Hospitality Quarterly, 60,* 237–248.
Campbell, J.W. (2015). Identification and Performance Management: An Assessment of Change-oriented Behavior in Public Organizations. *Public Personnel Management, 44,* 46–69.
Campbell, J.W. (2016). A Collaboration-based Model of Work Motivation and Role Ambiguity in Public Organizations. *Public Performance and Management Review, 39,* 655–675.
Campbell, J.W. (2018). Felt Responsibility for Change in Public Organizations: General and Sector-specific Paths. *Public Management Review, 20,* 232–253.
Campbell, J.W. (2020a). Red Tape, Rule Burden, and Legitimate Performance Trade-offs: Results from a Vignette Experiment. *Public Performance & Management Review, 43*(4), 741–765.
Campbell, J.W. (2020b). Workgroup Accord and Change-oriented Behavior in Public Service Organizations: Mediating and Contextual Factors. *Journal of Management & Organization, 26*(5), https://doi.org/10.1017/jmo.2018.42.
Campbell, J.W., and Im, T. (2016a). Perceived Public Participation Efficacy: The Differential Influence of Public Service Motivation across Organizational Strata. *Public Personnel Management, 45,* 308–330.
Campbell, J.W., and Im, T. (2016b). PSM and Turnover Intention in Public Organizations: Does Change-oriented Organizational Citizenship Behavior Play a Role? *Review of Public Personnel Administration, 36,* 323–346.
Campbell, J.W., and Im, T. (2019). Exchange Ideology, Performance Pay, and Pay Satisfaction: Evidence from South Korean Central Government. *Public Personnel Management, 84,* 584–607.
Campbell, J.W., Im, T., and Jeong, J. (2014). Internal efficiency and turnover intention: Evidence from local government in South Korea. *Public Personnel Management, 43*(2), 259–282.
Cerit, Y. (2017). The Mediating Effect of LMX in the Relationship between School Bureaucratic Structure and Teachers' Proactive Behavior. *Leadership and Organization Development Journal, 38,* 780–793.
Chen, C.-A., and Bozeman, B. (2012). Organizational Risk Aversion: Comparing the Public and Non-profit Sectors. *Public Management Review, 14,* 377–402.
Coursey, D., Yang, K., and Pandey, S.K. (2012). Public service motivation (PSM) and support for citizen participation: A test of Perry and Vandenabeele's reformulation of PSM theory. *Public Administration Review, 72*(4), 572–582.
de Geus, C.J.C., Ingrams, A., Tummers, L., and Pandey, S.K. (2020). Organizational Citizenship Behavior in the Public Sector: A Systematic Literature Review and Future Research Agenda. *Public Administration Review, 80,* 259–270.
do Nascimento, T.T., Porto, J.B., and Kwantes, C.T. (2018). Transformational leadership and follower proactivity in a volunteer workforce. *Nonprofit Management and Leadership, 28*(4), 565–576.
Ehrhart, M. G. (2004). Leadership and Procedural Justice Climate as Antecedents of Unit-level Organizational Citizenship Behavior. *Personnel Psychology, 57,* 61–94.
Fernandez, S., and Moldogaziev, T. (2013). Employee Empowerment, Employee Attitudes, and Performance: Testing a Causal Model. *Public Administration Review, 73,* 490–506.
Fernandez, S., and Rainey, H.G. (2006). Managing Successful Organizational Change in the Public Sector. *Public Administration Review, 66,* 168–176.
Fuchs, S. (2011). The Impact of Manager and Top Management Identification on the Relationship between Perceived Organizational Justice and Change-oriented Behavior. *Leadership and Organization Development Journal, 32,* 555–583.
Garg, S., and Dhar, R. (2017). Employee Service Innovative Behavior. *International Journal of Manpower, 38,* 242–258.

Ha, S.-B., Lee, S., Byun, G., and Dai, Y. (2020). Leader Narcissism and Subordinate Change-oriented Organizational Citizenship Behavior: Overall Justice as a Moderator. *Social Behavior and Personality*, *48*, 1–12.

Hassan, H. A., Zhang, X., Ahmad, A.B., and Liu, B. (2020). Public Service Motivation and Employee Change-supportive Intention: Utilizing the Theory of Planned Behavior. *Public Personnel Management*. First published online on July 27, 2020 at https://doi.org/10.1177/0091026020934515.

Homberg, F., Vogel, R., and Weiherl, J. (2019). Public Service Motivation and Continuous Organizational Change: Taking Charge Behaviour at Police Services. *Public Administration*, *97*, 28–47.

Hvidman, U., and Andersen, S.C. (2016). Perceptions of Public and Private Performance: Evidence from a Survey Experiment. *Public Administration Review*, *76*, 111–120.

Katz, D., and Kahn, R.L. (1978). *The Social Psychology of Organizations*. New York, NY: Wiley.

Kaufmann, W., and Feeney, M.K. (2012). Objective Formalization, Perceived Formalization and Perceived Red Tape Sorting Out Concepts. *Public Management Review*, *14*, 1195–1214.

Kaufmann, W., Borry, E.L., and DeHart-Davis, L. (2019). More Than Pathological Formalization: Understanding Organizational Structure and Red Tape. *Public Administration Review*, *79*, 236–245.

Langer, J., and LeRoux, K. (2017). Developmental Culture and Effectiveness in Nonprofit Organizations. *Public Performance and Management Review*, *40*, 457–479.

Lebel, R.D., and Patil, S.V. (2018). Proactivity Despite Discouraging Supervisors: The Powerful Role of Prosocial Motivation. *The Journal of Applied Psychology*, *103*, 724–737.

Li, N., Guo, Q.-Y., and Wan, H. (2019). Leader Inclusiveness and Taking Charge: The Role of Thriving at Work and Regulatory Focus. *Frontiers in Psychology*, *10*, 2393.

Li, R., Zhang, Z.-Y., and Tian, X.-M. (2016). Can Self-sacrificial Leadership Promote Subordinate Taking Charge? The Mediating Role of Organizational Identification and the Moderating Role of Risk Aversion. *Journal of Organizational Behavior*, *37*(5), 758–781.

Liang, H.-L., and Yeh, T.-K. (2019). The Effects of Employee Voice on Workplace Bullying and Job Satisfaction. *Management Decision*, *58*, 569–582.

Liu, B., Yang, K., and Yu, W. (2015). Work-related Stressors and Health-related Outcomes in Public Service: Examining the Role of Public Service Motivation. *American Review of Public Administration*, *45*, 653–673.

López-Domínguez, M., Enache, M., Sallan, J.M., and Simo, P. (2013). Transformational Leadership as an Antecedent of Change-oriented Organizational Citizenship Behavior. *Journal of Business Research*, *66*, 2147–2152.

Luu, T. (2018). Discretionary HR Practices and Proactive Work Behaviour: The Mediation Role of Affective Commitment and the Moderation Roles of PSM and Abusive Supervision. *Public Management Review*, *20*, 789–823.

Marinova, S.V., Peng, C., Lorinkova, N., Van Dyne, L., and Chiaburu, D. (2015). Change-oriented Behavior: A Meta-analysis of Individual and Job Design Predictors. *Journal of Vocational Behavior*, *88*, 104–120.

Marinova, S.V., Cao, X., and Park, H. (2019). Constructive Organizational Values Climate and Organizational Citizenship Behaviors: A Configurational View. *Journal of Management*, *45*, 2045–2071.

Marvel, J.D. (2015). Unconscious Bias in Citizens' Evaluations of Public Sector Performance. *Journal of Public Administration Research and Theory*, *26*, 143–158.

Miao, Q., Newman, A., Schwarz, G., and Cooper, B. (2018). How leadership and public service motivation enhance innovative behavior. *Public Administration Review*, *78*(1), 71–81.

Moon, M.J., and Bretschneider, S. (2002). Does the Perception of Red Tape Constrain IT Innovativeness in Organizations? Unexpected Results from a Simultaneous Equation Model and Implications. *Journal of Public Administration Research and Theory*, *12*, 273–292.

Morrison, E.W., and Phelps, C.C. (1999). Taking charge at work: Extrarole efforts to initiate workplace change. *Academy of Management Journal*, *42*(4), 403–419.

Moynihan, D.P., and Pandey, S.K. (2010). The Big Question for Performance Management: Why Do Managers Use Performance Information? *Journal of Public Administration Research and Theory*, *20*, 849–866.

Organ, D.W. (1988). *Organizational Citizenship Behavior: The Good Soldier Syndrome*. Lexington, MA: Lexington Books.

Organ, D.W. (1997). Organizational Citizenship Behavior: It's Construct Clean-up Time. *Human Performance*, *10*, 85–97.
Organ, D.W., Podsakoff, P.M., and MacKenzie, S.B. (2005). *Organizational Citizenship Behavior: Its Nature, Antecedents, and Consequences*. Thousand Oaks, CA: Sage.
Osborne, S.P. (2013). A Services-influenced Approach to Public Service Innovation? In S.P. Osborne and L. Brown (eds), *Handbook of Innovation in Public Services*. Chetlenham, UK and Northampton, MA, USA: Edward Elgar Publishing, pp. 60–71.
Ostroff, C., Kinicki, A.J., and Muhammad, R.S. (2012). Organizational Culture and Climate. In N.W. Schmitt, S. Highhouse, and I.B. Weiner (eds), *Handbook of Psychology*. New York, NY: Wiley Online Library, ch. 24.
Pandey, S.K., and Wright, B.E. (2006). Connecting the dots in Public Management: Political Environment, Organizational Goal Ambiguity, and the Public Manager's Role Ambiguity. *Journal of Public Administration Research and Theory*, *16*, 511–532.
Pandey, S.K., Coursey, D.H., and Moynihan, D.P. (2007). Organizational Effectiveness and Bureaucratic Red Tape: A Multimethod Study. *Public Performance and Management Review*, *30*, 398–425.
Park, S., and Jun, J.S. (2018). The Impact of Proactivity, Leader–member Exchange, and Climate for Innovation on Innovative Behavior in the Korean Government Sector. *Leadership and Organization Development Journal*, *39*, 130–149.
Perlow, L.A., Gittell, J.H., and Katz, N. (2004). Contextualizing Patterns of Work Group Interaction: Toward a Nested Theory of Structuration. *Organization Science*, *15*, 520–536.
Perry, J.L., and Vandenabeele, W. (2008). Behavioral Dynamics: Institutions, Identities, and Self-regulation. In J.L. Perry and A. Hondeghem (eds), *Motivation in Public Management: The Call of Public Service*. New York, NY: Oxford University Press, pp. 56–79.
Perry, J.L., and Wise, L.R. (1990). The Motivational Bases of Public Service. *Public Administration Review*, *50*, 367–373.
Piatak, J., Mohr, Z., and McDonald, J. (2020). Rule Formalization, Gender, and Gender Congruence: Examining Prosocial Rule Breaking for Internal and External Stakeholders. *International Public Management Journal*. First published online on August 19, 2020 at https://doi.org/10.1080/10967494.2020.1790445.
Potipiroon, W., and Faerman, S. (2020). Tired from Working Hard? Examining the Effect of Organizational Citizenship Behavior on Emotional Exhaustion and the Buffering Roles of Public Service Motivation and Perceived Supervisor Support. *Public Performance and Management Review*. First published online on March 24, 2020 at https://doi.org/10.1080/15309576.2020.1742168.
Pratt, M.G. (1998). To Be or Not to Be: Central Questions in Organizational Identification. In D.A. Whetten and P.C. Godfrey (eds), *Identity in organizations*. Thousand Oaks, CA: Sage, pp. 171–207.
Qian, J., Song, B., Jin, Z., Wang, B., and Chen, H. (2018). Linking Empowering Leadership to Task Performance, Taking Charge, and Voice: The Mediating Role of Feedback-seeking. *Frontiers in Psychology*, *9*. https://doi.org/10.3389/fpsyg.2018.02025.
Randall, M.L., Cropanzano, R., Bormann, C.A., and Birjulin, A. (1999). Organizational Politics and Organizational Support as Predictors of Work Attitudes, Job Performance, and Organizational Citizenship Behavior. *Journal of Organizational Behavior: The International Journal of Industrial, Occupational and Organizational Psychology and Behavior*, *20*, 159–174.
Ritz, A. (2011). Attraction to Public Policy-making: A Qualitative Inquiry into Improvements in PSM Measurement. *Public Administration*, *89*, 1128–1147.
Ritz, A., Brewer, G.A., and Neumann, O. (2016). Public Service Motivation: A Systematic Literature Review and Outlook. *Public Administration Review*, *76*, 414–426.
Ruck, K., Welch, M., and Menara, B. (2017). Employee Voice: An Antecedent to Organisational Engagement? *Public Relations Review*, *43*, 904–914.
Scott, P.G., and Pandey, S.K. (2005). Red Tape and Public Service Motivation: Findings from a National Survey of Managers in State Health and Human Services Agencies. *Review of Public Personnel Administration*, *25*, 155–180.
Shim, D.C., and Faerman, S. (2017). Government Employees' organizational citizenship behavior: The impacts of public service motivation, organizational identification, and subjective OCB norms. *International Public Management Journal*, *20*(4), 531–559.

Shim, D.C., Park, H.H., and Eom, T.H. (2017). Street-level Bureaucrats' Turnover Intention: Does Public Service Motivation Matter? *International Review of Administrative Sciences*, *83*, 563–582.

Stazyk, E.C., and Goerdel, H.T. (2011). The Benefits of Bureaucracy: Public Managers' Perceptions of Political Support, Goal Ambiguity, and Organizational Effectiveness. *Journal of Public Administration Research and Theory*, *21*, 645–672.

Sun, X., Wu, M., and Chen, Q. (2019). Ego Depletion and Self-control: The Moderating Role of Public Service Motivation. *Social Behavior and Personality*, *47*, 1–14.

Tang, T.L.P., and Liu, B.-C. (2011). Does the Love of Money Moderate the Relationship between Public Service Motivation and Job Satisfaction? The Case of Chinese Professionals in the Public Sector. *Public Administration Review*, *71*, 718–727.

Thompson, V.A. (1977). *Modern Organization*. Tuscaloosa, AL: University of Alabama Press.

Townsend, K., Dundon, T., and Loudoun, R. (2015). The Front-line Manager's Role in Informal Voice Pathways. *Employee Relations*, *37*. Accessed on July 7, 2021 at https://www.emerald.com/insight/content/doi/10.1108/ER-06-2014-0060/full/html.

Van der Voet, J., Kuipers, B.S., and Groeneveld, S. (2016). Implementing Change in Public Organizations: The Relationship between Leadership and Affective Commitment to Change in a Public Sector Context. *Public Management Review*, *18*, 842–865.

Van Dyne, L., and LePine, J.A. (1998). Helping and Voice Extra-role Behaviors: Evidence of Construct and Predictive Validity. *Academy of Management Journal*, *41*, 108–119.

Van Dyne, L., Kamdar, D., and Joireman, J. (2008). In-role Perceptions Buffer the Negative Impact of Low LMX on Helping and Enhance the Positive Impact of High LMX on Voice. *The Journal of Applied Psychology*, *93*, 1195–1207.

Van Loon, N., Kjeldsen, A.M., Andersen, L.B., Vandenabeele, W., and Leisink, P. (2018). Only When the Societal Impact Potential is High? A Panel Study of the Relationship between Public Service Motivation and Perceived Performance. *Review of Public Personnel Administration*, *38*, 139–166.

Vigoda-Gadot, E. (2007). Leadership style, organizational politics, and employees' performance: An empirical examination of two competing models. *Personnel Review*, *36*(5), 661–683.

Vigoda-Gadot, E., and Beeri, I. (2012). Change-oriented Organizational Citizenship Behavior in Public Administration: The Power of Leadership and the Cost of Organizational Politics. *Journal of Public Administration Research and Theory*, *22*, 573–596.

Walker, R.M., and Brewer, G.A. (2009). Can Public Managers Reduce Red Tape? The Role of Internal Management in Overcoming External Constraints. *Policy and Politics*, **37, 255–272**.

Wang, Q., Zhou, X., Bao, J., Zhang, X., and Ju, W. (2020). How Is Ethical Leadership Linked to Subordinate Taking Charge? A Moderated Mediation Model of Social Exchange and Power Distance. *Frontiers in Psychology*, *11*. https://doi.org/10.3389/fpsyg.2020.00315.

Williams, L.J., and Anderson, S.E. (1991). Job satisfaction and organizational commitment as predictors of organizational citizenship and in-role behaviors. *Journal of Management*, *17*(3), 601–617.

Williams, A.M., and Bland, J.T. (2020). Drivers of Social Engagement: Employee Voice–Advice Sharing Relationship. *Review of Public Personnel Administration*, *40*, 669–690.

Yang, F. (2017). Better Understanding the Perceptions of Organizational Politics: Its Impact under Different Types of Work Unit Structure. *European Journal of Work and Organizational Psychology*, *26*, 250–262.

Yang, K., and Kassekert, A. (2010). Linking Management Reform with Employee Job Satisfaction: Evidence from Federal Agencies. *Journal of Public Administration Research and Theory*, *20*, 413–436.

Zeng, H., Zhao, L., and Zhao, Y. (2020). Inclusive Leadership and Taking-charge Behavior: Roles of Psychological Safety and Thriving at Work. *Frontiers in Psychology*, *11*, 62.

Zhang, X., Qian, J., Wang, B., and Chen, M. (2020). The Role of Reward Omission in Empowering Leadership and Employee Outcomes: A Moderated Mediation Model. *Human Resource Management Journal*, *30*, 226–243.

24. Stressed versus motivated public employees: a systematic review of the motivation and stress literatures through a contextualized job demands-resources model

Rick T. Borst

INTRODUCTION

Within public administration, not unlike in other fields, many studies have been devoted in the last few decades to the question of what causes job stress and what motivates public employees (respectively, e.g., Giauque et al., 2013, and Harari et al., 2016). While the stress and motivational processes are interrelated and can even strengthen one another, models of work motivation and job stress have largely ignored each other until recently (Bakker and Demerouti, 2014). The most illustrative example is the enormous body of scientific articles on Public Service Motivation (see, e.g., the meta-analyses of Parola et al., 2019; Harari et al., 2017; Homberg et al., 2015) with only a few of them focusing on stress as a possible outcome of Public Service Motivation (Giauque et al., 2013; Van Loon et al., 2015).

The recent attention for the interrelationship between job stress and (Public Service) motivation in the field of public administration is the result of the increasingly popular Job Demands-Resources (JD-R) theory. The JD-R theory bridges well-known motivating models, including the two-factor theory and the job characteristics model, and stress models, including the demand-control model and the effort-reward imbalance model (Bakker and Demerouti, 2014). While the JD-R theory is developed in the context of job and organizational psychology, it can be applied to all work environments and tailored to specific occupations. The theory is also increasingly applied in public administration (e.g., Borst et al., 2019b; Giauque et al., 2013). However, the application of the JD-R model in public administration is widely scattered with some studies focusing on predominantly perceived job stressors and stress (i.e., burnout) among public servants (Hsieh, 2012; Jensen et al., 2017), while others focus predominantly on perceived job motivators and resulting motivational states (i.e., work engagement) (Borst et al., 2019b). Therefore, by systematically reviewing studies from top quality public management and human resources management (HRM) journals,[1,2,3] this chapter will present a structured and integrative overview of the JD-R theory and its contextualized version in the public sector.

This chapter is divided into three main sections. In each section, the general ideas of the theory will be described first, followed by the application in the public sector context using literature from public administration. The first section focuses on the building blocks of the theory: various job stressors and job motivators that will lead to (enduring) stress (i.e., burnout), and motivating states (i.e., work engagement). Also, the more recent third building block including personal motivators and personal stressors that can instigate motivational states and stress will be discussed. The second section focuses on the two basic processes lying at the heart of the JD-R theory: the motivating and stress processes that connect the stressors/motivators with the states of stress and motivation (Schaufeli, 2017). In the third section, the interactions between the job/personal motivators and job/personal stressors are described. The chapter ends with a conclusion and a discussion including the relevance of this overview for theory and practice as well as future research directions.

THE BUILDING BLOCKS

The JD-R model builds on established classical stress models including the Karasek's Job Demands-Control (-Support) model (JDC(S); Karasek, 1979; Karasek and Theorell, 1990) and the Effort-Reward Imbalance model (ERI; Siegrist, 1996) as well-established motivation models including the two-factor theory (Herzberg, 1966) and the job characteristics model (Hackman and Oldham, 1980). Two building blocks are central in these models: job stressors/job motivators on the one hand and states of stress/motivation on the other hand.

The stress models laid the foundation for the building blocks of the JD-R model related to the states of stress and job stressors/job motivators. However, these stress models are widely criticized nowadays. The JDC model is criticized because it only focuses on psychological stressors and only one job motivator (control; decision latitude), and the ERI model is also criticized because it focuses on a different cluster of job motivators (rewards; salary, esteem reward, and security/career opportunities) but ignores the importance of other already validated motivators by the JDC (Bakker and Demerouti, 2014). While the JDCS model extends the study of job motivators with (colleague/supervisor/organizational) support measures, and the ERI introduces the importance of personal motivators (overcommitment), the models remain criticized due to the overconfidence that with only a few variables all possible working environments can be analyzed. Moreover, the measurement instruments show no good discriminant validity, providing problems for the validity of the building blocks in practice (Bell et al., 2017).

Equal to the stress models, the motivational models laid the foundation for the building blocks related to motivational states and job motivators extended upon in the JD-R model. In the two-factor theory a distinction is in general made between extrinsic job motivators (including company policies, supervision, salary, interpersonal relations, and working conditions) and intrinsic job motivators (including achievement, recognition, nature of work, responsibility, and advancement). As a follow up, Hackman and Oldham (1980) developed the job-characteristics model. Within Hackman and Oldham's (1980) theory, five core job motivators are developed (skill variety, task identity, task significance, autonomy, and feedback) that should prompt three critical psychological states (meaningfulness, responsibility, knowledge about results) and inherently several motivational states. Although these models also lay important foundations for the building blocks of the JD-R model, they are criticized due to their one-sided attention for work motivation and assumption that the specific variables hold across all possible work environments (Bakker and Demerouti, 2014).

To overcome these critiques, the JD-R model is developed which combines both the stress and motivational building blocks: states of stress/motivation and job stressors/motivators. Moreover, the model is developed in such a way that it also builds in the possibility to contextualize the model to specific work environments such as the public sector.

General JD-R Perspective: States of Stress and Motivation

The first building block of the JD-R theory is composed by the various states of respectively stress and motivation of employees. There is no general agreement about the meaning of the term stress. According to stress researchers, stress might, for example, refer to a set of physiological, cognitive and/or emotional reactions that individuals generate when they face environmental conditions such as (potential) threats or opportunities (e.g., Lazarus and Folkman, 1984). The reactions, as well as the conditions in the workplaces that lead to these reactions, are therefore frequently called the stress process. While some scholars draw this further by stating that the whole process in itself is stress (Barber et al., 2013), zooming in on this process it is more logical to refer to the physiological, cognitive, and/or emotional reactions by employees as stress. Especially because the working conditions are referred to as a distinct construct (i.e., job stressors) that lead to reactions (Barber et al., 2013).

While the reactions in itself can be conceptualized as stress, these reactions in scientific terms are called strains. Also within the JD-R model these stress reactions are indeed labeled job strains (Bakker and Demerouti, 2014). Within the general JD-R literature many job strains have been tested throughout the years (see for an overview Schaufeli and Taris, 2014). However, burnout has become the representative concept for job strains in the JD-R model. Burnout is a chronic state of work-related psychological stress that is characterized by exhaustion (i.e., feeling emotionally drained and used up), mental distancing (i.e., cynicism and lack of enthusiasm), and reduced personal efficacy (Schaufeli, 2017).

While burnout has become the representative concept of strain in the JD-R model, it needs to be stated that it does not fully grasp the concept of strain. Firstly, other stress researchers show that the stress responses can be acute (i.e., short-term) or chronic (i.e., long-term) (Barber et al., 2013). Burnout clearly covers merely the chronic dimension. Other short-term dimensions are, for example, increased heart rate and attention problems. Secondly, the classic JD-R model suggests that burnout is a form of psychological strain leading to various other negative 'outcomes' including most often health-related outcomes (Schaufeli, 2017). In practice though, it is rather difficult to state that negative health-related outcomes are not strains in themselves; ill-health is, for example, equated with burnout as one of several strains (Bakker and Demerouti, 2017; Taris et al., 2017). Consequently, other stress scholars make a more explicit distinction in (physical) health (also called physiological), psychological, and behavioral strains and further divide these three large groups into acute and chronic strains (stress responses) (e.g., Barber et al., 2013). Translated to the JD-R model, this model mainly emphasizes the psychological side of strains with its main focus on burnout.

Not unlike stress research, there is also no general agreement about the term motivation. However, in the context of the JD-R model, work engagement has become the representative concept for motivation (Bakker and Demerouti, 2017). When work engagement emerged, it was defined as a 'persistent, positive affective-motivational state of fulfillment in employees that is characterized by vigor (i.e., high levels of energy and resilience), dedication (i.e., experiencing a sense of significance, pride and challenge), and absorption (i.e., being fully concentrated and happily engrossed in one's work)' (Maslach et al., 2001, p. 417). While the definition changed somewhat to 'a positive, fulfilling psychological state' (Schaufeli and Taris, 2014) the motivational characteristics are clear, without stating that it is exactly the same as motivation (Macey and Schneider, 2008). Indeed, the most recent figures of the JD-R model frame work engagement as the central concept to conceptualize motivation (Bakker and Demerouti, 2017).

The above discussed states of stress (burnout) and motivation (work engagement) are nowadays integrated in the concept named psychological well-being (Bakker and Oerlemans, 2011). From a classical point of view, psychological well-being at work is often broadly described as the unidimensional overall quality of an employee's experience and functioning at work (Warr, 1987). However, more multidimensional approaches including states of stress and motivation are proposed nowadays (Schaufeli and Taris, 2014). Also in the JD-R model a multidimensional conceptualization of psychological employee well-being is often applied which makes a distinction between (non-)energetic/motivational and (un)pleasant forms of psychological well-being (Bakker and Oerlemans, 2011; Bakker et al., 2011).

The (non-)energetic and (un)pleasant forms of psychological well-being are integrated via the circumplex model of psychological well-being (Bakker and Oerlemans, 2011; Bakker et al., 2011). This model emphasizes that states are not isolated entities but instead are interrelated based on the two neurophysiological systems of pleasure and activation/motivation (Bakker et al., 2011). Using this model, scholars position work engagement in the quadrant of high activation/motivation and high pleasure and burnout in the opposite quadrant of low activation/motivation and low pleasure (Bakker and Oerlemans, 2011). Due to these opposite interrelationships between states of stress and motivation, a thorough discussion takes place whether these are exactly the two opposite sides of the same coin. During the introduction of the JD-R model, burnout was indeed operationalized as being disengaged (Schaufeli and Taris, 2014). However, over the years many studies have conjointly tested work engagement and burnout, showing that employees not feeling burned-out does not mean that they feel engaged (Bakker et al., 2011). States of stress and states of motivation are therefore two sides of the same, albeit imperfectly shaped, coin instead of exact opposite counterparts (Bakker et al., 2011).

The coin is also imperfectly shaped as there are not two, but four quadrants. While job satisfaction typically represents the state of low activation/motivation and high pleasure, workaholism typically represents the state of high activation/motivation and low pleasure. Job satisfaction only plays a minor role in the JD-R model because it is not acknowledged as an energetic/motivational state but rather as a state of relaxation and contentedness. Accordingly, scholars argue that job satisfaction could just as well lead to passive employees without much initiative (unmotivated; Borst et al., 2019b). As a result, it is not an ideal type of motivation like work engagement. Moreover, workaholism plays a somewhat larger, but still relatively minor role in the JD-R model as well because it is a state of negative motivation. Within the JD-R literature, workaholism is often defined as the tendency to work excessively hard and being obsessed with work, which manifests itself in working compulsively (Bakker and Oerlemans, 2011). As a result, it is not a clearly defined ideal typical form of stress/demotivation like burnout. Hence, job satisfaction and workaholism receive less attention in the JD-R literature.

Contextualized JD-R Perspective: Public Servants' States of Stress and Motivation

Also within the context of the public sector, there is increasing attention for the study of the four well-being indicators (e.g., work engagement and workaholism: Borst et al., 2019a; burnout: Hsieh, 2012; Van Loon et al., 2015; job satisfaction: Cantarelli et al., 2015). Besides job satisfaction, the public administration literature also discusses and conceptualizes these states of stress and motivation using the JD-R model and well-being. However, due to the peculiarities of the public sector, several scholars suggest that the presence of especially the pleasant and energetic/motivational state work engagement and unpleasant and non-energetic/stressful state burnout are slightly different in the public context (e.g., Borst et al., 2019a; Fletcher et al., 2020).

Borst et al. (2019a) show that the pleasant and energetic/motivational state work engagement is the highest among (semi-)public employees in healthcare and education. It is argued that work engagement especially measures the experienced work meaningfulness and purposefulness by employees and these are relatively more often experienced by (semi-) public employees than other employees. Indeed, in particular (semi-)public personnel might see their work as a calling because they try to improve the quality of life of citizens/clients (Borst and Lako, 2017) and therefore experience purposefulness and meaningfulness in their work.

While scholars show that work engagement is relatively the highest among (semi-)public sectors, Hsieh (2012) argues that its unpleasant and non-energetic/stressful counterpart burnout is also relatively the highest in these sectors. The concept of burnout had its roots in care-giving and service occupations because the core of their work and organizational characteristics are aimed at emotional relations (Maslach et al., 2001). It is argued that stress is primarily determined by work and organizational characteristics rather than by individual predisposition and personal factors (Giauque et al., 2012). As a result, particularly human service professions in the (semi-)public sector have to deal with emotional demands which often induce emotional exhaustion (Hsieh, 2012). Emotional exhaustion is the primary dimension of burnout which is known for its specific stress-related reaction to the overwhelming emotional demands imposed by the organization. Hence, emotional demands make public sector workers feel drained, used up, and depleted of enthusiasm and energy to face another day (Hsieh, 2012).

In contrast to the explicit contextualization of work engagement and burnout to the public sector, job satisfaction and workaholism are predominantly generally applied by scholars in public administration. Through their meta-analysis, Cantarelli et al. (2015) indeed argue that their peer-reviewers requested for further contextualization of job satisfaction in the public sector to gain a more fine-grained image. Interestingly though, Borst et al. (2019a) do show in their meta-analysis that the job satisfaction and work engagement of public servants are relatively much more correlated. In addition, they also show that the rate of workaholism and work engagement of public servants is also much higher correlated than of employees in other sectors. From these results it can be deduced that, especially in the public sector, states of stress and states of motivation are to a large extent related. The general proposition from the JD-R model and the circumplex model that these states should be studied conjointly therefore seems to be confirmed, at least for the public sector.

Based on this theoretical discussion, it can be questioned what is empirically known about these building blocks of the JD-R model in the (semi-)public sector context. Especially because it might be the case that psychological literature has studied one or more of these states of stress/motivation using a (semi-)public sample, without explicitly contextualizing the JD-R model to the public sector (Borst et al., 2019a). As a result, all studies have been systematically studied. Based on the literature review of all studies, the descriptives about the states of stress and motivation in the (semi-)public sector are given in Table 24.1.

As Table 24.1 shows, the variations in states of stress and motivation across sectors varies considerably in some cases. Firstly, the level of burnout is as expected relatively higher in the semi-public sector than in government and social security. Looking at the dimensions though,

Table 24.1 Descriptive states of stress and motivation in the (semi-)public sector

	Government (N = 53)		Healthcare/education (N = 174/112)		Social security (N = 59)	
	Count[a]	Mean[b]	Count[a]	Mean[b]	Count[a]	Mean[b]
Burnout	3	2.76	36	2.92	9	2.72
Cynicism/Depersonalization	5	2.72	83	2.63	17	2.89
Emotional exhaustion	15	3.28	146	3.39	34	3.23
Low competence	3	2.46	53	2.11	9	2.45
Work engagement	17	4.92	69	5.18	18	5.08
Vigor	7	5.30	29	5.16	8	5.02
Dedication	6	5.43	24	5.35	7	5.13
Absorption	4	5.18	18	4.80	5	4.29
Job satisfaction	17	4.80	63	4.48	9	4.29
Workaholism	1	4.01	4	4.37	0	–
Working excessively	0	–	3	3.33	0	–
Working compulsively	0	–	3	3.81	0	–

Notes:
[a] Count is the amount of studies.
[b] All means are transformed through linear transformation to a 7-point scale (1–7) in line with most scales. Means are not sample-size corrected.

emotional exhaustion is indeed also higher in the semi-public sector than in the other sectors but feelings of depersonalization and inefficacy are relatively lower in the semi-public sector. Secondly, the general level of work engagement is also relatively higher in the semi-public sector in line with expectations. However, looking at the specific dimensions, all dimensions are scored the highest in the public sector and by far the lowest in the social security sectors. Thirdly, the level of job satisfaction is equal across the public and semi-public sector but much lower in the social security sector. Lastly, workaholism is higher in the semi-public sector than in the public sector but there are too little studies to definitively conclude this.

General JD-R Perspective: Job and Personal Stressors/Motivators

The second building block of the JD-R model is composed by the various job and personal stressors/motivators. According to the JD-R model, all working environments can be modeled using two different categories, namely job stressors (i.e., job demands) and job motivators (i.e., job resources). In general, job stressors are factors that cost energy to deal with, while job motivators are factors that give energy. Moreover, according to the JD-R model, these working environments develop in interaction with personality characteristics (Schaufeli and Taris, 2014). As a result, all personality characteristics in the JD-R model are modeled using personal motivators (i.e., personal resources) and personal stressors (i.e., personal demands). In general, personal motivators are defined as the 'psychological characteristics or aspects of the self that are generally associated with resiliency and that refer to the ability to control and impact one's environment successfully' (Schaufeli and Taris, 2014, p. 49). In contrast, personal stressors are defined as 'the requirements that individuals set for their own performance and behavior that force them to invest effort in their work which are inherently associated with physical and psychological costs' (Bakker and Demerouti, 2017, p. 279). While these general descriptions of the model are insightful, the descriptions of all these categories became more and more fine-grained since its introduction about 18 years ago. Therefore, respectively job stressors, job motivators, personal motivators, and personal stressors will be further elaborated upon below.

While early JD-R studies defined job stressors as rather unidimensional as those physical, social, or organizational aspects of the job that require sustained physical or mental effort, more multidimensional fine-grained approaches to job stressors exist nowadays. Although many multidimensional groupings of stressors are proposed, the most fairly known grouping is the one making a distinction between quantitative stressors (also termed overload or work pressure) and qualitative stressors. The group qualitative stressors is in turn further divided into cognitive (e.g., role conflict/ambiguity, complexity, qualitative workload), emotional (e.g., harassment, emotional dissonance, interpersonal conflicts), and physical (e.g., heavy lifting, unfavorable shift work schedule) clusters (Taris et al., 2017; see for a large overview Schaufeli and Taris, 2014). Increasingly, a separate third cluster of organizational stressors is also distinguished which include amongst others downsizing, bureaucracy, and reorganizations (Schaufeli, 2017). This multidimensional approach is helpful for seeing the forest for the trees as well as for the development of adjusted and focused interventions to specific groups of stressors (Schaufeli, 2017). Next to this multidimensional approach, another multidimensional approach of job stressors has become even more well known within the JD-R model.

The second well-known multidimensional approach builds on the proposition that not all job stressors have exclusively negative effects (Van den Broeck et al., 2010). Indeed, several studies showed that some job stressors appeal to employees' curiosity, competence, and thoroughness which inherently challenges them to reach goals. As a result, they are labeled as challenging job stressors which yield opportunities for growth and development (Bakker and Demerouti, 2017; Van den Broeck et al., 2010). This cluster of stressors opposes the classical viewpoint of the JD-R model that there are merely hindering job stressors which always hinder employees' work goal achievement and well-being. Based on these insights several JD-R studies empirically confirmed that many emotional and organizational stressors are usually experienced as hindering stressors by employees while various cognitive stressors including workload and time pressure are usually experienced as challenging job stressors (Van den Broeck et al., 2010).

While challenging stressors have some motivational potential, the real environmental motivational characteristics in the JD-R model are the job motivators. More specifically, job motivators are assumed to play either an intrinsic motivational role because they foster employees' growth, learning, and development (i.e., basic human needs), or an extrinsic motivational role because they are instrumental in achieving work goals (Borst et al., 2019b). Not unlike job stressors, multidimensional groupings of job motivators in the JD-R model also exist. The most fairly known grouping makes a distinction between job motivators located at the level of the organization at large (e.g., pay, career opportunities, organizational support), the interpersonal and social relations (e.g., supervisor and co-worker support, team climate), the organization of work (e.g., role clarity, participation in decision making), and at the level of the task (e.g., skill variety, task identity, task significance, and autonomy; Bakker and Demerouti, 2007).

Besides the above-mentioned environmental characteristics, personality characteristics can also have motivational potential. While personal motivators receive increasing attention in the JD-R model, systematic research is still missing (Schaufeli and Taris, 2014). It is suggested that the motivational potential possibly varies across different types and different combinations of personal motivators (Schaufeli and Taris, 2014). Still, based on a conceptual review of the JD-R literature, an increasing number of scholars make a distinction between trait personal motivators and state personal motivators (Schaufeli, 2017). These differences are based on the theoretical state-trait continuum between unchangeable hardwired traits such as intelligence, and highly variable and influential states including moods and emotions (Luthans and Youssef, 2007). Trait personal motivators in the JD-R model are therefore often defined as relatively stable psychological characteristics. Examples of the most studied trait personal motivators in the context of the JD-R model are the big five personality traits (extraversion, intellectual autonomy, conscientiousness, agreeableness, and emotional stability). In contrast, state personal motivators are somewhat more malleable psychological characteristics. The most studied ones in the JD-R model are psychological capital including its constituents of efficacy, hope, optimism, and resiliency (see for an overview Schaufeli and Taris, 2014).

Due to the increasing attention to personal motivators, its counterparts have been noticed by JD-R scholars as well. The study of personal stressors is one of the newest endeavors in the JD-R model with only some first empirical studies. It is suggested that especially trait personal stressors including negative poles of the big five such as emotional instability could be relevant personal stressors (Lorente Prieto et al., 2008). Moreover, performance expectations about one's own performance and perfectionism could also be forms of personal stressors (Bakker and Demerouti, 2017). However, as Bakker and Demerouti (2017) noticed, studies show that these personal stressors positively relate to work engagement indicating that these factors might be challenging personal stressors. In other words, performance expectations seem to internally challenge employees to increase their effort to meet expectations. Some first indications therefore show that personal stressors could be demanding but also challenging which point to multidimensionality just like the other stressors and motivators in the JD-R model.

Contextualized JD-R Perspective: Public Servants' Job and Personal Stressors/ Motivators

Within the (semi-)public sector, there is increasing attention for the job and personal stressors/ motivators. However, only a few cases apply the JD-R model by actually taking into account the peculiarities of the public and/or semi-public context (e.g., Borst, 2018; Borst et al., 2019b; Fletcher et al., 2020). As a result, Fletcher et al. (2020, p. 23) argue in their literature review on the relationship between JD-R and work engagement that the evidence 'very rarely focuses on delineating and examining sector-specific resources [i.e., motivators]' and that there is a 'lack of effort to identify specific public sector demands [i.e., stressors].' The evidence that does provide more insights in contextualization of the JD-R model is focused on three sector-specific motivators/stressors that will be discussed below: Attention for red tape as a job stressor, Public Service Motivation (PSM) as a personal motivator, and emotional stressors including pupil/student misbehavior and patient misbehavior/harassment.

Several scholars introduced red tape as a hindering job stressor in the JD-R model (Borst, 2018; Borst et al., 2019b; Cooke et al., 2018; Quratulain and Khan, 2013). It is a hindering stressor because the encountered rules, regulations, and procedures by public servants are experienced as pointless yet burdensome (Borst et al., 2019b). Moreover, red tape is at the same time an organizational stressor when placed in the other multidimensional typology of job stressors. Studies have examined red tape in the subsystems of personnel, procurement, information finance, and communication which show that red tape is deeply rooted in the complete organization (meta-analysis: Blom et al., 2020a). Indeed, Schaufeli (2017) shows that the equivalent factor bureaucracy is an organizational stressor in the JD-R model. Consequently, red tape is a hindering job stressor on the level of the organization in a public sector contextualized JD-R model.

Next to red tape, PSM is also introduced in the JD-R model as a trait personal motivator (Borst, 2018; Cooke et al., 2018). According to Bakker (2015), PSM is a relatively stable, higher level key psychological resource that is only subject to slow change. It refers to the predisposition of individuals to serve the public interest. It is a trait personal motivator in the JD-R model that indicates the willingness of public servants to engage in sacrificial behavior for the good of citizens without reciprocal benefits for themselves (Borst et al., 2019b). However, not all dimensions of PSM are equally important as personal motivators across contexts. Borst (2018) shows that particularly compassion is a personal motivator of semi-public employees including teachers and healthcare personnel, while commitment to the public interest and the attraction to public policymaking are mostly personal motivators of public employees in government and social security.

These variations in the height of personal motivators is also visible with the emotional stressors including pupil/student misbehavior and patient misbehavior/harassment. These factors are both emotional stressors which are specifically contextualized to semi-public organizations. For example, patient harassment is particularly an emotional stressor among healthcare employees (Bakker and Demerouti, 2007; Xanthopoulou et al., 2007) while pupil/student misbehavior is an emotional stressor among educational employees (e.g., Bakker et al., 2007). In line with the attention for these forms of emotionally demanding misbehaviors in the JD-R model, there is increasing attention for misbehavior of citizens or other clients in the public sector context as well (Tummers et al., 2016). These misbehaviors can vary from verbal aggression, sexual harassment, to physical aggression and threats. As these misbehaviors increase in public contexts, Tummers and colleagues (2016) suggest that the JD-R model should be used to analyze whether aggression indeed is also an emotional stressor in line with pupil and patient misbehaviors.

Although it is visible that these motivators and stressors are increasingly introduced in the JD-R model, it is still rather questionable how many studies actually apply these in general, and in what sectors in particular. The contextualized review of Fletcher et al. (2020) makes, for example, no distinction between public and semi-public organizations, but also no distinction between PSM as part of the JD-R model or other models. Moreover, only one well-being outcome is studied: work engagement. In addition, within the review of Schaufeli and Taris (2014) it is only mentioned that pupil misbehavior and harassment by patients are stressors in the JD-R model without mentioning anything about the frequency of analyses. As a result, all studies have been systematically studied. Based on the literature review of all studies, the descriptives about the job/personal stressors and job/personal motivators in the public sector, semi-public sector, and social security are given in respectively Tables 24.2, 24.3, and 24.4.

As Tables 24.2, 24.3, and 24.4 show, the general job stressors/motivators are studied frequently in all (semi-)public sectors but the sector-specific ones are relatively understudied. Especially in the semi-public sector, many studies can be found that analyze general job stressors and motivators. In this semi-public sector also sector-specific stressors are studied often, including emotional demands, patient misbehavior, and pupil misbehavior. However, in the other sectors, sector-specific stressors and motivators are understudied including emotional demands, client aggression, PSM, and red tape. Interestingly, studies aimed at red tape in the

JD-R literature are also almost non-existent in the semi-public sector. Moreover, only a few personal motivators/stressors are studied throughout the sectors but this line of research is also still neglected.

THE TWO BASIC PROCESSES

The building blocks of the JD-R model will be connected in this section. Firstly, job stressors will be linked with strains through the stress process, and the job motivators will be linked with the motivational states though the motivational process. Secondly, these processes in the JD-R model will be contextualized to the public sector.

General JD-R Perspective: Motivational and Stress Process

The motivational and stress process in the JD-R model are two separate but also interrelated processes. Originally, the JD-R model was developed to describe the process of how only burnout comes into existence. Two processes were distinguished. On the one hand, employees can become exhausted through a process of dealing with long-term excessive job stressors from which employees do not adequately recover. On the other hand, employees can become less motivated (also called disengaged by some scholars) due to a lack of job motivators (Schaufeli and Taris, 2014). These processes were respectively called the stress process and (de)motivational process of burnout and both lead to lower performance. Although these processes can be described separately, they both lead to burnout, suggesting the interrelationship between the processes (both low job motivators and high stressors can lead to burnout).

This interrelationship between processes became more separated, however, in the revised model where work engagement was introduced as the positively framed counterpart of burnout reframing the motivational process. In this revised model, it is assumed that burnout is a two-dimensional construct of exhaustion and depersonalization and job stressors affect both. In the renewed stress process, the JD-R model explains that job stressors lead to strains such as burnout, which in turn lead to various negative outcomes (mostly health-related outcomes) (Schaufeli and Taris, 2014). At the same time, in the renewed motivational process, job motivators lead to states of motivation such as work engagement, which in turn lead to various positive outcomes such as performance and organizational commitment. The idea that job motivators only play a negative role (demotivation) was in other words discarded and became the basic construct of a process in its own right: the motivational process (instead of merely a demotivational process).

Although the revised JD-R model brought some clarity due to the more clear separation of the stress and motivational process, it also brought some ambiguity. While according to the JD-R model 'stress responses' are strains (including burnout) that lead to 'negative outcomes' (including mostly health-related outcomes), in practice it is rather difficult to state that negative health-related outcomes are not strains in themselves (burnout, e.g., also has a health-related component) (Taris et al., 2017). The same applies to the separation between positive outcomes and motivational states. As a result, the most recent version of the JD-R model makes a less clear distinction between health outcomes and strains, and between positive outcomes and motivational states (Bakker and Demerouti, 2014). The newest JD-R model instead frames performance as the only clear outcome of various strains and states of motivation (Bakker and Demerouti, 2014).

To understand in turn the mechanisms behind the stress process and motivational process, most often the conservation of resources (COR) theory and self-determination theory (SDT) are integrated in the JD-R model. According to the basic principles of the COR theory, employees need to invest job/personal motivators/resources to protect against the loss of job/personal motivators, recover from past losses, and gain future job/personal motivators (Hobfoll, 2001). For example, to resolve a difficult work problem, the employee can ask the supervisor for help (investment of a job motivator) but wins time for him/herself (gain of a job motivator), or the employee invests time for him/herself (investment of a job motivator) to help preserve his/her autonomy (gain of a job motivator) (Dimoff and Kelloway, 2016). However, when the investment does not lead to another motivator, an employee needs to quickly find other motivators to not lose more motivators such as the personal motivator self-esteem (Dimoff and Kelooway, 2016). The increasing loss is called the loss-spiral which laid the basis for the stress-provoking process in the JD-R model. In contrast, next to the protection of motivators, employees can also accumulate motivators. Llorens et al. (2007) found, for example, that autonomy fosters self-efficacy beliefs (gain of a personal motivator), which in turn increase levels of engagement. This laid the basis for the motivation process in the JD-R model.

Moreover, as a macro theory of human motivation, the SDT posits three universal basic psychological needs (autonomy, competence, relatedness) that stimulate the motivation of employees. As a result, these basic psychological needs are integrated in the JD-R model as mediators between job stressors/motivators and the stress/motivational states to understand how the motivational and stress process work (Schaufeli and Taris, 2014). For example, interpersonal and social motivators lead to feelings of relatedness which leads to work engagement. Multiple studies indeed found job motivators satisfy these basic needs, whereas job stressors preclude their satisfaction, resulting in respectively work engagement and burnout (Schaufeli and Taris, 2014).

Contextualized JD-R Perspective: Motivational and Stress Process in the (Semi-)Public Sector

As already mentioned above, only a few cases apply the JD-R model by actually taking into account the peculiarities of the public and/or semi-public context. It was argued that sector-specific stressors/motivators were understudied as was shown in Tables 24.2, 24.3, and 24.4. Not surprisingly, the related stress and motivational processes of these sector-specific job stressors/motivators are also relatively understudied (e.g., Borst, 2018; Borst et al., 2019b; Fletcher et al., 2020). Maybe more surprising though is that the effects of the more generalized job motivators/job stressors are also barely modified to the public sector while it is argued that these effects might be moderated by boundary conditions (Borst et al., 2019a). Borst et al. (2019a) show that public contextual factors including formalization, political control (versus market control), and hard to measure goals are boundary conditions in the JD-R model that might moderate or mediate the influence of generalized motivators/stressors on states of stress and motivation.

These boundary conditions are based on the idea of the institutional context. An institutional context consists of regulative, normative, and cultural-cognitive elements that constrain the behavior and attitudes of individuals through determining, respectively, the rules of the game, the values deemed important, and the way of doing things, also known as institutional logics (Scott, 2001). In other words these boundary conditions can be regulative, normative, or cultural-cognitive elements. Several scholars argue that the public and semi-public institutional contexts are often demarcated merely based on the regulative boundary conditions as influencers of the behavior and attitudes of their employees (Borst, 2018; Van Loon, 2015). Indeed, one of the most studied regulative boundary conditions that is ingrained in the public and semi-public institutional context is formalization. Due to the accountability of public organizations, personnel policies including empowerment and financial incentives are highly formalized and inherently restricted. As a result, the motivational process related to the job motivators on the level of the organization at large are restricted in the JD-R model (Borst et al., 2019b). This is also confirmed by Borst et al. (2019b) in which it was shown that a cluster of organizational level motivators had a far lower significant relation with the motivational state work engagement than task and relational level motivators.

However, recent research starts to take into account normative boundary conditions of the institutional context as well (Borst, 2018; Kjeldsen, 2014; Van Loon, 2015). One of these boundary conditions is aimed at the effects of the difference between people-changing and people-processing values on the motivational and stress process in public and semi-public organizations. (Semi-)public organizations with mainly people processing values have limited contact with clients and only change the status or location of a user by applying the relevant legal framework (Kjeldsen, 2014; Van Loon, 2015). In contrast, (semi-)public organizations with mainly people-changing values have more intense and longer enduring contacts with an identifiable client group aimed at bringing changes in the status of these clients (Van Loon, 2015).

Applied to the JD-R model, scholars found that the motivational process of the dimensions of the personal motivator PSM significantly differs between organizations with mainly people-changing values versus people processing values (Borst, 2018). Due to the long and enduring contacts with clients, compassion is stronger related to work engagement among people-changers than people-processors. In contrast, commitment to the public interest and attraction to public policymaking are stronger related to work engagement among people-processers due to their relation with the values of legal framework development. Moreover, scholars show that due to the relatively high societal impact potential in people-changing organizations (due to the values of long contacts and status-changing of clients), PSM leads to higher states of stress because employees with high PSM easily overreach their mental and physical motivators (Van Loon, 2015). In contrast, scholars show that due to the relatively low societal impact potential in people-processing organizations (due to the one-off contacts), employees with high PSM also become more stressed because their job does not allow them to fully use their PSM and inherently become frustrated (Van Loon, 2015).

Due to the specific peculiarities of public organizations mentioned above, the boundary conditions might influence the motivational and stress processes. However, it is questionable how strong the effects really are due to the limited attention for these processes (Fletcher et al., 2020). Again, Fletcher et al. (2020) is the only recent overview, but it focuses merely on the motivational state work engagement. Moreover, it combines the sectors together while the exact point is that values might differ between these sectors due to their difference in processing and changing focus. As a result, all studies have been systematically studied. To start with,

Table 24.2 shows the relations between stressors/motivators and states of stress/motivation studied in the public sector.

As Table 24.2 shows, quantitative and cognitive stressors are in some cases challenging stressors and in some cases demanding stressors as there are both positive and negative relations with the states of stress and motivation. In contrast, the emotional stressors and organizational stressors are unambiguously hindering as they are negatively related to states of motivation and positively related to states of stress. Also, all job motivators and personal motivators are unambiguously positive for the motivation and negative for the job strain of public servants. Looking at the public sector-specific stressors and motivators, red tape indeed is unambiguously negatively related to work engagement. In contrast, the results for PSM are somewhat more ambiguous. PSM does not always significantly decrease burnout among public servants, nor significantly increase job satisfaction. To compare the results with other sectors, Table 24.3 shows the relations between stressors/motivators and states of stress/motivation studied in social security (army, police, fire departments, and prisons).

Table 24.3 shows that quantitative and cognitive stressors are in some cases hindering and in some cases challenging stressors for the employees in the public social security sector. This is in line with the results in the public sector. Moreover, all job motivators and personal motivators are unambiguously positively linked to the motivation and negatively linked to the job strain of public servants. Interestingly though, looking at the results of the social security sector-specific emotional stressors including emotional demands and client aggression, the results are more ambiguous. Emotional demands and client aggression are frequently insignificant in relation to the work engagement of public servants meaning that public servants do not become demotivated due to these emotional stressors. Still, almost all studies do show that these stressors increase strains including burnout. Whether these emotional stressors also vary in their relations with states of stress and motivation in the semi-public sector is presented in Table 24.4.

Table 24.4 shows that quantitative and cognitive stressors are also in the semi-public sector in some cases hindering and in some cases challenging stressors. Moreover, the job motivators and personal motivators are also clearly positively related to states of motivation and negatively related to states of stress. In line with the social security sector, the influence of emotional stressors increases states of stress but the influences on states of motivation are ambiguous. Still, other semi-public sector-specific emotional stressors including pupil misbehavior, parents pressure, and patient misbehavior are undoubtedly negative as they increase states of stress and decrease states of motivation.

INTERACTIONS BETWEEN MOTIVATION AND STRESS PROCESSES

In this section the interrelation between the motivation and stress process in the JD-R model are discussed. Thereafter, what is known about these interrelations in the context of the (semi-) public sector will be discussed.

Table 24.2 Descriptive stressors/motivators and relations with states of stress/motivation in the public sector

Antecedent	Total N	Burnout Pos.	Burnout Neg.	Burnout Weak	Work engagement Pos.	Work engagement Neg.	Work engagement Weak	Workaholism Pos.	Workaholism Neg.	Workaholism Weak	Job satisfaction Pos.	Job satisfaction Neg.	Job satisfaction Weak
Quantitative job demands	53	2	0	1	2		1	1			3	3	4
Time pressure/deadlines/work fast etc.	7	1					3					3	1
Workload	10	4	1	0	2	2	3					3	
Role ambiguity	4	3										3	
Role conflict	8	4				4				1		2	1
Work–life conflict	8	5				2	1					3	3
Job insecurity	2					2							
Task complexity	2	2									1		
Bullying	2					2							
Red tape	3					3							
Supervisor support/LMX/leadership styles	15		9	1	6						4		
Social support/TMX/community	15		9		9					1	3		
Organizational support/trust/fairness	16		1		8						7		
Performance feedback	3		2		1		1						
Developmental opportunities	4			1	3								1
Job autonomy	9		5		4						1		
Job control	13		3		1					1	7		
Meaningfulness	4				3					1			
Goal/role clarity/specificity	3		1		2					1			
Rewards/promotion	4		1		3								
PSM	6				4						2		1
Attraction to public policy making	3			1	1								
Commitment public interest	3		1		2								
Compassion	2		1		1								
Self-sacrifice	2		1	1	1								
Self-efficacy	3		1		2								
Strengths use	2		1		2					1			
Proactive	2				2								

Table 24.3 Descriptive stressors/motivators and relations with states of stress/motivation in social security

Antecedent	Total N	Burnout Pos.	Burnout Neg.	Burnout Weak	Work engagement Pos.	Work engagement Neg.	Work engagement Weak	Workaholism Pos.	Workaholism Neg.	Workaholism Weak	Job satisfaction Pos.	Job satisfaction Neg.	Job satisfaction Weak
Quantitative job	59	4			1							4	
Demands													
Workload	9	9	1		2	1	1					2	1
Overtime	3		1	2			1						
Cognitive demands	5	3		1	2		1						
Physical demands	3	2				1	1						
Role ambiguity	2	1	1			1	1						
Work conflict	6	1				2	1						
Work–life conflict	11	11				3	1					1	1
Job complexity	4						2						
Client aggression	4	3		1			1						
Emotional demands	9	8			1		4						
Organizational demands	3		2			1							
Supervisor support/LMX	22		13	1	15						5		
Social support/TMX/community	20		13	1	10						1		
Organizational support	10		4		4						4		
Developmental opportunities	5		3		4						1		
Job autonomy	8		5		3		2				2		
Job control	15		5		4		2				8		
Meaningfulness	3		1		3								
Job variety	3		1		1						2		
Reward	2		1			1	1						
Communication/participation	5		2		3						2		
Self-efficacy	5		3	1	2								
Self-esteem	2		1		1								
Optimism	2		2										
Resilience	2		2		2								
Conscientiousness	2		2		1								

Table 24.4 Descriptive stressors/motivators and relations with states of stress/motivation in semi-public sector

Antecedent	Total N 174/112	Burnout Pos.	Burnout Neg.	Burnout Weak	Work engagement Pos.	Work engagement Neg.	Work engagement Weak	Workaholism Pos.	Workaholism Neg.	Workaholism Weak	Job satisfaction Pos.	Job satisfaction Neg.	Job satisfaction Weak
Quantitative job demands	24	16			1	2	5					10	1
Workload	79	54	3	4	1	9	9	2				8	8
Time pressure	24	16	3			3	6					8	1
Cognitive demands	24	15		4	2	4	4	2				6	3
Physical demands	17	11		3		4						2	2
Role ambiguity	15	12		2		4						2	2
Job complexity	3	1		2								1	
Work conflict	35	29		2		11	1	1				8	3
Work–life conflict	37	25		1		9	5	2				13	2
Job insecurity	18	5		4		3	2				1	8	1
Pupil misbehavior	11	10				5							
Parents pressure	3	3		1								1	1
Patient misbehavior	13	12		1		1	1					1	
Bullying	4	3				1						2	
Emotional demands	42	33		2		9	4	2				5	2
Deep acting	8	2		5			1					1	1
Surface acting	11	8			2								2
Supervisor support/LMX	75	46	8		30		1		2		25	1	2
Social support/TMX/community	92	55	7		31		2	1	2		31		2
Organizational support/justice/fairness	40	18	2		12				1		22		
Developmental opportunities	29	10	1		17						6		
Job autonomy	51	29	6		20						12		
Job control	89	52	8		20		4			2	40		1
Meaningfulness	17	1	2		6						10		
Job variety	6	3			6						1		
Goal/role clarity/specificity	11	8	1		5			3			2		
Feedback	3	5			6						7		
Reward/promotion	21	11	2		4		4				7		
Communication/participation	16	7	3		9					1	6		1
Predictability	4	1			1						1		

370 *Research handbook on motivation in public administration*

Antecedent	Total N 174/112	Pos.	Burnout Neg.	Weak	Work engagement Pos.	Neg.	Weak	Workaholism Pos.	Neg.	Weak	Job satisfaction Pos.	Neg.	Weak
Self-efficacy	29		17		12		1			3	3		
Self-esteem	3		1		3						1		
PsyCap	3		1		2						1		
Optimism	7		4		4								
Resilience	5		3		2								
Emotional intelligence	4		2	1	2								
Perfectionism	2	2											
Imposter	2	2	1									1	
Hope	2		1		1								

General JD-R Perspective: Buffering and Coping Mechanisms

While the stress process and motivational process can be explained as separate processes, in practice they are not isolated. More concretely, the JD-R model shows that both personal and job motivators can also buffer the stress process by mitigating the negative effects of job stressors on the states of motivation and stress (Schaufeli and Taris, 2014). Moreover, these job and personal motivators can also exacerbate the positive consequences of challenging stressors for the states of stress and motivation (Schaufeli and Taris, 2014). The COR theory can be used to explain this buffering mechanism: when employees have enough personal and/ or job motivators to deal with the job stressors at hand, the job stressors will not lead to lower motivation nor higher stress.

Next to the buffering mechanism, the JD-R model also shows that coping mechanisms exist. In line with COR theory, it is argued in the JD-R model that employees need job and personal motivators to cope with job stressors. Consequently, job stressors do not have to be detrimental for states of motivation as long as employees have enough motivators. In fact, it is argued that job motivators can increase in their motivating effect when job stressors are high.

Contextualized JD-R Perspective: Buffering and Coping in the (Semi-)Public Sector

Not unlike in the general JD-R literature, both the buffering and coping mechanisms are also studied in the (semi-)public sector contexts. There are, however, two interesting findings in these contexts that added to the knowledge about these interactions.

Firstly, several scholars studied emotional stressors in the healthcare sector as these are particular stressors in this context. In line with general JD-R studies, these scholars found that job and personal motivators moderate the relations between job stressors and the states of stress and motivation. In contrast with these general studies though, these scholars found that the negative consequences of emotional stressors in the healthcare sector are buffered better by emotional motivators such as emotional intelligence (De Jonge and Dormann, 2006). An explanation is given through the development of the Demand-Induced Strain Compensation model (DISC). The DISC model assumes that emotional motivators are better aligned with emotional stressors than other kinds of motivators, which in turn will have an additional enhancing buffering effect. This is called the double matching principle which is indeed confirmed in the context of healthcare (De Jonge and Dormann, 2006).

Secondly, although the context-specific stressors including red tape are scarcely studied, Borst et al. (2019b) showed that red tape increases the coping effect of resources on work engagement. The study showed that the motivational effect of work-related job motivators increased due to red tape. As a result, states of motivation additionally increased. More studies are necessary though to further elaborate on these findings.

CONCLUSION AND FUTURE RESEARCH SUGGESTIONS

The aim of this chapter was to give a structured and integrative overview of the (interrelations between) motivation and stress process in the public sector by means of the JD-R theory. It can be concluded that while the JD-R model has not been widely used in public administration research, its applicability in the public context is confirmed by many other studies from other disciplines. Based on the systematic literature review three overall conclusions can be drawn.

Firstly, the states of stress and motivation are increasingly studied in the (semi-)public sector context. In total, more than 400 studies are available in the context of the JD-R model that analyzes these attitudes. What can be concluded from these studies is that in general, burnout and work engagement are higher in the semi-public sector than in the public and social security sectors but looking at the dimensional level, the results are much more diverse. What is particularly interesting is that the dimensions of work engagement are the highest in the public sector but by far the lowest in the social security sector. Also job satisfaction is by far the lowest in the social security sector. At the same time, workaholism, as a state in between stress and motivation is understudied so no conclusions can be drawn about this state. In conclusion, the most striking is the relatively low states of motivation (i.e., work engagement and job satisfaction) among employees in the social security sector.

Secondly, the systematic literature review shows that many general job stressors and job motivators are studied but the sector-specific job and personal stressors/strains are still understudied. Examples are red tape (only three), PSM (only six), but also client aggression and workplace aggression (both zero studies) as possible job stressors in the public sector. Moreover, personal motivators and personal stressors in general are barely studied. Interestingly though, based on the studies that do study the sector-specific stressors, it can be concluded that not all stressors are as hindering as expected. The states of motivation from semi-public servants and public servants in social security are, for example, not hindered due to emotional demands The same applies to PSM. PSM is not always as destressing and motivating as expected. At the same time, only a few studies are conducted focused on these sector-specific stressors/motivators.

Thirdly, the interrelations between stressors and motivators are increasingly studied but the JD-R model is relatively unable to clearly explain how various kinds of job stressors and job motivators interact and subsequently lead to various states of strain. The JD-R theory in public administration research is still predominantly used to test (causal) relationships between stressors/motivators and states of stress and strain, but that paints a too simplified picture. For example, it can also be assumed that there are further feedback loops than studied so far. States of stress might, for example, retroactively influence personal motivators or other motivational states. The recent interest in job crafting that links engagement to resources confirms these reversed causalities. The DISC model and COR theory provide some interesting avenues to study these feedback loops but these are still understudied in public administration research.

These three overall conclusions lead to matching future research suggestions. Firstly, the JD-R model needs to become more institutionalized in public administration literature to better understand the stress and motivational processes among (semi-)public servants. This institutionalization of the JD-R model can be reached when public administration studies focus more closely on contextual, cultural, and institutional characteristics of the various public sector organizations, including cultural and institutional differences (e.g., according to types of organizations or types of public services delivered); organizational climate; public management reforms; and finally several personal and job characteristics such as red tape, emotional labor, and PSM.

Secondly, to better understand the interactions between stress and motivational processes, more psychological theories including the COR theory and the DISC model need to be integrated and tested in public administration literature. Moreover, to analyze the possible reversed causalities between stressors/motivators and states of stress/motivation, more experimental research and time series analyses could be conducted. In addition, more qualitative research might be conducted to further explore the theoretical foundations of the empirical findings. In this way, it would not only be possible to establish causal links between job/personal stressors/motivators, and states of stress/motivation but also better explain the how and why of these relationships.

NOTES

1. Using key words related to the JD-R model, I searched the PsycINFO database which includes almost all publications in the field of psychology. In addition I searched the following public administration journals: ROPPA, PPM, IJPA, JPART, PAR, PMR, IPMJ. All studies can be found through: https://osf.io/7eqar/?view_only=61df534525d542838d65d5ee027ada85.
2. Based on the following inclusion criteria: empirical quantitative study, focused on JD-R theory and some well-being outcome, 100 percent (semi-)public sector sample, English.
3. Coding was based on the only two earlier meta-analyses that made a distinction between sectors (Blom et al., 2020b; Borst et al., 2019a): Organizations are defined as either public or semi-public on the basis of the following three formal characteristics: ownership, funding, and authority (Rainey, 2009). Public organizations are government-owned, are mainly publicly funded and the political authority is dominant over the economic authority, meaning that public managers' authority is dependent on and subjected to political decision making. These formal characteristics allow for considerable variety. On the one hand, there are the national police and army, which are fully public on all three criteria. On the other hand, in many countries, government-funded and mandated services are increasingly provided by organizational networks involving public, not-for-profit, and private organizations. An example of such a not-for-profit organization providing public services is the Salvation Army which operates in many countries to provide relief and social care to people in need. An example of institutional variation is provided by healthcare providers: in the UK the National Health Service represents all three formal criteria, while in the Netherlands healthcare is provided by organizations that are legally private bodies with a public task. These organizations who *mainly* fit the three formal characteristics are therefore defined as semi-public: education and human health services. Moreover organizations that *completely* fit the three characteristics are therefore unambiguously defined as public: public administration and compulsory social security.

REFERENCES

Bakker, A.B. (2015). A job demands-resources approach to Public Service Motivation. *Public Administration Review*, 75, 723–732.
Bakker, A.B., and Demerouti, E. (2007). The job demands-resources model: State of the art. *Journal of Managerial Psychology*, 22, 309–328.
Bakker, A.B., and Demerouti, E. (2014). Job demands-resources theory. In P.Y. Chen and C.L. Coopers (eds), *Work and wellbeing: Wellbeing a complete reference guide* (Volume III). Chichester: Wiley-Blackwell, pp. 37–64.
Bakker, A.B., and Demerouti, E. (2017). Job demands–resources theory: Taking stock and looking forward. *Journal of Occupational Health Psychology*, 22, 273–285.
Bakker, A.B., and Oerlemans, W. (2011). Subjective well-being in organizations. In K.S. Cameron and G.M. Spreitzer (eds), *The Oxford handbook of positive organizational scholarship*. New York, NY: Oxford University Press, pp. 178–189.
Bakker, A.B., Hakanen, J.J., Demerouti, E., and Xanthopoulou, D. (2007). Job resources boost work engagement, particularly when job demands are high. *Journal of Educational Psychology*, 99, 274–284.

Bakker, A.B., Albrecht, S.L., and Leiter, M.P. (2011). Work engagement: Further reflections on the state of play. *European Journal of Work and Organizational Psychology, 20*, 74–88.

Barber, L.K., Smit, B.W., and Shoss, M.K. (2013). The case of Mondays: Examining workplace rumors about stress. In D.J. Svyantek and K.T. Mahoney (eds), *Research in organizational sciences. Received wisdom, kernels of truth, and boundary conditions in organizational studies.* Charlotte, NC: IAP Information Age Publishing, pp. 27–75.

Bell, C., Johnston, D., Allan, J., Pollard, B., and Johnston, M. (2017). What do Demand-Control and Effort-Reward work stress questionnaires really measure? A discriminant content validity study of relevance and representativeness of measures. *British Journal of Health Psychology, 22*, 295–329.

Blom, R., Borst, R.T., and Voorn, B. (2020a). Pathology or inconvenience? A meta-analysis of the impact of red tape on people and organizations. *Review of Public Personnel Administration*, first published online on May 31, 2020 at https://doi.org/10.1177/0734371X20924117.

Blom, R., Kruyen, P.M., Van der Heijden, B.I.J.M., Van Thiel, S. (2020b). One HRM fits all? A meta-analysis of the effects of HRM practices in the public, semipublic, and private sector. *Review of Public Personnel Administration, 40*(1), 3–35.

Borst, R.T. (2018). Comparing work engagement in people-changing and people-processing service providers: A mediation model with red tape, autonomy, dimensions of PSM, and performance. *Public Personnel Management, 47*, 287–313.

Borst, R.T., and Lako, C.J. (2017). Proud to be a public servant? An analysis of the work-related determinants of professional pride among Dutch public servants. *International Journal of Public Administration, 40*, 875–887.

Borst, R.T., Kruyen, P.M., Lako, C.J., and de Vries, M.S. (2019a). The attitudinal, behavioral, and performance outcomes of work engagement: A comparative meta-analysis across the public, semipublic, and private sector. *Review of Public Personnel Administration*, first published online on June 3, 2019 at https://doi.org/10.1177/0734371X19840399.

Borst, R.T., Kruyen, P.M., and Lako, C.J. (2019b). Exploring the Job Demands–Resources Model of work engagement in government: Bringing in a psychological perspective. *Review of Public Personnel Administration, 39*, 372–397.

Cantarelli, P., Belardinelli, P., and Belle, N. (2015). A meta-analysis of job satisfaction correlates in the public administration literature. *Review of Public Personnel Administration, 36*, 115–144.

Cooke, D.K., Brant, K.K., and Woods, J.M. (2019). The role of Public Service Motivation in employee work engagement: A test of the Job Demands-Resources Model. *International Journal of Public Administration, 42*, 765–775.

De Jonge, J., and Dormann, C. (2006). Stressors, resources, and strains at work: A longitudinal test of the Triple Match Principle. *Journal of Applied Psychology, 91*, 1359–1374.

Dimoff, J.K., and Kelloway, E.K. (2016). Resource utilization model: Organizational leaders as resource facilitators. In W.A. Gentry and C. Clerkin (eds), *Research in occupational stress and well-being: Vol. 14. The role of leadership in occupational stress.* Bingley, UK: Emerald Group Publishing, pp. 141–160.

Fletcher, L., Bailey, C., Alfes, K., and Madden, A. (2020). Mind the context gap: A critical review of engagement within the public sector and an agenda for future research. *The International Journal of Human Resource Management, 31*, 6–46.

Giauque, D., Anderfuhren-Biget, S., and Varone, F. (2013). Stress perception in public organisations. *Review of Public Personnel Administration, 33*, 58–83.

Hackman, J.R., and Oldhamh, G.R. (1980). *Work redesign.* Reading, MA: AddisonWesley.

Harari, M.B., Herst, D.E.L., Parola, H.R., and Carmona, B.P. (2016). Organizational correlates of Public Service Motivation: A meta-analysis of two decades of empirical research. *Journal of Public Administration Research and Theory, 27*, 68–84.

Herzberg, F. (1966). *Work and the nature of man.* Cleveland, OH: Holland.

Hobfoll, S.E. (2001). The influence of culture, community, and the nested-self in the stress process: Advancing Conservation of Resources theory. *Applied Psychology: An International Review, 50*, 337–370.

Homberg, F., McCarthy, D., and Tabvuma, V. (2015). A meta-analysis of the relationship between Public Service Motivation and job satisfaction. *Public Administration Review, 75*, 711–722.

Hsieh, C.-W. (2012). Burnout among public service workers. *Review of Public Personnel Administration*, *34*, 379–402.
Jensen, U.T., Andersen, L.B., and Holten, A.-L. (2017). Explaining a dark side: Public Service Motivation, presenteeism, and absenteeism. *Review of Public Personnel Administration*, first published online on December 9, 2017 at https://doi.org/10.1177/0734371X17744865.
Karasek, R.A. (1979). Job demands, job decision latitude, and mental strain: Implications for job redesign. *Administrative Science Quarterly*, *24*, 285–308.
Karasek, R., and Theorell, T. (1990). *Healthy work: Stress, productivity and the reconstruction of working life*. New York, NY: Basic Books.
Kjeldsen, A.M. (2014). Dynamics of Public Service Motivation: Attraction-selection and socialization in the production and regulation of social services. *Public Administration Review*, *74*, 101–112.
Lazarus R.S., and Folkman S. (1984). *Stress, appraisal and coping*. New York, NY: Springer.
Llorens, S., Schaufeli, W., Bakker, A., and Salanova, M. (2007). Does a positive gain spiral of resources, efficacy beliefs and engagement exist? *Computers in Human Behavior*, *23*, 825–841.
Lorente Prieto, L., Salanova Soria, M., Martínez Martínez, I., and Schaufeli, W. (2008). Extension of the job demands-resources model in the prediction of burnout and engagement among teachers over time. *Psicothema*, *20*, 354–360.
Luthans, F., and Youssef, C.M. (2007). Emerging positive organizational behavior. *Journal of Management*, *33*, 321–349.
Macey, W.H. and Schneider, B. (2008). The meaning of employee engagement. *Industrial and Organizational Psychology*, *1*, 3–30.
Maslach, C., Schaufeli, W.B., and Leiter, M.P. (2001). Job burnout. *Annual Review of Psychology*, *52*, 397–422.
Parola, H.R., Harari, M. B., Herst, D.E.L., and Prysmakova, P. (2019). Demographic determinants of public service motivation: A meta-analysis of PSM-age and -gender relationships. *Public Management Review*, *21*, 1397–1410.
Quratulain, S., and Khan, A.K. (2013). Red tape, resigned satisfaction, public service motivation, and negative employee attitudes and behaviors. *Review of Public Personnel Administration*, *35*, 307–332.
Rainey, H. (2009). *Understanding and managing public organizations* (4th ed). San Francisco, CA: Jossey-Bass.
Scott, W.R. (2001). *Institutions and organizations* (2nd edn). Thousand Oaks, CA: Sage.
Schaufeli, W.B. (2017). Applying the Job Demands-Resources model. *Organizational Dynamics*, *46*, 120–132.
Schaufeli, W.B., and Taris, T.W. (2014). A critical review of the job demands-resources model: Implications for improving work and health. In G.F. Bauer and O. Hämmig (eds), *Bridging occupational, organizational and public health: A transdisciplinary approach*. Dordrecht, Netherlands: Springer, pp. 43–68.
Siegrist, J. (1996). Adverse health effects of high-effort/low-reward conditions. *Journal of Occupational Health Psychology*, *1*, 27–41.
Taris, T.W., Leisink, P.L.M., and Schaufeli, W.B. (2017). Applying occupational health theories to educator stress: Contribution of the Job Demands-Resources model. In T.M. McIntyre, S.E. McIntyre, and, D.J. Francis (eds), *Educator stress: An occupational health perspective*. London: Springer, pp. 237–260.
Tummers, L., Brunetto, Y., and Teo, S.T.T. (2016). Workplace aggression. *International Journal of Public Sector Management*, *29*, 2–10.
Van den Broeck, A., De Cuyper, N., De Witte, H., and Vansteenkiste, M. (2010). Not all job demands are equal: Differentiating job hindrances and job challenges in the Job Demands–Resources model. *European Journal of Work and Organizational Psychology*, *19*, 735–759.
Van Loon, N.M. (2015). Does context matter for the type of performance-related behavior of public service motivated employees? The relationship between PSM and multiple dimensions of self-reported performance-related behavior in various service providers. *Review of Public Personnel Administration*, *37*, 405–529.
Van Loon, N.M., Vandenabeele, W., and Leisink, P. (2015). On the bright and dark side of public service motivation: The relationship between PSM and employee wellbeing. *Public Money and Management*, *35*, 349–356.

Xanthopoulou, D., Bakker, A.B., Dollard, M.F., Demerouti, E., Schaufeli, W.B., Taris, T.W., and Schreurs, P.J.G. (2007). When do job demands particularly predict burnout? *Journal of Managerial Psychology, 22*, 766–786.

25. Worked to a crisp: 'realistic' and 'symbolic' stressor effects on burnout
Adam C. Green

INTRODUCTION

Work stress comes in many forms. Competing for a promotion, joining a new work group, being given unrealistic goals, changes in leadership, and scrutiny from the media are all examples of ways in which employees can experience stress from their job. Sources of stress, or stressors, can lead to emotional exhaustion, cynicism, and reduced feelings of efficacy at work, which are the three components of 'burnout' (Maslach et al., 2001). When employees experience burnout, they often disconnect from their work and become highly unproductive with their tasks. Burnt out employees are likely to either quit their job or engage in a number of counterproductive work behaviors in response. Work performance can thus be aided by examining this relationship between stressors and burnout. This chapter posits the following question about stressors and burnout: Do all work stressors contribute equally to burnout, or are there some stressors which contribute more strongly to burnout than others? To address this question, this chapter uses a social psychological lens to identify types of stressors which are most influential in leading to burnout. Specifically, this chapter uses Integrated Threat Theory (Stephan and Stephan, 2000) to distinguish between 'realistic' and 'symbolic' stressors, which are likely to differentially contribute to burnout. This chapter is laid out in the following structure.

1. Integrated Threat Theory is introduced and summarized. Realistic and symbolic threats are defined with examples of each.
2. 'Threats' are redefined within the organizational context, such that threat is conceptualized as a form of stressor when considering the workplace. Examples of these stressors are presented. Symbolic stressors are contrasted with realistic ones to postulate that symbolic stressors more efficiently contribute to burnout than do realistic stressors.
3. Organizational and external factors which might enhance or mitigate exposure to symbolic stressors are described, as well as individual differences which are likely to affect how well a given employee can deal with symbolic stressors.
4. Directions for future research are proposed.

INTEGRATED THREAT THEORY

'Threat,' in psychological terms, is our reaction to perceiving potential harm, and plays a powerful role in human psychology. Threat is useful to humans in that it allows us to avoid dangerous situations in which we can be harmed and has served us well in the past when avoiding dangerous animals (including dangerous humans). However, an extensive body of studies have found threat to be a main source of prejudice between groups of people (e.g., Steele, 1997; Stephan and Stephan, 1985, 2000, 2017). Threat to one's immediate safety is an obvious and intuitive way to conceptualize threat, but there are multiple types of threat which people experience. Stephan and Stephan's (2000) Integrated Threat Theory suggests that 'realistic' and 'symbolic' threats are two distinct varieties of threat which people can perceive as coming from another person or group of people.

Realistic threats threaten the existence or economic/political power of the self or of one's ingroup. The term 'ingroup' refers to any group of which one considers themselves a member (originally used to describe racial/political groups by Tajifel and colleagues, 1979; its definition has since expanded in the broader literature). Note that the term 'realistic' threat, here, does not refer to likelihood that a threat occurs, but rather refers to direct threat to one's, or one's group's, well-being. Examples of realistic threat sources include potentially losing one's job to someone else, an increase in crime in one's immediate vicinity, or one's favored party losing power in government. These sources of threat coincide with the common definition of what constitutes threat, and as such are relatively straightforward to understand in terms of their consequences, which involve the loss of safety, economic power, or political power at either the individual or group level.

Symbolic threats threaten the worldview of the self or one's ingroup. Symbolic threat can be induced by challenging someone's self-identity (Rudman et al., 2007) or beliefs (Stephan et al., 2000). Examples of symbolic threat sources include restrictions on one's religious freedoms, a coworker endorsing negative beliefs about one's ethnicity, or one having to talk to someone who strongly disagrees with them about a political topic. In short, these threats may not impact the well-being of one's group or self directly, but they can affect one's sense of self-identity and even an entire group's image for its members.

Integrated Threat Theory has been used to explain why minorities continue to be treated poorly in the US and other countries, including ethnic, sexual, and other minorities (Velasco González et al., 2008; Stephan and Stephan, 1985, 2000, 2017). Majority group members have rated ethnic minorities as posing both realistic and symbolic threat. These include realistic threats to jobs, safety, and political power, as well as symbolic threats to the dominant culture (e.g., bilingual education or cultural integration) (Steele, 1997; Velasco Gonzalez et al., 2008). Majority group members have rated sexual minorities as sources of primarily symbolic threat to what constitutes 'right' or 'wrong' (Riek et al., 2006), though realistic threat can also be perceived in the form of sexually transmitted diseases (e.g., AIDS) or through sexual attacks against women and children (e.g., transgender women attacking cisgender women and girls in women's bathrooms). These groups, along with others, are perceived as posing a threat to the majority group, and are the victims of prejudice and discrimination as a result.

While Integrated Threat Theory was created to address intergroup conflict, these types of threat are easily applied outside the context of larger groups (e.g., ethnicity or gender). Realistic threat is easily conceptualized in a general context. For example, the threat of a car crash, running low on money to pay bills, or the threat posed by a wild animal are each ways in which realistic threats can present themselves. Symbolic threats can also occur in a general context. For example, debating with another person about a contentious moral issue (Green, unpublished thesis data; see also Fisher et al., 2017), being presented with evidence that one's previously held belief is wrong, or witnessing one person victimizing another in an 'immoral' way. These examples can lead to the idea that one's values are under attack. To the extent that they do so, these examples constitute symbolic threats to one's worldview, beliefs, and/or morals.

THREAT IN ORGANIZATIONS: STRESSORS AND BURNOUT

In the context of organizational behavior, sources of threat are known as 'stressors.' Work stressors are anything job-related which causes stress to an employee (e.g., Chen and Spector, 1992). If work becomes sufficiently stressful, an employee can experience burnout, which is a combination of emotional exhaustion, cynicism, and low job efficacy (Maslach et al., 2001). Stressors can range from promotion competitions to a change in leadership to being ordered to do something unethical. Any stressor, when viewed through the lens of Integrated Threat Theory, can be seen as having realistic and/or symbolic components.

Consider the following stressors and their respective realistic and symbolic components:

1. An employee must meet a monthly quota for product sales, or risk losing their job.
2. A manager is pressured by their supervisor to persuade an employee to retire early, even though that employee loves their job and wants to keep working.
3. A police officer is assigned to police an anti-police violence protest.
4. An Environmental Protection Agency (EPA) employee must enforce new policies which harm the environment by allowing pollution of rivers.

Each of these stressors can produce varying levels of realistic and symbolic stress:

1. The possibility of the employee losing their job is very much a realistic stressor. However, it is also possible that the employee's sense of self relies, at least partly, on their ability to sell products and/or to make money. If that is the case, the risk of losing their job could also become a source of symbolic stress.
2. Pressure to force an employee into retirement can be a source of realistic or symbolic stressors. If the manager does not force the employee to retire, it may damage the chances for promotion or incur punishment (a realistic stressor). Conversely, forcing the employee into retirement may violate the stated values of the organization or the personal ethical beliefs of the manager (a symbolic stressor).
3. A police officer in this position faces the possibility that the protest may turn violent or that they could lose their job for behaving in a certain way (both are realistic stressors). They also face inherent symbolic threat in that the protesters are protesting police, which is an attack on the officer's self-identity (a symbolic stressor).
4. The EPA employee is certainly faced with a symbolic stressor, in that they are tasked with enforcing policies which run contrary to what they believe to be the purpose of their organization. They may be very capable of performing their task, but the difference between their personal beliefs and the actions they must take is a strong source of symbolic stress.

Given these examples, it should be clear that jobs each come with their own set of stressors, a notion which has long been assumed in literature on work stressors (e.g., Chen and Spector, 1992; Hatton et al., 1999). However, demonstrating that realistic and symbolic stressors exert differential effects on burnout, through the burnout components of emotional exhaustion, cynicism, and low job efficacy, is necessary to provide purpose to this theoretical distinction.

Realistic work stressors, such as job insecurity or being denied a promotion, can lead to anger, fear, and anxiety. Realistic stressors are functional in nature, and can be conceptualized as stressors which inhibit one's ability to succeed in their job. These stressors are primarily concerned with either achieving a goal or not achieving it. When considering their effect on burnout, realistic stressors primarily influence only job efficacy. If one is unsuccessful in completing their job or receives poor performance feedback (primary realistic stressors), the result is either that the employee redoubles their effort and perseveres or that the employee reacts negatively by giving up or decreasing the extent to which they rely on their work for personal fulfillment, both symptoms of job inefficacy (Maslach et al., 2001). While job inefficacy is one component of burnout, simply feeling less rewarded by, or capable of doing, one's job is not likely to be sufficient to lead an employee to experience burnout.

Symbolic stressors, such as witnessing unethical behavior or fulfilling a duty which goes against one's values/beliefs, can lead to a more complex set of responses. Cognitive Dissonance Theory (Festinger, 1962) holds that people strongly dislike cognitively contradictory thoughts, particularly about themselves. This includes when people engage in behaviors which contradict their beliefs, which forces one to do one of three things: change their actions to match their beliefs, change their beliefs to match their actions, or to tolerate the mismatch between their actions and beliefs. Each of these are possible outcomes of symbolic stressors. Consider the EPA employee from the earlier example. That employee can respond to their task of enforcing policy which contradicts their own beliefs or the organization's stated mission by doing one of three things: (1) they can change their actions to match their beliefs by quitting their job, (2) they can change their beliefs to match their actions by finding a reason why this particular policy is not so bad, or (3) they can tell themselves that they are just doing their job and keep enforcing the policy. The first option does not lead to burnout, as quitting precludes it. The second option requires one to compromise their beliefs by rationalizing away their own belief-violating actions, though people are generally adept at doing this, so, in most cases, this option is not likely to contribute significantly to burnout. The third option sustains one's cognitive dissonance, which can become a constant source of symbolic stress. Those who engage in this third option can become emotionally exhausted, cynical about the purpose of their job, and may receive less satisfaction from their job. This hits all three of the major components of burnout. In these cases, where an employee endures sustained or acute symbolic stress which they are unable to reconcile, burnout seems to be especially likely. Burnout, in turn, leads to an increase in turnover intention (i.e., intention to quit) and a host of counterproductive work behaviors, including gossip, theft, interpersonal conflict, and withholding information, among many others (Aronsson et al., 2017; Devereux et al., 2009; Jahanzeb and Fatima, 2018).

Figure 25.1 presents the theoretical model proposed in this chapter. While the model shows symbolic and realistic stressors as being separate, most stressors will have components of both types of stress. Thus, the model can most effectively be utilized by considering the magnitude of each type of stress a given stressor poses. Some stressors may be primarily realistic in nature, while others are primarily symbolic, though this can depend on organizational context and individual differences.

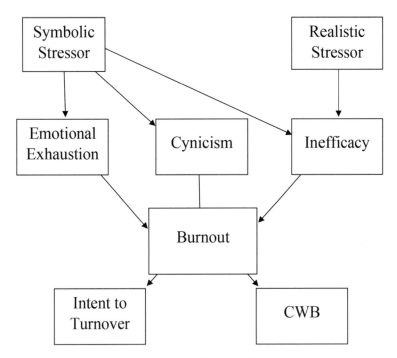

The proposed model of stressors' respective effects on burnout, through the constructs of emotional exhaustion, cynicism, and job efficacy, as well as the negative outcomes of turnover intention and counterproductive work behavior, which stem from burnout.

Figure 25.1   *Stressor path diagram: the proposed model of stressors' respective effects on burnout, through the constructs of emotional exhaustion, cynicism, and job efficacy, as well as the negative outcomes of turnover intention and counterproductive work behavior, which stem from burnout*

SYMBOLIC STRESSORS: ORGANIZATIONAL AND INDIVIDUAL FACTORS

Given the proposed influence of symbolic stressors on burnout, it is prudent to examine the environments in which they are most common, as well as the various individual factors which may enhance or minimize these effects. The following organizational factors are proposed to influence the presence or impact of symbolic stressors: organization sector (public versus private), leadership change, and public opinion. The following individual factors are proposed to influence the presence or impact of symbolic stressors: perceived organizational support, preference for hierarchy, work as part of one's identity, and personal ethics. Each of these factors will now be discussed in relation to symbolic stressors.

Public organizations can be defined by providing goods/services which are in the public interest, and are generally not concerned with making a profit (Rainey et al., 1976). Private organizations provide goods/services which the public, or other organizations, purchase, and are generally concerned with profit. However, the distinction between private and public has become less defined in recent years, as 'public' organizations contract out many duties to private organizations (privatization) while 'private' organizations are beholden to public laws and have taken public money to assist in their continued operation (e.g., banks, auto-makers, etc.). For the purposes of this chapter, 'public' organizations are defined as organizations which are not concerned with profit, while 'private' organizations are defined as organizations which compete with other organizations in a market to obtain profit.

Employees of private organizations compete for promotions through performance and generally have less job security due to the lack of private sector unionization. Additionally, their goals are clear: fulfill your job duties in order to help the organization generate more profit. These are each primarily realistic stressors. That being said, symbolic stressors can occur in private organizations. The earlier example of a manager being tasked with forcing an employee into retirement presents a source of symbolic stress. However, in most circumstances private organizations present primarily realistic stressors to their employees. Employees of public organizations, on the other hand, are more likely to be members of unions (providing job security), are not forced to compete with one another for promotions as often, and have the overarching task of providing their service/goods as effectively as possible. This dynamic suggests lower incidences of realistic stressors. Conversely, symbolic stressors can occur easily in public organizations. Public organizations are concerned with providing a service/good as effectively as possible (governance can be considered a service). Directives on what the organization's service/good is, and how to provide it, are sources of contention and stress for employees. For example, Immigration and Customs Enforcement (ICE) agents have been ordered to separate migrant children from their parents and detain them indefinitely (Aguilera, 2020). The agents themselves are not at risk, but being tasked with separating and confining children is likely a symbolic stressor for many agents. Stressors can be both strongly symbolic and realistic for public employees. For instance, United States Postal Service (USPS) workers were faced with the sabotage of their mission through removal of mail boxes and mail sorters shortly before the 2020 Presidential election, which was conducted mostly through mail-in voting due to the COVID-19 pandemic (Broadwater, 2020). This was presumably a symbolic and realistic stressor for USPS employees, as they were being used as a political instrument and were facing budget cuts which threatened their livelihoods. While the election mail was largely delivered on time due to strict prioritization by USPS, the after-effects of the election included massive backlogs of bills, letters, and other important mail for USPS customers (Naylor, 2021).

The presence of leadership change can also create symbolic stressors. A change in leadership can result in changes to the organization's goals, values, and expectations of its employees. These changes may alienate some employees, who do not agree with the new direction the organization is heading. This can serve as a symbolic stressor for those employees, as they are now tasked with fulfilling goals and adhering to values not consistent with what existed before. This is particularly the case for public employees of organizations where leaders are appointed by partisan elected officials. After an election, the former leaders of the organization may be replaced by new leaders who have completely opposite views for how the organization should best serve its purpose. Lower-level employees, in these cases, must endure this change, and experience confusion and stress because of it.

Public opinion can also be a symbolic stressor for employees. Negative public perception is a major external symbolic stressor. Public organizations are again most impacted by this, as organizations such as the police, Immigration and Customs Enforcement (ICE), and bureaucracies as a whole suffer from public image problems at the time of this writing. Employees of these organizations are the targets of public scorn from large sections of the population and blamed for misdeeds and inefficiencies of government. Private organizations are also impacted by public perception, though generally to a lesser degree. Employees of organizations which have violated ethical standards or have negative reputations can experience a conflict between their role as a worker and their membership of a negatively perceived organization, which is a symbolic stressor.

When considering the relationship between symbolic stressors and burnout, individual differences between employees enable some employees to avoid burnout for a longer period of time, while others may burn out relatively quickly. Several factors which may affect this relationship, either as a resource for the employee to draw upon or as a personality difference which insulates or exposes an employee to symbolic stress and/or burnout.

Perceived organizational support, defined as the extent to which an employee perceives their organization supports them in their work (Eisenberger et al., 1986), functions as a resource which protects against burnout by providing emotional resources to employees (Cheng and Yi, 2018; Kurtessis et al., 2017). While employees may be experiencing symbolic stress from their work, perceived organizational support can balance out their emotional resources and stave off burnout. Employees with low perceived organizational support, on the other hand, may react to symbolic stressors poorly in that they quickly become emotionally exhausted, cynical about their role in an organization that does not support them, and can lose meaning or confidence in doing their job.

Another resource of which employees vary in is their amount of preference for hierarchy, which is defined as the personal preference for systems which are highly hierarchical in structure (Friesen et al., 2014; Hudson et al., 2019). This construct, while primarily studied in intercultural or ethnic contexts, is a natural fit for organizational research, as organizations differ in their structure, and employees differ in the workplace environments in which they perform well. Here, high preference for hierarchy can influence the relationship between symbolic stressors and burnout by allowing employees to adjust their beliefs to match the actions tasked to them by authority figures. That is, those who prefer hierarchy would be better able to resolve the cognitive dissonance which symbolic stressors can create, as discussed earlier in the chapter. Conversely, those who do not prefer hierarchy are unlikely to use hierarchy as an excuse for changing their beliefs to match their actions and would then be more likely to sustain cognitive dissonance by continuing to perform tasks which go against their beliefs, which could then lead to burnout.

Symbolic stressors are stressors which stem from conflict with one's ideals, beliefs, or morals. Employees have been shown to vary on the amount that they consider their professional and personal identities to overlap (Pratt et al., 2006). Thus, it follows that the degree to which an employee bases their self-identity or self-worth on their job would influence the extent to which they are sensitive to symbolic stressors. Those who incorporate their work into how they view themselves are the most likely to be sensitive to symbolic threat. Conversely, those who view their work as more separate from themselves (i.e., work is something they do, rather than who they are) are less likely to care whether their personal beliefs are violated due to the separation between their 'self' and the organization they work for. For example, two doctors work in the same department of the same hospital. One doctor views their job primarily as one where they perform surgery and treat patients in exchange for a salary, while the other doctor considers saving people their life's work and prides themselves on their ability as a healer. Now, consider that these doctors are forced to decide who gets a ventilator when the hospital runs out of them during the COVID-19 pandemic (a type of symbolic stressor). The latter doctor would likely be much more affected by having to make this decision than the former, as the former would focus more on the fact that they are making a choice in order to perform their job well, while the latter would experience this decision as a failure on their part to live up to their self-image as a healer.

Finally, individuals have been shown to vary in the extent to which they care about certain aspects of morality. One conceptualization of morality proposes five different moral 'foundations': Harm, Fairness, Loyalty, Authority, and Purity (Graham et al., 2013). Each of these aspects can be violated in different ways in general contexts (e.g., discrimination based on race violates the Fairness foundation), or in the context of organizations. For example, the foundation of Harm can be violated by a manager being tasked with firing an employee who is the sole breadwinner for their family. Similarly, the foundation of Fairness can be violated by being subjected to discrimination due to gender, age, ethnicity or another characteristic. The foundation of Loyalty can be violated by an employee's manager refusing to honor a promised raise or bonus. The foundation of Authority can be violated by a whistleblower reporting unethical behavior by their organization to a media outlet. Lastly, the foundation of Purity can be violated by being subjected to unsanitary working conditions.

According to this theory, employees differ in their sensitivity to violations of these moral foundations (i.e., the degree to which they value each foundation). Some employees may be particularly sensitive to violations of Fairness, while others may be particularly sensitive to violations of Authority. Additionally, employees may vary in the total amount of sensitivity they possess towards moral violations in general. These differences lead to two theoretical proposals. First, employees who are particularly sensitive to a given type of moral violation should perceive those kinds of moral violations as more powerful symbolic stressors than those who are not as sensitive to those violations. Second, those who are more sensitive to moral violations in general will experience more symbolic stress overall due to the moral violations.

This list of potential moderating factors for the relationship between symbolic stressors and burnout is certainly incomplete. However, this provides a starting point when placing an individual employee in their work context, with the goal of predicting burnout based on the presence of symbolic stressors.

FUTURE RESEARCH

The idea that workplace stressors contribute to burnout has been studied extensively (e.g., Aronsson et al., 2017; Chen and Spector, 1992; Maslach et al., 2001). However, this chapter emphasizes the potential for identifying which stressors are most likely to lead to burnout, and in which organizational and individual contexts.

Future research into symbolic and realistic stressors should first focus on verifying the existence of two types of stressors in the workplace which fall into either a functional ('realistic') category or an ideological/ethical ('symbolic') category. However, the possibility exists that stressors can be broken down further into more categories. For example, the healthcare profession has been frequently studied in relation to burnout (e.g., Gillespie and Melbie, 2003; Shanafelt et al., 2002). The emotional stress which results from treating dying patients is an extremely potent stressor. One could argue that this would be a form of symbolic stressor in that a physician/nurse would not be in 'danger' as a result of another person's suffering. One could also argue that mental pain is no less 'realistic' than physical pain, and that this emotional stress would constitute a realistic stressor. Alternatively, this type of stress stemming from emotional hardship could belong to its own category of stressor. This question requires attention during the early stages of this avenue of research.

Once the categories of stressors have been defined, the next step is to examine their unique contributions to burnout. According to the theoretical model diagramed earlier in this chapter, symbolic stressors should contribute to all three of the components of burnout (to varying degrees based on the specific stressor), while realistic stressors should primarily impact only the component of inefficacy. As such, symbolic stressors should be stronger contributors to burnout than realistic stressors.

After establishing the crucial link from stressors (particularly symbolic ones) to burnout, it next becomes important to consider the contexts in which these stressors are more or less prevalent and more or less impactful to employees. Organizational and individual factors, possibly beginning with those listed in this chapter, should be examined as either insulating or exacerbating contextual elements. The addition of these factors should serve to enhance the accuracy with which burnout can be predicted and is thus a logical and necessary next step in this process.

Finally, developing recruiting, training, or supporting techniques which serve to protect against burnout by mitigating either the frequency or impact of work stressors seem to be the primary ways to apply the results of this line of research. Recruiting employees who are less affected by symbolic stressors, providing coping skills through training, and providing support to those employees faced with difficult situations in their jobs are each potential methods of reducing burnout. However, the specific content of these interventions and techniques will be informed by the results of the future research, and as such are still just topics of conjecture in this chapter.

If this line of research is found to be fruitful, managers can utilize the knowledge and techniques produced by it to better protect their employees from burnout and remain more productive and satisfied in their work lives.

REFERENCES

Aguilera, J. (2017) ICE is detaining children despite court order and COVID-19. https://time.com/5878909/children-ice-covid-19-detention-court-order/. Accessed August 17, 2020.

Aronsson, G., Theorell, T., Grape, T. et al. (2017). A systematic review including meta-analysis of work environment and burnout symptoms. *BMC Public Health*, *17*, published online on March 16, 2017 at https://link.springer.com/article/10.1186/s12889-017-4153-7.

Broadwater, L., Fuchs, H., and Corasaniti, N. (2020). Postal service warns states it may not meet mail-in ballot deadlines. https://www.nytimes.com/2020/08/14/us/politics/usps-vote-mail.html. Accessed August 15, 2020.

Chen, P.Y., and Spector, P.E. (1992). Relationships of work stressors with aggression, withdrawal, theft and substance use: An exploratory study. *Journal of Occupational and Organizational Psychology*, *65*, 177–184.

Cheng, J.C., and Yi, O. (2018). Hotel employee job crafting, burnout, and satisfaction: The moderating role of perceived organizational support. *International Journal of Hospitality Management*, *72*, 78–85.

Devereux, J.M., Hastings, R.P., Noone, S.J., Firth, A., and Totsika, V. (2009). Social support and coping as mediators or moderators of the impact of work stressors on burnout in intellectual disability support staff. *Research in Developmental Disabilities*, *30*, 367–377.

Eisenberger, R., Huntington, R., Hutchison, S., and Sowa, D. (1986). Perceived organizational support. *Journal of Applied Psychology*, 71, 500–507.

Festinger, L. (1962). Cognitive dissonance. *Scientific American*, 207, 93–106.

Fisher, M., Knobe, J., Strickland, B., and Keil, F.C. (2017). The influence of social interaction on intuitions of objectivity and subjectivity. *Cognitive Science*, 41, 1119–1134.

Friesen, J.P., Kay, A.C., Eibach, R.P., and Galinsky, A.D. (2014). Seeking structure in social organization: Compensatory control and the psychological advantages of hierarchy. *Journal of Personality and Social Psychology*, 106, 590–609.

Gillespie, M., and Melby, V. (2003). Burnout among nursing staff in accident and emergency and acute medicine: A comparative study. *Journal of Clinical Nursing*, 12, 842–851.

Graham, J., Haidt, J., Koleva, S., Motyl, M., Iyer, R., Wojcik, S.P., and Ditto, P.H. (2013). Moral foundations theory: The pragmatic validity of moral pluralism. In P. Devine and A. Plant (eds), *Advances in Experimental Social Psychology* (Vol. 47). Boston, MA: Academic Press pp. 55–130.

Hatton, C., Emerson, E., Rivers, M. et al. (1999). Factors associated with staff stress and work satisfaction in services for people with intellectual disability. *Journal of Intellectual Disability Research*, 43, 253–267.

Hudson, S.K., Cikara, M., and Sidanius, J. (2019). Preference for hierarchy is associated with reduced empathy and increased counter-empathy towards others, especially out-group targets. *Journal of Experimental Social Psychology*, 85, at https://doi.org/10.1016/j.jesp.2019.1038713871.

Jahanzeb, S., and Fatima, T. (2018). How workplace ostracism influences interpersonal deviance: The mediating role of defensive silence and emotional exhaustion. *Journal of Business and Psychology*, 33, 779–791.

Kurtessis, J.N., Eisenberger, R., Ford, M.T., Buffardi, L.C., Stewart, K.A., and Adis, C.S. (2017). Perceived organizational support: A meta-analytic evaluation of organizational support theory. *Journal of Management*, 43, 1854–1884.

Maslach, C., Schaufeli, W.B., and Leiter, M.P. (2001). Job burnout. *Annual Review of Psychology*, 52, 397–422.

Naylor, B. (2021). Postal service delivered vast majority of mail ballots on time, report finds. https://www.npr.org/2021/03/09/975198962/postal-service-delivered-vast-majority-of-mail-ballots-on-time-report-finds Accessed November 15, 2021.

Pratt, M.G., Rockmann, K.W., and Kaufmann, J.B. (2006). Constructing professional identity: The role of work and identity learning cycles in the customization of identity among medical residents. *Academy of Management Journal*, 49, 235–262.

Rainey, H.G., Backoff, R.W., and Levine, C.H. (1976). Comparing public and private organizations. *Public Administration Review*, 36, 233–244.

Riek, B.M., Mania, E.W., and Gaertner, S L. (2006). Intergroup threat and outgroup attitudes: A meta-analytic review. *Personality and Social Psychology Review*, 10, 336–353.

Rudman, L.A., Dohn, M.C., and Fairchild, K. (2007). Implicit self-esteem compensation: Automatic threat defense. *Journal of Personality and Social Psychology*, 93, 798.

Shanafelt, T.D., Bradley, K.A., Wipf, J.E., and Back, A.L. (2002). Burnout and self-reported patient care in an internal medicine residency program. *Annals of Internal Medicine*, 136, 358–367.

Steele, C.M. (1997). A threat in the air: How stereotypes shape intellectual identity and performance. *American Psychologist*, 52, 613–629.

Stephan, W.G., and Stephan, C.W. (1985). Intergroup anxiety. *Journal of Social Issues*, 41, 157–175.

Stephan, W.G., and Stephan, C.W. (2000). An integrated threat theory of prejudice. In S. Oskamp (ed.), *Reducing Prejudice and Discrimination*. New York, NY: Psychology Press, pp. 23–45.

Stephan, W.G., and Stephan, C.W. (2017). Intergroup threat theory. In Y.Y. Kim (ed.), *The International Encyclopedia of Intercultural Communication*. Hoboken, NJ: Wiley, pp. 1–12.

Stephan, W.G., Diaz-Loving, R., and Duran, A. (2000). Integrated threat theory and intercultural attitudes: Mexico and the United States. *Journal of Cross-cultural Psychology*, 31, 240–249.

Tajfel, H., Turner, J.C., Austin, W.G., and Worchel, S. (1979). An integrative theory of intergroup conflict. In M.J. Hatch and M. Schultz (eds), *Organizational Identity*. New York, NY: Oxford University Press, pp. 56–65.

Velasco González, K., Verkuyten, M., Weesie, J., and Poppe, E. (2008). Prejudice towards Muslims in the Netherlands: Testing integrated threat theory. *British Journal of Social Psychology*, 47, 667–685.

26. What happened to you? Understanding trauma and motivation in the public service workplace

Heather Getha-Taylor and Morgan D. Farnworth

INTRODUCTION

In the last decade, trauma has received increasing attention as a harmful, endemic public health problem (Becker-Blease, 2017; Magruder et al., 2017). Put simply, trauma is the emotional response to suffering, occurring as a result of violence, abuse, loss, and other adverse experiences (Substance Abuse and Mental Health Services Administration, 2014). In the United States, most individuals experience at least one life-threatening or violent situation during the course of their lives (Goldstein et al., 2016; Kilpatrick et al., 2013; Ozer et al., 2003). Importantly, exposure to trauma can impact health and wellbeing across a lifetime; these include poor physical and mental health outcomes (Anda et al., 2006; Felitti et al., 1998; Monnat and Chandler, 2015), fewer economic resources (Caspi et al., 1998; Covey et al., 2013; Zielinski, 2009), and adverse social outcomes (Kim et al., 2010; Messina and Grella, 2006). The widespread incidence of trauma and its deep impacts on American society resulted in intentional efforts to create trauma-sensitive service delivery systems, designed to be responsive to the needs of trauma survivors (Purtle and Lewis, 2017; Unick et al., 2019). These organizational reforms, however, are aimed at recipients of public services, and little scholarly attention is devoted to the impacts of trauma on the public service workforce. Despite receiving systematic treatment in other disciplines, including psychology, behavioral health, education, criminal justice, and social work, public administration has yet to examine the organizational impacts and considerations for managing a trauma-exposed workforce.

In response, this chapter introduces the concept of trauma and explores its implications for public employee motivation. Because of its complex and enduring nature, trauma may influence motivation through multiple pathways. Employees may be drawn to public service as a result of their own trauma (Evans and Evans, 2019): acting as a 'wounded healer,' public servants leverage their lived experience with adversity to empathize with clients and to better provide public services. In this vein, the public sector may attract a workforce with higher incidence of trauma exposure. Conversely, public servants, especially in front-line positions, may be exposed to trauma 'on the job,' while employed by public organizations (Anne Dombo and Whiting Blome, 2016; Carmassi et al., 2020; Ricciardelli et al., 2018). Public sector occupations in emergency response, healthcare, law enforcement, and social services are characterized by high job stress and frequent exposure to trauma. Otherwise, public employees may also experience vicarious trauma, by virtue of serving clients who have themselves experienced traumatic events (Anne Dombo and Whiting Blome, 2016). For these reasons, understanding trauma and its implications is a timely and important task.

Leveraging research across multiple disciplines, we present existing conceptualizations of trauma, describe contributing factors to trauma among public sector employees, and review the impacts of traumatic experiences—tailored to public management scholars and practitioners. This chapter also applies these insights to public employee motivation. Through the lens of trauma-informed public service, we argue that exposure to trauma may influence motivation in meaningful ways. We provide a framework for future trauma-informed scholarship to explore this relationship, while offering practical guidance to implement a trauma-sensitive public management approach.

DEFINING TRAUMA

While definitions vary across discipline, the concept of individual trauma (or traumatic stress) encompasses both the traumatic event and its resulting impacts. In simplest terms, trauma is the mental, emotional, and physiological response to a harmful event (Kimberg and Wheeler, 2019; Substance Abuse and Mental Health Services Administration, 2014). A more nuanced definition of trauma emphasizes 'the three E's' of individual trauma: events, experience, and effects.

> Individual trauma results from an event, or series of events, or set of circumstances that is experienced by an individual as physically or emotionally harmful or life threatening and that has lasting adverse effects on the individual's functioning and mental, physical, social, emotional, or spiritual well-being. (Substance Abuse and Mental Health Services Administration, 2014, p. 7)

Potentially traumatic events are numerous, including, for example: physical, sexual, and emotional abuse; living with a family member with mental health or substance use disorders; sudden or unexplained separation from a loved one; witnessing death or violence; experiencing discrimination, or living in an unsafe neighborhood (Goldstein et al., 2016; Kilpatrick et al., 2013; Kimberg and Wheeler, 2019; Straussner and Calnan, 2014). Conversely, traumatic events can impact entire communities or racial/ethnic groups, such as natural, environmental, and health disasters; war and terrorism; human trafficking and exploitation; systematic oppression, poverty, mass incarceration, and police violence (Bor et al., 2018; Magruder et al., 2017; Straussner and Calnan, 2014). Criteria for trauma in the *Diagnostic and Statistical Manual of Mental Disorders*, 5th edition (DSM-5) emphasize the broad nature of trauma, defining trauma exposure as direct experiences, witnessing a traumatic event, learning of a traumatic event experienced by a loved one, or repeated exposure to the details of a traumatic event (American Psychiatric Association, 2013). That is, traumatic events encompass those experienced first-hand, as well as vicarious, second-hand exposure to harm (Pearlman and McKay, 2008). Exposure to trauma may be acute (short-lived) or complex—involving recurring, chronic exposure to severe traumatic events over time (Courtois and Ford, 2009; Kimberg and Wheeler, 2019). Trauma can also be historical, affecting entire communities over multiple generations (Bor et al., 2018; Gone, 2013; Sotero, 2006).

Traumas that occur during childhood, referred to as Adverse Childhood Experiences (ACEs), are particularly harmful and enduring. Early adversity impacts development in parts of the brain responsible for empathy, problem solving, impulse control, and the body's threat response (Anda et al., 2006; Felitti et al., 1998; Straussner and Calnan, 2014). Long-term impacts of ACEs include worse self-rated health and more functional limitations (Monnat and Chandler, 2015; Springer et al., 2007), greater risk of diabetes and heart attack (Felitti et al., 1998; Monnat and Chandler, 2015), increased likelihood of mental health and substance use disorders (Goldstein et al., 2016; Springer et al., 2007), and premature death (Brown et al.,

2009). Scholarship also identifies adverse social outcomes associated with childhood trauma, such as lower adult socioeconomic status (Covey et al., 2013; Zielinski, 2009), higher rates of unemployment (Caspi et al., 1998), and higher risk of incarceration (Kim et al., 2010; Messina and Grella, 2006).

At any age, trauma exposure can lead to adverse health and social outcomes. Trauma is highly individualized: not everyone that experiences a traumatic event develops longer-lasting impacts. The effect of trauma is dependent on an individual's own perception of a traumatic event, their level of exposure and individual risk factors, and the broader social, political, and cultural context in which the event occurs (Magruder et al., 2017; McLaughlin et al., 2013; Straussner and Calnan, 2014). Exposure to traumatic stress, whether first- or second-hand, can cause disorientation, impaired awareness and judgement, hypervigilance, and the use of health-harming coping mechanisms (Levin et al., 2011; Pearlman and McKay, 2008; Straussner and Calnan, 2014). While these impacts are short-term for most, with human resilience buffering the effects of trauma (Bonanno et al., 2007), traumatic stress can develop into post-traumatic stress disorder (PTSD). This is a more persistent form of traumatic stress, affecting between 6 and 12 percent of the US population (American Psychiatric Association, 2013). Individuals with PTSD often re-experience the traumatic event (e.g., flashbacks, nightmares), resulting in irritability, risk-taking behaviors, being more easily startled, and difficulty sleeping or concentrating (American Psychiatric Association, 2013). Importantly, individuals who have experienced trauma may have behavioral symptoms and maladaptive behaviors; these are misapplied survival skills learned from coping with adverse experiences, whether occurring in childhood or as an adult. In the face of such behaviors, it may be tempting to ask: '*What is wrong with you?*' but it may be more important to ask: '*What happened to you?*' (Jennings, 2007).

PATHWAYS OF TRAUMA EXPOSURE IN THE PUBLIC SERVICE WORKFORCE

Unfortunately, trauma is incredibly prevalent across the United States. While there is no comprehensive national surveillance of trauma exposure, epidemiological assessments find that a majority of adults—between 69 percent (Goldstein et al., 2016) and 90 percent (Kilpatrick et al., 2013)—report at least one potentially traumatic event during their lifetime. Focusing on childhood trauma, considering its especially detrimental impacts, Merrick and colleagues (2018) find that 62 percent of adults in the United States experienced at least one traumatic event in childhood and that 25 percent of all adults had three or more adverse childhood experiences (Merrick et al., 2018). To be clear, public employees do not exist within a vacuum; given the prevalence of trauma across the United States, it is likely that large portions of the public service workforce similarly have experienced at least one traumatic event in their lifetimes.

To compound this issue, public employees may be at particular risk of experiencing trauma as a result of their occupation. Government employees, especially those in front-line positions, are regularly exposed to traumatic events, including first responders (Berninger et al., 2010; Clohessy and Ehlers, 1999; Molnar et al., 2017; Ricciardelli et al., 2018) and, especially in the context of the COVID-19 pandemic, healthcare workers (Carmassi et al., 2020). Each of these high-stress occupations involves, sometimes on a daily basis, direct exposure to trauma: witnessing death and human suffering, treating severe illness or injury, and caring for individuals who have experienced trauma. At minimum, contending with life-and-death work situations on a daily basis can be a source of burnout (Valcik and Benavides, 2017). Notably, research in this area finds that PTSD rates are higher for healthcare workers (Carmassi et al., 2020), firefighters (Berninger et al., 2010), and ambulance workers (Clohessy and Ehlers, 1999) as compared to the general US population.

In addition to direct exposure to traumatic events on the job, individuals may also experience indirect trauma, also known as vicarious trauma, or second-hand exposure to suffering (Molnar et al., 2017; Pearlman and McKay, 2008). Many public sector occupations involve repeated exposure to the details of traumatic events or work directly with trauma survivors, such as mental health providers (Cieslak et al., 2013), correctional officers (Bezerra et al., 2016), child welfare and social workers (Anne Dombo and Whiting Blome, 2016), and judges and attorneys (Levin et al., 2011; Vrklevski and Franklin, 2008). Much like direct trauma exposure, vicarious trauma impacts emotional, physical, and overall wellbeing (Levin et al., 2011; Molnar et al., 2017). In fact, the most recent diagnostic criteria for PTSD was updated to include recurring exposure to the details of traumatic events as potentially triggering the disorder (American Psychiatric Association, 2013). Even when exposure does not lead to PTSD, individuals in the 'helping' or empathetic professions describe vicarious trauma as compassion fatigue, or the 'cost of caring' (Figley, 2013).

Beyond the nature of the work, public employees can experience traumatic events as a result of workplace characteristics and interpersonal dynamics. For example, sexual harassment can be a significant source of trauma, especially when it involves a threat to physical integrity or financial wellbeing and concerns regarding the unpredictability of the harasser's behavior (Avina and O'Donohue, 2002). Even more, government employees may be the target of anti-government violence or other forms of occupational violence crime unique to the public sector (Nigro and Waugh, 1996). Other potential sources of workplace traumatic stress include bullying, racial and gender discrimination (Straussner and Calnan, 2014), and work overload in high-stress environments (Bezerra et al., 2016).

Despite the pathway of trauma exposure—whether direct or indirect—its implications of managing a trauma-exposed workforce are numerous. Employees, as a result of their public service work, may develop trauma-related symptoms, including, among others: fatigue and poor sleep (Clohessy and Ehlers, 1999; Straussner and Calnan, 2014), impacts on interpersonal relationships (Bezerra et al., 2016; Clohessy and Ehlers, 1999; Pearlman and McKay, 2008), difficulty with emotional regulation (Pearlman and McKay, 2008; Straussner and Calnan, 2014), avoidance behaviors (Levin et al., 2011), hyperarousal and reactivity (Cieslak et al., 2013; Vrklevski and Franklin, 2008), and difficulty functioning at work (Berninger et al., 2010; Magruder et al., 2017). For these reasons, understanding and addressing trauma among public employees is a critical priority.

INTERDISCIPLINARY INSIGHTS ON TRAUMA

The concept of trauma has received systematic treatment in other disciplines; however, public administration has yet to contend with the relationship between trauma and public service. Scholars and practitioners identified occupational violent crime as a threat to US government employees (Nigro and Waugh, 1996), noting the importance of the working conditions and management policies in protecting employees. While occupational violent crime is of great concern, public employees are exposed to trauma in other ways, by virtue of serving the public. Drawing from other scholarly areas, we explore insights on the organizational impacts and management implications of a trauma-exposed workforce. While existing scholarship examines the individual and organizational impacts of trauma, these efforts are generally siloed by discipline.

From psychology, Bezerra et al. (2016) reviewed the literature on psychological distress and work stress among correctional officers. From their work, we learn that stress among these workers is high, especially when they do not have the necessary resources and support to carry out their work. While the literature on this topic acknowledges the impact of organizational stressors, recommendations about individual psychological responses 'are seldom useful against persisting or overwhelming organizational stressors' (Bezerra et al., 2016, p. 2144). It is clear that organizational investments must also be made to improve work conditions for these front-line workers.

From the business management literature, we learn that investing in employee health and wellness just makes good business sense: it is linked to optimal organizational performance (Grossmeier et al., 2016). It is also a cost saving measure: a failure to invest in employee health and wellbeing can be linked to increased costs of health insurance, absenteeism, low morale and disengagement, and turnover (Lowe, 2020). However, organizations must be intentional about their investments, which includes determining the return on employee health investments. Contemporary organizations often track such returns via metrics such as improvements in factors such as employee satisfaction, engagement, turnover, and retention (Lowe, 2020).

From the health literature, we find that trauma-informed directives are more focused on service delivery recipients than on employees. For example, the TICOMETER assessment was developed by Bassuk and colleagues (2017) to measure trauma-informed care in the context of health and human services. The instrument includes items to measure five domains: (1) building trauma-informed knowledge and skills, (2) establishing trusting relationships, (3) respecting service users, (4) fostering trauma-informed service delivery, and (5) promoting trauma-informed procedures and policies (Bassuk et al., 2017). The goal of the assessment is to understand how trauma-informed practices impact client outcomes.

From the social work literature, we learn that social service agencies are largely unaware of the relevance of trauma-informed care as it relates to staff (Wolf et al., 2014). While social service agencies may have policies and procedures in place to ensure that core elements of *safety, choice, empowerment, collaboration,* and *trustworthiness* are in place for services to clients, these same policies are 'few and far between' as it relates to staff (Wolf et al., 2014, p. 119). The Trauma-Informed Climate Scale-10 (TICS-10) developed by Hales and colleagues (2019) represents an advancement in that it is designed to assess staff perceptions of safety, trust, choice, collaboration, and empowerment within a human services context (Hales et al., 2019). It can be used to identify areas of organizational strength and also areas for improvement.

Together, these interdisciplinary insights provide a foundation for understanding of the value of incorporating a trauma-informed lens to public service practice. Specifically, these findings highlight the need for, and the value of, investing in employee wellbeing. Further, these findings reveal a gap: the principles of trauma-informed care have primarily been directed at clients of social services, not employees. Finally, to fully address the impacts associated with occupational trauma, both individual and organizational resources and interventions are needed.

PUBLIC ADMINISTRATION AND TRAUMA

According to Guy and Newman (2016, p. 206), public service is a 'relational enterprise' that requires a human touch, including attention to the emotional labor required in citizen services (Guy and Newman, 2016, p. 206). Contemporary public service must be responsive to human needs: both the needs of citizens and the public servants who serve them. However, this premise was not always assumed. The inadequacy of public administration to address critical societal problems was at the heart of the New Public Administration (NPA) movement of the late 1960s and early 1970s. NPA reformers pushed administrators to act as change agents to better serve a changing society (Marini, 1971). This was, according to Zimring (1971, pp. 230–1), a significant break from 'value-free' or 'value-neutral' administrative norms that emphasized economy and efficiency as dominant bureaucratic values (Marini, 1971). Rather, bureaucracy should be an instrument for achieving the goals of social justice and equality.

While there was broad agreement with the need for NPA, Thompson (1975) raised an objection. As one of the lone voices of opposition, Thompson argued that the movement introduced inappropriate bureaucratic discretion which threatened public sovereignty. Further, he argued against compassionate administration. While there are certainly needs for compassionate treatment, Thompson contends that public organizations and their employees are 'incapable of becoming personally and deeply involved' (Thompson, 1975, p. 9). Understandably, this perspective may be seen as tone deaf to the needs of communities. However, when considering public employees, Thompson has a valid point. Indirect trauma and compassion fatigue are risks associated with working for a responsive bureaucracy.

Traditionally, one of the defining features of bureaucracy, according to Weber (1946), is its impersonal nature: 'the more bureaucracy is "dehumanized" the more completely it succeeds in eliminating from official business love, hatred, and all purely personal, irrational and emotional elements which escape calculation. This is the specific nature of bureaucracy and it is appraised as its special value' (Weber, 1946, p. 216). The scientific management movement, best known by the work of Frederick Taylor and the 'one best way,' also worked to minimize the human nature of public work through the pursuit of neutral, value-free management practices. Yet, the human relations movement, including the work of scholars such as Frederick Herzberg, Abraham Maslow, and Douglas McGregor, was a clear rejoinder that removing the personal aspects of organizations is neither recommended nor is it possible.

Today, there is a broader recognition of the affective dimensions of public administration (Guy and Mastracci, 2018; Hsieh et al., 2012). Public human resource management scholars and practitioners understand that chronic stress negatively affects employee performance and is therefore a concern for public organizations (Berman et al., 2019). While there are a variety of legal frameworks in place such as the Occupational Health and Safety Act (OSHA), the Americans with Disabilities Act (ADA), and the Family and Medical Leave Act (FMLA), these are just starting points for acknowledging the importance of public employee health. Applying these frameworks in practice has more often focused on legalistic interpretations of employee health (e.g., Bradbury and Jacobson, 2013) and less on overall employee wellbeing. As our understanding of employee wellbeing evolves, so should our policies and programs (Lowe, 2020).

MOTIVATING PUBLIC EMPLOYEES: A TRAUMA-INFORMED APPROACH

Motivating public employees is critical, given their connection with citizens and the potential impact of their work. However, motivation is a challenge in an environment when resources are constrained and public service is undervalued. While textbooks on public management typically address the topics of employee health and motivation, they often do so separately rather than exploring their connection. Yet, this connection is captured in one of our field's most fundamental and enduring ideas: Maslow's (1943) hierarchy of needs (HON) theory.

In popular representations of HON theory, the motivation to achieve and reach one's potential is only possible when more basic needs are met (Maslow, 1943). That is, the workplace context must meet basic needs (like health and safety) before more complex ones, including belonging and love, esteem, and self-actualization, can be realized. HON is often represented as a pyramid, implying that one need must be completely satisfied before moving to a higher level (Bridgman et al., 2019; Michel, 2014). However, these categories are not mutually exclusive, and the depiction of HON theory as such is related to marketing rather than empirical rigor (Bridgman et al., 2019). A HON that better reflects its indigenous origins—informed by Maslow's fieldwork with the Blackfoot Tribe (Michel, 2014)—emphasizes the interdependent domains of cognitive, physical, emotional, and spiritual needs (Blackstock, 2011). Importantly, trauma-informed care gives equal emphasis to physical and emotional safety alongside other core values, like trustworthiness, choice and control, collaboration, and empowerment (Fallot and Harris, 2006; Hales et al., 2019).

Further, trauma can serve as a potential explanation that is unexplored and potentially impactful. While our collective understanding of trauma has grown, we have paid insufficient attention to the impacts of trauma on employees who are involved in the delivery of public services in the United States. As noted in this chapter, there are many forces that contribute to public employee stress, which may also represent sources of trauma, including: interpersonal relationships, workload pressures, and stressful work tasks, as well as perceptions of organizational justice or fairness (Denhardt et al., 2018). While there are a number of organizational options for helping employees cope with these issues, recommendations often focus on individual efforts (such as enhancing coping skills). It is important to remember that individual interventions do not address the broader causes of stress and trauma.

Goh and colleagues (2016) note that the emphasis on individual wellness behaviors omits a critical factor: the impact of the work environment on employee health. Such factors as loss of control and lack of social support contribute to levels of stress that adversely affect employee health outcomes including increased risk of cardiovascular disease, depression, and anxiety (Goh et al., 2016). Organizational interventions must also be pursued, including giving workers the necessary autonomy, resources, and support to effectively manage their work demands which influences continued motivation (Lowe, 2020). This approach illustrates trauma-informed care or trauma-informed practice, which is 'grounded in understanding and responding to the potential impacts of trauma and creating opportunities for people to rebuild a sense of agency and control' (Unick et al., 2019, p. 135).

The core principles of trauma-informed care are reflected in the Substance Abuse and Mental Health Service Administration's four R's (2014):

- *Realizing* the widespread impact of trauma

- *Recognizing* the signs and symptoms of trauma among clients and staff
- *Responding* by integrating knowledge about trauma into practice and policy
- *Resisting* re-traumatization.

If public servants incorporate these principles into practice, the expectation is that these values will also support an environment which cultivates motivation. Unfortunately, despite growing evidence of workplace stress as a serious and potentially traumatic issue, 'most employers have not addressed the root causes of stress, burnout, work-life conflict, harassment, toxic work environments, and other contributors to reduced employee well-being' (Lowe, 2020, p. 59). Specifically, organizations have not done enough to understand and intervene to improve the 'psychosocial' work environment which includes the way work is organized, the way jobs are designed, the workplace psychological experience, and workplace relationships (Nigro and Waugh, 1996).

These elements are of particular concern in a public sector environment that prizes performance indicators of motivation, like regular employee engagement surveys (Byrne et al., 2017). It is critical to remember that employee engagement and employee wellbeing are linked and complementary goals. Healthy and safe employees are more engaged and a psychologically healthy workplace contributes to employee engagement (Lowe, 2020). In the public sector's push for improved engagement, how are managers and organizations matching employee investments to support continued motivation? Also, how are scholars investigating these efforts to build trauma-informed motivation theory and provide generalizable insights?

TRAUMA-INFORMED RESEARCH RECOMMENDATIONS

Our knowledge of occupational trauma in public service, including its effects on workers, is in its infancy. This gap represents a rich area for future investigations.

First, what is the relationship between public service motivation (PSM) and exposure to trauma? Does exposure to trauma as a result of public service work, whether first-hand or vicariously, augment empathy and increase PSM? Or does it lead to burnout and decrease PSM? How might the relationship between PSM and occupational trauma be impacted by organizational context and available supports?

Second, are employees drawn to public service as a result of their own first-hand trauma, as suggested by Evans and Evans (2019)? Those employed in public service organizations may choose to leverage their own lived experience, including exposure to trauma, as a form of expertise (Merritt et al., 2020). In the context of behavioral healthcare, Merritt and colleagues (2020) found such organizations employ individuals with mental health issues or substance use disorders *because of* their lived experience to enhance client-provider trust, foster a client-centered organizational model, and improve service delivery.

Third, are certain public service occupational groups more prone to direct or vicarious trauma? Does the cultivation of individual resilience help mitigate the adverse impacts of direct or indirect occupational trauma? How can public organizations help cultivate resilience (Bonanno et al., 2007), or emotional grit (Guy and Mastracci, 2018), to help improve employee effectiveness in front-line jobs? What are the most promising strategies for enhancing resilience? What are the most promising organizational strategies for mitigating occupational trauma in public service?

PRACTICAL RECOMMENDATIONS FOR TRAUMA-INFORMED PUBLIC SERVICE

While there is much to be learned about the extent of trauma exposure in the public service workforce and its impact on motivation, public organizations can incorporate trauma-informed principles into the delivery of public service. Trauma-informed care is a non-clinical, systems approach; it focuses on prevention rather than treatments for individual trauma (Bassuk et al., 2017; Jennings, 2007; Unick et al., 2019). This underscores the importance of a comprehensive systems approach to understanding, recognizing, and mitigating the impacts of trauma for both clients and public employees. By developing an organizational structure and culture that is responsive to the needs of trauma survivors, public organizations can help buffer the impact of trauma experienced by public servants. Integrated with the core goals of trauma-informed care, we present a set of recommendations for public agencies and public managers to foster resilience and build a trauma-informed public service.

First, public agencies should take care to train and educate all employees and managers on trauma and its impacts. This ensures that all individuals within the organization have the same level of understanding around trauma. Research has shown that agency efforts, such as the implementation of trauma-informed training, influence the effectiveness of trauma-informed care (Unick et al., 2019; Wolf et al., 2014). Topics of particular interest to public servants include the sources of first-hand or vicarious trauma, the relationship between traumatic stress and health, and how public organizations can foster resilience (Fallot and Harris, 2006; Guarino et al., 2009). These concepts should be reinforced in regular team meetings, alongside opportunities to discuss self-care strategies, engage in self-care practices, and debrief after traumatic events. To ensure regular, ongoing training and education around trauma, public organizations may establish an internal trauma team or workgroup (Guarino et al., 2009).

Importantly, public organizations must take care to ensure the safety of employees. As a foundational need (Maslow, 1943), safety is ensuring the emotional and physical wellbeing of individuals. Workplace safety can be enhanced by respecting the privacy and boundaries of employees, enforcing zero tolerance policies for sexual harassment and bullying, providing physical and mental health benefits and time off, and ensuring that common areas, bathrooms, and outside grounds are well lit. Further, public organizations can promote transparency and trustworthiness by providing accurate job descriptions, offering task clarity and consistency, and maintaining interpersonal boundaries. Successful managers also provide clear lines of communication, regular direction and feedback, and a formal system for addressing concerns, conflicts, and complaints. Interestingly, a failure to meet the mental health needs of public employees, especially those in high-stress occupations, can deteriorate trust between employees and the government, their employer (Ricciardelli et al., 2018). In this way, an organization's commitment to safety and trust are intrinsically linked.

Additionally, choice and empowerment remain core areas of action for public organizations. Despite strict hierarchical lines, public organizations can take care to include employees in decisions that affect them, provide opportunities for professional development and career advancement, and encourage employees to express their concerns. Through hiring competent supervisors and managers who can guide, support, reinforce, and develop staff, public organizations can not only motivate employees, but empower them. Finally, public organizations can adopt collaborative systems and processes. Organizations can facilitate interpersonal communication between workers, between staff and managers, and throughout the agency's hierarchy. Similarly, public organizations can develop work teams to enhance morale, social support, and interdependence across work tasks.

CONCLUSION

This chapter advances two key ideas. First, while our collective understanding of trauma has grown thanks to contemporary attention to this topic across disciplines, we have paid insufficient attention to the impacts of trauma on staff who are involved in the delivery of public services. This chapter provides details to explain why this approach is lacking and how to move forward in addressing this gap. Second, this chapter explains that focusing the discussion of trauma only at the individual level ignores broader, organizational forces which should also be acknowledged and addressed. To advance this goal, this chapter provides specific recommendations for organizational change.

At the time of this writing, the COVID-19 pandemic is a major source of stress and also represents a potentially traumatic event for workers across sectors. According to the *Total Worker Health Employer Guide* (2020), a variety of factors related to the pandemic are impacting employee wellbeing, including: overwhelming media coverage which affects mental health; business closures or downsizing which impacts financial wellbeing; limits on social gatherings which increase loneliness and isolation; disruptions to daily routines that hinder physical wellbeing, increasing family demands and caregiving responsibilities; and new challenges related to healthcare access and supply availability (*Total Worker Health Employer Guide*, 2020).

Given this list of significant impacts of the pandemic on health and wellbeing, it is perhaps unsurprising to learn that this event is having a much more pervasive influence than previous 'mass traumatic' events. For example, there is evidence that depression is three times greater than before the pandemic (Ettman et al., 2020). These findings suggest a challenging road ahead for society as it grapples with the economic and psychological impacts of the pandemic. These challenges will undoubtedly impact public employees, particularly those who experience direct or vicarious trauma of the COVID-19 experience (Carmassi et al., 2020).

Fear, anxiety, social isolation, and loneliness are some of the most prominent issues which are expected to be more pronounced for front-line workers like healthcare providers or first responders (Centers for Disease Control and Prevention, 2020). While this chapter highlights the importance of comprehensive approaches to trauma-informed care, the Centers for Disease Control and Prevention's advice for coping is focused on individual worker efforts, advising employees to monitor themselves for stress symptoms and build personal resilience.

This chapter's message is that managing motivation in a trauma-informed manner requires not just individual responses, but also organizational ones. This requires, however, a changed perspective on the part of public managers and the organizations they lead. Specifically, it requires an acknowledgement that what impacts one member of the organization impacts everyone. In the words of Dr. Nadine Burke Harris, when it comes to trauma, *'The single most important thing that we need today is the courage to look this problem in the face and say, "this is real, and this is all of us."'*

REFERENCES

American Psychiatric Association. (2013). *Diagnostic and statistical manual of mental disorders* (5th edn). American Psychiatric Association.

Anda, R.F., Felitti, V.J., Bremner, J.D., Walker, J.D., Whitfield, C.H., Perry, B.D., Dube, S.R., and Giles, W.H. (2006). The enduring effects of abuse and related adverse experiences in childhood. *European Archives of Psychiatry and Clinical Neuroscience*, 256, 174–186.

Anne Dombo, E., and Whiting Blome, W. (2016). Vicarious trauma in child welfare workers: A study of organizational responses. *Journal of Public Child Welfare*, 10, 505–523.

Avina, C., and O'Donohue, W. (2002). Sexual harassment and PTSD: Is sexual harassment diagnosable trauma? *Journal of Traumatic Stress*, 15, 69–75.

Bassuk, E.L., Unick, G.J., Paquette, K., and Richard, M.K. (2017). Developing an instrument to measure organizational trauma-informed care in human services: The TICOMETER. *Psychology of Violence*, 7, 150–157.

Becker-Blease, K.A. (2017). As the world becomes trauma-informed, work to do. *Journal of Trauma and Dissociation*, 18, 131–138.

Berman, E.M., Bowman, J.S., West, J.P., and Van Wart, M.R. (2019). *Human resource management in public service: Paradoxes, processes, and problems*. Washington, DC: CQ Press.

Berninger, A., Webber, M.P., Cohen, H.W. et al. (2010). Trends of elevated PTSD risk in firefighters exposed to the World Trade Center disaster: 2001–2005. *Public Health Reports*, 125, 556–566.

Bezerra, C. de M., Assis, S. G. de, and Constantino, P. (2016). Psychological distress and work stress in correctional officers: A literature review. *Ciência and Saúde Coletiva*, 21, 2135–2146.

Blackstock, C. (2011). The emergence of the breath of life theory. *Journal of Social Work Values and Ethics*, 8, 1–16.

Bonanno, G.A., Galea, S., Bucciarelli, A., and Vlahov, D. (2007). What predicts psychological resilience after disaster? The role of demographics, resources, and life stress. *Journal of Consulting and Clinical Psychology*, 75, 671–682.

Bor, J., Venkataramani, A.S., Williams, D.R., and Tsai, A.C. (2018). Police killings and their spillover effects on the mental health of black Americans: A population-based, quasi-experimental study. *The Lancet*, 392, 302–310.

Bradbury, M.D., and Jacobson, W.S. (2013). A new era of protection against disability discrimination? The ADA Amendments Act of 2008 and 'regarded as' disabled. *Review of Public Personnel Administration*, 33, 320–339.

Bridgman, T., Cummings, S., and Ballard, J. (2019). Who built Maslow's pyramid? A history of the creation of management studies' most famous symbol and its implications for management education. *Academy of Management Learning & Education*, 18, 81–98.

Brown, D.W., Anda, R.F., Tiemeier, H., Felitti, V.J., Edwards, V.J., Croft, J.B., and Giles, W.H. (2009). Adverse childhood experiences and the risk of premature mortality. *American Journal of Preventive Medicine*, 37, 389–396.

Byrne, Z.S., Hayes, T.L., and Holcombe, K.J. (2017). Employee engagement using the federal employee viewpoint survey. *Public Personnel Management*, 46, 368–390.

Carmassi, C., Foghi, C., Dell'Oste, V., Cordone, A., Bertelloni, C.A., Bui, E., and Dell'Osso, L. (2020). PTSD symptoms in healthcare workers facing the three coronavirus outbreaks: What can we expect after the COVID-19 pandemic. *Psychiatry Research*, 292, 113312.

Caspi, A., Wright, B.R.E., Moffitt, T.E., and Silva, P.A. (1998). Early failure in the labor market: Childhood and adolescent predictors of unemployment in the transition to adulthood. *American Sociological Review*, 63, 424–451.

Centers for Disease Control and Prevention. (2020). *Employees: How to cope with job stress and build resilience during the COVID-19 pandemic*. Centers for Disease Control and Prevention. Retrieved May 1, 2021 from https://www.cdc.gov/coronavirus/2019-ncov/community/mental-health-non-healthcare.html.

Cieslak, R., Anderson, V., Bock, J., Moore, B.A., Peterson, A.L., and Benight, C.C. (2013). Secondary traumatic stress among mental health providers working with the military: Prevalence and its work- and exposure-related correlates. *The Journal of Nervous and Mental Disease*, 201, 917–925.

Clohessy, S., and Ehlers, A. (1999). PTSD symptoms, response to intrusive memories and coping in ambulance service workers. *British Journal of Clinical Psychology*, 38, 251–265.

Courtois, C.A., and Ford, J.D. (2009). *Treating complex traumatic stress disorders: An evidence-based guide*. New York, NY: Guilford Press.

Covey, H.C., Menard, S., and Franzese, R.J. (2013). Effects of adolescent physical abuse, exposure to neighborhood violence, and witnessing parental violence on adult socioeconomic status. *Child Maltreatment*, 18, 85–97.

Denhardt, R.B., Denhardt, J.V., Aristigueta, M.P., and Rawlings, K.C. (2018). *Managing human behavior in public and nonprofit organizations*. Thousand Oaks, CA: CQ Press.

Ettman, C.K., Abdalla, S.M., Cohen, G.H., Sampson, L., Vivier, P.M., and Galea, S. (2020). Prevalence of depression symptoms in US Adults before and during the COVID-19 pandemic. *JAMA Network Open*, 3, e2019686.

Evans, C., and Evans, G.R. (2019). Adverse childhood experiences as a determinant of public service motivation. *Public Personnel Management*, 48, 123–146.

Fallot, R.D., and Harris, M. (2006). Trauma-informed services: A self-assessment and planning protocol. Washington, DC: Community Connections.

Felitti, V.J., Anda, R.F., Nordenberg, D., Williamson, D.F., Spitz, A.M., Edwards, V., Koss, M.P., and Marks, J.S. (1998). Relationship of childhood abuse and household dysfunction to many of the leading causes of death in adults. *American Journal of Preventive Medicine*, 14, 245–258.

Figley, C.R. (2013). *Compassion fatigue: Coping with secondary traumatic stress disorder in those who treat the traumatized*. Philadelphia, PA: Routledge.

Goh, J., Pfeffer, J., and Zenios, S.A. (2016). The relationship Between Workplace Stressors and Mortality and Health Costs in the United States. *Management Science*, 62, 608–628.

Goldstein, R.B., Smith, S.M., Chou, S.P. et al. (2016). The epidemiology of DSM-5 posttraumatic stress disorder in the United States: Results from the National Epidemiologic Survey on Alcohol and Related Conditions-III. *Social Psychiatry and Psychiatric Epidemiology*, 51, 1137–1148.

Gone, J.P. (2013). Redressing First Nations historical trauma: Theorizing mechanisms for indigenous culture as mental health treatment. *Transcultural Psychiatry*, 50, 683–706.

Grossmeier, J., Fabius, R., Flynn, J.P., Noeldner, S.P., Fabius, D., Goetzel, R.Z., and Anderson, D.R. (2016). Linking workplace health promotion best practices and organizational financial performance: Tracking market performance of companies with highest scores on the HERO Scorecard. *Journal of Occupational and Environmental Medicine*, 58, 16–23.

Guarino, K., Soares, P., Konnath, K., Clervil, R., and Bassuk, E. (2009). Trauma-informed organizational toolkit. Rockville, MD: Center for Mental Health Services, Substance Abuse and Mental Health Services Administration, and the Daniels Fund, the National Child Traumatic Stress Network, and the WK Kellogg Foundation. Retrieved May 7, 2013.

Guy, M.E., and Mastracci, S.H. (2018). Making the affective turn: The Importance of feelings in theory, praxis, and citizenship. *Administrative Theory and Praxis*, 40, 281–288.

Guy, M.E., and Newman, M.A. (2016). Emotional labor: The relational side of public service. In R.C. Kearney and J.D. Coggburn (eds), *Public human resource management: Problems and prospects* (6th edn). Newbury Park, CA: Sage, pp. 198–207.

Hales, T., Kusmaul, N., Sundborg, S., and Nochajski, T. (2019). The Trauma-Informed Climate Scale-10 (TICS-10): A reduced measure of staff perceptions of the service environment. *Human Service Organizations: Management, Leadership and Governance*, 43, 443–453.

Hsieh, C.-W., Yang, K., and Fu, K.-J. (2012). Motivational bases and emotional labor: Assessing the impact of Public Service Motivation. *Public Administration Review*, 72, 241–251.

Jennings, A. (2007). Models for developing trauma-informed behavioral health systems and trauma-specific services. Alexandria, VA: National Association of State Mental Health Program Directors, National Technical Assistance Center for State Mental Health Planning.

Kilpatrick, DG., Resnick, H.S., Milanak, M.E., Miller, M.W., Keyes, K.M., and Friedman, M.J. (2013). National estimates of exposure to traumatic events and PTSD prevalence using *DSM-IV* and *DSM-5* criteria: *DSM-5* PTSD prevalence. *Journal of Traumatic Stress*, 26, 537–547.

Kim, M.M., Ford, J.D., Howard, D.L., and Bradford, D.W. (2010). Assessing trauma, substance abuse, and mental health in a sample of homeless men. *Health and Social Work*, 35, 39–48.

Kimberg, L., and Wheeler, M. (2019). Trauma and trauma-informed care. In M.R. Gerber (ed.), *Trauma-informed healthcare approaches: A guide for primary care*. Cham, Switzerland: Springer International Publishing, pp. 25–56.

Levin, A.P., Albert, L., Besser, A., Smith, D., Zelenski, A., Rosenkranz, S., and Neria, Y. (2011). Secondary traumatic stress in attorneys and their administrative support staff working with trauma-exposed clients. *The Journal of Nervous and Mental Disease*, 199, 946–955.

Lowe, G. (2020). *Creating healthy organizations: Taking action to improve employee well-being*. Toronto: University of Toronto Press.

Magruder, K.M., McLaughlin, K.A., and Elmore Borbon, D.L. (2017). Trauma is a public health issue. *European Journal of Psychotraumatology*, 8, 1375338.

Marini, F. (1971). *Toward a new public administration*. San Francisco, CA: Chandler Publishing.

Maslow, A.H. (1943). A theory of human motivation. *Psychological Review*, 50, 370–396.

McLaughlin, K.A., Koenen, K.C., Hill, E.D., Petukhova, M., Sampson, N.A., Zaslavsky, A M., and Kessler, R.C. (2013). Trauma exposure and posttraumatic stress disorder in a national sample of adolescents. *Journal of the American Academy of Child and Adolescent Psychiatry*, 52, 815–830.

Merrick, M.T., Ford, D.C., Ports, K.A., and Guinn, A.S. (2018). Prevalence of Adverse childhood experiences from the 2011–2014 behavioral risk factor surveillance system in 23 states. *JAMA Pediatrics*, 172, 1038.

Merritt, C.C., Farnworth, M.D., Kennedy, S.S., Abner, G., Wright II, J.E., and Merritt, B. (2020). Representation through lived experience: Expanding Representative bureaucracy theory. *Human Service Organizations: Management, Leadership and Governance*, first published online on August 3, 2020 at https://doi.org/10.1080/23303131.2020.1797969.

Messina, N., and Grella, C. (2006). Childhood Trauma and women's health outcomes in a California prison population. *American Journal of Public Health*, 96, 1842–1848.

Michel, K.L. (2014). Maslow's hierarchy connected to Blackfoot beliefs. Retrieved May 1, 2021 from https://lincolnmichel.wordpress.com/2014/04/19/maslows-hierarchyconnected-to-blackfoot-beliefs/.

Molnar, B.E., Sprang, G., Killian, K.D., Gottfried, R., Emery, V., and Bride, B.E. (2017). Advancing science and practice for vicarious traumatization/secondary traumatic stress: A research agenda. *Traumatology*, 23, 129–142.

Monnat, S.M., and Chandler, R.F. (2015). Long-term physical health consequences of adverse childhood experiences. *The Sociological Quarterly*, 56, 723–752.

Nigro, L.G., and Waugh, W.L. (1996). Violence in the American workplace: Challenges to the public employer. *Public Administration Review*, 56, 326–333.

Ozer, E.J., Best, S.R., Lipsey, T.L., and Weiss, D.S. (2003). Predictors of posttraumatic stress disorder and symptoms in adults: A meta-analysis. *Psychological Bulletin*, 129, 52–73.

Pearlman, L.A., and McKay, L. (2008). Understanding and addressing vicarious trauma. Retrieved on July 8, 2021 from https://www.headington-institute.org/resource/understanding-vt-reading-course/.

Purtle, J., and Lewis, M. (2017). Mapping 'trauma-informed' legislative proposals in U.S. Congress. *Administration and Policy in Mental Health and Mental Health Services Research*, 44, 867–876.

Ricciardelli, R., Carleton, R.N., Groll, D., and Cramm, H. (2018). Qualitatively unpacking Canadian public safety personnel experiences of trauma and their well-being. *Canadian Journal of Criminology and Criminal Justice*, 60, 566–577.

Sotero, M.M. (2006). A conceptual model of historical trauma: Implications for public health practice and research. *Journal of Health Disparities Research and Practice*, 1, 93–108.

Springer, K.W., Sheridan, J., Kuo, D., and Carnes, M. (2007). Long-term physical and mental health consequences of childhood physical abuse: Results from a large population-based sample of men and women. *Child Abuse and Neglect*, 31, 517–530.

Straussner, S.L.A., and Calnan, A.J. (2014). Trauma through the life cycle: A review of current literature. *Clinical Social Work Journal*, 42, 323–335.

Substance Abuse and Mental Health Services Administration. (2014). *SAMHSA's concept of trauma and guidance for a trauma-informed approach* (HHS Publication No. (SMA) 14-4884). Substance Abuse and Mental health Services Administration, US Department of Health and Human Services.

Thompson, VA. (1975). *Without sympathy or enthusiasm: The problem of administrative compassion*. Tuscaloosa, AL: University of Alabama Press.

Total Worker Health Employer Guide: COVID-19 Edition. (2020). Retrieved on July 8, 2021 from https://hwc.public-health.uiowa.edu/wp-content/uploads/TWH-Employer-Guide_COVID-19-Edition.pdf.
Unick, G.J., Bassuk, E.L., Richard, M.K., and Paquette, K. (2019). Organizational trauma-informed care: Associations with individual and agency factors. *Psychological Services, 16,* 134–142.
Valcik, N.A., and Benavides, T.J. (2017). *Practical human resources for public managers: A case study approach.* Philadelphia, PA: Routledge.
Vrklevski, L.P., and Franklin, J. (2008). Vicarious trauma: The impact on solicitors of exposure to traumatic material. *Traumatology, 14,* 106–118.
Weber, M. (1946). *From Max Weber: Essays in sociology,* edited and translated by H.H. Gerth and C.W. Mills. New York, NY: Oxford University Press.
Wolf, M.R., Green, S.A., Nochajski, T.H., Mendel, W.E., and Kusmaul, N.S. (2014). 'We're civil servants': The status of trauma-informed care in the community. *Journal of Social Service Research, 40,* 111–120.
Zielinski, D.S. (2009). Child maltreatment and adult socioeconomic well-being. *Child Abuse and Neglect, 33,* 666–678.
Zimring, B. (1971). Comment: Empirical theory and the new public administration. In F. Marini (ed.), *Toward a new public administration: The Minnowbrook perspective.* San Francisco, CA: Chandler Publishing, pp. 225–232.

PART V

CONCLUSION

27. Conclusions: where does motivation research in public administration go from here?

Randall S. Davis and Edmund C. Stazyk

In the Introduction to this *Handbook* we noted that, despite public administration scholars' long-standing interests in examining employee motivation, few have attempted to comprehensively chronicle motivation research (but see Wright, 2001). We also argued that while existing attempts to examine the motivational landscape in government organizations have encouraged increased scholarly dialogue, they are also relatively narrow in scope. As such, we endeavored to compile chapters from several established and emerging authors with interest in examining the motivation puzzle from various vantages. Given comparatively limited efforts to identify and organize the central features of motivation research in public administration, we asked our contributors to share perspectives regarding the state of scholarship and chart a course for future generations of scholars.

Additionally, our Introduction sought to describe the vast intellectual terrain examining motivation in public administration with the intent of roughly categorizing motivation research. The issues examined by authors in this *Handbook* generally explore four themes including: theoretical foundations, sector-specific facets of motivation, the role motivation plays in human resources management, and how motivational factors influence work behavior. These chapters make clear that 'homegrown' theories developed in public administration still shape many scholars' intellectual efforts. Yet, it is also clear that 21st-century scholarship has expanded to include theories and concepts that traverse disciplinary boundaries.

As such, in this concluding chapter we attempt to take stock of the contributors' thoughts and articulate what we believe we have learned about the current state of motivation scholarship in public administration. We also attempt to summarize fruitful avenues for future research.

THE CURRENT STATE OF MOTIVATION SCHOLARSHIP IN PUBLIC ADMINISTRATION

Although issues related to employee motivation have consumed significant scholarly attention in public administration throughout its history, one could arguably trace the 21st-century expansion of motivation research to a few seminal articles published in the 1990s and early 2000s. First, as we noted in the introduction, Perry and Wise (1990) developed the concept of public service motivation (PSM). The development of PSM, according to Perry and Wise (1990), emerged to address personnel challenges emanating from reduced trust in governing institutions and the tarnished reputation of public service. Specifically, Perry and Wise argued that the presence of specific categories of motives predicted one's predisposition to self-select into public service and invest significant personal effort toward attaining publicly oriented goals. Perhaps equally importantly, Perry (1996) developed an operational definition in 1996, which served as a springboard to propel PSM research into the 21st century (see also Perry and

Hondeghem, 2008). As we argued in the Introduction, PSM research has facilitated significant discussion regarding employee motivation public administration. Yet, this research tends to emphasize a relatively narrow set of motivational factors internal to the individual while minimizing other plausible motivators—many of which are extrinsic to the individual—relevant for work motivation.

Second, Robert Behn (1995) sought to articulate the central questions that should shape public administration inquiry in the 21st century. The 'motivation question,' according to Behn (1995), asked 'how can public managers motivate public employees (and citizens too) to pursue important public purposes with intelligence and energy?' (p. 319). Behn's (1995) formulation of the motivation question enhanced the breadth of motivation research by focusing on a broader constellation of motivators and emphasizing the prescriptive aspect of motivation research. Moreover, he illustrated that different disciplinary traditions, primarily those of economics and psychology, influenced how researchers framed motivation questions. Examining employee motivation from specific disciplinary traditions encourages scholarship to focus on different clusters of motivators, which expands scholarly debate through evaluating competing hypotheses (see, e.g., DiIulio, 1994).

Finally, shortly after the turn of the 21st century, Wright (2001) sought to broadly synthesize the motivation literature in public administration in an effort to develop a more fully specified model of work motivation. Similar to Behn (1995), Wright (2001) broadly defined motivation research to include any examination of 'direction, intensity, and persistence of work-related behaviors desired by the organization or its representatives' (p. 560). The breadth of this definition allowed for connecting multiple streams of research in public management under the motivation umbrella. This piece represented perhaps the most comprehensive treatment of motivation in public administration at that time. Importantly, Wright's work laid the foundation for future scholars by demonstrating connections between disparate research streams.

These late 20th and early 21st-century pieces examining motivation helped frame the intellectual foundation of motivation scholarship in public administration in the 21st century. The chapters included in this *Handbook* illustrate that multiple generations of scholars recognize the central importance of public administration's historical roots, but also acknowledge that motivation research can reasonably profit from leveraging interdisciplinary inquiry to expand knowledge. Given these aims, debates over the proper specification of work motivation models have taken on some unique characteristics in public administration. First, many researchers in the field seem to agree that factors embedded in political environments influences a public organization's capacity to adequately motivate employees. Second, public managers confront resource constraints that compromises the ability to offer high powered, extrinsic rewards at levels comparable to private organizations. Finally, given public managers' relative inability to leverage extrinsic rewards, public administration scholars have tended to focus on motivation theories that do not rely on tangible rewards.

The chapters included in this *Handbook* address many of these unique characteristics in their attempt to explore state of motivation scholarship in public administration. To that end, each contribution addresses at least one of the following questions, and many contributions speak to more than one:

1. How do unique features of public and nonprofit organizations' institutional contexts influence employee motivation?

2. What is the interrelationship between intrinsic and extrinsic motivational factors, and how can managers leverage these disparate factors?
3. What factors encourage variation in individuals' responses to similar motivational factors (put another way, what shapes one's preferences for a given reward)?
4. How can new or expanded concepts inform motivation research, and where do they fit into broader motivational processes for public organizations?

Although we categorize the chapters in this *Handbook* into four broad categories, these questions cut across sections. Moreover, the chapters illustrate that public administration scholarship has progressed significantly in the first two decades of the 21st century. In our opinion, the public administration research community has developed much more nuanced answers to these questions, and the authors represented in this *Handbook* have expanded on earlier research to build research programs that inform theory and practice. Below, we briefly summarize what this *Handbook* teaches us about each of these questions.

The Institutional Context Question

Public management scholars frequently assert that public and nonprofit organizations must operate under unique institutional constraints relative to their private sector counterparts. To some extent, researchers correctly distinguish organizations' motivating potential based on unique institutional constraints and environmental exigencies. Indeed, multiple chapters within this *Handbook* analyze public distinctiveness. The most common refrain is that public organizations operate within a broader political environment fraught with competing stakeholder interests. A lack of political consensus compromises employee motivation because it can create conflicting expectations, constrain managers' ability to employ certain motivational tools, compromise the efficacy of certain motivators, reshape the flow of financial resources, and limit the ability of an organization to exert appropriate control over employees.

However, it is also valuable to note that many of the environmental features public organizations confront also influence private organizations, but to a different degree. As the boundaries between sectors blur, scholars will likely recognize similar environmental constraints influence employee motivation in for-profit organizations. As Bozeman (1987) famously observed, all organizations embody public characteristics to some degree. Particularly in the early 21st century, it seems that few organizations are immune from political trends. In this regard, we believe that public administration has developed insights that can inform those interested in generic management.

Many of the new and expanded concepts discussed in this *Handbook* likely apply to all organizations. As such, we believe these chapters are valuable because they seek to refine our understanding of the 'political' environment and seek to more precisely measure elements of politics with the capacity to influence organizational performance. In our estimation, future research can use the theories and concepts presented here to better operationalize politics as it relates to organizational operations. Scholars can then apply these theories and concepts to reinvigorate interest in cross-sector comparative studies. Indeed, several authors included should be considered the leaders in this field of research, and each has the capacity to influence research in disciplines outside public administration.

The Intrinsic Motivation versus Extrinsic Incentives Question

High degrees of contention continue to characterize scholarly debates regarding the relative efficacy of intrinsic versus extrinsic motivators. Several of the selections within this *Handbook* at least hint at the distinction between these two clusters of motivators. On the one hand, many students of public administration assert that factors beyond the control of managers limit their ability to leverage extrinsic incentives to motivate desired behaviors at work. It is also possible, as many of the chapters suggest, that the application of extrinsic incentives will undermine—or crowd out—an individual's internal drive to invest effort in achieving work tasks. Given these challenges, public administration research often emphasizes intrinsic motivators as the most useful way to encourage effort, persistence, and intensity at work.

On the other hand, outside the field of public administration, the debate regarding the extent to which extrinsic incentives undermine intrinsic motivation is far from settled (e.g., Cameron, Banko, and Pierce, 2001). It is equally plausible that extrinsic rewards possess no inherently negative properties, and can reasonably coexist with intrinsic motivation. Given that the institutional dynamics discussed above may well characterize the availability of incentives for public organizations, public administration scholars have conducted far less research on the potential compatibility of extrinsic incentives and intrinsic motivation. Yet, some chapters presented in this *Handbook* lay the foundation for making similar arguments.

Importantly, many of the contributors to this *Handbook* examine issues at the forefront of this debate. A more nuanced argument asserts that extrinsic incentives, indeed, serve important purposes for public organizations. Admittedly, certain situational constraints may increase the probability that incentives and intrinsic motivation are at odds. Yet, the motivating potential of extrinsic motivators such as pay, promotion, or job security should not be patently dismissed as irrelevant to the motivation equation for public and nonprofit organizations. Many of the authors here chart a course for more sophisticated examinations of the relationships between extrinsic incentives and intrinsic motivation. Neglecting incentives as a central piece of the motivation puzzle likely offers an incomplete view of work performance. Public administration scholarship could certainly capitalize on the institutional features of public and nonprofit organizations to address elements of this debate.

The Individual Variation Question

The factors and processes that govern human motivation are part of a multifaceted and complex system. The chapters in this *Handbook* illustrate that attempts to include all relevant factors into a single model are likely untenable. Moreover, as many of the authors conclude, one need not assume that employees will express uniform attitudes and behaviors in response to the same motivator or even the same category of motivators. When evaluating the extent to which a specific motivator elicits a given attitude or behavior, scholars must account for myriad organization-level and individual-level differences. The authors of these chapters are remarkably effective at illustrating the complexity of motivational processes and have taken significant strides toward accounting for the various factors from which individual differences are derived.

Contemporary motivation research in public administration acknowledges that employees will differ in how they understand, experience, and appraise the demands levied on them by the organization. Not only does accounting for these differences offer a more holistic picture of work motivation, but it also offers practical insights into matching individuals to jobs well suited for their unique predispositions. Many of the chapters examining sector choice and human resources management systems occupy this research space. For example, it is reasonable to conclude that strategic job design can foster recruitment and retention. However, job design efforts are better likely to succeed when organizations account for what individuals expect from work and properly match individuals to jobs designed to match their expectations.

Many authors have also situated motivational variables in broader theoretical perspectives to account for these individual differences. For example, examining employee behavior through the lens of stress theories represents an emerging research trend in public administration scholarship. In this regard, many contributors to this volume are on the cutting-edge of motivation research. Stress theories offer valuable insights into motivational processes because they treat behavior as a response to the emotional byproducts of one's interpretation of specific work demands. Theories of stress, appraisal, and emotion offer an abstract explanation for how specific work demands contribute to behavior via emotion while accounting for the unique predispositions and expectations of individuals. Understanding this complexity can certainly contribute to better designed jobs and a higher probability of properly selecting employees for a given set of tasks. Additionally, scholars have weighed the relative merits of objective and subjective indicators for relevant motivational concepts. Both objective and subjective measures are important, yet, objective measures tend to marginalize the relevance of employees' subjective interpretations and objective measures may constrain researchers' ability to convey actionable research recommendations to practitioners. In the process of measurement revision, scholars should not shy from refining both objective and subjective measures which are, in our opinion, the key to advancing public sector goal research.

In our estimation, nearly all chapters in this *Handbook* speak to this theme either explicitly or implicitly. As such, future research seems well poised to develop prescriptive recommendations for public managers interested in building a highly motivated workplace. Moreover, it appears that many of the chapters have coalesced on a common set of theories to examine individual-level behavioral differences in response to various motivators. Future research should now turn to testing these theories using more precise measures of task demands, personal characteristics, and emotional responses to identify the boundaries of these theories.

The Question of New and Expanded Concepts

The final question addressed in many chapters involves the degree to which our field requires new and/or expanded concepts to adequately understand work motivation in public and nonprofit organizations. As we articulated in the Introduction, and many authors articulated, PSM represents one of the few theories native to public administration. Developing a native motivation theory in public administration has distinct advantages. For example, it explicitly accounts for institutional differences across sectors and acknowledges that an individual's unique dispositional proclivities can shape expectations and guide behavior. Nevertheless, PSM has been the subject of some degree of conceptual critique (Bozeman and Su, 2015). Many of the chapters in the *Handbook* assert that the introduction of new and refined concepts can, to some degree, mitigate the conceptual overlap between PSM and other variables central to motivation.

At a minimum, the authors included here comment on several newer or more refined constructs including fairness, trauma, altruism, organizational identity orientation, and community-oriented sense of responsibility among others. The authors' inclusion of these concepts indicates the belief that each covers somewhat different conceptual terrain as compared to PSM. Indeed, many may well address some of the theoretical and methodological concerns with the current body of knowledge on PSM. From our perspective, however, introducing new concepts serves another, perhaps more important, purpose. New concepts serve to fill gaps in understanding that we have not yet been able to resolve using more traditional concepts and theories. A thorough examination of these ideas may well afford public administration research the opportunity to better speak to practitioners and help enhance motivation in the 21st-century workplace.

The chapters of this *Handbook* also invest some intellectual effort toward articulating a more unified theory of work motivation in public and nonprofit organizations. The locus of new and expanded concepts in a unified theory may well be a matter for debate. However, to the extent that these concepts add to our ability to explain and predict human behavior, new research can uncover precisely how they expand our current understanding of work motivation.

CONCLUSIONS

The chapters included here clearly illustrate the importance of addressing the four broad questions articulated above. Yet, public administration researchers can invest additional effort to fully address each. For example, examining the institutional context in which motivational processes are embedded is valuable, however, future research can refine variables and concepts meant to assess institutional and political environments. Moreover, the theories employed to generate institutional hypotheses cut across disciplines. Yet, it seems that since Behn (1995) first formulated the 'motivation question' psychological theories have become the most frequently used lens to examine work motivation in public management. To some extent, this suggests that contemporary research focuses predominantly on how institutional features, broadly construed, fit within a meta-theoretical framework designed to explicate psychological processes centered on human cognition, appraisal, and affect.

Nevertheless, the public administration research community should not rule out alternative theories based on economic explanations of human behavior. The explanatory capacity of theories of political control, which are often rooted in agency theory, can inform our understanding of why individuals choose to invest a specific degree of effort toward accomplishing work tasks. Arguably, these theories may have more to tell us about the specific factors that diminish motivation. Although psychological theories have become more pronounced, it is clear that current research has not completely discarded motivation hypotheses derived from political and economic theory. We believe that enhanced application of these theories can contribute to triangulating research findings and creating robust recommendations for enhancing motivation within public organizations.

While economic and psychological theories are predicated on different assumptions and often tested with different methodological tools, we may not have to assume that these theories are empirically at odds. Admittedly, some research—particularly PSM research—has been established as a countervailing force to rational choice perspectives. Yet, both these perspectives can inform our understanding for how and why workers behave as they do. It may be valuable to discard the assumption that individuals are either public spirited altruists or self-interested. Instead, it seems more reasonable to assume that individuals are sometimes altruists and under other conditions decidedly self-interested. In other words, we see no need to assume away human complexity, rather the research community should seek to evaluate it through adequately specified and theorized models. Future research can empirically evaluate that expectation empirically.

We also believe that the vast majority of motivation research in public administration examines the favorable aspects of organizational behavior. One could argue that the early emphasis on PSM encouraged generations of researchers to focus heavily on prosocial organizational behaviors. We do not dispute that understanding the origins of organizational citizenship behaviors, prosocial actions, and altruism inform how we understand an organization's performance potential. Examining only favorable aspects of organizational behavior, however, creates at least two challenges. First, counterproductive behaviors constitute a sizable proportion of employee activity within organizations. Second, related to the first challenge, given the disproportionate focus on positive behavioral outcomes, a significant proportion of research assumes that properly situating work within a given motivational context will encourage those with counterproductive tendencies to become productive, prosocial employees.

As Wright (2001) pointed out, many researchers are inclined to treat productivity as a proxy for motivation. In our opinion, this emphasis misses the observation that counterproductive behavior is motivated by the same processes that drive productive behavior (Spector and Fox, 2002). As such, the question of individual variation becomes even more critical for two reasons. First, managers should not assume that a given work environment will encourage favorable behavior for all employees. Second, and perhaps more importantly, it forces researchers and managers to admit that a productive, altruistic employee can become counterproductive and aggressive if conditions change. Public administration scholars have not adequately confronted this complexity.

We do not pretend to have comprehensive answers to these questions. Rather, our goal was to accumulate a body of scholars to comment on where research currently stands and where it should move forward. These challenges notwithstanding, the authors contributing to this *Handbook* have invested significant effort to chart a path forward for future generations of scholars. There is certainly more work to be done, but we know significantly more as a result of the important work of these authors. We would like to extend our gratitude to our chapter authors, and encourage our readers to heed their calls for high quality research.

REFERENCES

Behn, R.D. (1995). The big questions of public management. *Public Administration Review*, 55, 313–324.
Bozeman, B. (1987). *All organizations are public: Bridging public and private organizational theories.* San Francisco, CA: Jossey-Bass.
Bozeman, B., and Su, X. (2015). Public service motivation concepts and theory: A critique. *Public Administration Review*, 75, 700–710.
Cameron, J., Banko, K.M., and Pierce, W.D. (2001). Pervasive negative effects of rewards on intrinsic motivation: The myth continues. *The Behavior Analyst*, 24(1), 1–44.
DiIulio, J.D. (1994). Principled agents: The cultural bases of behavior in a federal government bureaucracy. *Journal of Public Administration Research and Theory*, 4, 277–320.
Perry, J. L. (1996). Measuring public service motivation: An assessment of construct reliability and validity. *Journal of Public Administration Research and Theory*, 6, 5–22.

Perry, J.L, and Hondeghem, A. (2008). *Motivation in public management: The call of public service.* New York, NY: Oxford University Press.
Perry, J.L., and Wise, L.R. (1990). The motivational bases of public service. *Public Administration Review, 50,* 367–373.
Spector, P.E., and Fox, S. (2002). An emotion-centered model of voluntary work behavior: Some parallels between counterproductive work behavior and organizational citizenship behavior. *Human Resource Management Review, 12,* 269–292.
Wright, B.E. (2001). Public-sector work motivation: A review of the current literature and a revised conceptual model. *Journal of Public Administration Research and Theory, 11,* 559–586.

Index

accountability
    teachers 264, 268
    unreserved fund balance management 184, 186, 187, 188–90
achievement motivation, theory of 28
activation theory 238
Adams, J.S. 40
administrative presidency 12–14
administrative systems and structures 73
adverse childhood experiences (ACEs) 388–9
affect
    and relational approach 302
    and social exchange 297–9, 302
affect-based trust 297
affective motives 148
age, and motivational crowding 45
agency decision-making 183
Aguado, N.A. 287
Alexy, O. 42
altruism and altruistic motivation 46, 50–51, 201–2, 206–8, 212
ambiguity, goals 80–81, 82–3, 84, 255
Anastasopoulos, J. 21
Andersen, L.B. 43
appointees (presidential) 12, 13, 16, 18, 21
appraisal (psychological process) 162–3
Arendt, H. 309
Aryee, S. 298
Asseburg, J. 31–2
atomistic fallacy 15
autonomy 10, 14, 59, 61, 62, 63

Bakker, A.B. 355, 356, 357, 359, 362
Barigozzi, F. 149
Barzelay, M. 236–7
basic psychological needs theory (BPNT) 29–30, 63, 65–6
Bassuk, E.L. 391
behavioral public administration (BPA) 20–21
behavioral public administration (BPA) and employee motivation 27–8
    conclusion 34–5
    experiments in research on public service motivation (PSM) 30–32, 33–4
    psychological theories in research on public service motivation (PSM) 28–30, 32, 34
    unanswered questions 33–4
behaviorism 74
Behn, R.D. 403
beliefs 202, 209, 317, 378, 379, 380, 383–4
Bell, A.B. 112
Bellé, N. 31, 32, 42–3
Bertelli, A.M. 45
Bezerra, C. de M. 391
Blader, S.L. 299–300
Borst, R.T. 253–4, 358, 362, 364, 365
Bottomley, P. 94
Bottorff, L.J. 110
Boyd, N. 202, 208–9
Brehm, J.O. 18
Brewer, G.A. 31, 32, 220–21
Brewer Jr., G.A. 31, 32
Brickson, S.L. 323, 326
Bright, L. 285–6
Brincker, B. 210
Brito, D.T.D. 94
Brown, K.M. 175
budget-maximizing theory 15
buffering mechanisms 371
Buiatti, C. 95
bureaucracy 10–12, 392
bureaucratic motivation, political economy of, *see* political economy of bureaucratic motivation
burnout 129, 240, 254, 356, 357, 358–9, 363, 366, 367–70
burnout, 'realistic' and 'symbolic' stressor effects on 377
    future research 384–5
    integrated threat theory 377–9
    symbolic stressors: organizational and individual factors 381–4
    theoretical model 380–81
    threat in organizations 379–80
Burns, P. 288–9
Burr, R. 238, 239
Bush (George H.W.) administration 13
Bush (George W.) administration 219, 266

Cantarelli, P. 43
career interest in government 284
    declining 284–5
    predictors of 285–6

and public service motivation (PSM) 286
  role of graduate education 286–9
Carpenter, D. 16, 19
Carter administration 221
causality orientations theory (COT) 61–3
centralization 342, 343
challenging job stressors 360
Chalmers, J. 176–7
change-oriented organizational citizenship behavior (OCB) 336–7
  discussion and conclusion 347–9
  nature of 337–9
  organizational context 340–44
  in public organizations 339–40
  public service motivation (PSM)-based model 344–7
character ethics 309
Chen, G. 178
childhood trauma 388–9
Chingos, M.M. 177
Christensen, R.K. 31, 32, 113
Chu, H.Y. 94
Chun, Y.H. 79
circumplex model of psychological well-being 357
civil service, *see* merit principles (US federal civil service)
Civil Service Reform Act of 1978: 13, 223
Clark, R.L. 176
Clinton administration 221
cognition-based trust 297
cognitive dissonance theory 380
cognitive evaluation theory (CET) 58, 59–60, 65
collective bargaining 160
collectivist organizational identity orientation (OIO) 321, 322, 323, 326, 328, 330, 331, 332, 333
Colquitt, J.A. 296, 297, 298
command incentives 48
Community Experience Framework 209, 210, 211
compassion 129, 392
  US federal civil service 223, 225, 226, 227, 228
compensation in for-profit, nonprofit and public organizations 137
  distribution of wages between sectors and within workplace 144–5
  implications for public administration scholars and practitioners 149
  non-monetary incentives 147–9
  sector differences in determinants of wages 140
  wage determination in public sector 142–4, 146

wage determination theory/models 138–40, 141–2
  see also pay; pay-for-performance
competence 59, 63
completion-contingent rewards 42
comprehensive annual financial reports (CAFRs) 184, 186–92, 193, 194, 195–6
Congress 11–12, 16–17
conjoint survey experiments 20
conservation of resources (COR) theory 364, 371, 372
contingent models 52
contingent rewards 42–3, 52
Contreras-Pacheco, O.E. 93
control orientations 62–3
Conway, E. 254
coping mechanisms 371
Cordery, J.L. 238, 239
corruption, Latin America and Caribbean 91, 94, 98, 99
Costrell, R.M. 173, 174
COVID-19 pandemic 259, 396
creativity 239
crowding in 39, 51
crowding out 29–30, 65, 148, 205; *see also* motivational crowding
culture
  clan 211
  developmental 341
  and job design 253
  Latin America 98–9
  organizational 209, 211, 324, 341–2, 346
  and self-determination theory (SDT) 66
cynicism about organizational change (CAOC) 255

Dal Bó, E. 94
Davis, R.S. 81, 82–3, 154, 157, 158, 162
de Cremer, D. 300–301
Deci, E.L. 40, 42, 57, 58–60, 61–3, 106
deferred retirement option plans (DROP) 173–4
defined benefit (DB) pension plans 169, 170–71, 172, 173, 174, 175, 176–7, 179
defined contribution (DC) pension plans 169, 171–2, 176–7, 179
Delton, A.W. 106
demand-induced strain compensation (DISC) model 371, 372
Demerouti, E. 355, 356, 357, 359
developmental culture 341
digital work design (DWD) 244
DiIulio Jr., J.D. 19
distributive justice 294, 298, 300, 301
diversity 129
document analysis (as qualitative method) 111

donative labor theory 126

education
    graduate, role in career interest in government 286–9
    teachers' pensions and retirement 173–4, 175, 177
    and wage determination 141–2
    see also teachers' motivation and systems for recruitment, retention, and evaluation
effort-reward imbalance (ERI) model 40, 355
emotional demands and exhaustion 358, 359, 379, 381
emotional empathy 207–8
emotional stressors 362, 366, 371
emotional support 383
emotions 297–8, 361
employee health and well-being, investing in 391
employee voice 254
employee/work engagement 253–4, 356–7, 358, 359, 363, 365, 367–70, 372, 394
employer branding, and public service motivation (PSM) 31–2
empowerment 301, 395
endogeneity 105
engagement-contingent rewards 42
equity 40, 293, 294
ethical behavior 31, 113, 308–9
ethics, prosocial and public service motivation (PSM) 307–8
    comparison of PSM and prosocial motivation 311
    conclusion and future research 316–18
    definitions 310–11
    Latin America 99
    nonprofit sector 314–16
    overview of links between 311–13
    public sector 313–14
    study framework 308–10
Every Student Succeeds Act (ESSA) 264
excitement motivation (EM) 210
executive politics, motivation in 12–14
experience, and wage determination 141
experimental research and qualitative methods 105–6
    conclusion 115
    document analysis 111
    experimental research, review of papers 111–13
    in-depth interviews 109–10
    methodological framework 113–15
    motivation 106–8
    motivational crowding 51
    observational studies 110–11
    pretest-posttest design 112

    public service motivation (PSM) 30–32, 33–4, 110, 111, 112–13
    qualitative research, review of papers 108–11
    sampling 108–9, 111–12
    vignette designs 112–13
external regulation 61
extrinsic goals 63–4
extrinsic incentives and rewards 125–6, 127–8, 147, 148, 205, 405; *see also* motivational crowding
extrinsic motivation 58–9, 107
    teachers 265–7, 268–9, 270–71, 277–8
    see also self-determination theory (SDT)

Faerman, S. 298
fairness, *see* justice and employee performance
family-oriented motivation, teachers 272, 273, 274–5, 276, 277
feedback 43–4, 50, 270
Feinberg, R.A. 60
Fletcher, L. 361, 362, 365
for-profit sector, *see* private (for-profit) sector
formalization 342–3, 365
Fullagar, C.J.A. 161
fund balance management practices, *see* unreserved fund balance management practices in US counties

Gagné, M. 57, 58
Gates, S. 18
gender, and extrinsic motivation 45
generally accepted accounting principles (GAAP), compliance with 188, 189, 190, 191, 192, 194
Giauque, D. 257–8
goal ambiguity 80–81, 82–3, 84, 255
goal conflict 15–16
goal-setting theory, *see* goals, as a driver of public sector motivation
goals
    clarity of 160
    extrinsic 63–4
    intrinsic 63–4
    and prosocial motivation 206
    sector differences 77–8, 79, 143–4
goals, as a driver of public sector motivation 71–2
    conclusion 85
    designing goals 75–7
    future directions and considerations 83–4
    goal ambiguity and clarification 79–83
    history and background of goal-setting theory 74–5
    importance of goals to organizations 72–3
    institutional constraints 77–8
goals contents theory (GCT) 63–4

Golden, M.M. 15, 18–19
Goldhaber, D. 177
Gorina, E. 175
governance, pension plans 172, 177–8, 179–80
Government Accounting Standards Board (GASB) 187
government careers, interest in 284
   declining 284–5
   predictors of 285–6
   and public service motivation (PSM) 286
   role of graduate education 286–9
Government Finance Officers Association (GFOA) 183, 186, 187–8, 192, 193, 195–6
government sector, *see* public (government) sector
graduate students, career interest in government, *see* government careers, interest in
Grant, A.M. 241
group engagement model 300–301, 303
guerrilla government 20–21
Gulick, L. 73

Hackman, J.R. 50, 237–8, 242, 245, 250, 355
Hales, T. 391
Hayes, M. 80
Haynie, J.J. 298–9
He, W. 296
health, *see* burnout; burnout, 'realistic' and 'symbolic' stressor effects on; job demands-resources (JD-R) model; stress; trauma; well-being
hierarchy, preference for 383
hierarchy of needs theory 393
high-performance HR practices (HPHRP) 257
Hoang, T. 175
Hollibaugh Jr., G.E. 20–21
Hou, Y. 185
Hsieh, C.-W. 358
Huberts, L.W. 308, 312
human capital 142
human resource management (HRM)
   and job design 257–8
   and motivational crowding 49–50
   and public service motivation (PSM) 99
   and unions 160
   US federal civil service 220, 221, 222
   see also other-regarding concepts
Humphrey, S.E. 238, 242

identified regulation 61
identity
   and affect 302
   moral 309, 311–12
   organizational identification theory 348–9
   orientation, individual 322, 324
   prosocial 311
   public service 310
   self-identity 378, 383–4
   social 209, 299–300, 310
   theory 324
   see also organizational identity orientation (OIO)
impersonal orientations 62, 63
inclusion 129
individualistic organizational identity orientation (OIO) 321, 322, 323, 326, 327, 329–30, 331, 332, 333
information and communication technologies (ICT) 243–5
informational justice 294–5, 296, 297, 301–2
ingroup 378
innovation, and extrinsic motivation 43
institutional context 404
   job demands-resources (JD-R) model 364–5, 372
   and job design 253–4
instrumental motives 148
integrated regulation 61
integrated threat theory 377–9
integrity violations 308, 312–13
interactional justice 296
interest groups 14
internalization 61, 65
interpersonal context 44, 298, 347
interpersonal dynamics, and change-oriented organizational citizenship behavior (OCB) 343–4
interpersonal justice 294–5, 296, 297, 300, 301–2
interviews, in-depth (as qualitative method) 109–10
intrinsic goals 63–4
intrinsic motivation 29, 41–2, 107, 144–5, 147, 298, 405
   teachers 265–6, 267, 269, 270–71, 277–9
   see also self-determination theory (SDT)
introjected regulation 61
involvement in workplace, and job satisfaction 238–9
Ippolito, R.A. 176

Jacobsen, C.B. 43, 48
jigsaw management 18–19
job characteristics
   definition of 160
   and job design 50, 237–9, 242–3, 250, 258–60
   relational 256–7
job characteristics model (JCM) 237–9, 242, 250, 251, 252, 355
job demands-control (JDC) model 250–51, 355

job demands-control-support (JDCS) model 355
job demands-resources (JD-R) model 239–40, 251, 254, 354–5
    conclusion and future research 371–3
    descriptive stressors/motivators 367–70
    general perspective 356–7
    interactions between motivation and stress processes 366, 371
    job and personal stressors/motivators 359–61
    motivational and stress process 363–4
    motivational and stress process in (semi-)public sector 364–6
    public servants' job and personal stressors/motivators 361–3
    public servants' states of stress and motivation 357–9
job design 234–5, 245–6, 249
    cultural and institutional contexts 253–4
    definition and origins 250–51
    discussion and future research 258–60
    enduring challenges in 243–5
    and goal ambiguity 255
    and human resource management (HRM) 257–8
    integrative approaches 242–3
    job characteristics, resources, and demands 237–41
    and motivation 237–43, 252–8
    and motivational crowding 44–5, 50
    and organizational changes and reforms 255
    and organizational climate 254
    perspectives 235–7
    political context 256, 260
    and red tape 256
    relational 241–2
    and relational job characteristics 256–7
    and work outcomes 251–2
job satisfaction 146, 238–9, 241–2, 357, 358, 359, 367–70
job sectors
    attraction vs. socialization debate 124
    characteristics/values 125–8, 130
    justice and employee performance 302
    public service motivation (PSM) 122–4, 130
    recruitment and retention 128–9
    see also sector differences
job security 126, 143, 144
Johnson, R.W. 173
justice and employee performance 293–4
    approaches to linking 295–301
    conclusion 303–4
    forms of organizational justice 294–5
    future research 301–3

Kasser, T. 63

Kettl, D.F. 221
Kim, D. 173–4, 175
Kinsella, C. 288
Kish-Gephart, J.J. 308–9
Klein, F.A. 94
Kloutsiniotis, P.V. 258
Koestner, R. 62–3
Krause, G.A. 16, 19

Lane, J. 313
Langer, J.A. 323
Latham, G.P. 72, 74–7, 83, 85
Latin America, *see* public service motivation (PSM) research, Latin America
Lavigna, B. 50
Lazarus, R.S. 162–3
leader-member exchange 296, 343–4
leaders, relational approach 300–301
leadership
    change, as symbolic stressor 382
    and change-oriented organizational citizenship behavior (OCB) 343–4
Leete, L. 144–5
Leitner, M. 42
Leon-Cazares, F. 94
Lewin, K. 206
Linos, E. 31, 32
Locke, E.A. 72, 74–7, 83, 85
locus of causality 60, 62
locus of control 62
locus of self-definition 322
loyalty and competence 21

machine learning (ML) 21
Mallinson, D.J. 288–9
market, competitive 138–9
market failure 139
Mascarenhas, A.O. 94
Maslow, A.H. 147, 393
Masterson, S.S. 296
Meier, K.J. 15
mentorship, teachers 269–70
merit principles (US federal civil service) 219
    conclusion 227–9
    data and methods 222–4, 232–3
    findings and discussion 224–7
    negative orientation of civil service reform 220–21
    research propositions 222
merit system 293
Meyer-Sahling, J.H. 31, 32
Mihail, D.M. 258
Mikkelsen, K.S. 95
Millennials, recruitment and retention 128–9
Miller, G.J. 19

minority groups 378
mission attachment 128
Moe, T.M. 14–15
Moloney, K. 94
moral foundations 384
moral identity 309, 311–12
moral licensing theory 34
moral reputation 21
morality 308
Morgeson, F.P. 236, 238, 242
Mostafa, A.M.S. 94, 257
motivation
    definitions of 158
    individual variation 405–6, 408
    new and expanded concepts 406–7
    as research topic 1, 402–8
    scholarship approaches and challenges 154–5
    typology of 106–7
'motivation question' 403
motivational crowding 39, 65–6
    conclusion 52
    determinants of 44–5
    early theoretical conceptions 39–40
    empirical findings 41–4
    future research 51–2
    implications for public sector management 47–51
    and public sector 45–7
    recent theoretical conceptions 40–41
Munnell, A.H. 144, 174
Mussagulova, A. 100

Nef, J. 91
New Public Administration (NPA) 392
New Public Management (NPM) 255
Nguyen, D.T.N. 255
Nixon administration 13
No Child Left Behind Act (NCLB) 264, 266, 268
non-monetary incentives 147–9
nonprofit sector
    career interest in 284, 285, 286
    characteristics/values 126–7, 130, 315–16, 317–18
    compensation 137, 139–40, 143, 144–5, 146, 148–9
    and completion-contingent payments 42
    ethics, prosocial and public service motivation (PSM) 123, 124, 307–8, 314–16
    lack of competitive market 139, 143, 146
    and organizational identity orientation (OIO) 323, 333
    recruitment and retention 128–9
    see also sector differences
norm-based motives 148

Nowell, B. 202, 208–9

Obama administration 266–7
observational studies (as qualitative method) 110–11
Oldham, G. 50, 237–8, 250, 355
Olsen, A.L. 31, 32
'option value' model (pensions) 173
Organ, D.W. 338
organismic integration theory (OIT) 58, 60–61, 64–5, 66
organizational ambiguity 255
organizational behavior (OB) 258, 408
organizational changes and reforms, and job design 255
organizational citizenship behavior (OCB) 94, 123, 207, 208, 209, 257, 338–9; see also change-oriented organizational citizenship behavior (OCB)
organizational climate, and job design 254
organizational context
    and change-oriented organizational citizenship behavior (OCB) 340–44, 345–7
    and public service motivation (PSM) 257, 345–7
organizational culture 209, 211, 324
and change-oriented organizational citizenship behavior (OCB) 341–2, 346
organizational identification theory 348–9
organizational identity 300
organizational identity orientation (OIO) 321–3
    future OIO research and practice in public administration 333–4
    local government manager study 329
    measuring, in public sector 325–33
    National Cross Sector Organizational Studies Project (NCSOSP) 329
    pilot studies 326–9
    qualitative responses to questionnaire items 326, 327–8
    research related to motivation and public administration 323–5
    results of studies 329–33
organizational justice, see justice and employee performance
organizational politics 344, 347
organizational reputation 21
organizational structure, and change-oriented organizational citizenship behavior (OCB) 342–3, 346
organizational support 129, 383
organizations
    definitions of 72
    and goals 72–3, 76–8, 79–85

interpersonal context 343–4
and prosocial motivation 310–11
and public service motivation (PSM) 310
and stressors 381–3, 391
threat in 379–80
values 209
other-regarding concepts 201–3
altruism 206–8
conclusion 212–13
prosocial motivation 206
public service motivation (PSM) 203–6
sense of community responsibility (SOC-R) 208–11
summary of 204
Ouyang, Y. 21
overall (global) justice 295, 298

Paarlberg, L. 50
Pandey, S.K. 79, 80
Parker, S.K. 234, 235, 236, 250–51, 252
pay
    fair, importance of 128
    for-profit sector 127–8
    and intrinsic motivation 41–2
    and motivation 125–6, 221
    nonprofit sector 126–7
    public sector 46–7
    and public service motivation (PSM) 48
    see also compensation in for-profit, nonprofit and public organizations
pay-for-performance 45, 48–9, 148–9, 266–7, 268
'peak value' model (pensions) 173
Pecino, V. 254
Pedersen, L.H. 210
Pedersen, M.J. 31, 32
Pendleton Civil Service Reform Act of 1883: 223
pensions, *see* public pensions and public sector employment
perception 44
performance
    and change-oriented organizational citizenship behavior (OCB) 336, 337–40, 347–8
    expectations 361
    factors influencing 158
    and goal ambiguity 80–81, 82–3, 84
    high-performance HR practices (HPHRP) 257
    and job characteristics 238
    measures, improving 279
    orientation 341
    pay-for-performance 45, 48–9, 148–9, 266–7, 268
    relationship with public service motivation (PSM) 31, 99

teachers 264–5, 266–71, 277–9
    see also justice and employee performance
performance-contingent rewards 42–3
performance management 206, 254
performance-related pay, *see* pay-for-performance
Perry, J.L. 1, 48, 92, 122, 148, 160, 203, 223, 402
person–environment fit 30, 80, 205
person–organization fit 258
personality 208, 359, 360–61
Pfiffner, J.P. 16
Pinder, C. 75
planning 73
Pliscoff, C. 94–5
Podgursky, M. 173, 174
policy disruption 13
political context 256, 260, 404
political economy of bureaucratic motivation 10
    bureaucracy 10–12
    conclusion 22
    critical assessment 17–19
    executive politics 12–14
    future agenda 20–21
    problematic assumptions 14–17
political theory 407
Porter, L.W. 160
POSDCORB 73
post-traumatic stress disorder (PTSD) 389, 390
Potipiroon, W. 298
power 10
    of unions 159–60, 161, 163
presidents 12–14, 16, 17–19, 21
pretest-posttest design 112
principal–agent theory 11–12, 13–14, 15–16, 17–19, 265, 266
private (for-profit) sector
    characteristics 127–8
    compensation 137, 138–40, 143, 144–5
    and organizational identity orientation (OIO) 323
    and realistic stressors 382
    and symbolic stressors 381–2, 383
    unionization in 155–7
    see also job sectors; sector differences
procedural justice 294, 296, 297, 298–9, 300, 301–2, 303
productivity 138, 145, 149, 158, 408
professional development, teachers 269–70, 278–9
prosocial behavior 122–3
prosocial identity 311
prosocial motivation 27–8, 202, 204, 206, 212, 256–7; *see also* ethics, prosocial and public service motivation (PSM)
psychological needs 364

psychological processes, governing motivation 162–3
psychological theories
 basic psychological needs theory (BPNT) 29–30, 63, 65–6
 predominance of 407
 in research on public service motivation (PSM) 28–30, 32, 34
psychological well-being 209, 357; *see also* well-being
public good 50–51, 348
public (government) sector
 characteristics 125–6, 130
 compensation 46–7, 137, 139–40, 142–4, 146, 148–9
 ethics in 313–14
 lack of competitive market 139, 143, 146
 and motivational crowding 45–51
 non-monetary incentives 147–8
 and organizational identity orientation (OIO) 323, 325–33
 public sector motivation 122–4
 and realistic stressors 382
 recruitment and retention 128–9
 and symbolic stressors 381–3
 see also goals, as a driver of public sector motivation; public pensions and public sector employment
public interest 125, 311–12, 313–14, 315–16, 316–17
 commitment to (US federal civil service) 223, 225–6, 227, 228
public management approach 20
public opinion 382–3
public pensions and public sector employment 168
 conclusion and future research 178–80
 effect of pension systems on public employees 170–72
 empirical evidence 172–8
 importance of public pensions 169–70
public policy, and motivational crowding 50–51
public sector motivation 122–4
public service identity 310
public service motivation (PSM) 147–8, 201–2, 203–4
 and altruism 207
 attraction vs. socialization debate 124
 and career interest 286–7
 and challenging work environments 210
 and change-oriented organizational citizenship behavior (OCB) 337, 344–7, 348
 cultivating 205–6
 definitions of 201, 310

experimental research and qualitative methods 30–32, 33–4, 110, 111, 112–13
graduate students 284
hiring for 204–5, 212
and human resource management (HRM) 99, 257–8
and institutional context 253–4
and job characteristics 252, 259–60
and job demands-resources (JD-R) model 362, 365, 366
job sector distinctions 122–4, 125, 130
and justice 298, 302
measurement of (US federal civil service) 223, 225–9, 232
and motivational crowding 48, 50, 51
and organizational context 257, 345–7
and pay 48
and performance 31, 99
vs. prosocial motivation 28, 311
as research topic 1, 402–3, 406–7, 407–8
and self-determination theory (SDT) 64–6
teachers 271–2, 273–4, 275, 276–7
and trauma 394
see also behavioral public administration (BPA) and employee motivation; ethics, prosocial and public service motivation (PSM)
public service motivation (PSM) research, Latin America 89
 achievements and lines of scholarship 97–8
 background, public administration 90–92
 conclusion and recommendations 99–101
 country-based studies 93–5
 cross-country studies 95–6
 gaps 98–9
 review 92–6
publication, underrepresented regions 100–101

qualitative methods, *see* experimental research and qualitative methods
quandary ethics 309
'quit cost' 169–70, 171

Rainey, H. 78–80, 81–2, 125
rapport-building, interviews 109–10
rational choice theory 11, 14, 17
Rattrie, L.T.B. 253
reactions (stress) 356
Reagan administration 13, 18–19
realistic stressors 379–80, 380–81, 382, 385
realistic threats 378
recruitment 128–9
 for altruism 208
 and merit principles 220

and motivational crowding 49–50
and other-regarding concepts 212
and pay 144
and pensions 174, 179
for public service motivation (PSM) 204–5, 212
for sense of community responsibility (SOC-R) 210
see also teachers' motivation and systems for recruitment, retention, and evaluation
red tape 79, 253–4, 256, 302–3, 343, 361–2, 371
regulation 29, 61
relatedness 59, 63
relational approach (justice and performance) 294, 299–301, 301–2, 303
relational job characteristics 256–7
relational job design 234–5, 241–2
relational organizational identity orientation (OIO) 321, 322, 323, 326, 327, 329–30, 331, 332, 333
retention 128–9
and pay 144
and pensions 175–7, 179
see also teachers' motivation and systems for recruitment, retention, and evaluation
retirement age 171, 175, 177
Richter, A. 244
Ripoll, G. 309, 311–12
Ritz, A. 95
role theory 239, 251
rule-based control mechanisms 47
rule sum 160
Rummel, A. 60
Ryan, R.M. 57, 58, 59, 60, 61–3, 106
Ryan, T.A. 74

safety 395
sampling 108–9, 111–12
Sanabria-Pulido, P. 93
Schaufeli, W.B. 356, 357, 359, 360–61, 362
Schott, C. 311, 312
Scientific Management Movement 73
sector differences 154–5
determinants of wages 140
goals 77–8, 79, 143–4
motivational crowding 45–7
see also job sectors
Selart, M. 42
Selden, S.C. 220–21
self-actualization 147
self-determination theory (SDT) 29, 40–41, 57–8, 106–7, 203, 364
background and overview 58–9
basic psychological needs theory (BPNT) 29–30, 63, 65–6

causality orientations theory (COT) 61–3
cognitive evaluation theory (CET) 59–60, 65
conclusion 66–7
goals contents theory (GCT) 63–4
organismic integration theory (OIT) 60–61, 64–5, 66
in public employee motivation research 64–6
self-esteem 41
self-identity 378, 383–4
self-interest 19, 313, 345
self-management efficacy 239
self-reporting bias 110
self-sacrifice 207, 223, 225, 226, 227, 228
Sell, A. 106
sense of community (SOC) 209, 210, 211
sense of community responsibility (SOC-R) 202, 204, 208–11, 212–13
sequential behavioral paradigms 34
slack resources, *see* unreserved fund balance management practices in US counties
Smith, C.A. 162–3
Snyder, M.M. 96
social and health outcomes of trauma 388–9
social desirability bias/effect 109–10
social equity 129
social exchange approach (justice and performance) 294, 295–9, 301–2, 303–4
social identity 209, 299–300, 310
social self 299–300
socialization practices by unions 161–2
sociotechnical systems 250
state functioning and role, Latin America 90–91
Stazyk, E.C. 80, 81, 82–3, 154, 162
Steijn, B. 27–8
Stephan, C.W. 378
Stephan, W.G. 378
Stewart, L.M. 185
strains 356, 363–4, 366, 372
street-level bureaucrats 256–7, 259, 303
stress 162–3, 239–40, 251, 252, 254, 406; *see also* burnout, 'realistic' and 'symbolic' stressor effects on; job demands-resources (JD-R) model; trauma
students, career interest in government 284–9
symbolic stressors 379, 380–85
symbolic threats 378–9

Taris, T.W. 356, 357, 359, 360, 361, 362
tax compliance 50
Taylor, F.W. 73, 235–6
Taylor, J. 241
Teacher Incentive Fund (TIF) 266–7
teachers' motivation and systems for recruitment, retention, and evaluation 264–5